Case Studies in Spirit Possession

Contemporary Religious Movements:
A Wiley-Interscience Series

Edited by IRVING I. ZARETSKY

EDITED BY

Vincent Crapanzano
Vivian Garrison

Case Studies in
Spirit Possession

A WILEY-INTERSCIENCE PUBLICATION

JOHN WILEY & SONS New York · London · Sydney · Toronto

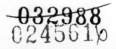

Library of Congress Cataloging in Publication Data:

Main entry under title:
Case studies in spirit possession.

   (Contemporary religious movements)
   "A Wiley-Interscience publication."
   Includes bibliographies and index.
   1. Spirit possession—Case studies.　I. Crapanzano, Vincent, 1939–　　II. Garrison, Vivian, 1933–

BL482.C37　　　　　　133.4′26　　　　　　76-26653
ISBN 0-471-18460-8

Printed in the United States of America

10 9 8 7 6 5 4 3 2 1

Contributors

Vincent Crapanzano is an associate professor in the Department of Comparative Literature, Queens College of the City University of New York. He taught previously at Princeton University (1970–1974). He received an A.B. from Harvard College (Philosophy, 1960) and a Ph.D. from Columbia University (Anthropology, 1970). Research interests are ethnopsychiatry, theories of interpretation, and anthropology of religion and literature. He has done fieldwork among the Navaho and among the Hamadsha of Morocco. Publications include *The Fifth World of Forster Bennett*, New York: Viking, 1972; *The Hamadsha: a Study in Moroccan Ethnopsychiatry*, Berkeley: University of California Press, 1973; "Saints, Jnun, and Dreams," *Psychiatry*, **38:** 145–159, 1975.

Vivian Garrison is an assistant professor in the Department of Psychiatry, New Jersey Medical School, College of Medicine and Dentistry of New Jersey, and a senior research associate in the Department of Anthropology, Columbia University. She has previously held teaching and research appointments at Yale University, Department of Psychiatry (1969–1972), and Albert Einstein College of Medicine and Dentistry (1965–1969, 1972–1974). She received a B.A. from New York University (Spanish and Psychology, 1960) and a Ph.D. from Columbia University (Anthropology, 1972). Research interests are urban social structure, community mental health, and folk healing systems. She has done fieldwork in urban neighborhoods of New York and New Jersey. Publications include "Sectarianism and Psychosocial Adjustment: A Controlled Comparison of Puerto Rican Penetecostals and Catholics," in I. I. Zaretsky and M. Leone (Eds.), *Religious Movements in Contemporary America*, Princeton: Princeton University Press, 1974; with C. M. Arensberg, "The Evil Eye: Envy or Risk of Seizure, Paranoia or Patronal Dependency?" in C. Maloney (Ed.), *The Evil Eye*, New York: Columbia University Press, 1976; with C. S. Thomas, "A Case of a Dominican Migrant," in L. Bryce-Laporte and C. S. Thomas (Eds.), *Contemporary Perspectives on Alienation*, New York, Praeger, 1976; with C. S. Thomas, "A General Systems View of Community Mental Health," in L. Bellak and H. H. Barten (Eds.), *Progress in Community Mental Health*, Vol. III, New York: Bruner-Mazel, 1975.

CLIVE S. KESSLER is an assistant professor of anthropology at Barnard College (1970–present) and was previously a lecturer at the London School of Economics and Political Science (1969–1970). He received his B.A. (Anthropology, 1965) from the University of Sydney and his Ph.D. (Anthropology, 1974) from the University of London. Research interests are religion and symbolism, and peasant movements. He has done fieldwork in Kelantan, West Malaysia. Recent publications are "Islam, Society and Political Behavior . . . ," *British Journal of Sociology*, **23** (1972): 33–50; "Muslim Identity and Political Behavior in Kelantan," in W. R. Roff (Ed.), *Kelantan: Religion, Society and Politics in a Malay State*, Kuala Lumpur: Oxford University Press, 1974.

JOAN D. KOSS is an associate professor of anthropology at the University of Puerto Rico (1967–present) and a postdoctoral fellow in the Department of International Health, University of California, San Francisco (1974–present). She previously taught at Temple University (1965–1966) and the University of Pennsylvania (1964–1965). She received a B.F.A. from Temple University (Fine Arts, English and Philosophy, 1955), and M.A. and Ph.D. degrees from the University of Pennsylvania (Anthropology, 1959 and 1965). Research interests are child socialization, psychosocial aspects of religion, comparative healing systems, and art and creative processes. She has done fieldwork in Trinidad, Puerto Rico, Philadelphia, and the Virgin Islands. Publications include "Therapeutic aspects of Puerto Rican Cult Practices," *Psychiatry*, **38** (1975): 160–171; "Artistic Expression and Creative Process in Puerto Rican Spiritist Cults," in J. Blacking (Ed.), *The Performing Arts: Music, Dance and Theater*, The Hague: Mouton, 1977.

JUNE MACKLIN is professor and chairman of the Department of Anthropology, Connecticut College (1956–present) and a visiting associate professor in the Department of Psychiatry, New Jersey Medical School, College of Medicine and Dentistry of New Jersey (1975–1976). Research interests and fieldwork experiences have been folk medicine among Mexicans and Mexican-Americans, Spiritism in Latin America, Mexican-Americans in the urban North of the United States, and Spiritualism in the United States. Publications include *Cultural Change and Structural Stability in a Mex-*

ican-American Community, New York: Arno Press, 1976; with Ward Canel, *The Human Nature Industry*, Garden City, New York: Anchor Press, 1973; "Belief, Ritual, and Healing: New England Spiritualism and Mexican-American Spiritism Compared," in I. I. Zaretsky and M. P. Leone (Eds.), *Religious Movements in Contemporary America*, Princeton: Princeton University Press, 1974; "Folk Saints, Healers, and Spiritist Cults in Northern Mexico," *Revista/Review Interamericana*, **3** (1974): 351–376; with N. R. Crumrine, "Structural Development and Conservatism in Three North Mexican Folk Saint Movements," *Comparative Studies in Society and History*, **15** (1973): 89–105; with N. R. Crumrine, "El Nino Fidencio: Un Estudio del Curanderismo en Nuevo Leon," *Anuario Humanitas 1967*, Monterrey, N.L., Mexico: Centro de Estudios Humanisticos, Universidad de Nuevo Leon, pp. 529–569.

ALICE LOUISE MORTON has worked as an anthropologist for the Social Science Research Council (1974–1975) and has taught at Cook College, Rutgers University (1973–1974), and the Bolton Institute of Technology, Bolton, Lancashire, England (1972–1973). She received a B.A. cum laude from the University of California, Los Angeles (Sociology, 1967) and a Ph.D. from the London School of Economics and University College (Anthropology, 1973). Specialties are social anthropology, ritual, human ecology, and Ethiopian studies, and she has done fieldwork in Ethiopia on the changing position of Ethiopian women and spirit possession cults. She is author of "Mystical Advocates: Explanation and Spirit-Sanctioned Adjudication in the Shoa Galla Ayana Cult," in Marcus (Ed.), *Proceedings of the First U.S. Conference on Ethiopian Studies*, East Lansing, Michigan: Committee on African Studies, Michigan State University, 1975, and has translated works by Sperber and Bastide from the French.

GANANATH OBEYESEKERE is a professor of anthropology at the University of California, San Diego (1972–present). He has also taught at the University of Sri Lanka (1958–1966 and 1968–1972) and at the University of Washington (1967–1968). He received a B.A. from the University of Sri Lanka (Literature, 1956) and M.A. and Ph.D. degrees from the University of Washington (Anthropology, 1958 and 1964). Special interests are social and psychological anthropology, sociology of Buddhism, ecstatic religion, and social theory and the ethnology of South and Southeast Asia. He has done extensive fieldwork in Sri Lanka and South India. Publications include *Land*

Tenure in Village Ceylon, Cambridge: Cambridge University Press, 1967; "Theodicy; Salvation and Rebirth in a Sociology of Buddhism," in E. R. Leach (Ed.), *Dialectic in Practical Religion,* Cambridge: Cambridge University Press, 1968; "Sinhalese-Buddhist Identity in Ceylon," in G. de Vos and L. Ross (Eds.), *Ethnic Identity: Cultural Continuities and Change,* Palo Alto, California: Mayfield, 1975; "The Impact of Ayurvedic Ideas on the Culture and the Individual in Sri Lanka," in C. Leslie (Ed.) *Asian Medical Systems,* Berkeley: University of California Press, 1976.

ESTHER PRESSEL is an associate professor of anthropology at Colorado State University (1968–present) and a postdoctoral fellow (NIMH) at Ohio State University (1975–present). She received a B.S. degree from Pennsylvania State University (Chemistry, 1959) and an M.A. (1964) and Ph.D. from Ohio State University (Anthropology, 1971). Specialties are African and Afro-Caribbean studies, psychobiological anthropology, and language and culture. Current research interests are the psychobiological aspects of altered states of consciousness. She has done fieldwork in Brazil. She is coauthor (with J. H. Henney and F. Goodman) of *Trance, Healing and Hallucination: Three Field Studies in Religious Experience,* New York: Wiley, 1974.

RAYMOND H. PRINCE, M.D., is a professor of Psychiatry at McGill University (1959–present). He has also taught and done research in Nigeria (University College, Ibadan, 1957–1959 and 1961–1963) and in Jamaica (University of the West Indies, Kingston, 1967–1969). He is author and editor of numerous papers and volumes in transcultural psychiatry and on the religious experience. The most recent and most relevant here include (as editor) *Trance and Possession States,* Montreal: R. M. Bucke Memorial Society, 1968; "Cocoon: an Interpretation of the Concern of Contemporary Youth with the Mystical," in I. I. Zaretsky and M. P. Leone (Eds.), *Religious Movements in Contemporary America,* Princeton: Princeton University Press, 1974; and "The Problem of 'Spirit Possession' as a Treatment for Psychiatric Disorders," *Ethos,* **2** (1974): 315–333.

LUCIE WOOD SAUNDERS is professor and chairman of the Department of Anthropology, Lehmann College of the City University of New York (1965–present). She also taught at Bard College (1963–1965). She received an A.B. (English) from Sweet Briar College and a

Ph.D. from Columbia University (Anthropology, 1959). Specialties are cultural anthropology and the Middle East. She has done fieldwork in Tobago and Egypt and has done interaction chronograph research in a state mental hospital. Recent publications are "Aspects of Family Organization in an Egyptian Delta Village," *Transactions of New York Academy of Sciences*, **30**, 1968: 714–721; "Um Habiba: an Egyptian Village Mother," in E. Fernea and B. Bezirgan (Eds.), *Middle Eastern Women Speak for Themselves.*

ANDRAS ZEMPLENI is currently doing fieldwork among the Senufo of the Ivory Coast (1972–1976). He received Diplômes de Psychologie Pathologique, Sociale, et Expérimentale from the University of Paris (1958–1961) and the Doctorat de Troisième Cycle (University of Paris, 1968). Specialties are ethnomedicine and social anthropology. He has also done fieldwork among the Wolof of Senegal (1962–1966) and the Moundang of Tchad (1969). He has taught at the University of Paris X, Nanterre (1968–1971). Recent publications are "Milieu Africain et Développement," in *Milieu et Développement*, Paris: Presses Universitaires de France, 1970; with A. Adler, *Le Baton de l'Aveugle, Divination, Maladie et Pouvoir Chez les Moundang du Tchad*, Paris: Itermann, 1972; "Pouvoir dans la Cure et Pouvoir Social," *Nouvelle Revue de Psychanalyse*, 1973; "De la Persécution et la Culpabilité," in *Prophétisme et Thérapeutique*, Paris: Hermann, 1975.

Foreword

With this book the anthropological study of possession states has finally come of age. As one of the authors in this volume points out, a major function of anthropological approach is to render intelligible the cultural and individual meaning of a performance. Now we have for the first time a collection of full-length studies that do just that for possession performances.

Possession studies have thus come a long way since T. K. Oesterreich published his exhaustive survey in 1921. The studies he reviewed were almost exclusively descriptive. Observers were dazzled by the flamboyance and bizarreness of the performances. Although Oesterreich devoted over a hundred pages to examples of voluntary possession in which individuals *seek* possession, he was at a loss to give any satisfactory explanation of why such a state would be desirable! It was not until the 1940s that anthropologists such as Ashton (1943) and Kuper (1947) began to discuss the idea that ritualized possession states were about the only way in which women in many cultures could escape from impossible home situations or achieve social prestige. The authors of the 1950s, such as Leiris (1958), Mischel and Mischel (1958), and Messing (1958), began to see other positive features such as the cathartic effects of acting out otherwise forbidden behavior and the supportive value of membership in the cult group. But these early studies and the spate of others that soon followed restricted their analyses to the social and cultural level, with very little reference to individuals. When case histories were provided (Kennedy, 1967; Jilek and Todd, 1974), they were very brief and were used largely to exemplify the kinds of illnesses or other problems dealt with. The present work's presentation of detailed case histories demonstrates that possession states are intelligible at the level of the individual, both as a response to adult life situations and, in some cases, as a consequence of childhood relationships and experiences.

In many ways these individual case histories strengthen and add flesh to the bare bones of earlier studies. It is remarkable, for example, how this present series supports the earlier insights concerning prestige roles for women. Twelve of the fifteen cases presented involve women, and the theme of female powerlessness, as well as the manner in which possession phenomena permit both temporary and long-term increases in women's power and control, is conspicuous in most of the histories. It is probably no accident that this current wave of interest in possession phenomena coincides with the current wave of feminism in the Western world, and that the field has been especially interesting to women anthropologists, as the list of references in this volume will confirm.

These intensive studies lend support also to the findings of the extensive statistical analyses of the Ohio State University group. From their study of some 480 cultures, they concluded that possession trance was much more likely to be found in complex and hierarchical cultures, and among these, cultures with excessively rigid roles were particularly likely to favor possession trances (Bourguignon, 1973). It is interesting that all the cases presented here involve members of such cultures; and several, such as the example from Sri Lanka (Obeyesekere) and the case of Dawit (Morton), provide beautiful illustrations of how possession permits a degree of elbow room for those encased in cultural straitjackets.

These studies have particular relevance for the psychological understanding of possession states. Many early observers, particularly those with a medical or psychiatric background, but also some anthropologists (Linton, 1958), saw nothing but psychopathology in these states. Why was this so? The psychopathological label makes sense in the context of nineteenth century psychology. When medical men observed dissociation in Western individuals, it was almost always in circumstances in which it was used as a mental mechanism to avoid a personal problem of some sort. There was often the suspicion of conscious intention, or malingering. It most often appeared in so-called hysterical patients (hysteria was thought by many to be linked with the uterus in some way and therefore only occurring in women!). But many prominent psychologists, including Charcot (1825–1893) and Janet (1859–1947), regarded it not as a mental mechanism, but as a weakness in the integrating power of the nervous system; dissociation resulted from insufficient mental energy to hold the person together. Dissociation therefore was seen as either faking or as a pathological manifestation in itself, and it was natural that when dissociation was seen in ritualized forms among non-Western peoples it was regarded in the same light.

Today the accusation of faking is still sometimes heard, but most psychologists who take the trouble to examine the cross-cultural literature must conclude that dissociation is real and that it can be a healthy mental function. That fact that large proportions of many populations are able to dissociate in itself suggests this view (Lee, 1968; Belo, 1960). It is true, of course, that dissociation can be put to self-defeating ends, but then so can sleeping and eating! Do these case studies support the dissociation-can-be-healthy point of view? For the most part they do. It is true that Mohammed (Crapanzano) and Dawit (Morton) do not seem particularly competent individuals. But most of the others are as competent and self-actualized as their peers. Some, like Mama Azaletch (Morton) and Rita (Macklin), seem to be of superior competence.

But for me the most interesting aspect of this volume is the light it sheds on the therapeutic value of these performances for individuals with frank psychiatric disorders. It has commonly been held that ritualized possession is of therapeutic value largely because it provides periodic release from tension by catharsis of dammed-up and socially unacceptable impulses. Using this cathartic model, it is seen that Mohammed (Crapanzano) can maintain his mental stability by periodically removing the charge from his masochistic urges by slashing at his head during *Hamadsha* performances. Most psychoanalysts, of course, would hold that this procedure is inferior to analysis because the subject must repeatedly undergo this catharsis; the masochistic impulses have not been analyzed to their childhood roots and therefore cannot be permanently laid aside. This is characteristic of religious ritual in general when it functions as psychotherapy; religious ritual is periodic and cyclical.

But this catharsis interpretation does not do full justice to the diversity and complexity of the phenomenon. For example, it is not helpful in interpreting the therapeutic effects in the many cultures where it is the healer and not the patient who becomes dissociated. This situation also presents difficulties for those who, like Sargant (1957), hold that the therapeutic effect of trance lies in its wiping the mental slate clean and in increasing the patient's suggestibility. Again, in these circumstances it is the healer and not the patient who would be subject to the brainwashing, which doesn't seem right! One common explanation is that when the healer becomes the mouthpiece of the gods or spirits, his suggestions gain enormously in power. He then has greater ability to command away the patient's symptoms by suggestion. Several case studies in this volume suggest, however, that there may be other therapeutic factors at work, some of them closely akin to those of modern psychotherapy.

Garrison provides us with an explicit comparison of the diagnostic and treatment procedures of *Espiritistas* in New York and of a psychiatrist working with the same patient. Her conclusion is that the approach of the *Espiritistas* and of psychotherapy are identical, or nearly so. This is an interesting but, in my view, a highly debatable claim.

We can perhaps usefully divide the problem into two parts. The first has to do with the theoretical aspects of why people behave as they do; the other, the practical aspect of the treatment or correction of deviant behavior or disproportionate distress. Strupp (1973) has recently made this important distinction for psychotherapy. He feels that psychoanalysis has made a major contribution to our understanding of human development and the intelligibility of the whole spectrum of neurotic and psychotic disturbances; but he believes that psychoanalysis as a mode of treatment leaves much to be desired. According to Strupp, Freud made the grave error of believing that the patient's understanding of the causes of his neurosis would automatically result in its cure. On the contrary, Strupp feels that when psychoanalysis does result in therapeutic effects, it is due to other factors, such as shaping, suggestion, and coercion on the basis of a powerful personal relationship.

Garrison argues that there is considerable similarity between the treatment systems of mediums and psychotherapists on both the theoretical and the practical levels. For her, the psychotherapists' superego is equivalent to the *Espiritistas'* protective spirit who rewards and punishes and guides; the ego is the "individual spirit"; the id is equivalent to the base or ignorant spirits. The only major difference, she feels, is that for the *Espiritistas* the good and bad points exist outside the individual's skin, while for the psychoanalyst all three components, ego, superego, and id, are within the individual. Other anthropologists have tried to make similar kinds of comparisons to show that psychoanalysis has discovered nothing new. Wallace (1958), for example, drew attention to the similarity between the Iroquois' dream theory and that of Freud. For both, dreams represented wishes of the soul, and in both views illness ensued if the wishes were not gratified or come to terms with. Horton (1961) pointed out the similarities between the psychoanalytic view of the unconscious and the beliefs held by many West African groups in the contract between the self and his heavenly double. Presumably one could take many other cosmologies and draw more or less valid parallels with psychoanalytic formulations about the self and the origins of conflict. For me, the important and distinguishing aspect of the psychoanalytic formulation is that the unconscious aspects are regarded as the results of the individual's early family relationships. No other system that I know of understands the importance of childhood experiences in the genesis of adult behavior and illness. For me, such differences are of the order of the difference between alchemy and chemistry, or between astrology and astronomy, or something like the difference between a belief in clairvoyance and the invention of television!

What about treatment methods? Here again Garrison emphasizes the similarities between the two systems. She makes us aware of the considerable degree of psychological awareness in the *Espiritistas'* management of the case of Maria. This is true. When Maria came to the medium and to the psychiatrist, she denied any problems in her relationship with her husband. Then the spirit, speaking through a medium, told her that she hated her husband, and she was led to admit that this was correct and that indeed she had had fantasies of cutting his head open with a meat cleaver! She was also brought by the mediums to admit to her difficulties with men in general and to face up to the fact that her husband had a severe physical illness. From what we know of other non-Western healing approaches, there is much more psychological mindedness in the *Espiritistas'* approach than in most others (Prince, 1964). This is perhaps related to the location of the *Espiritistas* in the middle of New York City, where the surrounding culture includes strong awareness of the psychogenesis of psychiatric problems. For me, however, the more interesting and important point in the comparison lies in a difference between the two systems: the rapid shift of the *Espiritistas* into a social relationship with their patients. For orthodox analysts this socializing would be thought undesirable in that it would obfuscate transference relationships. In the *Espiritista* system this back and forth shift between the authoritarian ritual relationship and the egalitarian social relationship has significant therapeutic implications. An important function of this spirit display technique, as illustrated in a number of these case studies, may well be this forcing of the client into the realm of personal relationships; a forcing through the patient's massive denials and mistrusts. Subsequently, the subject having once been broached on the authority of the spirit, the healer can take up the question and discuss it frankly with the patient during the informal social relationship.

To conclude, it seems to me that the theoretical formulations of the spirit systems discussed in this book are significantly different, and that they have less truth value than Western psychoanalytically oriented theories. On the other hand, as regards therapy, I believe many of these case histories reinforce the view that possession states and other non-Western healing techniques are very worthwhile approaches to treating troubled people. The insights drawn from these case histories represent an important advance in our understanding of why this should be so.

RAYMOND PRINCE, M.D.

Mental Hygiene Institute
Montreal, Canada
September 1976

Acknowledgments

The editors of this volume would like to thank all the contributors for their cooperation in preparing these case histories. We would also like to thank Jane Kramer and Conrad Arensberg for their editorial comments and assistance, and Doris Maria Rivera and Dorothy A. Reisman for typing and editing various sections of the manuscript.

VINCENT CRAPANZANO
VIVIAN GARRISON

New York, New York
September 1976

Contents

Case Studies in Spirit Possession

Vincent Crapanzano

Introduction

For ages the army of spirits, once so near, has been receding farther and farther from us, banished by the magic wand of science from hearth and home, from ruined cell and ivied tower, from haunted glade and lonely mere, from the riven murky cloud that belches forth lightening, and from the fairer clouds that pillow the silvery moon or fret with flakes of burning red the golden eve. . . .

James Frazer, *The Golden Bough* (1958, p. 633)

In the left foreground of Peter Paul Rubens' *The Miracle of Saint Ignatius of Loyola,* originally commissioned—and completed—around 1618 for the Jesuit Church in Antwerp and now hanging in the Kunsthistorisches Museum in Vienna, a nearly naked man lies contorted on his back, well below the maudlin, passive figure of the saint who stands before an altar with his right hand lifted in a gesture of blessing. The man is in a state of catalepsy. His limbs, even his toes, are rigidly ex-

1

tended; his muscles are bulging and taut; his right hand clenches the cord which bound him and from which he has convulsively broken loose. His head hangs back, supported by a naked youth. His face is grotesque: mouth open and frothing, lips blue, forehead deeply furrowed with veins protruding. His pupils have rolled back, revealing the whites of eyes which seem to stare out emptily at the viewer. The man is possessed.

Above him a woman, typical of Rubens' large, fleshy women, has fallen back in a epileptoid seizure into the arms of three spectators who attempt to constrain her. Her neck is hideously swollen. Indeed, as Charcot and Richer (1887) have observed in their *Démoniaques dans l'Art*, "il a fallu de la part de ce maître un grand respect de la vérité pour n'en rien atténuer, et pour consentir à cette hideuse déformation des lignes du cou." The woman's mouth is open; her tongue protrudes; her nostrils are dilated; her pupils are hidden under her upper eyelids. She pulls violently at her hair with her right hand, and tears her dress open with her left. She too is possessed.

Despite the painter's intention of cataloguing at least some of the miracles of the saint, as told in Ribadineira's *Life of Saint Ignatius* (Smith, 1969), the figures of the possessed are the dramatic center of the painting. The saint himself looks up toward heaven. To his right stand nine Jesuits, presumably those who went to Rome with him in 1538 to obtain permission to found their order; the first is Saint Francis Xavier. With two exceptions, the Jesuits' gaze is drawn down magnetically to the possessed. Saint Francis alone maintains an expression of resigned beatitude. The others are struck with awe and fear, with fascination. The crowd surrounding the possessed look either to the saint for a miracle or stare with the same frightened fascination at the possessed. Only the figures in the right foreground—two mothers bearing children to the saint, and the man from Barcelona whom Saint Ignatius forced to confess before he hung himself—appear unmoved by the spectacle of possession. They are lost in their own miracles.

Rubens has captured the dramatic power of the possessed. The exorcist himself and, for that matter, the demons who fly off through the sunlit nave of the cathedral, are of lesser importance in his painting. He has also captured—and this is most important for our purposes—the fascination which has characterized the Westerner's response to the spectacle of spirit possession. This fascination is compounded of the attractive and the awesome, the familiar and the unfamiliar, the pleasing and the fearsome. It corresponds to the Greek *deinos* which, according to Rudolph Otto, may mean "evil or imposing, potent and strange, queer and marvelous, horrifying and fascinating, divine and demonic, and a source of 'energy' " (Otto, 1950, p. 39). It is the experience of the uncanny—"that class of the terrifying", as Freud (1963b, p. 20) has described it, "which leads back to something long known to us, once very familiar." It is also the experience, *angstvoll* to be sure, of our own possibility, our desire perhaps for extinction within the other. Freud (1963b, p. 49) observed that in epilepsy and madness, ascribed in the Middle Ages to demonic influence, the ordinary person sees "the workings of forces hitherto unsuspected in his fellow-men but which at the same time he is dimly aware of in a remote corner of his own being."

Euripides, in *The Bacchae*, has given us perhaps the first, certainly the most complete, recorded description of this fascination with the possessed (Euripides, 1958). (It should be recalled that in the apocryphal *Book of Tobit* Tobias fell in love with Sarah and "yearned deeply for her" without ever having seen her, when he learned that he himself would not succumb to the demon who had killed her previous seven husbands on their wedding night.) Pentheus, King of Thebes, at first denies any other interest in the Baccantes than one which is politically necessitated: he must be rid of the stranger who has wrought orgiastic frenzy on the women of his city. All too strenuously, Pentheus refuses the Bacchantes the validity of their experience. "Priestesses of Bacchus they claim they are, but it's really Aphrodite they adore" (ll. 224–225).[1] He derides the blind seer Teiresias and his own grandfather Cadmos, who had bequeathed the kingdom to Pentheus, for going to join the Bacchic rites: "Go worship your Bacchus, but do not wipe your madness off on me" (ll. 343–344). Yet he listens to the report of his messenger, who saw the rites on Mount Kithaeron:

> First they let their hair fall loose, down
> over their shoulders, and those whose straps had slipped
> fastened their skins of fawn with writhing snakes
> that licked their cheeks. Breasts swollen with milk,
> new mothers who had left their babies behind at home
> nestled gazelles and young wolves in their arms,
> suckling them (ll. 695–701).

They performed miracles; they resisted attack and capture.

> Unarmed, they swooped down upon the herds of cattle
> grazing there on the green of the meadow. And then
> you could have seen a single woman with bare hands
> tear a fat calf, still bellowing with fright,
> in two, while others clawed the heifers to pieces . . .
> And bulls, their raging fury gathered in their horns,

> lowered their heads to charge, then fell, stumbling
> to the earth, pulled down by hordes of women
> and stripped of flesh and skin more quickly, sire,
> than you could blink your royal eyes (ll. 735–747).

They rushed to the valley:

> They snatched the children from their homes. And when
> they piled their plunder on their backs, it stayed in place,
> untied. Nothing, neither bronze nor iron,
> fell to the dark earth. Flames flickered
> in their curls and did not burn them (ll. 734–758).

They were immune, too, to the spears and swords of the angered villagers whose lands they had razed. The messenger affirms his belief in the god Dionysus. Pentheus orders his men to attack. Yet, finally, the hand of the stranger Dionysus releases Pentheus' fascination with obsessive furor. It will be his end.

> Pentheus if you are still so curious to see
> forbidden sights, so bent on evil still,
> come out (ll. 812–814).

He now would pay a great sum to behold the Bacchantes. Even the cynical Dionysus can only question: "Why are you so passionately curious?" (ll. 813). "Of course," answers Pentheus in one of the most psychologically revealing lines of the tragedy, "I'd be sorry to see them drunk—" (ll. 814). He admits then to Dionysus' suggestion that he craves sugh a sight: "I could crouch beneath the fir trees, out of sight" (ll. 814). He craves, too, the sensual pleasure of the spectacle, even the flight into frenzy. Indeed, Bernfeld (1928) has observed in his psychoanalytic study of fascination that a primitive attempt at mastery of intense stimuli consists in the primitive ego's imitating that which is perceived; perceiving and changing one's body according to what is perceived were apparently originally one and the same thing!

However we understand this fascination with the spirit possession, as a revival of repressed infantile complexes or a reconfirmation of primitive beliefs once surmounted (the two sources of the uncanny, according to Freud), or as the allure of Evil or even the temptation of Satan (for so the fascination has been interpreted in Western theological thought), the spectacle of spirit possession has driven Western man to produce the most lurid descriptions of possession as well as the most abstract, objectivistic, indeed rarefied, analyses of the condition. "The majority of anthropological writers on possession," I. M. Lewis (1971, p. 26) has observed, "have been equally fascinated by its richly dramatic elements, enthralled—one might almost say—by the more bizarre and exotic shamanistic exercises, and absorbed in often quite pointless debates as to the genuineness or otherwise of a particular trance state." Both the luridly descriptive and the objectivistic texts—they are polar types, heuristically employed here—must be regarded as products, defensive perhaps, of the fascination that is felt before the possessed. They serve both to (re-)create the experience the author wishes to convey and to separate him from it; simultaneously they serve an evocative and exorcistic function. They are not, however, lone incantations; they speak within a tradition and are constrained by it. They are also constrained by the "real"—inevitably, if paradoxically, interpreted through the traditional idiom. The breaking out of this closure—the hermeneutical circle, as it has been called in the literature of interpretation—is perhaps the single most romantic, irrealistic quest of the anthropologist, bringing with it the threat of madness and chaos, or, to speak in the less mythic and more anodyne idiom of anthropology itself, the threat of cultural disorientation and unanchored relativism. The response to the threat is, of course, a conservative retrenchment within the language of tradition.

One need only compare Edward Tylor's description of the possessed, essentially an imaginative construct which nevertheless served as a type-construct for generations of anthropologists and students of religion, with, say Cyril of Jerusalem, a fourth century Christian author, to appreciate the extent to which the traditional Western idiom of possession has affected the presentation of possession, its distinguishing features, and hence its classification.

Cyril: the unclean devil, when he comes upon the soul of man . . . comes like a wolf upon a sheep, ravening for blood and ready to devour. His presence is most cruel; the sense of it most oppressive; the mind is darkened; his attack is an injustice also, and usurpation of another's possession. For he tyranically uses another's body, another's instruments, as his own property; he throws down him who stands upright (for he is akin to him who *fell from heaven*); he perverts the tongue and distorts his lips. Foam comes instead of words; the man is filled with darkness; his eye is open yet his soul sees not through it; and the miserable man quivers convulsively before his death. (Oesterreich, 1966, p. 7)

Tylor: The possessed man, tossed and shaken in fever, pained and wrenched as though some live creature were tearing or twisting him within, pining as though it were devouring his vitals day by day, rationally finds a personal spiritual cause for his sufferings. In hideous dreams he may even sometimes see the very ghost or nightmare-fiend that plagues him. Especially when the mysterious unseen power throws him helpless on the ground, jerks and writhes him in convulsions, makes him leap upon bystanders with a giant's strength and a wild beast's ferocity, impels him, with distorted face and frantic gesture, and voice not his own nor seemingly even human, to pour forth wild incoherent raving, or with thought and eloquence beyond his sober faculties to command, to counsel, to foretell—such a one seems to those who watch him, and even to himself, to have become the mere instrument of a spirit which has seized him or entered into him, a possessing demon in whose personality the patient believes so implicitly that he often imagines a personal name for it, which it can declare when it speaks in its own voice and character through his organs of speech; at last, quitting the medium's spent and jaded body, the intruding spirit departs as it came (Tylor, 1958, p. 210).[2]

More recent accounts than Tylor's 1871 presentation could be given to demonstrate the continued use of the traditional ethico-religious idiom in describing the possessed in purportedly scientific studies. Aidan Southall, for example, describes a possessed woman in the following words:

One woman began to be very violently taken, jumping about the floor on her knees and approaching the fire, her whole torso shaking, her shoulders flexed forward and shuddering, her head lolling madly round and round and side to side as if head and neck were a ball on a piece of string. As her knees were on the edge of the red-hot embers and her head practically knocking into them, another woman fended her off from them. Then the other who had been shaking on her knees seemed suddenly and forcefully propelled from inside and in a moment the two possessed women were in a fierce grapple with their arms, as if wrestling, while still on their knees. Both would again have been in the fire but for the other woman fending them off. Others shouted at them "You have killed one enough!" . . . and they seemed to recover their normal senses enough to stand up and violently abuse one another: "You are a Lendu! Shit! Arsehole!" and so on. The "dancing" continued. The same one again became violently possessed, jumping round on her knees, and then it was as if some sudden inner force propelled her straight through the door outside, threw her on the ground full length and rolled her over and over on the bare earth of the compound, up the slope to the edge of the grass. There she lay still, then walked quivering back to the hut and stood inside the door quivering uncontrollably from head to foot. . . . (Southall, 1969, p. 234).[3]

Southall's description of the séance continues for several more pages. Admittedly, the external demon, accepted as real and evil by Cyril, acknowledged as an interpretive strategy by Tylor, is replaced here by a "psychologically more satisfying" simile: "as if some sudden inner force propelled her. . . ." The description, if for no other reason than the use of quotation marks around "dancing", is ethically charged, judgmental.

This is not to fault Southall—I too have made a choice here and elsewhere in my selection of quotations—but to call attention to those idiomatic presuppositions that influence the texts, descriptive or theoretical, we produce and from which we draw conclusions. Concern with the moral qualities of the possessing demon (Jeanmaire, 1951), with voluntary versus involuntary possession (Osterreich, 1966; Lewis, 1971; Pressel, 1974; *et al.*), with glossolalia, or speaking in tongues (Goodman, 1972), with orderly versus disorderly, learned versus unlearned (Sargant, 1964; 1974), somnambulistic versus frenetic possession (Belo, 1960), with possession versus mediumship or prophecy (Firth, 1967),—these concerns, however significant they may be in any given possession context, all have deep roots within the Western tradition. Such traditional concerns and stylistic maneuvers can be illuminating, but they can also produce a kind of blindness.

Spirit possession, in one form or another, is reported throughout the world. Bourgignon (1973) has found that in a sample of 488 societies in all parts of the world, 437 (90%) are reported to have one or more institutionalized, culturally patterned forms of altered states of consciousness; 251 (52%) of these societies associate such experiences with spirit possession. It is likely that in those societies where spirit possession is not reported in the ethnographic literature, possession, were it explained, would immediately be understood. Even in the Western world where, except in certain fringe religions and esoteric cults, possession no longer "occurs," it serves nevertheless as a very powerful metaphor for the articulation of that range of experience in which the subject feels "beside himself," not fully responsible for his own condition, as in extreme love, intense hatred, tantrums, furor, excessive courage, compulsive ideation, the *idée fixe*, obsessional acting out, and, of course, fascination itself. Indeed, particularly in those states in which the individual feels great remorse—guilt—for an act he has committed, there is on occasion a longing for an authentic, believable, idiom of possession; to the Westerner "liberated" from its constraints, spirit possession may symbolize a magical route of escape from the burden of responsibility accompanying an ideology of intense individualism that is contradicted daily in the "real" world.

Granting this metaphorical extension, spirit possession may be defined for our purposes as *any altered state of consciousness indigenously interpreted in terms of the influence of an alien spirit.* Although it is conceptually necessary, as Wallace (1959) and Bourgignon (1970; 1973) have stressed, to distinguish between the psychobiological conditions of the possessed and the (cultural) interpretation of the state of possession, it is important to recognize that the interpretation affects the structuring and evaluating of the psychobiological state itself.

An altered state of consciousness is understood here in Ludwig's terms as

those mental states, induced by various physiological, psychological, or pharmacological manoeuvres or agents, which can be recognized subjectively by the individual himself (or by the objective observer of the individual) as representing a sufficient deviation, in terms of subjective experience or psychological functioning, from certain general norms as determined by the subjective experience and psychological functioning of that individual during alert, waking consciousness (Ludwig, 1968; 1969).

Characteristics of such altered states of consciousness, listed by Ludwig, include alterations in thinking such as disturbances in concentration, attention, memory, and judgment as well as an impairment in reality testing and a marked tendency toward archaic modes of thought, a disturbed time sense, loss of control, changes in emotional expression (ecstatic and orgiastic feelings, detachment, etc.), changes in body image, perceptual distortions, changes in meaning or significance such as an increased evaluation of subjective experiences, ideas, and perceptions, a sense of the ineffable, feelings of rejuvenation, and hypersuggestibility.

The altered state of consciousness most frequently associated with possession is "trance," defined by the *Penguin Dictionary of Psychology* as "a condition of dissociation, characterized by the lack of voluntary movement and frequently by automatisms in act and thought, illustrated by hypnotic and mediumistic conditions" (as quoted in Lewis, 1971, p. 38). M.J. Field writes, referring principally to Ghana:

The possessed person is in a state of dissociated personality whereby a split-off part of the mind possesses the whole field of consciousness, the rest being in complete abeyance. Splitting of the stream of consciousness into parallel streams is familiar to anyone who can "do two things at once" such as playing the piano and simultaneously planning a summer holiday. . . . It is the total banishment of all but one stream which is the essential feature of dissociation (Field, 1969, p. 3).

Field's contention that the essential feature of dissociation is "the total banishment of all but one stream" of consciousness remains questionable. The underlying reality described by possession is, as Jaspers

(1959, p. 615) notes, manifold. It includes, but is certainly not limited to, such experiences as the *Verdoppelungserlebnis*—the doubling of the ego consciousness—which seems to characterize what Oesterreich (1966) calls the "lucid form of possession." In such possession states the possessed does not lose consciousness of his usual personality. He "is the passive spectator of what takes place within him," and is quite capable of remembering the "terrible spectacle" (Oesterreich, 1966, p. 40).

It should be added that the term dissociation, so frequently used to describe trance and possession trance more generally, has, according to Partridge (1958), its etymological root in the Latin *socius*, companion or associate, which is probably akin to the Sanskrit *sakka*, a companion, and from which are derived the English *social*, *society*, and so on. *Dissociare* in Latin means to disjoin oneself from. Dissociation, then, has at least etymological connotations of a removal, a disjoining from the social, from—possibly—the socially constructed world of everyday life. Certainly most trance states are associated with a removal from the normal cues and rules of sociability; the trancer is lost from his socially constructed self.

The interpretation of such altered states of consciousness in terms of spirit influence is, of course, a cultural construct which varies with the particular belief system prevalent in the culture. The definition of spirit possession offered included not only cases in which the spirit was believed to take possession, to inhabit, a human subject, or "mount," but also those cases in which the subject was believed to be attacked by, married to, or in some way influenced by the spirit to produce the alteration of consciousness. The definition includes, to use the idiom of Catholic theology, both states of possession and obsession. It also includes those states, heuristically distinguished by Raymond Firth (1967, p. 296) as "spirit possession," "spirit mediumship," and "shamanism." By spirit possession, Firth understands "phenomena of abnormal behavior which are interpreted by other members of the society as evidence that a spirit is controlling the person's actions and probably inhabiting his body." Spirit mediumship refers to "the use of such behavior by members of the society as a means of communication with what they understand to be entities in the spirit world." "To be capable of such use," Firth adds, "the behavior of the person possessed by the spirit must be intelligible or able to be interpreted; this implies that it must follow some fairly regular, predictable pattern, usually of speech." Shamanism "applied to those phenomena where a person, either a spirit medium or not, is regarded as controlling spirits, exercising his mastery over them in socially recognized ways." Such a system of classification, however useful it may be for some analyses, imposes on the reality of spirit possession, as both editors of this volume have observed it, a conceptual rigidity that distorts the essential fluidity of interpretation and consequent (verbal and behavioral) articulation of the phenomena. Often the human victim of the spirit moves—if not in one séance, then throughout the course of his relationship with the spirit—in and out of all three states. Nonmediumistic trances, after the initial onset, are usually as regular and predictable as mediumistic ones. Emphasis on control may well be more important to the Western observer than to the native, who may find the question of control meaningless!

Too rigid a definition also precludes the recognition of spirit possession as a powerful—authentic and believable—metaphor for the description of other conditions not usually associated by the Western observer with altered states of consciousness, especially not with trance. Possession metaphors were used (not in an unfamiliar manner) in Morocco, for example, for extreme rage, sexual excitement, love, prolonged erections, morbid depressions, and on occasion for those conditions that Jean-Paul Sartre would call bad faith, in which the subject did not want to accept the consequences of his or her own desires. The "extensions" of possession are too intimately connected with the possession syndrome to be ignored, especially in considering the role possession plays for the individual. As we suggest further on, the dynamics of spirit possession, in the restricted sense, may be regarded as the metonymization of a metaphorical relationship, to the limit of identity.

Spirit possession is an unquestioned given in the world in which the individual believer finds himself. It provides him with an idiom for articulating a certain range of experience (Firth, 1967; Obeyesekere, 1970). By articulation, I mean the act of construing, or better still constructing, an event to render it meaningful. The act of articulation is more than a passive representation of the event; it is in essence the creation of the event. It separates the event from the flow of experience, from what Alfred North Whitehead saw as "merely the hurrying of material, endlessly, meaninglessly." It gives the event structure, thus precipitating its context, relates it to other similarly constructed events, and evaluates the event along both idiosyncratic and (culturally) standardized lines. Once the experience is articulated, once it is rendered an event, it is cast within the world of meaning and may then provide a basis for action.

The act of articulation requires a vehicle for articulation, an idiom, which must be distinguished from a medium of articulation such as spoken language, gesture, a behavioral sequence as in ritual, theater, or the serving of dinner, or some endopsychic process. Although the idiom is probably structured as language, it is more than language insofar as the term is used daily in its restricted sense and in linguistics. It is perhaps more closely related to *Sprache* as it was used by Herder, von Humboldt, and other nineteenth and twentieth century German philologists and field theorists (Schaff, 1973) and to *discours* as it is used by such structuralists as Henri Lefebvre (1971). Within the idiom are embedded traditional values, interpretational vectors, patterns of association, ontological presuppositions, spatiotemporal orientations, and etymological horizons. The idiom itself is composed of elements—*cultural units* in David Schneider's (1968) usage—that are interrelated in a systemic manner and obtain their meaning through this interrelationship much as the minimal units of meaning in language obtain their meaning through their relations of similarity and opposition to other minimal units. The idiom is not, however, *culture* as it is commonly used by anthropologists. Rather it provides the basis for those schemata by which reality is interpreted. Such schemata, which can probably be reduced to a series of propositions about reality, form the basis for what the anthropologist calls culture and, within a more restricted domain, the psychologist calls personality (Crapanzano, 1975).

The possessing spirits are principal elements within the idiom of spirit possession. They are, as was mentioned earlier, givens within the world of the believer and subject to an often complex logic or grammar. Whatever their ontological status, their existence is no more questioned than is the existence of their human (and occasionally animal) carriers. Actually, the human and animal carriers are, within the idiom, equally principal elements—a point frequently ignored by Western scholars who despite even a sensitivity to cultural difference are seldom able to extend this sensitivity to the most basic ontological assumptions of their taken-for-granted world. To render a complete picture of the spirit possession idiom, it would be necessary to include not only a description of the spirits, their associations, and interrelationships, but also a description from within the idiom of their carriers, and *their* associations and relationships. In other words, it would be necessary to render explicit the demonology and anthropology of the system.

The important point for our purposes is the consensually validated, and often ritually confirmed, belief in the existence, the facticity, of the spirits. The implications of this status must be fully grasped if we are to understand the articulatory function of spirits and spirit possession in its own terms, and to resist the reduction and consequent distortion of the spirit idiom into a second idiom, the "psychological" idiom, in which we in the modern Western world feel more comfortable. The spirit idiom (I should really say spirit idiomata, for there are undoubtedly significant variations in the idiom throughout the world) provides a means of "self-articulation" that may well be radically different from the self-articulation of the Westerner (Lienhardt, 1961). Much of what is articulated in the West as within the individual may be articulated as outside the individual in those societies in which the spirit idiom is current (Pouillon, 1972; Garrison, Chapter 10). It is well to remember Lichtenberg's observation (quoted in Béguin, 1946): "As we do not know exactly the location of our thought, we can place it where we want."

The spirits as consensually validated and ritually confirmed existents exterior to the individual are not projections in the traditional psychoanalytic sense of the word, as many psychoanalysts have asserted (Freud, 1963a; Mars, 1946). For the psychoanalyst, projection "appears always as a defence, as the attribution to the other—person or thing— of qualities, feelings, or desires that the subject refuses or fails to recognize (*méconnait*) in himself" (Laplanche and Pontalis, 1973, p. 347). Thus there can be projection only where there has been introjection. If the spirits *qua* exterior existents serve as a means for the articulation of what the Westerner would regard as within him as outside him, then strictly speaking there can be no projection of what was within outside, for there was no within to begin with!

Such a radical view is obviously intolerable to the modern Western sensibility, yet this view has suggested itself to many anthropologists and other Westerners who have worked with the spirit possessed. We must distinguish carefully here between the phenomenology of experience, including the experience of the self, and the articulation of experience, including the articulation of the self. The effect of the latter upon the former must always remain hypothetical. The difficulty of keeping the phenomenology separate from the articulation results from the necessity of suspending disbelief in our everyday encounters with others in our world. We assume that what the other articulates is what the other experiences or, for some reason, is hiding from us or even masking from himself. The confusion of these two domains can be found in the psychoanalytic tradition itself and may in fact account for the acceptance of such explanatory constructs as the unconscious as real.

Projection and articulation by means of spirits are both essentially metaphorical processes (Wagner, 1972). In projection, the other is the vehicle for the qualities, feelings, and desires—the tenor of the metaphor, in I. A. Richards' terms (1936)—that are within the self. The movement is essentially centrifugal, from inner to outer. In articulation through spirits, the spirit too is the vehicle for such qualities, feelings, and desires, or at least their motivation, but here the tenor is located outside the individual from the start. In spirit possession itself, the movement is the very opposite of projection. It is centripetal, from outer to inner, literally but not psychoanalytically speaking, introjective.

Of utmost significance in both metaphorical acts is the status accorded the vehicle within the idiomatically structured and evaluated universe of the individual. A Western paranoid, for example, who believes himself pursued by secret agents makes as much use of the idiom at his disposal as does a Wolof tribesman of Senegal who believes himself hounded by a particular ancestral spirit. Both articulate feelings of persecution within their idiom and suffer, so to speak, the consequences of that idiom. In the one instance, to cite the most striking difference of consequence, the secret agents are not generally recognized as existing in the particular context by anyone other than the paranoid and those about him whom he has conned into accepting his persecutory beliefs. In the second instance, the ancestral spirits are generally recognized to exist and to hound their progeny in almost any context. This difference may well be immense in its consequences. Where the persecutory order (to use Marie-Cécile and Edmond Ortigues' [1966] expression) is collective, the relationship between the persecuted individual and others within his world is different from where the persecution is considered idiosyncratic and fantastical. In the first instance, the individual may not suffer the same social isolation, loneliness, feelings of abandonment and desertion as in the second (Silverman, 1967). By affording a substitution of a "culturally constituted fantasy" for an "idiosyncratic pathological one," the possession idiom, as Obeyesekere (1970) has suggested, may well minimize, in extreme cases, the possibility of a "psychotic loss of contact with the outside world" and ego-disintegration. The "persecuted" individual may be plunged into an idiomatic system that involves the possibility, even the inevitability of therapeutic intervention. Indeed, his initial persecution is transformed into an initiation into a (new) symbolic order. He learns to speak the language of spirit possession; he submits himself to its pertaining logic.

I do not mean to suggest here that the idiom of spirit possession is more conducive to cure than is the "psychological" idiom of the modern Western world. Both have their successes and failures, however "cure" is defined. Nor do I mean to suggest that spirit possession is a form of paranoia or of any other mental disorder. In my experience—and as should be evident from the contributions to this volume—the spirit possessed are not reducible to any single psychiatric diagnosis even within a single culture (see Messing, 1959, for example). The idiom may be used in a multitude of situations—the exact parameters of which must be determined both within a single culture and cross-culturally—by individuals of various personality types with differing levels of ego integration and adaptive responses to their environment. In some instances, spirit possession may be seen as a sign of evident pathology by the Western investigator; in others, as in the case of Dawia, for example, in my own contribution to this anthology, as a successful adaptive response by a relatively well-integrated personality to a particular (stressful) situation. To emphasize "pathology," "mental disorder," "psychosis," and "neurosis" in cases of spirit possession, as Devereux (1956) and Silverman (1967) have done, is to raise what is essentially a misleading, though culturally expectable, response to an "uncanny" encounter. However "ego-syntonic" they may be to the investigator, such diagnoses may well blind us to the dynamics of spirit possession. The question that must be asked is this: What, besides a protective shield, do we gain from calling a shaman a schizophrenic (Silverman, 1967), an individual possessed by a spirit a paranoid (Ortigues, 1966), a neurotic (Freud, 1963a; Wallace, 1966), or an hysteric (Freed, 1964)?

The initial "persecution," or initiation into the spirit idiom, may be conceived of as an articulatory act. (It is a thrust into the symbolic order much as the infant's first words are a thrust into language.) This initiation frequently takes the shape of a dramatic illness—paralysis, mutism, sudden blindness, or such contrary behavior as nursing the feet of a newborn infant. It should be remembered that even in the case of such dramatic illnesses the diagnosis of possession—and possession symptoms—is not necessarily immediate (Young, 1975). A diagnosis of spirit possession and the consequent structuralization of the ailment may be but one option within the "medical" system of a particular society. The initial thrust may be far less dramatic. The neophyte, like Habiba in Saunders' contribution to this volume, may simply have been in attendance at a possession ceremony when he was suddenly seized by a spirit. Often such "slippages" into the spirit idiom are articulated in retrospective accounts in a stereotyped manner. Many Moroccans who were possessed by a she-demon named 'A'isha Qandisha reported that their first experience of possession occurred in a ceremony during which they mocked the possessed or the she-demon herself. (Such stereotypical stories—Dawit's and Mama Azaletch's stories in Morton's contribution are excellent examples—put a stop to questioning and, much like Freud's dream symbols, to free association.) The illness itself is a most eloquent symbol, for not only does it focus attention on the possessed—Something must be done!—but it is also inchoate and requires definition. Such definition occurs through a variety of diagnostic procedures and attempts at cure.

The initiate must become situated within the new symbolic order of the spirit possession idiom just as the child must learn (as Jacques Lacan [1966] maintains) his position within the symbolic order through resolution of the Oedipal crisis. He must learn to be possessed and to appease or satisfy the possessing spirit; that is, to articulate essentially inchoate feelings, of persecution or inferiority, of fear or bravado, of hatred or love, in terms of his local idiom.

At this point a distinction must be made between those cases of spirit possession in which the aim of cure is the permanent expulsion of the possessing demon and those which aim to create a symbiotic relationship with the spirit (Jeanmaire, 1951; Crapanzano, 1973; Wallace, 1966; Messing, 1959). Jeanmaire, the French classicist, has suggested that these different aims reflect different attitudes toward the demon. Where the demon is considered as essentially evil, permanent expulsion is the aim of therapeutic intervention; where the demon is considered as essentially amoral, the aim is the creation of some sort of "working relationship" with the demon that often involves the demon's conversion from a malevolent into a benevolent spirit and his carrier's entrance into a possession cult. Such possession may even be desired. However, even in cases where the aim is the permanent expulsion of the demon, the exorcism may fail to permanently rid the human carrier of his spirit. Such recidivism is frequently reported in Western literature (Osterreich, 1966; Huxley, 1952). In his analysis of the seventeenth-century painter Christoph Haitzmann, Freud (1963a) notes (but, in my opinion, does not give due consideration to the fact) that Haitzmann ends up in a monastery where he is subject to visions if not seizures.

The learning of the language of spirit possession has both a technical and a symbolic side. Technically the spirit possessed must learn to be possessed—to enter trance, to carry out expected behavior gracefully, and to meet the demands of his spirit. In fact, almost all reports of spirit possession stress the fact that the novice is usually clumsy and must learn to be a good carrier for his spirit (Métraux, 1959). Symbolically, the spirit possessed must learn to situate himself within the idiom; that is, to structure and evaluate his experience in terms of the idiom at his disposal. Such a self-situating may proceed by trial and error, as in Zempleni's case of Khady Fall, in which the Wolof priestess learns only after a long resistance to her call her own position within the world of the *rab* spirits—a world which mirrors symbolically the lineage structure of her social world. Or it may proceed through the guidance of a curer, as in Obeyesekere's case of Somavati or Garrison's of Maria. Often the possessed is incorporated into a cult and given the possibility of becoming a curer in his or her own right (see Minfouga Nicholas,

1972; Lewis, 1971, Crapanzano, 1973; Zempleni, Morton, Obeyese-kere, Pressel, Garrison, this volume). The movement from initial illness to final incorporation within a cult is often accompanied by an indeterminate period in which the possessed resists the call of the spirit and suffers depression, extreme alienation, dissociation, and even fugues. Such a period, analogous in many respects to what mystics refer to as the dark night of the soul (Underhill, 1961), may be symbolized as a period of wandering or, as one of my Moroccan informants eloquently put it, "my life in the cemeteries" (see the cases of Khady Fall, Rita M., and Dawit in this volume).

Although the spirit idiom structures inchoate feelings (Dodds, 1966; Lienhardt, 1961; Cassirer, 1946), it must be flexible enough to afford idiosyncratic accommodation to the individual and his situation, as well as to temporal changes in him and his situation if it is to "take." The idiom may be composed of a highly elaborate demonology, as in Sri Lanka, Brazil, or Haiti, or its spirits may be ill-defined and highly ambiguous as are the *jnun* in North Africa. In either case, the spirit characters are not so well developed as to discourage individual elaboration and specification. Such elaboration and specification, however idiosyncratic and fantastical they may seem to be, result from a complex "negotiation of reality" between the possessed and those about him. Such "negotiations" occur not only within the formal diagnostic and therapeutic contexts so well documented in the papers by Obeyesekere, Kessler, and Garrison, but also in the less formal contexts of everyday life that are much more difficult to document. Often the particular characteristics and demands of the possessing spirit are made manifest during exceptional experiences such as dreams or visions. However private such experiences may be, they, or at least their enunciation, occur within a social setting and are addressed to an other. The dream, the vision, or the altered state of consciousness lends rhetorical force to the pronouncements.

The character and demands of the spirits reflect two different functions that the spirits serve within the possessed's articulation of experience. On the one hand, they mirror some portion of the individual or some significant (introjected?) figure in his experience that he may refuse to recognize or accept; on the other hand, they may be a means of articulating desires that are unacceptable to someone in his position. The distinction here is not analytical; it is one of emphasis. In the one instance (to borrow a metaphor from Clifford Geertz [1966]) the articulatory function of the spirit is essentially scalar; in the second, vectorial. (Compare Geertz' "moods" and "motivations.") The distinction is also implicit in Freud's theory of projection. As Laplanche and Pontalis

(1973, p. 348) have observed, Freud's theory of paranoia contains an ambiguity in his use of projection:

The differences in the conception of the mechanism of paranoia allows us to distinguish two meanings of projection:

a.) In a sense comparable to the cinematographic meaning: the subject sends out an image of that which exists in him in an unconscious fashion. Here projection is defined as a mode of misapprehension (*méconnaissance*), with, correlatively, the apprehension (*connaissance*) in the other precisely of that which is misapprehended in the subject;

b.) As a quasi-real process of expulsion: the subject thrusts out of himself that which he does not want and subsequently finds it anew in the external world. Here, one can say, schematically, projection is defined not as 'not wanting to know' but as 'not wanting to be.'

The first perspective, the authors conclude, relates projection to an illusion; the second roots it in the originary split between the subject and the external world. Without pursuing the relationship between these two modes of projection and the Freudian-Lacanian distinction between repression and foreclusion (*Verdrängung* and *Verwerfung*), I suggest that both modes are reflected in the conception of the spirit with a specific character—the scalar mode—and particular desires—the vectorial mode. The latter is more intimately connected with the relationship between the spirit and his carrier than is the former, in which the relationship remains inarticulate (forecluded!) to a certain extent. "The identities are encapsulated, insulated from one another, each permitted its share of fulfillment," as Wallace (1966, p. 145) has observed.

Both modes reflect two different functions the spirits serve for the possessed. From the point of view of character, the scalar mode, spirit possession and its cure are concerned with questions of identity (Monfouga-Nicolas, 1972; Wallace, 1966), often sexual identity. Hausa women who find themselves in a masculine role as curers earning a livelihood are often possessed by distinctly feminine spirits (Monfouga-Nicolas, 1972); more often women appear to be possessed by male spirits, as a gesture of assertion (Lewis, 1971). In Pressel's study (this volume), João, a man with distinct homosexual tendencies, is possessed by a female spirit. From the standpoint of the spirit demands, the vectorial mode, spirit possession is concerned with conflict resolution (Firth, 1967). I should repeat that neither mode, however, is entirely distinguishable from the other, for in the final analysis, character can be reduced to desire and desire to character. Nonetheless, emphasis on the two modes appears to vary from idiom to idiom and in their usage by the individual within any idiom.

The spirits are not, however, simply random refractions of the individual and his desires, as are Usener's "momentary deities." ("These beings do not personify any force of nature, nor do they represent some special aspect of human life; no recurrent trait or value is retained in them and transformed into a mythico-religious image; it is something purely instantaneous, a fleeting, emerging and vanishing content, whose objectification and outward discharge produces the image of the 'momentary deity!' [Cassirer,1946, p. 18]) They must resonate with the idiomatically structured and evaluated world—the *Umwelt,* or at least the *Mitwelt,* of the phenomenologists—in which the individual finds himself. According to Mary Douglas (1970), the evaluation of trance as positive or negative will vary with the articulateness of social structure. Trance-like states "are feared as dangerous where the social dimension is highly structured, but welcome and even deliberately induced where this is not the case" (Douglas, 1970, p. 74). The spirits, too, must be subject to the transformations that obtain in that world. To cite but one superficial example, again from Morocco: the whimsical, arbitrary, and essentially untrustworthy she-demon 'A'isha Qandisha resonates with certain common, or at least stereotypic, experiences that Moroccan men have with their women, especially their wives. One of 'A'isha Qandisha's victims must transform her, usually through a possession ceremony, from a faithless and malevolent spirit into a trustworthy and benevolent one if he is to rid himself of her persecution, just as a husband, stereotypically, must domesticate his wife into her role as faithful and helpful spouse (Crapanzano, 1973).

The spirits as elements within the spirit idiom are in essence polysemic. They refer not merely to psychological reality but to social reality as well and, if Levi-Strauss (1963) should happen to be right, to physiological reality too. "The idiom in which these personal phenomena of anxiety, conflict, illness and recovery was couched," Firth (1967, p. 329) writes in the conclusion to his study of Tikopian spirit mediumship, "was one in which the physical and psychological syndrome of trance was described in terms of social constructs, including notions of spirit owners and spirit actions" (see also Harris, 1957; Lewis, 1971; Kessler, this volume). From his essentially sociological perspective, not untinged by Puritan ethic, Firth adds that "the process of finding the solution to personal problems" was

converted to social use and made to serve the needs of others. Moreover, the Tikopians, by giving persons subject to psychological disturbances a social job to do, enabled them to use the therapy they purported to apply to others to find their own self expression.

Thus spirit idiom serves to synthesize the psychological and sociological aspects of human existence.

At a formal level of analysis, the transformation effected within the spirit idiom appears to be isomorphic with the metaphor-metonymy transformations within any linguistic system (Jakobson and Halle, 1971; Lacan, 1966). Spirit possession may be conceived as a complex series of transformations of (usually negative) metaphorical statements into (occasionally positive, at least ritually neutral) metonymous ones in a dialectic play of identity formation. Manifestly, the spirit often represents what the possessed is not—men are possessed by women, women by men—or does not desire (Métraux, 1959; Bastide, 1958). The Moroccan male victim of 'A'isha Qandisha is most assuredly not a female nor even feminine; the chaste Haitian woman possessed by the promiscuous Ezili–Freda–Dahomey is most assuredly not subject to promiscuous desires! The carrier's identity and desires are the opposite of the spirit's. During possession, however, the carrier becomes nearly identical with his spirit. The Moroccan male comes as close to being 'A'isha Qandisha, a woman, as is possible; the Haitian woman as close to being Ezili, a promiscuous if not whorish flirt, as is possible. A negative metaphor is transformed into a positive metonym even to the limit of identity within—and this permits the transformation—*a very special context.*

Possession appears to collapse at least temporarily the defining other—the spirit's carrier—by which the other is constituted in a dialectic of identity formation (Mead, 1956; Sartre, 1963a, 1963b; Yap, 1960). That such a dialectic often involves possession by spirits of a sexual identity opposite to that of the carrier reflects the fact that "male" and "female" are very potent symbols of otherness in identity formation. Insofar as the spirits are "collectively" fixed, or the relationship between carrier and spirit is fixed, the possessing spirit offers a "convenient" stability in the dialectics of identity formation that is not found in ordinary, everyday social transactions. This may be of "therapeutic" advantage. It too is an essentially conservative gesture (Sartre, 1963a).

The *very special context,* of course, is not precipitated by the carrier but by the spirit. This is significant because it points to the rhetorical force of the possession idiom. However the elements within the idiom resonate with the individual and his world; however constraining the logic or grammar of the idiom may be, the idiom provides a powerful rhetorical strategy for the definition of self and world (the scalar mode), and the manipulation of others (the vectorial mode)—a stragegy whose motivation lies outside human control but requires human redress. The rhetoric of spirit possession may be used for self-aggrandizement and self-assertion (Firth, 1967), the realignment of marital relations (Lewis, 1971; Messing, 1959; Barclay, 1964, and nearly all the contributions to this volume), an escape from an unpleasant situation (Métraux, 1959; Pressel, this volume), the immediate control of persons around the possessed during possession ceremony (Mischel and Mischel, 1958), self-chastisement (Crapanzano, 1973), the attainment of intimate though fleeting interpersonal relationships desired by the carrier but prohibited socially in the nonpossessed state (Mischel and Mischel, 1958), the desire for a specific object (Harris, 1957), and the assertion of rights among the socially marginal, especially women (Lewis, 1971). It seems that, uncovering the rules which govern such definitions and manipulations requires detailed, contextually sensitive analyses of individual cases of spirit possession. To us, epidemiologically derived generalizations of spirit possession such as I. M. Lewis' (1966; 1971) seem less convincing than his analyses of the strategy of spirit possession in specific instances. As Wilson (1967) suggests, the data upon which they are based may be subject to other interpretations. What must be generated are not sociological generalizations that are essentially static if not tautological, but context-specific rules of identity formation and manipulation that are basically dynamic.

Although the present anthology had its origins in the editors' fascination with spirit possession, it also grew out of their discontent with many, but by no means all, of the "texts" thar have been produced on the subject. However exciting the florid descriptions of possession may seem at first, after a time they become tediously repetitious; however ingenous many of the interpretive arguments about the causes, incidence, and cures of possession may be, they often seem overgeneralized—an evasive gesture, away from the reality that both editors, and presumably the other contributors to this anthology, experienced in their own work. As in so much anthropology, there seemed to be a quantum jump from the minutiae of ethnographic description to the generalities, commonalities, and universals of ethnological speculation, without even a proper theory of the relationship between particular and universal. The middle ground seemed largely barren. Overall, an adequate account of exactly what possession meant and what role it served for the individual living in a world where possession was believed possible seemed to be missing. In other words, the literature lacked material that would illuminate spirit possession in all its complexity and enable a theoretically sophisticated, substantively adequate, self-critical approach to the phenomenon.

In the hope of contributing to a dynamic approach to spirit possession, the editors first arranged a symposium on case studies in spirit possession at the 1973 meetings of the American Anthropoligical Association in New Orleans and then for the publication of this anthology, with additional contributions from anthropologists who had not participated in the symposium. Our aim was not to provide a theoretically homogeneous set of articles on spirit possession throughout the world—this would have been a falsification of the phenomenon under study, the material on hand, and the anthropological enterprise itself—but to offer a set of papers revealing the multidimensionality of the phenomenon and the diversity of approaches by which it can be studied, even within the limits set by the case history approach.

Cases are reported from Malaysia, Sri Lanka, Egypt, Ethiopia, Senegal, Morocco, Brazil, Puerto Rico (on the island itself and in New York City), and the United States. Approaches, always difficult to define, range from the social anthropoligical to the psychological, from the psychoanalytic within the tradition of culture and personality to the French Freudian tradition, from the phenomenological to the strategic, from the interactionist to the cultural. Without exception, all the contributions are essentially eclectic; they are the product of a struggle to make sense of spirit possession and yet remain faithful (at least substantively) to the possessed. In this I believe they have succeeded. Each in its own way engages the reader not in the impersonal flush of ethnographic detail characteristic of the monograph but in the ethnographically enriched lifeworld, the *Lebenswelt,* of the possessed.

The importance given to the individual, however, varies from contribution to contribution. And it is probably fair to say that all the contributors wrestled with the case history approach itself. Despite a long tradition of collecting life history material and somehow molding it into case histories, anthropologists have never been altogether at ease with the individual case history. In part this is also a consequence of the formal constrictions imposed on living field data by the essentially Western genre of the case history. Indeed, this genre—not to mention the genres of ethnography—has until recently been considered, if considered at all, as essentially transparent, and the full implications of generic formulation on the material of anthropological and psychological research have yet to be explored (Crapanzano, 1974; Marcus, 1074; Conkling, 1975).

Implicit within the case history genre are certain fundamental, cultural presuppositions about the boundaries of self, the relation of the individual to the collectivity, the importance of such "endopsychic" phenomena as dreams, hallucinations, visions, and body apperceptions, the shape of the past (and the future), its falling into some, usually chronological, order, and the use made of the past as explanation or justification for the present, if not as symbolic matrix for articulation of the present and future. Such presuppositions may well run counter to the biographical articulations—or better still the articulations of self— that are expressed in ahistorical, mythopoetic, or spirit-oriented cultures. "Data concerning family life," the Ortigues note in their description of taking an anamnesis among the Wolof and other Senegalese tribesmen, "seems to us to be lived and remembered without being organized in a time oriented in a manner of 'European' time. Each event is reported for itself, as completely closed and is not related to what preceded it and what followed it. The remembered past seems here less heavy, less important" (Ortigues, 1966, p. 39). The fact of biography may in fact be the ethnographer's assumption; his biographies, life histories, and case histories may be the product of *his* question. The question itself may well impose a new *prise de conscience* on the informant which, however satisfying to the ethnographer, and even to the informant, is nevertheless a distortion of "unquestioned" cultural reality. Or, in the words of Andras Zempleni, a contributor to this volume, who has been most cognizant of the status of the discourse upon which life histories are built,

where no "personal demand" of, say, recovery exists, it is the demand of the ethnographer that structures the interview. And this demand, which generally attempts to gather, if not information, at least "a live experience" or "a view from within" of "religious facts" rarely can sustain the effort of a turning inward, into the self, which would enable the informant to express himself as a private individual.

Spirit possession provides the individual with an idiom for self-articulation which is oriented differently from the essentially internalized, past-suffused psychological idiom of the Western world from which the case history itself developed.

In "A Connecticut Yankee in Summer Land," Joan Macklin confronts the question of the "normality" of a possession trance medium in contemporary New England. She argues that "the trance and *her* [the medium's] set of assumptions can be regarded as the end products of a normal social, cultural, and historical process." However peripheral Spiritualism may be in the United States, Macklin argues its basic assumptions and the aspirations of its practitioners are very much a product of the American value system, dominated by a mechanistic view of the universe and by the partially contradictory beliefs about the

equality of man and his perfectability. (She follows Cora Dubois here.)
In fact, even "the spirits appear to be inner-directed Nineteenth century individuals and counsel accordingly!" Rita M., the subject of Macklin's paper, is a "scientist *manqué*," and her successes, Macklin writes,
result precisely from her failure as a scientist. "She combines the orderly, predictable, and replicable with the unique, non-recurrent, and
individual." She—Spiritualism—boundary-hops between the empirical
and the transcendent with the consequence that she and Spiritualism
are anomalous. "They are not crazy, but also not quite mainstream."

Macklin prefaces her cultural analysis with a psychological one, in
which she argues that from a psychiatric point of view it is possible to
view Rita M. as a psychopathological personality (cf. LaBarre, 1969).
"At least she can be said to be coping with life's problems with primitive
or perhaps even childish methods." Macklin's point here is not to favor
a psychiatric approach but to contrast two different sets of assumptions
by which the same data can be interpreted. Both, curiously, arise from
the same cultural tradition. Implicit in Macklin's approach is a self-critical stance—a stance which most of the papers in this volume try to
preserve insofar as they remain faithful to their subject and resist the
reduction of the idiom of the possessed to that of the investigator.

What is striking to me about Macklin's presentation and psychological analysis of Rita M. is the similarity of so much of what Rita M. says
about herself, and Macklin in turn says about her, to the more exotic
cases in the volume. "Nineteenth century" though the spirits in Macklin's account may be, they appear often enough as embarrassingly
transparent figures of compensation and as refractions (to use Jung's
term) of Rita M.'s shadow.

Supported by a band of diverse spirit guides, which is orchestrated by an all-
caring, all-knowing, and constantly attentive monk control, she is able to become whatever she wishes by complementary projection: an all-powerful and
wise male; a well-educated male doctor whose credentials are impeccable; a
mischievous child, center of attention which she herself never had; a high-
born, self-indulgent and powerful Egyptian woman; *etc.* By supplementary
projection she can also foist onto the spirits the unacceptable attributes she
finds in herself: the engaging child spirit also is irresponsible; the Egyptian was
not only selfish, she also wilfully destroyed those who crossed her.

This transparency of symbolism, to cite one similarity, occures in most
of the other cases reported here. There is also in Rita M.'s account of
herself a kind of "savvy," almost an insight into the "psychological"
symbolism of her spirits that recalls a similar "savvy" I observed among
my own Moroccan informants. This savvy is reminiscent too of the

savvy often displayed by hysterics in the understanding of their own symptoms. Although the possessed—and the hysterics too for that matter—may even precariously approach a boundary, they are careful not to boundary-hop.

Doubtless Andras Zempleni's "From Symptom to Sacrifice: The Case of Khady Fall" is both ethnographically and theoretically the most complex contribution to the volume. Zempleni, who was one of a team of researchers working under the direction of Henri Collomb on mental disorder in Senegal, uses a theoretical perspective recently dubbed by the *Yale French Studies* (Mehlman 1972) as French Freudian, and little known among either anthropologists or psychoanalysts in the United States. Although he is clearly influenced by Jacques Lacan, the founder of the movement, and more particularly by the Ortigues, who worked in Senegal with him, Zempleni's approach is considerably more sober and, despite the evident difficulties of translation, clearer than that of many other French Freudians. His article was first publshed in French in *L'Homme* in 1974, and appears here in English for the first time.

Through a minute analysis of the Wolof priestess Khady Fall's articulation of her life history, Zempleni traces her development into a successful possession-curer. The *rab* and *tuur* ancentral spirits enable her to articulate and integrate her *position*—I would write "identity" were it not for the psychological overtones of the word—within the complex lineage-structured world, with its conflicting demands, in which she finds herself. "The determining characteristics of the spirits inherited by Khady—their ethnic origin and religion—repeat the essential features of the lineages to which she herself belongs." They become signifiers of descent and affinity for her and enable her to resolve her personal problems on the "demonic stage." Her domestic altars to these spirits provide a "screen on which are projected, in condensed form, her family history and her own biography." Her story is organized

like a destiny tenaciously held to myth, and not like a psychological or family novel. This destiny is recounted in a series of discrete episodes—one is tempted to say in scenes and acts—that refer, in the manner of coded messages, to the unconscious positionings of the narrator.

As in the other cases in this volume, and in cases reported elsewhere in the literature, illness is "the first if not the exclusive reason for renewing the alliance with the spirits."

The bodily space is invested and pervaded by the ambivalent ancestral sign. The *rab* love the very one they punish for having neglected them; they "inhabit" and "torment" those by whom they have chosen to be honored. Possession, here, is a vacillating inscription, with the body, of the ancestral signifier.

The body becomes the medium of symbolic transformation which is replayed periodically in possession ceremonies. In the case of Khady Fall in an order closely integrated with the obtaining lineage structure, and elsewhere in a less structured manner, the aim of the ceremony is not the permanent expulsion of the spirits but the creation, or the renewing, of an alliance with the spirit which, whatever its psychological function—prestige, self-assertion, and so on—serves to articulate the individual as both more and less than he or she is. As Pouillon (1972) suggests, it is ultimately a question of the "location" one learns to assign to what is not I.

Zempleni, anxious to demonstrate the applicability of the psychoanalytic investigation of the individual in a field situation, has based his analysis on the retrospective accounts of his informants. Such a "text" is produced by the encounter between the ethnographer and his informant and cannot be considered as having a referent any more "real" than those in the utterances of any psychoanlytic patient—of anyone, strictly speaking. Sensitive as Zempleni is to the status of his text, and to his own position in its production, I feel that he has not given sufficient attention to his own "liberating" role in his demand on Khady. The position granted *Alamdu*, the European *rab*, may reflect Khady's transference and also, *non sine pudore dico*, the liberating position of the European within her life. Perhaps this "liberation" also affects the importance of her fetish object, *Sajinne*.

In Lucie Wood Saunder's "Variants in Zar Experience in an Egyptian Village" and in my own Moroccan case of Mohammed and Dawia, emphasis is placed on the multiple uses of spirit possession within a single cultural context. Saunders contrasts the *zar* possession of two women of different social status: Azziza, married to a rich villager and, as such, isolated within her household from more frequent interchange with the peasant women of the village, and Habiba, a peasant woman. For Azziza, possession plays a dominant role in her everyday life. She says that she is continually aware of her spirit's presence, that she dreams about her from time to time, and that she cannot even do certain ordinary things to beautify herself, such as putting henna on her hands, without first seeing the spirit. She interprets "not feeling well" in terms of the displeasure of her spirit, her "underground sister." (cf. Leiris, 1958). For Habiba, possession appears to have been a temporary interlude by which, after a very difficult first marriage, she was able to gain her second husband's attention and respect. Her behavior at the *zar* ceremonies was never extreme, the reality of her trance problematical, and she never associated her possession with a particular traumatic event. She could not even give an account of an initial experience of possession. Nevertheless, she did interpret a painful wrist in terms of the spirits and underwent the appropriate curing ceremony.

In the cases of both Azziza and Habiba, and in the cases reported by Lewis (1971), spirit possession enables the modification of a husband's behavior or at least "the testing and savoring" of an improvement. (This role also appears in other cases here; e.g., Rita M.'s husband was "touched by a spirit.") In the case of Mohammed and Dawia, possession regulates a marriage on the point of breakup over the death of a son and the birth of an unwanted daughter. "These events," I write, "are mediated by the presence of a *tertium quid,* the demons, who are external to the participants but impose their will on them." The demons not only (re-)structure the marital situation but serve as biographical orientation points and correlatives for feelings and emotions that extend beyond the situations which precipitated the possession. My emphasis here is on the rhetorical force of possession. Dawia, whose possession is in psychiatric terms reactive, situationally determined, makes use of her husband's spirit idiom—an idiom which articulates "deeper," long-standing feelings of inadequacy, a fragmented identity, and unacceptable desires—to regulate her marriage. Articulation of the central events that precipitated the marital crisis in terms of spirits preserves the marriage by "casting out" tensions and hostilities, resentment, guilt, and anger onto the demonic stage, *die andere Szene,* in Freud's words.

The spirit idiom does not, however, always provide a successful stage for the deflection of interpersonal tension. Alice Morton notes, for example, in "Dawit: Competition and Integration in an Ethiopian Wuqabi Cult Group," that when Dawit's moroseness and withdrawal, his spirit's harshness, and his own disagreeableness became extreme, those about him in the cult group to which he belonged "began to attribute his withdrawal to personal, psychological causes." This behavior may well have resulted from Dawit's ambiguous status as a man, not even a womanish man, in an essentially female role. She notes, too, that possession by *wuqabi* (*zar*) spirits was not always agreeable to the possessed, and that many of the possessed whom she interviewed had tried without success on various occasions to escape from even the benign accommodations they had made with the spirits. There is, Morton notes, "real social—as well as financial—cost to being possessed, unless the possessed individual is able to become a professional healer."

Dawit himself was a sort of healer. He was not on his own, however, but lived in the compound of Mama Azaletch, a cult leader reminiscent of Khady Fall. Speaking of the zar-possessed more generally, Morton observes, that if they show no signs of improvement with treatment, they are likely to be relegated by their families to possession cult groups where they are forced to rely more and more heavily on other members of the group, especially on a leader who may very well be exploitative. (See Field, 1970, for a study of such groups in Ghana and Devereux; 1966, for the role of suggestion by such groups and their leaders in trance and hypnosis).

While there are sanctions which can be brought to bear against spouses or against kin and affines if they become exaggerately exploitative, the bale wuqaba [the cult leader] who exploits his or her group members in an extreme fashion—while subject to desertion by them—always has the power and authority of the spirits to back up his or her actions.

Possession may actually become a form of enslavement not only to the spirit but to the cult leader.

Dawit's isolation resulted not from his possession, but apparently from familial ostracism over an allegation of incestuous relations with a maternal aunt. He fell into the possession idiom. It served as a means of articulating his relations with Mama Azaletch and her group and maintaining his sexual identity. "His problem seems to have been not one of sexual inadequacy," Morton writes, "but rather appropriate channeling of sexual adequacy both before he became a member of the wadaĝa group and afterward. . . ." After an inappropriate flirtation during a ceremony (the accusation of which calls to mind the accusation of incest by his family) Dawit's possession required redefinition for him to be successfully reintegrated into the cult group.

Somavati, the Sinhalese female subject of Gananath Obeyesekere's "Psycho-Cultural Exegesis of a Case of Spirit Possession in Sri Lanka," was drawn through her possession into a cult group which provided her with a substitute kin group: "a group with whom she could interact freely and on whom she can depend." Somavati's exorcism, according to Obeyesekere, served symbolically, at least, for her to reestablish her damaged authority relations; it effected not only a catharsis—a means to express repressed sexual and aggressive drives—but, by articulating her conflict in terms of spirits, demons, and deities, it brought about a realignment of her relations with her family. She was given the possibility of "play." As Obeyesekere observes, importantly, the "critical period of the 'cure' lies in the post-ritual period." Somavati is afforded the opportunity to become a priestess. Although she goes through the investiture, she does not pursue the career, allegedly because she has no room

for a shrine in her crowded quarters, but probably because she has neither the intelligence nor the resources required for the role. Besides,
Obeyesekere argues somewhat mechanically, granted the possibility of
play, her sexual inhibitions are relaxed.

Obeyesekere's approach to possession is, in his own terms, that of
"psycho-cultural exegesis"—"an attempt to render intelligible the sociocultural context in which possession occurs and the manner in which
the personal experience of possession is expressed with a set of standardized cultural meanings." His interest lies in "how cultural meanings are manipulated by the individual to express personal needs and
emotions." Accepting what is, in my opinion, a somewhat mechanistic
view of psychoanalysis—and an overly "constructed" view of Somavati's
personality development—Obeyesekere attempts to account for the origin of Somavati's possession and the success of her cure in both psychodynamic and situational terms. Her possession, he is careful to remind
us, is "not a psychotic, or nervous breakdown in the Western sense." It
was "culturally 'timed' and expressed in a prescribed demonic idiom."
Not only did it result from accumulated psychological pressures, it was
also an attempt to cope with these pressures.

Somavati's spirits, like those of Rita M., Dawia, and several of the
other subjects of the papers in this book, are clearly symbolic refractions of significant figures—imagos is perhaps the more appropriate
word—in her life. Somavati could, for example, "through the demonomorphic representation of her grandmother" (a woman to whom she
had been "sold" when she was only a few months old and from whom
she was arbitrarily removed when she was seven), "expresses her hatred
for this lady, her hostile oral rage, and above all direct that oral rage
against a 'hated' (and loved) person, her mother." Such representation,
Obeyesekere observes, might also revive her mother's own guilt at having renounced her daughter.

Obeyesekere's focus on the individual as the subject of psychocultural exegesis is a welcome antidote to the focus on the generalized personality—"the indefinite abstract subject," in Zempleni's words—which
most culture and personality studies have treated. His recognition,
however, that many of the problems of the individual are "culturally
generated" through socialization is an equally important antidote to the
particularism inherent in the case history approach. The standard ritual has not developed fortuitously. "It can be presumed that it was
designed to cope with the pressing psychological conflicts that are
found in the local population." The psychological problems and conflicts, Obeyesekere reminds us, are finite too.

In "Conflict and Sovereignty in Kelantanese Malay Spirit Seances,"

Clive Kessler relates spirit possession to I. M. Lewis' thesis that possession is found most frequently among people of inferior, marginal, ambiguous, or problematic status, especially women, and that it provides them with a "means whereby underlings, beset by social strain, may protect their interior status, bid for attention, or, by threatening to cause embarrassing disruptions, induce their superior to honor the obligations inhering in their admittedly unequal relationship" (Kessler's summary; Lewis, 1971).

Kessler examines the use of the possession idiom by women of three different statuses: (1) newlyweds who escape from an arranged marriage; (2) older married women who wish to preserve their marriages; and (3) widows and divorcees of middle age. He presents two paradigmatic cases from his sample: Mek Mas, an older married woman who managed through possession to preserve her marriage; and Mak Su Yam, a widow for whom possession functioned simply as a catharsis. By drawing attention to herself and her dilemma, and by symbolically overcoming her male foe (her husband) during the possession seance—significantly by dancing the *bersilat,* the male dance of self-defense—Mek Mas was able to preserve her social position at least temporarily, thus discouraging her husband from seeking a new wife. Her husband "had seen, at the performance, how isolated he was, and what substantial support there was for Mek Mas, especially when her retaliatory assault was enthusiastically applauded." (Kessler's emphasis on the communicational aspect of the possession ceremony is noteworthy.) In Mek Su Yam's case, the possession could not alter the "fundamentally ambiguous social position" from which her symptoms stemmed.

Kessler's paradigmatic cases expose the situational logic of Kelantanese possession but do not raise the question of the subjective articulation of the situation by the possessed. He writes, for example: "To counter an unwanted possessive husband and the unwillingness of her kin to counter divorce before it seems inevitable the reluctant young wife, unable directly to stage an embarrassing scene, has one principal recourse for ending her arranged marriage. She becomes sick. . . ." Kessler seems to employ here, at least implicitly, a rather ad hoc theory of motivation, implying purposive if not calculated behavior where such "purpose" and "calculation" may well be precluded by the spirit idiom itself.

The main thrust of Kessler's paper is, however, to relate the possession idiom to the sociopolitical one. He argues that the idiom of possession is not exclusive: "It links illness and possession to other power-laden contexts from which it derives." The richly symbolic healing seances "enact an allegory of personality and polity."

Beset by social pressures and psychic conflict the patient, then is apparently depicted as an arena of faction disputes and of rival tendencies.

The "disputes" and "rival tendencies" result because they—their potential is always endemic—have been unchecked in person, as in polity, by reason (*akal*). It is the sovereignty of reason that the healer seeks to restore, Kessler observes, through the accretion of spiritual essence (*samagat*) and the expulsion of disruptive emotions (*nafsu*). Kessler's emphasis is on the "person," as articulated within the multilayered idiom of possession, politics, and personality in Kelantan, and reminds us that to comprehend possession it is necessary to understand not only the demonology of a people but their anthropology as well.

Stressful situations, Esther Pressel argues in "Negative Spirit Possession in Experienced Brazilian Umbanda Spirit Mediums," may produce involuntary and uncontrolled negative possession in even experienced mediums. She argues that the progression, observed by Lewis and Bourgignon among others, of possession from a primary phase, in which the medium's behavior is involuntary and uncontrolled to a secondary phase in which he learns to control his disorderly spirits, may reverse itself under especially disturbing circumstances. Thus an experienced medium, Cecilia, one of the two subjects Pressel discusses, suffered negative possession when a granddaughter was born with a cleft lip and a niece from the country moved into Cecilia's already overcrowded quarters. (Cecilia's initial involuntary and uncontrolled possession also was caused, according to Pressel's interpretation of Cecilia's retrospective account, by stress resulting from her husband's bizarre behavior—he fought with his employees, fired them, and lost his business—his taking a mistress, and the death of two of his three children.) João, her second subject, a less controlled medium with marked homosexual tendencies, suffered negative possession when he had work problems or when he was sexually baited. What constitutes a stressful situation is, in Pressel's observational approach, essentially of her own determination. Implicit if not always explicit in her formulation is the rhetorical function of such involuntary possession.

Joan Koss' "Spirits as Socializing Agents: A Case Study of a Puerto Rican Girl Reared in a Matricentric Family" addresses itself to the deepest psychological ties of the belief in spirits and spirit possession—to the very problematic of our own psychological idiom. Anna lives with her father as wife, according to Koss, "without apparently the least pang of guilt or intrapsychic conflict over the inappropriateness of their actions given definite social, moral, and legal prescriptions against incestuous relations." Anna was raised in a fatherless world in an isolated household by five sisters, including her mother, who conferred in secret nightly with the spirits of their deceased parents. Anna does not even learn the identity of her father until she is twenty-one years old and, within three weeks of meeting him, (she seeks him out) she and her father become lovers. What troubles Anna, according to Koss, and presumably her father, are "usual marital problems" and the ambiguity of her status vis-à-vis others within her world.

Koss argues that Anna's deceased grandfather, in spirit form, was "her paternal authority and the ultimate referent for her most basic notions of 'correct' behavior." The sisters deferred constantly to their grandfather for authority, and Anna herself as a child had experiences, visions, of him that were confirmed by her mother and aunts. The paternal image, Koss suggests, is split for Anna between her disembodied grandfather, who bore the role of "psychological" father, and her real biological father. Her relationship with the latter, Koss suggests, may be understood if we accept a Freudian view as an effective means of resolving "a host of conflicts stemming from her illegitimacy, her controversial and painful existence as the result of well-advertised immorality on her mother's part, the extreme restrictiveness on sexual intimacy imposed by her maiden-aunt socializers, and her desire for a physical father due to a fatherless childhood brought about by her mother's wrongdoing." However, Koss refuses such a reduction without at least entertaining a second possibility, a second idiomatic construction of the events that is "more faithful to a Puerto Rican culturally constituted reality."

This view would consider the real possibility that the spirit grandfather did take on an objective existence for Anna as a child. . . . The spirit grandfather, as a principal socializing agent in Anna's life, reinforced the strict morality imposed by her maiden aunts and became the source of her conceptualization of "father," since he was "father" to all the women around her.

The man she is living with, Koss argues, though recognized by Anna as father in terms of the cultural definition of the word, has "none of the attributes of 'father' as she experienced those attributes during her tender years."

However this may be, the Western reader cannot but ask whether Anna is not particularly well defended, even by the spirits of her deceased grandfather, from guilt over incest. The particular form of her account of her past may itself be an evasive if not a defensive maneuver, a neutralizing verbal positioning of herself within the world of her contemporaries. She would have worn a button, "Incest is for all the Family," had her father/spouse not stopped her.

In "The Puerto Rican Syndrome in Psychiatry and Espiritismo," Vivian Garrison compares in detail two working systems of healing, that of Espiritismo as practiced by Puerto Ricans in New York City and that of psychoanalytically oriented psychotherapy as practiced in several New York hospitals where Garrison has worked. Her approach is not reductionist. In order to avoid the built-in "psychological" bias of the usual investigations of folk therapy that use the "scientific" and "objective" language of contemporary psychology and psychoanalysis, Garrison seeks to compare the two "languages" in terms of a third "etic" one composed of "anthropological concepts insofar as they have been developed, ordinary English, and arbitrary symbols." She is careful to note that

the terms in Spiritism as in psychodynamic theory take their meaning from the total complex of concepts that make up one or the other of these two systems of thought. No terms from either system can, therefore, be directly equated with a term from the other.

Nonetheless, Garrison finds striking similarities in the conceptualization of self (e.g. *protecciones,* or wise, helping but also punishing spirits; *causas,* or ignorant molesting spirits; and *proprio ser,* or one's own spirit in whatever state of ignorance or wisdom it has achieved across successive incarnations approximate the superego, id, and ego) and in the evolution of cure (levels of possession approximate levels of psychological significance). The most striking difference in the two languages is, of course, the physical location attributed to the concepts. Indeed, Garrison's insistence on the term "concept" merits note; for she argues that the spirits serve essentially a conceptual function, that their existence is not more concrete than that of the ego, superego or id for the Western psychotherapist. Although the spirits' existence, and their exact nature, is disputed among the mediums, no medium would say they do not exist. Here we have an example of the same confusion, culturally validated in this instance, of a phenomenologically descriptive term with an explanatory construct that I argued earlier was responsible for the frequent reification of the explanatory constructs in psychoanalysis.

Garrison's detailed comparison of the two systems is organized around the case of Maria, a Puerto Rican woman who suffered an *ataque de nervios* at work, was recommended for psychiatric therapy, and, instead, underwent treatment by an *Espiritista.* The *ataque de nervios,* or Puerto Rican Syndrome as it is frequently called in the literature, is generally characterized by a partial loss of consciousness, convulsive movements, hyperventilation, moaning and groaning, profuse salivation, and aggressiveness to self and others. It is sudden in onset and termination. From a psychiatric point of view, it is a "dissociation in an attempt to disown undesirable impulses associated with anger and/or aggression as well as sex." For the Espiritista, Maria's attack was initially diagnosed as *brujeria* (witchcraft)—later diagnoses were also made—and Maria was recommended for "development" of her spiritual faculties. For Garrison, the spiritualist's treatment involves the restructuring of an essentially involuntary regression, produced at least in part by stressful conditions, into a regression in the service of the ego.

I should like to note here, with specific regard to Garrison's paper, that the treatment of Maria—as frequently in the treatment of the possessed in other parts of the world—is not directed only to the possessed. Other members of the possessed's social world who may show no manifest symptoms of pathology are involved in the treatment as well. Insofar as the case history approach focuses on the individual, it tends to distort the focus of possession and its treatment, which may have less to do with the individual, however he is defined, than with a larger interpersonal unit. Such therapies are often sociocentric, and not patient-centered as in the modern Western world.

In his study of Jean Genet, Jean-Paul Sartre compares the poet-dramatist's embodiment of the Other to the Ethiopians' relationship with the zar spirits that possess them. For Sartre, ethnographically naïve, these spirits are nothing less than the self of the possessed objectified and rendered sacred. He writes:

For right-thinking people, Genet embodies the Other. And as he has fallen into their trap, he embodies the Other in his own eyes too. But this Other, who has been installed in him by decree of society is first a *collective representation* of which it has all the characteristics. Fixed and intangible, it cannot be reduced to the contingent movement of an individual consciousness. It is Genet himself, but *with another nature*. It is *sacred* Genet haunting the everyday soul of profane Genet (1963b, pp. 162–163).

For the Westerner, the spirit possessed, representative of "another cultural tradition," embodies the Other in its most extreme, most exotic, most alien form. Such an Other must remain distinct from us, or be reduced to one of us. We cannot afford Genet's luxury, limiting and destined to failure in any case. The dialectical drama between the possessed and his spirit, between (human) self and (spirit) Other, may well provide an allegory for the confrontation between the ethnographer and his people, between modern man and the primitive. The question of where the spirits lie, of who is possessed by whom, may be simpler to answer in this context but of more significance.

NOTES

1. This line and those from the the *Bacchae* are reprinted by special permission from the University of Chicago as publisher from Euripides, *The Bacchae*, William Arrowsmith, translator, © by the University of Chicago from volume four of *The Complete Greek Tragedies* (University of Chicago Press, 1958/1960).
2. Reprinted by special permission of John Murray (Publishers) Ltd. from E. B. Tylor, *Religion in Primitive Culture.*
3. Reprinted by special permission of Aidan Southall and Routledge & Kegan Paul Ltd. (Africana) from "Spirit Possession and Mediumship among the Alur" in *Spirit Mediumship and Society in Africa* edited by J. Beattie and J. Middleton (London, 1969).

REFERENCES

BARCLAY, HAROLD B.

1964   *Buuri al Lamaab: A Suburban Village in the Sudan.* Ithaca: Cornell University Press.

BASTIDE, ROGER

1958   *Le Condomblé de Bahia.* Paris: Mouton.

BÉGUIN, ALBERT

1946   *L'Ame romantique et le Rêve: Essai sur le Romantisme allemand et la Poésie française.* Paris: Jose Corti.

BELO, JANE

1960   *Trance in Bali.* New York: Columbia University Press.

BERNFELD, SIEGFRIED

1928   "Uber Faszination." *Imago* 14: 76–87.

BOURGIGNON, ERIKA

1967   "World Distribution and Patterns of Possession States." In *Trance and Possession States,* R. Prince (Ed.). Montreal: J. M. Bucke Foundation.

1970   "Ritual Dissociation and Possession Belief in Caribbean Negro Religion." In *Afro-American Anthropology: Contemporary Perspectives,* Norman E. Whitten and J. F. Szwed, (Eds.). New York: Free Press.

1973   "Introduction: A Framework for the Comparative
              Study of Altered States of Consciousness." In *Religion,
              Altered States of Consciousness, and Social Change,* Erika
              Bourgignon (Ed.). Columbus, Ohio: Ohio State Univer-
              sity Press.

CASSIRER, ERNST
1946   *Language and Myth.* New York: Dover.

CHARCOT, J. M. and PAUL RICHER
1887   *Les Démoniaques dans l'Art.* Paris: Adrien Delahaye et
              Emile Lecrosnier.

CONKLING, ROBERT
1975   "Expression and Generalization in History and Anthro-
              pology." *American Ethnologist* **2:** 239–250.

CRAPANZANO, VINCENT
1973   *The Hamadsha: A Study in Moroccan Ethnopsychiatry.*
              Berkeley: University of California Press.
1974   "The Writing of Ethnography." Paper read at the An-
              nual Meetings of the American Anthropological Associ-
              ation, Mexico City.
1975   "Saints, Jnun, and Dreams: An Essay in Moroccan Eth-
              nopsychology." *Psychiatry* **38:** 145–159.

DEVEREUX, GEORGE
1956   "Normal and Abnormal: The Key Problem of Psychiat-
              ric Anthropology." In *Some Uses of Anthropology: Theoret-
              ical and Applied.* Washington, D.C.: The Anthropo-
              logical Society of Washington.
1966   "Cultural Factors in Hypnosis and Suggestion: An Ex-
              amination of Some Primitive Data." *International Journal
              of Clinical and Experimental Hypnosis* **14:** 273–291.

DODDS, E. R.
1966   *The Greeks and the Irrational.* Berkeley: University of Cal-
              ifornia Press.

DOUGLAS, MARY
1970   *Natural Symbols: Explorations in Cosmology.* London: Bar-
              rie and Rocklieff.

EURIPIDES
1958   "The Bacchae." Translated by William Arrowsmith. In
              The Complete Greek Tragedies, vol. 4, David Grene and R.
              Lattimore (Eds.). Chicago: University of Chicago Press.

FIELD, M. J.
1969   "Spirit Possession in Ghana." In *Spirit Mediumship and
              Society in Africa.* John Beattie and J. Middleton (Eds.).
              London: Routledge and Kegan Paul.

1970   *Search for Security: An Ethnopsychiatric Study of Rural Ghana.* New York: Norton.

FIRTH, RAYMOND

1967   "Individual Fantasy and Social Norms: Seances with Spirit Mediums." In *Tikopia Ritual and Belief.* Boston: Beacon.

FRAZER, JAMES G.

1958   *The Golden Bough: A Study in Magic and Religion* (one-volume abridgement). New York: Macmillan.

FREED, STANLEY A. and RUTH S.

1964   "Spirit Possession as Illness in a North Indian Village." *Ethnology* **3:** 152–171.

FREUD, SIGMUND

1963a   "A Neurosis of Demoniacal Possession in the Seventeenth Century." In *Freud: Studies in Parapsychology,* P. Rieff (Ed.). New York: Collier Books.

1963b   "The Uncanny." In *Freud: Studies in Parapsychology,* P. Rieff (Ed.). New York: Collier Books.

GEERTZ, CLIFFORD

1966   "Religion as a Cultural System." In *Anthropological Approaches to the Study of Religion,* M. Banton (Ed.). London: Tavistock.

GOODMAN, FELICITAS D.

1972   *Speaking in Tongues: A Cross-Cultural Study of Glossolalia.* Chicago: University of Chicago Press.

HARRIS, GRACE

1957   "Possession 'Hysteria' in a Kenya Tribe." *American Anthropologist* **59:** 1046–1066.

HUXLEY, ALDOUS

1952   *The Devils of Loudun.* New York: Harper and Row.

JAKOBSON, ROMAN and MORRIS HALLE

1971   *Fundamentals of Language,* 2nd rev. ed. The Hague: Mouton.

JASPERS, KARL

1959   *Allgemeine Psychopathologie.* Berlin: Springer Verlag.

JEANMAIRE, H.

1951   *Dionysios: Histoire du Culte de Bacchus.* Paris: Payot.

LABARRE, WESTON

1969   *They Shall Take Up Serpents: Psychology of the Southern Snake Handling Cult.* New York: Schocken.

LACAN, JACQUES
1966   *Ecrits*. Paris: Seuil.

LAPLANCHE, JEAN and J.-B. PONTALIS
1973   *Vocabulaire de la Psychanalyse*. Paris: Presses Universi-
                       taires de France.

LEFEBVRE, HENRI
1971   *Everyday Life in the Modern World*. New York: Harper
                       and Row.

LEIRIS, MICHEL
1958   "La Possession et ses Aspects théâtraux chez les Ethio-
                       piens de Gondar." *L'Homme* I.

LEVI-STRAUSS, CLAUDE
1963   "The Effectiveness of Symbols." In *Structural Anthropol-
                       ogy*. New York: Basic Books.

LEWIS, I. M.
1966   "Spirit Possession and Deprivation Cults." *Man* **1:**
                       307–329.
1971   *Ecstatic Religion: An Anthropological Study of Spirit Posses-
                       sion and Shamanism*. Baltimore: Penguin.

LIENHARDT, GODFREY
1961   *Divinity and Experience: The Religion of the Dinka*. Oxford:
                       Clarendon.

MARCUS, STEVEN
1974   "Freud's Dora." *Partisan Review* **41:** 12–23, 89–108.

MARS, LOUIS
1946   *La Crise de Possession dans le Vaudou*. Port-au-Prince: Im-
                       primérie de l'Etat.

MEAD, GEORGE HERBERT
1956   *On Social Psychology*. Chicago: University of Chicago
                       Press.

MEHLMAN, JEFFREY (special Ed.)
1972   *French Freud: Structural Studies in Psychoanalysis*. *Yale
                       French Studies* 48.

MESSING, SIMON D.
1959   "Group Therapy and Social Status in the Zar Cult of
                       Ethiopia." In *Culture and Mental Health*, M. K. Opler
                       (Ed.). New York: Macmillan.

MÉTRAUX, ALFRED
1959   *Voodoo in Haiti*. New York: Oxford.

MISCHEL, WALTER and FRANCES

1958   "Psychological Aspects of Spirit Possession." *American Anthropologist* **60:** 249–260.

MONFOUGA-NICOLAS, JACQUELINE

1972   *Ambivalence et Culte de Possession: Contribution à l'Etude du Bori Hausa.* Paris: Anthropos.

OBEYESEKERE, GANANATH

1970   "The Idiom of Demonic Possession: A Case Study." *Society, Science, and Medicine* **4:** 97–111.

ORTIGUES, MARIE-CÉCILE and EDMOND

1966   *Oedipe africain.* Paris: Plon.

OESTERREICH, T. K.

1966   *Possession, Demonical and Other, Among Primitive Races, in Antiquity, the Middle Ages, and Modern Times.* Secaucus, N.J.: University Books.

OTTO, RUDOLPH

1950   *The Idea of the Holy,* 2nd ed. New York: Oxford.

PARTRIDGE, ERIC

1958   *Origins: A Short Etymological Dictionary of Modern English.* New York: Macmillian.

POUILLON, JEAN

1972   "Doctor and Patient: Same and/or Other? (Ethnological Remarks)." *Psychoanalytic Study of Society* **5:** 9—32.

PRESSEL, ESTHER

1974   "Unbanda Trance and Possession in São Paulo, Brazil." In *Trance, Healing, and Hallucination: Three Field Studies in Religious Experience,* F. Goodman, H. Henney, and E. Pressel (Ed.). New York: Wiley.

RICHARDS, I. A.

1936   *The Philosophy of Rhetoric.* Oxford: Oxford University Press.

SARGANT, WILLIAM

1964   *Battle for the Mind.* London: Pan Books.
1974   *The Mind Possessed: A Physiology of Possession, Mysticism, and Faith Healing.* Philadelphia: Lippincott.

SARTRE, JEAN-PAUL

1963a   *Saint Genet: Actor and Martyr.* New York: Mentor.
1963b   *Search for a Method.* New York: Knopf.

SCHAFF, ADAM

1973   *Language and Cognition.* New York: McGraw-Hill.

SCHNEIDER, DAVID M.

1968   *American Kinship: A Cultural Account.* Englewood Cliffs, N.J.: Prentice-Hall.

SILVERMAN, JULIAN

1967   "Shamanism and Acute Schizophrenia." *American Anthropologist* **69:** 21–31.

SMITH, GRAHAM

1969   "Rubens' Altargemälde des hl. Ignatius von Loyola und des hl. Franz Xaver für die Jesuitenkirche in Antwerpen." *Jahrbuch des Kunsthistorishen Sammlungen in Wien* **65:** 39–60.

SOUTHALL, AIDAN

1969   "Spirit Possession and Mediumship among the Alur." In *Spirit Mediumship and Society in Africa.* John Beattie and J. Middleton (Ed.). London: Routledge and Kegan Paul.

TYLOR, E. B.

1958   *Religion in Primitive Culture.* New York: Harper and Row.

UNDERHILL, EVELYN

1961   *Mysticism: A Study in the Nature and Development of Man's Spiritual Consciousness.* New York: Dutton.

WAGNER, ROY

1972   *Habu: The Innovation of Meaning in Daribi Religion.* Chicago: University of Chicago Press.

WALLACE, ANTHONY F. C¡

1959   "Cultural Determinants of Response to Hallucinatory Experience." *A.M.A. Archives of General Psychiatry* **1:** 74–85.

1966   *Religion: An Anthropological View.* New York: Random House.

WILSON, PETER J.

1967   "Status Ambiguity and Spirit Possession." *Man* **2:** 366–378.

YAP, P. M.

1960   "The Possession Syndrome: A Comparison of Hong Kong and French Findings." *Journal of Mental Science* **106:** 114–137.

YOUNG, ALLAN

1975   "Why Amhara Get Kureynya: Sickness and Possession in an Ethiopian Cult. *American Ethnologist* **2:** 567–584.

ZEMPLENI, ANDRAS
    1974   "Du Symptome au Sacrifice: Histoire de Khady Fall."
                            L'Homme **14:** 31–77.

June Macklin

A Connecticut Yankee
in Summer Land [1]

INTRODUCTION

Lately, social scientists have been able to regard spirit possession and its associated phenomena as possibly being within the range of normal behavior but only as long as it occurred in cultures other than our own.[2] When found in American society, trance states and spirit possession seem much more acceptable if they occur in "subcultural" ethnic groups such as Mexican-American, Puerto Rican, or American Indian: urban villagers, who cannot quite sort out what is natural and what is supernatural, and whose *Weltanschauungen* are innocent of the Enlightenment, the Industrial Revolution, and the scientific method.

Phenomena that we treat with anthropological solemnity and interest as long as they are reported from Africa, Burma, the Caribbean, or Latin America, become risible at best and deviant at worst when they manifest themselves in New England among middle-class white Americans.[3] Here, it is quite easy to look upon the possessed trancers as "sick."

In this chapter I propose: (1) to present in detail the case of Mrs. Rita M., a white, middle-class possession trance-medium from New England; (2) I shall then interpret these data (Analysis I), applying a set of assumptions which anthropologists share with many other social and behavioral scientists, and which lead us to the conclusion that she is irrational and unscientific, perhaps even a psychopathic personality; (3) I shall than reexamine the same case history (Analysis II) to demonstrate that the trancer and her set of assumptions can be regarded as the end products of normal social, cultural, and historical processes. Therefore she is, like most other Americans, a scientist *manqué:* her faith in science, its methodology and techniques is unlimited. Finally I shall suggest that her success with her many clients accrues precisely from her failure as a scientist: she combines the orderly, predictable, and replicable with the unique, nonrecurrent, and individual; through ritual possession she effects the union of the eternal with the temporal.

The methodology utilized in collecting the data for this chapter will be detailed as an integral part of the argument advanced in Analysis II. Suffice it to report here that life history data were collected (on tape) from nine certified Spiritualist mediums. These mediums represent two national Spiritualist organizations, which currently (1975) have commissioned a total of twenty mediums to practice in the state of Connecticut. Data from mediums of both certifying groups are included, for while details of belief vary among Spiritualists, most organizations share similar declarations of principles. The case of Mrs. M., in most respects, may be taken as paradigmatic of mediumship in American Spiritualism.

MRS. RITA M.: THE WOMAN AND HER WORKS

Mrs. Rita M., 65, is a possession trance-medium and ordained minister of the National Spiritualist Association of Churches of the United States of America (N.S.A.C.). The N.S.A.C. is the "largest and most conservative" (Judah, 1967, p. 63) national Spiritualist group in the United States, and was organized in Chicago in 1893. It can charter churches, certify ministers, mediums, and spiritual healers, conduct courses on the "science, philosophy and religion" of Spiritualism as well as sponsor Spiritualist camps.[4] As Judah has pointed out (*loc. cit.*), the N.S.A.C. "boasts of having the highest standards for mediums" requiring of minister-mediums that they be members of a N.S.A.C.-affiliated church for a year, train for at least two years to become licentiates, spend a year lecturing, and take both written and oral examinations prepared by the National Board. Reportedly Mrs. M. is the only medium in Connecticut with the ability to go into trance, [5] be possessed by a spirit, and so communicate with beings in the Summer Land, a term many Spiritualists use interchangeably with Spirit Land.[6] This gift, one of the physical "phases" of Spiritualist mediumship, is defined as "total unconsciousness on the part of the medium of events passing in the mundane world," and is "superinduced by an external spirit intelligence whose personality becomes dominant and uses the organism" of the medium primarily for speaking. This dominating "intelligence (a spirit which has once lived in mortal form)" (Spiritualist Manual, 1967, p. 54) usually is referred to as the medium's "control."

Born in Vermont in 1909 of first-generation immigrant parents—a French-Canadian mother and an Italian [7] father—Mrs. M. is the sixth of nine children, and the last of four girls born to the family.

A short, compact, energetic, intelligent woman, she is very articulate and employs an extensive vocabulary, especially for one with only eight years of formal education. She is carefully coiffed and groomed, and stylishly attired. Apt analogies spring readily to her mind and assist her in presenting spirit messages interestingly and vividly. She is self-confident, euphemistic, and optimistic. She laughs easily at the idea that some people think she is an "odd duck, a spook chaser." She reports that her psychic gifts tend to run in the family, her mother, her maternal grandmother, and her paternal great-grandmother having had similar abilities, although not to the same degree that she has. Her first encounter with the world of spirits occurred when she was four or five years old, and she adds: "nine out of ten mediums will tell you that they had experiences in their early childhood." She gives the impression of being a warm, nurturing woman, and frequently addresses her clients as "dear." She speaks comfortably of the spirit world and usually refers to her "band" of spirit guides conversationally as "they." Other members of her family have also adopted this form of reference, regardless of their involvement in Spiritualism. "They" also direct the ways in which she helps others organize their lives.

Suffering from a spiritual illness at nineteen, she was helpless in the face of her "call" to become a medium. When she protested that she did not want to be a medium, that she wanted to live a "normal" life, she was told by another medium that it was not what *she* wanted, it was what "they" wanted. Currently she lectures on Spiritualism and brings "messages" from spirits in the Summer Land to congregations in various Spiritualist churches. In the New England area most such churches do not have a medium-in-residence but function with a system of guest mediums who travel the circuit. She has participated in several of the Chatauqua-like summer camps sponsored by Spiritualists, and conducts a weekly group session or "circle" to help those wishing spiritual development. She has been giving private "readings" since she developed as a medium, and now "reads" for from 600 to 800 different people a year. "They" insignificantly influence how she organizes her time and energy, as well as how she organizes her self, her past, present, and future.

Mrs. M.'s family moved from Vermont to Connecticut when she was about four years old because of her father's work as a railroad section foreman. She now lives in the town in which she grew up, and has never lived outside of New England.

She recalls her first mediumistic experience, a nocturnal vision of a small girl kneeling near her bed, as frightening. This occurred when she was about five or six, and would have coincided with the birth and infancy of her youngest brother. Her "favorite" brother was three years her junior, and the last boy another "two or three years younger; I don't quite remember." She perceives herself as having been unusual, something of a "loner" who liked to read a great deal.

I was a kind of dreamer. I lived in a world of my own. I don't mean I was odd. I had friends, but books fascinated me. My sister, the one next to me, was more of a tomboy and I was more of the quiet type, and my father used to laugh at me. They would have to chase me away from the kitchen table when they wanted to use it, and I'd walk right through to the other room, never taking my eyes off the book. My father would say, "Here comes the priest; here comes the priest." I always had a book; as far back as I can remember, I read. But I was only able to finish grammar school, although I was a very good student. I don't say that to be egotistical, but I never had to study much: if I read something once or twice, I had it. I think I did well because I did all this reading on the side.

She continued to see spirits in the home, and would ask her mother repeatedly who they were, not realizing that her mother didn't see them: "They looked real. They had clothes, and they looked like flesh. There was nothing ghostlike or vaporish about them. This continued for about two and a half years" (i.e., until she was about six or seven). Mrs. M. concludes: "My mother must have thought she was raising somebody that was a little off," and adds that she learned not to talk about what she saw because her brothers used to torment her, saying, "You're crazy. You belong in the bug house!"

When she was eight or nine, illness kept her out of school for an entire year. She was pale and had no color and although no blood tests were run, she was supposed to have been suffering from anemia:

I was never so bored in my whole life! Of course, I read a lot, but you cannot read all day without cessation. I was on a diet of grape juice, no vinegar, and no salt, but I stole salt when my mother wasn't looking. Finally she caught me, and said that I might as well eat what I wanted to. If I was going to die, I would just have to die. I gradually got better and went back to school that next year.

Illness, her own and that of members of her family, was to play an important role in her subsequent social and psychological development.

Her mother suffered from severe and frequent headaches, unsuccessfully seeking relief from "doctor after doctor. My father spent a lot of money on her. They'd give her medication and they'd say this and that. She was in her fifties when they discovered that she had a tumor in her womb—and after an operation, her headaches went away." Because of her mother's poor health, Mrs. M. had always helped with the housework, doing all of the ironing (27 shirts a week) by the time she was eight or nine years old.

Her next indication that she was destined for a distinct role in life came when she was about twelve. She began to have what she refers to as her

floating away spells. I would actually have the sensation of floating. I know now that it's called cataleptic clairvoyance or astrotraveling. It could happen anywhere. I could have been washing dishes, and I'd all of a sudden be looking at different cities or different country scenes. One time I remember looking down, seeing a big building, and I know now that what I saw was Westminister Abbey, although I didn't know it then.

Events in her mundane world were not as attractive as her "floating away" travels.

It is clear that she saw the feminine roles available to her as restrictive, and that she did not have the power to alter the frustrating situation in which she now found herself. Her resentment grew:

I wanted to go to the academy, and then to college to become a teacher or a nurse. But my mother informed me that I was not going to do that. She had the idea that if a girl was out of her mother's sight overnight, she was apt to get into trouble. They also wouldn't let me go directly to commercial school because one of my older sisters tried it and quit. I got stubborn and said that if I couldn't do what I wanted to, then there's no sense in my going to high school. I decided that I was going to work. I got a job in the five-and-ten. It didn't last very long because my mother had these terrific headaches, and so I had to come home. The longest I ever worked in covered employment [i.e., with Social Security benefits] was three months. Every time she got sick, I'd have to come home and take care of her.

Mrs. M.'s relationship with her father was also quite strained at this time. She refers to her upbringing as "strict," her father being particularly awesome, powerful, and occasionally unjust, a mercurial figure.

I was afraid of my father. He was a hard man and a hard-working man. We had three big gardens plus we owned our own home. He used to get up about half-past four or five o'clock in the morning. Believe me, after nine o'clock at night, you didn't open your mouth. He used to swear. And if there was anything I hated, it was that swearing. I used to say, I can't stand a person that swears. I just can't stand it. I used to hate him. It's a terrible thing to say, but I did, I hated my father. I thought he was the meanest man. He was undemonstrative. Ours was not a family to show affection. I never saw him kiss my mother, either.

Mrs. M. documents further her inability to please a demanding, but unrewarding father, and the conflicts within the family:

By the time I was about twelve, thirteen, or fourteen, I had all the work in the house to do because the last of my older sisters married and left home. My mother would be flat on her back and I'd see her tear her hair because her headaches were so severe. But, let me forget to put something on the table. Or, if something wasn't there just the way Pop wanted, he'd start raving. I was just a kid, I'd cry. I was very sensitive.

But we can see that even then, the young Rita was beginning to become more self-assertive, and was ready to challenge even such a powerful, arbitrary, paternal authority:

One day, George—my favorite younger brother—came home, and I told him to go get some Italian bread, because Dad would not eat American bread. George didn't come home until after Pop had had his supper with no bread. I'm shaking in my boots, you know. I'll never forget it. Pop went out and he cut a switch. George came in and Pop laid it onto him and gave him one good crack: he was really in a temper, really furious! And without thinking—I was sitting at the table—I jumped out of the chair, grabbed that whip out of his hand, and broke it up into about five pieces with zoom, zoom, zoom! I couldn't stand to see him hit George. I was about fourteen or fifteen then, and without thinking what I was doing because I was scared of my father. He brought his hand up as if to strike me. Then he dropped his hand, and walked into the other room. My mother told me afterward, "I thought he was gonna knock you clean across the room. I don't know what ever possessed him not to give it to you." *I* think it was daring of me to jump up and break that whip up. I admit George deserved it. But I couldn't stand to see it, 'cause I was sensitive anyway, and I hated to see anyone get a lickin! To this day, I don't know where I got the courage to do it.

The unfairness of the world to the young and female was very apparent to Rita: the girls would plead for the privileges granted their brothers, but were denied them. Their father always refused, saying, "That's different." Rita comments (laughingly): "We got that constantly, and I used to think, 'Why was I born a girl?' He was strict with the boys too, though, and if they did something wrong, he'd give them a walloping." Her sister Madeline, immediately her senior, volunteered: "Italian men, that's the way they were brought up, that they were boss, and you did what they told you."

Mrs. M. was ready to challenge not only paternal authority, but also that of the religious hierarchy:

I really believed in the Catholic Church and knew the acts of faith, hope, charity, the whole business. I learned what I was supposed to learn. But I remember, in the second grade of school, they were teaching us about the beatitudes. I think that it came to the one that *the meek shall inherit the earth.* I raised my hand and asked: "How do you know that is true?" The nun said, "You sit down and keep still. You stay after school." I was terribly shy; for me that was a terrible punishment. She made me kneel on the seat, after the kids left school. She said, "You're not supposed to ask those questions. You're supposed to accept them." I persisted, "But how *do* you know that?" She said, "Now, you're not supposed to ask that. Don't you do that again, or else you can go home and stay there." I can remember questioning at that young age. I was not accepting everything that they said.

When she was eighteen, Mrs. M. married a man of Italian extraction. Her marriage ended her aspirations for a professional career in teaching or nursing. She continued to challenge her father during her early married life despite her fear of him. When he criticized her for going to the Spiritualist church, she told him that she had a

mind of my own. I'll believe the way I want. He said that I was brought up a Catholic and I was supposed to stay a Catholic. He said that that's the way his mother brought him up and that's the way he'd believe until the day he died. Then I asked him that if his mother told him that the sun would never shine again, would he believe her? He said, "By God, I would." I told him that I wouldn't be a damn fool enough to. We went round and round.

She added, offhandedly, that her oldest sister was her father's favorite, "his baby," but when he and her mother finally had to go to live with one of the children during the last twelve years of their lives, it was she whom he chose.[8]

She began to move further into her mediumship after her first son was born. She was then nineteen, had had a "hard time," had suffered from a delayed delivery, and they had to deliver him with instruments. She was in labor from Tuesday until Friday.

I carried him nearly eleven months. It sounds impossible, but I did that with both my children. The night that I started in labor, I saw my sister's face come into the room. That was my sister, Blanche [next to the oldest], who had passed on from the flu when she was pregnant. I saw her face come up in the corner, but it didn't frighten me. I didn't feel that she had come for me. Then my son was very sick when he was little, the first year of his life. I went through a lot of torment with that, but he got over it. From the time he was about three months old was when psychic things began to happen more and more to the point where I wasn't feeling well. I went to doctor after doctor. I had terrible stomach trouble. I'd have days I couldn't eat. Sometimes I'd go three days without even drinking water. I was, of course, looking for a physical cause. I realize that if psychiatry was as prevalent then as it is today, they would have sent me to a psychiatrist first thing. They said I was nervous, but I told them there wasn't anything to make me nervous.

The problems with the baby continued, since nothing agreed with him. Mrs. M. reports that although she had "loads of milk, there was no richness to it. I couldn't nurse him. They fed me beer. That was like giving me poison." Still her son did not respond, and the formulas provided for him did not work either. She finally gave him up for dead. "I fell apart and told my mother that he was going to die, and that was all there was to it."

She and the baby were living at her parents' home at this time, because her husband was away working in New York State:

It was a terrible time. I had reached the breaking point. I was nothing but a skeleton, skin and bones. The baby cried day and night. I'd sit up in bed and hold him across my chest to keep him from waking my father up. The minute I put him down after he was asleep, I'd get down on my back and he'd start to cry. Up I'd come again I had no more than two hours sleep for a long time. My mother would take him at seven in the morning. It was a strain for my father. When he wanted to sleep, well, don't make any noise to wake him up. I was so afraid of waking him that I was under a strain all the time there. When Sonny was about four and a half months old, we finally got him straightened out so that he was gaining weight.

The tensions—familial, marital, and maternal—in Mrs. M.'s life continued to mount, compounded by the death of her sister Blanche. Now about nineteen, she began to see things again, as she had before. On one occasion after she and her husband had retired, she saw a man dressed like a padre next to her son's crib. On another, she saw a woman whom her mother was later able to identify from the description as being her great-grandmother. She began to fear for her sanity, and her husband considered her "crazy." He reports that he would come home and find her cowering in a corner, weeping. She hadn't told him of her earlier experiences at the time they were married because she was afraid he would think that she was a "little bit off."

As her son began to "straighten out," Mrs. M. became more and more aware of her spirit presences:

I was afraid to stay in the house alone. My husband was a great one for going out. He used to go out and bowl, gamble, play cards—anything that took him out of the house. I was home an awful lot alone. My son was about eight to ten months old. My husband was a good worker, but you couldn't keep him home. That's the funny part, it didn't bother me that much because I loved to read. If he was home, I'd read anyway. We wouldn't have much of a conversation. That was the days before we had television and I wasn't keen on radio. As far as his going out, that didn't bother me. But I got to the point where I was so nervous because I felt eyes on me all the time. It felt like somebody staring at me. So I'd sit in the kitchen with my book and pray to God that my son wouldn't wake up, so I wouldn't have to go into a dark room. I was in terror because it felt like there were eyes on me all the time. I'd sit with my eyes glued to that book, turn the pages and try to concentrate. It got to the point where I got real nervous and my mother got concerned. I told her there was nothing wrong with me except that I was afraid to be alone, and that I was "seeing things."

In the following event, it is possible to see how the distraught Rita began to move more specifically toward her mediumship, to shift from one belief system (Catholicism) as she received instructions about another (Spiritualism). Her mother, worried about her exhausted, fearful daughter, took her to visit an acquaintance who also was a card reader and medium (Mrs. M. says that she was unaware of her acquaintance's special abilities at the time). This woman identified Mrs. M. as a potential trance-medium, telling her that "someday you are going to go under control" (i.e., under the control of the dominating spirit intelligence mentioned earlier).

I must have been about nineteen and a half then. I looked at her; I didn't know what a trance-medium was. She explained to me that under certain circumstances you can make contact with the spirit world. I told her, "You can't make

me believe that. It's contrary to everything I believe as far as my religion is concerned." She merely replied, "You'll have your proof someday."

The next step in her development is quite dramatic:

Within a month, my sister[i. e., the third-born daughter] became ill. I went
down to her house to help her out. I had fed and bathed her four children and
my own son, and sank exhausted onto the closed toilet seat in the bathroom,
the children's soiled clothing in my hands. Suddenly a figure was in front of
me, dressed in a monk's habit, and the face cowled so that one could not see it.
This figure stood a table's length away from me. I was petrified. The light was
on in that room, so it was illuminated. I said, "Oh my God, don't show me your
face." I thought that if I saw a face, I'd faint dead away. In the meantime, all
the kids had gone to sleep. The figure flashed out. Right where the figure had
come, these eyes came and stood about a foot and a half from me. The eyes
were brown. They had the most kindly look I've ever seen on anybody's eyes.
They stood in front of me and just stared right into mine. I couldn't take my
eyes away if you paid me a million dollars.

I was so scared that I couldn't move anyway. All of a sudden, after staring at
me for a few seconds, they flashed off. They came again in the corner of the
room up over the sink, looked at me, and all of a sudden they were gone. Then
over the sink in little blue chip diamonds, it started to form this thing. It
spelled out my initials, R. A. (A.'s my maiden name). I saw them etch it. By the
time that was finished, I had gotten hold of myself. I went out of the house flying. Down the stairs I went. I didn't bother taking the clothes. They stayed
right there. I went out of the house and onto the porch. I got myself in the
corner with my knees up against my chest. I'm in the corner of the house and
I'm just rigid, I'm so scared. It's a good thing that the kids didn't wake up.
They could have screamed bloody murder; I wouldn't have gone back into the
house.

After I had been out there about a half hour—holding myself rigid, visualiz-
ing it over and over again, scared to death—my husband stepped onto the
porch. He looked over and said, "What are you doing there?" That's all he had
to say. Suddenly I was laughing, crying, shaking, I went hysterical. He didn't
know what the devil had happened. He ran in the house, wet a towel and
mopped my face with it. He got me up. I just cried and cried, and shook, and
laughed. I just didn't know what I was doing. Finally, after fifteen to twenty
minutes, he got me calmed down.

Rita next returned to her mother's medium friend. Her indoctrina-
tion continued:

She knew about that spirit's visit, and told me that I shoudn't have been so
frightened, that it was only my 'guide,' and that someday he would put me
under "control." I told her I didn't want to see anything like that, but she

responded that what I wanted didn't matter; it is what "they" wanted that counted.

So it was that her main "guide," "control," or "gatekeeper" put in his first appearance. All-wise, all-knowing, kind, and benevolent, her faceless monk will be attached to her and no one else as long as she is in the "earth plane." He is not here because he was ordered to come by spirit authorities with more power than he has; rather he is here working with and for her because he has chosen to come. He has been willing to sacrifice his own development and progress in Spirit Land in order to work for and protect her. Because of his previous development and the universal nature of his being, he is able to advise and to "bring through" a client's own "loved ones" [9] from Spirit Land.

Now that her spirit guide had been identified by another medium, her anxiety and concern to learn more about the spirit world, trance-mediumship, and Spiritualism intensified. She obtained as many books as she could on psychic phenomena, as well as those in the field of psychiatry, because she still had very little idea of what trance was. All of the eight other Spiritualist mediums interviewed report that once their potential had been identified by an established medium, they began to read and investigate the literature on such phenomena. The model of mediumship exhibited by celebrated individuals such as Emanuel Swedenborg (1688–1772) and D. D. Home (1833–1886) [10] is well known to them all.

Still unconvinced that *she* would go under trance, Mrs. M.'s fears continued:

The only thing that I wanted was a logical explanation as to how you went under trance. Would I feel different? Would I be odd? A few months later I began to get "weak spells." I couldn't eat; even water wouldn't stay in my stomach. I felt as though the blood was going out through my toes, like I was dreaming; it just felt like a drain. I couldn't understand what it was. I would walk the floor. My lips would be all puffed up from my biting on them and hurting myself. I'd dig my fingernails right into my hands to hold myself together. I was afraid of what was happening. I didn't know it, but I was fighting control. I didn't know anybody I could tell this to. This went on for months, and the result was that I was becoming extremely nervous. So my mother insisted on my going to the doctor and, of course, he couldn't find anything wrong with me. I couldn't tell the doctor that I was afraid of going under control because they would put me down in the state [mental] hospital. This went on for approximately nine months. I felt terrible.

It would appear that Mrs. M.'s mother was able to adapt selectively to the Spiritualist belief system and still remain a Catholic. Actually her shift meant that she no longer punished her daughter for being "different."

I lived near my mother and I used to go up there and help her do her work every day. I went up on a Monday and didn't feel good. I had just had a rotten day. She was a great tea drinker, and we sat down and had a cup of tea. On Thursday, I told my mother, "Ma, I come up here every day, but there is something wrong with my head. I come up here, we sit down to have a cup of tea, but I don't remember the afternoon." She said, "Oh, that's all that's bothering you?" I said, "What do you mean? There's got to be something wrong with somebody like that. Am I losing my mind?" She said, "No, you've been under control for three days," I said, "I've been *what?*"

She told me that we were talking about average things when all of a sudden my eyes closed; I slumped; my voice changed, and she said I started to talk. I told her things relative to her people that she didn't even know about herself. She took a special trip to Vermont to find out if they were accurate. I looked at her and said, "Ma, you mean that that's all there is to it? I never felt anything, going or coming." It was because of the change in my voice that she knew *I* wasn't talking to her. And it was proof enough to her that I was under control, because I told her things about her family that she herself did not know. She tested me regularly because she wasn't convinced of the reality of it as first.

In her attempts to understand her mediumship, Mrs. M. became more interested in the Spiritualist church in her town, and occasionally attended services. She was told repeatedly by every medium who came to work on the platform of this church, "You belong up *here*." [That is, on the platform as a medium. One or more such identification has occurred at every Spiritualist service on which I have data.[11] One can see how these comments, from an already established medium and reinforced by the wisdom and insight of "enlightened" spirits, would be hard to ignore.] Mrs. M. decided to set further tests to adduce additional "proof" for herself. She asked a local trance-medium of wide reputation to check her. "I went under control, and when I came back to myself she told me that I had a decided gift, and urged me, 'Go on with it. You'll never be sorry.'"

In the meantime she suffered a miscarriage, but nonetheless was determined to have another baby. She did not want her first son to grow up spoiled as the result of receiving too much attention. She ultimately did conceive and gave birth to another son when her firstborn was five years old. Again she had a difficult delivery:

That's when the doctors told me to let somebody else have the babies. "You're taking your life in your hands." I didn't want to have any more children, not after two experiences like that, nor did my husband. The baby was born at home, so he was with me right straight through it. When I expressed my disappointment at not having a girl, my husband said, "You ought to thank God that you don't have a daughter to go through the hell you just did."

After suffering from an ovarian infection at twenty-six, Mrs. M. underwent a complete hysterectomy at twenty-nine.

By the time she was twenty-two, Mrs. M. had passed the written and performance tests required to become a fully licensed medium. Although she was occupied mainly with the rearing of her children during the following decade, her mediumship and spirit presences were prominent in her life. Her separation from the Catholic Church became complete, although this precipitated more battles with her father.

Mr. M. had never been too enthusiastic about his wife's work as a medium: "In fact, I think that he thought I was about to go down the river in a little padded cell." He remained a skeptic until he too was touched by a spirit during one of his wife's spiritual development sessions in which he was a participant. He already had been told by one of his wife's "guides" that he had a good healing gift, and that a Blackfoot Indian was acting as his control. But when he was touched by a spirit, he cried and sobbed uncontrollably. ("You'd think it was a woman," commented Mrs. M.)

Mrs. M. had been told that she would one day be able to work out of control, but says that she is grateful now that she cannot work any other way, as she is so "supersensitive," and that having to be conscious of the problems of others would bother her greatly. She says that she is aware of others' problems now only if they choose to recount them to her after she comes out of control. She observes that mediums who are partly conscious have to be very careful of what their own minds suggest: [12]

There are over-gullible people, over-impressionable people, who imagine all kinds of things. They can become over-imbued with the idea of mediumistic ability and go overboard with it. I always have to guard against that in an unfoldment group. But *my* consciousness is completely blotted out: I just drop "me" away; I take a sip of water—it seems to have a natural purifying influence—relax, and empty my mind, and my guide takes over.

Her life continued to be a stressful one, and the world of spirit continued to be directly involved in her career. Her favorite brother was killed at twenty-six in an automobile accident between the births of her two sons. Later the spirit of that favored eldest sister returned through another medium, urging her to go through ordination to become a minister of the Spiritualist faith as well as a licensed medium. Mrs. M.

ultimately complied with the request, and at forty-two (in 1953) was ordained, when her children were grown. Now an ordained minister-medium, she was as fully accredited in her career as one could be.

In addition to serving churches in the New England area, and Spiritualist summer camps, she continues to sit one evening a week with a group of people who want to develop spiritually. She guides and directs them, and validates what they "get": it is considered to be evidential if *she* sees the same thing that one of them sees. She also can prevent the developing individuals from attracting negative personalities from spirit.

As the *Spiritualist Manual* points out (1967:43), "Well-developed mediums . . . . learn how to prevent these [bad] spirits from controlling or confusing them by directly asking aid from the guides whom they have learned are worthy of absolute trust. . . . . Undeveloped, undisciplined mediums [are] the sport of the lower spirits. . . . Once when Mrs. M. was sitting with a group, she saw repeated flashing of red lights. She immediately inquired whether or not everyone was all right; she then dismissed the circle for that evening, interpreting the lights as a warning from her trusted monk. And she has had to exorcise such "low spirits" on a few occasions.

Mrs. M. asserts proudly that she has never advertised, has never had a card printed to announce her abilities. People hear of her by word-of-mouth, or call her for an appointment after seeing her "work" on the public platform in a Spiritualist church. She books four appointments a morning five days a week throughout the year, except for the Florida vacation which she takes annually, staying in the South for a period of four to six weeks. Her services are so much in demand that she usually is booked up for at least two months in advance.

ANALYSIS I
"The weird sisters,
hand in hand . . . ."

Shakespeare, *Macbeth*, Act I Sc. 3

As Thomas Szasz (1970; p. 191) has pointed out, the "act of classification is an exceedingly significant event." The data from the human life set out above could be classified and organized to present Mrs. M. as a psychopathic personality, or at least as a case of arrested development. The pathogenic dynamics seem clear. By employing a series of defense mechanisms thoughout her life, she has been able to reduce and control magically the tensions created by a series of interpersonal conflicts. Although she is coping with the various problems of living and helping others to cope, she could be judged to be suffering

impairment of psychological, social, and cultural functioning. To anyone familiar with the literature [13] on possession trance-mediums, the
details appear to arrange themselves in an all-too-familiar pattern.

Parent-Child Relationships

The relationships between the girl, Rita, and her parents seem not to
have been conducive to the forming of a healthy personality. Her
mother, ill, ineffective, and powerless in the family, was unable to meet
her love needs, or provide her with an acceptable model for womanhood. Nonetheless, the mother's very illness was effective in controlling
Rita's behavior, who could never make plans for her own self-actualiza-
tion because the mother's needs took priority. At several stressful times
in Rita's life, her anxiety expressed itself somatically, a clear indication
of her identification with her mother's mode of handling problems.
Until her parents' deaths, within a few months of each other when Rita
was fifty-one, their demands limited her self-determination. It was also
only after they made the "transition known as death" that she was able
to devote five mornings a week to giving private "readings," as she still
does.

It seems clear that her relationship with her father was also highly
unsatisfactory. Born into a situation where he already had a favorite
girl "baby," she tried to serve him well, but succeeded only in invoking
his unpredictable and often unjust wrath. He attempted to undo his
unjustness with money, not love: Once when he had beaten her for an
imagined impudence, and realized it, he gave her fifty cents and gruf-
fly asked her to stop crying. She remembers that she had to wear stockings for three days to cover the welts on her legs caused by the whipping. She was explicit about her desire to be a boy, for males are
powerful, self-determining, and come equipped from birth with privileges which were not hers, at least not as a child. Her need to be distinctive, to be an individual and her persistent human conviction that
she was unique, were violated constantly (e. g., as when she was not
permitted to attend commercial school because an older sister had performed poorly—which implied, "You are all alike.") Such parent/child
relationships are found quite uniformly among the families of all of the
Spiritualist mediums interviewed. All have referred to their upbringing
as "strict," and described their parents as undemonstrative with each
other and with their children.

In Mrs. M.'s case, having a controlling spirit monk makes it possible
for her to manage what might be considered her Oedipus-Electra complex, although it is a somewhat mutilated resolution. She now has an

all-loving, all-protecting father figure with whom she can identify. Sexless on both conscious and unconscious levels (he is a celibate monk, and she is always aware of his presence because she sees the skirt of his habit), he also is willing to sacrifice the most important goal (spiritual progress) a spirit or a human being could have in order to work for her. Her own father would not even sacrifice his sleep when she was nursing a sick child. She explicitly denies sexual titillation where her guide is concerned, saying that it is a

purely aesthetic [sic] relationship. It has no foundation in the physical aspect at all, except he does possess me and take over. If I had any guide around me that was "feeling me up," I would feel that I was with a very low vibratory force.

Fully aware of the mechanism of projection, Mrs. M. observes that some mediums do indulge in

wishful thinking. A woman called me, said she had had very psychic experiences, and that she had had sexual relations with her spirit guide. I just listened to her with amazement and told her I didn't want to get involved. I felt that if she was in touch with any forces at all, it would have to be with the very lowest. I'm not saying it's impossible, but I doubt that something like that could happen. She was middle-aged, unmarried, and I think that a medium—man or woman—can attach too much importance to the guide; this is probably a substitute for an unhappy marriage, or for not being married. It can be almost like an imaginary lover. Some mediums that I have known will refer to their guides in the same way that someone else might refer to God, which is wrong.

When possessed by the monk's spirit, Mrs. M. is transformed into the powerful, privileged male she longs to be, and he also provides the opportunity for education which her own father denied her. The *Spiritualist Manual* (1967; p. 82) observes: "We often receive, through mediums of moderate education, communications which plainly come from a trained and educated mind." The official interpretation is that here is "strong evidence that the message does not originate with the mediums, but comes from without." Mrs. M. would agree, but adds that because of her limited education, spirit had to put her through a training period in order to get her ready for the "work":

For example, the word "infinitesimal." I would hear it and hear it going through my head, and other words that did not have any meaning for me. Finally, I would go and look them up in the dictionary. I needed those words in order to be able to convey the message that spirit wanted to send through me.[14]

It requires little insight to see that this is a surrogate father who behaves the way she always wished that her own father had behaved: kind, exclusively devoted to her by choice, always there at moments of stress, while still encouraging her to be an individual, to be herself. The *Spiritualist Manual* (1967; p. 56) explicitly recognizes this, affirming that "the relation of the medium to the manifesting intelligence is. . .sometimes that of a child to a wise and loving parent. . . ."

Sibling Relationships

Relationships with siblings also emerge as problems to be solved for all the mediums surveyed for this chapter. Becker (1973; p. 4) remarks

Sibling rivalry is a critical problem that reflects the basic human condition . . . children . . . so openly express man's tragic destiny: he must desperately justify himself as an object of primary value in the universe; he must stand out,. . . show that he counts more than anything or anyone else.

Eight of the nine mediums were born somewhere in the middle of large families.[15] Therefore most of them had to fight for parental attention and affection already in short supply. These problems seem to have been especially difficult in the case of Mrs. M. She felt herself to be unique from early childhood. She reports that her mother was both exasperated and impressed by her visions and prophecies; however, an older sister (third-born daughter, three years her senior) comments today that she knew nothing of these abilities, and "considered Rita just the same as the rest of us."

Early in life, Mrs. M. learned skill in the secrecy, deceit, and manipulation so characteristic of the political maneuvering of middle children (e. g., she learned not to tell anyone of her visions, to play ill to avoid unpleasant situations, to violate the doctor's diet by stealing salt, and to conceal from her husband her mediumistic experiences). Her behavior during the year she apparently suffered from anemia might be seen as regressive, as a futile effort to command the attention she so desperately desired. As Rita recalls her vague symptoms, she began to recover after her mother decided not to give her any more special attention (e.g., insist on the special diet), announcing that if Rita was going to die, she would just have to die. Other evidence of her attempts to attract attention is reflected in the nickname "Magpie," given her by her siblings because she talked so much.

One can see something of the competitive, exhibitionistic, manipulative sibling pattern carried over into the relationships mediums have with each other. Without exception, all nine mediums deny that they want attention themselves but project this desire onto other mediums, some of whom they denounce as "poseurs" and "actors." [16] All mention the jealousy rampant among them at the same time that they deny their own jealousies. ("There is room for all of us.") Unwarranted attention given young mediums, which they "can't handle," is liable to put them in the state hospital. The State Secretary of the National Spiritualist Association in Connecticut comments: "Professional jealousy in mediumship is very widespread; *that is the ruination of Spiritualism*" (his emphasis).

All must contend with the bit of Spiritualist philosophy which propounds the idea that inspired communications from the

spirit world are not necessarily infallible truths, but may partake of the imperfections of the mind from which they emanate and . . . are subject to misinterpretation by those to whom they are given (*Spiritualist Manual*, 1967, p. 46).

So mediums can pit their omniscient, omnipotent guides, as well as their own more advanced spiritual development, against that of any other medium. They need accept the authority of no one else, neither other mediums, nor other presumed sources of spirit inspiration.

Not even the client for whom the spirit message is intended necessarily knows better than the medium. If a client rejects a message or says he doesn't understand it, the medium usually insists impatiently: "I can't change it, that's the way I get it. Think about it; ask your mother." Or: "Perhaps it is for the future then. Remember what I said."

Weston La Barre (1969, p. 146) states that the charismatic cult leader he studied exhibits all the characteristics of the "urethral personality: Flamboyance, exhibitionism, dramatic flair, sensitivity to and preoccupation with the opinion of others . . . slyness, ambition, and quick temper." All these characteristics, combined with upward social mobility—"he must stand out"—are to be found in mediums who have turned to Spiritualism to gain power when their fantasized goals—love and attention of parents; specialized knowledge; control over their own and other's lives; "to count for more than anyone else"—are thwarted.

Stress, Authority, and Mediumship

Stressful periods in the mediums' lives set the stage for the entrance of spirit beings. Mrs. M. saw her first vision when she suffered most acutely from sibling rivalry. Her "floating away" spells at twelve magically made it possible for her to escape the stress of total responsiblity for managing the house, and effortlessly transported her to an exotic fairyland filled with marvelous sights, while she left her material body in the kitchen scrubbing the dishes or ironing shirts.

Before she actually went under control, Mrs. M. primarily employed the defense mechanism of withdrawal. In their feeling of uniqueness, and being compelled to secrecy because they were so misunderstood, our budding mediums—and many spiritually "gifted" religious figures, such as Western La Barre's snake-handling cult leader—constructed worlds of their own into which they could withdraw, worlds without stress: "that only world which gives pleasure and gratifies his Pleasure Principle, his own narcissistic psyche." (La Barre, 1969; p. 150)

A loner in a world populated with people visible only to her, Mrs. M. could anticipate the arrival of a favorite uncle (who always gave her a dime when he came) when others hadn't an inkling that he was coming. She learned early how to gain control over her world, a world in which parents are strict, busy, hard-working, and too tired to expend energy understanding the "craziness" of a child suffering from what they considered to be an overactive imagination.

From the outset, constant conflict with the authority figures in her life created stress and caused her to experience anxiety. Mrs. M. sees herself as having been always a curious, independent, questioning person who had confidence in her own mind and her own ability to think through the illogical ideas being thrust at her by an arbitrary adult world. "The meek shall inherit the earth? How do you *know* that?" She thinks of herself as having been a six-year-old willing to take on the Roman Catholic Church and its sacred books. Of course, it was a way of punishing her father who insisted, with the Church, that she should accept without question that which parents and Church told her, even if it went contrary to all of her sensory perceptions. (She was meek and seemed not to be heiress to the earth.)

She was prepared to find in Spiritualism a compatible religion which presents God as an impersonal power labeled Infinite Intelligence rather than as an authoritative father figure who demands unquestioned allegiance but promises very little in emotional dividends.

As a daughter, helpless to punish an unjust father effectively, she was later to find solace in knowing that "sin and wrong-doing will necessarily bring remorse and suffering that would be difficult to describe in words. . . ." (*Spiritualist Manual*, 1967, p. 39). Spiritualism emphasizes individual responsibility for obtaining Heaven on Earth.

Once she had gone under "control," she became much more self-assertive, but now under the guise of spirit direction. Under trance, she can abdicate ego controls temporarily, while her monk deals with the exigencies of the world. We see that he appeared to succor her at a time when she was questioning her competence as a wife, mother, and daughter.[17] Her child was ill, and the milk she had for him was not rich enough; her husband was frequently out of the house; and her father continued to be angry with her for persisting with the "nonsense" of Spiritualism.

As a married woman, she continued to challenge the authority of the Catholic Church aided by her protecting monk. The stress she felt over her conflict with the Church was somewhat mitigated when the spirit of a dead priest came through her mediumship and told her Catholic mother that there was nothing wrong in being a medium, or in consulting one. The only reason the Church has to inveigh against them, he explained, is because the ignorant laity is so gullible that it would stop supporting the Church and begin to worship and pray to the medium. With this message from Spirit Land, he not only exonorated Mrs. M. but pointed out the threat that charismatic figures have always constituted to legitimate, established authority; namely, how to routinize the gnostic vision, once direct communication with the Truth has been achieved? Her husband ("he's a lousy Catholic") gleefully related that the local parish priests were quite worried about her at one time and pressed upon him books for her to read, shouting at him: "We're the only ones who can communicate with the next world; we are the ones chosen to know."

Mrs. M. rose to the position of vice-president in the State Spiritualist Association of Connecticut, but a difference of opinion with other state officials about the Board's responsibility ("Not one of 'em had the backbone of a spider") caused her to sever this connection. Currently she is affiliated directly and only with the national organization.

Mrs. M. also felt ready—with the support of spirit—to challenge other major knowers, "chosen ones," in American society. She had reason to lack faith in medical practitioners when she was growing up: an infant sister died of an uncured abscess; her mother suffered mysterious, incapacitating headaches which could not be diagnosed; a brother, fatally injured in an automobile accident and lying comatose in the medically prescribed diet when she was nine, and nonetheless recovered; the doctors could not cure her son's problem, and it took her mother's folk knowledge to do that; and they could not find out what was wrong with her or treat her when she was suffering before going under control. She understood from spirit inspiration that her favorite frother, fatally injured in an automobile accident and lying comatose in a hospital, had suffered from a "torn brain," a diagnosis which astounded the attending physician. He inquired: "Young woman, how did you know that?" And now her guides sometimes give medical advice contary to that suggested by the medical doctors of the Earth Plane, and they're usually right.

That perceived power over the real world is one of the strengths of Spiritualism is apparent: a male medium in his late sixties recalled that he was first attracted to Spiritualism as a child because his father's boss, a highly successful man, never made a business decision without first consulting his own (the boss's) clairvoyant sister. So it was evident to the boy that the mediumistically endowed woman had power over all of them: her brother, the highly successful boss; his employees, including the informant's father; and finally over the boy himself, until he too was able to develop into a powerful medium.

Clearly, when stress occurred in the life of Mrs. M., whether occasioned by sibling, parental, or other authority conflicts, her mediumistic abilities manifested themselves. Thus she was able to redefine and reorganize events in such a way that she maintained at least a modicum of control over these critical relationships. She emerges as a powerful, competent figure, able to do, to create a satisfactory, gratifying world in which as she says, "Thoughts are things." Equally magically, she has the power to undo the consequences of painful thoughts and events for both herself and her clients.

The Band in Summer Land

The magical control a Spiritualist medium is able to exercise over the world is seen in the nature of the elevated, progressive spirits with whom he or she carries on transactions. By the mechanism of both complementary and supplementary projection, a medium is able to create a fantasy world inhabited by beings who not only bring power, but over whom one literally and symbolically has control. Mrs. M.'s gatekeeping monk steps in when, as she puts it, "I drop 'me' away." A guide in whom she has complete confidence, he admits or excludes all other spirits. And those other carefully selected spirits become the loci of unadmitted, inappropriate, or unfulfilled desires, repositories of a medium's fears and aspirations. Possessed, the medium must be heeded, having become an eloquent and authoritative instrument of other voices and other times. Offenders among the living on the Earth Plane are brought to heel, siblings outmaneuvered, and parents punished by prescient spirits. Furthermore, one's patricidal rage or jealous anger are now characteristics of spirits that must take responsibility for such unacceptable aggressiveness. For example, Nadaena comes to Mrs. M. She is the selfish, formerly self-indulgent, willful spoiled ruler's daughter who had "done away with people who displeased her." This

spirit seems clearly to represent the willful, rebellious Rita who imagi-
natively did away with those who angered her: through Nadaena she is
able to express her unconscious wish to kill her hated father, and the
demanding youngest brother (a wish she made explicit in one interview). Now Nadaena (Mrs. M.?) returns, having expiated her sins after
many thousands of years in the world of spirit. Nadaena temporarily
takes over Mrs. M.'s ego control, comes through and urges clients "to
make use of their abilities, make use of their lives, and be considerate
of others." Contrite and virtuous, she works at undoing all of the mur-
derous thoughts Mrs. M. once had, for her "particular forte is to try to
get people to better themselves and not be selfish as she was."

The little spirit girl, Daisy Bell, permits the acting out of the indulged baby role, one in which Rita's needs for the attention she never
had and the nurturance she desired can be satisfied. Daisy Bell is mischievous, frivolous, and tactless: she "tells all" with impunity. Such
child spirits are familiar from disparate parts of the world such as
Brazil and Burma: Pressel (1974, p. 192) interprets the function of
these spirits as permitting mediums to act out needs of the baby role,
while Spiro (1967, p. 221) tells us that Burmese shamans are able to
express their dependency needs in a "highly regressive identification"
with a baby girl *nat*. He adds that "the shaman expresses his dependency, making claims, as it were, on the nurturance of all who watch
him."

Mrs. M. also is helped by Dr. Denton, whose voice reportedly is altogether different from hers: it is deeper and he employs a different
"phraseology." Clearly a projection of her own aspirations for formal
credentials, his degree is honorary and he acts as the liaison between
her and the Council members in Spirit Land. He usually appears when
she is working in a "circle" of people, and speaks often of the Council.
She assumes that the Council oversees the band of spirits which come
to her. She reemphasizes that the spirits in one's band "elect" to come
to the medium's assistance, and must be advanced spirits in order to be
able to take such a position.

Mrs. M. was able to undo her guilt over her hostile rejection of the
Catholic Church (when the priestly spirit communicated through her
and exonerated her), and one of her spirit band also can be regarded
as undoing the hostility implied by her lifelong questioning of established religion:

There is a Bapist minister; his discourses are all very religious, more on the
order of the personal application of things and their oneness with God and all
this sort of thing. He told how he *had* been very active in his church, but *that he*

realized he didn't know the full scope of religion, that he had only accepted it, as the textbook said [my emphasis].

Not only does the spirit band permit one magical control of the world. One is also able to manipulate other spirits, spirits of those who have made the transition recently, over whom one had very little control when they were on the Earth Plane. In Mrs. M.'s case, her father's spirit returned and

stood right beside my bed. That was the biggest shock of my life. I didn't expect him, being the type of man he was. I thought that if anybody would come back, it would be my mother. But it was my father who put in an appearance first.

She is causing the angry, rejecting father to undo all of his denials of the validity of Spiritualism.

Magical undoing of parental injustice is epitomized in the following account, told me by a sixty-seven-year-old male medium:

We always called my father the Boss, never Father or Dad. Well, after he died he came back just as he was in life, just like a bull in a china shop, blustering and giving the orders. I told him, "You think you're still alive; well, you're not! You're not the boss any longer. I'm the boss, now. And don't you come back until you can behave yourself, and conduct yourself civilly." When he did return, he came back on his knees—*on his knees*—humble, and asking forgiveness [his emphasis]. The medium added, I was never one to take orders, even to this day. I've always given them, all my life, and it was difficult to be brought up so strictly. In fact, my mother was so strict that many times I stood between her and my sister to protect the sister. There wasn't a very good feeling there for a son to do that. But she [i.e., the mother] comes in beautifully now (spiritually) and works with both me and my wife (who also is a medium). She came back and apologized for the difficult times we had had. *This relieved a great deal of pressure* [emphasis added].

"The Medium is the Message" [18]: The Power of the Word

Other evidence that Spiritualist mediums attempt to exercise magical control of their worlds is to be found in their use of language. Zaretsky (1974, p. 189) observes that Spiritualist churches share with other American metaphysical movements, such as Christian Science and New Thought churches, a belief in the inner power and meaning of words, and Judah (1967, p. 17) considers this importance attached to words as "one of the defining attributes of Spiritualist churches when compared with orthodox denominations." Zaretsky (1974, p. 190) goes on to say that Spiritualists speak of the power of the spoken word in both the religious and secular spheres; they claim that words "once uttered, have the power to create or effect [sic] the referent which they symbolize." Mrs. M. often commented that "Words are things," or used its variant, "I believe that thoughts are things, you know. . . ." This gives the speaker control [19] over people, spirits, and things in his world. A part of the power, uniqueness, and superiority which Mrs. M. sees in herself resides in her ability to manipulate thoughts: these can be sent to others to communicate, to heal, and to control. Her mastery over the symbolic world of language is impressive, as was mentioned earlier. Her conversation is interlaced with correctly used and pronounced words such as "emulate," "cessation," "infinitesimal," "imbued," "embryonal," "vicarious," and "detrimental." It might be pointed out that although she is blunt about the hatred she felt for her father because of his strictness and unfairness, she actually first mentioned (and repeatedly stated) that she hated him because he swore; that she couldn't tolerate.

The use of euphemisms is endemic in Spiritualist publications and on the platform; for example, no one is poor, just suffering from an "impecunious condition." Such emphasis on verbal gentility bespeaks a whole world of upwardly mobile people who have faith that the Word will permit the speaker to transcend the social, educational, and economic limitations by which he is circumscribed. And the Word finally permits transcendence of that ultimate limitation, Death: one only makes a "transition."

The Medium Gives the Message

Finally trance-mediumship permits one not only the power to redefine and manipulate his own reality, but also gives him the authority to foist that distorted reality onto others with whom he has transactions. Mrs. M. was asked by an acquaintance who knew of her mediumistic ability to visit his wife, who had been committed to the state mental hospital after having been apprehended rushing about the streets, incoherent, in the pouring rain. The woman, an only child, had always had a very difficult relationship with her mother. The mother, now dead, returned in spirit to continue her harrassment. In order to cope with the accusing, critical voice of her mother, the patient had been attending a spiritual development class run by a male medium. He urged her to forgive her mother, to listen and accept what the mother was saying. (The mother was continuing her in-life denigration of her daughter and her daughter's husband, saying that he was a philanderer, that he had married her for her property, that he now had put her in a mental institution, and that the daughter—the patient—was herself a fool, etc., etc.) Mrs. M. inquired if she had told the doctors about the voice. The patient exclaimed: "Do you think I'm crazy? They'd lock me up for good!" Mrs. M. continues:

I began to visit with her regularly, for perhaps two and a half months. I talked with her about her mother, and I said, "Forgive her, yes, you should do that. But for heaven sakes, don't listen to her! Ignore her! When her voice comes, read, knit, crochet, anything! But keep busy—and don't listen!" I tried to give her a different slant on her own reactions. You *can* shut out evil influences. Of course, I asked the guides to stay with her and help her. When she left there, she had no more problems.

Mrs. M., like R. D. Laing, found a malicious parent, intelligibility, and praxis in what was otherwise considered to be human pathology. But once Mrs. M. had drawn the patient into her own world, and helped her to accept her own "psychotic vision as authentic," they both had declared "war on the world view of normal consensus" (Sedgwick, 1971, p. 15).

Hand in hand, medium and client walked into the well-organized, but weird, land of Spirit.

Summary, Analysis I

The paradigmatic case of Mrs. M., a possession trance-medium, presents us with an individual whose emotional needs were frustrated from the outset. The fourth girl (and sixth of nine children) of hard-working, strict, first-generation immigrant parents, she had to struggle throughout childhood, girlhood, and young womanhood for self-realization. Her aspirations to pursue an acceptable feminine career in teaching or nursing were thwarted by the demands of family responsibility. She had to leave school at thirteen, submit to paternal authority (which was at times arbitrary), care for an incapacitated mother, younger siblings, and the home. Mrs. M. was rebellious against institutionalized authority as early as she can remember, but was powerless to change her situation without the help of intervening spirits from the Summer Land.

Supported by a band of diverse spirit guides orchestrated by an all-caring, all-knowing, and constantly attentive monk control, she is able to become whatever she wishes by complementary projection: an all-powerful and wise male; a well-educated male doctor whose credentials are impeccable; a mischievous child, center of attention which she herself never had; a high-born, self-indulgent and powerful Egyptian woman; and so forth. By supplementary projection, she can also foist onto the spirits the unacceptable attributes she finds in herself: the engaging child spirit also is irresponsible; the Egyptian was not only selfish, she also wilfully destroyed those who crossed her. Utilizing the mechanism of projection, Mrs. M. and the other mediums surveyed here transcend their immediate limitations, personal and environmental, and ultimately have the power to transcend the universal human problem: Death.

To conclude that Mrs. Rita M. is a psychopathological personality may be overstating the case, but clearly she can be said to be coping with life's problems with primitive or perhaps even childish methods. Not only is she herself adjusting in this fashion, but this neurotic woman also is organizing the lives of other borderline cases with the same magic wand.

ANALYSIS II
"Though this be madness,
yet there is method in't."

Hamlet, Act II, Sc. 2

Spiro might well have been describing New England mediums rather than Burmese shamans when he suggested that the "initial recruitment experience, ... as well as persistence in [the role] are both motivated by the desire to satisfy. . . . frustrated needs: sexual, dependency, prestige, and for want of a better term, Dionysian" (Spiro, 1967, p. 219). He adds that the "psychopathological elements" in their shamanistic/mediumistic behavior are temporarily resolved by the "intermittent activation of the role" (Spiro, 1967, p. 226). So as was demonstrated in Analysis I, one could classify those recruited to become shamans in Burma or mediums in New England as "persons suffering from either pathological or at least pathogenic symptoms," and conclude that it is by "becoming shamans [read: mediums] that they are saved from psychopathology" (Spiro, 1967, p. 228).

However, if the act of classification is a highly significant event because it is a manifestation of human power to create categories rather than discover them, as Szasz (1970, p. 190) suggests, how can we be certain we have been putting "spiritualists and shamans" in the right class? The data from the life and works of Mrs. Rita M. could be classified and organized to present her as well within the range of normal and healthy as set out by the American value system. Looked at this way, she is a figure in the mainstream of American life, or at least is striving to become one. Neither she nor Spiritualism is innocent of the Enlightenment, the Industrial Revolution, and the scientific method.

Spiritualism grew out of the main challenge of the nineteenth century, namely, the conflict which the rise of science (and materialism) presented to religion (and to spiritualism). One of the first metaphysical movements to be fostered by that challenge, Spiritualism shared many ideas in common with the other such groups. These ideas, "already existent in pre-nineteenth-century American thought, were reinforced in the nineteenth century, and formed a cultural milieu which has continued as a part of the American scene to the present." (Judah, 1967, p. 22) The confrontation is epitomized by the comment of one nineteenth-century observer who pointed out in 1886:

We learned that we were not men, but protoplasm. We learned that we were not spirits, but chemical combinations. We learned that we had laid up treasure in the wrong places. We learned that the drama of 'Hamlet' and the 'Ode to Immortality' were secretions of the gray matter of the brain (Carter, 1971, p. 89).

There are many excellent studies of the cultural and social upheaval fomented by "the spiritual crisis of the gilded age" (Carter, 1971) and several others which examine the crisis with particular reference to the birth and development of Spiritualism.[20] I do not propose to summarize them here, but an examination of the specific ways in which Mrs. M. is interpreting, applying, and promulgating the value system which crystallized out of nineteenth-century American thought is germane to our discussion.

Spiritualism and American Values

Twenty years ago, Cora Du Bois (1955, p. 132 ff) adumbrated the basic premises underlying the American value system. These are still operative (cf. Hsu, 1972). First, Du Bois points out, we—scientist and layman alike—believe ourselves to be living in a mechanistic world of which man is the master. Since this world was created by the Great Mechanic and set in motion according to Natural Law, it is neither random nor capricious, but orderly and knowable. The little human machines which inhabit it have not only the ability but the obligation to make an effort, to work at knowing and mastering it and ourselves as well. As Floyd Matson (1966, p. 14) says, ". . . the universal pattern of rigid determinism, or mechanistic causation, applied to human nature as plainly as to physical nature." Not only are we dealing with a machine that "ticks along like clockwork—now and hereafter. It is a very optimistic machine in every way. With perseverance and better understanding of natural laws, even the mechanism of death may be unlocked, reassembled and reversed" (Cannel and Macklin, 1973, p. 167).

Specifically, the God of the metaphysical movements was regarded as a utilitarian deity who granted the desires of those who followed and used his spiritual laws. (Judah, 1967, p. 28) So it is not surprising to learn that one of the principles of Spiritualism states that one "makes his own happiness or unhappiness as he obeys or disobeys Nature's physical and spiritual laws" (*Spiritualist Manual*, 1967, p. 37). The manifestations of spirits and the like, which orthodox religions accepted as "supernatural," were redefined by Spiritualists as being phenomena which conform to the regularities of Natural Law. No caprice, disorder, or irregularity is to be found in Summer Land either. So Mrs. M.'s reasoning is not necessarily "primitive," nor a reflection of "traditional, magico-religious" thought. She, like Robin Horton's African religious expert (1970, p. 134), assumes a "basic modicum of regularity" in the behavior of the spiritual agencies at work behind observed events. And, as Horton goes on to point out, the expert "who diagnoses the intervention of a spiritual agency is also expected to give some acceptable account of what moved the agency in question to intervene" (1970, p. 136). Mrs. M. also provides us with such accounts. The cause of the aberrant behavior of the institutionalized woman she treated was a mother's nagging spirit; the proof that this was the cause, and that bizarre behavior was the effect of spirit intervention was empirically clear: the woman's problems began when she accepted her mother's voice and ceased when she stopped listening to it.

Furthermore, Du Bois (1955) tells us, Americans subscribe to two more basic premises which are inherently contradictory: we believe that all men are created equal, while holding at the same time that man is perfectible. This contradiction is also embodied in Spiritualist philosophy. So it is that all of the mediums in the sample under consideration claimed on the one hand that all humans are endowed by Natural Law with some psychic abilities (so in that we are equal), while on the other hand, they believe that they alone had been born with a gift. Without exception, all knew of gifted relatives in their backgrounds, from which one could infer that they perceived a legitimate claim on a genetically bestowed ability that made them special, more sensitive instruments. Thus they were acknowledging with the mainstream American that while all are created equal, some do have special talents which can be perfected; one can emerge as a unique individual: not everyone who applies to medical school is admitted; some are more intelligent than others; not everyone gets into art school; some are more talented than others; and so on.

Work emerges again as a specific instrumental value through which Americans strive not only to master a mechanistically conceived universe but also to reach the goal of their own perfectibility. Official Spiritualism and Mrs. M. completely endorse this value. We have seen how Spiritualism provided the means for Mrs. M. to improve herself educationally, as well as providing a specialized role akin to teaching when that latter avenue for achieving perfection was blocked. The *Spiritualist Manual* (1944, p. 131) emphasizes the value of work explicitly, stating that while there are idlers in the lower spheres who do not feel the necessity of working, ". . . on the spirit plane, all are workers, even the children; and there are beautiful children there, many of them taken out of the slums of earth life, out of the homes of poverty and degradation—little outcasts or waifs—taken to that spirit plane and trained for work. . . . They desire to work" (*Spiritualist Manual* 1944, p. 132). So everyone works in the spirit world without drudgery and "hard, fierce competition. . . ." Spirits and thus mediums know it is a "truth that man not only is immortal but is limitless in his . . . achievements as he unfolds, advances, and rises, step by step, through *self-effort, self-culture* and growth to the uttermost bounds of power and possibility" (*Spiritualist Manual,* 1944, p. 133).[21] Clearly each person must be self-reliant and make an individual effort in order to move toward perfection, for "Everybody will have to do his own work, though there are helpers and teachers all along the way." (*Spiritualist Manual,* 1944, p. 134).

As noted, most of the spirits that are sufficiently elevated to act as teachers and guides are either foreign or autochthonous Americans (cf. Macklin, 1974; Hallowell, 1967) and are therefore outside the society and its members whom they have come to scold, correct, advise, and help. They are, nonetheless, redolent of a peculiarly nineteenth-century bouquet. They are invariably optimistic: "Any elevated spirits," says Mrs. M., "would know whether or not the person was able to accept a pessimistic message. It is only common sense that they wouldn't bring through a message which would upset someone very badly, even if it were true." Furthermore, the spirit teachers always counsel in terms of the values of a stable society and plump for the reestablishment of traditional family and marital relationships: "You still care for that guy, don't you?"; or, "Stop nagging him; try a little harder to please him." The spirits appear to be inner-directed nineteenth-century individualists and counsel accordingly: "Be yourself! Your mother means well, but you must assert yourself; she's coming through to apologize."

Interestingly enough, even the hard-working mediums, for whom no task should be impossible, did not and do not challenge the existing power structures of American society. As we have seen, frustrated though she was by the social system in which she found herself, powerless Rita M. was able only through trance to transform herself temporarily into a knowledgeable commanding presence, with whom others—including males with institutionalized authority—had to reckon. Furthermore, spirit guides who direct spiritualist mediums fall into the category that I. M. Lewis (1970, 1971) has termed "peripheral": they are not "morally charged powers held to be responsible for upholding public morality" (1970, p. 204). Many are representatives of societies and cultures alien to that of the medium and her clients. They even may be frivolous and a little silly.[22] As is true of the spirits found in the diverse areas from which Lewis (1970) draws his data,[23] our spirits regularly expressed a "marked predilection . . . for women in general, and . . . for certain depressed and despised categories of men"[24] (1970, p. 294). Lewis points out that the men must permit the existence of such cults, and that "both men and women are more or less satisfied: neither sex loses face and the official ideology of male supremacy is preserved." (1971, p. 86).

Thus it seems clear that Mrs. M. and her spirits share with the rest of us the view that we occupy a universe that can be understood and that life is a problem to be solved: With the help of knowledgeable experts—talented, trained scientists, mediums, and progressed spirits—we too can understand and cope. We too can approach perfection by applying ourselves optimistically and by accepting direction from those better prepared than we. Progress is inevitable both here and in the hereafter, if we desire it and make the effort to achieve it.

All of these basic American and Spiritualist premises about the nature of the universe and the nature of man and his relationship to the universe are epitomized in one cheerful paragraph from an article entitled, "How You Can Succeed" (Smith, 1970, p. 5), gleaned from the official publication of the N.S.A.C.:

Nothing is impossible to honest, *hard work.* Even genius is an infinite capacity for hard work. This includes research, digging for truth, even seeking, reading biographies, autobiographies, psychology, sociology, philosophy, ... stories of the lives of successful people, to see what makes them *"tick,"* and what their ideas were of success, and what were the results. . . . making a success of life is much like raising a good garden or baking a good cake. . . . But *you must follow the directions,* or you can have an unsuccessful *product* (my emphases).

The basic American premises and the values accompanying them are stated explicitly by Reverend Smith. Implicitly, she characterizes the method by which her readers can produce an ideal garden, cake, or human life.

On Method: Scientists and Spiritualists

Charles Matson tells us that by the end of the eighteenth century Newton's method, "the method of causes and mechanisms, had become standard procedure throughout the respective sciences" (1966, p. 15). Sensory perception was the sole source of the true knowledge about the "real" world. "What could not be stretched or shrunk to fit its procrustean framework [i.e., the giant mechanism] was simply not 'phenomena' at all. . . . it was only superstition, a kind. . . . of fallacy of vision which the scientific lens would soon correct, and which meanwhile might better be disregarded" (Matson, 1966, p. 11). Although the deterministic Newtonian model has been considerably modified by physical scientists, practitioners of the human sciences remain strongly, if uneasily, attached to this paradigm. With other social scientists who move in the world-taken-for-granted of Western culture, I too consider that there is one way to know: observe, count, and measure objectively; reason inductively, generalize, and replicate the research. I approached Mrs. M. with a "scientific" notion of what was "real" as opposed to "simulated" trance and, like my colleagues, "suspect" that my subject is not in "real" trance because her trancing behavior is so stereotyped. But we have learned recently that even those behaviors expressed in trances induced by the use of hallucinogenic drugs are controlled and stereotyped.[25]

The "scholarly" paradigm in Analysis I does not accept the existence of spirit forces, but sees religion "as a haven for the maladjusted, a compensatory mechanism for misfits." Religion is a symptom. As Harvey Cox (1974, p. 14) wryly observed in a recent review of a book dealing with marginal religions: "Regardless of what informants tell [social scientists] about faith and what it means to them, the investigators always know better." So eager are we to convince our colleagues of the validity and reliability of our data that the usual scientific paper follows a highly predictable format: a declaration of methods and techniques follows hard upon the statement of hypothesis. I include a discussion of my methodology and techniques here because they represent an integral part of the argument that the American social scientist, layman, and medium alike share basic epistemological premises and methods.

The 1975 National Spiritualist Association of Churches *Year Book* informs us that a total of 532 mediums were commissioned [26] by the organization for that year in the United States. Of those, 144 were men, 374 were women, and the sex of the remaining 14 cannot be inferred from their given names. My data are based on a 43 per cent sample of the mediums in Connecticut, representing two licensing Spiritualist organizations (this happens to be nine mediums). I used a structured interview schedule and a tape recorder to get eighty-four hours of uniform, comparable data from them, information which I had previously inferred to be significant from the paradigm constructed for such phenomena by earlier researchers. The tapes were meant to insure that I would hear what was really said, not what I was prepared to hear and remember. I wanted to remain an objective observer, an "innocent bystander," [27] as I had been trained to do. I considered the reality of spirits to be untestable by scientific methods.

Clearly, however, Mrs. M. also accepts scientific assumptions. She visits other mediums for her own readings because, as she puts it, "I just want proof of spirit." She receives constant proof from others that she is in touch with spirit. When clients apologize for having been skeptical of what Mrs. M. said while under trance, she says "I tell them they owe the guide an apology, not me." Her methodology is positivistic, as was that employed by William James (1969), E. B. Tylor (Stocking, 1971) and Gardner Murphy (1970): she hears, sees, and feels the spirits speak to her, appear to her, and touch her. She can replicate these phenomena every time she goes under trance. She observes that other mediums, under the same controlled circumstances, can also replicate such phenomena.

So scientist, layman, and medium alike share a faith in positivism, "an outlook which exalts the sciences as providing the only valid tools for acquiring knowledge of the world . . . and hold them [i.e., the sciences] to be based largely on the process of induction from occurences in the visible, tangible world" (Horton, 1973, p. 297).

Evidence is very important to Mrs. M.: "I want to be sure that I'm not being misled by my own mind; there are those who become overimbued with their own ideas, it is not really spirit coming through to them." So she maintains a skeptical, antidogmatic attitude, constantly seeking proof that her results are both valid and reliable. Spiritualism officially encourages (*Spiritualist Manual*, 1967, p. 42) every person to be open always to restatement as growing thought and investigation reveal new truth "so that every individual is free to follow the dictates of reason." Mrs. M. values inductive reasoning and frequently scoffs at the interpretations of spirit communications given by other mediums, saying that they "just go against common sense, they're just not logical, and therefore could not have come from Spirit Land." Science, at least in the popular mind, is rational and open; its practitioners are supposed to be constantly questioning their own assumptions and tentative conclusions.[28]

Furthermore, in the knowable but nonetheless complex mechanistic world we inhabit, one needs specific training in the techniques, methodology, and content of his field to become an expert whose knowledge is authoritative. So it is that even a gifted medium must serve an apprenticeship, and receives certification only after having been measured and tested. Identified early by practicing mediums already certified to recognize special abilities, the developing medium must normally sit in a circle of spiritual "unfoldment," where—even as do other professionals in our society—he or she acquires the proper vocabulary and sets of attitudes. The medium must pass both a written examination and a practicum, showing that he not only has an intellectual grasp of the principles of Spiritualism, but that he himself is a sufficiently tuned instrument to be able to vibrate in harmony with the spirit plane and be a receiver of messages for those attending services.

So the credentialing system of "scientific" careers is paralleled by the licensing associations of Spiritualist mediums. The latter do not enjoy the degree of professionalization of some other careers, however, as there is no "elite segment of society which has been persuaded that there is some special value in its work" (Freidson, 1970, p. 72). The nature of its source of knowledge, being rooted in the individually received messages of the medium, also militates against control by an elite: schism is inherent in a system that enjoins its practitioners to be always open to restatement as new truths are revealed. Accrediting Spiritualist bodies look askance at the licenses granted by others, regarding them as less demanding than their own. They speak of others with the disdain a physician might employ when referring to a chiropractor. The credentialing system carries on right into Summer Land, as we have seen, where one can continue to work and learn and honorary degrees are conferred on the deserving. Effectively, they convert themselves into knowledgeable technocrats. As Carter concludes, "If Spiritualism was right . . . salvation was not a matter of being 'born again,' but only of learning a new technique" (1971, p. 103).[29]

If the central human problem is not one of misery but of meaninglessness, then that has also been solved by Spiritualist assumptions:

"Man is not a speck floating in an incomprehensible universe, he is part of a perfectly orderly process which moves all things and all life in exquisite precision" (Hirst, 1970, p. 12), or in Albert Einstein's oft-quoted words, "God wouldn't play dice with the Universe."

The Great Mechanic is in his heaven, all is right with the earth plane, but will be even better in Summer Land, where everyone is at his prime. Babies grow to that point, the old and infirm revert to what had been their best physical and mental state: a traditional heaven. For most Americans, the "uncertain trumpet" hasn't yet blown the sour note of chance.

If then, the scientist, layman, and medium do share basic premises, methods, and techniques for organizing Chaos, why must Mrs. M. acknowledge that others regard her as a "bit off," an "odd duck, a spook-chaser"? Why is it that in recent years she and Spiritualism have been unable to persuade an elite segment of society that there is some special value in their work? The answer seems to lie in the "conceptual boundary-hopping" (Gellner, 1973, p. 176) which Mrs. M. does with ease: she (and Spiritualism) have moved the existence of spirits from the category of untestable to that of testable. But the scientific world view, as Ernest Gellner has argued so cogently (loc. cit.), insists on orderly and regular conduct from concepts as well as from people. Mrs. M. also hops boundaries in regarding spirits as superior knowers, guides to intelligibility as well as human conduct. The boundary delineating "proper" sources of knowledge and "proper" experts was fixed by the turn of the century. By refusing to recognize the scientifically determined boundary between the empirical and the transcendent, Spiritualism and its mediums have become anomalies: they are not crazy, but are also not quite mainstream.

EPILOGUE

Mrs. M. remembers a prophecy her monk offered through her instrumentality long ago: many children would be born, he said, in the coming generation with greater spiritual gifts than had ever been known before. Now she sees this coming to pass. Perhaps as the attack mounted against scientism—science become religion—grows, we may come to appreciate an entire dimension of human experience with which scientific methods cannot cope, and which scientists do not wish to examine. Science is committed to its fallible paradigms, as William James noted: "Orthodoxy is almost as much a matter of authority in science as it is in the Church," and he observed that if scientific men of his era (e.g., Helmholtz, Huxley, Edison, and Pasteur) were to embrace clairvoyance, thought transference, and ghosts, we would all "stampede in that direction" (quoted in Carter, 1971). Ernest Becker (1973, p. 284) is willing to put faith in the behavioral sciences on the same level as the mystical, asserting that modern man "buries himself in psychology in the belief that awareness all by itself will be some kind of magical cure for his problems," and adds: "We might say that modern man tried to replace vital awe and wonder with a 'how to do it' manual."

Although Mrs. M. and her fellow mediums are attempting to emulate the scientific model, and Spiritualist literature constantly cites those same heroes of science to bolster their arguments, perhaps they offer something science cannot. As a medium, she repeatedly emphasizes our human uniqueness, allows for the individual case, and urges that we are neither pawns in a huge chess game, nor merely cogs in a great, complex machine, masterminded and manipulated by experts. One can affect his own destiny, and his own acts of will do make a difference. Although Mrs. M. is a technician, she also is an artist: she knows that she was born with a gift and has the authority which accompanies this conviction.

Andrew Greeley and William McCready (1975, p. 12) argue that self-transcending mystical experiences are "widespread, almost commonplace, in American society today." As William James observed: "The existence of mystical states absolutely overthrows the pretension of nonmystical states to be the sole and ultimate dictator of what we may believe." Replicability has been dethroned. Examinations of this dimension of our humanness have become best sellers; witness the popularity of the books of Carlos Castaneda. A century of living the "myth that this is a mythless age" has compelled us to deny our own patterns of traditional thinking.

Mrs. M. and Spiritualism offer to some an occasional moment of transcendence over both self and death. She would agree with Becker (1973, p. 285) ". . . that a project as grand as the scientific-mythical construction of victory over human limitation is not something that can be programmed by science." Or, with Hamlet, perhaps we can conclude, "There are more things in heaven and earth, Horatio, than are dreamt of in your philosophy" (Shakespeare, *Hamlet:* Act I, Sc. 5).

NOTES

1. Fieldwork among Spiritualists has been conducted sporadically during the past seven years, with the intensive interviewing for this paper being carried out between December 1974, and March 1975. I would like to thank

Florence Gittens for her able assistance in interviewing; Francis Owens, Secretary of the Connecticut State Spiritualists Association, and Molly Owens for invaluable guidance; Evelyn Cowan and Arlene Freudenstein for their generous cooperation; Drs. R. E. Kent and John MacKinnon for critical readings of earlier drafts of the paper; and Ward Cannel for his help in conceptualizing and organizing the data. A very special thanks goes to the Reverend Calista Rita, without whose time, energy, humor and wisdom, the paper could not have been realized. A Connecticut College grant assisted with typing expenses.

2. Torrey (1974) deals with this shift from regarding all "spiritualists and shamans" as sick, to seeing them as the most healthy and intelligent individuals in their respective societies. In particular, says Torrey, the behavior associated with spirit possession has been labeled "hysterical" or "deviant" by social scientists.

3. Zaretsky (1974, p. 217) notes that Spiritualism and present-day varieties of Spiritualist churches in the United States have not been of great interest to social scientists. As investigators who accept Western culture without understanding its theoretical foundations (Horton, 1970, p. 134), we probably are ensconced in the viewpoint of modern industrial mass society which holds that altered states of consciousness are "not approved and supported but considered deviant, pathological, suspect" (Bourguignon, 1974, p. 243)—and therefore not worthy of our time and energy.

4. Many of these camps were established as early as the 1880s, and still attract mediums and adherents from many states and Canada during a given season. The mediums function in the various daily religious services (e.g., healing, sermons, and the bringing of messages through from the spirits) as well as conducting sessions for small groups of people ("circles") seeking spiritual development, and giving private "readings" for those seeking them. Formal courses in the history, philosophy, and practice of Spiritualism are also offered. At Camp Chesterfield, Indiana, one of the oldest (established in 1886), better-known camps, there is a resident staff of more than 25 mediums, and two or three "guest workers" are invited to serve during the two-month summer season. Most staff mediums have their own homes on the camp grounds, and hang out shingles which announce the "phases" of their psychic abilities (e.g., clairvoyant; healer; trance-medium; direct voice; psychic artist; materialization; psychometrist, etc.). Camp Chesterfield also boasts three small hotels, a cafeteria, gift shop, and "book nook." The latter distributes an eclectic selection of books on all psychic phenomena as well as predictions for the coming year as dictated by the spirits to one or more mediums. There is also a museum of Spiritualist memorabilia. The 1975 *Year Book* of the N.S.A.C. lists a total of thirteen such camps operating their auspices in the United States; other licensing organizations conduct their own. I have been a sometime participant-observer in two: Camp Chesterfield and the Ladies' Aid Society Camp in Connecticut.

5. For purposes of this paper, I shall accept the definition of trance given by the subject, her clients, and the *Spiritualist Manual:* she is in trance when she and her clients say she is. The *Manual* (1967, p. 54–55) describes this phase of mediumship as that "in which there is a total unconsciousness . . . of events passing in the mundane world. This state is superinduced by an external spirit intelligence [a spirit which has once lived in mortal form] whose personality becomes dominant and uses the organism of the medium for the purposes of writing or speaking, usually the latter . . . the medium passes from a state of outward consciousness into one resembling natural sleep. . . . The medium never once acknowledged to me (or others, to my knowledge) any consciousness or memory of what occurs while she is under trance.

Anthropologists studying the subject in other parts of the world also find it difficult to define trance. It has been remarked of certain West African societies that most possessed persons conveniently come out of trance at dinnertime. Horton (1962) reports that the Kalabari insist rather strongly on the reality of dissociation and on the inability of the priest to remember what happens to him during possession, while Spiro (1967, p. 207) asserts ". . . most instances of alleged possession observed by me showed no indications of trance and in many cases the culturally stipulated signs of possession . . . appeared to me to have been simulated rather than genuine. Still, I cannot be sure of this." My own observations of Mexican and Mexican-American mediums in trance conform with Spiro's. Yet mediums, clients, and public agree that the medium is in trance. In any case, the differences between full consciousness and the various altered states of consciousness have recently (cf. Ludwig, 1966, p. 255) come to be regarded as a matter of degree rather than as discrete. Even the aspiring Yanamamo shaman, functioning under drug-induced trances must be able to exercise control over himself, and present stereotyped "proper" possessed behavior; otherwise, he will not be permitted to continue his shamanistic apprenticeship.

6. The term Summer Land apparently comes from Andrew Jackson Davis, considered by most American Spiritualists to have been their first philosopher. He authored many books (most of which reportedly were spirit-inspired and came to him while he was in trance) including *A Stellar Key to the Summer Land,* published in 1867. His works, more mentioned than read by modern Spiritualists, are almost inaccessible.

7. From a village five miles outside Naples. He came to the United States at nine, and lived with an older brother. Mrs. M. never came to know her paternal relatives, nor did she learn to speak Italian.

8. Mrs. M. wanted me to make it very clear to readers that it was only as a child that she hated her father, at a time when she was in no position to understand the problems of the adult world. She asserted, upon reading the transcript, that they later got along very well, even when they were living under the same roof.

9. "Loved ones" refers to spirits of one's relatives and friends. The unique vocabulary of Spiritualists is used throughout this paper with translations being given only where I felt it was necessary for clarity. For a masterly linguistic analysis of Spiritualist argot, especially as it relates to the social organization of Spiritualist churches, see Zarotsky (1970, 1972, 1974).

10. Among mediums, the story of the effeminate, Scottish-born, apparently illegitimate Daniel Dunglas Home is well-known. Perhaps the most convincing medium to have appeared in the history of modern Spiritualism, this child of a long line of seers is an ideal type of medium: subject to fainting spells in his childhood, he experienced spirit manifestations at four, had an excellent memory, and attracted rowdy poltergeists to the house of an aunt who reared him. He seemed to have had all the gifts, or *phases*, of spiritualism including levitation. He was reportedly also an excellent "natural" actor: lionized by such notables as Elizabeth Barrett Browning, Napoleon III, the King of Bavaria, and other royal heads of state, he hobnobbed with the aristocracy of several countries and married a Russian countess. If the power of spirit could bring fame, money, prestige and a felicitous marriage, even to the lowly-born such as Home, can it not do as much for mediums of this century?

11. A total of thirty-nine public sessions over the past six years, managed by seventeen different mediums.

12. The *Spiritualist Manual* (1967, p. 55) asserts that there are "comparatively very few trance-mediums," although it is acknowledged that this "phase is superior for lectures and speeches." Because the medium is presumed to be completely entranced, his own consciousness is unable to alter or question "the verity of the statements" being brought through by the spirit intelligences.

13. Cf. Bourguignon (1965); Colson (1969); Doyle (1926); Garbett (1969); Harner (1973); James (1969); Middleton (1969); and Tambiah (1970).

14. The *Spiritualist Manual* (1967, p. 56) concurs: "The intelligences acting upon [the mediums] are almost invariably of a superior character, and therefore, must mold the organism, by constant use for the expression of higher forms of thought."

15. The medium who did not fit this pattern (the first of a two-child family) was born to a mother who already was a member of a Spiritualist church.

16. In fact, many Spiritualist mediums have been in show business in one capacity or another. Zaretsky found this to be the case, and it is true of nearly half the mediums (four) I have interviewed. Several others report having participated with enthusiasm in amateur or school theatricals.

17. Her case is strikingly parallel to those presented by Lewis (1971, p. 190–191) in his discussion of possession by peripheral spirits: "In peripheral cults the catchment area of possession is so circumscribed that those who occupy marginal social positions are strongly at risk. . . . The keenest recruits and the most committed enthusiasts are women who, for one

reason or another do not make a success of their marital roles, or who having fulfilled these roles, seek a new career in which they can give free rein to the desire to manage and dominate others."

18. Zaretsky's felicitous title for his doctoral dissertation (1970).

19. "But why do men name things? . . . To gain control over the thing named and more generally, over one's power to act in the world. The act of naming or classifying is intimately related to the human need for control or mastery." (Szasz, 1970, p. 196)

20. Cf. Doyle (1926); Hardinge (1970); James (1969); Judah (1967); Podmore (1902); Thurston (1933); and Zaretsky (1970).

21. It is interesting to note that in the 1967 edition the emphasis on work and reference to "little waifs," has been removed. Perhaps this is in response to shifts in value orientations as the hedonistic gained ascendance, and the importance of work declined somewhat during the late 1960s and early 1970s.

22. In fact, a strong rebuttal of Spiritualism has been the triviality of spirit messages. Carter asks if we are to infer that "perhaps . . . the only ghosts who took the trouble to come back and talk to us were those with nothing better to do?" (1971, p. 243).

23. Southern and Eastern Africa, and Northern India.

24. Nationally women outnumber men 2½ to 1 as licensed N.S.A.C. mediums. I have been told repeatedly by Spiritualists in both Connecticut and Indiana that the males who have become mediums or are developing are "effeminate," or "Well, not really homosexuals, maybe, but not very masculine, either." For example, one widow, a medium of 40 years standing, whose husband also had been a medium, remarked that they used to attend national N.S.A.C. meetings annually, and her husband was always complaining, "Where are your real men? I certainly don't see any here!" At Camp Chesterfield, I was told that "You'll find it out sooner or later, so we may as well tell you that most of the male mediums are 'gay.' " Although this seems to be a widely shared emic view, I have no independent quantifiable evidence. No one could offer a folk explanation as to why male homosexuals should be especially attracted to mediumship, and my evidence does not warrant a structural analysis. Among licensed healers nationally, men do outnumber women (151 males to 128 females). These proportions also corroborate Zaretsky's findings, (1974, p.175). Lewis comments: ". . . structural analysis demonstrates that treatment accorded those who fall in such 'peripheral' social categories enhances even if only temporarily, position and status." (1970, p. 295; 1971, p. 86)

25. See Note 5 above.

26. In Connecticut, a total of 19 (one has since died) were commissioned, five men and fourteen women. Reportedly there are also three mediums licensed by the Universal Church of the Master (a Spiritualist organization with headquarters in California), two of whom are included in my sample.

I have four hours of taped interviews with each of eight mediums apart from my main subject. From her, I have on tape six hours of public performances and twenty hours of in-depth interviewing. I also taped interviews with her husband, her sister, and the medium who validated her ability. Add to that twenty hours of tape that Mrs. M. permitted seven different clients to make during private readings over a period of four years, during which she had no idea that these tapes would be used for research. Therefore one can conclude safely that these latter are in no way distorted because of investigator contamination. (I do have her permission, as well as that of her clients, to refer to them.)

27. But as Matson tells us, even "among atomic physicists . . . there are no innocent bystanders; the act of observation is at the same time unavoidably an act of participation" (1966, p. 127).

28. Gellner (1973, p. 165), citing the influential Thomas Kuhn, points out that "scientific inquiry does not range freely amongst boundless alternatives, as the popular image suggests, but, at any given time, is constrained by the currently dominant 'paradigm,' whose hold only weakens at the time of major scientific revolutions."

29. This point of view puts our recent enthusiasm for the transcendental in a new light. Marvin Harris (1974, p. 250) makes much the same telling point when he says that Carlos Castaneda's Don Juan is a technocrat whose knowledge carries no moral burden. Castaneda's "relationship to Don Juan unfolds in a moral wasteland in which technology is the supreme good, even if he and his teacher eat 'buttons' instead of pressing them." Raymond Pince (1974, p. 263) agrees, commenting that transcendental meditation is "simply a technique for accomplishing peace of mind, an increased ability to mobilize one's energy and to be more effective in the world . . . [it] can be learned quickly and painlessly."

REFERENCES

BECKER, ERNEST

1973   *The Denial of Death.* New York: The Free Press, a Division of the Macmillan Company.

BOURGUIGNON, ERIKA

1965   "The Self, the Behavioral Environment, and the Theory of Spirit Possession." In *Context and Meaning in Cultural Anthropology.* Melford E. Spiro, Ed., pp. 39–60. New York: The Free Press, a Division of the Macmillan Company.

1974   "Cross-Cultural Perspectives on the Religious Uses of Altered States of Consciousness." In *Religious Movements in Contemporary America*. Irving I. Zaretsky and Mark P. Leone, Eds., pp. 228–243. Princeton, NJ: Princeton University Press.

CANNEL, WARD and JUNE MACKLIN

1973   *The Human Nature Industry: How Human Nature is Manufactured, Distributed, Advertised and Consumed in the United States and Parts of Canada*. Garden City, NY: Anchor Press, Doubleday and Company, Inc.

CARTER, PAUL. A.

1969   *The Idea of Progress in American Protestant Thought, 1930–1969*. Philadelphia: Fortress Press.

1971   *The Spiritual Crisis of the Gilded Age*. DeKalb, Il: Northern Illinois University Press.

COLSON, ELIZABETH

1969   "Spirit Possession among the Tonga of Zambia." In *Spirit Mediumship and Society in Africa*. John Beattie and John Middleton, Ed., pp. 69–103. New York: Africana Publishing Corp.

COX, HARVEY

1974   "The Country is Full of Ideolects." A review of *Religious Movements in Contemporary America*. Irving I. Zaretsky and Mark P. Leone, Eds., Princeton, NJ: Princeton University Press. *The New York Times Book Review*, pp. 13–14, December 22.

DOYLE, ARTHUR C.

1926   *The History of Spiritualism*. New York: George H. Doran.

DU BOIS, CORA

1955   The Dominant Value Profile of American Culture. *American Anthropologist*, **57:** 1232–1239.

FREIDSON, ELIOT

1970   *Profession of Medicine: A Study of the Sociology of Applied Knowledge*. New York: Dodd, Mead & Company.

GARBETT, G. KINGSLEY

1969   "Spirit Mediums as Mediators in Valley Korekore Society." In *Spirit Mediumship and Society in Africa*. John Beattie and John Middleton, Eds., pp. 104–127. New York: Africana Publishing Corp.

GELLNER, ERNEST

1973   "The Savage and the Modern Mind." In *Modes of Thought*. Robin Horton and Ruth Finnegan, Eds., pp. 162–181. London: Faber & Faber.

GREELEY, ANDREW and WILLIAM MCCREADY
1975   "Are We a Nation of Mystics?" *The New York Times Magazine*, p.12. January 26.

HALLOWEL, A. I.
1967   "The Backwash of the Frontier: the Impact of the Indian on American Culture." In *Beyond the Frontier: Social Process and Cultural Change*. Paul Bohannon and Fred Plog, Ed., pp. 219–345. Garden City, NY: The Natural History Press.

HARDINGE, EMMA
1970   *Modern Spiritualism in America*. New Hyde Park, NY: University Books.

HARNER, MICHAEL J.
1973   "The Role of Hallucinogenic Plants in European Witchcraft." In *Hallucinogens and Shamanism*. Michael J. Harner, Ed., pp. 123–150. New York: Oxford University Press.

HARRIS, MARVIN
1975   *Cows, Pigs, Wars & Witches: the Riddles of Culture*. New York: Vantage Books, Random House, Inc.

HIRST, RONALD L.
1970   "What Are You Doing for the N.S.A.C.? In *The Summit of Spiritual Understanding*. Cassadaga, Fl: The National Spiritualist, p. 12, November.

HORTON, ROBIN
1962   "The Kalabari World-View: An Outline and Interpretation." *Africa*, **XXXII** (3): 197–220.
1970   "African Traditional Thought and Western Science." In *Rationality*. Bryan R. Wilson, Ed., pp. 131–171. New York: Harper Torchbooks, Harper & Row.
1973   "Levy-Bruhl, Durkheim and the Scientific Revolution." In *Modes of Thought*. Robin Horton and Ruth Finnegan, Eds., pp. 249–305. London: Faber & Faber.

HORTON, ROBIN and RUTH FINNEGAN
1973   Introduction. In *Modes of Thought*. Robin Horton and Ruth Finnegan, Eds., pp. 13–62. London: Faber & Faber.

HSU, FRANCIS L. K.
1972   "American Core Value and National Character." In *Psychological Anthropogy*. Francis L. K. Hsu, Ed., pp. 241–266. Cambridge, Ma: Schenkman Publishing Company, Inc.

JAMES, WILLIAM
1969   *William James on Psychical Research.* Gardner Murphy
                       and Robert O. Ballou, Eds. New York: Viking Compass
                       Edition, The Viking Press, Inc.

JUDAH, J. STILLSON
1967   *The History and Philosophy of the Metaphysical Movement in
                       America.* Philadelphia: The Westminister Press.

LA BARRE, WESTON
1969   *They Shall Take Up Serpents: Psychology of the Southern
                       Snake-Handling Cult.* New York: Schocken Books.

LAING, R. D.
1967   *The Politics of Experience.* New York: Ballantine Books.

LEWIS. I. M.
1970   "A Structural Approach to Witchcraft and Spirit-Pos-
                       session." In *Witchcraft Confessions and Accusations.* Mary
                       Douglas, Ed., pp. 293–310. London: Tavistock Publica-
                       tions.
1971   *Ecstatic Religion, An Anthropological Study of Spirit Posses-
                       sion and Shamanism.* Middlesex, England: Penguin
                       Books Ltd.

LUDWIG, ARNOLD M.
1968   Altered States of Consciousness. In *Trance and Possession
                       States.* Raymond Prince, Ed., pp. 69–95. Montreal: R.
                       M. Bucke Memorial Society.

MACKLIN, JUNE
1974   "Belief, Ritual and Healing: New England Spiritualism
                       and Mexican-American Spiritism Compared." In
                       Religious Movements in Contemporary America. Irving I.
                       Zaretsky and Mark P. Leone, Eds., pp. 383–417. Prince-
                       ton, NJ: Princeton University Press.

MATSON, FLOYD W.
1966   *The Broken Image: Man, Science and Society.* Garden City,
                       NY: Anchor Books, Doubleday and Company, Inc.

MIDDLETON, JOHN
1969   "Spirit Possession among the Lugbara." In *Spirit Me-
                       diumship and Society in Africa.* John Beattie and John
                       Middleton, Eds., pp. 220–231. New York: Africana Pub-
                       lishing Corp.

MURPHY, CARDNER with the collaboration of LAURA A. DALE
1970   *Challenge of Psychical Research: A Primer of Parapsychology.*
                       New York: Harper Colophon Books, Harper & Row.

NATIONAL SPIRITUALIST ASSOCIATION OF THE UNITED STATES OF AMERICA
1944   *Spiritualist Manual.* Washington, D. C.

NATIONAL SPIRITUALIST ASSOCIATION OF CHURCHES OF THE UNITED STATES OF AMERICA
1967   *Spiritualist Manual.* Milwaukee, Wis.
1975   *Year Book.* Cassadega, Fl: Southern Headquarters National Spiritualist Association of Churches.

NELSON, GEOFFREY K.
1969   *Spiritualism and Society.* New York: Schocken Books.

PODMORE, FRANK
1902   *Modern Spiritualism.* Vols. I & II, New York: Charles Scribner's Sons.

PRESSEL, ESTHER
1974   "Umbanda Trance and Possession in São Paulo, Brazil." In *Trance, Healing, and Hallucination: Three Field Studies in Religious Experience.* Felicitas D. Goodman, Jeannette H. Henney, and Esther Pressel, Eds., pp. 113–221, New York: Wiley.

PRICE, LUCIEN (ED.)
1956   *Dialogues of Alfred North Whitehead.* New York: Menton Books.

PRINCE, RAYMOND H.
1974   "Cocoon Work: An Interpretation of the Concern of Contemporary Youth with the Mystical." In *Religious Movements in Contemporary America.* Irving I. Zaretsky and Mark P. Leone, Eds., pp. 255–271. Princeton, NJ: Princeton University Press.

SEDGWICK, PETER
1971   "R. D. Laing: Self, Symptom and Society." In *R. D. Laing and Anti-Psychiatry.* Robert Boyers, Ed., pp. 1–50. New York: Perennial Library, Harper & Row.

SMITH, ENID S.
1970   "How You Can Succeed." In *The Summit of Spiritual Understanding.* Cassadga, Fl: *The National Spiritualist,* pp. 5–8, November.

SPIRO, MELFORD E.
1965   "Religious Systems as Culturally Constituted Defense Mechanisms." In *Context and Meaning in Cultural Anthropology.* Melford E. Spiro, Ed., pp. 100–113. New York: The Free Press, a Division of the Macmillan Company.

1967   *Burmese Supernaturalism: A Study in the Explanation and Reduction of Suffering.* Englewood Cliffs, NJ: Prentice-Hall Inc.

STOCKING, GEORGE W., JR.
1971   "Animism in Theory and Practive: E. B. Tylor's Unpublished Notes on Spiritualism." In *Man: The Journal of the Royal Anthropological Institute,* **6:** 88–104.

SZASZ, THOMAS. S.
1970   *Ideology and Insanity: Essays on the Psychiatric Dehumanization of Man.* Garden City, NY: Anchor Books, Doubleday and Company, Inc.

TAMBIAH, S. J.
1970   *Buddism and the Spirit Cults in North-East Thailand.* London: Cambridge University Press.

THURSTON, HERBERT, S. J.
1933   *The Church and Spiritualism.* Milwaukee, WI: Bruce Publishing Company.

TORREY, E. FULLER
1974   "Spiritualists and Shamans as Psychotherapists: An Account of Original Anthropological Sin." In *Religious Movements in Contemporary America.* Irving I. Zaretsky and Mark P. Leone, Eds., pp. 330–337. Princeton, NJ: Princeton University Press.

ZARETSKY, IRVING I.
1970   *The Message is the Medium: an Ethno-Semantic Study of the Language of Spiritualist Churches.* Ann Arbor, MI: University Microfilms.
1972   "The Language of Spiritualist Churches: A Study in Cognition and Social Organization." In *Culture and Cognition: Rules, Maps, and Plans.* James P. Spradley, Ed., pp. 355–396. San Francisco: Chandler Publishing Company.
1974   "In the Beginning Was the Word: The Relationship of Language to Social Organization in Spiritualist Churches." In *Religious Movements in Contemporary America.* Irving I. Zaretsky and Mark P. Leone, Eds., pp. 166–219. Princeton, NJ: Princeton University Press.

Andras Zempleni

TRANSLATED BY KAREN MERVEILLE

From Symptom to Sacrifice:
The Story of Khady Fall

Psychoanalytic study, more concerned with speculating about the contents of *Totem and Taboo* than with investigating its methods, ignored for a long time the demands of its own practice as it continued to interpret "primitive" socioreligious facts. Even with Roheim, and the first direct field work, the approach of psychoanalytic anthropology still consisted of an exegesis of certain societies' collective productions (e. g., myths, rites, beliefs, and social institutions) in order to formulate statements about an abstract subject or about individuals who would never have the opportunity to express themselves within an analytic field. This approach established the culture as its measure rather than the individual and, even theoretically, ignored the position that the individ-

Reprinted by permission of the Ecole des Hautes Etudes en Sciences Sociales and by Editions Mouton from *L'Homme,* **14** (1974): 31–77

ual might and should occupy within the context of his society. Doubtless, establishing psychoanalytic clinics outside the Western world
allowed analysts to meet a few such individuals, but a dialogue was possible only with those who, to use the words of *L'Oedipe africain* [1], could
"formulate a personal demand"; those who could negate themselves in
relation to the traditional or, more particularly, the socioreligious determinants of their own society. Thus sociocultural change revealed itself as the determining condition for psychoanalytic practice. At the
same time, those who stayed in the bush—and the uses they continued
to make of their rites, religions, family relations, and beliefs—remained
inaccessible to clinical study and could only occasionally be reconsti-
tuted through the deformed image of a new kind of individual.

In religious anthropology the same problem exists but in a different
light. Despite some remarkable exceptions [2] and reiterated professions
of faith, ethnographers seldom describe religions in terms of their specific use by social groups and individuals. In field work both ethnographer and informant are frequently accomplices in the abuse of
generalizations, if not in a common negation. The ethnographer is concerned with the description of "religious facts," which he tends to consider as the constituent elements of a religious system. He is rarely
prompted to trace the variation of these facts—representations, rites,
and symbols—to their diversity of use and to the personal history of his
informants. This very diversity provides him with what he considers to
be variants or versions; divergences that tradition has adopted from a
common origin for obscure reasons. The ethnographer's true interlocutor is found at the mythical site of this origin—"the Yoruba,"
"the Dogon," the Third Person, the indefinite subject in whom all acts,
beliefs, feelings, typical and nontypical attitudes, the "variants" and
"versions," find their common denominator. And the informant, even
if he has not been explicitly urged to do so, will readily accept the comfortable position offered him by the ethnologist's imaginary. * By
speaking in the calm space offered him by the neuter pronoun, the in-

---

* The imaginary (*imaginaire*) is one of the three orders introduced into psychoanalytic
terminology by Jacques Lacan. It refers essentially to the perceptive and hallucinatory
(image-producing) function and contrasts with the symbolic (*symbolique*), the discursive
function, and the real (*réel*), that which is real for the subject. In his work on the mirror
stage (roughly between the ages of six and eighteen months) Lacan postulates the primary alienation of the infant from himself, as through a mirror, and his consequent dis-
covery of self. The mirror image (*image de semblable*) provides the ground for all subsequent identifications. It provides, too, intrasubjectively for the fundamentally
narcissistic relationship between subject and ego and intersubjectively for the dual relationship. See Lacan, 1966 and Laplanche and Pontalis, 1973, in the reference section to
the Introduction, for further details [Editor's note].

formant can invoke the voice of his ancestors or his social group to mask his own subjectivity. Better yet, whatever in his discourse on spirits, magic, and domestic rites is related to his personal history, to his identifications, and to his words as an individual can only gain a narcissistic dividend—the prize of conformity. Why should he refuse a game that he cannot lose? A game which immediately gives the singularity of an articulated narrative for the generality of a polyvocal society and leaves us with a monotonous, fragmented or lifeless coherent description.

The fact that the autobiographies and "life histories" may have been meant to ease the ethnographer's conscience does not necessarily free them from this speech arrangement nor from ponderous descriptive exoticisms. For where no "personal demand" of, say, recovery exists, the demand of the ethnographer structures the interview. This demand, which generally attempts to gather, if not information, at least "a live experience" or "a view from within" of "religious facts," [3] rarely can sustain the effort of a turning inward toward the self that would enable the informant to express himself as a private individual. In the following case study, I wish to show that the position of the ethnologist (and of his interlocutor) are not necessarily incompatible with the requirements of a coherent clinical approach. If he cannot analyze the subject's fantasies through their transformations in a transference relationship, he can, under certain circumstances, employ alternate methods.

Khady Fall, the possessed Wolof priestess who is about to tell her own story, related her life in a series of episodes which she considered the essential moments of a fate that was willed by her *rab* (her personal allies or the ancestral spirits of her lineage). We will see in the course of her narrative that the *rab* she names occupy well-defined symbolic positions in her life history and carry out specific functions which can be clearly articulated. I realized early that the analysis of these positions and functions—or more generally, of the use of religious "signifiers" in the process of solving a personal problem, quite common in itself but expressed in the *rab*'s idiom—could only be made in a situation distinct from the ordinary interview. For Khady, as opposed to those who had hospital consultations, [4] the *rab*'s idiom or, in a larger sense, the traditional language of persecutory interpretation, [5] was the only acceptable "psychological" level of expression. Psychoanalysis defines this level of expression in terms of projection and inversion of aggressive drives.[6] Khady could say whatever she wished on this level, [7] aside from what would have forced her to recognize her own desires in the will of the *rab,* and would have obliged her to assume her individual fate. Thus the fundamental rule I tried to follow throughout the interviews was to remain within the limits that this form of expression set for her discourse. Whenever I interrupted and asked her to clarify or elaborate some detail of her story, I did so in the language of the possessed and the Wolof cult of the *rab*. If, very occasionally, I offered an "interpretation," I refrained from using any psychological vocabulary. Insofar as possible I also tried not to glean any general information about ancestral spirits or possession rites. Although Khady's domestic shrine (shown in the Appendix) served as a veritable "interview guide" at the beginning, I soon learned to consider this symbolic space as a kind of projection of her personal history that should be explored as such by my questions.[8] All this presupposed a certain familiarity with the "field" and a certain kind of relationship with Khady.

I first saw Khady at a *ndǝp* session at Fass.[9] I had already been working for some time with a team of psychiatrists, psychoanalysts, and sociologists, who were attempting a new approach to the phenomena of mental disorders in Senegal.[10] My task was twofold. First, I was to provide the clinician with whatever useful information I could find concerning those concepts of illness, etiological representations, and therapeutic rites that he encountered in his daily practice and could not understand. Second, I planned to undertake a monographic study of the traditional system of interpretation of mental disorder among the Wolof and the Lebou. As this system is composed of four major levels of interpretation—ancestral spirits (*rab*), witchcraft (*dɔmm*), interpersonal magic (*ligêêy*), [11] and Islamic spirits (*jinne-seytaane*)—I had to call on four kinds of specialists, and among them the officiants of the possession cult. The mistress of the order of the possessed to which Khady belongs made no secret of her distrust when she first received me. It required about a year of regular attendance at the ceremonies of her congregation before she permitted me to witness the reputedly secret rites and consented to answer my questions in public. Little by little the idea of a collaboration between the "doctors" of the hospital and the traditional healers was beginning to make headway in her congregation as in the other congregations of Cap-Vert.[12] Khady and her colleagues came to think of me as one of the "doctors" who perhaps didn't believe in the *rab* but who, by their mere presence, were ready to testify to the effectiveness of their practices: a testimony that is essential to any therapy requiring and manipulating the collective consensus.

We became better acquainted under these conditions. Ismaila Samb, my interpreter (I understand Wolof but speak it poorly), knew Khady. Both of us had done her some small favors, such as driving her home in the car, getting medicine for her rheumatism, and taking her to the hospital (where she was diagnosed for high blood pressure).[13] These errands earned us her sympathy. She asked us to her house, introduced us to Mamadou Diop, her healer husband, and invited us to attend the domestic rites of the sick under her care. This reception encouraged us, and shortly thereafter we paid her several "greeting calls" and returned a few times to question her about her *rab* and spirit possession. One day, to explain a detail, she took me to the enclosure where her shrines were located and began to enumerate the names, qualities, and origins of her *rab*. Then, on the spur of the moment, she told a story concerning the personality of these spirits. After that I felt I had to change my approach, and asked her in a separate interview to talk about her shrines and her personal history. Thus the rhythm of our conversations, one or two a week and always at her house, was established (despite her reticence, which showed itself in broken appointments and a dubious unavailability). Soon we became intimate enough for her to call me *suma taalibe*, "my pupil", [14] and for me to respond *suma yaay*, "my mother". Jokes played an important part in our conversations. They probably served as a compromise to conceal whatever remained of our mutual distrust: mine, in regard to the "authenticity" of her story, and hers, as to my belief in the *rab* and my true intentions.

Ultimately the motives I had set forth from the start—the welfare of the sick, the need to become better acquainted with traditional methods of treatment to improve Western techniques—carried little weight compared to one essential question: did I or did I not believe in the powers of the *rab*, in the authenticity of their actions both in her life and eventually in mine? If not, why did I insist that she tell me her "secrets?" Probably none of the answers I tried to give to this underlying question really satisfied her. She had nothing more to go on than a vague suspicion of my disbelief and my unspoken desire to make use in my "practice"—nonexistent, of course—of the bits and pieces of knowledge she had revealed to me. Nonetheless this situation in which, though I remained unacknowledged, I had to serve as support for her belief, sharply distinguished our conversations from those undertaken at the hospital. Indeed, the mere act of consulting a doctor or a psychoanalyst should be considered as a break in the persecutory shaping—and in the traditional treatment—of the illness. The sick person and his family who consulted a European therapist (whatever the color of his skin) would not ask him to support or even assert the patient's belief but, at the very most, to arbitrate his relation to the belief of the others within his own ambiguous position, between one form of organization that he had already rejected (based on the persecution pattern) and another which he had not yet assumed (based on the interiorization pattern). Thus the words spoken in this kind of relationship—those related to associations, beliefs, dreams, visions, representations—are neither comparable to, nor have the same goal as, those used by a priestess such as Khady to narrate her "successful" experience of being possessed.

Let us return to the conversations. Regardless of whether the process so subtly analyzed by O. Mannoni as "I know, but just the same . . ." [15] came into play, these conversations also had an incentive quite free of my relationship to Khady. Her pleasure in evoking the events of her past was no doubt reinforced by the presence of two experienced witnesses, my interpreter and her husband. Generally we spent the first hour (out of two or three) in greetings and exchange of news. Then we resumed the thread of the narrative from the previous session, and Khady began to speak. Her most characteristic procedure was to associate one episode with another, one dream with another, without bothering about sequence or chronology. When she ran out of material, I would intervene and ask her to be more explicit about specific data. [16] Later I used this data in writing her biography, and regretted that my material could not lend itself to a more rigorous analysis. [17]

All told we had about twenty interviews. Occasionally I offered Khady small gifts, money, or kola nuts, which she shared with her husband. It would have been shocking for a friend and *taalibe* not to have done so.

In the following pages I shall first give a short synopsis of the cult of the *rab* and of the relationship between illness and spirit possession; then I shall present Khady, her house, her domestic shrines, her *rab*, and her genealogy. Finally I shall deal with her narrative or, one might say, her autobiography. The passages in brackets are my commentaries or interpretations, which I summarize and elaborate upon slightly in the last section.

THE CULT OF THE *RAB*

Within the cult of the *rab* lie traces (not always dependable) of the ancient family religion of the Wolof and Lebou who were converted to Islam in great numbers toward the end of the nineteenth century. The cult is practiced today by women and a few men within their lineage or in congregations of the possessed. *Tuur* and *rab* are ancestral spirits. In the origin myths, the *tuur* [18] is a spirit of water and uncultivated land who concluded an alliance that could be transmitted from one generation to the next with the founding ancestor of a lineage. This lineage (generally uterine) was thus paired with the invisible line formed by the descendants of the *tuur*. Yet, for adepts of the cult, the *tuur* takes his features from both ancestral figures and spirit imagery. Her name is always preceded by the epithet *maam*, meaning "grandfather, ancestor." His attributes are well known to the lineage segment, neighborhood, or village to which he is attached and which renders constant homage to him.

The dividing line between *tuur* and *rab* [19] is not quite clear. The *tuur* are *rab*. When the *rab* are regularly honored, they become *tuur*. Their difference can only be understood in terms of the degree of alliance seniority. On another level, however, the *rab* cannot be assimilated with the *tuur*. An ancestral spirit, he is also a component, a "companion," or double of the visible person. If he is actualized (through illness) and is named (during the rites of spirit possession), he is then integrated into the spirit world acknowledged by the group. This spirit world replicates the official society. Thus the *rab*—like the *tuur*—have a name, sex, religion, ethnic origin, caste status, profession, and personality. The distinction between Muslim spirits (*seriñ*) and pagan spirits (*ceddo*) is particularly important in ritual.

Generally the *rab* live in the *xamb,* a domestic shrine composed of a pestle stuck in the ground, a stone gathered near the sea, and two earthenware containers. One container has a wide opening and is filled with water and three roots; the other, turned upside down, is pierced in the middle of its base. The number of *rab* that the owner can claim determines, approximately, the quantity of shrines within the enclosure. Here, each Monday and Thursday, offerings are made of milk, *nak* (sweetened millet mixed with milk) or chewed kola nut by the *boroom tuur,* the "*tuur* master," or the *boroom rab.*

In such a domestic enclosure the *ndəpkat,* [20] like those possessed ordinarily, carry out their personal and family rites. Their title indicates membership in one of the congregational groups charged with organizing the three major rites of spirit possession: *ndəp, tuuru,* and *samp.* These rites, whose common sequence reproduces, in reverse order, the ancient Wolof marriage ceremony, [21] are in no way rites of exorcism. Their aim is not to expel the spirit but to conclude an alliance with the spirit. The sick person is first swabbed with milk—"mothered"—by the *ndəpkat* gathered at his house. Next, he is "measured" (*natt*) and made to fall into a state of semiconsciousness, favorable to the naming of his *rab.* The spirit, once it has been named, is "brought down" (*wacce*) from the patient's body and transferred to the domestic shrine where the *rab* will receive regular offerings. The *tuuru* rite (addressed to a spirit who has already been located and identified) and the *ndəp* (organized on behalf of anonymous and errant *rab*) are followed by dances of spirit possession performed in public. These dances are absent in the *samp* ("to fix, to plant"), a discrete ceremony without music or possession seizures, most frequently addressed to Muslim *rab* and held in the intimacy of the possessed man's or woman's home.[22] Here the first concern of the celebrants is fixing the spirit within its domestic setting.

ILLNESS

Illness is the first if not the exclusive reason for renewing the alliance with the spirits. The bodily space is invested and pervaded by the ambivalent ancestral sign. The *rab* love the very one whom they punish for having neglected them; they "inhabit" and "torment" those by whom they have chosen to be honored. Possession here is a vacillating inscription, within the body, of the ancestral signifier. Sometimes it indicates the descent into an imaginary, narcissistic reality of body-to-body (or, more exactly, body-within-body) struggle, with all the implied dangers of primitive fusion, abolition of symbolic reference, and loss of identity. Other times it indicates a body condition which, according to its symptoms (reversible paralysis, asthenia, amenorrhea, remittant fever), serves as a signifier that can be turned into a medium of exchange within the circuit of gifts and debts that bind the possessed's own family to his or her *rab*. The final effect of this rite that establishes or reestablishes the symbolic exchange, by gaining access to the name of the *rab*, varies from one case of possession to another. In all cases, however, it is characterized by the transformation, and not the suppression, of the corporeal inscription. It is witnessed by the ritualized crisis of possession—the offering of the self—which the "cured" initiate must address to his allies periodically. This crisis might well be called a metaphor of that which cannot be symbolized in their relationship.

The possession "syndrome," confirmed by tradition and frequently evoked in the biographies of *ndəpkat,* is characterized by the prevalence of depressive forms. Anorexia and loss of weight, mutism and withdrawal, problems with the locomotive faculties, and apathy are the most recurrent signs of this general shrinking of the communicative functions often observed among the possessed. Those who are hospitalized frequently complain of repeated and painful coenesthetic disorders often linked to problems of reproduction. These patients show evidence of a profound transformation in their actual corporal experience and in the wealth of their parasensory and dream experiences.[23]

The foregoing indications are periodically inverted in preinitiatory, unritualized seizures. Mutism gives way to logorrhea, immobility to an anxious agitation, apathy to overflowing demonstrations of affection. Those familiar with the sick person recognize the prodromal symptoms of these seizures, often spectacular and normally ending in a fall (*daanu*). They help him through the crisis in a simple, straightforward way, while remaining continuously attentive. Their relaxed attitude probably explains why experiences involving such corporeal dislocation are undergone with great ease.

KHADY FALL

Her House

Colobane is located near the center of Dakar. It is a transitional area located between the chaotic misery of the slums that border the Autoroute and the relative affluence of the Medina and Sicap districts. An ill-reputed flea market which most people in the neighborhood avoid is held there daily. Khady Fall lives not far from this market on a sandy, barely shaded street which the neighborhood women follow each day on their way to the public fountain. Her brick-colored wooden house, patched here and there with odd boards and bits of sheet metal, is indistinguishable from the other neighborhood dwellings. It opens onto an inner courtyard which Khady shares with three other families living in the same "square." None of these families are related to her.

One enters the house by a door into a main room which serves as parlor and bedroom. The furntiure and the setting are familiar: a big bed covered with a pile of white and colored fabrics, a couple of armchairs with wornout, green plastic covers, a brazier, enameled washbasins, rolled up prayer mats, an old radio set. The room is orderly and cool, the air perfumed with incense that is burned each evening. Only the walls reveal the occupant's identity. As is the custom in this milieu, the walls are covered with Muslim colored prints and all kinds of photographs. But the expressive stiffness of the Koranic figures, the provocative, solemn aspect of the great marabouts, the slightly comic decorum of the family portraits form a remarkable contrast to the exultant dynamism of those pictures that represent Khady as *ndɔpkat* or as simply possessed: in one, she is smiling in the midst of female officiants who surround a sacrificial ox; in another, she is dressed in full attire and dancing inside a circle of spectators who, fully absorbed, are leaning toward her; in yet another, she looks wild-eyed and points at an invisible enemy. The cult objects are ornaments hanging on the wall (a

cap with mirrors, an oxtail, and an amber necklace) further accentuate
the incongruity of the setting.

The adjoining room, which serves as a kitchen, is nearly empty. A
back door leads to the "showers": an enclosure where the members of
the family wash and urinate. To the right of this enclosure, running
the length of the bedroom, the domestic shrines are lined up in a row.
They are screened from the street by a high fence of woven straw. The
passerby can see nothing but the tops of the three emerging baobab
trees.

Her Household

Khady has no children of her own. Aissa, four years old, and Astou, six
years, the two little girls who live with her, are adopted. Moussa, the
twelve-year-old schoolboy who sleeps in the kitchen, is the son of one of
her nieces who is married to a farmer. She has agreed to take care of
the boy while he is at school.

Mamadou Diop, her present husband, does not object to the boy for
he too has no children of his own. He is a man of sixty, tall, gaunt,
bearded, and always dressed in a "boubou" and a faded cap of indistinguishable colors. He is a healer, whose clientele is mainly local, and his
earnings are low but regular in contrast to the fees collected by his wife.
He wants to be recognized as lettered, as a marabout, as a "good Muslim" for reasons evidently related to his wife's activities. But he is better
acquainted with the ancient forms of Wolof, Serer, or Peul magic than
with the Arab science of writing or Koranic verse. He is very well informed about "*rab* illness," possession rites, and the remedies employed
by Khady. When she is away or otherwise unavailable, he takes her
place quite readily, without abandoning, however, that condescending
reserve of the Muslim male confronted with "women's business." He
never tried to interfere with or influence my interviews with Khady. On
the contrary, his rare interruption, always concise and technical, helped
to clarify them.

Khady's appearance reveals nothing of her past or of her illnesses.
Her medium height, her corpulence (accentuated by the bulk of her
brightly colored dresses), her heavy limbs, her hair (arranged in a
quantity of small braids), her feet dyed with henna, her enveloping
presence are all typical of the aging Wolof woman. Her face is intelligent, her features delicate. Rather than hardening her expression,
the three oblique scars across her face seem to harmonize with her
somewhat prominent cheekbones, her dark and lively eyes, and her
thick lips that are always quick to smile. Her features and movement,

her malicious look and lively mimicry are reminiscent of the young woman's beauty; one would not think that she is close to sixty.

Her Domestic Shrines, Her Rab

At Khady's age, *ndɔpkat* clientele is secure. Each Monday and Thursday, the days of the cult, Khady receives her former patients who come to "wash" themselves on their personal shrines, as well as her neighbors who consult her regularly about their children or their troubles, and the new recruits whom she has met at a relative's house or during her order's rites of possession. On these days her house is bustling with people. The visitors are first received in the bedroom. When the preliminary conversations are over, Khady leads them to the enclosure where the *xamb* are located in order to begin the offerings and to administer baths and remedies.

She has no apparent difficulty in finding her way around the enormous disorder of pottery containers, pestles, and iron rods half buried in the ground. The *xamb* of her former patients—fourteen in all—are set up along the edge of the rectangular enclosure. Her own shrines are in the center, close to the three baobab trees dedicated to her Serer *rab* and *tuur*.

The three *tuur,* who are inherited from her ancestors and who comprise her principal allies, are all placed to the east of the row of baobabs. The baobabs themselves are oriented on a north-south axis.[24]

	Name	Characteristics
INHERITED TUUR (principal allies)		
maternal (NORTH)	*Ardo*	Peul, pastoral nomad, Moslem
EAST		(*seriñ*)
paternal (SOUTH)	*Maam Ngesu*	Wolof, warrior, pagan (*ceddo*)
	Ndeban	Serer, pagan
ACQUIRED RAB (secondary allies)		
	Xoye	Serer, "brother" of *Ndew*
	Wargi Ndiaye	Serer, bard of *Ndew*
WEST	*Ndew*	Serer, pagan, second-born twin of *Ndeban*
	Diogoy Wali	Serer, "brother" of *Ndew*, native of the Sin region
	Ndiaga Umi Sore	Serer, *lawbé* companion of *Ndew*
	Boury Diouf	Serer, fisherman, native of Sangomar
	Alamdu	European (*tubaab*), ship captain

The shrines of *Ardo* are located toward the north. He is the Muslim Peul shepherd who has been "following" his (Toucouleur) matrilineage for five generations. Toward the south are the pottery containers of *Maam Ngesu,*the Wolof *tuur* of Khady's father, and those belonging to *Ndeban,* the Serer spirit who "entered" her father's family during the marriage of one of his ancestors to a Serer woman.

The seven *rab* Khady acquired herself, who are her secondary allies, are located toward the west. They are all "infidels," pagans (*ceddo*). *Ndew, Ndeban*'s twin brother, is their leader.[25] He "commands" four other Serer *rab:* his "brothers *Xoye* and *Diogoy Wali,* his "griot" * *Wargi Ndiaye,* and *Ndiaga Umi Sore,* his *lawbē* (bushel-maker) companion. But *Ndew* has no power over *Boury Diouf,* a fisherman *rab,* nor over *Alamdu,* Khady's European *rab.*

The Origin of Maam Ngesu, the Paternal Tuur

All these figures do not enter individually into Khady's story. *Maam Ngesu, Ardo,* and the twins *Ndew* and *Ndeban* are the veritable actors of her drama, with *Maam Ngesu* in the leading role (often in an obscure manner). For Khady, this ally of her father commands her other *tuur* and *rab,* and her sacrifices and offerings are first directed to him. It is he whom she invokes at night to diagnose the complaints of her patients. Again, it is *Maam Ngesu* whom she associates with her *gallaj,* or most precious "fetish," *Sajinne,* without which she could neither cure nor attend the possession rites.

Sajinne is a large ox horn stuffed with powdered roots and other medicines. The black mass that blocks its opening, which Khady calls its "head," is a voluminous ball studded with cowries and decorated with red pearl necklaces. The three little goat horns that are fixed in this bull like small pointed teeth are entwined with threads. The beak of an egret and the skull of another bird (*tox*) blackened with blood hang from these threads. Khady does not know how, when, or why *Sajinne* was made by her paternal ancestors, who in turn passed the "fetish" on

---

* The griots (Wolof, *gewɛl*) are musicians, singers of praise, reciters of genealogies, tellers of tales of kings and warriors, play-actors, acrobats, and buffons who are attached to free-born lineages whose history they know and relate. In former days the griots accompanied warriors to battle and urged them on with martial songs; they acted as court jesters to kings and had the right to mock and insult anyone. They were reputed for their drunkenness, licentiousness, and magic and were long resistant to Islam. They were not buried in the ground or thrown into the sea, for if they were, it was thought, the crops would fail and the fish die. They were buried in hollow baobab trees, and even today the griots are buried in a separate section of a cemetery. See David P. Gamble, *The Wolof of Senegambia* (London: International African Institute, 1967) [Editor's note].

to her. It feeds on blood, she says, and has its own gill. When it refuses to cure a patient, it becomes very heavy, so heavy that Khady cannot lift it. *Sajinne* is incomparably more powerful than her other *gallaj*, the "bald head," or jackal head,[26] for example, which protects her from witchcraft.

Thus *Sajinne* has all the ill-defined characteristics of a fetish object. It is neither an emblem nor some "symbol" of *Maam Negesu*.[27] And yet, Khady associates it with this *tuur* whose origin is given in the following twin myth.

A long time ago, twins were born. The one who came out first was a boy. The second did not show himself right away. He continued to appear as a scrap of placenta (*and*, "placenta," "companion"). The old people of the village hid him in a granary to shield him from the looks of the curious. Some time later, he transformed himself into a snake. The old people then ordered his twin brother to go to him regularly to seek advice. In exchange, he was given meat, blood, and milk. In this manner, the snake grew up in the granary. One day, he came down and settled in the hollow trunk of a *Ngeer*[28] tree which stood near the village. From then on, meat, milk, and *nak* (sweetened millet) were placed at the foot of the tree. Much later, a piece was cut from the tree for making a war drum which was called *Jigul Jamm*, "which brings misfortune on peace.

The double birth, the placenta's metamorphosis into a snake,[29] the setting up of an elementary structure of exchange (twin brother—*rab*—the village elders), the appearance of the village tree, are constant themes in *rab* mythology. For Khady, however, this origin myth is incomplete without the founding legend which tells us that the twin brother was the founder of the royal patrilineage of the Fall family from Cayor, of which she herself is a distant descendent:

Maam Ngesu's twin brother was called Gnoku Fam. He was born at Fam Kunda, in Soss country. A great hunter, he wore a gold earring in his right ear. One day he went out to hunt. His dog followed him. *Maam Ngesu* was with him. He walked for a long time toward the west. One morning, he discovered he was in Cayor. The inhabitants of this country asked him his name. "My name is Gnoku Fam, I come from Fam Kunda", he answered. But the people didn't understand very well and called him Fall. Answering his request, they gave him land on the very place which became Mboul, the capital of Cayor. He married and later became king.

The following is implied in this account: the Soss hunter Fam would never have become the Wolof farmer Fall and still less the king of

Cayor without the protection of his powerful and invisible twin, *Maam Ngesu,* who in turn became the tutelary spirit of Mboul,[30] capital of the Cayor kingdom.

Her Family, Her "Heritage"

From then on, we enter the time of repetition. Each alliance that a descendant of Gnoku Fam forms with the *rab* re-presents this original pact of the lineage with the "double" of its founding ancestor. The story of *Maam Ngesu* is thus the primordial reference within the family's symbolic system.

As opposed to the usual practice of *rab* inheritance through the female line, Khady's paternal ancestors are said to have "transmitted" this *tuur* from father to elder son. Thus he is said to have "followed" the lineage until the death of Birama Fall, Khady's father, who had six wives. Yaga, the youngest son of the third wife, and Aliou, the eldest of the fourth, first inherited the shrines of *Maam Ngesu* (Figure 1). It was only after the death of Aliou that the *tuur* began to "visit" Khady, the daughter of her father's fifth wife. She has a full brother, Ngouda.

As we have seen, the Serer *tuur, Ndeban,* entered the lineage through Tyoro Fall, the Serer wife of Birama Fall's great-grandfather. After that, he is said to have followed the same "road" as *Maam Ngesu* (Figure 1).

On the maternal side, the tuur *Ardo* is transmitted along the female line. He first passes from mother to daughter, then from Maty Kane, Khady's mother, to Ibrahima Diouf, the "cousin." Khady in turn inherits the *tuur* from this cousin (Figure 2) in dramatic circumstances.

The maternal lineage is of Toucouleur origin. It is not accidental that it is represented by a Peul spirit.[31] In Khady's narrative this lineage, as well as its *rab,* has pronounced Muslim characteristics. This is its Islamic side.

The paternal ancestors are Wolof, like their principal *tuur.* The Fall warriors, as well as *Maam Ngesu* and *Ndeban,* are the "infidels" (*ceddo*) of the family mythology. This is its pagan side.

Thus the determining characteristics of the spirits inherited by Khady—their ethnic origin and religion—repeat the essential features of the lineages to which she herself belongs. And we will see that her domestic shrine is the screen on which are projected, in condensed form, her family history and her own biography.

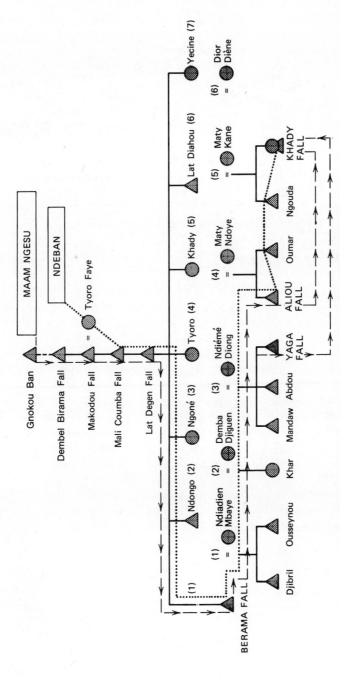

Figure 1. The paternal relatives and their *tuur* (*Maam Ngesu* and *Ndeban*).

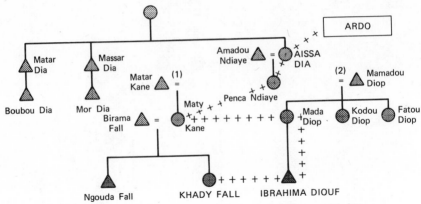

Figure 2. The maternal relatives and their *turr* (*Ardo*).

KHADY FALL'S NARRATIVE

Although Khady did not tell me her story in the (approximately) chronological order I later adopted, she definitely made me feel that her life could be arranged in three major periods:

- the one in which she lived under the sign of her very early election by the spirits and during which she stubbornly resisted the call of her *rab;*
- the one she now calls her time of "travels," that is, her initiatory illness which ended with the building of her first domestic shrine;
- and the one, finally, in which she committed herself, of her own free will, to priesthood, served her apprenticeship and began treating the sick.

I

"I knew that I would have to receive this heritage. But I did not want it."

ELECTION AND RESISTANCE

The Broken Shrine

The earliest event she remembers takes place in Diabass, the Wolof-Serer village near Dakar where she was born. Her father is the well-known chief of a neighboring village. She is two or three years old:

I'd been given a stick. I was a child and didn't pay attention to anything. I swished the stick around and hit the "canari" (the pottery containers on the shrine) that belonged to Yacine Faye, a Serer neighbor. The "canari" broke. The women started to shout. I fainted. My mother came running to breastfeed me but I didn't want to eat. They went to fetch my father. He listened to the people and told his relatives: "Go ahead, take her away if she's dead!" He, in turn, shut himself up in his *xamb;* he went to work.[32] When he came out, he told the people: "I see that my child is not dead." He saddled his horse and, as soon as he arrived in Diabass, he called for *laman* Sobel [the Serer chief]:

MY FATHER: I told you not to eat my child!

THE LAMAN: No, nobody tried to eat your child. She broke Yacine Faye's "canari" and the *rab* are attacking her.

YACINE FAYE: Birama Fall, I know that your *rab* are strong. But this time your child won't recover unless you kill a red ox for *Ndew* and for myself. You are to put the child on the back of the ox and she must carry a winnowing-basket on her head.

The father, puzzled at first, soon understood that the owner of the broken shrine demanded the name-changing rite, the *ndəp-layu.* He accepted. On the day of the sacrifice, Khady was baptized *Yacine* in honor of the injured possessed. Even now, the people of Diabass still call her by this name. And the *rab* who lived in the shrine, the Serer *Ndew,* has never left Khady since then.

[As we can see, the first tie that binds Khady to this *Serer rab* is characterized by a challenge to her father. Birama Fall, in his capacity as magician and name-giver, is driven into a corner by the very ones he treats as witches. His knowledge fails him and his will is thwarted once his daughter has been promised to the spirits.]

In the following years, Khady falls ill several times. Each time her father manages to cure her on the shrines of *Maam Ngesu.* At the age of eight or nine, her mother places her in charge of a relative from Mecke.[33] Khady has hardly arrived in this village when she is struck with "paralysis." Her neck is "broken," she has "very big eyes," and "she is so ugly to look at" that she is covered with pagnes. Her mother, in Dakar at the time, comes to fetch her. On the way back, Khady has convulsive fits and has two "falls," one immediately after the other. The marabout consulted by her mother is categorical: "The *rab* say that she must be taken home this same day, otherwise she will die." They return home in great haste.

A Child is Beaten: Pregnancy and Mutism

Around the age of sixteen, Khady is married to Samba Fall, a paternal relative. She becomes pregnant. In her fourth month she witnesses a scene under the village tree:

Ke Diakho, an important person in the village, tied a young boy to a tree and started beating him. He struck him so hard that I started to cry and then fainted. I was carried to my house. I had a dream. A boy asked me where the marabout was. I showed him the room where my family had lodged a *seriñ* (a marabout). Then I saw the marabout himself. He told me Ke Diakho had fallen from a camel and was dead. I woke up. The women explained to me that the child was Ke Diakho's griot. He had beaten him because the child had stolen something from him. During my sleep, my mother tried to separate them, but the man did not want to listen to her. He made the child get on his camel and took him off into the bush.

Khady's dream continued to intrigue her. She tried to get details from her husband:

Why did this child and this marabout come to see me in my dream?
Because you had seen the boy get a beating.
No, that's not true, since the marabout told me that Ke Diakho was dead!

The whole story was cleared up the next day but, first, something alarming happened: Khady woke up mute. She could not say a single word. The people were busy commenting on this event, when a boy came to "call the marabout" to the bedside of Ke Diakho who "was throwing up fat" (i.e., he was a witch). The *seriñ* had barely arrived on the spot; already the sorcerer's body was getting stiff and a few moments later, he died.
[Barring the question of witchcraft, which endangered her as well (because she was pregnant), Khady had thus foreseen and predicted everything. But her prophesy caused her to become mute. In fact, the only explanation she can give for her muteness is the imprudence with which she had revealed her dream to her young husband: "I stayed like that for four months because I had told my dream to Samba Fall."
In short, she is telling us that her "illness" was not punishment for her ambivalent feelings on witnessing the cruel treatment of the boy.[34] It was only the price the *rab* made her pay for her gossip. The *rab* had revealed the future to her because they loved her. But she had not understood that she should refrain from divulging their message as long as she had not yet accepted their alliance, had not yet asked for and

submitted to the appropriate rites. The penalty imposed upon her by the spirits was proportionate to her misappreciation (*méconnaissance*): she had been deprived of the very possibility of betraying their secrets.]

The Twins or the Sign from Maam Ngesu

Speech is restored to her with the help of a possessed Serer woman. Her delivery is approaching and, as is customary, she consults a marabout on the subject of the birth: "You're going to have twins," says the marabout, "the first shall be a boy, but the second will have the appearance of an *and* (placenta, "companion")."

Khady gives birth, with these words still fresh in her mind, and this is what she sees: "The first is a boy, he's like all other boys. But the second is not quite a human being (*nit*). Both are stillborn."
[The *rab* is the invisible twin, the double of the person (*nit*).[35] Khady suddenly finds herself in the position of her female ancestor in the family myth: the origin myth of *Maam Ngesu*. She now has definite proof that the *rab* wanted to stir her to the depths of her soul.]

Yacine and the Killing of the Snakes

During her next pregnancy, she tries to avoid this danger. In order to appease *Ndew,* the Serer *rab* whom she suspects is responsible for her bad luck, she *gives the name Yacine* to the little girl who is born. Her delivery takes place normally, and the child grows up in good health. One day Khady goes to the field with her husband to dig peanuts:

> When the sun rises, I put Yacine down in the shade of a tree and I go back to work. Suddenly, it's as if I had received a blow. I jump up and turn around: I see three snakes surrounding Yacine. I shout, I want to run off . . . then, I run toward the child. But the snakes don't want to go away. Then, my husband comes up and kills all three of them with his machete.
>
> I put Yacine on my back, and we start back to the village. To get there we have to cross a river channel. We're just going into the water when I see a snake lying quietly on the river's edge. My husband calls to a Serer who's standing on the other side: "Do your snakes act like that?" "No," says the Serer, "but perhaps they're our companions." So, my husband gets out of the water and kills the snake.

The four snakes were *rab,* of course. Samba Fall, the husband, had been clearly warned. The spirits did not take long to retaliate. A few days later a man fell on Yacine "accidentally" and the child died on the spot.

The Bowels are Cut: Sterility

But the *rab*'s vengeance was to go still further. The very day of Yacine's death, Khady explains, they "cut my bowels"[36]: "I cried out, I even heard the noise it made . . . then, they wet my feet. It was as if they'd poured water over my feet."

She was terribly scared and, with her mother's help, she did everything that might "satisfy" the spirits. But they were no longer disposed to forgive her. On that day she became sterile.[37]

[Today Khady feels that she has paid this way, heavily, for her husband's mistake. The *rab* blamed her, their elect, for she did not want to listen to their call. "I knew," she says, "that I would have to receive this heritage, but I didn't want to accept it."]

The Mother's Sacrifice

Soon after her divorce from Samba Fall, for whom she could no longer bear children, Khady falls seriously ill from a kola nut which her mother had bought from a family slave. She has violent stomachaches and vomits continuously. Nothing, not even the treatments of the quickly identified witch,[38] help to ease her discomfort. Her mother offers a goat to the *rab* in vain. Maty Kane then begins praying desperately to God, asking to be taken in Khady's stead. Her wish is fulfilled. Khady is cured; a month later, her mother dies of an unknown illness.

[Khady did not tell me how she reacted to this event. Neither did she say how Birama Fall acted at the death of his fifth wife. She was always very circumspect when it came to her father's words or actions. But there is evidence that leads me to suppose that her father died at about the same time, leaving his *rab* heritage to his sons, Aliou and Yaga Fall.]

Toward the "Great Illness"

After losing her mother, Khady settles in Dakar. She is about twenty-three when she marries Aliou Gaye, a young man who already has one wife. One day the *rab* warn her that her mother-in-law and her co-wife are plotting with a Sosse marabout to "work" her with magic: they want to prevent her husband from giving her money. Khady warns Aliou of their intentions. At pay time she sees that their magic has indeed succeeded and divorces him.

One day, she pays a visit to a "sister" from Thiaroye who has just sacrificed a goat to her *rab*. During the night, Khady's own *rab* "show" her a black goat and "claim their share." The next morning, she wakes up "paralyzed," with "her feet joined." These disorders last for less than a week. They disappear under the effects of the sacrifice that a *ndɔpkat* offers to her *rab*.

After her divorce, she lives in the house of her full brother, Ngouda. Again, she is pursued by the spirits. In the course of a "baptism" ceremony, she generously distributes money among the griots. Suddenly she receives a "blow on the head." She cries out, thrashes about, and falls on the ground. For several days she suffers from insomnia and headaches. The marabout whom she consults states that "her *rab* do not agree with the *rab* of Ngouda Fall." Yet they have the same mother and father.

[Khady is between twenty-five and thirty years old when these events take place. Her initiatory illness is about to begin. What should be retained, within her discourse, of this first and most remote period in her life? The organization of her discourse is not by any means chronological. Each episode is like the punctuated highpoint of a fate in which Khady reinscribes her past.

This fate demands that she accept her father's heritage and assume her origins by submitting to the ancestral spirits. The voices of the *rab* proclaim: "You are our chosen one, our future ally, and that is the reason why we cause your illness." But Khady—and this is the leitmotiv of her narrative—rejects the spirits' offer; she does "not want to accept the heritage." Her body pays the price for her refusal. Her "paralyses," her recurrent crises, her mutism, her stillborn children, and her sterility fill the void that results from her inability to pronounce the word of alliance.

The *rab*'s idiom enables her to articulate this refusal. She does not directly express her resistance to the law of her paternal family, to her father's law. Yet her question is there, marked, from the episode of the broken shrine onward. Her first alliance with *Ndew,* the Serer spirit, is tied up under the sign of the defeat of her father's power. Her "arranged" marriage with Samba Fall, a paternal relative, is the tragic moment in which she loses her fertility. She—*the rab*—do not want this marriage. They take away her power of speech, for they are the judges and spokesmen of her own aggressive fantasies. The *rab,* those implacable intermediaries, enable her to express what she imputes to her husband as well as her self-accusations regarding her daughter's death and the tragedy of her own sterility.

The Serer *rab* appear as symbolic support for her resistance to the paternal tradition. Ndew, in whose honor she receives and gives the

name of Yacine, is totally her own. The day she finally accepts him as
the "twin" of *Ndeban,* the *tuur* of her father's ancestors, she has overcome a great deal.]

II

"A grand-daughter does not escape her ancestors. Come give us something to eat and
drink."

Initiatory Illness

No doubt to free herself of the magic that caused her last divorce,
Khady next marries Mor Dia, an old marabout who belongs to her maternal family.[39] For three years the couple live together peacefully.
During the fourth year, for some unknown reason, Khady suddenly
leaves their home. Her husband sends a messenger to call her back.
She sends him away. Then, Mor Dia asks for a divorce, and Khady con-
sents.

Her "Travels"

Scarcely a few days after this decision, the *rab* appear to her in human
form and pronounce the following sentence:

Wəret   mbaa   nga   wêêt   ni   Maty Wade!
Leave! (go out!) otherwise you   will waste   like Maty Wade!
                               away alone

[*Wəret* and *wêêt* are two complementary procedures in Wolof magic.
The first compels the individual to leave his or her house and, if the
agent of the magic desires it, to wander about aimlessly like a bird.[40]
The second has a contrary effect: it immobilizes and isolates the individual to the point that he or she loses all pleasure in life, all
sociability.[41] Both are known to be deadly magic.]

Khady obeys this injunction—without exactly knowing who Maty
Wade is, although the name reminds her of her maternal Toucouleur
ancestors—she leaves Dakar and seeks refuge with a "sister" at Mbour.
Mor Dia joins her there and pleads with her to return with him, but she
remains inflexible. A fortnight later she gathers up her belongings and
returns to Dakar. But there is nothing to be done; she cannot stay. She
leaves again, first for Diabass, and then goes to a maternal aunt at Kaolack. She is hardly settled there when she wants to leave—is compelled

to leave. She flees to Mbake, an important Mouride center, then to British Gambia. Actually she does not remember all her travels. "For three years," she tells me, "I was like a carrier pigeon. It was the *rab* who pushed me on. They were telling me: 'Go! Leave for such and such a place!' And I would pick up my belongings and leave."

From Magic to Ardo

However, despite this commanding need to "travel," she finds the means to marry a fouth time to Djugo Tall, a chauffeur. Soon after they marry, Djugo has to leave for the army. She is alone, in Kaolack, when Mamadou Mbake, the great Mouride marabout, calls for her:

"I have had a dream for you," the marabout tells her. "I saw you being shot at. The bullet went straight through your right shoulder, through your chest, your thighs, and your ankles, and then it fell to the ground. After that, the people wanted to tie you with a gold chain. But I took hold of the chain and told them: 'This is not the time to tie her up.' Now you must prepare balls of *nak* and distribute them among the beggars!"

Khady follows the marabout's advice, without giving much thought to the meaning of the dream. But when she is about to hand out the last ball of *nak*, she stops short: "I felt the shock; it was as if I'd received a blow in my heart . . ." She is taken to the Kaolack infirmary. Once again Khady is "paralyzed," her "hands are on her back," and her eyes are "blinded." The doctors admit their inability to treat her condition, and she is taken home. [For Khady, this episode and the "travels" are closely related. We should remember that it was to escape magic that she had married Mor Dia, the old marabout. But by resisting, on two occasions, this relative's efforts toward reconciliation, she exposes herself to (instead of benefiting from) his magic. The words of the *rab* ordering her departure (*wɔret mbaa nga wêêt* . . .) and the compulsive nature of her "travels" seem to agree with the hypothesis that she is under the effect of a powerful *ligêêy* (magic spell).[42]

Khady, however, rejects this hypothesis whenever I suggest it. She insists upon the *rab* version and, more specifically, blames *Ardo*, her maternal *tuur*: "It was *Ardo*, the nomad shepherd, who forced me to travel."

She says this despite the fact that she is contradicted by the dream of the marabout Mbake. At first she seems invulnerable: the bullet went straight through her.[43] She is protected therefore, either by her *rab* or by the Muslim God. Then the situation is reversed, and we see her under the magic spell. Being tied with a chain is a common metaphor

in Wolof *ligêêy*.[44] She is not invulnerable, or, rather, she cannot be effectively protected *by her rab*, but only by Islam—*by the marabout*—who
has the power not only to inhibit magic but also to perform it. "This is
not the time to tie her up," says the marabout, as if he were in charge
of her aggressors.

The consequences of the dream clarify its contents even further. The
marabout orders Khady to perform a "charity" (*sarax*), which is something entirely different from an offering made to the *rab*. It is an act of
human mercy, a counterpart of divine charity, while the offering made
to the spirits is an act of exchange. God does not keep accounts, on a
basis of parity, as the *rab* do with the gifts that they receive. The spirits
never order food to be distributed outside their circle of allies. Neither
are they appeased by the fact that Khady has, in addition, been advised
to "make the *sarax* with *nak*," their ritual food. From then on, according
to Khady, it becomes clear why they are attacking her. They warn her
that the food is theirs by law, that they are "following" (*topp*) her, and
that she should not "seek her luck elsewhere."

This time, the marabout's words are implicitly challenged. It is her
rab's possessive love that makes her ill and not the magic, which refers
her to Islam. Both conflict and message are clear enough. First as a
being chosen by the *rab*, and second as a Muslim, Khady finds herself at
the crossroads of two paths of identification with her mother. She is
tempted by the protective power of the marabouts—hence her marriage to Mor Dia, the maternal relative who represents the "Islamic
side"—but she feels she is expressly called to order by her *rab*, by
Ardo, who is equally her mother's *rab*.]

Ardo's Messenger: Maram Galaw Tayba

Thus, once again, Khady is seriously ill. She consults several healers in
Kaolack but their treatment hardly improves her condition. Accompanied by her husband (the fourth), she now starts a tour of the best
boroom tuur. At Kaffrine, the famous Mor Ndaw sacrifices a sheep in
honor of her *rab*, but warns: "For you, a *samp* [45] is needed, and it
wouldn't be any help if I made one here. You must make it in the very
place from which you come." Khady does not heed his advice. Feeling
somewhat better, she goes directly to see a Gambian *boroom tuur*. This
healer goes still further than his predecessor: "Your *rab* is a *rab* that
heals,[46] you must build him a house." And he too recommends the return to her native land: the *rab* are attached to their soil, it is there that
the shrine must be built.

The course of events accelerates. One night, while in a border village, Khady has a dream. *Maram Galaw Tayba,* one of the *rab* belonging to her maternal grandmother, Penda Ndiaye, "appears" before her:

He came with a goat's head. He wanted to place it on top of my eyes. I told him: "Do you want to hurt me?" He answered me: "No, I'm *Maram Galaw Tayba,* I've come to see you." Then he said very distinctly: "A granddaughter does not escape her ancestors [*maam*].[47] Come, give us something to eat and drink!"

[For Khady, this dream is the decisive moment that marks the end of her peregrinations. The *rab* came, she tells me, on behalf of *Ardo* who had been responsible for her "travels." The goat's head was the sacrific he had been asking her to make for a long time. She had had to "blind herself" in order to come to this realization.]

Thus her memory inscribes the confused epic of her "travels" in a closed period strictly fixed at each extremity by a key phrase, the "hallucinatory" injunction that decided her departure and the dream message that ordered her return.

Departure, travel, return. . . . She recalls this period as one of ambulatory madness, of a blind and compelling urge to transgress the fundamental rules of both her caste and society: restraint in travel, reserve in behavior and speech, attachment to the native soil and "passive" self-control.[48] She seems to consider this "travel" period as a kind of counterpart to the first period of her life, characterized by immobility, mutism, and "paralysis."

The fact that Khady blames *Ardo* (her mother's Peul ally) for her wanderings is indicated clearly by the metaphor organizing these episodes and by her process of identification with her mother (which these wanderings instigate): "I went from place to place as if under the influence of my mother's nomad rab." This attitude, however, is somewhat modified by a detail in her narrative.

The spirit who orders her return is neither *Ardo* nor the indeterminate subject ("they," "the *rab*") that had enjoined her to leave. It is *Maram Galaw Tayba,* the *rab* messenger, who invites Khady to submit to the law of her ancestors. This call to transmit messages of defiance, of rivalry or—as is the case here—of authority.

Maram Galaw Tayba is the female *tuur* of Tayba Ndiaye, a place near Khady's native village. There she is known as the ally of the founder of the patrilineage (Matar Ndiaye) and is associated throughout the region with the Ndiaye, and never, it seems, with the Fall.[49] Consequently it is highly probable that this spirit is the *paternal tuur* of Khady's *maternal* grandmother, Penda Ndiaye, and that the latter "received" this *tuur* from her agnatic Wolof or Lebou ancestors.

If we reintroduce Khady's inherited *rab* into this interplay of transmissions, we have the following pattern (Figure 3).

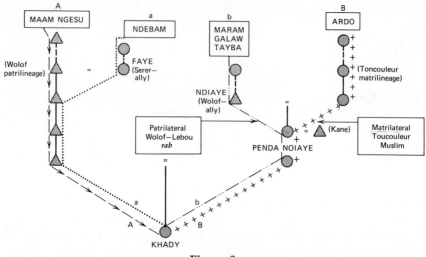

Figure 3

We can now begin to understand what the naming of the messenger *rab* implies for Khady, for the symbolic elaboration she undertakes at the conclusion of her "travels."

Ardo (Figure 3, B), who sends the dream message, is the signifier of Khady's "milk" tie to her mother's Toucouleur and Muslim matrilineage, and of her incorporation in a kinship group. In naming this "originary tuur" [50] of the lineage, she can claim her descent, namely, as "granddaughter" of her maternal ancestors. She can do this, however, only in a position of imaginery identification with her mother, without acknowledging her debt to the father who engendered her.

Maram Galaw Tayba (Figure 3, b), the female messenger, appears as the first indication of that acknowledgment. This *tuur,* who is the grandmother's paternal, Wolof, and probably "infidel" *tuur*—in a relationship parallel to Khady's with Maam Ngesu [51]—is the symbolic representative of those allies to whom the matrilineage owes its existence and, consequently, of the ally to whom Khady owes her own birth. In naming this messenger as *Ardo's* spokesman, Khady's dream indicates the place of the "fathers": in the beginning of her maternal ancestry and, by metonymy, the place of *her* father in her identification with her mother.

This designation inscribes a cleavage and thereby prepares for the articulation of both the paternal and maternal signifiers.

The First Samp

Khady, with the messenger's words still fresh in her mind, immediately sets out in the direction of her native land. But first—is it still a resistance or simply a misunderstanding?—she stops at Diourbel and then at Rufisque, where she falls ill once again. The pain is so great that she feels her "head splitting in two." She is taken to Dakar and it is there, around 1940, that her first *samp* takes place.

This *samp*, however, is not without difficulties. The first try fails because her present husband, who is a "good Muslim," doesn't want any music played, [52] and in the midst of the ceremony, deprived of drums, the body of the *ndɔpkat* directing the rite, "begins to swell." It is deduced that Khady's *infidel rab (ceddo) "require drums."* Nevertheless, a second *ndɔpkat* carries out still another rite without music. This results in her having "violent pains in the legs." She begins the rite once again, and this time the *rab* seem to accept the sacrifice.

[This first and fragile alliance with the *rab* concludes the second period of Khady's life. During this period her development takes a decisive turn.

Her discourse turns upon the question of religious affinity and upon the search for a means of identification with her mother. By questioning her relationship to the Islam of the marabouts and to the religion of ancestral spirits, she discovers the mediating role played by the Muslim *rab* that she has inherited from her maternal ancestors. She is able to renew the link with her father's "heritage" by referring to this (Muslim) rab belonging to her mother.

She had already entered into an ambiguous dialogue with the representatives of Islam before beginning her "travels." Everything she does seems to indicate that she sought their protection to escape the *rab*. She marries Mor Dia and thus expresses her preference for the power of the marabout over the power of the *rab*, and as a precaution against magic. When she describes her peregrinations as if they were under the influence of a Muslim *ligêêy*, what she blames elsewhere on the *rab*, she seems to impute to Islam. She claims this to be true, clearly enough, in the episode regarding the *"nak* charity." It is for having "sought her luck" with Islam that she is called to order by her *rab*.

What does this search, this call to order, and this final alliance with the Muslim spirit mean to her? By turning toward Islam she remains true to her mother's profession of faith that saved her from death. But

she must also recognize in the religion of the marabouts a direction
that would free her from the fate of submission (a submission extolled
by the voice of the *rab*) and from the female condition prescribed by
family traditions. Does she not also seek, within Islam, an illusory autonomy, the points of identification that might allow her to mask her
indebtedness toward the *rab*? Be this as it may, the final compromise
reflects the troubled ambiguity of her efforts. When she accepts the alliance with *Ardo,* the Muslim *rab* who is also inscribed in her mother's
history, she can live momentarily with the illusion of having to choose
and of not having chosen. Finally, however, the voice of the spirits for-
bidding her equivocation is stronger than everything else. As the messenger spirit proclaims, a granddaughter does not escape her ancestors.]

III

"I inherited this knowledge from my ancestors!"

Accession to Priesthood and to a Therapeutic Role

The first rite was offered to the Muslim *Ardo.* But it also had to honor
the pagan twins *Ndew* and *Ndeban,* for it was these Serer "infidels" who
had insisted upon music. Thus they returned to claim their due.

The Pagan Spirits "Demand Drums"

One Monday morning, Khady found her shrines knocked down and
her tree roots torn out of the ground.[53] She immediately caught a
rooster for sacrifice in order, she says, to avert danger. But just as she
was about to slit the bird's throat, she became frightened and let go of
it. She asked a man to make the sacrifice instead. After he had completed the sacrifice, Khady felt a "blow on the head." Soon she had to
be put to bed; her body was burning with fever and pain.

She then called on the service of a *ndɔpkat* from Rufisque,[54] who sacrificed a goat. For the first time, drums were played. But her recovery
did not last long. A few days after the *samp,* she awoke with a severe
itch and a feeling of irritation: "as if red pepper had been put into my
eyes." She was quick to recognize the cause of her troubles. She went to
the *ndɔpkat* and directly accused him of having stolen the tree roots
from her freshly built shrines: "Women should not have knowledge
(*xam-xam*)!" said the healer. *"I inherited this knowledge from my ancestors!"*

was Khady's reply. After a heated dispute, Khady went home and, for the first time, decided to consult her cousin Ibrahima Diouf.

[This is another significant stage in her story. Ibrahima, the son of one of her mother's uterine sisters, is at the peak of his career as a healer. Not only does he consider himself the legitimate guardian of *Ardo,* but he also withholds, without any justification, part of Khady's paternal heritage. It remains unknown how and why the *Sajinne* came into his possession.]

Ibrahima uses this "fetish" [55] to diagnose his cousin's condition. He advises Khady to "drive a certain person out of her house" and to undergo a *ndəp* for a period of eight days. She did not tell me how she accomplished the delicate task of "driving out" her husband (to whom her cousin was evidently referring), but she did describe in detail her first one-week *ndəp,*[56] which took place under Ibrahima's immediate direction. After this rite she felt strong and healthy.

Ardo, Ndew, and *Ndeban* have finally and fully accepted the pact. It must, however, be consolidated by repeating the sacrifices at Diabass on ancestral ground. Khady decides to accomplish this after a dream in which young circumcised men appear to her. She organizes a rite that lasts three days, and she distributes the sacrificial meat on the shrines of her three *rab.*

The "Hospital" Stone and the Vulture Head

From then on, she no longer has any of the violent attacks she was subject to in her youth. She begins to learn the profession of *ndəpkat,* hesitantly at the start, but then with more and more assurance. Her first teacher is her cousin. Other *boroom tuur* succeed him in the course of a rather long period (4–5 years) which Khady considers her years of apprenticeship. At the beginning of this period, two events make a strong impression on her teacher.

At the death of Khady's father, the family shrines had been "divided" among Aliou and Yaga Fall on one side, and Ibrahima, the cousin, on the other. Aliou was the principal heir. For a while, the brothers left their "share" beneath that baobab of the lineage which Khady likes to call the "hospital," because, she says, so many people have been cared for beneath that tree. Later, each of the brothers took his "share" away.

Thus the "hospital" was empty when Khady had another dream about her *rab.* She saw human shapes and then she heard a voice: *"Now is the time to retrieve what has been left in someone else's care!"*

In the morning, she went to consult the neighborhood seer.

THE SEER (a woman):   *You yourself know things that I don't.*
KHADY: *No,* I know nothing, *I'm young.*
THE SEER: *You must go and retrieve your share beneath the baobab tree!*
KHADY: My brothers have already taken everything.
THE SEER: *No! Your share is the stone that the* rab *have buried underneath the tree.*

Ibrahima reached the same conclusion. At his insistence, Khady agrees to visit the spot. She takes along a family slave:

I told him to dig under the baobab tree. He digs and digs, but I see nothing. The hospital is already almost uprooted, but I still see nothing. Then I hear a voice which tells me "That one mustn't see us!" [57] I order the slave to leave the tree and I take up the hoe [*daba*] myself. Immediately I strike against something hard. I take it out. It's the stone. I wash it, wrap it in my pagne, and carry it home with me. There's nobody around. Then I pour milk in a gourd and place the stone in the milk. . . . I told all this to Ibrahima. He was astonished: "Why did you put it in milk?" "Because it must have been hungry!" "You're downright clever!" he told me. [58]

During this same period, and under similar circumstances, Khady recovers another "part" of her paternal heritage: *Bopp u taan,* or "vulture head," which she now wears against her chest. [59]

I was gathering peanuts. Suddenly I heard a noise. I turned around and there was *Bopp u taan* lying on the ground. I picked it up and went to see my uncle [one of her father's brothers]. He told me: "You're lucky, this is the head that belonged to your father. He told me you would be his heiress. But, do you have the courage to keep it?" I answered yes. He then began to work on *Bopp u taan* with verses and powders. He gave it back to me.

["I know, I don't know . . . it's me, it isn't me": Khady constantly wavers between these two positions. One of them in narcissistic: she is the cherished granddaughter, the innocent one chosen by the *rab,* who discovers the treasure buried in the ground and receives a gift fallen from heaven. The other position is phallic: she is already the knowledgeable *boroom tuur* who proves her capacity to honor her father's heritage both by her wisdom (immersing the stone in milk) and by her courage (in keeping the vulture's head).

How can we define these two positions? First it is the *rab* who notify her of her right to the heritage. It is they who provide her with the emblem and instruments of her new power. Khady herself "knows nothing." She does not take her father's heritage; she receives it. Pushed back beyond her father, this heritage is denied as the symbolic equivalent of "the place of the father." [60] For as long as her ancestors send her this heritage, she possesses "the courage to keep it." Through the voice of her *rab* she can express what she feels as ineluctable and menacing in her pursuit of this new power, which challenges her insofar as she is her father's daughter and places her position of rivalry with her brothers.]

The First Ndəp and the "Moving" of the Rab

Thus it is not without reason the Khady's first disagreement with her cousin Ibrahima comes soon after the episode with the stone. They still trust one another at the time Khady organizes and directs her first *ndəp* at Diabass. But Ibrahima becomes reticent when Khady decides to transfer her *rab* to Dakar.[61] She ignores her cousin and performs the rite for this event. *Ardo, Ndew,* and *Ndeban,* and their Serer companions "leave" her native land.

This "departure" of the *rab* coincides with the first appearance of *Maam Ngesu.* Her account is confused here. Her father's *tuur* supposedly began to "visit" her at her brother Aliou Fall's death. She had difficulty walking and suffered from headaches and chest pains which, she claims, were cured by her fifth, and present, husband. After a series of rites, *Maam Ngesu* is supposed to have definitely entered her *xamb.*

Alamdu, the Ship's Captain

Her collection of *rab* is now almost complete. Only *Alamdu,* the European, is missing.[62] This is how she describes him:

> He's a ship's captain. I can see him in dreams. He's dressed in white, all in white. He wears medals and a cap with gold fringes. He always wants to take me out to sea on his ship. I had bought compound at Thies, but *Alamdu* doesn't want me to go there because Thies isn't by the sea.

One night she dreamt about Alamdu's ship and about her dead brothers:

> He made me get on his ship. In the cabin I found all my dead brothers. They were well-dressed and in good health. Aliou took hold of my arm: "Where are

you going?" I said: "I'm going to see *Alamdu*." When *Alamdu* touched me on the shoulder, another brother cried out: "Let her go!" The *rab* answered him: "No, I don't want to let her go! She's Maty Kane's daughter!" Then, I heard a voice that said to me: "Go and pour milk on his costume!" I took milk and poured it over him. *Alamdu* laughed. He gave orders for the ship to depart.

[Here again, we come upon the subject of Khady's brothers and of her identification with her mother. The "dead" brothers in Khady's dream are all members of the paternal family to which she herself, by right, belongs. Only Aliou Fall, the father's principal heir, is named. The "brothers" intervene on two occasions to prevent her from seeing her *rab*. They forbid this relationship whose sexual undertones are quite evident.[63] But their opposition—inasmuch as they represent paternal law—provokes the *rab's* reply: "No, I don't want to let her go, she's Maty Kane's [her mother's] daughter!" Implied in this sentence is another: "She's not only the daughter of [her father] Birama Fall." In short, everything takes place as if Khady were affirming her right to deal with the *rab* in her mother's name. By identifying herself with Maty Kane, she can face her father's sons.

These words, consequently, are pronounced by the *rab* and not by Khady; by the European *Alamdu* and not by the Peul *Ardo*, the Wolof *Maam Ngesu*, or the Serer *Ndeban*. One can easily understand why the paternal spirits were excluded. But why not *Ardo*, her mother's rab? Is he or is he not eliminated because he represents the father's world within the world of the mother. Or, to put it differently, because he plays the role of symbolic mediator—the Mediator between the Islamic and the pagan, between the maternal and paternal traditions—in Khady's story?

Alamdu, the European, is free of this ambivalence.[64] His position is outside the two family traditions; even outside the ancestral cult. His function may very well be that of a neutral, a term of delimitation by which Khady expresses her final autonomy (congruous with her adhesion to the religion of the *rab*).]

The Conquest of the "Fetish" Sajinne

As *Ardo* is the mediator between the *rab*, Ibrahima, the maternal cousin, is the mediator between men. Khady tells how she detached herself from this "false" brother after she dreamt of her own dead brothers.

Once in Dakar, she becomes a well-known *ndɔpkat*. She takes care of the sick, both in her own house and in that of her order at Fass. She is still missing one object, however: the formidable *Sajinne*. This "worked horn," as we have seen, belonged to her brother Aliou before Ibrahima Diouf captured it.

One day Khady goes to visit her cousin. When she arrives there, she has a dream in which she sees a leg of mutton. "Who has slaughtered a sheep in your house?" she asks Ibrahima, but her cousin doesn't answer. Offended, she goes to stay with a relative who lives in a nearby village. There she learns the following news: Ibrahima's sister-in-law is seriously ill; she has one crisis after another.

Her cousin seems to understand what is happening. "I know," he says, "why Khady mentioned a leg of mutton. She must organize the *ndəp* for this woman." Khady, when contacted, first claims incompetence: "I can't, all my *gallaj* ("fetishes") are in Dakar; all I have is *Bonko.*" [65] "It doesn't matter," Ibrahima replies, "you can take *Sajinne.*" She accepts the offer and the ceremony begins.

In the midst of the rite, Ibrahima's wife takes a spectacular fall. The drums are stopped. Ibrahima, furious, accuses Khady: "It's you who made my wife fall!" And he picks up both *Sajinne* and the gourd filled with roots that he had lent to his cousin. But Khady does not concede; she replaces *Sajinne* with her *laar* (oxtail) and continues the rite.

Two weeks later, the woman has another seizure and Khady is asked to come and treat her. But she does not answer the call. First she needs a dream: "The woman sinks into the sand, up to her neck. I grab her by the ears and pull her out. A voice tells me: 'You must kill a red rooster, you must hold a *nak* charity.'" On awakening she goes to her cousin's house.

IBRAHIMA: It's my wife Kumba. She wanted to leave us.
KHADY: I know. I saw her yesterday. It was I who pulled her out of the sand.
IBRAHIMA: I think it's the epidemic fever.
KHADY: No! Give me a red rooster and fetch your wife, I'm going to hold the *wacce.* [66]

The cure is rapid and Ibrahima's defeat total. Several days after the rite, he says to Khady: "Now, I'm ruined. It's you that has the knowledge. Now everything is yours." And Khady retorts: "You tried to ruin me. You tried to take away the *Sajinne* and the medicine gourd. You thought I was going to abandon everything. You were wrong."

Her cousin did not object when Khady took the *Sajinne* with her to Dakar. Before his death, some months later, Khady had a dream in which she perceived *Ndofèn*, one of his Serer *rab*, accompanied by *Ardo:*

"I see Ibrahima's people, he's going to die very soon," she told her husband early in the morning.

[Thus Khady's story ends with the conquest of the fetish object to which she attributes a substantial part of her therapeutic powers. *Sajinne* "heals" insofar as she knows how to manipulate him. She heals insofar as *Sajinne* agrees to serve or, at least, to inspire her. The ("worked") horn is endowed for her with intentionality.[67] Despite the fact that it is associated with *Maam Ngesu,* it does not express the *tuur's* will. One might say that its obscure origin and the uncertain circumstances of its transmission (from the paternal lineage to the matrilineal "cousin") are indications of its relative autonomy in relation to the family determinants.[68] This autonomy suggests that it functions quite differently from the emblems, shrines, and cult objects attached to the ancestral spirits.]

ANALYSIS AND ABSTRACT

From the preceding it is evident that Khady's entire story is organized, from the incident of the broken shrine to the conquest of the horn, like a destiny tenaciously held to myth, and not like a psychological or family novel. This destiny is recounted in a series of discrete episodes—one is tempted to say in scenes and acts—that refer, in the manner of coded messages, to the unconscious positionings of the narrator. First, I shall try to recapitulate the evolution of these positionings, occasionally basing my analysis on the analysis of Khady's case history by Maud Mannoni.[69]

The narrative is structured, as we have seen, in three major periods. The leitmotiv of the first period is a refusal. Khady rejects the family tradition of the *rab,* which she feels to be coercive, decrepit, yet dangerous. She does not want the "heritage," the submissive fate proclaimed by the voice of the *rab.* Her somatic symptoms, "paralysis," mutilation, muteness, are the price she pays for this refusal. They serve as substitutes for the sacrifices claimed by the spirits.

Who, precisely, are these spirits? In the inaugural episode Khady receives the name of Yacine and is promptly dedicated to *Ndew,* the Serer *rab,* whose shrine she had broken. This nomination—her earliest memory—confirms the failure of her father's magic power. Here we have the first indication of what may become essential. For it is not mere chance that the Serer *rab* immediately appear as those who Khady claims were both hostile, and loving, to her as an individual. These *rab* who caused her father's defeat—and relate, according to the psychoanalyst, to the castration of the father—already reveal themselves as the principal authors of her illness and suffering, and as the privileged signifiers of her fate as possessed.

Ambivalence with respect to the power of this father is the dominant theme of the first period. One cannot speak of Khady's "refusal of her heritage" without referring it to the adjacent incestuous fantasies, notably in the episode of mutism and in the scene of the child beaten by the sorcerer-father. Nevertheless, this ambivalence—a vague concept in itself—enters her narrative only in and through the idiom of the *rab*. Khady's "imaginary" immediately arranges these *rab*, under the influence of her family situation, in a specific manner.

This situation is atypical. In the Wolof family, the *rab* are generally transmitted from woman to woman and transmission along the uterine line is clearly predominant. In her own family, the *rab* are the father's prerogative, the prerogative of the men of her paternal lineage, while those of the maternal lineage assert themselves as the spokesmen of Islam. For Khady, dealing with the *rab*—whoever they be—is, first, dealing with the power of her father and of his paternal lineage.

Thus we should be able to clarify the predominant role played in Khady's story by the Serer *rab* (seven out of ten spirits represented by her shrines, I recall, are Serer) by considering the position they already occupy within the tradition perpetuated by her father; or, more exactly, by considering the position of the Serer spirit whom Khady selected (among others, no doubt) from the paternal tradition (of which we have no direct knowledge and no present concern).

The *tuur Ndeban* is one of four terms in the symbolic structure already shown in a more detailed form (Figure 3) and which, once again, we return to (Figure 4).

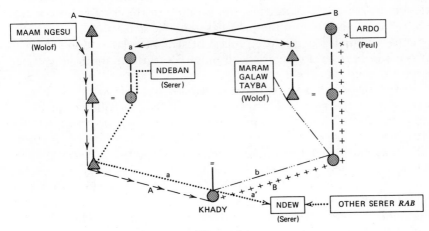

Figure 4

In this symbolic structure

- A (*Maam Ngesu*) and B (*Ardo*) indicate Khady's double relationship to or, one might say, her double incorporation in groups of descent and filiation: her father's patrilineage and her mother's matrilineage.
- a (*Ndeban*), the spirit introduced into the patrilineage by the Serer wife of the father's great-grandfather, and b (*Maram Galaw Tayba*), the messenger *rab* introduced into the matrilineage by the Wolof husband of the mother's grandmother, together indicate the internal boundary, the very condition of this incorporation or relationship insofar as it originates in the incest taboo and in the rule governing alliance

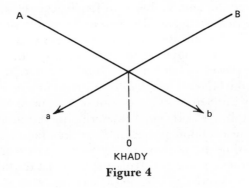

Figure 4

Formally, *Ndeban* (a) is to *Maam Ngesu* (A) what *Maram Galaw Tayba* (b) was to *Ardo* (B): the symbolic representative of the allies—the others' allies—at the origin of the agnatic ascendants and thus the signifier that designates, through metonymy, the position of the mother and of the maternal relatives within the paternal symbolic structure.

Once Khady has begun the process of symbolic elaboration—the key process in her development—a becomes B's signifier for A, and b becomes A's signifier for B.

At this stage in her story, however, Khady has not yet begun this articulation. To her the *rab* are not named allies, signifiers that could refer her to other signifiers, but only imaginary instances bent on destroying her fecundity, and on preventing her from being a mother. The only spirit that has already been named by her is *Ndew*, the *rab* whom her earliest memories associate with an aggressive act (the breaking of the shrine) that provoked her father's defeat; who appears to her to be in complicity with the other, unnamed Serer *rab*, since he does not protect her from their repeated aggressions; who becomes the "master" or "big brother" of the other Serer *rab,* when they have been named and introduced into her shrines, [70] with the exception of *Ndeban* who is designated by his name and whom Khady considers as the *elder twin of Ndew.*

This forms a singular twinship: *Ndeban,* the elder of the two, could only have punished Khady for her unconscious desire to escape the rule and prohibition under his authority, whereas *Ndew,* the younger, punishes her for her unjustified aggressiveness toward her father. One might say that this twinship, this unity in duality, is the remarkably appropriate mnemonic trace of her ambivalence rooted in her incestuous fantasies.

The death of her daughter, of her twins, and her sterility are, from what she tells us, the work of the Serer *rab.* It is as if they were penalizing her for her marriage to Samba Fall, her paternal relative, that was "too close." And in his relationship to the (Serer) spirits of the river channel, the young man surrenders nothing to the father. He defies them; he kills them and Khady is punished. This shifting about reveals another aspect of the forces at play. "I will not accept the heritage," she tells us, "because I refuse to take upon myself the faults that my paternal relatives, the men, have committed toward the spirits." But these spirits are not to be misled. As representatives of her ambivalent attitude toward her father, of her desire to seize masculine power, they direct their reprisals against her. They kill her daughter Yacine, whom she had vainly dedicated to *Ndew,* and make her sterile despite the rites performed by her mother. They even refuse Maty Kane's sacrifice of her life, for the want to deal with Khady alone or, as M. Mannoni says, with what refers to her castration.

We come now to the second period, in which both her mother and father are already dead. Khady's crisis will reach its climax before she discovers a way of resolving it. This way lies through identification with her mother, first experienced as a possession by and then as an alliance with *Ardo,* the *rab* of the maternal lineage. How does she arrive at this, and what does the mediation of this *rab* signify? In the preceding period, as we have seen, she struggled in an imaginary relationship with her father and the masculine figures of her paternal lineage. Does she not, at the birth of her twins, go so far as to raise herself to the position of the mythical ancestor who gave birth to both *Maam Ngesu* and the founder himself? Since she cannot conclude an alliance with the spirits—in other words, occupy her position within her lineage— she finds herself on the verge of delirium.[71] This delirium is about to assume, with her "travels," and acute character. Yet it heralds the outline of the answer to her essential question, one she could never state other than in the idiom of the *rab:* how can I accept myself as my father's and my mother's daughter, and what is my place among my father's heirs, my paternal brothers?

Her dream about Alamdu, the European *rab,* gives the most explicit answer to this question. Khady, seduced and seducer in turn, behaves as a sexual being. And the ship captain's reply to the dead brother's gesture of prohibition designates, in an unambiguous manner, the direction that she has chosen: "No! I won't let her go. She's Maty Kane's daughter!"

Returning to the period before her "travels," the way that leads to an identification with her mother is still lost in the mist of her search for religious affinities. Islam or the *rab?* Islam against the *rab?* Islam as a means of avoiding the *rab?* This seems to be her dilemma at the time of her second marriage to the marabout, Mor Dia. Actually she is already betrayed by both the dilemma and the remarriage. For there is a striking reversal in her conjugal relation. While her first husband, Samba Fall, was a young paternal relative, a "brother" figure who attacked the *rab,* her new husband, Mor Dia, is an old maternal relative, a "father" figure who defends Islam. How is one to understand this reversal and this detour into the world of Islam? What is Khady seeking by placing herself under the protection of a "good marabout," other than an illusory escape from the circle of wish-and-reprisal in which she had been imprisoned by her *rab?* What does she seek, for the duration of a marriage, if not the denial of her "heritage"? And what does she hope to find in Islam—her mother's faith and the faith of her maternal ancestors—other than a means of identification that would enable her to mask her debt toward the paternal *rab?*

We already know how her endeavors failed but now we must discover why. One of the most significant developments in her story seemed, to us, the fact that the delirious epic of her "travels"—her initiatory illness—begins precisely with this failure and ends in the alliance with her mother's Muslim rab. The mother's name already appears in the "hallucinatory" injunction that determines her departure, which is apparently an escape from her husband. Khady speaks of her peregrinations as if they had been provoked by the magic of the marabouts, although she refuses to interpret them as anything other than the occult actions of the Peul nomad *rab.* This means in effect that the "good father" figures whom she believed she found in the uterine-marabout series now tend to reappear in the archaic and familiar aspect of the persecuting male.

This reversal, however, is not regression leading to a state of stagnation, to the "paralysis" that characterized the first period. During that period, two kinds of interpretations are given to her disorders: possession by the *rab* and attack by sorcery. Introduction of the theme of Islamic magic connotes a change in the level of relationships. As Edmond and Marie Cécile Ortigues have shown, the interpretation of disorders by means of this magic establishes a formal structure on a genital-phallic level (as opposed to the pregenital-oral level of sorcery-anthropophagy) that presupposes the genital couple. The position of the persecutor is determined, they say, by the position he holds within the Oedipal triangle.[72] In other words, Khady is no longer involved in a deadly confrontation with the changing aspects of a power that bears the masculine sign; rather, she is already engaged in an evolving process whereby her position, as daughter of both her father and her mother, is (phallically) at stake.

If this is indeed the meaning of her development, it inevitably leads to the elaboration of a symbolic structure or, to put it differently, to the articulation of the paternal and maternal signifiers. Khady rests in the imaginary for as long as she remains with the marabouts, these delusive fathers, these "uncles" whom she finds again in the Islamic world associated with her maternal lineage. Later, they become her new persecutors. Moreover, she is condemned to return to those that represent the origin of her desire, the ancestral spirits. She must become the designator of her father's position within her mother's history; she must identify with her mother while acknowledging her debt toward her father. This is the meaning of the nomination of *Maram Galaw Tayba* (b) and of the sacrifice Khady finally makes to *Ardo* (B), her mother's Muslim *tuur*.

After this, one can understand why this syncretic spirit occupies a pivotal position in her initiation. He is the symbolic mediator between Islam and the religion of the *rab*, of the two traditions to which she must adjust in order to define herself; only he can serve as support for formulating a compromise between the two. This compromise is announced by the presence of the messenger *rab* (A's signifier for B) as a necessary and decisive step toward the assumption of her father's heritage.

At the beginning of the third period, however, a series of events apparently threatens to upset everything. The Serer and paternal *rab* reenter her life, en masse, as if offended by Khady's denial during her Islamic period. It is as if the alliance with *Ardo* had not the importance we have just given it, since the "infidels," *Ndeban* (a) and *Ndew* (a'),—the reunited twins—rise again and strike her in order to claim their rights. However, upon examining her narrative, this does not represent a return to her past. These spirits, she tells us, "demand drums," music and dance—the characteristic signs of homage rendered to the *ceddo rab* (infidels), to those *rab*, precisely, who were excluded from the first rite by Khady's "good Muslim" husband. Clearly she does not waver in her determination to conclude the alliance; she only tells us how her last attempts failed so as to mask the true extent of her commitment. For the insistent return of the infidel *rab* indicates how this alliance obliges her to recognize her debt toward her paternal ancestors. It obliges her no longer to pay the price of her refusal with her body's symptoms, but to claim her right to the heritage by sacrifices to the spirits. Her entire progress might be summarized in her exchange with the healer who had made the drums sound for the first time: "Women should not have knowledge!" "I've inherited this knowledge from my ancestor."

The opening of the third period is clearly motivated by her quarrel with this healer. For the first time, Khady asserts herself as one who possesses inherited knowledge and is not simply destined to submission and misfortune. It is this assertion that propels her from the position of a sick or simple possessed person to that of therapist. For the first time, too, she confronts a man in the domain of "*rab* knowledge" and decides to consult her maternal cousin Ibrahima, the guardian of *Ardo*. Both the assertion and the decision introduce the dominant theme of this last period: the rivalry with her brothers.

This first important factor: Khady claims the knowledge of her ancestors. Maud Mannoni analyzes this highly significant moment:

What counts in this experience is less a hypothetical cure than the access Khady gains to a certain form of clairvoyance and knowledge. The knowledge emerged at the same moment that desire stirred and brought into play its very functioning that, until then, had been imprisoned in fantasy. It is in the suffering body that the basis of this knowledge was stored: it was this body that had to enter a whole meaningful dialectic system (removing itself from its stillborn children, alienating itself in its different parts) before it could situate itself within the field of desire. And the notion of sacrifice and mutilation served as vector to secure the other's presence within the network of desire [. . .] It is by realizing her desire that Khady awakes to her function as healer. Once she has sufficiently committed herself, she is free to reintegrate desire in its cause.[73]

For us, however, this interpretation (prescribed by a method of demonstration which we shall not analyze here) presents the problem of general statements arrived at too quickly. We should first attempt to discover what it means to Khady to search for "knowledge of the *rab*" and to accede to therapeutic functions. For although it is true that in traditional therapy the victim of an illness acquires *ipso facto* a certain control over the illness and that the "cure" often implies a certain knowledge, this does not mean that every possessed Wolof covets the therapeutic power of *ndɔpkat*.

When Khady embarks on the conquest of this power, she is told: You're only a woman! But now she can answer: I know that, but it's as such that I revindicate my rights. This means that she is no longer imprisoned in the web of her old imaginary identifications with the masculine figures of her paternal lineage, but is already on the way to a symbolic identification with her *legatee* brothers and, beyond them, with her dead father.

She can thus "reintegrate desire in its cause," we quite agree, provided that it is specified that her search for the "knowledge of the *rab*-that-heal" [74] is the necessary and ultimate result of her search for a position relative to the men of her patrilineage. It is these men who apparently have always transmitted the "heritage" buried under the baobab tree which Khady has maliciously called the "hospital." Everything would have been different if the "heritage" had come, as with most of the Wolof women, from her relatives along the uterine line. It may even be said that her story illustrates, in an exemplary fashion, the effects of the socioreligious evolution of the Wolof country, where the cult of the *rab* has become "women's business" ever since the men gradually adopted (at least outwardly) the Koranic faith.

We must leave the task of verifying these hypotheses to comparative clinical study [75] and go on to the second question: Khady's rivalry with her brothers. Edmond and Marie-Cécile Ortigues describe the "African Oedipus complex" according to three essential traits. First the authors claim, the symbolic function of the father remains attached to the ancestor, and this ancestor, and thus the father, are "unequable." Oedipal rivalry is thus systematically shifted to the "brothers," who polarize the aggressive drives projected and inverted in the form of persecutory reactions. Finally, the resolution of the Oedipus complex is conditioned by identification with the "brothers," provided that their rivalry is overcompensated by a very strong solidarity within the age group. [76]

Needless to say, this theory clarifies only the general context of the final phase of Khady's development. The authors quoted above describe the Oedipus complex of the boy and give the "brother" concept its widest extension, as a category of generation. For us, it is important to understand more fully the relationship of a woman, Khady, to three given individuals: Aliou and Yaga Fall, her father's two heirs, and Ibrahima, her "uterine" cousin, who maintains the cult of the maternal *tuur*.

First it must be noted that although Ibrahima is constantly in the foreground, the story's fundamental reference point is to the first two figures. For Ibrahima is to the brothers what *Ardo* is to the paternal spirits. Whereas his origin relates him to the mother's world, his practice designates him, within that world, as the representative of the father's religion. Ibrahima performs the function of mediator between the two worlds exactly like the syncretic spirit he serves as guardian.[77] For Khady he is a transference figure with all the ambiguity of a "big brother"—alternately protector and persecutor, in whom she finds support for expressing whatever enters into her rivalry with her brother-heirs.

Ibrahima completes Khady's initiation and her early apprenticeship. Yet the relationship between teacher and pupil is nearly reversed from the outset, from the time the *rab* inform the neophyte that the moment has come to recover "her heritage" (the stone buried under the "hospital," and the vulture's head that had miraculously dropped on the field). In both these episodes Khady was caught between two positions: the narcissistic one of the simple candidate who receives her "share" of the heritage without having asked for it, and the phallic one of *rab* mistress (*boroom rab*) who knows that milk must be given to the stone and who feels "strong" enough to keep the vulture's head. We have also seen that the first position enabled her to anteriorize her father's heritage; that is, to act, as if she were not taking but receiving it through ancestral providence. It now seems evident that the first position, which remains that of the *rab*'s victim, exists to conceal and to justify the second: her desire to assert herself by confronting, without compromise, her paternal brothers. Her "share" had been "entrusted" to these brothers, the *rab* say: Khady accuses them of having "taken everything" in her hypocritical dialogue with the woman seer, who has good reason to believe neither in Khady's "youth" nor her ignorance. Among these brothers Khady now finds a place guaranteed by her dead father's words, reported to her by her paternal uncle: "You are lucky, this is the head that belonged to your father. He said that you were to become his heiress."

She knows that she has taken the last decisive step in recovering the symbols of her heritage by directing her first *ndǝp* and, even more, by taking the risk of "moving" her *rab* to Dakar. Despite her teacher's (Ibrahima's) reticence, she chances this reputedly delicate undertaking with the clear intention of establishing herself as healer in the capital. The spirits no longer object to this act of independence which, nevertheless, removes them from their ancestral soil.

At the death of her brother, Aliou,—an event that earlier would have caused, a fortiori, a drama now occurs discreetly—the primordial *tuur, Maam Ngesu,* begins "visiting" Khady and "enters" her shrines at the cost of a mild illness. This in turn is relieved by a small number of sacrifices. Thus Khady is no longer alloted merely a new "share" of the heritage, but the very name she believes now permits her to claim her entire ancestral paternal inheritance.

These sacrifices to the founder's mythical twin conclude the process of symbolic elaboration that began with the dream message. We can now retrace the different steps of this process by recalling the order of rab nominations, given that rab are signifiers of filiation (A and B) and of alliance (a and b) that have permuted according to the following rules (Figure 5).

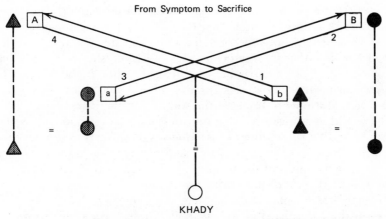

Figure 5.   From symptom to sacrifice.

Mamed *Rab*	Maram Galaw Tayba	Ardo	Ndeban	Maam Ngesu
Signifier	b	B	a	A
Signified	A	a	B	b
	Maam Ngesu	Ndeban	Ardo	Maram Galaw Tayba

The fact that each of the spirits named by Khady has thus been permuted in the position of signifier and signified at specific moments in her development allows us to say that this cycle of nominations is a proper symbolic elaboration. For the cycle to begin, one *rab* had to present himself as the "messenger" of another—as the signifier of another signifier. For the cycle to close, this other *rab* had to be integrated within it.

Can we say, however, that the cycle is really closed? Does the story of the "granddaughter" actually resolve itself in the perfect symmetry of this kind of symbolic construction? Or can some indication of Khady as subject, as the author of the construction, be found? To determine this, we need only examine the pattern of her shrines.

Those spirits who have actual twin shrines at their disposal, [78] those whose nomination and integration have been *confirmed by ritual,* are *Maam Ngesu, Ndeban, Ardo,* and *Ndew.* Neither the hollow brick nor the container without medicine, belonging to the European *rab, Alamdu* (to whom I shall return) constitute an "operative" shrine. [79] The Serer *rab* related to *Ndew*—who sometimes inhabit Khady during possession rites, and whom she then uses to serve her simplest interests [80]—are only represented by pestles and various objects placed around the pottery containers belonging to their "master." As for the messenger, *Maram Galaw Taybe,* she is not represented among the shrines. If I had questioned Khady about the reason for this omission, she would no doubt have scoffed at my incorrigible naivete. Why should she "fix" in her *xamb* a spirit who only speaks for the others, who does not come to "blind her" but only to transmit the will of her ancestors?

She would have answered that this messenger never had a messenger of her own; that the signifier of A (*Maam Ngesu*) for B (*Ardo*) never entered the category of the signified; that *Maam Ngesu* was the final result of her "travels" and not the beginning of a new period in the continuously repeated cycle of permuting *rab* names.

Nevertheless, to play and complete the game, she had to reserve a place on the chessboard of the symbolic family structure. But did she not exchange one piece for another as well? Do we not discover, in place of the missing *rab,* whose shrine she had broken long ago, one who is not her family's ally but is a figure of her personal fate? *Ndew* is the term that designates both the origin and the author of this construction.

Can we say that the game is now definitely completed? Is it true that Khady's identification with her dead brother is the ultimate result of her development? Has she managed to find a certain balance in her life by becoming a healer? We must now discuss how the last two episodes of her narrative leave these questions open.

The first episode, like the second, refers to a symbolic element outside the family tradition. *Alamdu,* the European *rab,* who receives Khady and her dead brothers in his ship's cabin, is a kind of false ancestral spirit. The *Sajinne* horn which she manages to "snatch" from her cousin is a "fetish" of uncertain origin. The ill-defined position, linking this *"rab"* to the "fetish," can be seen in the pattern of the shrines: the horn's place is within the hollow brick that serves as shrine to the European spirit.

The dream with *Alamdu,* as was mentioned earlier, sums up this important postulate in Khady's development: she had to identify with her mother in order to take her place among her paternal brothers. But it also contains another message inverted to the limit. The dead brothers forbid Khady to form a sexual relationship with an "unbelievable" figure who escapes their control and their domain. This spirit who is "unbelievable" because of his contrasting "infidel" splendor and his Koranic name (a maternal reference) acclaims his partner as a sexual being and as her mother's daughter. In short, Khady makes him say: "In trying to identify myself with my mother's side, I have found two kinds of references. The first—*Ardo,* the messenger, my cousin—refers me to the law, to my father's heritage. The other—Islam?—refers me to what, within myself, would free itself of this law and this heritage. But this is an impossible desire. . . ." This impossible desire is what the "unbelievable" *Alamdu* might stand for within Khady's spirit world: a kind of symbolic buffer.

Is the conquest of the *Sajinne* horn the beginning of a new stage in Khady's development, or does it simply indicate another boundary? Let us recall the facts. After a truly mystical battle that lasts several weeks, she manages to take the "fetish" away from her cousin. This is actually the last act in the drama that confronts her with her masculine rivals. Yet this act has nothing in common with those that precede it. Her rivals are no longer her paternal brothers but her master, her maternal cousin. The object of rivalry is no longer the heritage—the stone which, as her father's heiress, she rightfully recovers. Instead, it is the signifier of a knowledge that she acquires during a conquest, revealing her as a "more skillful" therapist than her teacher. She is no longer the innocent victim, chosen by the *rab:* a victim "allotted" this object as a reward for submission to the law that forbids her to surpass her brothers. She is now a healer and mistress over her *rab* whose knowledge entitles her to take possession of the object and to savor victory in her cousin's defeat.

The *Sajinne* horn, the badge of this knowledge and victory, is equally inscribed in the symbolic system that structures and encloses her entire discourse. It is inscribed, admittedly, as a limiting principle that refers her to the origin of her knowledge and powers. Through this fetish object, without which she can neither cure nor "see," Khady is related to the phallic signifier that designates her as a healer capable of manipulating the law of the *rab.* She is related to that obscure part of her ancestry which captured the force of the spirits, and to that obscure part of herself which she can neither express within the spirits' idiom nor assume as an individual. The *Sajinne* "fetish"—mirror and double—offers Khady the blurred reflection of what could not otherwise be expressed in her discourse. (see Appendix)

APPENDIX

The Baobab Trees

They define the north-south axis of the *xamb* and are dedicated to the Serer *rab Ndew*, *Ndeban* and *Xoye*. The bush next to *Ndeban's* baobab is called *Mbootal* (from *mboot*, "to carry on one's back"). Khady tells me that it "takes care" of the sick just like the *mbootal*, the initiatory father, took care of the circumcised in the ancient Wolof rite.

The Shrines and Objects of the Inherited tuur

Ardo:	his two pottery containers (I,5) and his nomad shepherd's emblems: *yet*, a forked stick (7), *giir*, a milk pail (2), and *gamba*, a small gourd (3).
Maam Ngesu:	his principal pottery container (II), his upside-down container that he "shares" with *Ndeban* (22), his warrior's emblem, the *xec*, or scepter (4).
Ndeban:	his pottery containers (27,22), his pestles (23,23a), and the stone that was found under the "hospital" (19).

The Shrines and Objects of the Acquired rab

Ndew (21,18), his "brothers *Xoye* (27), and *Diogoy Wali* (28), his "sorcerer" *Wargi Ndiaye* (29), his *lawbê* (bushel-maker) companion *Ndiaga Umi Sore*, whose "axe" is a stone blade (17) placed on top of the pottery container (18).

Boury Diouf, the fisherman *rab*, is represented by a river stone (30).

Alamdu, the European *rab*, has a shrine composed of a hollow brick (15) and a pottery container filled with water, but without tree roots (16).

The gallaj ("fetishes")

Sajinne (12), placed on top of Alamdu's "room" (15).

Bonko (13), a kind of double to *Sajinne* that Khady associates with the Bambara *rab* (belonging to her former patients; see below).

Bopp u tila (14), a jackal head which she also calls "bald head": an oval-shaped mass (20 cm), encrusted at one end with jackal teeth. It undoes magic and offers protection from anthropophagic witches (*dɔmm*).

Miscellaneous Objects

Khady uses the *xor*, a shell (26), and the *mbatu*, a calabash ladle (6), for bathing her patients. She keeps *bajin*, the horns of sheep and goats she has sacrificed (8), and bottles of eau de cologne (10) she has used in offerings of incense to the Muslim *rab*. Finally, the three pestles reinforced with iron rods (24,24a,24b) and the iron cane (25) are ves-

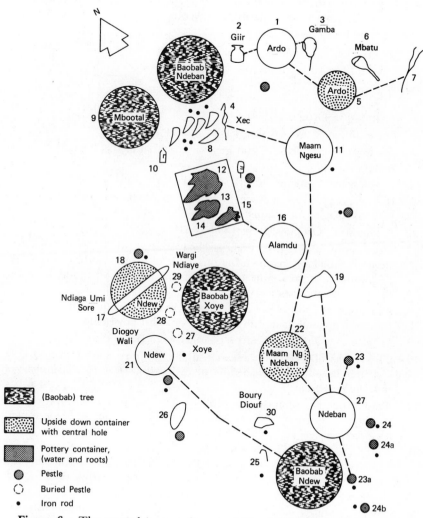

Figure 6. The central (personal) part of Khady Fall's domestic shrine.

tiges of the rites she carried out in order to keep alive (*danc*) *nit-ku-bon* children (cf. Zempleni and Rabain, 1965).

The Shrines of Former Patients

There are fourteen in all and they are placed north and west of the enclosure. Among their owners (all of whom are women), three live abroad and one was hospitalized (in 1964) in the neuropsychiatric ward at Fann. Among the *rab*, I numbered eight Lebou (two of them Muslim), three Bambara (all Muslim), one Wolof, one Peul and one Mulatto (the *tuur* of the island of Gorea).

NOTES

1. E. and M-C. Ortigues, 1966.
2. For example, V. W. Turner, 1968.
3. For an historical account and general appraisal of this method, cf. L. L. Langness, 1965.
4. At the neuropsychiatric ward at Fann (Dakar).
5. It is necessary, as we shall see, to distinguish also the role of sorcery, interpersonal magic, and Islamic spirits.
6. E. and M.-C. Ortigues, 1966, Chapter III.
7. Much more, in any case, than psychiatrists and psychologists usually assume. We shall see that by using this mode of expression Khady is able to communicate a great variety of problems, relationships, and situations common in clinical practice.
8. And not as a set of object and symbolic relationships to be used to "illustrate" the general data of my research on spirit possession.
9. *Ndəp:* possession rite (cf. infra, p. 10); Fass: a Dakar district.
10. The results of this team research, under the direction of Professor H. Collomb, have been published in the review *Psychopathologie africaine*, and in *L'Oedipe africain.*
11. Transcription of Wolof words. The graphic representation employed and its Internal Phonetic Association equivalent: ē = e (closed); e = ɛ (open); ə = ə (central); c = c(ty); j = ɟ (dy); x = x (kh); ñ = ŋ (palatal).
12. This idea, defended by Professor Collomb, seems to have been very profitable to both the psychiatrists, who wished to be informed about traditional therapies, and to the sick, who continued to practice them outside the hospital.
13. Unlike the other *ndəpkat*, who came to the hospital spontaneously, and who felt honored by an interview with the chief doctor, Khady never con-

sented to make a display of her knowledge and, even less, of her personal history.

14. Term used by marabouts and healers to designate their disciples.

15. O. Mannoni, 1969.

16. The difficult task of reconstituting chronologic references in African biographies has been remarked upon and analyzed by M.-C. and E. Ortigues.

17. This would have enabled me to give an account of Khady's associations and would have been based on the raw material of the interviews. After several attempts I abandoned this type of analysis, which presupposes a different kind of relationship and a different interview situation.

18. From the verb *tuur*, "to pour, to spill" (milk offering).

19. From *rab*, "animal".

20. *Ndɔp*, "to cover"; *kat*, agent suffix.

21. Cf. A. Zempleni, 1967.

22. Most men prefer this discrete rite which spares them the disapproval (mitigated, to be sure) of the Islamic community.

23. See the case studies published in *Psychopatholigie africaine* and *L'Oedipe africain*.

24. Figure 6 in the Appendix indicates the arrangement of the shrines and objects as I found them in the *xamb* in 1964.

25. *Ndew* and *Ndeban* are names of Serer twins. *Ndew* is the younger.

26. *Bopp u tila:* an oval-shaped mass the size of an ostrich egg, studded at one end with jackal's teeth.

27. The emblem of *Maam Ngesu* is the scepter (*xec*) of the ancient Wolof warriors. It is found near his shrines (cf. Fig. 6, no. 4).

28. *Guiera senegalensis.*

29. The Serer call their ancestral spirits *fangol*, "snake." The *rab* ("animal") can easily metamorphose into a snake, a gray lizard, or other reptile.

30. As his song-motto recalls: *Maam Ngesu Mboul, wali na, ragal bu ko dêgg daw.* "*Maam Ngesu,* (he from) Mboul was present, the timorous one, upon hearing him, flees."

31. For the adepts of the cult of the *rab*, as for most of the Lebou and Wolof from Cayor, the Peul and Toucouleur are related in many ways: origin, language, geographic proximity, and religion orthodoxy.

32. *Ligêêy:* good or bad magic; in this case, the practice of divination or clairvoyance.

33. A custom practiced on a large scale. The child may be entrusted to a paternal or maternal relative whom one wishes to honor or, in the case of sterility, to console. The two little girls living with Khady too are "entrusted" children.

34. The essential themes of "A child is beaten" are easily recognized in this episode, which is arranged around the fantasy of being beaten by the sor-

cerer-father. In the story, he is opposed by the mother and, above all, by the marabout, that is, by Islam.

35. The two basic components of the Wolof *nit* are the *fit,* or vital force located in the liver, and the *rab.*

36. According to Wolof belief, the child is conceived in the *butit bu juur,* in the "bowel that gives birth." Its rupture results in sterility.

37. A premature rupture of the amniotic sac or an early miscarriage? The nature of this accident is not clear.

38. Probably the *galaxndiku:* the victim drinks the water with which the sorcerer has gargled in his own mouth.

39. He is said to be the cousin of Aissa Dia, Khady's maternal grandmother (cf. Figure 2).

40. In which case the procedure is called *nawtal,* "making fly." The magic preparation is known under the more current term: *gênne,* "going out, making out."

41. See the detailed description of these prodedures in A. Zempleni, *Interpretation et therapie traditionnelles du desordre mental chez les Wolof et les Lebou,* ms., 1968, Chapter IV.

42. Any Wolof healer would give this interpretation. It should be noted that aimless wandering is one of the chief signs of an attack by magic.

43. A semiconventional expression of invulnerability among the ancient Wolof warriors. It is frequently employed by the patients in the psychiatric ward at Fann.

44. "To have attached someone" (*tak*) often means "to have worked on someone" (*dañu ko ligêêy*), "something has been done to someone with magic."

45. Rite of building the domestic shrine.

46. He confers therapeutic powers unto his ally. The *rab* of the ordinary possessed do not "heal."

47. *Maam:* grandparent, ancestor in a broad sense; an epithet that precedes the names of the *tuur.*

48. See, notably, B. Ly, 1967.

49. Personal communication from J. Irvine, an American ethnologist who lived in this village.

50. *Tuur u cosaan.*

51. This would not have been true of the *rab* which Matar Kane, the mother's Toucouleur father, might have transmitted to his daughter and, in turn, to Khady. For this ally belongs to the world symbolized by *Ardo.*

52. Muslim *rab*—the men, that is—prefer the discretion of rites without music and, most of all, without public dances of possession. In contrast to the "infidels," they prefer the *samp* to the *ndɔp.*

53. These roots, whose symbolism is quite elaborate, are buried in the foundations of the shrine.

54. Today, a wealthy marabout of that town. He told me very little about Khady.

55. Cf. supra, pp. 98–100.

56. The eight-day *ndəp* always requires the sacrifice of an ox, and the three-(or four-)day *ndəp* that of a sheep or goat.

57. I.e., "he is a sorcerer."

58. The stone is now in her *xamb* (figure 6, no. 19). It is associated with the shrine of *Ndeban*. The sick sit on this stone when taking their bath.

59. An oval-shaped mass wrapped in leather, which she wears at the end of a long necklace.

60. E. and M.-C. Ortigues (1966, chapter IV) emphasize this equivalence in the case study of Talla—the only one that may be compared with Khady's—and show how the symbolism of castration can be expressed through the idea of inheritance.

61. The spirits are attached to their native soil. They leave it only at the price of a specific rite which the possessed call, in the Franco-Wolof jargon, the "déménagement des *rab*."

62. And two other spirits who have no specific shrines. *Yangoti* is a griot. Thanks to him, Khady is able to collect alms during the rites. *Jaxay* is the eagle-acrobat; his piercing look and beating wings—mimed by Khady—drive away the sorcerers.

63. The "captain" wants to take Khady with him in his ship, to be alone with her. The manner in which she spills milk over the clothes of the *rab* has nothing in common with the serenity of an offering. *Alamdu's* laughter is anything but customary behavior among the *rab*.

64. His name comes from the Koranic expression alhamdulilaahi, "I thank God." Thus he seems to be associated with Islam. Still a European *rab* is, by definition, an "infidel."

65. A kind of double to *Sajinne* (cf. Figure 6, no. 13).

66. Rite of "bringing down" (*wacce*) the spirit (cf. *supra*, p. 10).

67. "If it refuses to heal, it becomes very heavy." This intentionality or real existence is what defines the horn as a fetish-object.

68. *Alamdu,* the European *rab,* and *Sajinne,* the "fetish," occupy similar positions in this respect. In the *xamb* (Figure 6), the horn is placed on top of *Alamdu's* shrine. Can this be mere coincidence?

69. After a first and manuscript version of this work (cf. M. Mannoni, 1970: 187–193). On the whole, this analysis seems to me correct; more correct, in any case, than the comparison made between the case history of Khady and that of Mary, a patient at Kingsley Hall, who has related her personal experience in M. Barnes, 1973.

70. Namely, *Xoye* and *Digoy Wali,* the "brothers" of *Ndew; Wargui Ndiaye,* his "sorcerer"; *Ndiaga Umi Sore,* his "*lawbê* companion" (bushel-maker caste). (See the Table of the *rab, supra,* p. 16.)

71. A delirium according to Wolof standards, which admits all kinds of "ideas," "visions," "voices," and parasensorial experiences, provided they are confirmed by a ritual alliance with the *rab*.

72. E. and M.-C. Ortigues, 1966, p. 254.

73. M. Mannoni, 1970: 192–193.

74. That is, of the "infidel" *rab* on the paternal side. Muslim spirits do not usually "heal." The expression is frequently employed by the *ndɔpkat*.

75. A series of studies which would systematically relate the socioreligious structure (past and present) of the subject's family to the clinical material obtained under similar interview conditions.

76. E. and M.-C. Ortigues 1966, Chapter III.

77. It goes without saying that Ibrahima has other *rab,* as is indicated by Khady's dream predicting his death.

78. A pottery container turned upside down, with a central hole, of another pottery container, filled with water and tree roots, and a pestle stuck in the ground.

79. Apt to serve in the rites that Khady performs either to treat her patients or to maintain her own condition as therapist.

80. For instance, to solicit money when she is possessed by *Wargi Ndiaye, Ndew*'s "sorcerer."

REFERENCES

BARNES, M.

1973   *Voyage a travers la folie.* Paris: Le Seuil.

IRVINE, J.

1972   "Strategies of Status Manipulation in the Wolof Greeting," *Conference on the Ethnography of Speaking.* University of Texas (unpublished).

LEVI-STRAUSS, C.

1958   *Anthropologie structurale.* Paris; Plon.

LANGNESS, L. L.

1965   *The Life History in Anthropological Science.* ("Studies in Anthropological Method"). New York, Chicago, San Francisco: Holt, Rinehart & Winston.

LY, B.

1967   *L'honneur et les valeurs morales dans les societes wolof et toucouleur du Senegal.* Unpublished thesis, Paris.

MANNONI, M.

1970   *Le psychiatre, son "fou" et la psychanalyse.* Paris: Le Seuil.

MANNONI, O.

1969   *Clefs pour l'imaginaire ou l'Autre Scene.* Paris: Le Seuil.

ORTIGUES, E. and M.-C.

1966   *L'Oedipe africain.* Paris: Plon.

TURNER, V. W.

1968   *The Drums of Affliction. A Study of Religious Process among the Ndembu of Zambia.* London: Oxford University Press.

VALABREGA, J. P.

1967   "Le probleme anthropologique du phantasme." In *Le Desir et la perversion.* Paris: Le Seuil.

ZEMPLENI, A.

1966   "La Dimesion therapeutique du culte des *rab. Ndop, tuuru et samp*, rites de possession chez les Lebou et Wolof," *Psychopathologie africaine* **II** (3): 295–439.

1967   "Sur l'Alliance entre la personne et le *rab*, dans le *ndap*," *Psychopathologie africaine* **III** (3): 441–451.

ZEMPLENI, A. and J. RABAIN

1965   "L'Enfant *nit-ku-bon.* Un tableau psychopathologique traditionnel chez les Wolof et les Lebou.", *Psychopathologie africaine* **I** (3): 329–443.

Vincent Crapanzano

Mohammed and Dawia: Possession in Morocco

For the possessed, possession is real. However it manifests itself—in trance, in acute hysterical dissociation, in schizophrenic reactions, in multiple personality, in tantrums, or in love—possession provides an existential validation for the belief in a class of spirits who are able to enter and take control of a human being or animal. The belief that one has been or can become possessed is an important determinant of the subjective life of the individual and of his behavior. The state of possession itself enables the possessed to express and communicate, in a symbolic fashion, a range of subjective experiences or psychological dispositions, and to demand an appropriate response. The fact of having once been or of being presently possessed enables the possessed and those around him to explain certain experiences that extend well beyond the limit of the "possession state" as it is classically understood.

The spirits or demons capable of entering and seizing control of an

141

individual serve more than an explanatory function.[1] They enable the possessed to articulate a range of experiences which the Westerner would refer to as "inner," "psychological," or "mental." They are what I have called elsewhere symbolic-interpretive elements (Crapanzano, 1973a, 1975). They both symbolize certain psychological dispositions and offer immediately an interpretation in a manifestly non-psychological idiom. They may even evoke the dispositions as T. S. Eliot's objective correlatives evoke the feelings and emotions associated with them (Eliot, 1960). They are not projections in the psychoanalytic sense of the word but givens in the world of those who believe in them. Insofar as these symbolic-interpretive elements are part of a system—demonology—they are subject to the logical constraints and evaluations of that system and thus serve to structure and evaluate (the articulation of) the dispositions accordingly. The dispositions are articulated, if not actually cast, on a stage external to the individual in a collective rather than an individual idiom.

The fact that the dispositions are articulated on an external rather than an internal stage in collective terms has certain important consequences. Insofar as subjective experience is expressed in terms of spirits external to the individual, subject to systemic constraints believed in by the individual and those around him, the locus of the individual's selfhood appears to be differently oriented and the dimensions of individuality appear to be differently determined for him than for the Westerner (Crapanzano, 1975). We might expect, for example, that the individual's sense of personal responsibility would be different. Psychological dispositions associated with a breach in the individual's moral code—dispositions that the Westerner would express in terms of guilt—might well be articulated in terms of spirits (Crapanzano, 1972). The individual does not chastise himself, as the Western depressive does, but is chastised by the spirit.

Not only does the articulation of psychological dispositions in terms of symbolic-interpretive elements affect the orientation of self and the determination of individuality, it also affects the relations that obtain between the possessed and those around him. The possessing spirit serves as a mediator, a *tertium quid,* between the possessed and the other (cf. Girard, 1961). Dyadic relations become triadic, and there is a consequent depersonalization and generalization of these relations. They are removed, so to speak, from the idiosyncratic plane of reality and "projective reality," subject to the constraints of language, to another plane, *die andere Szene* in Freud's sense, the demonic, subject to the constraints of the demonology (Mannoni, 1969). The interplay between self and other is cast not in the *real* but in the *imaginary* (Lacan, 1966).

The symbolism differs essentially from the symbolism of the neurotic or psychotic in that it is collective rather than individual. Relations so articulated persist where, were they articulated on the plane of reality, they would perish.

In this chapter I illustrate the role that possessing spirits and possession play in the articulation of life experience. I will examine the life histories of Mohammed, a Moroccan Arab man possessed by a she-demon named 'A'isha Qandisha, and Dawia, Mohammed's wife, possessed by a he-demon, Shaykh al-Kanun, believed to be 'A'isha Qandisha's husband. I will be concerned specifically with one sequence of events that are associated in their minds and form an episode in their lives. The episode is bounded by the death of their son Gueddar and Dawia's entry into the Ḥamadsha brotherhood. 'A'isha Qandisha and Shaykh al-Kanun play an important role, at least in their present-day articulation of the events.

The material I present is biographical. It is not based on actual observation of the events themselves but on Mohammed and Dawia's recollection of them. Thus my analysis is not of the events as they occurred but of their articulation by the two primary participants about fourteen years after their occurrence. Of the past, the events speak to the present (van den Berg, 1955). Their expression is determined by the present-day situation of the participants, including the other—my wife and myself in the case in point—whom they address. It is shaped by that "conversation," described by Peter Berger and Hansfried Kellner, which sustains the shared world of a married couple.

Furthermore, it is not only the ongoing experience of the two partners that is constantly shared and passed through the conversation apparatus. The same sharing extends into the past. The two distinct biographies, as subjectively apprehended by the two individuals who have lived through them, are over-ruled and reinterpreted in the course of their conversation. Sooner or later, they will tell all—or, more correctly, they will tell it in such a way that it fits into the self-definitions objectivated in the marital relationship. The couple thus constructs not only present reality but reconstructs past reality as well, fabricating a common memory that integrates the recollections of the two individual pasts (Berger and Kellner, 1970, p. 62).

I will argue that it is precisely Mohammed and Dawia's present-day articulation of the events, if not their past articulation of them, in terms of 'A'isha Qandisha, Shaykh al-Kanun, and possession that enables them to construct a world in which the maritally disruptive effects of the death of a son and the birth of an unwanted daughter are mollified. The events are mediated by the presence of the tertium quid, the demons, who are external to the participants but impose their will on them. These demons and the relations they impose not only structure the marital situation, past or present, but also fit within the participants' articulation of the remainder of their biographical experience. They serve then as biographical orientation points and correlatives for feelings and emotions that extend beyond the situation at hand. In this fashion, they may be said to symbolize these feelings and emotions.

'A'ISHA QANDISHA, SHAYKH AL-KANUN, AND THE ḤAMADSHA

'A'isha Qandisha and Shaykh al-Kanun are *jnun*,[2] a class of spirits created before man and composed of vapor and flame. 'A'isha Qandisha is famous throughout northern Morocco; Shaykh al-Kanun and the fact of his marriage to 'A'isha Qandisha is not so well known. Although the jnun are usually imperceptible to man's ordinary senses, they may render themselves visible in a variety of forms. They are said to have names and hence sexes, but the names of only a few are commonly known. Although the jnun are not necessarily evil or harmful, they are usually avoided, because they are considered to be whimsical and arbitrary, capricious and revengeful, quick-tempered and despotic, and, therefore, potentially dangerous at all times. If they are wounded or insulted, they are quick to retaliate by striking their adversary or taking possession of him. (The symptomatology of the victims of the jnun range from feelings of general malaise and mild depression to sudden blindness and complete paralysis of the limbs and face.) Most often the man or woman who has injured a jinn is quite ignorant of his or her misdeed. Men and women who are angry or frightened or who are in a liminal period associated with a change in social status are particularly liable to attack. Treatment of a jinn's victim may aim at its permanent expulsion or, as in the case of the victims of 'A'isha Qandisha and other named jnun, at the establishment of a symbiotic relationship in which the jinn is transformed from a malevolent into a benevolent spirit (Crapanzano, 1971, 1973a). The jinn's victim becomes a follower (*tabi'*) of the jinn. The jinn may require the follower to obey seemingly arbitrary commands—wearing certain colors, burning special incense, or performing a trance dance (*ḥadra*) to a specific musical phrase or melody (*riḥ*). These symbiotic cures are performed by members of such popular Islamic brotherhoods as the Ḥamadsha, of which Mohammed and Dawia are devotees (*muḥibbin*).

The character and attributes of Shaykh al-Kanun, like those of most other male jnun, are not elaborated, while those of 'A'isha Qandisha are well developed. She is said to appear either as a beauty or a hag but always with the feet of a camel or some other hooved animal. In her ugly aspect she is black and has long, straggly hair, pendulous breasts, and elongated nipples. She likes red and black, black benzoin, and the music of the Ḥamadsha. Lalla 'A'isha, as she is sometimes called, inspires fear in all Moroccans who are familiar with her. She is always libidinous, quick-tempered, and ready to strangle, scratch, or whip anyone who insults her or does not obey her commands. She demands absolute and unquestioning obedience from her followers. I have heard them refer to her as "our mother." 'A'isha Qandisha is also said to enter into marriage with men by seducing them before they discover her identity.[3] She may require her "husbands" to wear old and dirty clothes and never cut their fingernails; she often restricts their sexual activities. A man's only safeguard against 'A'isha is to plunge an iron or steel knife into the earth before succumbing to her. Like other jnun, Lalla 'A'isha appears in dreams and visionary experiences, often as a woman familiar to the dreamer or visionary, but always having the name 'A'isha.

The Ḥamadsha, who specialize in the trance cure of 'A'isha Qandisha's victims, trace their spiritual heritage back to two Moroccan saints of the late seventeenth and early eighteenth century, Sidi 'Ali ben Ḥamdush and Sidi Ahmed Dghughi. They may be divided into three principal groups: the descendants of the saints, who do not usually dance; the professional Ḥamadsha, who perform the cures; and the devotees (muḥibbin) who attend their ceremonies. The Ḥamadsha are notorious for their practice, during their trance dances, of slashing their heads with knives and halberds or bashing them with jugs of water and iron balls. Their trances are not understood in terms of some sort of mystical union with the Divine, but in terms of the jnun, most frequently 'A'isha Qandisha, and of the saints they venerate. The blessing, or baraka, of the saint enables the Ḥamdushi[4] to enter trance; the violent, frenetic phase of the trance, called jidba, in which the acts of self-mutilation occur, is usually interpreted as possession by 'A'isha Qandisha or another jinn. The trancer mutilates himself to please the she-demon and to force her to leave him. As I have shown elsewhere, the cures involve an intricate restructuring of the relationship between the she-demon and her victim (Crapanzano, 1971). 'A'isha is transformed from a malevolent into a benevolent spirit who keeps her victim in good health and fortune as long as he follows her commands. The breach of these commands is associated with a breach in the victim's moral code, with an inability (in the case of a man) to live up to the ideal standards of male behavior.

THE EPISODE

Mohammed and Dawia's versions of the episode differ in a number of significant details, although both include the following important facts. Dawia left Mohammed to watch over their eighteen-month-old son, Gueddar. Gueddar knocked over a kettle of boiling water and was burned so badly that he died three days later. Mohammed invited the Ḥamadsha and slashed his head violently; he continued to dance with them very often. Dawia disapproved of Mohammed's head-slashing. After Gueddar's death, she was bitten by a scorpion on her way home from one of the dances at which Mohammed mutilated himself. A few months later Dawia gave birth to Khadija, a daughter. Mohammed, who had wanted a son, was disappointed. Dawia threw water on a fire five days after Khadija's birth and was struck by a jinn. Mohammed slashed his head on Khadija's name-day celebration. On the Feast of Sheep (*'ayd l-kabir*) Dawia was struck again. She fell to the ground, talked nonsense, and either refused to nurse Khadija or nursed her feet. She did not respond to the treatment of a *fqih,* or teacher-magician. The leader of a Ḥamadsha team was called in, and he played different melodies on a guitar (*ganbri*) for three days until he was able to find the one to which Dawia's jinn responded. The Ḥamadsha were summoned, and a black he-goat was sacrificed. Dawia was made to drink the goat's blood. She danced the trance dance for the first time in her life, and was cured. She claims to have been struck by Shaykh al-Kanun, the Shaykh of the Brazier.

Mohammed's Account of the Episode

Although Mohammed mentioned the death of his son at one of our first meetings, he did not tell me that he had been looking after the baby at the time of the accident. Even after I had known him for more than six months, Mohammed was very evasive, as the following excerpt from my field notes illustrates:

I cried once when I lost my son. In 1952, a child was born after Fatna [his eldest daughter]. He was next to the boiling water. It fell over on him and burned him, his whole right side. We took him to the hospital, but there was nothing to be done. He was one and a half years old.

I had asked Mohammed if he had ever cried as an adult. We had been talking about men and women who cry in trance. Mohammed had explained that it was a style of trance for those who do not slash their heads. "It is like hitting the head for them." Later in the interview he told me that Dawia had nursed Gueddar when she was pregnant.

His mother was pregnant and nursed him. She did not tell this to the doctor. The milk is poison then. A month after conception, the milk becomes poison. . . . .

Mohammed was referring to the prevalent belief that the milk of a pregnant woman is poison to her children.

Mohammed often confuses the first time he slashed his head, probably after his discharge from the army in 1944, with his performance of the trance dance after his son's death. He remembers the performance as the one in which he slashed more violently than he had ever done before or has done since. He associates this performance, and others after Gueddar's death, with Dawia's illness.

The first time Dawia danced, she was sick for three months. I used to dance the trance dance, but Dawia didn't. There was a saint called Sidi M'hamed. When Dawia was sick, I took her there. We found a team [of Ḥamadsha] there—about sixty people. There was a ball game. I heard the trance dance as I was playing and went to it. I danced with the halberd [shaqria]. I hit my head very hard, and my whole body was covered with blood. Dawia refused to go with me or wash my clothes. We had a mule. I climbed on the mule. I told Dawia to climb on too, but she refused because I was all covered with blood. She walked, barefoot, and was bitten by a scorpion.[5] I said, "Well, here is your blood. Why did you laugh at me?" She was sick for three days from the scorpion. I had taken a razor blade and scratched the place where she was bitten. . . . One day the village headman [muqaddim] called out that there should be no fires outdoors. He saw Dawia had already lit a fire in the oven. She tried to put it out. Something hit her. I didn't think that she was sick, but during the Feast of Sheep we sacrificed our sheep, and the moment she took a piece of meat she threw herself against the wall. Something had taken her. Then I knew something was wrong. Khadija was three months old. I went to get a fqih. He found Dawia hidden under the covers. He began to read the Koran. He saw Dawia get up and thought he was reading the right passage. But Dawia slapped him.[6] He left right away. I looked for another fqih. Dawia told him to leave or she would slap him too. Then I knew that she was possessed [maqiusa]. I went to Moha. He is dead now. He was an oboe player [ghiyyat].[7] He came with his guitar. He looked for a Koran. When he went into the room, he put it at Dawia's feet. She could not have seen it, but she cried out: "Take your book away. Take your book away." Then he knew she was possessed.

Moha played the guitar for Dawia until he found her melody. He invited his team and Dawia danced. "Since then," Mohammed said proudly, "she dances the trance dance and is possessed."

Mohammed describes his condition at this time. We were discussing dreams about 'A'isha Qandisha and his problems with her:

[When did you first have problems with her?] I dreamed a lot about a woman called 'A'isha and others who were probably 'A'isha. [Cuts off conversation.]
[What happened then?] I had to sponsor nights [ceremonies]. If I didn't, something would happen. She is in all houses.
[Indicates with a gesture that she is in his house.] There are some houses where she always is. Others, only sometimes. [When were your first problems?] "In 1954 [sic] when Khadija was born. At that time Dawia was sick. Each night 'she' came to me. I sent someone to Moha. He stayed with Dawia for three days. Dawia dances to his air. I dreamed of 'her.' A night was necessary. I made two nights for 'her.' " [Mohammed appears confused and very nervous.]

Dawia's Account

Dawia, a more consistent informant, does not appear to have the same need to preserve the episode's symbolic superstructure.

There was a boy, Gueddar, who died. He came after Fatna. He was cross-eyed. When he was born, he was born in a caul. . . . His eyes were crossed, and his pupils were white. He grew quickly. Once, his father took him to be registered—he was one-and-a-half and looked four. Once we went to Meknes [they were living in the country] to live but we didn't stay. I wanted to return to my village. We stayed only three months. It was harvest time. I left Guedder with his father. "Watch the child," I said. "I am going to get water at the fountain." Mohammed was making tea. The kettle was on the brazier, full of boiling water. The boy did not see well. Mohammed was not paying attention. Gueddar knocked over the kettle. The boiling water spilled all over him, from shoulder to foot. The child had neither finger- nor palmprints. When we were in Meknes, a woman gave him some cake and then kissed his hand. The moment she took his hand, she took away his blessing. Three days later he was burned, and three days after that he died. We had gone to the doctor.

Dawia explained that children born without finger- and palmprints are considered to have a lot of baraka; people who are cross-eyed are said to be able to find buried treasure. The woman in Meknes had wanted Gueddar's baraka. Gueddar also had bad luck, she added, because they had abandoned the family custom of shaving a child's head and leaving his pigtail in the saint's tomb. They had had Gueddar's head shaved in Meknes. At his burial, near their ancestral saint's tomb, Dawia found a ten-franc piece and two beads from a necklace—an indication that her next child would be a girl. She says that she was not pregnant at the time of Gueddar's death but conceived six months later.

Dawia claims that Mohammed had frequently slashed his head before they were married, but that only after Gueddar's death did he first extend an invitation to the Ḥamadsha. He hit his head with particular violence on that occasion. Dawia also stresses the fact that Mohammed did not report Gueddar's death to the authorities because he did not want to lose his dependency allowance from the French government. (He was on a pension.)

Mohammed's head-slashing also recalls to Dawia how she became a Ḥamdushiyya.

We were at Sidi M'hamed. Mohammed, my sister, and I were eating. There was a team there. Mohammed saw the team and left his meal and went to them, and I was angry. It was the *musem* [annual pilgrimage to a saint's tomb]. The team was big, very big. There was a crowd of people, men and women, performing the trance dance. They touched shoulders [when they danced]. I didn't like that. I went over to watch. There was a Khalifi [a member of a saintly lineage from the Gharb]. They have pigtails. He pulled me into the dance. He made me lie on my stomach, and he walked on my back [to give me baraka]. He said, "Dawia get up. That which you have long sought from Allah you will receive today." When I got up, I saw Mohammed hitting his head with a halberd. I was upset after the Khalifi made me fall. I insulted him. I said to my sister, "Look at the people! What do they do? They are stupid. They are crazy [ḥummaq]."

Dawia watched the Ḥamadsha all day. When it was time to leave, she refused to get on the mule with Mohammed because he was all covered with blood.

There were many girls and women, walking and dancing. Each time Mohammed saw me tired, he stopped and said, "Come, get on." I walked. I didn't want to get on. I was barefoot. Suddenly a scorpion gave me a terrible bite on the foot. I was nearly dead. Mohammed and my sister stopped. They tied my leg so that the poison would not rise, and they took a razor blade and scratched a little on the spot where the scorpion had bitten me. Mohammed said, "Now, you will get on the mule." I still refused. My sister carried me on her back. We walked a little, and then my sister got tired. Mohammed got off the mule, and I got on. We arrived home. I was unable to eat for three days. My foot was swollen. When I was sick, my mother said, "Well, it is your fault. Why didn't you listen to Mohammed? If you continue to refuse, perhaps you will die." Since then I have always feared Mohammed and I began to love the Ḥamadsha. Every time Mohammed invited them, I made good meals, but I still didn't dance. Soon, after the birth of Khadija—I was already pregnant at the pilgrimage—two months later, after the harvest, Khadija was born. She was five days old, and my mother, who was a midwife, was not at my house. It was very hot and the wind was strong. The village headman called out, "If anyone starts a fire outside, he'll have a year of prison." Mohammed had brought a bucket of water. When I heard the headman, I threw the water on the brazier.[8] It was two days before the Feast of the Sheep.[9] We sacrificed a sheep. I washed up all the blood. I was a little sick and didn't eat anything until nightfall. Then we prepared skewers of meat. We began dinner. I was alone with Khadija and Mohammed. I took a piece of bread to pick up the meat, and my hand stopped on the plate. I do not remember what happened. Mohammed said later that I fell and talked to myself and tried to cry "tai bah bah" [nonsense syllables]. Mohammed was afraid. He went to get my mother. My mother came and saw me. My eyes were popping out to here. [Points to cheeks.]

Mohammed brought one fqih, who stayed the night, and then in the morning, a second.

He came and read the Koran, but I gave him a slap. I said, "Will you go? Or do you want me to scratch out your eyes?"

The fqih left, and Dawia began to nurse Khadija's feet. Mohammed got Moha.

I do not remember his coming. Mohammed was afraid of me. Ever since I threw water on the fire, he thought that as the jnun attacked me, they would perhaps attack him.

Moha played for Dawia for three days and then she was taken to her mother's house, for fear that there was a jinn in her own.[10] She was made to drink the blood of a goat sacrificed for her, a common Ḥamadsha practice.

The moment I drank the blood, I saw 'A'isha and her husband dancing the trance dance. He spoke to me in Jews' language. 'A'isha looked like a Muslim but she also spoke to me in the Jews' language. He sang my trance (ḥal), but I did not understand. . . . They were happy because they had drunk some blood and felt good.

Dawia claims that with the exception of 'A'isha's hands, which were like camel's feet, the she-demon looked just like her. "If you had shown me a picture of 'A'isha at that moment, I would have said it was Dawia."
     Dawia was then given unsalted meat (massus).[11] She ate half, and Moha left the rest where she had thrown the water.

There was a friend, a true Ḥamdushiyya, in the team. She took water and threw it on the ground and then led me to the trance dance.[?] She threw the water because 'A'isha is always in the ground and loves water and mud. She did this so that 'A'isha would leave the ground.

The Hamdushiyya helped Dawia dance.

'A'isha and her husband were on each side of me. I was afraid they would enter me again.

Then, after a break for tea, Dawia danced alone to the music of the guitar. She saw 'A'isha and her husband as Muslims.[12]

They were dancing in front of me. They were both in blue jallabas. They were happier as Muslims. When they were Jews they were happy, but they always had their eye on me—the illness.

On a later occasion Dawia describes Mohammed's reaction to Khadija's birth in the following manner:

When I was pregnant with Khadija, I knew I should have a boy, but I did nothing because it comes from Allah. When she was born, Mohammed came in and was a little sad but said nothing. On the seventh day, at the name-day cele-bration, he slashed his head. Mohammed, at Khadija's birth, as is our custom, kissed Khadija and touched my cheek and said O.K. During the first seven days, I was a little sick. I threw water on the fire before the seventh day. I was hit by a jinn then, but it [the sickness] came little by little. I had a fever. I was sicker then than after the birth of my other children. After the seventh day, Mohammed said, "I am sorry we had a daughter. Now we have a problem." When Khadija was twenty-five days old, Mohammed declared her birth and the death of his son. He did not exactly say that it was my fault but he suggested it. "If it had been a boy, we would not have had any problems." [Mohammed refers here to the fact that he had not declared Gueddar's death.] He did not hit me, but he often said, "Ah, I am sorry." Even now he says it. He bothered me a lot. "I do not like this," he screamed at me. He got very angry. It was true he went to other women. He told me so, laughing. It was true. I was hit by the jinn three weeks after the birth of Khadija. When I was possessed [maquisa], Mohammed no longer talked about the problem of Khadija. He was much gentler. He came to me and said, "Ah, I am sorry that I screamed at you, that I bothered you. . . ." He kissed my cheeks and said, "Do not suffer. You will be cured." He knew it was because of his yelling that I was sick. And he cried and wept next to me. Even though I was sick, even though he yelled, I think that all he says is not from his heart.[13]

THE CHARACTERS: MOHAMMED

In 1968, at the time of my research, Mohammed was living in a shanty-town on the outskirts of Meknes with his wife and their seven children. (His eldest son, his child by his first wife, lived in the Rif.) He is in his late forties, a thin, coffee-colored man with exceptionally bright brown eyes. His bearing is military, and he frequently makes use of military expressions in his conversation. He is nicknamed "the sergeant." Mohammed spent nearly two years in the French army during World War II before he was discharged because of an injury suffered on the Tunisian front. One of his fingers was blown off and a second paralyzed. He does not seem much concerned about his injury but he does take particularly good care of his fingernails.[14] They are a sign that he does not have to work. He lives on a pension from the French government. (He bought his present house with compensation money for his war injury, which he finally received in 1966; it is one of the better houses in his neighborhood.) Although he occasionally seems embarrassed by the fact that he lives in a shantytown, he has never seriously considered working to improve his situation. His embarrassment may be due to the fact that Fatna, a primary school teacher, keeps nagging him to move to the more fashionable medina of Meknes.

Mohammed's military bearing is really the only thing about him that suggests a soldier. He does not impress one as having either the strong and aggressive or the decisive and disciplined character of a military man. He is actually a somewhat slow, indecisive, cautious person of moderate intelligence. He is usually gentle, and immediately likeable. Like many Moroccans of his background, he is quick to form dependency relations with people in superior positions and feels betrayed when his needs are not met. Occasionally he has exceptionally violent tantrums during which he beats his wife and children.[15] Once, just before he and his family made their permanent move to Meknes, he was arrested because of a fight in which he bit off his opponent's nipple. Unlike most Moroccan men, he actively participates in the tantrum fights that many of his female neighbors have over their children. He and his family joke about his extreme rage, in which he forgets himself. This rage, they claim, is produced by the swelling of a special vein, the *hasham,* which causes the rage, the *hashamiyya,* in the blood to mount to the head. It is the hashamiyya, and not the man, who is responsible for his acts during such an enraged state.[16] "The hasham does not like anything that is not just."

Mohammed was born in a small village in the Gharb in 1924 or 1925. His parents were fellahin who trace their ancestry back through a local saint, Sidi Gueddar, to Sidina Omar, the prophet's caliph. When Mohammed was about six, his father, Hassan, divorced his mother, Dawia. Mohammed, who finds the subject of his father's divorce almost too painful to talk about, is not sure exactly when the divorce took place. He knows only that it was before his circumcision at the age of seven.

His mother remained in the village until the war. Then she disappeared. "I have no idea if she is alive or dead," Mohammed said once with tears in his eyes.

My mother went away after my father divorced her, and I went into the army. I put a request for information about her on the radio. They asked for her twice, but we never heard a thing. My mother comes from Fez. She is not here. I do not know if she is alive or dead.

Mohammed does not resent his father for divorcing his mother. Divorce is a man's prerogative.

After his divorce Hassan married 'A'isha, a divorced woman with one son, and subsequently had four sons and two daughters by her. Mohammed did not, and still does not, get along with either his stepmother or her sons. 'A'isha appears to have favored her own children at Mohammed's expense.

[How did you get on with your step-mother?] I was never in agreement with her. There were always problems. She did not want me in the house because I was not her son. Did you ever want to hit her? Yes. [He laughs.] She used to make me do woman's work.

'A'isha apparently used to report his disobedience to her husband, who beat Mohammed violently, often throwing him to the ground. On at least one occasion, Hassan tied Mohammed up before beating him with a stick. Mohammed's father, now senile, appears always to have been dominated by 'A'isha. He is not permitted even now to eat at Mohammed's about their treatment of his father. He is proud that he became a Ḥamdushi house. Mohammed's present relations with his half-brothers and sisters are as poor as those with his stepmother. He does not admit to any jealousy or resentment, but he gossips about them and complains about their treatment of his father. He is proud that he became a Ḥamdushi before they did. He claims to have cursed his eldest brother over money matters, and he holds this curse responsible for his brother's illness.

Mohammed spent his childhood in the country. He slept in the same room with his mother and father until their divorce, and then in a room with his paternal grandmother. He remembers his father beating him once when he wet his bed. He was circumcised comparatively late.

I remember when I was circumcised. I did not think it was going to happen. I thought I was the favorite son and was going to a feast. . . . I was given a good jallaba and a burnous, and was put on a horse and led around the village. I was taken to the mosque, and then home. The barber was hidden in the room so that I wouldn't see him. When I was brought in, two men held me tightly. The barber came and sharpened his scissors. [Demonstrates.] He took the foreskin and put a little bit of sheep manure under it and twisted the foreskin around it. This was to protect the head [*ras*, glans]. He cut it with a single stroke. And the skin jumped off, and I jumped. I cried terribly. A woman put me on her back and danced in front of the oboes. The woman danced with me a little. She did this so that I would forget the pain. The barber had put on medicine [had, in fact, pushed the bleeding penis into a freshly cracked egg to which a little rabbit dung had been added]. I stopped crying. They sacrificed a bull for me. They made a lot of bread and invited a lot of people and had a feast. I sat in a corner. The guests gave me money: one thousand francs, five hundred francs, two hundred francs, one hundred francs. [He is very nervous and is beginning to free associate.] The feast lasted all day. On the second day they put medicine on me. I remained in bed all day. The third day I walked a little. If a woman is menstruating, she is not clean and cannot look at the boy because then the wound will not heal. The scissors were really hard. When he cut, I jumped in the air. I thought I would kill him. I thought that had I been big, I would have killed him. Who can look at a person who has caused you blood and pain? No one can take that. There are people who are not circumcised until they are big and then they run away. I thought at the beginning that he had cut it off.[17]

Mohammed played with other boys at the river and attended the traditional village school for a short time—he is able to sign his name—and then became a shepherd.

He masturbated and, like many other country boys, he indulged in homosexual play, mutual masturbation and anal stimulation without penetration, and acts of bestiality with goats, mares, mules, and cows.

There were times we wanted to take a cow without its calf. Then the cow does not want it because it will be separated from its calf. We would take off our clothes. One boy gets under the cow, he rubs a little manure on himself, and knocks at the cow's udders. The cow thinks it is its calf, and then the rest of us can go in. . . .

Mohammed is not particularly ashamed of either his homosexual or bestial relations. They are expected of adolescent boys, especially in the country.

When Mohammed was still in his early teens, his family moved to Meknes. He held several odd jobs, but was never apprenticed to a master artisan. In 1942 he joined the army—"My father was poor so I joined up,"—and was wounded nearly two years later. After his discharge in 1944, he returned to the country. His first sexual experience with a woman was in the army.

It was in Meknes. It was Sunday. The company went to the brothel. I watched my buddies go in with the whores but I couldn't. I was alone. I was fixed to the spot like a tree. There were two women, a Muslim and a French one. They came to me, and each one pulled at me. It was the French one who won out. "Come, come, you have nothing to fear," she said. I had confidence in her but not in the Muslim woman. She put me to bed. She took off all my clothes. She put my penis in her mouth. I was scared. I thought she'd bite it off. The moment I saw my penis in her mouth, I was scared. When she saw my penis was hot, then she took me in the Muslim way. She kept saying, "Come! Come!" I was afraid, but the moment I saw my penis in her vagina, I began to move. After I finished, she gave me one hundred francs.

Mohammed had intercourse with other prostitutes and with fellow recruits during his military service, but he never again had fellatio. "I felt cornered," he said. "It was like a second circumcision. I bit myself on the arm." Moroccans of his background do not practice oral intercourse. Fellatio is considered French, and not Muslim; there are many jokes, suggestive of castration, about it.[18]

Upon his return to the country, Mohammed was married to Zahara but divorced her as soon as she was pregnant.

When she got pregnant, she didn't like me any more. This often happens to women who are pregnant for the first time. She wouldn't even stay in my house. I waited two months because I thought that she might change her mind. She didn't. So I went to the judge and got divorced. . . . I was tired of her behavior. I didn't get the bride price back.

The child, a son, lived with his mother until he was five and then with Mohammed's maternal grandfather.

Mohammed had not wanted to marry Zahara. He wanted Dawia, whom he had known since she was born, but Dawia's father had refused him on the grounds that she was too young for marriage. After he divorced Zahara, Mohammed ritually shamed Dawia's father into accepting his proposal by publicly sacrificing a sheep for him. They were married in a year, when Dawia was twelve. Three years later, Dawia gave birth to Fatna. While she was pregnant, Mohammed left her and—apparently without divorcing Dawia—married a third woman, lived with her for three months, divorced her, and returned to Dawia. A year later Dawia gave birth to Gueddar and then to Khadija. The family moved to Meknes where the other children were born. When I last saw Mohammed, in the summer of 1973, he said that now he would have no more children, and this saddened him.[19] He dotes on his grandchildren.

In recounting his personal history, Mohammed first refers to 'A'isha Qandisha after describing Gueddar's death. His relationship with the Ḥamadsha, however, goes back to the time he was a shepherd in the country. Even before that he had seen the Ḥamadsha perform. Fear of punishment for having let two goats fall into a river—and, in another version for having lost them and five sheep—appears to be the incident for a dream which Mohammed associates with his having become a Ḥamdushi.

When I was eleven or twelve, I was a shepherd. One day I saw my flock nearing the river. Two he-goats fell in. I went to the river to get them out, and after I had saved them, I climbed out of the river and fell unconscious. The invisibles [the jnun] are often in rivers. I was sick for a month. I was fainting all the time. I could not tell night from day. One night I dreamed that two men came to my place. One was in a *darbala* [a tattered outer garment] and the other in clean clothes. I was with several children at the river's edge as the two men approached. There were four or five children. When the men came up to me, the man in the darbala wanted to stab me with a knife. The man in the clean clothes—his name was Bushta—and the man in darbala began to fight, and I ran away. When I awoke the next morning, I saw that I was a man and was no longer sick. A few days later a neighbor invited the Ḥamadsha. I heard the music and danced with them and was then completely cured.

Relating the dream on another occasion, Mohammed added, "The moment I danced the trance dance, I felt better. Since then I dance and hit my head with the halberd. And when my father watches me making the trance dance, he says, "My son will soon die." According to Mohammed the man in the darbala is a jinn; Bushta is the saint Moulay Bushta. "When I was eight years old," Mohammed explained, "I had saved twenty-five centimes and wanted to buy something, but a friend of my father's took me to Moulay Bushta, and I gave my money to the saint. I think that it was he who saved me." He holds 'A'isha Qandisha responsible for several dreams about rivers that he associates with the dream he related. His associations, as I have shown elsewhere, suggest that illness, equated with femininity, is an escape from punishment by the father. Insofar as this escape is identified with being a woman, it is unsatisfactory. The Ḥamadsha cure restores his manhood (Crapanzano, 1975).

Since Gueddar's death Mohammed has been a regular devotee of the Ḥamadsha. Although he claims to have powers of curing victims of the jnun, he has consistently refused to become a member of a team. "I wouldn't be a member. I don't want to leave my house empty and not know what is happening to my children." Mohammed attends the annual pilgrimage to the Ḥamadsha saints, and he visits their shrines and the shrine to 'A'isha Qandisha when there is an illness in the family. On these pilgrimages he is relieved of depression, paresthesia, chest pains, and difficulties in breathing. He is also relieved by the trance dance. Unlike some Ḥamadsha, Mohammed has considerable difficulty in entering trance. His melodies must be played perfectly. If they are not, he becomes irritable and is not satisfied. His body becomes sore, his limbs stiff, and he feels very depressed until he has another opportunity to dance. He usually does not remember his trance experience. "I see nothing in front of me but the oboe (ghita), the drum (tabil), and the recorder (nira).[20] When I dance I listen to what the oboe and the drums are saying." It is my impression that he usually does not mutilate himself until another dancer does so first.

Mohammed tries to invite the Ḥamadsha at least once a year, but he often does not have enough money to do so. During the nine months I spent with him, however, he did invite them twice: once because Dawia had fallen sick and once to celebrate the recovery of his abducted daughter (Kramer, 1971). He does perform the trance dance much more frequently—at least once a month and on occasion two or even three times a week—and usually he slashes his head. Like other devotees he is compelled (by 'A'isha Qandisha) to dance whenever he hears his special melody. Mohammed actually responded to three melodies in 1968 and to four by 1973.[21] I have noticed that he usually manages to attend ceremonies when he is anxious or depressed. He is very offended by the suggestion of a relationship between the trance dance and sexual intercourse.

Mohammed considers himself *maqius* by 'A'isha Qandisha. "Maqius" may be translated as either possessed or struck by a jinn. According to Mohammed, the jinn may enter the body but need not always be there. "Sometimes she squeezes my knees or my back or my shoulders. She moves all the time." For Mohammed "maqius" seems to mean that he is in intimate association with 'A'isha Qandisha, who may either protect him, strike him, or possess him. He holds her responsible for feelings of sudden dizziness, for headaches, for difficulties in breathing, for his depressions, the success of his curse on his eldest stepbrother, for inconsequential chance events, his curing ability, and certain of his dreams. 'A'isha Qandisha, he claims, has recently given him the power to see the jnun.

Three years ago I started to see them. I see them like I see people. I see them everywhere, even next to cars.[22] The first time I saw them, I saw . . . people flying and then I saw that they were different. . . .

[What happened that day?] The night before I had danced the trance dance and had not had enough,[23] and then in the morning I took a walk and saw them. Even now sometimes they punch me in the shoulder. I see them all the time. When? Even at night. I have told you this because I see them and I am not a seer [shuwwaf]. I have been friends [with the jnun] ever since I first saw them. Perhaps if I keep trying to be friends, they will give me my bread [the ability to become a seer]. . . .[24] I can feel them. They are always next to me.
[Even today?] Today I smelled incense when I was still in bed. I asked my wife if she smelled it. She did too. So we looked around and could find nothing.
[I don't understand.] They were the ones who burned it. Are they all the same? They change their faces all the time. They have many different colored bodies and eyes, mouths, wings, and horns. Sometimes their faces are like men and at other times like dogs.
[Are they men or women?] I can't tell. There is always one tight against the right and another tight against the left.[25] There are big ones and small ones. Old ones and young ones. Each person has two. The one on the right is like a man. He is big, and you see from heaven to earth. The one on the left is not so big. Only their faces are like people's.

Mohammed does not deny the role of 'A'isha Qandisha in his first attack by the jinn, but he holds her directly responsible for his condition since his son's death. He sees her during trance, and when he slashes his head, he sees her slashing her own head. He claims that he can see her not only in dreams but at other times as well.

Even without the trance (hal), I see her next to me. Even now—in the air, not on the ground.
[What does she look like?] She is difficult to describe. She changes. Sometimes she is red.[26] Sometimes she is black. I see two of her. If I look carefully, I see more than ten. . . . [When did you see her for the first time?] I saw her about four in the morning, and the second time at four in the afternoon. It is difficult to talk about her because she told me not to say anything. It is possible that she will sit down now on your notebook, and you will not see her. Most Ḥamadsha who say they see her are lying. They can only see her when they're asleep. If they tell you they see her when they're asleep, they're telling the truth. I see her often. I'd be able to see her on an airplane. She is always next to me.

Mohammed is often reluctant to talk about 'A'isha for fear of punishment. One night, after a discussion with me, he was "almost strangled by her."

DAWIA

Dawia is a handsome, articulate woman of thirty-six. She is proud of her marriage to Mohammed, and one senses in their presence unusual warmth and intimacy. Dawia was born in Mohammed's village. Her father was a fellah, and her mother bore twelve children, six of whom—all boys—died at birth. Dawia is the third eldest of five sisters; her surviving brother is the youngest child.

Dawia's life, as she articulates it, begins with her marriage to Mohammed. Her earlier memories concern Mohammed's visits and his first proposal. Her saddest childhood memories are of being sent out by her mother in a thunderstorm to bring in the sheep, and of being beaten by her father when she had cooked a meal badly. Her happiest memories are of receiving new clothes for the Festival of Sheep and for a pilgrimage to Sidi Gueddar.

My mother gave me new clothes. She said, "Come, we will go to the pilgrimage." I was not married yet. When I heard there would be a pilgrimage, I was very happy. Also very free. I walked all around near the trance dance. I ate candy and walked as long as I wanted to. I had never been so free.

Dawia immediately relates this event to "an even happier one": the day Mohammed asked for her in marriage. She remembers herself as her father's favorite; her mother was cruel to her; especially after the birth of a long-awaited son. She fought with her eldest sister until her father knocked their heads together; then they stopped fighting. She fought with her second sister, and still does. That sister is always telling her to divorce Mohammed.

Dawia's family invited the Hamadsha at least once a year to glean their baraka, but no one in the family performed the trance dance.

I saw people dance the trance dance and hit their heads even with jugs, halberds, and stones. The first time I saw someone hit his head—he was called Hassan—it was at my parents', and Mohammad also hit his head with a jug. I was very little, and he, Hassan, hit first with a jug and then with a pot. There was a lot of blood. I was frightened. I ran away, and so do most girls when they see that. I came back when the Hamadsha had stopped. My mother took me in her arms and said, "Don't be afraid. They are only dancing the trance dance. It is not serious." My oldest sister put me on her back.

Dawia remembers imitating the Hamadsha after their dances. "We let our hair down [27] and danced like the women, and the boys took little sticks and pretended they were knives."

Dawia recounts her life, from the time of her marriage to the present, in terms of Mohammed. The principal events are her pregnancies, sickness in her family, the move to Meknes, occasional pilgrimages, the trance dance, and her relationship with the jnun.

Mohammed first asked for Dawia in marriage when she was about ten.

When he left the army and returned to the village, he saw me. He loved me. He wanted to marry me. I did not know what to think about it. I did not even know what marriage was. I liked him very much. He always brought me candy. He was always there between my eyes.

After he married Zahara, Mohammed continued to visit Dawia's family, and he always brought her gifts, clothes, and toys. He said that he had been forced into marrying Zahara by his father. Zahara was so jealous of Dawia that on one occasion she tried to poison her. Mohammed noticed in time, and hit Dawia so that she would not come back to visit Zahara. "He hit me because he loved me so much and had seen that I was almost killed." When Dawia was a little older, her father started to arrange a marriage for her with another man.

I was there. I knew what was going on. I wanted to marry Mohammed but couldn't say anything. It would have been shameful. I loved Mohammed but could not tell the truth. Mohammed was nearly raised in our house, among the five girls. He was always fair. There were never any stories with him.

When Mohammed learned of this, according to Dawia, he threatened to kill her rather than let her marry another man. Dawia's father and mother did not approve of Mohammed because he slashed his head and because he had left his first wife when she was pregnant. When he took a second wife during Dawia's first pregnancy, Dawia's father would not let her return to him until he had divorced the other woman.

Dawia learned about marriage from her two older sisters. Whenever she saw Mohammed after his second proposal was accepted, she ran away and cried. She cried throughout her wedding. On the last night of the wedding:

I was in the room with a lot of women. Outside there was dancing and much noise. The women bothered me. They said, "Oh, he is coming. He is coming. He will put himself inside you. . . ." Mohammed came in and sat down and made tea. I still had the wedding hood on. I would not take it off. Mohammed gave me tea, and I refused it. He ate some bread and asked me to eat some. I said no. It was two in the morning. He took off my hood. I cried. I screamed. . . .

Mohammed tried to be gentle with Dawia, but finally had to force her onto the bed. He took off all her clothes except a white chemise.

He kissed me. I cried. He caressed me, and I pushed him away. He said, "I am only going to laugh with you. Do not be scared." When I saw his penis, I was scared. Then he made love to me. There was such pain. I cried. I cried. The pain was terrible. He tried many times. It took a long time.

Mohammed wrapped Dawia up, threw some candy into the room, as is the custom, and left.

Then the women entered. My sister took the [blood-stained] chemise and put it on her head and took it outside to dance with [in order to show all the guests that Dawia was a virgin]. The other women were next to me. They were eating the candy. They said, "Well, you guarded it well, but he succeeded in the end." They laughed, and I cried. My mother found me crying and hugged me and said, "Now your problems are over. Let us hope it will last all your life."

For over a month, Dawia was in pain every time Mohammed made love to her. She remembers these first weeks of marriage as the most terrible in her life.

Shortly after her menarche, and two years after her marriage, Dawia conceived Fatna.

I didn't know what was wrong. I vomited all the time. I couldn't drink tea. I went to my mother and asked what was wrong. "Perhaps you are pregnant," she said. Then I didn't love Mohammed any more. Each time he spoke to me, I cried. I thought of what would become of me: living in the country with all those children.

Dawia refused to sleep with Mohammed, fearing that she would conceive again each time he made love to her, and have a multiple birth. But she remembers him as gentle with her, even though he left her during that pregnancy.

Dawia and Mohammed's relationship seems to have remained fragile until Gueddar was born. Mohammed frequented other women. The family moved to Meknes after Gueddar's birth—Mohammed began to smoke kif then [28]—but returned to the country before his death. Dawia, far from her family, was not happy in Meknes. She was, and to some extent still is, suspicious of city life and its effect upon children. "They depart from the tradition," she says of city people. "They are not as close to their families. They marry different people because they are educated." But after Khadija was born, the family moved back to Meknes, and Dawia now considers herself a permanent resident of the city. Her primary identification, however, is still with her village, which she visits whenever she can. She claims that the fight in which Mohammed bit off his opponent's nipple was responsible for their move to the city. The French civil administrator put pressure on them to leave the village by threatening to block their compensation money if they did not send their children to city schools.

Dawia has been an active devotee of the Ḥamadsha ever since her first performance of the trance dance. Although she dances as frequently as Mohammed, like most female devotees, she does not mutilate herself. She has likened her feelings after a good trance dance to her feelings after making love well. She visits the Ḥamadsha saints and 'A'isha Qandisha's shrine during the annual pilgrimage, and whenever anyone in the family is ill. When her son, Abderrahim, was sick— he was suffering from convulsions—she took him to the saints' villages and promised them, and 'A'isha Qandisha, a sacrifice if he got better. She and Mohammed danced on this trip and invited the Ḥamadsha when Abderrahim recovered. Dawia performed the trance dance seven days after each of her children (since Khadija) was born because the dance relieves her depression. "A woman who has the jnun inside her," she explains, "is depressed after the birth of a child and needs the trance dance. She becomes depressed because she does not like blood." Dawia also danced when a daughter, Hadda, died five days after birth. She holds herself responsible for Hadda's death. She had eaten butter.

The followers of Sidi 'Ali do not eat butter.[29] So my daughter was strangled. He who is in me was not satisfied with me. To avenge himself, he killed my daughter. 'A'isha does not like butter. . . .

Dawia acknowledges the fact that sometimes, after a misunderstanding with Mohammed or a neighbor, she becomes sick. "I take a little henna [30] and mix it with water and drink it like soup," she says. "If the henna does not work, then I call in the Ḥamadsha."

Dawia has in fact only been struck once since her initial attack after Khadija's birth, in March 1968. She had dusted a mat into a drain. (Drains are a favorite spot for the jnun.)

I went into the kitchen. Someone grabbed my left big toe. I felt as though my foot was asleep. I could not move it. In the kitchen, there was a tea tray, a kettle of boiling water, and a brazier. Mohammed was praying. I cried. I fell. Mohammed caught me just in time, before I upset the kettle of boiling water. . . . I was in bed for two hours. My foot was still asleep. My last thought before falling—I saw a snake pass in front of my eyes. I woke up.

Dawia explained that the snake was a jinn. The next day she was attacked again, this time by something that looked like a dog. "Perhaps it was Shaykh al-Kanun disguised as a dog." Mohammed called the fqih who could do nothing for her. That evening, Mohammed fell sick. "He was hit by the same thing that hit me. He was hit in the eyes. He trembled with cold from eight until eleven-thirty." The next day Mohammed and Dawia went to the Ḥamadsha saints. Dawia dreamed there that Lalla 'A'isha came to her and took her by the hair and said, "You have come."

I said, "Yes, I have come." Lalla 'A'isha said, "Come to me." Then she dragged me by the hair to the spring. "Now wash yourself," she ordered. I washed, but the water was cold, very icy. When I washed, I ululated. Then I was awakened by someone [in the saint's tomb] who was possessed. Oh, I was sorry. I wanted to profit more from the dream and talk more to Lalla 'A'isha.

After the dream, Dawia and Mohammed returned to Meknes and sponsored a Ḥamadsha ceremony. Dawia explained that they had been attacked because they had not invited the Ḥamadsha when they moved into their new house.[31]

Dawia considers herself to be possessed by two male jnun: Shaykh al-Kanun and Musawi, both of whom love the same colors, blue and yellow. Dawia often confuses the two jnun.[32] She always wears their favorite colors, burns their favorite incense, and adheres to either of their commands.

Ever since I first fell into trance (ḥal), I loved these colors. When I wear them, all goes well in my body.

She has a rich sexual life with both her male jnun.

There are times that 'A'isha's husband comes to me [in a dream] just like Mohammed and sits down at my feet. He sleeps there. He is dressed just like a Muslim—jallaba, slippers, and a turban. When he comes in a dream he is always dressed, never naked. He comes just like Mohammed. He asks if I want to sleep with him. I accept and sleep with him. Sometimes he comes to the house and spends a lot of time there. Other times I find myself somewhere else. I think it is his house. When he makes love to me, he takes off his clothes. He is a Muslim and exactly the color of Mohammed. He looks just like Mohammed but a little heavier. I see myself. I am dressed up beautifully, like a bride. When I sleep with him, I am naked. . . . In my dreams we are not young. We are older. He is like a man who has returned from a long trip and sleeps with his wife. . . . I have much pleasure, and feel as though I have just been married. I am better satisfied with 'A'isha's husband than with a man; I am happy [fraḥana] afterward. Each time I am with him I see that I have on beautiful clothes.

Dawia explains that she is satisfied by 'A'isha's husband because he prepares her. "He carresses me and talks to me and laughs with me." Mohammed tends to be more perfunctory in his lovemaking. He does not remain inside her for long; he only kissed her on the genitals once, after a long trip. Dawia does, however, derive some pleasure from Mohammed.

At times, Dawia says that 'A'isha's husband comes to her when 'A'isha goes to Mohammed. She and Mohammed have joked about this.[33]

Sometimes Mohammed wakes up in the morning and tells me to get him some warm water [to cleanse himself]. I say, "Why wash? You have not slept with me." He says, "Last night I slept with a woman. I must bathe." I say, "That's ridiculous. You wake up and wash without having made love to me. . . ." Yes, I wash after I sleep with 'A'isha's husband. Mohammed laughs. He is amused by that.

At other times, Dawia denies that she and Mohammed have complementary relations with their respective jinn partners. She notes that she dreams of 'A'isha whenever she suspects that Mohammed is unfaithful to her. She has had several anxiety dreams about his marrying another woman.

Mohammed was married to another woman. I was screaming. I was crazy [hamqa] in the dream. I saw him. He entered with his new wife, and I went outside and yelled, "Let me leave. I will not stay." I saw him sleeping with her.

It is 'A'isha Qandisha who comforts her.

One night I saw 'A'isha. She said, "Do not suspect Mohammed. He is not thinking of that. You, both of you, are followers of Sidi 'Ali. I will not let you get divorced. When you see Mohammed like that, fear nothing. It is his *hal* [trance] that makes him like that."

DISCUSSION

Mohammed and Dawia's articulation of their personal histories, including our central episode, are not altogether comparable. Mohammed's story was told to me in fragments over a period of nine months; Dawia's was told to my wife within a few weeks' time as a running narrative, and it was told toward the end of our stay in Meknes. My wife had known Dawia, however, nearly as long as I had known Mohammed. She did not encourage as much free association as I did. Both of us had excellent rapport with Mohammed and his wife. They were our friends and the friends of our field assistant and his family.[34]

My relationship with Mohammed changed considerably with time. His invitation to the Ḥamadsha in March 1968 was the first "night" I attended. Mohammed was proud that he had provided my entry into the world of the Ḥamadsha. He felt it his responsibility that I be told the truth about the brotherhood; he was somewhat concerned, if not jealous, about my interviews with other Ḥamadsha, especially those of whom he did not approve. Over the months, as I learned more about the brotherhood, Mohammed began to confide in me. He looked forward to our "talks" and even initiated them on his own accord. He was developing a dependence on me, which I did not want to encourage for fear that he would take my departure as yet another abandonment. This dependence was stimulated by practical help that we were able to extend to Mohammed and his family (Kramer, 1971).

Mohammed must have experienced a certain ambivalence toward me as well. Sometimes he would arrive at an interview distracted, if not withdrawn and suspicious. At other times he would talk to me about the most intimate aspects of his past—seldom his present—or about such potentially dangerous matters as his relationship with 'A'isha Qandisha and the other jnun. Perhaps in talking about them he was asserting his superiority to, or at least his independence of, the *nasrani* who was always asking him questions. "It is difficult to talk about her ['A'isha Qandisha] because she has told me not to say anything. It is possible that she will sit down on your notebook, and you will not see her." Mohammed's confidences seemed, however, to lack the depth, the inwardness, that I have come to expect in Westerners. As he revealed himself, 'A'isha became more and more threatening. "I was almost strangled by her." Mohammed always preferred to keep me aloof, and distant, in order to confide in me. With the exception of asking me about circumcision once, he never questioned me about my life or beliefs.

Dawia's relationship to my wife was not one of dependence. She showed a geniune curiosity about my wife that Mohammed never did about me. She was pleased by my wife's attention and enjoyed her interviews and even her puzzlement over why she was asked such detailed questions about the obvious and the trivial. They were her equivalent to my interviews with her husband. Unlike Mohammed, who always emphasized the different, Dawia looked for the similar in my wife—in their common womanhood. Theirs was a relationship of sharing. Dawia was confident. Neither she nor Mohammed ever tried to use us to influence the other.

Still, I think it would be a mistake to consider the different shapes of
Mohammed and Dawia's stories solely in terms of their different in-
terlocutors. The fragmented character of Mohammed's story—and his
digressions which, however psychologically significant they may be, are
not always to the point—reflect a fragmented identity. His articulation
of his life experiences in terms of 'A'isha Qandisha and the other jnun,
and to a lesser extent in terms of the saints, Sidi Gueddar, Moulay
Boushta, and Sidi 'Ali ben Ḥamdush, enable him to express and structure his life in systemic terms external to himself. His inner life is immediately deflected outward onto that other stage which I have called
the demonic. His identity is not anchored within him but outside himself, in 'A'isha Qandisha. She becomes the principal element in the articulation of his personal history and, undoubtedly, in the interpretation of his present.

'A'isha Qandisha permits Mohammed the expression and even the
acting out of desires which he, as a man, would find unacceptable.
Thus conflicts are expressed in terms of male and female. Acceptable
desires are articulated in terms of himself or, on occasion, in terms of a
saint. Unacceptable desires are articulated in terms of 'A'isha Qandisha
and sometimes of other women including his wife. 'A'isha Qandisha is,
however, an ambiguous figure. She may appear as a beauty or a hag, as
benevolent or malevolent, as a seductress or a strangler. "Sometimes
she is red. Sometimes she is black." Yet she is never white. White is a
color Mohammed associates with goodness, piety, and prayer.[35] She
always has the feet of a camel, even in her most beautiful manifestations and she is always potentially dangerous, untrustworthy. She must
be controlled, but to be controlled she must be obeyed. Control involves enslavement. Mohammed must be as a woman in order to be a
man.[36] He is possessed by her, one with her, and is forced to slash his
head. "I see her with the iron in front of me," he explained. "Then I
want the ḥalberd."

'A'isha Qandisha reflects Mohammed's experience of other women
or, perhaps more accurately, his articulation of his experience of other
women. His relationship to women is one of ambivalence. He both
desires and fears them. The theme of castration runs through all his
dealings with women. His mother, Dawia, was good to him and then
abandoned him. He relates her disappearance to the war in which he
lost a finger. As is the custom in the Gharb, he was led to the circumcision by a woman, perhaps even by his mother or stepmother. His reaction to the circumcision was one of rage: "I thought that had I been
big, I would have killed him." He was betrayed. "I did not think it was
going to happen. I thought I was the favorite son and was going to a

feast. . . ." He thought that the barber had cut off his penis. His step-mother, 'A'isha,[37] reported his disobedience to his father who beat him violently. (His only escape from punishment was through illness.) She also made him do woman's work. He did not have confidence in the Muslim prostitute, and the French one took his penis in her mouth. "I was scared. I thought that she'd bite if off. . . . I felt cornered. It was like a second circumcision. I bit myself on the arm." His reaction to castration is to bite himself. To act as a man, he must mutilate himself. His rage is directed toward himself. It is perhaps no accident that Dawia finds his lovemaking perfunctory. Mohammed himself has told me that he does not like to remain inside a woman for very long. He never complained, however, of impotence.[38]

Mohammed's rage is not, however, always turned on himself. He has a violent temper; he beats his wife and children. He participates in the tantrum fights of his neighbors, who are women. His aggression is, in the psychoanalytic sense, oral. He bites off the nipple of his opponent in a fight. A cow is even deprived of her calf before intercourse. Her udders are knocked. 'A'isha, however, will not tolerate Mohammed's anger. If she is not obeyed, she will attack him, possess him. Illness, castration, circumcision, and head-slashing—all of these, identified with being a woman, are an escape from the burden of manhood. The desire least acceptable to him is the desire to escape manhood, to become a woman. Possession by a she-demon and head-slashing during the trance dance are compromise formations. Mohammed becomes a woman in order to become a man; and he does so not by his own volition but by the will of another, 'A'isha Qandisha, a woman with distinctly phallic traits: camel's feet, long fingernails, maenad-like curls, pendulous breasts, and elongated nipples.

The castrator is ultimately male. Mohammed's father Hassan, not present at his son's circumcision,[39] allows his penis to be cut; he beats him violently. Mohammed escapes from the man in the darbala, a jinn, who is later identified with 'A'isha Qandisha. He escapes through illness from his punishing father whom he remembers with little warmth, toward whom he shows no manifest hostility, and with whom he cannot identify. The saints too are distant in their sanctity and in their ability to work miracles. (Mohammed fled from Moulay Boushta in his dream.) They do not serve as models. It is, however, their baraka that enables him to enter the very trance in which he mutilates himself, in which he becomes one with 'A'isha Qandisha, and through which he finally becomes a man.

Dawia's life story, unlike Mohammed's fragmented history, is a more or less consistent narrative designed to evoke a response in her interlocutor. Dawia has a flair for the dramatic that she displays in even the minor incidents of everyday life. She is a storyteller. Despite the precariousness of her situation as a woman in Morocco, she is more confident than her husband. She talks on the "plane of reality." She has an edge on herself and is able to admit ambivalence in herself and others. She does not live in the constricted world of her husband; she does not have the same vested interest in maintaining a symbolic superstructure. She accepts the demands of the jnun and her responsibility in meeting them. They are elements in her world with which she must reckon. "Hadda died. It was my fault. . . . He who is in me was not satisfied with me. To avenge himself he killed my daughter." Often she takes delight in her relationship with the jnun. She has a sense of humor. Even 'A'isha Qandisha is less menacing for her than for Mohammed. She offers Dawia support.

Mohammed's narrative, deflected though it is onto the demonic stage is centered on himself. Dawia's life is centered on Mohammed. She is outer-directed. Her life begins with her marriage. Until then her memories are vague and confused, evoked only by questions; she was only twelve when she married. It is Mohammed's life, or, perhaps more accurately, her life as married to Mohammed, that provides the structure for Dawia's experience. Her fate is Mohammed's; Mohammed's is in 'A'isha Qandisha.

For Mohammed, the jnun serves to articulate desires which are unacceptable to him; for Dawia, they serve to regulate interpersonal relations. She is much more willing to accept desires and other aspects of her being-in-the-world that may not measure up to her ideal self-image. (However ideal this image may be, it is affected by her inferior status as a woman in Moroccan society—a status that Mohammed accepts in his vision and manipulation of her.) The jnun serve either as compensations for deficient interpersonal relations or to mediate relations that may be on the verge of collapse. On the one hand, Dawia's sexual relations—her relations, perhaps, in general—with Shaykh al-Kanun and Musawi are more satisfying than her sexual relations with Mohammed. On the other hand, she is struck exactly when her marriage to Mohammed is about to dissolve.

The episode I have chosen to investigate is central to Dawia's personal history. (It does not play the same role for Mohammed. He ignores it, or tells it in terms of his wife.[40] Dawia recasts her relationship to Mohammed in demonic terms. She learns to speak Mohammed's language. "The implicit problem of this (marital) conversation is how to match two individual definitions of reality," Berger and Kellner have written. "By the very logic of the relationship, a common overall definition must be arrived at—or the conversation will become impossible and, *ipso facto,* the relationship will be endangered" (1970, p. 61). Until Khadija's birth Dawia looked down on the Ḥamadsha. "Look at the people! What do they do? They are stupid. They are crazy," she tells her sister. She is angry at Mohammed for slashing his head. She refuses to mount the mule—to speak his language. She is bitten by the scorpion.

Mohammed refuses to accept responsibility for the death of his son. He tries to blame Dawia: she nursed Gueddar when she was already pregnant. (Dawia denies that she was pregnant. She did allow the woman in Meknes to give Gueddar the cookie and kiss his hand—to take his baraka.) Mohammed cries. Crying, at least in trance, is "like hitting the head." He slashes his head more violently than ever before. He does not punish himself; it is 'A'isha who makes him slash his head. His relations with Dawia deteriorate. He smokes kif and frequents other women. He angers Dawia. He claims that he left a ball game to dance; Dawia claims that he left their meal. He complains about the problems of registering Gueddar's death and the compensation money they will lose. The burden is placed on Dawia: she must bear a son, a replacement for Gueddar.

Dawia gives birth to a girl. Mohammed is disappointed. He says nothing about it for seven days, but Dawia knows. "When I was pregnant with Khadija, I knew I should have a boy." She is struck five days after Khadija's birth, putting out a fire in a brazier. This is no accident. Had Mohammed extinguished the fire, Gueddar would not have been scalded to death. She is in fact attacked by the Shaykh of the Brazier, the jinn responsible for Gueddar's death who looks just like Mohammed. (The Mohammed responsible for her son's death is cast out onto the demonic stage; she need not blame her husband.[41]) A few weeks later Mohammed complains about Khadija. "He did not exactly say it was my fault, but he suggested it," she says. "He bothered me a lot. 'I do not like this,' he screamed at me. He got very angry. It was true that he went to other women. It was true." Their marriage is about to collapse. Dawia is again struck by a jinn. She rearticulates her relationship with Mohammed in terms of the she-demon and her husband.

Mohammed no longer talked about the problem of Khadija. He was much gentler. He came to me and said, "Ah, I am sorry that I screamed at you, that I bother you. . . ."

He feared the jinn, at least according to Dawia. "Mohammed was afraid of me. Ever since I threw the water on the fire, he thought that as the jnun had attacked me, they would perhaps attack him." [42] She has learned to speak his language, but she has not forgotten her own—a point that Berger and Kellner ignore. "He knew that it was because of his yelling that I was sick." Dawia exhibits a savvy that Mohammed lacks.

Dawia has forced Mohammed to articulate their relationship in terms of 'A'isha Qandisha, the one woman who will tolerate no anger. She sees 'A'isha Qandisha as herself. "If you had shown me a picture of 'A'isha at that moment, I would have said it was Dawia." Mohammed himself, undoubtedly ignorant of his wife's trance vision, makes the same equation.

Each night "she" came to me. I sent someone to Moha. He stayed with Dawia for three days. Dawia dances to his air. I dreamed of "her." A night was necessary. I made two nights for "her."

It is not sure who the final "her" is—Dawia or 'A'isha Qandisha and all the women she reflects.

'A'isha Qandisha, Shaykh al-Kanun, and the jnun generally have very different meanings for Mohammed and Dawia. They serve different articulatory functions in their apprehension of their personal histories. As elements in a common idiom, however, as collective representations subject to systemic constraints, they enable more than the articulation of subjective life; they enable the articulation and rearticulation of ongoing human relations not simply by giving meaning to these events but by entering into them as third parties, as mediators, whose existence is reconfirmed for the believers whenever they take possession of a person. Whatever the truth of our central episode may have been, its articulation in terms of 'A'isha Qandisha and her husband enables both Dawia and Mohammed to preserve their marriage by casting out the tensions and hostilities, the resentment and anger, the acceptance and projection of guilt, caused by the death of a favored son and the birth of an unwanted daughter, onto the demonic stage. Thus Dawia and Mohammed are enabled to live together with greater warmth and more intimacy than I have observed in most Moroccan couples of their background.

NOTES

1. Although Wallace (1959), Bourgignon (1968), and others have correctly pointed out that possession is not a single, distinct psychophysiological

syndrome but an interpretation of a number of possible syndromes, they have failed (in my opinion) to consider adequately the role that interpretation as possession plays in the symptomatology and cure of the syndrome and in other facets of the possessed's subjective experience.

2. The masculine singular of *jnun* is *jinn* and the feminine singular is *jinniyya*.

3. The distinction between a follower and a husband of 'A'isha Qandisha is not clear-cut. A follower may become a husband, a husband a follower. Relations with the she-demon change over time.

4. *Ḥamdushi* is the masculine singular of *Ḥamadsha; Ḥamdushiyya* is the feminine singular.

5. 'A'isha Quandisha and the other jnun may take the form of a scorpion.

6. In conversation once Mohammed implied that it was not Dawia but that which was in her that slapped the fqih. For Mohammed, who prefers to think of Dawia as struck by the she-demon and not her husband, it was 'A'isha Qandisha who struck the fqih.

7. The oboe, or *ghita,* is one of the *Ḥamadsha* instruments.

8. Note that Mohammed refers to an oven fire in his account and Dawia to the fire in a brazier in hers. Gueddar was scalded by water boiling in a brazier.

9. Dawia sometimes identifies the Feast of Sheep with Khadija's name-day celebration during which the Ḥamadsha were invited. Detailed questioning revealed that the Feast of Sheep was in fact after Khadija's name day. The exact chronology is not clear.

10. Dawia explained that she did not want to go to her mother's house because she was afraid there would be a fire there. She claims that when she arrived there, there was in fact a fire. One of her younger sisters had been playing with matches.

11. Unsalted meat is frequently given to the victims of the jnun. The jnun are said not to like salt. Many Moroccans sprinkle salt on places where the jnun are said to gravitate before they go to bed.

12. Note the transformation of 'A'isha Qandisha and her husband from Jews to Muslims, from aliens to friends. This mirrors visually the transformation of the jnun during cures from malevolent to benevolent spirits (Crapanzano, 1971). Note also that Dawia does not at first understand Shaykh al-Kanun because he speaks the Jews' language.

13. Dawia implies not only that Mohammed does not mean what he says but also that he is not responsible for his words. Her "savvy" must not be considered "insight" in the psychoanalytic sense of the word, for she is not aware of the underlying dynamic of her "symptom formation."

14. 'A'isha Qandisha is said to force her husbands and some of her followers to let their fingernails grow. Mohammed resists; he does the opposite. He keeps them short. As a child he bit his nails and was punished by his father.

15. On at least one occasion, Mohammed tied up his daughter Khadija and beat her with a stick. On another, he beat Dawia up so badly for having given a loaf of bread to a neighbor that she went to court. Mohammed was found guilty, and Dawia then withdrew her charges. Khadija explains her father's anger in the following words:

> He flies into a rage and turns pale and does not know what he is doing. It comes on him from time to time. There is no reason for it. When I saw him starting to get mad, I used to go into the toilet and lock the door. Once, he was suddenly not himself. He turned pale and started saying things and looked around in all directions at once. He wanted his stick to beat me. I went into the toilet and stayed for hours. Then, when it was night, he turned off the lights so that I would come out. I was very scared but I stayed until he fell asleep. Then I came out and tiptoed into the bedroom and lay down. In the morning he had forgotten his anger and said, "I wasn't myself."

Upon questioning, Khadija implied that 'A'isha Qandisha was responsible. Khadija and her father have frequently fought. Sometimes they tickle each other until they cannot laugh. Khadija was thirteen or fourteen at the time.

16. Note again the shift of responsibility from the self.

17. When Mohammed had finished telling me about his circumcision, I asked him to tell me any story that occurred to him. He told me a long, rambling one about a beggar who overcame a king and married a beautiful woman. The beggar then became king.

18. On one occasion I told Mohammed about *vagina dentata* myths. He was frozen for a moment, then dully denied the existence of women with toothed vaginas. Finally he asked if such women existed in Europe and America.

19. Dawia claims that with Mohammed's help she is now employing magical birth control techniques.

20. These are Ḥamadsha instruments.

21. One of these melodies is the same as Dawia's. They do not, however, share the same colors or incense.

22. Mohammed always expressed considerable interest in my car.

23. That is, his jinn was not satisfied. Mohammed is usually anxiety-ridden when he has not had enough. He is distracted and moody, given to depression. His body is sore, and he has difficulty breathing. He suffers from tingling in his joints.

24. Mohammed was still not a shuwwaf in 1973.

25. Moroccans, like other Muslims, believe that there are two angels always at the side of every human being. The angel on the right keeps account of the human being's good deeds, the one on the left of his bad deeds. These are weighed on Judgment Day.

26. 'A'isha Qandisha's favorite colors are red and black.

27. During the trance dance, women let their hair fall.

28. Mohammed has not smoked kif in years.

29. This is one of the more idiosyncratic rules that Dawia follows. It is by no means universally accepted by the Ḥamadsha.

30. 'A'isha Qandisha is said to like henna. Henna seems often to be symbolic of blood. Just as Dawia drank the goat's blood, so she drinks henna.

31. I was not able to discover any other problem between Mohammed and Dawia at this time. They argued over whether or not they should spend the money for a ceremony after having spent so much for their house. Dawia did not want to. She was struck. Then Mohammed refused to sponsor the cermony for her. He was struck. The ceremony was given. Their relationship was restored. To look to the cause of the illness only in terms of a breach of ritual obligation, as Wittkower (1971) does, is to miss the role that rituals play in reconstituting interpersonal relations on the verge of collapse. The breach is a symbol for the interpersonal defect.

32. Shaykh al-Kanun and Musawi may parallel the two manifestations of 'A'isha Qandisha. The theme of transformation may be hidden here.

33. Mohammed never mentioned to me having sexual relations with 'A'isha Qandisha.

34. Our field assistant was present at most of our interviews with Mohammed and Dawia.

35. The following associations were elicited when I asked him to tell me what occurred to him when I said "white." "It is good, the white, because everyone dresses in white on Fridays. They say their prayers in white. White is a favorite color. White is worn by pious people. It is the color one should wear. There are many people who like it. In Morocco one wears all kinds of colors: white, black, and yellow. It reminds me of the Friday flag."

36. Mohammed's ambiguous sexual identity is well illustrated by the following sequence of drawings (Figure 1). I asked Mohammed to draw a man (time to completion, five minutes), then a woman (six and a half minutes), then anything he wanted to (four minutes), and finally himself (eight minutes). The last request took him aback and caused him great anxiety (as it had caused in my other Moroccan informants). Note in his self-portrait the presence of both male and female genitalia and the absence of bodily closure (as in his drawing of a woman). The depiction of ribs and knees was not unusual among my informants; that Mohammed only drew knees on his woman and on himself is, however, unusual. The hedgehog and the snake occur in Moroccan folklore. Mohammed had never made a drawing before.

37. There is an irony in the names of Mohammed's mother and stepmother, Dawia and 'A'isha. He is married to a Dawia and maqius to an 'A'isha. One cannot help but wonder whether his desire to marry Dawia was not in a sense symbolic of his desire to recover his "good" mother. Of course,

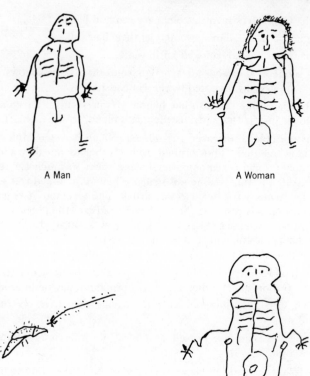

A Man   A Woman

A Snake Fighting a Hedge Hog   Self Portrait

Figure 1

Dawia was so young—ten at his first proposal—that she was less threatening perhaps than an older woman.

38. His potency may well be a defense against castration fears. The "phallic orientation" of Mohammed's sexuality is not untypical of other Ḥamadsha.

39. Fathers are not present at their sons' circumcisions.

40. Its reality is perhaps too painful for him. Gueddar is more than just a son; he is proof of Mohammed's manhood. His death is in a sense the death of Mohammed, Mohammed qua man.

41. It should be noted that years later, in March 1968, when Dawia was again struck, she saw a tea tray, a kettle of boiling water, and a brazier. Mohammed was praying.

42. When she is struck in March 1968, Mohammed is also struck.

REFERENCES

BERGER, PETER and HANSFRIED KELLNER

1970   "Marriage and the Construction of Reality; An Exercise in the Microsociology of Knowledge." In *Recent Sociology, No. 2: Patterns of Communicative Behavior*. H. P. Dreitzel, Ed., New York: Macmillan, pp. 50–72.

BOURGIGNON, ERIKA

1968   "Divination, transe et possession en Afrique transsaharienne." In *La divination*. Vol. 2. Andre Caquot and Marcel Leibovici, Eds. Paris: Presses Universitaires de France, pp. 331–358.

CRAPANZANO, VINCENT

1971   "The Transformation of the Eumenides: A Moroccan Example." Paper read at the annual meeting of the American Anthropological Association, New York City.

1972   "The Ḥamadsha." In *Saints, Scholars, and Sufis*. Nikki Keddie, Ed. Berkeley: University of California Press, pp. 327–348.

1973a   *The Ḥamadsha: A Study in Moroccan Ethnopsychiatry*. Berkeley: University of California Press.

1975   "Saints, Jnun and Dreams: An Essay in Moroccan Ethnopsychology." *Psychiatry* 38: 145–159.

ELIOT, T. S.

1960   "Hamlet and His Problems." In *Selected Essays*. New York: Harcourt, Brace, and World, pp. 121–126.

GIRARD, RENÉ

1961   *Mensonge romantique et vérité romanesque*. Paris: Grasset.

KRAMER, JANE

1971   *Honour to the Bride Like the Pigeon that Guards Its Grain Under the Clove Tree*. London: Collins.

LACAN, J.

1966   *Ecrits*. Paris: Seuil.

MANNONI, O.

1969   *Clefs pour l'imaginaire ou l'autre scene*. Paris: Seuil.

VAN DEN BERG, J. H.

1955   *The Phenomenological Approach to Psychiatry: An Introduction to Recent Phenomenological Psychopathology*. Springfield, Illinois: Charles C Thomas.

WALLACE, ANTHONY F. C.

1959   "Cultural Determinants of Response to Hallucinatory

Experience. *A. M. A. Archives of General Medicine*
1: 74–85.

WITTKOWER, E. D.

1971   "Transcultural Psychiatry." In *Modern Perspectives in
World Psychiatry.* John G. Howells, Ed. New York: Brun-
ner/Mazel, pp. 697–712.

Lucie Wood Saunders

Variants in Zar Experience in an Egyptian Village [1]

Zar is a term used in Egypt, the Sudan, Ethiopia, and the Arabian peninsula to refer to belief in possession by spirits and the ceremonies associated with this belief. The central theory of the *zar* is that spirit possession is manifested by illness which can be alleviated by propitiating the spirits through ceremonies that consistently include dance and trance behaviors. Other features which the *zar* shares with similar possession cults are that the spirits are peripheral to the major religious belief of the society and that the participants are predominantly women.

Many recent reports of the *zar* indicate that it has multiple functions, more than one of these usually being recognized by the members of a particular community (Barclay, 1964, pp. 196–208; Fakhouri, 1968, pp. 49–56; Lewis, 1971, pp. 71–79). Analyses of *zar* cults tend to assume or focus on a fairly uniform level of individual experience (e.g., Kennedy,

1967). Observation of *zar* participants in an Egyptian village suggests that the multiple social functions of the zar are related to considerable variation in the pattern, intensity, and goals of individual participation. This chapter examines the different ways two village women participated in the *zar* and the relationship between these differences and their domestic roles as defined for their respective social stratum.

The women are from a village I shall call Kafr al Hana. It is a medium-size community of about 2400 persons located in the central Egyptian delta near the Damietta branch of the Nile. The region is one of intensive and highly productive agriculture, with so dense a population that several villages of clustered mudbrick houses like those of Kafr al Hana are visible from its periphery. The village population includes a small number of landowners whose holdings enable them to hire agricultural workers and who also may have other sources of income, some owner-operators, and a great majority of persons with little or no land whose main income is derived from working for wages on estates or doing unskilled labor on contract outside the village. The landowner-employers, who do no physical labor, are described locally as rich and are distinguished in the village from all the others who identify themselves as *fellahin,* meaning that they cultivate the land themselves. The differences in access to resources affect food consumption, style of dress, domestic and public roles, and life expectations to some extent, though partible inheritance assures considerable mobility between the segments. Rich men are expected to aspire to be community leaders and to maintain a controlled, dignified bearing, assuming responsibility in village affairs and showing respect and courtesy to all. Their wives are expected to stay in the house during the day, refraining from public appearance on the street, in shops, in markets, or in quarrels. Fellahin women may work in the fields as well as the house, go on errands to shops and in the market, and are allowed to go about the village during the day. The domestic roles of rich and fellahin women differ in that the latter usually manage household funds, while husbands do this in rich households. Authority over rich women is transferred to their husbands at marriage, while it remains with the brother or father, if he is living, of a fellahin woman.

During 1961–1962, there were about forty women and a few men in Kafr al Hana who went to zar ceremonies regularly or occasionally. Villagers use the word *da',* meaning "beat," to refer to these ceremonies; and, while they understand the term *zar,* they say it is a word used by city dwellers to refer to the same practices. They do not usually distinguish *zar* spirits as a group from other kinds of spirits, and use the term *afarit* to refer to them as well as to other spirits such as those of particular places or ghosts. The possessing spirits with whom villagers are familiar include spirits of foreign origin, such as the Sudanese spirit and the Greek spirit, as well as a particularly violent spirit named the Red Djinn, a ship spirit, and the spirits of locally famous shaikhs (cf. Lewis, 1971, p. 32).

While belief in the existence of spirits is general in the village among men and women, and is seen as compatible with their Muslim religious convictions, the authenticity of zar spirits is a subject of controversy. All the leading men and most others disavow the possibility of possession publicly, yet reveal some degree of concealed belief in that they fear to disobey the spirits' commands to their wives. Former zar goers, men or women, also deny the reality of possession, although the depth of their disbelief is difficult to determine. Women who go regularly or occasionally or have never gone to the zar express belief that possession occurs. Thus most women do not publicly deny the possibility of possession, while most men do, and the behavior of both suggests an underlying reservoir of belief which may be maintained more easily because of the general understanding that other kinds of spirits exist, affecting people's welfare, and that any illness or misfortune may have spirit causes. Zar goers also vary in degree of participation, including those who showed total involvement during zar ceremonies and a continuing awareness of possession in their daily activities, persons who regarded the zar as therapy for a particular illness yet reacted intensely during ceremonies, and other regular participants whose possession appeared shallow in its penetration of their lives and in its manifestations during zar sessions.

Possession is suspected most often when a person is ill and the condition does not respond to other cures such as herbal remedies, removal of the causes of specific illness induced by the evil eye, or removal of the effects of sorcery, and locally available medical practice. The symptoms that the possessed experienced are described as including swelling of the legs or stomach, stomach pain, loss of appetite, barrenness and, most commonly, nervousness; some participants who had been to physicians said they had diagnoses of heart trouble, abscesses, and epilepsy. Less frequently, possession may be interpreted first from a dream or if a person goes into trance when hearing zar music.

Diagnosis of possession is made by the *shaikh* [2] who conducts zar ceremonies and also practices magical means of curing. He finds possession on the basis of the person's account of symptoms of illness or dream experiences, and he recommends the kind of ceremony a person should have. A possessed person responds with twitching or other uncontrollable movements to the tune associated with her particular spirit the first time she hears it at a ceremony, dances to it, and goes into trance, during which the spirit speaks through her expressing particular demands. Subsequently, a woman dances every time she hears the tune but she may or may not go into trance. There is no initiation period, and no formalized role difference between the most recent and the longest term participants. If a person's symptoms are not relieved by following the shaikh's initial recommendations, there is another consultation with him but there is never an elaborate diagnostic procedure to ascertain the particular spirit (cf. Messing, 1958).

Two different means of attending zar ceremonies are open to villagers, and they differ in some of the experiences they create for participants. They are alike in that music and individual dancing are their central features. One, which may be called the public zar, is held every Friday and is operated by the shaikh as a kind of business enterprise. It is attended by people from several villages, each of whom pays the shaikh 2 piasters (two-fifths of the daily wage of a woman agricultural worker in winter). The shaikh and his band of three men drum the songs associated with the different zar spirits while his wife sings parts of them, or she and the shaikh accompany the drummers with tambourines. The songs of the zar spirits are always described as sad songs. The Friday ceremonies are attended by men and women who dance in separate, undecorated rooms with the doors open between them. The shaikh and his band sit in the women's room near the door and the women sit on the floor, almost forming a circle around the empty central area. When the women first come in, they remove their black overdresses, though they do not usually do so away from their own homes.

The zar begins with the recitation of the Koran, then the musicians begin to play and some of the women rise to dance, covering their faces with white or black veils. They say they dance to those songs that arouse a trembling in their bodies, and this trembling is visible before they begin to dance. They say that numbness precedes this phase. A person must dance to the songs associated with his particular spirit, and may choose whether to dance to the other songs. Few of the spirits require special patterns of dancing to their songs, thus the dancers move very differently to the same song. Some women remain seated throughout their dance, moving their heads from side to side or shaking them up and down at speeds which accelerate with the tempo of the music to great rapidity. Others make sweeping movements with their arms and bodies only as they stand firmly in place; some sway while stamping their feet in place. In either seated or standing positions, some women move head, hands, and body together; others move head and hands with minimal body motion; still others move the head only. Several women stand with their hands against the wall and sway violently from side to side; a few kneel or sit and slap the floor hard with their hands as the music progresses. The more exaggerated movements are of the upper part of the body. The Red Djinn always requires violent movements, but in the general pattern younger women dance strenuously while older women move very slightly in response to the music. Each song lasts about ten minutes, and when it is nearly ended some women fall to the floor, or would fall if others did not support them. Their bodies begin to twitch as they fall, and some slap the floor with their hands as they lie there. Other participants come to them and cradle them in their arms, or pat their backs as they would pat small children who are ill. Those who go into trance speak in high voices, expressing the desires of their spirits for special objects such as food and jewelry. If any person present has the object desired by the spirit, it is lent to the woman in trance as soon as possible to indicate to her spirit that she will get it as soon as possible. After the woman has expressed the desires of her spirit, she slowly returns to a sitting position. The weekly zar ceremony lasts about three hours and ends when the shaikh ascertains that everyone present had a dance.

There are usually twenty-five to thirty people present at the public zar. None of the participants has a predominant role. Since people come from different villages, they know each other only slightly and there is a relatively low level of socializing.

The other type of zar ceremony that may be called private is held at the house of a possessed person and is arranged especially to meet particular demands of the spirit. This ceremony, referred to as sulha or reconciliation, directs attention to the woman who is holding it. The woman invites all zar participants in the village as well as her friends and kin. Everyone in the village who goes to the zar at all must attend, because if one hears the music and does not dance the spirit will be displeased. Each guest contributes money to the shaikh and his musicians play several songs, so that every person present dances at least once during the evening. The woman who is holding the zar dresses in her best clothes, is especially well groomed, and is called the bride. She may change clothes several times during the evening. The central feature of this ceremony is that late in the evening the shaikh brings a tray containing a cone of sugar, lighted candles, henna, and hard candies into the center of the room. The musicians play the song associated with the bride's spirit, and she dances around the tray holding animals or birds aloft in both hands while other women follow carrying more. The woman's spirit has specified the kind and number of birds or animals. Gradually the musicians lead her toward the oven room, and leave her there with several women who are kin or special friends. She disrobes, climbs into a pan on top of the oven, and one of the women kills the birds and animals so the blood runs over her. She rubs herself well with the blood, dresses, and returns to the main room as the guests gradually disperse.

There is a greater sociability at a private *zar* where all present know one another. The bride and her husband or kin bear the major expenses for musicians, sacrificial animals, sugar, candles, and rose water, which they sprinkle on the guests. A private *zar* may cost several pounds or more, thus minimally it amounts to as much or more than the monthly income of a fellahin household. While it is clearly more difficult for a fellahin family to accumulate funds for a private *zar,* they are held by women in both segments of the population.

The two women presented here show different types of involvement in the *zar* and it seems to have somewhat different meaning for each of them. I knew both of them well, having lived in the house of the first, Aziza, for six months, and the second, Habiba, was my closest village friend and associate during the period of field work. Aziza is a long-term participant in the *zar,* and her belief in her possession pervades her interpretation of her daily activities. She attends only private ceremonies, but seems deeply involved in the experiences of dance and trance. Habiba was a short-term participant in the *zar,* and her mode of participation appeared different. She did not interpret activities outside the context of the *zar* in terms of her possession, except for attributing minor physical problems to the spirit's displeasure. When she attended public *zar* ceremonies, she behaved as if she were going on a pleasurable expedition, and when she held a private *zar* the enjoyable aspects of dressing up and socializing predominated. The two women are like each other and all other women in the village in that they are excluded from public participation in village politics and government, as well as from most Muslim group rituals, since women's religious activity here is confined to private prayers, fastings, and listening to Koranic recitation from a distance. They differ in social position, which has significant effects on some aspects of their behavior and may lead to different kinds of problems to be resolved through the *zar.* Thus Aziza, whose husband is a village leader and considered rich, has little opportunity to develop interests outside her household because she is restricted to her house during the day. She cannot go to public *zars* or about the village to visit other people. Habiba, who is a fellaha, moves continually between her husband's house, that of her mother and her brother, and her neighbors'. She goes about the village freely, as well as on errands to other villages. Additionally, she like other fellahin women has greater authority in the management of household funds. The different experiences that Aziza and Habiba have with the *zar* are rooted in these social and domestic differences as well as in particular features of their personal histories.

Aziza, who was about thirty years old in 1961, had been possessed for about five years and was still possessed in 1965. She was a member of a leading family, her father and dead brother having been village head (umda). She expressed great affection for this older brother who died and for her remaining brother. Strong relationships between brother and sister are not unusual in the village, but that between Aziza and her brothers had been forged in especially difficult circumstances as they grew up. She and her brother described themselves as having had a harsh childhood; they had suffered greatly because their father had married a second wife, divorced their mother, and kept the small children with him. Their stepmother was exceptionally cruel in a role in which no kindness is expected. Incidents such as denial of choice foods to her husband's children, and the imposition of heavy work on them at too young an age are remembered markers in a series of hard years. The stepmother died before Aziza was married, then her father was paralyzed, and Aziza cared for him for the rest of his life. After he died, her younger brother took her on a long visit to Cairo and when she returned she was married to her father's brother's son. She and her husband were much older than most villagers at marriage, and were well disposed toward the match.

In 1961 there was little in Aziza's domestic and family relationships that would seem to generate continuing stress for her. She and her husband lived in one of the best houses in the village with their three sons and daughter. Since her husband hired people to cultivate for him and was also a salaried person, he had much free time and he spent more time talking with his wife than most village husbands of comparable social status. Occasionally he took his wife on trips for pleasure outside the village; on one occasion they went to the wedding of a kinsman in another village, and on another they attended the celebration of a holy man's birthday in another village. At home, Aziza's conversations with her husband showed a fairly equal give and take; she often initiated a topic of conversation with him and was always the more talkative of the two. Their children were still in school, with the exception of the fifteen-year-old son who was restless in secondary school, too young to react against parental authority. Her daughter was old enough to help with housework. The most recent traumatic event in her life was the marriage of her remaining brother to their dead brother's widow. She loved both brothers very much, and this marriage disrupted her relationship with her younger brother. Forewarned of the impending marriage in a dream, she interpreted it as taking something from the dead brother that he could not defend. She did not speak to her remaining brother for a year after his marriage.

Aziza said she became ill soon after her older brother died. She said people came to tell her that he was dead and she ran to his house. She could not cry or scream, but her stomach knotted and she fainted. After that she began to have strange dreams, and in one that has recurred since that time, she sees a black woman who has red hair with white streaks in it, sitting cross-legged and wearing a low-cut white dress. She runs after Aziza in the dream, then Aziza wakes up with a headache.

When Aziza began having these symptoms, her kinswomen and neighbors came to comfort her, and she tried locally available remedies including aspirin and coffee when her headaches were especially severe. Her husband was very concerned and took her to a physician in the district capital several times, but she was not relieved.

Convinced by the recurring dreams that a spirit was possessing her, Aziza went to a *zar* with a cousin and told the shaikh about her headaches and dreams. He explained that the dream of a black woman meant she was possessed by the Sudanese spirit, and recommended that she hold a ceremony of reconciliation (*sulha*) with the spirit for which she should have black drummers and sacrifice a black lamb.

Aziza did not know what to do about this recommendation because her husband had forbidden her to participate in the *zar* as some of their kinswomen did. Her discomfort continued, and she reasoned that she would follow a part of the shaikh's recommendation by making the animal sacrifice but she would not arrange for drummers. She would sacrifice a black lamb at the next feast and rub its blood over her body without making her husband suspicious. She did this and her symptoms subsided for a while. On subsequent feasts she was careful to buy black pigeons in addition to other meat and to kill them as sacrifice to the spirits, although no one knew that she used them in this way.

About a year later, she began to have a great deal of trouble with her stomach again; her dreams and the consequent headaches became more frequent and her legs began to swell. She realized that she would have to meet the other desires of the Sudanese spirit. Her husband was so concerned about her condition that he agreed to her holding a sulha, although he continued to say that he did not believe in spirit possession. After this *zar*, Aziza felt very well for a long period of time, and the shaikh told her that she needed to hold a *zar* only once every four years to satisfy the spirit.

Despite the long periods between her ceremonies, Aziza says she is continually aware of the spirit's presence. She continues to dream about her from time to time, and she feels that she cannot do certain things to beautify herself until she has seen the spirit do so first. She says that she does not put henna on her hands, for example, unless she sees the spirit do so. She says that the spirit has aged since she first saw her and is now almost an old woman. Aziza identifies the spirit with her underground sister and says that when she does not feel well her underground sister is expressing displeasure with her.

Aziza's case shows general characteristics of possession among *zar* goers and particular features that reflect her social position in the village and her role as a rich man's wife. The general characteristics include the concept that the possessing spirit will be appeased with consequent alleviation of her symptoms, and the perception of the origin of possession in a traumatic event. Her seeming identification of the spirit with her underground sister reflects the widespread belief among women especially that a spiritual double of every person is with him from birth, but Aziza was the only person I knew who identified the double with the possessing spirit. She was also the only person I knew whose spirit is a woman. Her social position was reflected in the spirit's demand that she hold private *zars* rather than that she attend the public one regularly. This made it possible for her to maintain the behavior appropriate to her social status by not going out during the day; the demand also reflected her ability to pay the greater expenses of a private *zar*. She also attended other private *zar* ceremonies held in the village. Her husband expressed the pressure the *zar* places on husbands when he said that he had spent 400 pounds to prove that the *zar* cures people. Attention to the sick is an essential means of showing concern for a person here, and it is also a way of demonstrating that one intends them no harm; thus a husband must support his wife's *zar* activity whatever his degree of belief or disbelief.

Zar ceremonies and beliefs are one of the few activities and interests outside the domestic context open to Aziza. The *zar* also offers one way that she can control her husband's behavior to some degree. That he recognized this is indicated by his remark that he had spent 400 pounds proving that *zars* cure people. He could not refuse to allow her to participate, however, because that would have been interpreted as saying he did not care about her health or her. Although Aziza seemed too deeply convinced of her possession for *zar* participation to be a conscious effort on her part to gain specific practical ends, she must have known it had this effect.

Habiba, who lived alone with her second husband, identified herself as a fellaha. She was about twenty-three years old in 1961 and had been going to the zar for about nine months, having started a few months after her second marriage. She had been her mother's favorite child and had been indulged throughout her childhood in the best clothes and food that her mother could afford. As a child she experienced a short period of distress when her mother was married to her stepfather, but this marriage was brief and his harshness was compensated for by her mother's continuing indulgence of her. Habiba's first husband had seemed a fortunate choice because of the socioeconomic position of his family, his youth, and good appearance, but the marriage was a change for her from an indulged status to a deprived one. Habiba and her first husband lived in his father's house, which is usual in the village, and she described her hardships there in some detail. She said that they never gave her enough to eat, yet they made her work hard in the fields. She was so hungry sometimes that she would ask a neighbor in the fields to cook her a piece of corn so she could have something to eat; after the birth of her first child, she was so hungry that she ate the grain which is placed in the tray for the ritual after childbirth. Finally Habiba asked her mother and her brothers to divorce her from her husband because of the harsh way his mother and he treated her. She did not ask to go to the zar during her first marriage because she knew that would have been refused.

Habiba stayed at her brother's house for three months after the divorce, then was married to her present husband who is much older than she. Her life with him contrasts sharply with her first marriage. This old husband, who is bent and stiffened by age and hard work, continually responds to her demands for fresh evidence of his considerations of her. He works on an estate thirty kilometers from the village and returns only once a fortnight, so Habiba has little housework to do and no agricultural work. She spends time with her mother at her brother's house, visits other women, and goes to market or other places with her brother. Like other peasant women, she is not restricted to the house during the day, and has more freedom in her use of time than most because of her husband's absence. In 1961 her major problem was that she had not become pregnant by her second husband, and she attempted to remedy this by all known means though she said she did not use the zar. Habiba, like other peasant women, had discretion in the management of household funds. She also owned a small piece of land which her brothers cultivated, giving her a share. At the end of her first year of marriage she entered into a business partnership with her brother and husband in buying a calf. Her brothers retained authority over her behavior after marriage, and her mother continued to support her in every problem situation with them or her husband.

Habiba went to the public *zar* frequently and danced to the songs associated with the spirit of the ship. Her behavior at the *zar* was never extreme, and she retained a high degree of awareness when showing trance behavior. She was self-conscious about her appearance while dancing because other participants and the shaikh sometimes laughed at each other and Habiba was clumsy, showing little sense of the beat of the music, though in daily life she was considered one of the handsomest women in the village.

Habiba explained that she wore a yellow dress to the *zar* because that pleased the spirit, and she pointed out how beautiful the dress was. She said that she became aware of her possession when she began to move to the music at a *zar,* but she never associated this awareness with a particular traumatic event nor could she give an account of an initial experience of possession. She knew that every person is born with a double but never made an association between the double and the possessing spirit. She also complained of disturbing dreams, although these never featured the spirit.

During the winter Habiba attributed her weekly *zar* participation to her painful wrist; when this was not alleviated, the shaikh suggested that she hold a private *zar* and then the subsequent ceremony at the end of forty days. Habiba's behavior during her preparations for the private *zar* could be best characterized as showing eager anticipation. She asked her husband and her mother for financial help, then invited all the women in the village so that the musicians would not be so expensive. She paid much attention to her clothes for the evening, putting two sets of them in order, admiring them, and anticipating how she would look in them. The purchases of candles, soap, sugar, and sacrificial animals for the occasion were also of engrossing interest for several days. Finally she expended great effort on cooking the meal for the musicians and the last people remaining at the *zar*. She spent the day of the event grooming herself, and during the *zar* she spent most of the evening moving graciously among the women, chatting with them, occasionally dancing, and changing her dress to suit certain songs, thus creating a new appearance. At the end she made the procession with the animals, circling the room seventeen times, then went into the oven room to kill them. In the days following the *zar*, Habiba, her kin, and friends discussed every detail repeatedly. She affirmed that she felt much refreshed by it, though she did not like having dried blood on herself and washed it off before the required week was over. She said that her wrist improved.

Habiba continued to attend the weekly zar after this, but four years later she no longer went, nor did she hold private ceremonies. She explained by saying that spirits do not really possess people, but people go to the zar to enjoy themselves. She continued to attend zars held by friends, to talk with others and listen to the music. By then, Habiba had a daughter by her second husband. She was successfully selling the products of her cow, and her relationship with her husband continued to be peaceful.

For Habiba, the zar seemed to be another way to gain her husband's attention and assert her importance as a wife whose wishes would be respected. Whether she experienced trance remains doubtful, and she never spoke of daily awareness of her spirit. Instead the zar seemed for her to be a recreation, giving pleasures more similar to those of a social gathering then a therapeutic session or religious ritual.

Two aspects of wives' domestic roles that are determined by the social stratum are pertinent to the explanation of Aziza's apparent deeper involvement in the zar and Habiba's early withdrawal from it. One major difference in the respective strata is the patterning of interpersonal activity implicit in the role of wife, a dimension of inquiry to which Arensberg and others have directed attention (Arensberg, 1972, p. 8). Aziza, like other women of high social status, has few opportunities to visit neighbors and none to socialize with them while doing work or errands outside the house because she must stay inside. Thus her pattern of interpersonal activity is sharply limited in terms of whom she may interact with, her opportunities to initiate interaction, and probably the frequency of her interaction with others. Habiba, like other fellahin women, can see and talk with other women in the fields or when she goes about the village on errands, and she visits her mother daily. Her latitude of interaction is increased because of her husband's absence from the village, so she spends more time with her mother or brother in his shop than most women would. The differences in patterning interpersonal activity among the rich and fellahin are not foreshadowed in child-rearing practices. Children in both strata are continually with other persons, first their mothers and then other children, so they seem to interact with others constantly. While rich wives undoubtedly react in varied ways to the constraints on their behavior, the zar is one response that is open to them. It has the immediate effect of increasing their range of interpersonal activity, as it does for all village women.

The differences in the jural and economic relationships of husbands and wives among the rich and the fellahin is the second significant factor in the different *zar* behavior of Aziza and Habiba. In Aziza's household as in other rich homes, financial matters are her husband's province, and this is reflected in her direction of her *zar* activity toward him. It is he who has to pay for her participation, accepting the demands of the spirit for sacrifices, private ceremonies, and Aziza's presence at other *zar* ceremonies in the village. This is the only sphere of her activity her husband does not control. He holds the funds of the household, manages her land, and she goes out only with his permission. Since authority over Aziza's behavior was conveyed to him at her marriage, rather than remaining with her brother, she cannot maneuver between the two of them in a conflict situation. Her institutionalized means of attaining her desires if they diverge from her husband's are the weapons of the subordinate, which include persuasion, sulking, cooking poorly, and relying on his concern for her well-being. In using any of these weapons, she lacks the immediate support of public opinion because of her relative isolation within her house. Aziza's role as a rich wife not only decreases her range of interaction outside the household but also focuses her resources on her husband. While the *zar* gives her an additional interest and enlarges her sphere of interpersonal activity, it also offers a means of modifying her husband's behavior. Such uses of the *zar* have also been noted in other reports. This relationship between *zar* activity and social status tends to be confirmed by the fact that most of the rich women in the village are involved with the *zar*.

Habiba, like other fellahin women, managed household funds and was beginning to establish her independent source of income through her partnership in owning an animal. Authority over her was retained by her brother when she married, and her husband had to refer disputes between them to her brother. Habiba had to ask her husband's permission to go out only when the expedition was an unusual one. Her mother was always her ally in any dispute with her brother or husband, and she sometimes enlisted one of the latter against the other. Something of the continued significance of her family or orientation is suggested by the fact that her mother as well as her husband gave funds for her *zar*. For Habiba, the *zar* seemed to be a way of testing and savoring the improvement in her marriage situation with her second husband. It served also to show the community the contrast between her previous situation as a deprived wife and her present treatment as an indulged one, even though her husband was old. *Zar* ceremonies were occasions for dressing up, a chance to hear music and dance, and provided an opportunity to play a central role at her private *zar*. Since Habiba's use of the *zar* did not derive from the long-term definition of her role, she withdrew as the managerial and mothering activities in her life demanded more time and attention. Years earlier her mother had followed the same course. She participated in the *zar* after she had been married for a few years and had children, but after her husband died and she became responsible for the financial maneuvering necessary to arrange her children's marriages, she withdrew completely, later attending occasionally for amusement.

I. M. Lewis has shown that there is a higher incidence of possession among women in societies that exclude them from social, religious, and political affairs, and that peripheral possession cults are essentially protest movements against dominant men that enable women to gain their ends by oblique means (Lewis, 1971, pp. 30–31, 85–92). The cases of Aziza and Habiba suggest that in such societies women whose roles are most limited are most likely to be deeply involved in possession cults. In Kafr al Hana, these are women in the higher social stratum. Although all women are excluded from public political and religious activities, fellahin women are less subject to their husbands in economic matters and in daily activity. They also have greater opportunity to maneuver in social relations, since authority over them remains with their families of orientation.

The different ways in which the two women participate in the *zar* reflect its different social functions. On the most overt level, it functions as a curing society. Beyond that it may provide sociability in a place where large gatherings are few, loneliness is abhorred, and interaction highly valued. It also offers the pleasure of dressing up to make a fine appearance, music which is appreciated but not heard regularly, the lights of candles, and the fragrance of rose water. In addition, it is one of the few group religious rituals open to women. In sum, the multiple functions of the *zar* permit women to react to it as a therapy, religious experience, or party, while using it for different ends in specific relationships.

NOTES

1. The field work on which this paper is based was done under the auspices of the Social Research Center, American University at Cairo. Sohair Mehanna al-Attawi of American University at Cairo, my co-worker, had a major role in research. I also thank Dr. Nadia Attif who helped me with an earlier version of this chapter and Dr. Diana Brown who helped me revise it.

2. The term *shaikh* is used to refer to a respected older man, a religious leader, or a specialist in magic.

REFERENCES

ARENSBERG, CONRAD.

1972   "Culture as Behavior: Structure and Emergence." *Annual Review of Anthropology,* **1:** 1–26.

BARCLAY, HAROLD.

1964   *Buurri al Lamaab: A Suburban Village in the Sudan.* Ithaca: Cornell University Press.

FAKHOURI, HANI.

1968   "The Zar Cult in an Egyptian Village," *Anthropological Quarterly* **41:** 49–56.

KENNEDY, JOHN.

1967   "Nubian Zar Ceremonies as Psychotherapy." *Human Organization* **26:** 185–194.

LEWIS, I. M.

1971   *Ecstatic Religion: An Anthropological Study of Spirit Possession and Shamanism.* Middlesex, England: Pelican Books.

MESSING, SIMON.

1958   "Group Therapy and Social Status in the Zar Cult of Ethiopia." *American Anthropologist* **60:** 1120–1126.

Alice Morton

Dawit: Competition and Integration In an Ethiopian Wuqabi Cult Group

Spirit possession is an option taken up by Ethiopians of many ethnic groups in their efforts to solve novel, as well as recurring, persistent, and complex personal and interpersonal problems. Many of the problems regarded as best dealt with in terms of possession and other kinds of spirit-related activity concern illness, but other sorts of problems are thought to be amenable to solution in these terms as well. Possession is both a traditional and a contemporary option for problem solving, frequently adopted by modern urban dwellers as well as by rural traditionalists. There are a variety of institutionalized possession cults in Ethiopia as well as a considerable incidence of individual possession in the domestic sphere, outside the context of organized possession cult groups (*wadağa*).

193

This case study concerns a man, Dawit, who was highly involved with possession in one small cult group.[1] Over a period of time, his involvement with this group and its leader became so great that he was effectively cut off from participation in the wider social field. Yet, throughout, his role within the group was problematic. As the case history shows, he passed through various stages of competition with other adepts, with the leader of the cult group, and finally—as the result of a lingering illness—came to be integrated into the group at a new level. Although this material could be treated in a variety of ways, the discussion which follows the presentation of the case will concentrate on the competitive and integrative aspects of the case.

WUQABI POSSESSION

The *wuqabi* cult is only one of the cults present in Addis Ababa and in the rest of central Ethiopia, although it is perhaps the most widespread, drawing members from most ethnic groups, both Christian and Muslim. The cult is organized around a set of beliefs in the power of spirits called *wuqabi* by cult members, and *zar* by outsiders (Lewis, 1971; Morton, 1973). These spirits are peripheral to the pantheon of Ethiopian Orthodox Christianity, although they are believed to be the creations of the Christian God. They are invisible, omniscient, capricious, and recalcitrant, and are thought to inhabit the ether over the whole Ethiopian Empire.

Their social organization mirrors that of earthly Ethiopians—some of them are Christians and some Muslims; others are Amhara, and still others are Galla, Tigrean, Somali, or Gurage. Their occupations—soldier, judge, priest, farmer, servant—are ranked in a hierarchy which resembles the mundane social structure.

It is believed that although these spirits are basically amoral, they may, if carefully courted and honored, be engaged by the possessed person in a mutually beneficial relationship of accommodation initiated (by the spirit) through the mode of affliction, but transformed into a condition of regularized, latent possession (in the person). Through this process of accommodation the spirit is persuaded to cease being amoral and potentially dangerous and to become benign. Accommodation relationships of this kind are usually arranged and mediated by possessed healers (*bale wuqabi*) who, through their own experience of possession by one or more of these spirits over a long period of time, are believed to have developed special expertise in dealing with the whole class of *wuqabi* spirits.

Although the *bale wuqabi* is seen as knowing more about these spirits than do the newly possessed, there is never a presumption that a *bale wuqabi* can achieve complete mastery over his or her own possessing spirits or over those possessing others. The *bale wuqabi* is vastly more skilled at dealing with spirits than are others, but is not in a definitive sense a master of spirits. In time, however, such a person is considered to develop special status vis-à-vis the whole class of *wuqabi,* thus gaining access to authority over other possessed individuals and their spirits based on the presumption of this special status.

Each named *wuqabi* spirit may have an infinite number of refractions. Thus each spirit can possess any number of human beings at will, and each possessing refraction may make slightly different demands for services and other behavior on the part of the possessed. Still, all refractions of a named *wuqabi* share a certain set of idiosyncratic tastes, preferences, and desires, so that there is said to be some consistency, for example, in the offerings that should be made to the many refractions of one spirit, or in the kinds of trance behaviors that the spirit will call forth in its "horses." To some extent these regularities permit the possessed healer to identify the spirit afflicting a newly possessed individual.

Insofar as it is a key concept in the ideology of *wuqabi* possession that these spirits are capricious and fundamentally unknowable, such regularities are regarded as mutable; any *wuqabi* refraction is likely to "change its mind," and begin to make new demands, or elicit new and unpredictable behaviors in the posessed person, as well as visiting the possessed with new kinds of afflictions. This unpredictability of the spirits is used as a major explanatory device when carefully negotiated relationships of accommodation between the possessed and the possessing spirit break down. Such breakdowns then are not necessarily always considered to be failures on the part of the possessed to live up to the terms of the agreement or on the part of the *bale wuqabi* to negotiate the compact properly.

According to the ideology of the cult, once a refraction of a *wuqabi* spirit begins to possess someone, the individual has no recourse but to accommodate the spirit. Possession is instigated by the spirits; people cannot choose spirits and cannot choose to be possessed. Similarly, only the spirit can decide to cease possessing a given person, and it is believed that this almost never happens. Initially the spirit indicates its interest in possessing an individual through the mode of illness or some other variety of affliction, to get his or her attention and to ascertain that its intentions will be taken seriously. In order that the affliction be redressed, the spirit must be honored by special offerings in ceremonies held at stated intervals. Ideally if such an arrangement is worked out quickly, the individual will recover from the affliction and the spirit, if treated well enough over time, will in turn come to protect the individual from the predations of a variety of evil spirits.

Ultimately, if the accommodation relationship is successful and maintained by both parties, it is believed that the individual will profit insofar as the spirit helps him or her to vanquish enemies, to make the right choices in a wide range of situations, and to predict the behavior of others. The person who is possessed by a satisfied *wuqabi* is supposed to become healthy, wealthy, and wise.

Primarily this idea of the inevitability of possession, and thus the need to regularize it through the establishment of an accommodation relationship, distinguishes *wuqabi* possession from "attacks" by other kinds of spirits, especially by several classes of evil spirits: *aganint, saytan,* and *ǧinn.* Whereas these malign spirits can eventually be exorcised or anathematized, *wuqabi* are impervious to such techniques and, to my knowledge, they are never tried once *wuqabi* possession has been diagnosed. This then is most characteristic of beliefs about *wuqabi* possession rather than the belief that a relationship with a possessing spirit can be profitable.

Although individuals can and do make arrangements with evil spirits that are said initially to be to their advantage, this is clearly regarded as immoral and sinful. It is also thought to be extremely dangerous, and the longer the relationship lasts the more likely it is that the spirit will visit terrible lasting afflictions on those who have contracted with it for special mystical powers. A similar toll is not believed to be exacted by accommodated *wuqabi* spirits which, as was mentioned earlier, are eventually thought to be rendered benign by the process of accommodation and turned into supporters of the moral and normative in human behavior generally.

It is important to note, however, that individuals are by no means always content to be possessed by these potentially benign and helpful spirits, and most of the case histories I collected in the field reflected this feeling. Individuals who had been adepts in *wuqabi* cult groups for as long as twenty years often indicated that they had tried at various intervals to escape from their possessing spirits. Either they changed cult groups, in the hope that a more effective *bale wuqabi* would be able to find alternate diagnoses for their ailments, or they refused to honor their obligations to the spirits altogether. However, according to these informants, such strategies were not successful. The spirits always "caught" them again, often visiting them with ever more severe illnesses until they were willing to honor their obligations, often at more inflated levels.

There is a real social, as well as financial, cost to being possessed, unless the possessed individual is able to become a professional healer. Such healer status is both financially and psychologically remunerative, and a successful *bale wuqabi* may become an important member of the local community. Although still regarded by the majority of the non-possessed as morally suspect, a successful possessed healer is regarded as a force to be reckoned with.

An individual who has remained an adept for a number of years, serving the spirits by serving the *bale wuqabi*, is in a markedly different position. Serving the spirits is costly in terms of time, emotional commitment, and money. The longer an individual is a cult adept, the greater the likelihood that he or she will become possessed by more and more spirits, and each spirit will require a range of services and offerings that are expensive in terms of money and time. While multiple possession is a sign of status within the cult, if this status cannot be enhanced sufficiently to lead to increased authority as an assistant leader, it is a losing game. Further, the greater the commitment of the adept to possession-related activities, the greater is his or her commitment to the *bale wuqabi* leader. If one successful cure has been worked by the healer, the adept is thought to owe the healer and his or her spirits a lifelong debt of gratitude. If a cure has not been successful, the adept will tend to act upon the belief that more must be done for the healer and his or her spirits in the hope that a cure will finally be achieved.

Thus, while it may be accurate analytically to point up the benefits of adept status in terms of increased ability to get the attention of others, increased access to special kinds of support, and the choices that adept status offers the individual for opting out of a wide range of "normal" social commitments, there are costs as well. It has been argued in the literature on possession in Ethiopia that by becoming cult adepts, women are providing themselves with a means for leaving their husbands, the traditional deprived status they have as wives in male-dominated households and as women in a male-dominated society (Lewis, 1971). However, it is also true that women, and some male adepts as well, once they are cut off from their spouses, children, kin and friends, are very much at the mercy of the leaders of the cult groups to which they belong. Since possession by *wuqabi* is not considered to be sinful or shameful, this might appear to be a contradiction. However, the contradiction is more apparent than real.

While possession by *wuqabi* is not shameful—it is not thought to be the fault of the possessed, and in any event, these spirits are not malign ones—it is expensive. Once the possessed has made demands for money, tolerance, and other kinds of support for the spirits from his or her spouse, immediate family, and others whose support can be mobilized, but still shows no signs of "normality," these people tend to consign the possessed to the cult, refusing to continue to accept the fact that the ante is always likely to be raised. The spouse may divorce the possessed "because of the spirits," take the children, and leave the possessed essentially well enough alone. The nuclear family will be reluctant to shelter the possessed since, if they do, they too will have to continue to pay for the involvement with the spirits and the cult. If the possessed moves to another area, it will soon become known that he or she is possessed, and the same problems of access to support may continue.

The possessed is then forced to rely increasingly on the other members of the cult group, and especially on the leader around whom the group is organized, since the other adepts are probably in a similar situation, and have little surplus money, time, or attention to devote to the problems of others. In these ego-centered *wadağa* groups, the relationship of each member to the leader is far more crucial than the relationships among the adepts. Although several adepts often go to live at the home of the *bale wuqabi* leader at the same time, they compete with each other for attention, and are less like the members of a corporate group or a voluntary association than like jealous siblings vying for the affection and attention of a parent.

In this context, individual adepts may become involved in new situations of dependence which may be even more binding than those they were initially involved in outside the cult group. Although there are sanctions that can be used against spouses or kin and affines if they become exaggeratedly exploitative, the *bale wuqabi* who exploits his or her group members in an extreme fashion, while subject to desertion by them, always has the power and authority of the spirits to back up his or her actions. Usually this authority can only be brought into question by questioning the leader's claim to possession by high-ranking *wuqabi*. Since this rarely occurs, however, the authority of the *bale wuqabi* is, for cult adepts, a kind of final authority (Knutsson, 1967; Morton, 1975). Thus participation in a cult group as an adept can lead to a situation of increased dependence, rather than create a venue for self assertion and independence or for status enhancement.

THE FIRST SETTING

It is nearly impossible to tell from outside the walls of a compound in Addis Ababa what sort of people live within it, whether they are Amhara or Galla, rich or poor, many or few. Mama Azaletch's compound was no exception; only at night, when one could hear the drumming and singing in honor of the spirits, was there any observable difference between her compound and those around it. Located in a typical neighborhood of Addis close to the center of town, the compound is more accessible than some. It faces a paved road near a much-used bridge, and is directly opposite a government high school, but it looks undistinguished from the outside. The walls, which are of mud mixed with straw, buckle here and there. The corrugated iron gate is poorly installed and often hangs ajar.

There are only two structures within the enclosure—a rectangular dwelling house divided into three sections, and an animal shelter. Both structures are situated in the far corner of the compound, so that the rest of the area, overgrown with sparse grass, appears larger than it actually is. Only two of the three sections of the house are occupied, and one can see into the third empty one in passing. The whole house looks dilapidated.

Across from the house, toward the opposite wall of the compound, is a stand of eucalyptus trees bordering a ravine. In the middle of the compound, under a large shade tree, a local priest gives reading classes to a small group of children. Aside from this group, there are few people visible in the compound. Usually two or three women, clustered in front of the door to the first section of the house, drink coffee or converse with those inside the house. They may occasionally have to shoo away several chickens scratching around morosely in the compound. Sometimes they take shelter from the sun under the roof of the animal shelter, as there are never any sheep or goats in it.

The residents of this compound are Mama Azaletch, her grandson, Haile, his wife, and their small daughter. Azaletch lives in the first section of the house, and Haile and his family live in the one adjoining hers. Also sharing Mama's part of the house, rather than living in the third, empty section, are Dawit and his eight-year-old son, Habte. Other people may come to stay for a day, a week, or a month, but these six people are the core of the residential unit which is bounded by the walls of the compound. Mama pays the rent for the entire place. The rent is very low, however, as there are no modern conveniences of any sort—no running water, electricity, or latrines. Mama meets the rent from the proceeds of her work as a *bale wuqabi*. This is also the fund from which she contributes to the support of Haile and his family, and Dawit and his son. She has no other income, and Haile only works part-time because he is in high school.

During the day, Mama holds consultations for the women of the neighborhood who come with their problems, asking her to call upon the spirits to intervene in their behalf. Although these women solicit her help and advice for a variety of problems, primarily they involve harrassing quarrels with other women, worrisome situations concerning health of their children and husbands, trying issues connected with work or lack of it, with love, and with successfully anticipating threatening future events. Usually each woman brings with her an offering of coffee, incense, or perfume, or twenty-five or fifty cents. This payment is offered to the spirits, and is accepted by Mama.

Dawit also shares Mama's consultations from time to time. He offers a somewhat different range of comment and advice which, when it contradicts that given by Mama, is thought to derive from the difference in identity and attitude of their respective possessing spirits. Rarely offerings are given directly to him in connection with their joint consultations. Those who come to have their dreams interpreted are more likely to ask outright for Dawit, and to give their offerings to him. Dream interpretation is something he and his spirit are thought to do better than Mama and her spirits.

Both men and women who come for consultations of this kind during the day are rarely invited into the house. Instead, they carry on their conversations with Mama and Dawit from outside. If they cannot be heard, one of the women who comes regularly to serve the spirits will act as a "repeater" (aggafari). This woman stands in the doorway and is often asked to restate remarks from both parties to the consultation. It is believed that since such a person, an adept in the wadağa group, is familiar with the likes and dislikes of the two bale wuqabi and their possessing spirits, she will be able to state people's cases more effectively than they could themselves.

Only adepts or other bale wuqabi are allowed into the house because it is the house (mosqet) of the spirits, who will be angered if people who haven't observed the ritual prescriptions of the cult are permitted to enter.

At the wadağa meetings, which are held five nights a week by this group, anyone who is allowed to enter the house must have observed the entrance rules during the entire preceding week. These rules prohibit the eating of certain foods, sexual intercourse, contact with the dead or with those who have attended funerals, quarreling, or other kinds of unseemingly behavior. Typically, at Mama's wadağas, only the five or six most experienced and devoted adepts—those who come also in the daytime to clean the house, boil coffee, and otherwise serve Mama and the spirits—are allowed to participate in the ceremony from inside the house. The others sit outside, clustered around the door or, if it rains, sheltering under the lean-to meant for animals. Usually ten to fifteen people participate from outside in this way. Some of them are less serious adepts; others have been told during consultations in the daytime that they must come to the *wadaǧa* for their cases to be heard directly by the spirits when they descend upon the *bale wuqabi*, who then become entranced. Occasionally they are joined by one of the devoted adepts who has broken a rule during the week and is hoping to escape notice by remaining outside the house.

MAMA AZALETCH

Mama is an Amhara and an Orthodox Christian.[2] She is an imposing woman, tall, large-boned, and slender. She always stands very erect, avoiding the slightly bent posture of many Amhara women who appear always to be on the verge of bowing. Her heavily lined face is usually framed by a red headscarf; underneath the scarf, her head is shaved. She wears an abundance of heavy silver jewelry of the type associated with poor peasants who cannot afford finer gold filigree work. She often wears tattered and rumpled clothes, especially when she is staying around the compound all day. Yet she manages by her very presence to make it seem as if she is dressed in the finest handwoven white cloth bordered with colorful embroidery; actually she has quite a store of these traditional national dresses as well as some more colorful "modern" dresses which she wears especially for the spirits. When Mama is attired in one of these outfits, she is immensely dignified and strikingly attractive. Although she appears to be a venerable sixty or so, it is likely that she is probably only about forty-five.

Mama says that she was born in Bale province, the daughter of an Amhara *neftegna* (soldier-colonist) who had been sent to that remote Galla area by Emperor Menelik II, in the late 1800s, during the last period of Menelik's expansion of colonial rule. She says that her father, a friend of the Emperor, was half Amhara from Gondar town and half Tigrean. Her mother, she says, was a beautiful Wolloyé woman from Yeddju in Wollo province, of a Muslim family. The mother became a Christian when she married Mama's father. Her family, according to Mama, held this against her. Curiously, Mama claims that she herself became a Christian only when she was possessed by *wuqabi*. Sometimes she says that one reason why she is ill, that is, possessed by these spirits, is because her mother's family is trying to get her to become a Muslim again, and has sent the spirits to trouble her. She continues her story:

In 1936, I was caught by a certain spirit. I ran away from my home in Bale to the desert, and there I lived in a cave. I would not see anyone or speak to anyone, and I became very wild. But there was one woman of high rank there who was interested in my case, and she would send her son to bring me beans and unsalted bread. I stayed there in that place, eating very little, and seeing no one, for four years and eight months. If they had tried to take me from that cave and put me in a house with other people, I would have broken any bonds and escaped back to the desert. It was the spirit that made me wild that way. This spirit still comes upon me sometimes, and then I have to throw off all my clothes and run outside, from the house and from the town.

Eventually I came back to myself, and to people. Then I came to live in Addis Ababa, and I was better for a time. Before that, I lived on the lands of Taye, of Arussi province, who had lands in Bale too. That is why I know him and his power. But when I came to Addis, the spirits still wouldn't leave me, and I would still jump and shout. That was around the time of the Italians [1936–1941]. And my husband grew tired of it. He is still alive, and he lives in Addis also. He was a hunter before we came here, but now he works at the slaughterhouse. I never see him, but I know where he is and what he does.

Once I tried to get rid of the spirits, after my first husband had left me. I went to Wolisso, to the place of the famous priest who cures people, [3] and I stayed there for seven days. And he said that I would be cured. That was nine years ago. At that time I was married, and I wore a lot of gold jewelry, and I chewed chat[4] more than I do now. That priest told me that I must put aside my gold and that I must not chew chat, and that I must not jump and shout when the spirits came, and that I would be cured if I did these things. But it was no good, and the spirits stayed with me.

This story of her life was told to us by Mama in public as well as in private. It is a highly stereotyped version of the possession career, especially insofar as it includes a flight into the wild, fasting in the desert, and renunciation of normal contact with family and others. The ineluctable nature of the possession itself is also presented in a highly stereotyped fashion. Unlike Dawit's story which follows, this tale resembles many other life histories of possessed individuals that were collected by us in the field.

Mama Azaletch often complained of the hardships which she had been subjected to because she was possessed. One of her bitterest complaints at the time we knew her was that the students from the local high school across the road from the compound would throw stones at her and at her house, and that they would come to the wadağas, at first saying they wanted the help of the spirits, but then causing trouble and angering the spirits. She said that she had told the police about the harrassment, but remarked that one had to be careful of the police because some people claimed the holding *wadaǧa* meetings was illegal. Actually a local police private was often to be found outside the gate of the compound when a *wadaǧa* was in progess, and it is possible that he was being payed some sort of protection, since he certainly never intervened in the meetings.[5]

At other times she would complain about her poverty and about being cut off from "normal" people. She said that if she had been able to keep a husband, now that she was old she would have someone to look after her, and would not always be worrying about money. She was worried about Haile, her grandson, who was about twenty years old, but still attending high school. She felt that he could use more money if only she could provide it. She was also worried about Haile's mother, her daughter, who lived in Debre Berhan in northern Shoa, and worked for a foreign family. During our contact with Mama, this daughter lost her job, as the foreigners went back home, and Mama then tried to send money to her as well.

Quite often, Mama was also clearly troubled about Dawit. She was very fond of him, as we shall see, and regarded him as her most devoted follower, as well as her most successful cure. The fact that she shared her house with him, despite the insinuating remarks of some of her neighbors and also, apparently, of some of the members of the *wadaǧa* group, may be interpreted in a number of ways. Although it is entirely possible, and though people hinted that it was the case, I doubt that Dawit had ever been her lover, and it seemed unlikely that he was her lover at the time we knew them. Most of the time she seemed to treat him like a spoiled and favored son. She certainly retained her status as head of the household and, as far as we could ascertain, had complete control over the money that both of them solicited from their clients. It was, at least in the beginning of our contact with them, her house, her compound, and her *wadaǧa* group. Apparently she was willing to share all of this with Dawit and to look after his young son, but she seemed quite clearly to wish to retain her position of authority and command.

DAWIT

Dawit, a man in his late twenties, is, like Mama, an Orthodox Christian. He is at least half Amhara. He is very thin, fine-boned, and of medium

height. By Ethiopian standards he is quite handsome, with the me-
dium-brown complexion admired by Amhara. He is very careful of his
appearance, and always wears clean clothes, preferably new ones.
Sometimes he dresses like a traditional Christian priest, with his long
hair enveloped in a white turban. Like a Christian hermit, he never
cuts his hair. This is also a trait associated with men who are possessed.
At other times, he wears the Somali cloth skirt and the colored turban
associated by Ethiopian Christians with Muslims, as well as with all
kinds of spirit-possessed healers. When he puts on this outfit, he wears
one gold earring, Muslim prayer beads around his neck, and always
something red. Invariably, he is clean-shaven and neat.

People in the neighborhood are afraid of Dawit. They make up accusations about him, saying that he is not really possessed at all. Some
say he is one of those who has made a deal with various evil spirits.
They accuse him of sleeping with the women in Mama's *wadağa*
group, and there are those who insist that he is Mama's lover as well.

He had been living in this compound for several years, but it was
hard to find anyone in the vicinity who knew him well or claimed to.
The people said that, like most *bale wuqabi*, he kept himself to himself
at home, and let the members of the group bring him news of others'
affairs. Nonetheless, these same people seemed to feel that he was a
bad neighbor (though they rarely said this of Mama), a potentially dangerous man, and someone to be avoided. This was true both of informants who liked Mama, and believed that she had some real mystical
power because of the *wuqabi*, and of those who thought that she was a
bit crazy and that most *bale wuqabi* were frauds.

Members of the *wadağa* group itself also appeared to be afraid of
Dawit, particularly of his moodiness. Although this moodiness was attributed to the spirits, and was actually one of the pieces of evidence
that the adepts used to substantiate their belief that he was possessed by
wuqabi, it was at the same time regarded by them as extreme and potentially dangerous. They implied that he could not be relied upon to
behave in an appropriate fashion, either under normal circumstances
or when his spirit had descended upon him and he was in trance.

As for Dawit himself, he was certainly not outgoing, and appeared to
cultivate this image of himself as unpredictable and both personally
and mystically dangerous. From the start, he was against our participation in the rituals of the group, and advised Mama either to keep us
away or to charge us exorbitant sums for the privilege of asking questions and watching what was going on. In time he changed his attitude,
eventually complaining that we did not pay enough attention to him
and to his spirit. When we in turn began trying once again to converse

with him and to ask him about his life and his spirit, he became extremely coy and seemed to enjoy teasing us with little bits of information, refusing to provide any complete information about himself. Later in the year, when he became very ill, he changed his attitude enough to ask our help in sponsoring his cure. Even then, however, he was unwilling to tell us his life story, although he was often present when others in the group, especially Mama, related various versions of it. What follows is the most complete version, told to us by Mama, with comment and additions from other women in the group who could remember when he first came to see them.

This version was related to us at least twice when Dawit was not present: once it was told by Mama when several of the women adepts were there; another time it was told by the eldest woman adept when no one else was there. It is not like the stereotyped stories of most possessed informants. However, this version does resemble that told to newcomers to the *wadaǧa* group and to the group as a whole on the occasion when Dawit's claim to authority was in dispute. On these latter occasions, Dawit was present. While it is true that the version of Dawit's initial encounter with the group that follows is standardized, there is reason to believe that the facts it relates are essentially true.

Dawit's grandmother had a stepdaughter. He lived in the same house with his parents and with this woman in Betcha, where he was born. Everything was fine, and he worked at the local cotton factory, saving money by living with his family. He had a young woman whom he was going to marry. She is the mother of Habte, but they never married in the end.

Once, someone came to the parents and accused Dawit of sleeping with his aunt. The family was very suspicious about it and confronted them, but they both denied it strenuously. Still the family was suspicious, and though they allowed him and the aunt to live with them, they wouldn't give either of them as much as a cup of coffee. They both begged them, and said again that it was not true, and asked who had accused them. But this did no good. The family said that they knew the truth, that it could not be otherwise, and they would not believe Dawit or the aunt.

Finally, it was too much. Dawit decided to leave, and he wanted his aunt to leave also. He was almost crazy with anger, and he thought he would throw himself in the river. Or else he would go far away, to Arussi province, where no one would know him and his shame. But in the end he decided to come to Addis Ababa, to stay with the children of his aunt. She did not come with him, but the children took him in to live with them.

He was all right in Addis, and they treated him well. But no one could tell him who had accused him of this crime, and he would brood about it. Some people in the neighborhood, who had heard his story, told him that he could find out who had accused him if he went to see a *bale wuqabi* called Tadesse, who lived in another part of Addis and was very powerful. Through the spirits, he would be able to find the answer to his question.

He went to that place to look for this Tadesse, but he could not find his house. He wandered all the day, asking people for him, but they didn't know Tadesse at all. Finally, at night, he was still looking, and he heard the drums at Mama's house. He asked the people there what it was, and they told him that it was Mama Azaletch, and that she had the spirits, and that perhaps she could help him. He said that he didn't care if she was not Tadesse, so long as she could answer his question, and he went in.

Up to this point, the account is fairly straightforward. Dawit, a literate young man, part Amhara, part Galla, living in a Galla area of Shoa province, is apparently well on the way to integrating himself into the local modernizing sector. He has a factory job, and is presumably saving money to get married. However, he is accused—rightly or wrongly—of committing incest, one of the worst of all traditional offenses. It is important that in this case, the traditional Christian definition of incest obtains, proscribing sexual relationships and marriage with anyone to whom one is related through seven ascending and descending generations, even including stepchildren of one's grandparents or of one's parents or, in fact even any siblings of those stepchildren who may not have beeen accepted into the same household (Morton, 1973). While it is not clear from the account whether the "stepdaughter" of Dawit's grandmother was actually his mother's own half-sister, this is not significant. If he had slept with his mother's own half-sister, it would have been worse, but even if the woman had a different father and mother, the fact that she was socially recognized as Dawit's mother's sibling makes it bad enough, and incestuous enough.

What is less clear from the story, as well as from subsequent accounts given by group members, is whether the accusation was justified. However, this is not crucial, as Dawit's main wish was to identify his accuser in order to confront him or her, and seemingly he wanted to use such a confrontation to get this person to retract the accusation, and also to exact some sort of retribution. Given stories of equivalent cases of incest accusations, Dawit may well have wanted to kill this person, or at least give him or her a violent beating. In any event, it is Dawit's enlisting the help of the spirits in his attempt to discover who had accused him of incestuous behavior that becomes crucial rather than, for example, a desire to prove his innocence.

When Dawit came to Mama's house, it was a Friday, and he found them having *wadağa*. When Mama's spirit asked him who he was, and why he was there,

Dawit told the story of his problem in Betcha, but maintained that he had been falsely accused. He asked the spirits to help him to find the identity of his accuser. But Mama's spirit objected, saying, "You did not come to see me, to beg me, you came looking for Tadesse." So Dawit kissed the ground, and said, "Yes, it is true, my master, but if you help me it is the same, if only I come to know who accused me. If you help me, I will boil coffee for you and I will serve you." But the spirit said, "Those men who serve me must be virgins, or my servants should be maidens, or old women or old men. So how could you serve me? Those who serve me must wash themselves and be clean. They must not go here and there, or be restless. Otherwise, they will become ill." And Dawit wept, and once again fell down and kissed the ground, and said that if Mama and the spirit helped him, he would do anything that they asked. And so the spirit relented, and now he has been here, serving the spirits for eight years, just like a woman.

At some point during these eight years spent at Mama's home, serving the spirit, Dawit was defined as possessed. It was decided by Mama and her spirit that he was possessed by the spirit *Mute Arba,* who is said to live in Guna, in Arussi. This is a male spirit and a Muslim, who likes the desert life, and is a giver of just decisions whether the client is rich or poor. *Mute Arba* is also said to distribute the money it receives from the possessed among the poor. It speaks in a strange voice, and wears a turban on its head (i.e., it causes these things in its "horse"). Apparently this spirit is believed to be more closely associated with the cult of *Gifti Arussi* [6] than are some other *wuqabi* spirits, which may be relevant to what follows.

In some ways Dawit was treated by all the members of the group as though he were the oldest, best-loved, and most important of the adepts. Even those women adepts who admitted to being afraid of him because of his moods and his harshness as a judge during the judgement phase of the *wadaǧa* ceremonies often said that he should be excused because he was sad and had suffered many injustices in the past. Less explicitly they seemed to indicate that he suffered, being constrained to act in an extremely circumscribed manner because of his involvement with the spirits, and as Mama's subordinate. It is not "normal," they implied, for a vigorous, handsome young man to be celibate or to have to defer to the will of an older woman who is neither his relative, his employer, or his landlord.

Yet in other contexts, and especially when outsiders were there, Dawit was treated like Mama's equal in leadership and sometimes— when it was his spirit that had descended and not hers—he was accorded more deference and respect than she. In the domestic situation, at least when we were the only strangers present, he was sometimes paid court by all of the women who came to visit and to work for the spirits. They tended to treat him as they would any other Ethiopian male who was a head of household, in terms of the personal services they performed for him, until Mama would remind them that they were there to serve the spirits and that they had other work to do. In terms of the respect accorded to him by those in and closely associated with the group, he clearly had much more authority than did Haile, Mama's grandson. It was difficult, however, for us to judge the nature of the relationship between these two men, since the latter kept to himself in his part of the house most of the time when Dawit was at home and awake, and never appeared at any of the *wadaǧa* meetings.

Habte, Dawit's son, was treatd by Mama and the group members the way that traditional Amhara treat foster children; that is, as something between an own child and a young servant. They told us that Mama was paying for him to go to "night school," but he must have gone only rarely, as he appeared never to miss any of the *wadaǧa* meetings. Though he always attended, and clapped and sang with vigor, he was largely ignored by the adults at these and other times.

It was hard for us to get Dawit's son to talk about himself or about his father. Partly this was because it is generally regarded as inappropriate to question a child; children of such a young age are thought to have little of importance to say. Partly, however, it was because Habte seemed to feel that we represented a danger to his father, and thus he said very little to us. He did tell us, however, that he believed that spirits and possession by them were a sickness, and that his father was very sick with it, as we could see. He offered that he himself was not possessed, and that his mother was not, so far as he knew. Of his mother he said very little only that she still lived in Betcha, and that although he missed her, he preferred to live with his father in Addis.

One of the main services that Dawit, being literate (unlike some ninety-five percent of the Ethiopian population at that time), provided to clients and adepts, other than the interpretation of dreams, was writing various kinds of "papers" for them. This, together with his occasional Christian priest's dress, made some people in the area think that he was a *däbtära,* an unordained church functionary who specializes in spells and amulets. Yet both Dawit and Mama always told new clients that amulets were useless or even bad, and that they were also forbidden by the government. They declared that once a client had started trying to solve his problems by going to a *däbtära,* it muddled things with the spirits, and a successful solution would then be much more difficult to achieve. On the other hand, Dawit and Mama were not against clients seeking the advice of other possessed healers, "since the spirits are the same." In fact, their professional rivalry seemed only to extend to specialists who claimed different kinds of mystical power than theirs. They would occasionally refer a client to another *bale wuqabi*, and seemed not to think that in this way they were helping the "competition."

Over a period of four months, we went to visit Mama and Dawit at least twice a week, once during the daytime consultations and again at night, to participate in the *wadaǧa* meetings. During this period, however, we saw relatively little of Dawit, except when he was in trance at night. Even though he stayed mainly within the compound during the day, he maintained his distance from us as well as from the members of the group. Sometimes, we were told, he would go out to collect rent on a house that he owned somewhere in Addis, but no one could or would tell us anything about how he and acquired this house, or why he didn't live there instead of staying on with Mama.

Much of the time he spent at home, Dawit spent in bed or behind the curtain in the main room of the part of the house he shared with Mama. He was often extremely withdrawn, even when several clients had come for consultations. Sometimes when these people greeted him or asked after his health he would refuse to answer; at other times, he would return their greetings but refuse to deal with their problems, saying that the spirit was not ready or that the spirit was somewhere else.

Whenever we asked Mama why Dawit behaved in this way, seeming to despise the clients and to avoid contact with anyone whenever possible, she would say that the spirits made him that way. Yet she would also make fun of his moods, and when he was not obviously listening she would express concern about his health. After about two months, she commented that he had been eating very poorly and would now only deign to eat dried beans and to drink coffee. He appeared to be living mostly on *chat*, and she commented that this and coffee were bad for the heart. Thus although these foods are associated with the spirits and with fasting, she was less impressed with his abstinence than she was concerned about his apparent addiction to *chat*.

During these same conversations, Mama invariably rehearsed to us at least part of the history of Dawit's arrival at her *mosqet*, and extolled his present virtue and the way he had devotedly served the spirits for so many years. The other women who were there would shake their heads over him, praising the power of the spirits who could bring such things to pass. Clearly this was seen as something unusual, and a true sign of the power of the spirits. Implicit in their remarks was the contrast between Dawit's obvious attractiveness as a man, the general unattractiveness of other men who were sometimes involved in this group, and the role that Dawit had been forced to play out of devotion to the cult—he had acted "like a woman." They indicated over and over again in more and less subtle ways that he was extremely exceptional in this regard, and that his devotion must be placing a considerable strain upon him. Thus he should be treated with acceptance and tolerance, even when his behavior was quite objectionable in terms of Ethiopian standards of politeness.

But one night, Dawit went too far. During the *wadağa*, there was a young woman sitting with him behind the curtain. Mama, who had come back late from buying the *chat* for the meeting, apparently did not realize that the woman was there and began to prepare for the cele- bration in her usual slow and casual manner. Suddenly the woman started to giggle, and everyone in the house—as well as those sitting outside close to the doorway—could hear her, and Dawit's low whisper- ing in reply. Although casual conversation is allowed between the say- ing of the initial blessings and the beginning of the drumming and singing that mark the real beginning of the *wadağa* celebration in honor of the spirits, such conversation should be quiet and decorous, lest the spirits become annoyed and refuse to "descend." For a *bale wuqabi* to sit behind the curtain giggling, laughing, and whispering with a woman is unseemly at best, and positively scandalous at worst.

Initially, although significant looks were cast from one adept to an- other, nothing was said by any of the other group members, and Mama, apparently oblivious, went off to another part of the house to change her clothes. But then, as the tension was building up, the woman who was hidden behind the curtain with Dawit started to in- sult Tashome, one of the quietest of the regular adepts, and the only other man in the group except Dawit. Tashome, outraged, told her to "mind her shopping," and stop disturbing decent people. She made a tart reply, and he was so offended that he quickly left the house and failed to return that night or for several days thereafter.

For a few moments things appeared to calm down, as others received their bunches of *chat* from Mama, who at this point was sitting outside the curtain. But then Dawit, in his spirit voice, asked one of the women who was participating from outside the house whether it was she who had accused him, early in the day, of being possessed by *aganint* (de- mons) rather than by *wuqabi*. The woman who had been addressed de- nied that she had made this very serious allegation, swearing her al- legiance to the spirits of the house and to their chosen servants, Mama Azaletch and Dawit.

Once again, everything seemed to quiet down. Then another woman, also outside, where she could not be seen, suddenly volunteered the information that it was the wife of Azaletch's grandson who had made the allegation against Dawit. (This woman, who seemed, like her husband, to ignore Dawit's presence in the house most of the time, was supposedly asleep next door. Nothing was heard from her or from Haile, however, although both of them were home that night.) At this point, Mama repeated a very dramatic rendition of her first encounter with Dawit, and again sermonized on his quality and excellence as a servant of the *wuqabi,* and his status as one beloved by the spirits, since he had given up so much to serve them.

Although this might have calmed the other adepts, and was clearly intended to do so and to restore confidence in Dawit's mandate from the spirits, it was not entirely successful. Interestingly, however, it may be taken as an indication that Mama felt she must defend the legitimacy of Dawit's authority, backed by the spirits, lest it be questioned more seriously and lead to the questioning of her own. Thus, despite having to accuse her grandson's wife, albeit indirectly, of lying and calumny, she chose to defend Dawit.

It is worth noting that this was the first time we participated in a *wadaǧa* where all the spirits of the house refused to "descend," either on Mama or on Dawit, or on the other adepts. In fact, the whole night was very tense, and neither of the two attempted cures—one of a small boy said to be "eaten" by a person with the evil eye, the other an infant who seemed to have bronchitis—was in any way successful. It was said that this was because people had been thinking evil thoughts and spoiling the tranquil atmosphere necessary to the spirits. Nevertheless the ceremony continued until after dawn, as usual, while the mysterious woman stayed behind the curtain.

This incident occurred in the third month of our contact with the group. During the following weeks, there appeared to be a subtle change in Dawit's relations with the adepts and with clients who came for consultations. Ultimately his attitude toward Mama changed as well. At first, it was only that his spirit became more and more harsh with the adepts during the judgment phases at *wadaǧas. Mute Arba* often told them that they were lax, that their spirits were not satisfied with the way they were behaving, and that they would begin to be ill again and unlucky. He began to harrass them, either when he was supposed to be in trance or when he was not, warning them that if they didn't provide him and his spirit with more and more costly offerings they would suffer further difficulties with their own spirits.

But if his pronouncements and judgments grew more harsh, over the next few months, the adepts and clients became braver, and started

to argue with him and with *Mute Arba*. This was something we had
never seen before. Formerly, whatever the judgment, the adept would
thank the spirit and then either choose to carry out its instructions or to
ignore them, risking retribution. But no one ever questioned the word
of the spirit directly either during or after the judgment.

Yet during this period they appeared suddenly to become markedly
argumentative. On one occasion, for example, there was a running
argument between a woman adept and *Mute Arba* that continued
throughout an all-night session. This woman, according to the spirit,
had been quarreling with another adept. As payment for quarreling
near the *mosqet,* and thus offending the spirits, *Mute Arba* demanded
that the woman give an offering of one dollar Ethiopian. But she refused, publicly, saying that the spirit was wrong and that it was not she
who had been quarreling. This was a novel event, and the others who
were present seemed as shocked as we were. They began to whisper to
each other and to predict that the woman would surely back down
quickly; yet she did nothing of the kind. At intervals for the rest of the
night, she and *Mute Arba* argued back and forth, she defending herself
and the spirit threatening her with a wide variety of terrible consequences. Just before dawn, in the last exchange, the spirit told her that
she would surely sicken and die if she did not soon bring a bull to be
sacrificed, and the woman in turn replied she was not afraid and that
they would all see what would happen.

While this instance of conflict within the group was singular in its duration and intensity, it was also typical of the kind of troubled interaction that became common during this period. Dawit became increasingly withdrawn, eating less and drinking more alcohol, saying that his
spirit wanted *araki* and that it must be provided. When he spoke to
people at all Dawit was markedly hostile, and if people were happy and
laughed about something he would dash out from behind the curtain
and demand to know why they were laughing at him.

Also, he began to complain that we had never paid enough attention
to him, and that we did not respect him or his spirits as much as we
respected Mama and hers. He told us that his spirit ranked equally with
hers, and that he too was the head of this house. Every time we came
for a *wadaǧa* or for a daytime visit he would reiterate these compliants,
becoming more and more hostile. Finally we offered to provide a sheep
and money for a feast on Saint Michael's day, a project that had been
discussed within the group but they felt would be beyond their means.
We agreed that this feast would be offered especially in honor of *Mute
Arba,* and said that a sheep of the appropriate color should be chosen.
Once we had actually handed over the money for the sheep to Mama,

Dawit became relatively gracious toward us and seemed placated if not satisfied.

But even at the feast, which was put on both for the Christian holiday and for the spirits, *Mute Arba* and Dawit were not satisfied. Dawit went into trance unexpectedly, and the spirit said it "would not let him eat" this food since it was not really meant properly for this spirit but rather for the others. Instead, the spirit demanded that Dawit be brought a bottle of *araki*. When this had been done, the spirit seemed to withdraw and Dawit began to talk to various people, wandering from group to group with the bottle in one hand and a whip in the other. For a while he seemed calmer, but then went into trance again, and the spirit again started to remonstrate with the people. It said that all of the women who had prepared the feast had conspired against it and that they would all be punished; the spirit would order Dawit to beat them all with his whip and make them very sick.

The women adepts became very upset, and begged the spirit to reconsider. Actually, the level of tension was so high that many of the people who had come to the feast but were not connected with the cult refrained from eating. This may have been partly because they thought it would be impolite to eat if one of the hosts did not, or because they believed Dawit was telling them indirectly that they were in danger of being poisoned. Many of the people got up to go when *Mute Arba* made his second announcement, but then some astute person began drumming and singing for the spirit. Dawit began to dance, pretending to whip the women, but actually only touching them lightly with his whip. After this at least six of the adepts became actively possessed, and the feast continued late into the evening.

Things went on this way for some time, Dawit becoming by turns ever more withdrawn and ever more hostile to everyone with whom he came in contact. When new clients came for consultations, he would sit behind the curtain chewing *chat* and apparently ignoring what they were saying. Then quite suddenly, he would begin to speak in his spirit voice, contradicting everything that Mama had been telling the client. Occasionally the arguments between the two spirits, relayed back and forth by an *aggafari,* became extremely heated and the clients became afraid. At other times the consultations would break down altogether, and the client would be told to come back another time.

Toward the end of the fifth month, when tension within the group had increased considerably, we were told when we arrived one day that Dawit had become very ill. He could not eat at all and he was coughing up blood. We were not allowed to see him but were asked to give Mama some money so that Dawit could be given special foods and herbal medicines could be purchased from a local specialist. In turn, we asked whether Dawit would agree to go to the hospital, which was very near the compound. Mama told us that she would consult with the spirits and ask whether Dawit could be taken to the hospital, but reminded us that we already knew that normally spirits do not permit the possessed to deal with "foreign" doctors. Dawit, overhearing our conversation, said that he felt so unwell that he would indeed consider going to the foreign doctors despite the spirits. If the spirits were going to kill him in the end, he said, he might as well go to the hospital to see what the doctors could do.

Dawit did not go to the hospital. Instead Mama called in a herbologist, saying that it was clearly not the spirits that were afflicting Dawit, so it must be the sort of illness that a specialist of another kind could deal with. Despite medicines taken internally, however, and other medicines spread on the swellings that were emerging under his arms, Dawit did not get better. After a week or two he became very pale and thin, continued to cough up blood, and grew so weak that he could scarcely get out of bed. We suggested he might be tubercular, but he disagreed. Despite our continued urgings, he refused to go to the hospital. Although on occasion Mama Azaletch told us again that this might be an option when all other means had been tried, and asked us for money to "save" against this eventuality, it became clear that his going to the hospital was no longer considered now that his illness was more severe.

Instead Mama called in a "needle-giver," a new kind of specialist who gives injections, supposedly of antibiotics but often of milk or water. Dawit was told by this man that he would be well within a week, although no diagnosis was given; instead he got worse and grew steadily weaker. On certain days he would seem a bit stronger and would sit up and talk to visitors. Sometimes he could even participate in the *wadaĝas,* which were still held, sitting propped up behind the curtain. Over the next two months, however, his condition did not improve, and Mama and the other members of the *wadaĝa* group grew more and more worried. Yet Mama was still insisting that it could not be a question of affliction by the spirits for if it were, she said quite simply, she would know it and would be able to manage it. And if it were something beyond the power of her own spirits, but still spirit-related, she would know whom to go to for help.

Unfortunately we were not able to follow developments closely at this point because we had gone to Guna-Ferekasa in Arussi province to participate in the semiannual ritual at the shrine of *Gifti Arussi*. While we were there, however, we encountered Mama Azaletch, who was there by herself. She was quite cordial and told us that she had come to get some advice about curing Dawit's illness, and that she was alone because they had not had enough money left after all the medicines were bought for Dawit for anyone else to make the trip with her. She told us that Dawit was too ill to come, but she seemed quite cheerful and said she had received assurances in Ferekasa that Dawit would recover. She had been told that he should be moved out of the house, since the dust and the air there were bad for him. She said that it seemed it might be a matter of the spirits after all, that they would see about it when she got back to Addis.

When we returned to Addis some weeks later and went to visit Dawit, we found that he was living in a tent at the far side of the compound near the the eucalyptus trees. All of the ritual paraphernalia were there with him, and there were fresh flowers stuck in a Coca-Cola bottle, an offering from one of the women adepts. Dawit seemed much gentler than before and was rather warm to us for the first time. He was still very feeble and could hardly raise his head to bow in greeting, but he was surprisingly cheerful. He showed us his swellings with some pride; they were still covered with rags soaked in medicine, but he admitted that this treatment hadn't done much good. Again we asked whether he would go to the hospital, and he said that this time he would if we could give him the money. We left the money with Mama, and returned in about a week to find that Mama had consulted the spirits again, who said that Dawit must not go to the hospital. Instead they had finally told Mama and the rest of the group that Dawit was possessed by a new spirit, and that this spirit was afflicting him to show him that it wished to be taken seriously and honored with the other spirits of the house.

This new spirit, which did not possess anyone else in the group, was called *'Offa,* and is associated with Galla, with the wild, with hunting, and with warriors and *shifta* (bandits). This spirit is considered particularly difficult to domesticate, and often refuses to "inhabit" houses that are built for it (cf. Morton, 1973).

When we went to the tent to ask Dawit about his new spirit, he told us that he was feeling much better now that he knew what was wrong, that he had used our money to buy some clothes for the new spirit, which had made it more pleased with him than before. Everyone seemed markedly more cheerful now that they had a new and convincing explanation for Dawit's illness, and they all began to say that surely now he would recover.

However, the next few times we visited him, we found that Dawit was not observably better physically, and that he again seemed depressed and withdrawn. At this time, Mama was very withdrawn as well, except when Dawit sulked and refused offers of food in his old curt style; then, for a moment, she would mock him in a quietly animated way. But her house was very bare, and she seemed more troubled now than she had before the explanation for Dawit's illness had been arrived at.

The next month Dawit was still ill, and still in bed in his tent most of the time. Ramadan was approaching, and it would soon be time for a semiannual pilgrimage to Guna-Ferekasa. This second pilgrimage, timed to coincide with the end of Ramadan, is primarily for Muslims, but Christians also come and attend the ceremonies, which last for about a week. As at the "Christian" celebration, people who are possessed and need help in regularizing their possession relationships, as well as others who have made vows to the shrine of *Gifti Arussi,* come from all over the Empire.

So it was decided that Dawit must go to Ferekasa this time, and because he was so ill several members of the group would have to go with him and Mama, to take care of him on the trip and during the celebration. In the end, after much bargaining, and with many doubts about the wisdom of sending him on a ten-hour journey by lorry or bus, we agreed to underwrite this trip. It was decided that we would meet the group in Ferekasa, where Dawit was to have a private audience with Taye, the saintly leader of the cult.

THE SECOND SETTING

Guna-Ferekasa, the home of Taye, is on the Arussi plain. It is a self-contained community built up by Taye, who owns the land in the district and supports a part of the local population. It is considered to be an important ritual center by Christians, Muslims, and religious traditionalists alike, and is renowned throughout Ethiopia.

Twice a year, Taye, the current incumbent leader of the cult, opens the area to pilgrims to the shrine of his great-grandmother, the Lady of Arussi (*Gifti Arussi*). At each of these two yearly pilgrimages we estimated that at least ten thousand people gather at Ferekasa to honor the memory of Woizero Shebash, the original leader of the cult, and to bring the offerings they have pledged to her memory or her power (*karama*) throughout the year, in return for her blessings, protection, and help. Although many of the pilgrims are not possessed, and do not think of these celebrations in terms of spirit possession at all, a majority of them come at least partly because they define themselves as actively or latently possessed by *wuqabi* and other kinds of spirits. They come to be cured of various ailments as well, either those thought to be caused by unaccommodated *wuqabi,* or those attributed to attack by various kinds of evil spirits. Those of high status are allowed to have special curing sessions with Taye himself, who treats them either in public or privately by subjecting them to the power of his blessedness, which is believed to derive from Allah. Others hope to be cured by the beneficial effects of bathing in the local spring waters, as well as simply by being in this sacred and ritually powerful spot. English-speaking informants described Ferekasa as a "central clearinghouse for the possessed."

Interestingly, many of the possessed pilgrims have never seen Taye, or know little or nothing about him. Yet they know the miraculous life history of Shebash and, in Shoa at least, the phrase *ye Taye karama* (the mystical power of Taye) is commonly heard throughout the year. The other tracts of land owned by Taye are also supposed to be especially powerful in the ritual sense, and on the trip from Addis Ababa to Ferekasa individuals become actively possessed at certain landmarks that are believed to be the boundaries of his property.

During the pilgrimages the local people build huts out of branches for the pilgrims to live in, selling this space for a moderate sum. Other pilgrims, especially Arussi Galla from the local area, bring their own tents, as do some of the wealthier pilgrims from the towns. Itinerant traders come early to set up stalls in the valley, selling all kinds of foods, as well as items typically offered to spirits and to saints such as incense, perfume, prayer beads, rugs, and colored cloth. In addition, people who have made specific vows bring with them offerings that they have promised, which range from gold to coffee beans, from costly carpets to the clothes off the backs of the poor. Anything given in good faith is accepted, according to the ideology of the cult, and all material goods received as offerings are said to be redistributed to the poor.

Transportation to the area from all parts of the Empire is provided by independent charter landrover, bus, and lorry, but a significant number of pilgrims come on foot, or on horses or mules. For at least a week before the celebrations begin, the road to Ferekasa is thronged with pilgrims in all varieties of regional dress, singing in almost all the languages of Ethiopia. When these masses of people get to Taye's land, they tend to camp or to rent huts in clusters, according to area of origin, so that the valley becomes a microcosm of the Empire.

During the day, and throughout the night, these groups of people dance in large circles led by a *bale wuqabi* or other mystical specialist from the home area singing in local dialect. Meanwhile, at one side of the valley, a constant stream of pilgrims take their offerings to the shrine of Shebash. Some of the possessed visit this shrine along with the nonpossed, but primarily they take their offerings to another "mosque" inside Taye's compound. At night they line up on the hill in front of this compound, waiting to take part in the wadaga which goes on all night, in shifts. This wadaga is run by the hadjis, who have been educated in the faith and sent to Mecca by Taye. Although it is said that people do not go into trance at these rituals, they do spend much of the time there testifying to the magical cures they have received as a result of the blessing and power of Taye.

At the pilgrimage perhaps a thousand of the most faithful are fed in groups. These individuals are called up to the compound on the hill on the morning after the fast has ended, and are fed honey by the hadjis. Taye blesses them for the coming year, addressing the people themselves part of the time and, the spirits that traditionally possess them in turn. He exhorts both the spirits and the possessed to honor the terms of the agreements they have maintained over the last year, and not to trouble one another, and to live peacefully together.

That evening there is a period when a chosen few, whose relatives or friends have made special representations to Taye or his retainers, are brought to the compound to be cured by exhortation and by the laying on of hands. During these ceremonies, some of which are carried on in public, Taye appears on the veranda of his house, and addresses the several hundred people who have been allowed within the fence to watch and to sing, to increase the efficacy of the cure. Still other more risky or complicated cures are attempted within the house, away from the eyes and ears of the masses of pilgrims.

DAWIT AT FEREKASA

Mama Azaletch had been hoping for this special kind of curing session when it was decided that Dawit should be brought to Ferekasa, and she had laid the groundwork for it when she had come alone earlier. Apparently at that time, some of Taye's retainers had promised that something could be done if they brought Dawit for the pilgrimage at Ramadan.

When we arrived, we found Mama, Dawit and Habte, Haile and several of the women from the wadaga group in Addis already established in two huts as near as possible to Taye's compound. They had made a fairly high bed of skins and blankets for Dawit so that he would be as far as possible from the damp of the ground. When we first entered the hut where he was staying, he was propped up in the corner, very still, and at first we were afraid he might not survive the journey after all. Mama told us that he had been extremely weak when they arrived, and had started vomiting blood. They were afraid that one of his swellings had burst internally, a sure sign that he would die. Still they hoped, through the power of Taye, which was so strong here where he himself lived, Dawit might still be saved.

On the next day, which was the first day of the celebration, Dawit was not much better, and everyone stayed in or near the huts praying for his recovery. There was a seriousness about the demeanor of them all that had been lacking before, even when Dawit had been at his worst in Addis. Apparently it seemed a bad omen that he had taken such a turn for the worse here at the very shrine of the cult whose leader was supposed to be able to cure him. Mama came and went quietly, trying to get in touch with the retainers who had originally promised to help her and Dawit and hoping to make them aware of the severity of the case.

The following day the feeding of special pilgrims with honey was to take place, and Mama came back at dusk to say that she and Dawit had been told to appear there, and perhaps later they would be able to return for more personalized attention.

The next morning Mama and Dawit, in their finest spirit clothes—Dawit all dressed in red for the spirit *'Offa*—went slowly up the hill to Taye's compound. At this point Dawit could scarcely walk, even though he was leaning very heavily on Mama, who was a strong woman. But they got there, among the last to arrive, and sat down on the grass among the others who had been admitted for this ritual in honor of the breaking of the fast. They and the others waited quietly while the *hadjis,* carrying large basins of honey, went from person to person, doling out a bit of honey into the right hand of each. After this, and the blessing which followed, Dawit and Mama descended the hill again, slowly, slowly, and went back to the huts where they were staying. When we went down to see them an hour or so later, Dawit told us he felt much better and that, thanks to the power of Taye, he felt he would soon be well. Although he was again lying propped up in bed in the corner and still seemed extremely weak, everyone seemed truly relieved, and the air of gloom that had hung about them all for so long began to lift.

On the fourth day, Dawit got up from his bed and managed the even longer uphill walk to the shrine of Shebash. But later that day, he collapsed and had to go back to bed again. Later still, he rose once more and went from one of the neighboring groups to another greeting people and receiving their blessings and wishes for his recovery. Finally, on the following day it was decided that Dawit was strong enough for the trip back to Addis Ababa, and Mama and the others prepared to leave. This was the last day of the formal celebration, and Taye's retainers had driven about the valley early in the morning blessing the people and asking them to go back to their homes until the next celebration.

The last we saw of Dawit, he was standing in the doorway of the hut ready to leave for home. He was dressed once again like a traditional Christian Amhara, all in white. He looked very thin and very pale as he stood surrounded by the other members of the group and supported by Mama. He bid us goodbye, thanked us in the name of the *wuqabi* for our help and for bringing him to Ferekasa, and wished us a good return trip. He assured us that he would now recover, as *'Offa* would now be pleased, and they would know how to honor this new spirit when they returned home. Everyone smiled and bowed, and we were politely dismissed. Although we would have liked to know what happened to Dawit in the end, due to a change in field site, we were never able to find out.

DISCUSSION

It should be clear at this point that our relations with Mama Azaletch and Dawit, though of relatively long duration, were rarely very close. Often we had to wait a very long time for answers to our questions, or explanations of interactions we observed, and sometimes neither was forthcoming. In part this was due to a belief most possessed Ethiopians appear to hold about the importance of secrecy in connection with anything relating to the spirits. In fact, one of the women adepts once said to me with considerable animation, "If you would ask me about something else, about cooking, or farming, or anything else, I would be pleased to tell you about it. I know that you are like a child—that your questions mean no harm—but if I tell you about the spirits I will become sick, and I am afraid."

Sometimes, however, we appeared to be more readily accepted, at least by Mama Azaletch and the other women. One way in which this was expressed was when we were finally told by all of them together about Dawit's "escape" from Betcha and his arrival at Mama's door. This was perhaps the turning point, and it did not come for several months. Later, we were accepted increasingly as members of the group, as opposed to new Ethiopian clients who were given the "full treatment" of mystification, important in maintaining the image of the *bale wuqabi* as a specially endowed, unapproachable, and clairvoyant individual chosen by the spirits to be invested with special powers.

Nevertheless, we never made much progress with Dawit. Although when he fell ill he included us in his general change to gentleness and politeness, he was never very outgoing, and seemed to have a real phobia about talking of himself, especially about his past. Whereas after a time, Mama would delight in boasting to us of the hard time she had had learning to accommodate her spirits, Dawit never said anything to us about the process by which he initially became defined as possessed, nor would he talk about his spirit and its idiosyncrasies. Thus almost all of the information about him that has been included here comes from direct observation or from accounts from Mama, the other women, or Habte, Dawit's son.

Certainly the status of Dawit's life history given above is problematic. Insofar as it is secondary material, it needs to be accepted cautiously. As a result, it is very difficult to make statements about the background to the observed case material with much certainty. Further, insofar as we have no account of the onset of Dawit's initial possession by *Mute Arba,* and almost no account of his later acceptance of intrusive possession by *'Offa* as the explanation for his illness, the comments that follow are offered only in a tentative way.

One thing that the others in the group commented on frequently was Dawit's moodiness and generally withdrawn attitude. While this was sometimes described as typical of all *bale wuqabi* and a sign of their intense involvement with spirits, it was also considered, in his case, to be exaggerated. If he was hostile to us in the beginning, as time passed, and his interaction with others became more and more troubled, he seemed to be hostile to everyone. However, it should be noted that at least part of the time, this moodiness, and the subsequent harshness, were attributed to the spirit *Mute Arba* and not to Dawit himself. Further, it should be mentioned that most *wuqabi* when speaking through entranced adepts or cult group leaders, speak harshly, exhorting their "horses" to give them more and costlier offerings, and castigating them for actual or imagined infractions of the rules of the cult or failure to live up to the terms of their respective accommodation agreements. Often these spirit speeches are extremely insulting, with the spirit cursing the possessed and threatening him or her with the direst of consequences that include ravaging illnesses, sterility, and even death.

From the observer's point of view, however, this is largely a matter of the style of the individual possessed person. Some spirits speaking through the trance of the possessed are childlike, meek, and cajoling. Further, an experienced *bale wuqabi* can exhibit a range of speech styles as well as of message content from the spirits without anyone inferring that the trance is simulated rather than real. (However, adepts sometimes claimed to be able to tell when a *bale wuqabi* was feigning trance, although this was accepted as necessary for the benefit of the others, that is, those who were not sufficiently sophisticated to catch on.) Yet at times it may be more effective, in terms of obtaining certain results from adepts and clients, if the *bale wuqabi* finds that the spirits refuse to "descend" despite everyone's supplications. This was the case on the evening when Dawit was flirting with the woman behind the curtain, and when he demanded to know who had accused him of dealing with demons.

While one might assume that the best way for him to counter such an accusation would have been to go into trance immediately and have his spirit speak very forcefully to all present, perhaps threatening them with dreadful consequences for lack of faith, what actually happened may have been more effective. That is, the failure of the spirits of Dawit or Mama Azaletch to agree to descend—and the concomitant failure of the spirits possessing the adepts to descend upon them—and cure the two patients who were the focus of this particular meeting appears to have been far more threatening, since ultimately the relationship of each group member to his or her possessing spirit depended on the relationship of the *bale wuqabi* to their respective spirits. In addition, this failure of all the spirits to descend was a convenient explanation of why the two patients, at least one of whom was clearly suffering from a physical ailment, could not be cured at that time.

Although the adepts and Mama were able to cope with Dawit's moroseness and withdrawal and to accept the idea that his spirit was harsh for its own—presumably justified—reasons, this only continued until he took it too far, especially at the feast on Saint Michael's day. In time he became increasingly disagreeable personally, and when he began to refuse food and to drink more and more *araki* everyone was obviously worried about the consequences. Although at first they held to the explanation that this was a matter of the spirits causing difficult behavior on Dawit's part, after this crisis they began to attribute his withdrawal to personal, psychological causes.

During this phase, when we asked most of the women possible reasons for his continuing estrangement from them, they told us: "He has been living here like a woman for so long. . . ." Thus the explanatory focus changed from Dawit as a person possessed by a spirit to Dawit, a man living an unnatural life for a man of his type—a young, virile fellow who had demonstrated his manliness by fathering a son. This explanatory phrase was spoken so often that it should be seriously considered, particularly because it was uttered with considerable sympathy.

Sex roles in Amhara society are very clearly defined, and expectations regarding proper male and female behavior seem to be accepted by members of both sexes. A proper Amhara man (and this applies to men of other ethnic groups as well, although there are some differences in degree) should be proud, aggressive, canny, secretive, and, in some important sense, disdainful of women and of women's concerns. He should in no way allow himself to be trifled with, and should err rather on the side of imagining insults and slights where there are none. In his relations with women, a young man should be selfish, demanding, stern, and very virile. A cult of masculinity centers around the notion of a man as tough, unsympathetic, and sexually potent, often measuring his success with women in terms of how much pain he can inflict on them in the course of sexual activity. All men, especially young ones, are expected to be promiscuous, and need not try to bind women to them by ties of affection but rather by admiration of their strength and by respectful fear.

Both men and women informants often told us that generally men prefer to deal with, talk to, and spend time with men, and women prefer to deal with, talk to, and spend time with women. A man who seeks the company of women exclusively is regarded either as a rake or a potential seducer of other men's wives. If he does not seem to seek sexual gratification from women but still prefers their company, he is regarded as womanish. A man of the latter sort, called a $s^{y}et$-a-$s^{y}et$ ($s^{y}et$ = woman) is thought to be someone who by nature should have been created a woman instead of a man. Some, but by no means all, of the men classified in this way are transvestites.

It is said that a man of this kind prefers the company of women because he shares their trivial concerns and interests: he is interested in dress, in cooking, in children, and in gossip. Once classified in this way, he is not regarded as a threat to the virtue of the women whose company he seeks, nor is he regarded as a homosexual. He may be liked well enough by men, but will not be taken seriously by them. He is consigned by other men to the world of women.[7]

According to informants, this sort of man is likely to get involved with *wadaǧa* groups, since these are good places to find women. Women may laugh at such men when they first claim to be possessed by spirits, but they come to accept them into their *wadaǧa* groups and take their claims to being possessed seriously when there is evidence to support them.

Dawit, however, was in no way a $s^{y}et$-a-$s^{y}et$. Nor did we ever hear anyone refer to him as such, even in jest. If anything, in the past, he seems to have conformed rather too closely to the Amhara model of rapacious behavior with respect to his relations with women. Otherwise it would be extremely unlikely that anyone could convincingly have accused him of incest. Such an accusation, when it is unjustified, is a deadly insult, and the proper and expected male response is an equally serious vengeance. Thus while incest may be an offense worth killing for, so is a false accusation of incest.

It is tempting to interpret Dawit's having waited until he was far from Betcha to announce his predicament to the spirits as a sign that he did not really wish to confront his accuser. It is equally tempting to regard the whole account of the accusation of incest as a sort of cover-up for feelings of sexual inadequacy. For not only did he leave home rather than confront an accusation of inappropriate sexual behavior, but he also agreed with the spirits that he would refrain from sexual activity altogether for a long period. Nevertheless, the preponderance of the data militate against this interpretation. His problem seems not to have been one of sexual inadequacy but rather of the appropriate channeling of sexual adequacy, both before he became a member of the *wadaǧa* group and afterward, especially in the instance involving the woman behind the curtain.

In every version of Dawit's life story that we obtained from others, the motivation attributed to his lengthy and devoted service to the spirits was his pressing need to know who had unjustly accused him of committing incest. Having failed in his attempts to identify this person by normal means, he turned to the spirits and apparently felt at the beginning that any source of mystical aid would be worth almost any price.

It is interesting, however, that he sought this mystical aid after he had left home, in Addis Ababa where he was unknown and where only his side of the story would be aired. Had he sought the aid of a local specialist in or near Betcha, he would have been able, for example, to purchase a spell or charm that would reveal the culprit. Presumably, had he wished to ask *wuqabi* spirits or even evil spirits for help, he would have been able to get an answer from a local specialist that would at least identify someone in the area, and this identification in turn could have been used by Dawit to substantiate his public accusation against some enemy. Yet Dawit seems not to have adopted any of these traditional options. Instead, he came to the spirits when he was far from home. Although he may have been a true believer in their power at that time, the majority of the comments of the other group members tends to deny such a view. Indeed, they stressed the fact that Dawit did not seem to care which spirits he contacted, and didn't know how to address them properly. They also implied that the had taken the spirits lightly when he promised to serve them, perhaps not believing that he would have to carry out his part of the bargain.

It is also noteworthy that in no version of this story of Dawit's first encounter with the spirits did he or others think he was possessed at the time. Instead, like the clients who came to him for consultations when he became a *bale wuqabi,* he was seeking mystical intervention from the spirits in a mode other than that of possession. In return for this intevention, he appeared willing to alter his behavior radically. The threat, should he renege, seems to have been that he would become possessed. Thus his choices were to remain ignorant of his accuser's identity, to adopt the role of a woman in a possession cult, or to become possessed.

Apparently Dawit began to learn about the spirits after he had come to live with Mama and her family, during the period when he was serving the spirits in the way that beginning adepts do. The main kinds of services required in this first stage of the adept phase of the possession career are quite menial, and are definitely considered "women's work." The new adept must pound and boil coffee, clean the house, cook food, and wait upon the *bale wuqabi* like a domestic servant. He or she may be allowed to warm the drums, to run errands, and to buy *chat* and other supplies destined for consumption "by the spirits," but otherwise the tasks are those involved in the running of any large household. With the possible exception of running errands and warming the drums, all of these tasks are done by women and not by men.

Amhara men are taught early to have contempt for domestic work. If small boys show too much interest in cooking or in other chores that their mothers perform in the house, they are quickly warned off and ridiculed until they lose interest. In a rural setting, they are sent off at an early age to herd animals with other boys and seem not to be encouraged to hang around the house, especially around the kitchen. (They are also kept from close contact with their sisters from a rather early age, since it is believed that the propinquity of any nubile girl or woman is such a temptation to any male that he is likely to succumb no matter what his relation to her.)

It must have been extremely demeaning for Dawit when he first got involved with Mama and the group to have to learn to perform women's tasks, to associate primarily with a group of women, and especially to live as the dependent of a woman to whom he was not related. Since he was apparently required by the terms of his agreement with the spirits to remain celibate as well, his perception of himself as a suitably masculine young man about to wreak vengeance on someone who had accused him—albeit falsely—of incest must surely have suffered some deterioration, if not a series of severe blows. This could well have been true even though those around him, who defined themselves as devotees of the cult, and therefore completely at the mercy of the spirits, might not have seen his position as completely unique or as ridiculous. It is also worth noting that by the time we encountered him, Dawit was doing none of these menial tasks and was instead being waited on more than Mama approved of.

Had Dawit come to be involved in the *wuqabi* cult through a more typical route of illness, subsequent diagnosis of possession, and inclusion in a *wadaǧa* group as an adept, the cost to his masculine self-image would have been considerably less. Already having defined himself as subject to the whims and demands of the spirits, and having been cured to some extent of the original affliction which had led to that self-definition, by participation in the cult group, he would have been able to realize a benefit that could be regarded as commensurate with the costs he had to pay for loss of prestige in the wider community. Further, had this been the case, he would probably not have had to make such a stringent agreement with the spirits possessing him. That is, he would not have had to come to live at the home of the *bale wuqabi,* could have carried on normal relationships with women, and avoided, almost entirely, the demeaning work of actual service. There were other men in this cult group whose experiences fitted this pattern.

Alternately, had Dawit been involved for some time in a possession cult group as an assistant *bale wuqabi,* and then set up business on his own as head of another group, he would have been in a position to take total command and to become the center of attention and devotion of a group of dependent women. As an autonomous leader, he would have been exercising an accepted prerogative if he trifled with women adepts or women clients from time to time, although this would have elicited some negative comments from outsiders.

This was not the case with Dawit. Even when he had come to be defined, and to define himself, as possessed—and even when his promotion in the hierarchy of the cult group was thus achieved—he was still quite clearly subordinate to and dependent upon Mama. His over-reaction to a variety of remarks, especially to what was essentially good-natured teasing, as well as the extremely harsh messages and decisions transferred through him by his spirit, were considered inappropriate for someone of his status in the group. Nevertheless they were effective insofar as some of the adepts and clients sometimes evinced real fear of him.

The incident with the woman behind the curtain, however, seems to have been too much. His prior and subsequent attempts at self-assertion were ultimately acceptable so long as he himself accepted a certain standard of behavior. But once he began to act like a "normal" man, instead of like one chosen by the spirits at least partly because of special qualifications of righeousness, a significant amount of hostility was evoked in those around him; he had ceased to play by the rules. Beyond this time, the adepts clearly appeared to begin to make a separation between what they could tolerate from Dawit's spirit when they were sure it was really the spirit acting and what they could tolerate from Dawit himself.

In the weeks after the nearly disastrous feast on Saint Michael's day, the level of tension in the group was extremely high, and it could have been anticipated that if Dawit did not change his behavior, he would often be accused of trafficking with devils rather than being possessed by the benign *wuqabi*. It is also possible that beyond a certain point Mama would not have been able to counter these accusations and her own clientele would have fallen off. Had she continued to justify and support Dawit while he continued to become increasingly disagreeable and erratic, it is possible that her own authority, backed by the control she had attained over her own and others' spirits, would have been questioned as well.

When there were only hints of such a situation developing, Dawit got sick. At first he was able to function and carry on his ritual duties. The rest of the time he was very withdrawn and clearly suffering from physical symptoms which were growing more acute. As his symptoms became more severe, and more dramatic, he became an object of sympathy and in turn became more gentle with others. The accusations against him seemed forgotten temporarily, and all the group members rallied to his support. This was so obvious that Mama got nervous and appeared genuinely jealous of all the attention shown to Dawit. Further, the severity of his illness seemed to fluctuate with remarkable ease, and in the beginning Mama was quite openly suspicious that Dawit was exaggerating his ailment.

This may be one of the reasons why she steadfastly refused to entertain the idea that his illness might be caused by intrusive possession by a new *wuqabi* spirit until all other options seemed closed. For if she made such a diagnosis, Mama would have shown that she took the illness very seriously, and would also thereby be providing Dawit with further claims to status and power within the group. This would have been true even though it would be Mama herself who diagnosed possession and negotiated the new accommodation relationship with the spirit intended to bring about a cure.

Thus before Dawit moved his tent into the compound, after Mama had returned to Addis from her trip to Ferekasa, she refused to consider such a diagnosis. Even after this move had been organized, based on the knowledge obtained during her trip, she remained nervous and apprehensive. While she was organizing the adepts to refurbish the compound, at least partly to keep them away from Dawit and his new spirit, she in turn became withdrawn and short-tempered. Meanwhile Dawit was treating the other adepts with markedly greater consideration.

Later, however, when his symptoms failed to respond to treatment, even after the diagnosis of possession by *'Offa,* she again took matters in hand, and began to organize the second group trip to Ferekasa, thus leaving herself the option that another diagnosis might be forthcoming, backed by the credibility of proximity to Taye and his mystical power. She knew the kinds of rituals to carry out in the interim and was in charge of furthering the negotiation of Dawit's accommodation with *'Offa* until they left. Finally it was she who could claim special relationships with Taye's retainers in Ferekasa, and she alone who might be able to arrange for a special curing session for Dawit when they arrived.

While it would be simplistic to argue that Dawit was not getting well on purpose, or that his illness was significantly psychosomatic from the beginning, he did appear to get better and worse with remarkable ease and felicity, depending on the attitude of others, especially that of Mama Azaletch. He seemed to alternate between more and less subtle assertiveness and partially feigned weakness, in an effort to find the right balance between the two. After the arduous trip to Ferekasa, however, it became apparent that he was really extremely weak, and perhaps in danger of dying. Then, perhaps for the first time, he seemed to be aware that he was now entirely dependent on the sufferance of Mama and the support of the members of her family and of the cult group who had made the trip with him.

They in turn seemed genuinely afraid that he would die, and stayed with him in the hut, refraining from participation in the lively and casual group *wadaǧas* that were occurring all around them in the valley. At this point his illness was clearly regarded as critical, and all the others did everything that they could to save him.

Interestingly, Mama's inability to arrange a special curing session for Dawit with Taye was not taken as a sign of failure on her part, either of worldly social influence or of mystical potency. Rather, the others said that Taye, who was blessed and powerful, must have decided that the feeding and blessing session to which Dawit and Mama were invited would be enough and that Dawit did not need further personal attention. This assumption was borne out by the fact that Dawit took a star-tling turn for the better almost immediately thereafter. Despite his collapse the next day, this radical improvement was taken by the others—and apparently by Dawit himself—not as a temporary remis-sion, but as a sign of a conclusive recovery that would follow a suitable period of convalescence. As far as they were concerned, he was cured.

Yet this cure, like others that are thought to derive from successful accommodations of initially intrusive *wuqabi* spirits, would depend on Dawit's successfully honoring his new spirit and, perhaps more impor-tantly, on the willingness of the whole group to accept this spirit into the house, to be honored by all for the indefinite future. Initially it was this allegiance to the spirits of the house, and acceptance of them as governing their own possessing spirits, that tied the members of the group to Dawit and to Mama Azaletch as well as binding them to one another.

Thus while the domestication and accommodation of *'Offa* provided Dawit with a further basis for self-assertion within the group, it also ul-timately increased his dependence on the other members since it was their willingness to take this new possession seriously and to honor the spirit, which would in part determine the success of that accommo-dation in time. According to the ideology of the cult, should they re-fuse this kind of support, the likelihood that he would fall ill again would increase greatly.

Having supported him during his illness, accepted the diagnosis of intrusive possession by *'Offa,* and participated in and witnessed his cure at Ferekasa, all of the adepts—but most especially Mama Azaletch—had made Dawit their own. Although we do not know what happened to them after the trip to Ferekasa, by the time we left them all the ele-ments existed for acceptance by them all of this newly defined rela-tionship of interdependence, sanctioned by the paramount mystical au-thority of Taye and *Gifti Arussi,* mediated by Azaletch, and centered around Dawit, who was now, perhaps for the first time, fully integrated into the group and into the *wuqabi* cult itself.

NOTES

1. The data reported here were gathered in the field in Addis Ababa, Ethi-opia, in 1969–1970. The research was carried out under the auspices of the Social Science Research Council of Great Britain, to whom grateful ac-knowledgment is made.

2. The Amhara are a Semitic people, six million in number who, together with the Tigreans, have formed the political majority in Ethiopia for several

centuries. They are, however, critically outnumbered by the Galla, or Oromo, a Cushitic people numbering eleven million. The majority of the Galla were brought into the Empire during the reign of Emperor Menelik II (1889–1913), when they were conquered or, in some instances, reconquered. The majority of Amhara are Ethiopian Orthodox Christians belonging to the established church of the Ethiopian Empire. Orthodox Christians account for forty percent of the entire Ethiopian population, an additional forty percent being Muslim, and the remainder either religious traditionalists or converts to Roman Catholicism or Protestantism.

3.   Wäldä Tinsay Gizaw is an Orthodox Christian ecclesiastic who, for some years, has run a highly popular series of faith-healing rituals at his home in Wolisso (Ghion). When I was in the field, he was still extremely popular, and it was said that he was supported by, and given gifts by, HIM Haile Selassie I. People of all ethnic groups and all social classes thronged to his rituals to be cured of various ailments, primarily perhaps to be exorcised. Wäldä Tinsay claimed at that time to have cured two million people (Giel et al., 1968; Morton, 1973).

4.   *Chat (Catha edulis)* is a drug chewed primarily by Ethiopian Muslims in certain regions. The chewing of *chat* is frowned upon by Orthodox Christians, as is the drinking of coffee, although only the most devout keep from drinking coffee. Chewing chat is an important element in Harari friendship group meetings, among Muslim men in Harar, and chewing *chat* together is thought to bind members of a *wadaǧa* group together in somewhat the same way. *Chat* and coffee are closely associated with *wuqabi* spirits, and Christian women—who would otherwise decline to chew *chat* out of shame—are enabled to do it if they are possessed by Muslim or even by Christian spirits, since the spirit demands it (cf. Morton, 1973; Waldron, 1974).

5.   Spirit possession cult group activity was technically illegal when this research was carried out. However, the law was rarely enforced, except when individual possessed specialists and other mystical healers were occasionally fined for "cheating" innocent people, claiming to be able to cure them or to foretell the future.

6.   *Gifti Arussi,* our lady of Arussi, is both the name given to an historic person, Woizero Shebash Yemer, and to a cult in honor of her power (*karama*). There are various stories told about the wondrous powers displayed by this woman during her life, and the cult and associated pilgrimages are nearly as popular with Ethiopians as are the faith-healing rituals of Wäldä Tinsay. According to the most commonly repeated legend about Wo. Shebash, and the founding of the cult, this woman, a worker of miracles, originally came from Yeddju, in Wollo province. From there, she is said to have gone to Harar, where some allege she was the lover of Ras Makonnen, the father of Haile Selassie I. At that time, according to the legend, she was still mortal and had not yet received the gift of miracles and of curing from Allah. After some adventures she returned to Yeddju, and then became able to make herself disappear and to cure people of all kinds of ailments. The fol-

lowing is a version of her life story, which describes the origin of the cult and the mythical mandate of the incumbent in 1969–1970, Kenyazmatch Taye:

When Wo. Shebash went from Yeddju on retreat, the road took her to a place with white grass and with green grass, and she was taken by the spirits to Kalalo. And the Lord Allah honored her. Being honored by the Lord is better than being honored by men, which comes through bribery and begging. But gifts from the Emperor and from God cannot be cancelled or taken away. I will tell you from the beginning to the end. The Lord is as vast as the ocean.

When Wo. Shebash came back from her retreat, it was on Friday that she came to Guna-Ferekasa. The place where she sat, and where she touched the ground with her staff at Guna-Ferekasa, there a tree called *koshim* grew. And then she came to live at a village called Karsa. When you pass that place today, you must stop and rest there. And all of the people and all of the animals came to worship her, and she did many marvelous things. And strange animals appeared, and were gentle, and people came from all over to see her and to be cured. But there were so many that she made them come twice a year, except for the first ones who knew her and were there in that place. And all the land became hers, and the people, and she cured them and made them well. And the Lord honored her, and she was a Saint.

And Wo. Shebash gave birth to a daughter, who gave birth to a daughter, And Shebash told her granddaughter that she was going to give birth to a girl. And she said that this child would have six fingers on each hand and six toes on each foot. And when this child was born, they saw that it was true, and they thought that this would be the successor of *Gifti Arussi.* But she said to them that this child was not theirs, but belonged to Allah. And it was true, and she died before she was married. And then Shebash said that her granddaughter would have a son, and that this son would belong to the people, and that he should be called *Getaye,* my lord, my master, and he could take her place. And then she died, at the end of the reign of Emperor Menelik. And we come every year to honor her on the anniversary of her death. Amen.

But Taye, when he was a child, was sent to live in the Palace, in Addis Ababa, because he was the child of the quality of the Amhara. And he was raised as a Christian, and he left the cult of *Gifti Arussi.* When he became a young man, having been educated, he was a member of the life guard of Ras Tefari Makonnen, when he was crown prince. And later, when Ras Tefari became emperor, and was Haile Selassie I, then Taye was in the imperial bodyguard. But then the Italians came, and he was a patriot, and he fought them, but they caught him and took him to Mogadishu, in Somalia, but they did not kill him.

And when he came back to Addis, and when the Emperor returned, he fell sick and was taken to the hospital. And he was burning with fever and was dying, and the foreign doctors could find nothing wrong with him. They wanted to let him go, for they could do nothing for him. But then one man, an imam, came to him in the hospital from Guna-Ferekasa, from the shrine of his great-grandmother, Wo. Shebash, and told him that he would surely die if he did not leave Christianity, and told him that he must come to serve Allah in Arussi, for the people needed him. And then he had a dream, and in the dream he saw that it was true; that he had the gift of Allah, and must go there and cure the people, and build the shrine.

But at that time he had to divorce his wife who was a Christian, and marry a woman who was a Muslim, and study Islam, and he had to become a Muslim. And he did all these things, and has been well ever since. He is never sick, and he never tires, and he helps all the people, those who live on his land, and those who come every year. And he helps the Christians and the Muslims alike. He has been given the gift of Allah and his spirit is the spirit of Allah, and it is that which controls the *wuqabi* and the *zar*, and the *g̃inns* and the devils, and it is this which cures the people. And he now has seventeen children, and he is forty-eight years old. Amen.

7.   There is little overt homosexuality in central Ethiopia. While male-male or female-female friendship is stressed, it is not thought to have sexual overtones except in very rare instances. Men who are friends embrace each other, walk arm in arm, and otherwise engage in a great deal of physical contact. Yet within the culture, there is no allusion made to homosexuality in this context. Repeated questioning of informants of both sexes elicited the view that homosexuality was not to be found in Ethopia, and observation across a wide range of occasions tended to confirm this view, at least insofar as overt instances are concerned. To some extent, however, the category of s^uet-a-s^uet may stand for latent homosexuality. Still, it is important to reiterate that this association is not overtly made by Ethiopians themselves. Further, it should be stressed that Dawit did not in any way conform to the model of the s^uet-a-s^uet and, in our view, did not conform to the Western model of homosexuality.

REFERENCES

GIEL, R. *et al.*
  1968   "Faith Healing and Spirit Possession in Ghion, Ethiopia." *Social Science in Medicine* **2.**

KNUTSSON, K. E.
  1967   *Authority and Change.* Göteborg, Sweden: Etnografiska Museet.

LEVINE, D. N.
  1965   *Wax and Gold.* Chicago: Chicago University Press, p. 249 ff.

LEWIS, I. M.

1971   *Ecstatic Religion.* London: Penguin Books.

MORTON, A. L.

1973   "Some Aspects of Spirit Possession in Ethiopia." University of London. Unpublished Ph.D. dissertation.

MORTON, A. L.

1975   "Mystical Advocates: Explanation and Spirit-Sanctioned Adjudication in the Shoa Galla Ayana Cult." In *Proceedings of the First U.S. Conference on Ethiopian Studies,* H. Marcus, Ed. East Lansing: Michigan State University Committee on Ethiopian Studies.

WALDRON, S.

1974   *Social Organization and Social Control in the Walled City of Harar, Ethiopia.* Unpublished Ph.D. Dessertation, Department of Anthropology, Columbia University.

Gananath Obeyesekere

Psychocultural Exegesis of a Case of Spirit Possession in Sri Lanka

PSYCHOCULTURAL EXEGESIS

Psychocultural exegesis is a technique for analyzing the behavior of informants in such states as spirit possession, mediumship, trance, and related conditions. These conditions are culturally structured insofar as the definition of the ecstatic seizure, the setting in which it occurs, the visions experienced by the patient, and the exorcism that follows (in spirit possession) have a standard form and a coherent meaning which render them intelligible to the community at large. Yet while the cultural form which embodies the ecstatic experience is a publicly intelligible one, the experience itself is highly personal, not one shared by the group. Ecstatic states are generally rare and experienced by only a few

Adaptation reprinted by permission of from *Contributions to Arian Studies*, **8** (1975).

in any community. Thus most forms of ecstatic religion, to use Lewis's term, are based on intensely personal experiences, though expressed in a cultural idiom and within a standard framework.

The experience here is not a communal, shared one. When I go to church or temple on a holy day, or to a horse race, or a football game, I participate in a cultural experience more or less in common with my fellows in the same congregation or audience. By contrast, the possession experience is not shared; yet the idiom and context of possession is comprehensible to others insofar as it is couched in terms of a larger shared culture. Thus it is radically different qualitatively from psychotic expression or fantasy that is both ego-alien and culture-alien, that is, out of touch with cultural reality. Possession involves an ego-alien experience, but is not culturally alien.

A successful exorcism and cure result in harmonizing the original traumatic experience with both ego and culture; thus ecstatic religion is both personal and cultural. One should add, however, that such personal experiences may be due to the intensification, in the individual case, of sociopsychological conditions endemic to the group. For this reason the group has learned through time to handle these experiences by standardizing them in a culturally acceptable manner.

In psychocultural exegesis I attempt to render intelligible the sociocultural context in which possession occurs and the manner in which the personal experience of possession is expressed within a set of standardized cultural meanings. Exegesis on both cultural and psychological levels involves the following:

1. The experiences of possession and possession behavior are related systematically to the social, personal, and cultural background of the patient.

2. Possession is followed by exorcism, in which the troublesome spirits are expelled from the body of the patient by a priest. The utterances and behavior of both patient and priest are explicated for their cultural meaning. The cultural symbols operative in the ritual are rendered intelligible.

3. Rendering the cultural meaning of a performance intelligible is what Geertz, following Weber, considers to be the major aim of anthropological interpretation. I go a step further. Exegesis aims also at elucidating the manner in which the personal experience is expressed in a cultural framework. Cultural meanings are manipulated by the individual to express personal needs and emotions. How this occurs is the major thrust of my analysis. In sum, psychocultural exegesis employs a

flashback technique: the events in the possession and exorcism are systematically related to the social, cultural, and personal background of the patient, rendering them intelligible from the point of view of both personality and culture.

It will be evident from the foregoing discussion that my notion of culture as a system of shared meanings is derived from Max Weber and those social scientists who have been influenced by him. But what about personality? Here I follow most culture and personality theorists and use psychoanalytic theory to unravel the intensely personal, affectively loaded, and often unconsciously motivated behavior of the individual experiencing possession.

Pyschoanalytic theory is useful for another reason. Freud himself was interested in relating personality to culture and integrating the level of personal experience with that of cultural meaning. *Future of an Illusion, Group Psychology and the Analysis of the Ego,* and "Obessional acts and religious practices," are of considerable interest and importance to the anthropological and sociological analyst of religion. The weaknesses in these works are well known, but let me emphasize their strengths: (*a*) First, Freud was concerned with the individual's social relationship to a deity or deities in the pantheon, which is a sociological problem. This is a parent-child relationship, based on an infantile model (Freud, 1957). (*b*) Man, in the face of hopelessness, despair, and suffering projects this infantile model into the cosmos and thereby achieves a sense of personal security. Thus projection is both a mechanism of defense and a system of security. (*c*) Ritual—a technique of interacting with the deity—is like the obsessional acts of neurotics, in that while the ritualized obsessional acts of neurotics are an attempt to cope with an idiosyncratic inner anxiety, the rituals of religion are culturally constituted mechanisms for channeling the anxieties and psychological problems common to a group.

These several strands in Freud's sociological thinking were superbly integrated into a single paradigm by Kardiner, in his notion of "projective systems": cultural structures, like religion, help channel the personal projections of individuals; these in turn arise as a result of common socialization experiences which produce generic psychological traits (basic personality structure) in a given population (Kardiner, 1945). Basic personality structure, resolves Durkheim's dilemma: religious projective systems are not products of a "collective consciousness," in Durkheim's sense (1915) but a product of psychological traits common to a group, and the genesis of these traits could be explained systematically rather than in an ad hoc manner in terms of psychoanalytic theory.

While Kardiner's paradigm resolved some of the methodological problems involved in the relationship between personality and culture, it also created new difficulties. One pertains to the use of any ideal typical constructs such as Basic Personality Structure, which may seriously distort or oversimplify the complexity of empirical reality. What is the incidence, distribution, and frequency of these personality traits in a given society? Whiting and his associates have operationalized Kardiner's scheme by isolating specific antecedent variables like a type of socialization practice; they then infer a psychological consequence of this practice, and predict the kind of projective system that the antecedent and intervening variables generate. Thus punitive socialization produces an aggressive rather than a benevolent pantheon of supernaturals (Lambert, Triandis, and Wolf, 1959; see also Spiro and D'Andrade, 1958).

While there are many merits in these approaches, they bypass the problem that interested Freud—the individual's relationship to the pantheon of deities. For example, cruel socialization may produce a pantheon of cruel deities, but how does the individual relate to them? What motivates him to relate to some and ignore others? Religious pantheons haven't the simple clarity of the Judeo-Christian tradition that Freud was impressed with in his study. Polytheistic religious pantheons, common the world over, have a bewildering array of supernatural beings, with highly variable attributes. In Buddhist Sri Lanka for example, the head of the pantheon is the Buddha and below him are *devas,* righteous gods, often addressed as father. But some of these "fathers" are more benevolent than others (e.g., Vishnu); other deities, like Dadimunda, are stern and punitive; still others, like Skanda, are handsome and demand filial piety from the worshipper. On the level of the group all persons in the culture believe in these deities, but some individuals may have a special relationship with one particular deity; thus the individual's selection of a deity from a large number in the pantheon is a problem of great significance for the sociology and anthropology of religion.

Let us compare briefly one variant of the Judeo-Christian tradition, Catholicism, with the Sri Lankan Buddhist pantheon. There is on the one hand God the Father whom everyone worships and supplicates. The analogous position in Buddhist pantheon in Sri Lanka is the Buddha himself. All persons in the culture concerned believe in the existence of their main deity and have a permanent continuous relationship with him. But take the next level of the pantheon, the saints in Catholicism and the *devas* (gods) in Buddhism. All persons believe in their existence but some select one or more from a larger pantheon for a special relationship(s), and it is these motives for selection that need explication. Finally, take the devils in medieval Catholicism and the demons in Sri Lanka. All persons believe in their existence but the individual's relationship with them is at best occasional, and some individuals may have had no relationship with them. And when it comes to undefined evil spirits such as ghosts, goblins, or *pretas* in Buddhism (the evil spirits of dead ancestors), the relationship with the spirit becomes an even more individual affair. One might conclude by saying that the individual's relationship with deities in the pantheon may be *permanent, continuous* (God, Buddha); *selective, continual* (saints, devas); *selective, occasional* or, may not exist at all (devils, demons, spirits). The cognitive belief in all these systems of worship is universal; the nature and intensity of the belief becomes more variable and selective as one approaches the lower ends of the hierarchy. Also, I believe that the motives of the individual become less structured, more variable, and less "modal," as we descend the supernatural hierarchy.

Now I can state the thesis of this chapter. This is a detailed examination of a case of an urban woman from Sri Lanka possessed by the occasional supernatural beings of the pantheon, demons and *prētas*. The demons are named beings having a position in the Sinhalese Buddhist pantheon, but the *prētas* (evil ancestral beings) must in a sense be created by each individual. The culture recognizes the existence of the category *prēta*, but why a particular *prēta* should possess a person is an individual matter. First we shall examine the psychological significance of the possession for the woman: what motivated her to choose these particular spirits from the pantheon and what psychological meaning do they have for her? Possession is followed by "cure"—an expulsion of the demons and *prētas* from the body of the patient in an exorcistic ritual. The ritual is a "standard one": other patients with different symptoms or illnessess must go through the same or a similar standard ritual. How is this standard ritual related to the individual patient? And how do patient and priest utilize the standard ritual to cure a particular case? It should be realized that both belief in spirits and the ritual are standard cultural beliefs and practices: how does the individual express his or her personal problem within a standard belief system? Through "psychocultural exegesis" the events in the possession episode and exorcism ritual are retrospectively related to the cultural background of the society and the personal and social background of the patient.

II

THE PATIENT

The patient, Somavati, age twenty-nine, was brought to my attention in early 1969, when she came to be exorcised by the *Kapurāla* (priest) of a shrine for the gods or *dēvas* located at Navala, a Colombo suburb which I was studying as part of a larger research project on curing rituals in Sri Lanka. I witnessed the whole ritual of exorcism, photographed it in detail, and tape-recorded it fully. I interviewed Somavati six times in several long sessions two months after her exorcism, and several sessions much later. I followed her case until September 1971, nearly two years after the exorcism. The personal and social background of the patient is derived from these interviews, cross-checked with information supplied by the *Kapurāla* and by her parents.

Somavati was the eldest daughter of a poor farmer belonging to the *goyigama* (cultivator) caste. Their original home was at Homagama, once a little village but now a town, about twenty miles from the city of Colombo. Her father, P. A. Pantis Singho, was one of fourteen siblings, and her mother who came from the nearby "village" of Talagala was one of seven siblings. These simple familial facts in the context of Sri Lanka's changing villages meant that whatever ancestral property existed had to be divided among siblings. This in turn resulted in fractions of land, causing indigence and all sorts of family disputes. Pantis Singho lived at Homagama until Somavati was twenty-three years old. He quarrelled constantly with his siblings and finally left his paternal village for good. Then he worked in the village of Kiriwattuduva, near his wife's ancestral home for three or four years as a rubber tapper on a small plantation owned by an Ayurvedic physician. When he lost this job he went to a small village near his paternal home as a laborer and cultivator of some *ande* (leased) paddy land. He stayed there for a little over a year then found employment in Boralasgamuwa, a suburb of Colombo. He lives there still in a small two-room house with his large family, excluding his eldest son but including Somavati and her two children. All of them except the three youngest siblings work as paid day laborers (average daily income per person is about U.S. $.75).

The following features of Somavati's family background are essential for understanding certain aspects of her illness and subsequent cure. (a) Her parents were ordinary peasants who had been thrown out of their village by an acute shortage of land. They lost their roots in their villages of origin and moved into a new situation as paid day laborers in economically unstable jobs, but not however on a starvation or near-starvation level. (b) The orginal homogeneous, kin-based villages from which they came have changed radically due to land shortages and rapid population growth. Some have sold their lands and moved out into urban areas. Some villages have been swallowed up by the encroaching tide of urban sprawl. The kind of kinship supports that were available to an individual in a more traditional village is practically nonexistent for Somavati's family. In other words alienation from the larger kin group is a characteristic feature of their lifestyle.

I shall now sketch the personal life history of Somavati. Her birth order in her family of orientation is summed up in Figure 1. Her birth

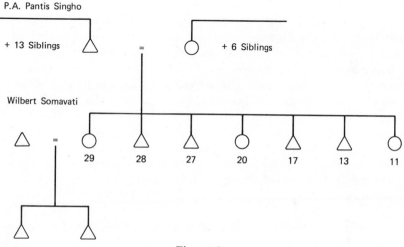

Figure 1

order typically poses certain psychological problems in any such family group: early weaning and shifting of maternal affection to the newborn (and desired) son. This problem was exaggerated in Somavati's case by certain unique life experiences.

In early infancy Somavati was given to her mother's mother for adoption. In late pregnancy her mother went to her grandmother's house for confinement and delivery. It is a common custom in patrilocally organized groups in Sri Lanka for the mother to go back to the parents on critical occasions such as childbirth and illness. However, when Somavati was a few months old she was given to the grandmother for adoption. Somavati's own words are worth quoting "I was not *himi* ('destined', 'entitled') for my mother, and she sold me to my grandmother." Rightly or wrongly, Somavati was absolutely convinced that her mother was given a cash payment by her grandmother. Real or fantasized, the sense of betrayal by the parents must have been strong. At this time her parents lived in the paternal village of Homagama, not too far from the grandmother's village, and visited her once in a while, but this could only have reinforced the jealousy toward her sibling, and her oral rage. Thus several events in her life history can be documented with some certainty: early weaning, betrayal by the parents, loss of parental love and separation from them, and adoption by the grandmother. It is probably true that Somavati's grandmother loved her deeply and provided enough gratification for her affective needs, but none of this could have prevented the trauma of early weaning associated as it was with separation from the mother.

She lived with her grandmother for seven years, and recalled this period as the happiest time of her life. Her grandmother showered her with affection, she liked to recall. When she was seven, her father brought her back home. The reason given was that grandmother was too old, but Somavati shrewdly recollected what was probably the real reason. Her brothers were growing up, her mother was pregnant with a fourth child, and she needed someone to look after the younger siblings. From that time onward her life was *karadara*, "full of difficulties." She had to look after her siblings, and was scolded and sometimes hit when she did not perform these tasks properly. She had to give up schooling at third grade (standard 3), so Somavati is not properly educated though she can read reasonably well and write with some difficulty.

It should be remembered that there is nothing unusual in elder siblings looking after younger ones in peasant families in Sri Lanka. What is unusual are the circumstances in Somavati's case—her being taken away from the security of her grandmother's home and thrust into a role for which she was unprepared, from being taken care of by her grandmother to having to take care of her "hated" siblings. She could recall her separation from her grandmother. She felt *dukkha* ("suffering"), and her grandmother cried and objected to her being taken away. "I also wanted to stay, but father took me away, as if by force." She also stated that she used to visit her grandmother often, but the old lady died when Somavati was about fourteen years old.

Somavati's life in her parental home seems uneventful until her marriage, yet these intervening years have considerable psychological significance. In Sinhalese socialization of females two factors stand out conspicuously. Firstly, there is a rigid sexual puritanism which is characteristic of the more urbanized areas such as Somavati's village. Consequently there is a total segregation of sexes and inhibition of sexual expression. For example, Somavati had no heterosexual premarital experience of any sort prior to her marriage, and her case is not unusual. In traditional villages there are opportunities for adolescents to indulge in petting, and interfemoral copulation in the adjacent jungles or near the bathing stream, but in the crowded, urbanized villages just beyond the suburbs of Colombo these opportunities are scarce. Schools, which are generally coeducational, help the development of romantic love affairs, but in Somavati's case this was not available. Parental control over young girls is also tight, and unchaperoned visits are not permitted. Somavati, like other girls of her background had no sex education at all; her parents, even on the eve of her marriage, never spoke to her about sex. This cultural attitude toward sex has one major consequence: repression becomes a major mechanism of defense for coping with sexual stimuli.

Secondly, the aggression drive is radically inhibited and controlled. The Buddhist norms of nonviolence are strongly believed in by the Sinhalese of this area. Somavati's grandmother, for example, was an extremely pious lady who regularly practiced meditation; she would literally not harm the mosquito that sucked her blood, but would gently brush it away. Thus ideas of nonviolence were inculcated into Somavati, as with others in the culture, very early. These values combined with notions of female modesty, decorum, and gentleness, have a further effect on personality: the establishment of repression as the major mechanism for coping with hostile and aggressive feelings stimulated no doubt in Somavati's case, as in other cases, by her environment; for example resentment toward the siblings she had to look after. For Sri Lanka I think it would be correct to say that the more urbanized the culture, the more entrenched repression becomes as an ego defense; less opportunities are provided for overt expression of sexual and aggression drives. The continued use of repression in this manner leads to certain expectable character traits in the female population: a propensity to hysteria, anorexia, widespread hypochondriacal tendencies, and somatization of conflicts. Western-trained doctors have coined a term for a major preoccupation of female patients visiting the outpatient department of government hospitals. They call it "A.P.R.", from *Atha Paya Rudava* ("hands-feet-pains"). These tendencies are widespread among the general female population, and cannot be considered the cause of spirit possession, for then every female must be afflicted with it. This is certainly not the case, since spirit possession only happens to a few. But if some of the modal psychological problems are intensified, or new stresses have to be coped with, then I believe conditions favorable to spirit possession may arise (Obeyesekere, 1970).

Take Somavati's socialization traumas of early weaning and parental betrayal. The oral rage that this experience no doubt generated cannot be expressed overtly or against objects or persons in the outer environment, since such expressions would be forbidden in her culture. They have to be repressed, and the repressions have to be consistently maintained. Or take her relationship with her grandmother; it was destroyed by the parents. She is given a servant role as caretaker of siblings and is punished if she fails in this role. The quantity of repressed rage against her parents and siblings must surely have been great, and must have entailed severe strains on the defenses of her ego.

At sixteen, Somavati decided to join a weaving school a few miles from her village. Her parents agreed, since she could get an income from this source that would help enhance the meager family budget. For the first time Somavati could get away from home and mix freely with members of her own sex. At weaving school she cultivated several friends with whom she could gossip and talk about the future. Even here the girls did not talk directly about sexual matters but indirectly, in romantic terms, they would talk about heroines in popular novels or films. Their gossip was not, however, all romantic cloud cuckoo land stuff. Somavati said that often they talked about the difficulties of a woman's life in Sri Lanka. They felt that a woman's lot was no good. "Look at our impure menstruation which forbids us to go to places of worship." They particularly emphasized their lack of leisure and their inability to go out alone. Apparently the wish to go alone somewhere—shopping or to films—was viewed as embodying freedom! Distrust of males and marriage were other topics discussed. Someone would give an instance of parents quarreling, and would say: "It is a pity if we too have to put up with this in marriage". Friendships, gossip, added income, and a temporary flight from home were all provided by the weaving school, which Somavati saw as a "good" period in her life.

At the weaving school Somavati met her future husband; she was eighteen and he twenty-five. He was a skilled mason from Galle in the Southern Province of Sri Lanka, and had come to Homagama to work for a government contractor. They soon became "friendly," and began to chat with each other in school, where he visited her. He met her parents and proposed marriage; they objected to it at first and told Somavati that he had no stable job and his home was far from theirs. The reasons for the parents' objection to what would seem to have been a "good match" are worth considering. People like Somavati's father are highly respectable peasants of the *goyigama* caste, who operate according to traditional marriage rules hardly applicable to their present economically indigent circumstances. For them a good marriage must either be with a kinsman (a cross-cousin) or, if an outsider, it must be a strategic marriage that helps forge an alliance between two kin groups. The latter has to be arranged with great care, hence the objection to the "hasty" proposal. But Somavati, who saw marriage as an escape from her home, persisted, and her parents finally relented.

She described her first night with her husband as *bayasāka*, "filled with fear and doubt." Her mother gave her no advice about sex, only about living with her husband in concord and amity. Her husband too was sexually inexperienced and failed to have intercourse on the first night. But the situation improved, and Somavati claimed to have enjoyed their sex life greatly. Initially they lived in a rented house in Kottava, about ten miles from her parent's home. Her husband had steady employment and was a good provider. She had their first child a year after marriage. Then—the details are unclear—things changed quite drastically.

It is indicative of the superficial nature of their premarital romance that Somavati had no idea that her husband drank. She learned this in the first week of her marriage. His drinking habits became much worse a year later and continued through the four or five years of their married life. Generally he drank in the evenings, almost never in the mornings. He mixed *ganja* (cannabis sativa) with alcohol, and in his drunken state he beat her. As time went on the beatings occurred independently of the alcoholic stimulus. Somavati says that sometimes he would strap her with his belt; at other times he would hit her with little or no provocation. If she wanted to go see her parents, he would assault her. "You don't need to go to your parents," he said. "If dinner is late, if there is too much salt in the food, or too little salt, I get beaten." Sometimes her neighbors, hearing her cries, intervened, but the results of their intervention were only temporary. Sometimes he abused the neighbors and told them to mind their own business. Somavati's life was not, however, a total misery. Her husband could be very good and loving at times and he was always a good provider. There was no cessation of their sex life either. Though Somavati denied ever having intercourse after episodes of beating, they continued to enjoy sex when he was in a "good mood."

My interviews with Somavati convinced me that she had a sadomasochistic relationship with her husband. In my first series of interviews with her, two months after her cure, she struck me as being somewhat "flat," almost affectless, constantly giggling. Some of this shyness is expectable in a Sinhalese girl interviewed by a male regarding her private life. It was as if on the one hand she enjoyed being interviewed on sex, and on the other resisted it as befits a "modest" woman. Her giggling increased when I asked her questions about her husband's brutality, and in several places in my notes I have commented that she seems to enjoy talking about it. Several events she mentioned in the interviews brought out the masochistic component in her personality. She never retaliated or objected to being beaten. Question: "When he hits you what do you do?" Somavati (laughs): "I don't do anything, I just wait." She cried, but did not even retaliate verbally. She did not talk about her husband's cruelty to her parents, or siblings, or friends. "Why burden my parents and friends with my problems," she said. Her parents eventually heard of her husband's cruelty from her neighbors and questioned Somavati, who admitted it. They also found out that he had a mistress; they asked Somavati to leave her husband and come home with them. Somavati was quite reluctant, but her father told her that if she did not leave Wilbert she could not expect them to support or look after her in the future. She finally relented and departed for her parents' home with her child. She was at the time four months pregnant. But Wilbert was not easily put off and visited her there and beat her a couple of times. Somavati's parents forbade Wilbert to visit her, and persuaded her to file for divorce. Meanwhile Wilbert informed the police that Somavati was kept "against her will" by her parents, but nothing came out of it. After five months she was granted a divorce by the Colombo South Magistrate. Wilbert visited her once after the divorce was granted, but never again.

Her passivity on being beaten, her reluctance to leave Wilbert, and the fact that she endured his cruelty for about four years strongly suggest that she wanted to be beaten. It is likely that she actually provided the requisite "provocations" by making his dinner late, putting too much or too little salt into his food, and so on. Other evidence of a projective nature indicated sadistic traits. For example, I asked her what were the items she most enjoyed in the newspapers she read, and she replied: "Funeral advertisements, court cases, like murder cases, where punishment is meted out by the courts." I asked her what types of punishment are appropriate for murder, and she replied, "the type of punishments that existed in the time of the Kandyan kings," that is, extreme physical torture. I asked her what type of punishment is appropriate for a minor offense like petty theft—a fine, or imprisonment, or whipping? "Whipping," she replied, "it is the only effective punishment." Note that this kind of sadism is close to masochism in its "passive" character: it is not expressed in direct outward reactions like the husband's, but in a vicarious enjoyment of cruelty.

It should not surprise us to see masochistic traits in Somavati's personality, if we consider the nature of her life prior to her marriage.

Repression of sex and aggression, we noted, were a common feature in Sinhalese females and produced anticipated character traits such as widespread hypochondria, and somatization of mental conflicts. In Somavati's case the amount of repressed aggression was much greater, and hence masochistic traits due to internalization of hostile rages were to be expected. To rephrase it: although there is a tendency toward masochism in normal (modal) females, in Somavati's case there is a full development of masochistic traits.

III

POSSESSION

In this section I will deal with Somavati's episode of spirit possession. I will first describe the events in her life that preceded this episode and then attempt a psychocultural exegesis of her spirit attack by referring it to Somavati's personal background sketched earlier. This I believe will help us understand fully the psychological significance of spirit possession for the individual.

Somavati's reluctance to leave her husband and join her parental household was based on both nonrational and rational factors; nonrational because the sadomasochistic relationship with her husband met the unconscious demands of her personality, and rational in that she would face economic insecurity in her father's household. Her husband was after all a good provider. Furthermore, it is likely that the return to her parents reactivated the trauma that resulted from an earlier event—her forceful removal from the security of her grandmother's home. But the deed was done, and Somavati finally severed all connections with her husband.

They were still living in her father's village at Homagama. At this time her father quarreled with his siblings, sold the little property they had, and went to live in Kiriwattuduve as a rubber tapper on a plantation owned by an Ayurvedic physician. This was a further strain for Somavati, since she had to give up her friends in the village and her kinsmen, always a source of security and support. She had also given birth to her second child, and it was impossible for her to go to work or to weaving school. They lived on the plantation belonging to the physician and soon the elder of her two brothers married and brought his wife to live in their already crowded household. Owing to interpersonal conflicts, the son and his new bride went back to his father's village in Homagama to live there with his father's kinsmen. During this whole period, of about twenty months since she had left her husband, Somavati had very little leisure, practically no money, and depended exclusively on parental support. She had no sex relations with anyone (indeed this would be almost impossible, given the circumstances in which she lived). Her parents also had no interest in getting her married. This new deprivation must have added to the strains already overburdening her. Then came the spirit attack.

The episode of demonic possession and attack occurred in an extraordinarily complicated manner. The Ayurvedic physician's wife's brother's wife was possessed by the *prēta* (evil ancestral spirit) of her husband's mother, Mary Nona. Let us call this couple X and Y. (X and Y lived in Poruvedanda, a village about six miles from Kiriwattuduve where Somavati lived.) Many exorcistic rituals were held to banish the spirit from the body of the woman (Y), but to no avail, since X and Y were very unpopular in the area and their enemies performed counter-magic to render the ritual ineffective. X and Y consulted a demon exorcist (*Kattadirāla*) from Talagala to cure Y's malady and banish the evil spirit Mary Nona. This exorcist, Louis Kattadirala, was from Talagala where Somavati's grandmother lived and in fact was her next door neighbor at one time. Louis the exorcist, suggested to X a way in which the ritual could be successful and capable of warding off counter-magic. The crucial part of the ritual, which consists of *jīvan* (making magically "live," or "active" a sacred thread), should be performed in the Ayurvedic physician's house in Kiriwattuduve away from enemy counter-magic. The physician agreed, and this part of the ritual was performed at his house in the late afternoon. Then Louis and the Ayurvedic physician rented a car and took the charmed thread to X's house in Poruvedanda to be tied on Y's wrist. Before they left the Ayurvedic physician asked Somavati to come to his house and keep his wife company, as she was "alone" with two young children and a servant. Somavati agreed and went to the Ayurvedic physician's house at 6 p.m. Her father cautioned her before she left: he said that the ritual being performed there was a dangerous one and she should not go. But Somavati felt obliged to help her father's employer, and thus her father could not seriously object to it.

"I was there for about one hour, chatting with the Ayurvedic physician's wife. I suddenly felt as if there was a big weight on my head and then I didn't see anything. . . ." She fell down unconscious. This was around 7 p.m. A message was sent to her father to say she was ill. Meanwhile she was given some water and she felt better. Her father arrived. She spoke to him and then fainted again and remained unconscious till around midnight. She was practically carried home. A message was sent to Louis Kattadirala, who arrived about 4 a.m. and tied a charmed thread around Somavati's wrist. She felt better, but as soon as Louis left (around 6 a.m.) she fainted again. Louis came back and tied an *āpa nūl* as "bond thread." *Apa nūl* is a charmed thread that wards off the spirit attack for a limited period of time specified by the priest: twenty-four hours, or three weeks, or three months, or longer. The spirit is held in "bond" as it were: after this period a larger ritual must be performed to banish the evil spirit.

The circumstances of Somavati's illness left no doubt that she was the victim of a spirit attack. The *āpa nūl* was to prevent a further attack for a three-month period when a larger ritual would have to be held to banish the spirit or spirits that plagued her. But the spirit was too powerful or the *āpa nūl* was not truly effective, for Somavati had several attacks during this three-month period. An exorcist had to come and tie another *āpa nūl*. These subsequent attacks occurred at about the same time as the initial attack (around 7 p.m.). She described the nature of these attacks:

My hands and feet grow cold; it is as if I don't possess them. Then my body shivers—shivers, and the inside of my body seems to shake. . . . This goes on and on . . . and if I hear someone talk I get angry. My rage is such that I could even hit my father and mother . . . this is how the illness starts.

She behaves like the evil spirit possessing her: she hoots, shrieks, runs all over, threatens to assault people and eat them up. "Kanava, kanava. . . . Kanava. . . . I will eat you up, eat you . . . eat you," she says in this state, shrieking and hooting. In this state she says she is Mary Nona, the same spirit that possessed Y.

Exegesis: Spirit Possession

In Somavati's personal history there were enough psychological strains to precipitate a "breakdown." Possession is not something alien to her: she, like other women of her background, has seen women who have been possessed by spirits. Thus cultural models for the emulation of the sick role have been available to her. Everyone also knows that it is dangerous for a young woman to be present in the house where a deadly ritual is being held. This was what prompted the Ayurvedic physician to ask Somavati to keep his wife company and also the reason for Somavati's father to caution her from doing precisely that. In a vague and probably undefined way Somavati wanted (unconsciously) to keep the physician's wife company. Moreover she left around 6 p.m., culturally defined as a *samayan velāva*, a time when evil spirits are out, and also, though the distance was short, she went alone. "Alone" in Sinhalese belief is a dangerous state; it makes a person vulnerable to demonic attack. Such an attack during a period of "aloneness" (physical and psychological) is known as *tanikam dōsa* "troubles of aloneness (caused by demons)." Somavati must surely have been aware of these cultural beliefs when she went out, and uneasy about them. Indeed, I do not believe that even a very brave person in her culture would have been free from anxiety. When she went to the house the topic of conversation with the physician's wife was the ritual. The physician's wife spoke of her sister-in-law's possession and how she used to run out of the house when she was ill. Meanwhile Somavati was aware that the *Kattadirāla* was at the house of the sick woman, probably tying the magic thread to bring the demon under control. The context for spirit attack was just right: the relevant cultural ideas were in her mind; she was full of anxiety; psychologically she was prepared for a "breakdown," to give up, so to speak, the burdens that pressed on her. Hysterical traits that she had as a consequence of the radical repression of the sex drive made her psychologically *capable* of being "possessed," getting into trancelike states of hysterical dissociation. However, her trancelike behavior did not occur immediately. Initially she was in a state of psychological aloneness (i.e., extreme anxiety), and an evil spirit visited her in this vulnerable state. The culturally anticipated consequence followed: unconsciousness. She woke up with the appropriate cultural stimuli: water, and later the tying of a thread by the priest. I have seen patients and priests fall "unconscious" on the floor during curing rituals; yet invariably they arise when charmed water is sprinkled on them. Somavati also got up when someone sprayed water on her, but she became unconscious again immediately because (I think) she realized that the "water" was ordinary water given by the physician's wife. However, when the priest arrived, sprayed charmed water and tied the thread, she became much better. Her behavior was exactly in accordance with the cultural definition of the situation. Again, the "automatic" nature of such behavior fits in with her hysterical disposition.

Spirit attack can take various forms: illness for example, or fainting spells. Possession (*āvēsa*) is one consequence of spirit attack where the spirit, in essence or in reality, resides in the patient. In Somavati's case the context favored an interpretation of possession, though Somavati had not yet manifested trancelike behavior. Furthermore, a spirit that is being banished from one patient may escape into the body of another; this is exactly what seemed to occur that day. It is likely that people who were gathered around the "unconscious" Somavati were expressing these and similar opinions regarding her illness. My knowledge of other patients with similar experiences suggests that these states of unconsciousness are not true blackouts: selected events in the outer environment are being "unconsciously" (in the psychoanalytic sense) noted by the patient (Obeyesekere, 1970, pp. 97–111). Moreover, during the brief period she got up (as a result of water lustration), she must have been aware of what happened to her and interpreted it as a demon attack, with possession as a possible consequence.

Thus Somavati had two or three fainting spells before full-blown possession occurred, and then she acted "like a demon." Thereafter no fainting spells occurred, but always the kind of behavior described earlier, generally around 7 p.m. In this state she confirmed the public expectation: she was in fact possessed by the spirit of Mary Nona (who had originally possessed patient Y).

Let us now examine the psychological significance of Somavati's possession. The possession by a spirit is something that she also, unconsciously, wanted to happen. It is not a psychotic or a nervous breakdown in the Western sense; the breakdown was culturally "timed" and expressed in a prescribed demonic idiom. It is a breakdown as a result of accumulated psychological pressures; at the same time it is an attempt to cope with these pressures by bringing them to the surface and acting them out. Aberle's view (1952) that Latah and Arctic hysteria are coping devices of the ego is also applicable in this case. The hostile, repressed feelings are expressed directly in the demonological idiom readily understood by the culture. Once possessed by a demon, a considerable leeway in behavior is possible: some patients, like Y, may run out into the streets; others might tear their clothes off, depending on the nature of the individual's inner problems. In Somavati's case several clear-cut psychological problems are expressed in her behavior while possessed:

1. Oral rage: shrieking, hooting, and threatening to eat people, are an expression of infantile rage against early weaning and deprivation of love.

2. Hatred toward parents who she feels have been responsible for this.

3. Generalized aggression: she threatening to assault anyone around, converting masochism and passive sadism into overt aggressive behavior.

These attacks then permit "abreactions" of repressed impulses. Before each attack the patient experiences "a heavy weight in the head" (*baragatiya*); but after acting out in this manner she collapses. When she gets up the heaviness (due perhaps to the strain of repressions kept under control) disappears, and she awakes as if from a deep sleep. Moreover, her ego is protected from the shameful unfeminine behavior she may have performed for two reasons. First, she has total amnesia for the actions performed during possession and the only information she gets is from her parents and siblings who witnessed them. Second, these family members are tolerant of her bizarre behavior, since it is not she but an independent demon who behaves this way. The woman is absolved from the responsibility for her actions. Thus a pattern of behavior has been established: whenever the strains become intolerable the patient gets possessed, acts out her impulses and, after a period of illness that may last for a couple of days, reverts to her normal role. The temporary relief experienced and the secondary compensations of attention and parental solicitude for her welfare reinforce that pattern of behavior.

Exegesis: Prētas

Somavati was possessed by the spirit of Mary Nona, who belonged to a class of evil spirits known as *prētas*. Who is a *prēta* and what is the significance of being possessed by a *prēta*?

In doctrinal Buddhism, any person excessively attached to the things of the world can on death become a *prēta*. But as this doctrinal idea is translated in Sinhalese behavior, a *prēta* is generally a near kinsman, often born in that state due to excessive love of the living. In the many interviews I have had with persons whose parents were born as *prētas* I have always been impressed by the fact that a person may say that his father or mother is a *prēta* and must be placated with impure foods. The same person may have spoken very highly of his father, and may even say that he is a *prēta* because his parents loved him too much. Psychologically, however, if not theologically, the conversion of a loved one into a miserable spirit surely illustrates a strong unconscious hatred for the dead person, a feeling that the actor refuses consciously to recognize. In fact in my many interviews with persons whose kinsmen had become *prētas*, not one person recognized the unusual, shocking nature of this concept, although to call someone a *prēta* in everyday parlance is a derogatory insult of the worst order.

Once the belief that a dead kinsman is a *prēta* has been created, certain consequences follow. One may make merit and transfer the merit to the *prēta* to help him achieve a better rebirth. If the *prēta* is a troublesome poltergeist he may have to be banished. Alternately, since the *prēta* is hovering about the human habitation he may "possess" one of the living. The psychology of possession by *prētas* may be more complex than the simple belief that one's ancestor is a *prēta*. For example, Y was possessed by the spirit (*prēta*) of her husband's mother. It may be possible that she was thus expressing an attitude not simply to the mother-in-law, but also to her husband, ("you son-of-a-prēta!"). Furthermore, like Somavati, Y also must surely have been using the *prēta* to express and act out her own unconscious impulses.

The context in which Somavati "fell ill" (according to cultural notions) was such that she had to seize upon the *prēta* most readily available—that of Y's mother-in-law, someone totally unknown to her. For the moment any demonic spirit could help her to escape from an intolerable life situation. But someone else's mother-in-law, although temporarily useful, cannot be as satisfactory as a near kinsman. Let us consider how another *prēta,* this time a near relation of Somavati, also came to possess her.

One day, soon after Somavati's illness, her father went to see Louis Kattadirala, the exorcist, and asked him: "Why did *you* do this to my daughter?" After a pause, Louis Kattadirala replied: "I didn't do it deliberately. I wanted to transfer the *prēta* from my patient [Y] to the physician's wife, but your daughter happened to be there and since she had a bad period [*apala*] the *prēta* seized her instead."

What is the significance of this (seemingly) extraordinary conversation between Somavati's father and the exorcist? To members of the culture this conversation is perfectly ordinary and expectable, but it requires interpretation for the Western reader. Earlier we noted that according to Sinhalese cultural beliefs a *prēta* can voluntarily move from one patient to another if the time is apposite. Another cultural view is that a *prēta* can be transferred from the body of one patient into another by an exorcist. This is a popular technique in exorcism, for the *prēta* will be quite willing to seize another patient rather than be trapped and captured by the exorcist and destroyed, which is what a true and complete exorcism by the *Kattadirāla* would entail. Somavati's parents, harrassed by the new problem on their hands, interpreted the events as a deliberate machination by Louis Kattadirala. Other events seem to confirm this: the patient became ill again as soon as Louis Kattadirala left the house. He subsequently tied an *äpa nūl* effective for a period of three months, but it did not work. The psychological reason for the *äpa nūl* not working is Somavati's (unconscious) resistance to cure. The cultural interpretation given by her parents is that Louis Kattadirala was himself responsible for this, and that is why he could not bring the *prēta* under control. My own guess is that Louis did nothing of the sort. However, even if he did it, why did he admit it? For one thing he would have realized that Somavati's father's explanation was a logically tight one, and denying it would be of no avail. Thus he admitted doing it but absolved himself of evil intention toward Somavati by saying that he wanted the *prēta* transferred to the Ayurvedic physician's wife, but because Somavati had an astrologically bad period, she became the victim. This admission had another important implication: Louis Kattadirala's skill and reputation as an exorcist would be enhanced. He could in fact do these powerful things. Somavati's father had to accept this explanation, but he insisted that the exorcist do something truly effective for his daughter. Louis Kattadirala agreed.

Three months after her first attack Louis Kattadirala performed a ritual for Somavati. The culmination of this ritual was the tying of a *Vishnu āgora yantra:* a copper plate with esoteric figures, consecrated to Vishnu, charmed 108 times, then rolled up into a talisman worn by the patient. Before this *yantra* could be tied on the patient, the *āpa nūl* she was already wearing had to be cut. As soon as this was done, however, the spirit, temporarily removed from its bondage, shook Somavati. During this possession state she said that the *āgora yantra* would be effective for only three months! It is clear that she was resisting: she did not want the exorcist to bring the spirit under control completely. The spirit (i.e., anthropomorphized traumas) had to be activated periodically to bring her some relief. Three months later she had another attack, a severely traumatic one, in which another *prēta* intruded into her person—the *prēta* of her dead grandmother!

This new event resulted in a total severance of social relationships between Somavati's family and that of Louis Kattadirala. Louis had a daughter who was also subject to possession by a *prēta*. Somavati's parents now believed that Louis had done it again, and transferred the *prēta* inhabiting his own daughter to the susceptible Somavati. I do not think there was any substance to this; retrospectively they also came to believe that Somavati's grandmother had possessed the exorcist's daughter since they were neighbors, and this *prēta* now possessed Somavati. All these interpretations were brought about by Somavati herself; in her "trance state" she said that Louis was responsible for her attack. Her unconscious motive was to belittle Louis and thus make her parents dispense with his services. In this she succeeded, for the parents were easily convinced that Louis was to blame and did not consult him further; the severance of social relationships was final.

The motives for choosing the mother's mother as *prēta* are relatively easy to explain if we look back into Somavati's life history. The mother's mother was a loved person, dearly so; yet in the infantile psyche she was also a hated person. She was responsible for removing Somavati from her own mother's breasts, and these simply could not be replaced by the grandmother. She had also "betrayed" Somavati when she was handed back to her parents. The infantile rage against the grandmother was probably very strong, but could not be expressed or even recognized because of the strong love she had for this pious lady. It is also interesting to note the full implications of Somavati's action for the salvation of her grandmother, according to Buddhism. Somavati's grandmother had been a pious lady and on all counts should have gone to heaven. By converting her into a *prēta* Somavati not only denied her this chance but put her into a situation of near-eternal misery and damnation. Such actions, which contradict her professed love, can be explained in terms of the psychoanalytic theory of ambivalence. Through the demonomorphic representation of her grandmother, Somavati could do several things: express her hatred for this lady, her hostile oral rage, and above all direct that oral rage against a "hated" (and loved) person, her own mother. She (i.e., the *prēta* in her) threatens to eat the mother ("kanava", "I will eat you"); her mother's own shock and pain must have been very great, for it is her own (dead) mother (as *prēta* inhabiting her daughter) who is saying all this. It is likely that this revives her own guilt at having renounced her daughter, for which her mother now threatens her in such a terrifying manner.

The Routinization of the Sick Role

For the next two years, from the last-mentioned possession to the point where she consulted the Kapurala at Navala, Somavati had about ten bouts of possession. I shall mention a few of the episodes for which I have information, and comment on their significance.

1. The first bout during this two-year period occurred when she went to a Buddhist temple at Talagala where a *pirit* (recital of sacred texts by monks) was being held. The attack lasted for a few days, and was controlled when the priest gave her some oil which had been made *jīvan* ("charmed," "made live"). This was very effective and for about nine months she was free of trouble.

2. Another attack occurred when Somavati's father lost his job on the Ayurvedic physician's plantation at Kiriwattuduve and the whole family moved to Malapalla, a village close to his parental village. An exorcist from that village came and tied a charmed thread (nūl). In her trance state Somavati said that the *sīma* (period of validity) for the thread was only three months. (In fact in every subsequent bout she

makes the same *sāstra* or "prophecy," which is accepted by all.) Thus the exorcist has no choice but to limit the period to three months.

3. After this three-month period the same exorcist tied a *Vishnu āgora yantra*, the same type of talisman that Louis gave Somavati. This was a powerful *yantra*, but its efficacy was also necessarily limited to three months. Yet in two days Somavati had another attack, broke the *āgora yantra*, and in a *sāstra* (prophecy) told everyone present that the younger sister of this exorcist had put *ūrutel* ("pork fat") around the house to render the talisman ineffective. In an interview, Somavati had this to say about this event:

My mother had gone to weed a rice field. My sister and I were alone in the house. A boy from the next house came into ours stealthily and put *ūrutel* right around the house. My sister says she saw the boy come in. I saw only a little bit of the oil on the top of an empty tar barrel near our kitchen. The very next day I fell ill again.

It is impossible to weed out fact from fiction in this account. My own impression is that the event did not take place in the manner described. It is likely that Somavati saw the boy—the son of the exorcist's sister—in her garden and saw some "oil" in the empty tar barrel, and in her fantasy she combined the two events. Again Somavati's motive was "resistance": to render the *āgora yantra* ineffective so that she could get possessed again. According to Sinhalese beliefs pork fat renders ritual and magic ineffective.

4. The exorcist came back and tied another thread, and this was effective for a month or so.

5. Now Somavati's father had to leave Malapalla where he had no stable employment, and he took a job as rubber tapper in Boralasgamuva, near Colombo. Although Somavati also had a job now in a nearby factory, the possession states increased in frequency: even a *pirit* ritual in a neighborhood temple, or news of such a ritual, would provoke an attack. She also had two new demons (not *prētas*) inhabiting her: Riri Yaka (Blood Demon) and Mahasona (the great demon of the graveyard). She informed her family of these two demons in several *sāstras* (prophecies) she uttered while possessed by them. She also mentioned that they had been put into her some time back by the same evil Louis Kattadirala. After one of her attacks a friend in the factory recommended that she visit the shrine we were studying.

Exegesis

Several important events happened during this two-year period. One of the most important was her possession as she listened to the *pirit* ritual at the Talagala Buddhist temple. According to Sinhalese beliefs all persons who are genuinely susceptible to demonic attacks cannot bear the sound of monks reciting *pirit* (sacred Buddhist texts sung as general blessings). A woman (or man) who gets possessed at *pirit* is confirmed in that particular role. In general these *pirit* rituals are held in a temple in the presence of a large congregation of villagers: the possession bout on such an occasion then occurs before the public eye, and Somavati's became publicly accepted as true possession, not a sham put-up job. Her sick role was thus publicly "legitimated."

The reason why *pirit* has this effect on patients is very simple. One of the major texts recited in pirit ceremonies is the *Ratana Sutta* where the Buddha quelled the demons who were devastating the city of Visala; another, the *Āṭānāṭiya Sutta,* also deals with demons and their banishment. The power of these texts are such that their recital excites the spirit residing in the patient, producing the expectable possession symptoms. These powerful cultural stimuli invariably produce the possession response in extremely hysterical women.

The frequency of the attack increased with critical changes in family residence. The economic uncertainty and changes in residence produced one attack. Then several occurred when they were in Malapalla, an alien village where Somavati's father had no stable job. Then they moved to Boralasgamuva where both she and her parents had jobs, but this was a totally new environment and they had no friends or relations there. At least Malapalla, though an alien village, was close enough to her father's village where her kinfolk lived. At Boralasgamuva the attacks became more frequent; new demons possessed her and she couldn't witness *pirit* rituals or even hear the word *pirit* uttered. She was confirmed in her role, and her attacks became regular, routinized. Her parents learned to live with it, and tolerate it.

One of the unconscious problems that Somavati had to face was the various exorcists who used to tie a thread or talisman and thus control the demon. She devised a technique for coping with this through the *sāstra* or prophecies she uttered while being possessed. Again the cultural belief facilitated this: the "being" that resides in the person (whether a god, demon, or *prēta*) can speak through its agent, and these statements would be "true." In some instances they would be prophecies (*sāstra*). Somavati then used *sāstra* for various ends; for example, to limit the efficacy of the talismans to three months. Even this period could be shortened, so that on one occasion she broke the talisman after two days and in her *sāstra* said that the exorcist's sister had used pork fat to render the talisman ineffective. Later, in her new residence at Boralasgamuva, she became even more confident. She became possessed regularly, and simply stated in her *sāstra* that the various exorcists that treated her were worthless; that their talismans were ineffective. Her parents had to look for new exorcists constantly.

Though Somavati's bouts had become routinized, accepted by her parents as more or less inevitable, their intensity did not diminish. Two demons from the formal pantheon were now inhabiting her. These demons are named beings, permanent members of the Sinhalese pantheon, unlike *prētas* who come and go, and are the souls of dead (greedy) persons. The demons are beings who live in a demon world and can inhabit a person only in essence, generally by casting a glance (*dishti*) at the patient. Thus it is possible for any particular demon to cast his glance at any number of people, and all these people will be imbued with his essence, which represents his full person. A *prēta*, by contrast, generally resides in one person, and if you capture him and put him away (e.g., cast him into the ocean) he will not bother you again. But a demon, when banished from the body of the patient, still lives (in the demon world) since what is banished is his essence, not his full person. Such a theory is necessary to explain the simple empirical fact that several persons in a given village or region may be afflicted by the same demon at the same time.

Several intriguing questions arise as to why Somavati chose these two demons. Why the necessity to be possessed by any more supernatural beings, when two *prētas* (Mary Nona and her grandmother) were in occupation of her body already? Why these two demons from about half a dozen other "popular" ones in the pantheon? What feelings are being expressed through these new demons who in their essence (*dishti*) have possessed her?

With the routinization of the sick role Somavati had more control both over her environment and over her possession. She could make her parents dispense with exorcists and bring new ones in; she could put on her attack and rationalize it culturally, for example, the pork fat episode. Indeed the whole mechanism of prophecy (*sāstra*) was firmly established as part of the sick role. It gave her a sense of power and self confidence; she could foretell events. Surprising as it may seem the routinization of the sick role implies that more ego control has been established in the timing and performance of possession. She could bring in new demons to express other problems of her personality. Through the *prēta* of her mother's mother she was directly expressing her oral rage against her mother's mother and her own mother; and indirectly against others—father and siblings. With the two new demons, her masochistic needs are being expressed: according to Sinhalese belief these two demons are horribly aggressive beings, totally malevolent and punitive. It is likely that she has transferred the attributes of her husband to these male demons who were tormenting her. Acting out is through *prētas:* acting in, through the demons. Somavati told me that these beings "torture her" (*vada denava*).

Why choose these two demons and not, for instance, Huniyan the demon of sorcery, and Kalu Kumara the demon of lust, also popular demons in the pantheon? Take Mahasona, "the great demon of the graveyard," who possessed her. In Sinhalese belief he is the most aggressive of the demons, and the most violent. It is no accident that of all the demons in the pantheon Mahasona is the one associated with physical beating: he hits people when they are alone and the marks of his hands appear on the back. He takes various apparitional shapes, the most popular one is when he suddenly accosts a person who is wandering alone. The victim looks up but Mahasona is so huge that his face can hardly be seen. Mahasona hits him in the back and he falls in a faint. It is likely that the psychogenesis of this cultural "vision" is the infant's perception of the cruel parent. Somavati, however, had no such experience with Mahasona: she seizes on one aspect of his character, the cruel, vindictive, punitive one.

Similarly with Riri Yaka, the blood demon, who possesses her. As his name signifies Riri Yaka is a bloodthirsty, vindictive demon. Moreover his birth in the human world, according to mythology, is most interesting: he tore his mother's breast, and killing her emerged into the human world as a demon. Somavati's identification with this demon is unmistakably clear: the experience of the demon and her own experience of being deprived of the mother's breast are isomorphic. The idiosyncratic personal experience of Somavati can be expressed through the cultural belief in Riri Yaka. Infantile traumas are being acted out in this manner. Indeed it is likely that the psychogenesis of this cultural belief lies in the trauma of early weaning that is probably widespread in the culture, as a result of continual production of babies, absence of a postpartum taboo, and the transference of maternal affection to new, rival siblings.

IV

EXORCISM

Some preliminary remarks are necessary if the reader is to follow the description and exegeses of the ritual of exorcism performed by the *Kapurāla* (priest) of the Navala shrine. Although the ritual for Somavati was a standard one, it was in a sense designed for the kinds of problems Somavati faced, since other women who also came for these cures had similar problems; for example excessive repression of sex and aggression drives leading to hysterical and sometimes masochistic traits. Some of her life experiences were somewhat unique—her sadistic husband, separation anxiety, and pronounced oral aggression. The ritual permitted considerable leeway in behavior, however, so that these problems could also be aired within the framework of the standard ritual. On the night of Somavati's exorcism there was another patient—a young, attractive female typist, middle class and English-educated, who worked in the Supreme Court in Colombo. Yet although she underwent the same formal ritual as Somavati, her behavior was strikingly different: she was quiet, reserved, and displayed none of Somavati's acting-out behavior. Her reserve was explained easily: she was not possessed by spirits. Enemies had practiced sorcery on her and made her ill. One part of the standard ritual was especially relevant for her: the cutting of the evil effects of sorcery. This part of the ritual was not important for Somavati. We shall focus exclusively on Somavati.

The shrine is located in Navala, a Colombo suburb, tucked away at the end of a quiet cul-de-sac. The priest lived in a small hut on the shrine premises; between his hut and the shrine is a sandy compound (the dancing arena) where most of the actions during exorcisms are performed. The clients were generally lower middle-class or working-class people, neither affluent nor generally indigent. There were three types of clients. First, those who came for prophecies or medical prescriptions during the daily seances held at 11.05 a.m., when the Kapurāla (priest) falls into a trance and becomes a vehicle for a deity. Second, there were occasional nightlong exorcisms like Somavati's. Third, there is a permanent core of clients who regularly visit the shrine. I call this regular congregation a "cult group," intensely involved in the activities of the shrine, social and religious, and with an avowed leader, the Kapurāla. Often those who constitute the cult group graduate through the first two "stages."

The major deities of the pantheon are represented here. The Buddha has a special shrine at the bō tree (*ficus religiosa*) in the compound. Inside the shrine are the following deities: Ishvara (Siva) the formal head of this group of deities, his sons Skanda and Ganesh; also Dadimunda, Vishnu, Vibisana, Saman, and the goddesses Kali and Pattini. They are represented in their shrine by their images, ornaments, and weapons. The supernatural hierarchy can be summed up as follows. In Sinhalese belief, the Buddha occupies the highest position in the pantheon and no ritual can commence without permission from him. The Buddha is viewed as totally benevolent, but since he is not alive he cannot intercede on behalf of persons or grant them favors. This is done by the gods (*dēvas*), who follow in the pantheon hierarchy. They are just deities, and will help persons; their attributes, however, vary, some for example being more stern than others, and some are superior to others. The demons are malevolent beings, and temporary altars for them are constructed in the outer edge of the shrine compound. The belief is that the demons are "servants" of the gods; the gods in turn are protectors of Buddhism. Demons must obey the gods. Originally all demons used to kill humans, but they have been quelled by either the Buddha or the gods and have been compelled to accept offerings from the public instead. The theory of curing here is that the gods will control and banish the demons and *prētas* from the body of the patient.

The priest here is a *Kapurāla,* one who officiates on behalf of the gods, unlike the *Kattadirāla,* the demon exorcists. The *Kapurāla* impersonates the gods; the *Kattadirāla,* the demons. The *Kapurāla* like the gods he personates is vegetarian, unlike the meat-eating, nonabstemious *Kattadirāla.* The former has also a higher social status corresponding to the superior nature of his cult.

Mention must be made of the kind of audience present on the night of the ritual, and the official actors. There were members of Somavati's immediate family, excluding the oldest sibling; the typist's parents and several relations; over a dozen members of the cult group of the Navala shrine; and well over twenty-five outsiders from the area who had heard that an interesting ritual was being held that night. The main ritual personnel were the *Kapurāla,* two assistants, and a drummer.

The ritual begins at 8:25 p.m. when the family of the patient (or patients) moves in towards the *dēvale* with offerings—baskets of fruit, sweets, flowers, and incense: the *Kapurāla* and his assistants are with them. The drummer beats his drum; Somavati shivers and hoots at this stimulus. In a few moments they are all inside the *dēvale,* facing the images of Siva, Vishnu, Kali, Pattini and Skanda. The *Kapurāla* himself shakes vehemently inside the small shrine before the image of Siva, with a basket of food in his hands. He sings songs in praise of the gods, and his assistants join in unison. The slight tremors in Somavati have subsided, and she is calm now; the drums are silent. When the *Kapurāla* sings songs on Skanda, Somavati starts shaking slowly, almost gracefully as if in a trance state. The time is 8:45; the singing is over, and the drums start again. The *Kapurāla* now starts shaking violently, and so does Somavati, imitating his movements. The *Kapurāla,* in this state, takes a shawl and gently fans the deities (their images). He then moves into the inner shrine where there is a large image of Vishnu, and fans this deity. He then comes back, and moves out into the dancing arena and blesses members of the audience. Meanwhile the patients and the family have placed their offerings on the altars; they come into the compound following the *Kapurāla*. They sit on mats with the others in the audience, but Somavati, still shaking, is in the dancing area with the *Kapurāla*. She tries to move toward the audience but the *Kapurāla* holds her by the hair and drags her to the center of the dancing arena. She moves slowly toward him. He still has a cane in his hand, in a trance, possessed by Skanda, while she is possessed by the evil spirits. She tries to go toward her seated parents, but he holds her by the hair again and brings her to the center of the arena.

The following dialogue ensues.

Kapurāla: Yes . . .
SOMAVATI: (rather contemptuously) Here I come and you can prove your worth, *Mr. Kapurāla.*
Kapurāla: Ha! Ha! Ha! Ha!
SOMAVATI: Get out you . . . I am not to dance with you, they say.
Kapurāla: That cannot be . . . emphatically . . .
SOMAVATI: (interrupting) I'm not to dance.
Kapurāla: (in stern tones) I order you who are inhabiting this mortal body to dance.
SOMAVATI: Not dancing. . . . Even if *one* goes away there are . . .
Kapurāla: Emphatically . . .
SOMAVATI: Not only I, there are three others along with me. All three must dance right here.
Kapurāla: Emphatically! Not only these three but all the hosts of demons and demonesses living in Sakvala rock must obey my beck. Emphatically, I am the Lord Skanda of Kadira-pura [Kataragama]. In the past haven't I ordered all de-mons—demonesses . . . to dance and I have with me pun-ishments I can mete out to them. Now today, at this time demons and demonesses have come to this Island of the Dhamma [Dhammadvipa, i.e., Sri Lanka]. But remember I am Skanda the Lord, and you must, yes, play.

She "plays" as instructed. The drums start beating faster and Somavati dances briskly, imitating the movements of the *Kapurāla*. Then she sees someone in the audience and hoots several times, and asks him to go away. But no one knows at this point who he or she is. Then in a thin, shrieking voice she says: "I am Mary. There are two others. Leave this place immediately (to the person in the audience not yet identified). . . . I came here for the love I had for my children. I am . . . oh! I'll depart. Listening? I am Alpi Nona [the grandmother]. It's that Louis who brought me here. I had gone to his daughter's house . . ." A member from the audience asks: Did you go there on your own?

SOMAVATI: I [Mary] was taken there. On the day of the ritual of exorcism at 6 p.m. I was taken there, listen. I will leave, I swear! Swear! Swear! By the gods! By the Buddha I swear! Swear! Swear! By the gods! Buddha! Swear, swear, swear, gods! Buddha, swear. . . . Yes I [Mary] did not worship the Buddha and the gods; protected my children, accumulated wealth, never went into a temple. Yes I [Alpi Nona] was taken there by that Louis. I will depart, I will, I swear by the gods, by the Buddha, I will depart.

Exegesis

Some exegeses of the preceding events are required before we proceed further in the description of the exorcism. What is occurring here is a drama significant on both cultural and psychological levels. On the other hand, there is the relationship between Somavati and the *Kapurāla* as they perform in the arena. More importantly, however, it is a morality play: the god Skanda is speaking through the *Kapurāla* and interacting with the *prētas* inhabiting the woman. There are at least two levels of interaction here: *Kapurāla* and Somavati; and Skanda and the *prētas*. The "I" in the speeches may refer to any of these persons.

The action takes place according to the cultural definition of the situation. Thus the god Skanda is the powerful deity, stern and handsome, the vanquisher of *asuras* (demons). He has a stick in hand, representing parental authority and discipline. The god himself affirms this (speaking through the *Kapurāla*) for the demons to hear, "most emphatically." Initially the spirits are reluctant to dance. Psychologically, this refers to Somavati's resistance: she is reluctant to be "cured"; and she goes toward her parents. Culturally, it refers to the reluctance of the demons, wayward beings, to be controlled by Skanda. The *Kapurāla,* stick in hand, pulls her by the hair with the other into the center of the arena: neither form of resistance is of any avail. The *prētas* speak up and identify themselves and the circumstances in which they possessed Somavati—validating and justifying before everyone present the interpretations the family had made regarding this case. That is, Mary Nona had been brought to the physician's house by Louis and possessed Somavati because it happened to be her bad period astrologically; and Alpi Nona her grandmother had possessed Louis' daughter, and Louis then transferred this *prēta* over to Somavati. Since the *prētas* themselves are speaking, everyone accepts this interpretation of the illness.

Finally there is the moral message communicated to the audience. Somavati acts out the *prēta* role exactly as the Buddhist texts define it: they are beings who, because of excessive love and attachment, have been reborn in this dreadful state. This is particularly true of Mary Nona who did not observe Buddhist worship regularly. The dreadful consequences of attachment (*tanha*), the root of all problems according to Buddhism, is vividly portrayed in the enactment.

The Exorcism Continued

The time is about 8:55 p.m. The patient jumps up and down in the arena; sometimes she has slower movements, dancing gracefully, moving the lower part of her body. The *Kapurāla* is also facing her, dancing with her, cane in hand. Her eyes shine with a strange look. Suddenly she goes toward the audience and sits down on a mat. The *Kapurāla* pulls her by the hair, and makes her dance again. An assistant brings a torch for the *Kapurāla:* Somavati hits this man and hoots. The *Kapurāla* gives her a bunch of coconut flowers: long tough strands of flowers like a whip. Somavati dances with the flowers in hand, hooting, and says: "I am Kalu Yaka [the black demon]." The *Kapurāla* takes her by the hair into the shrine, takes her up to the altar of each deity still holding her by the hair, and forces her head down on the altars, paying obeisance to the deities. Then he takes her outside to the *bō* tree and makes her pay obeisance to the tree (i.e., the Buddha).

Exegesis

Somavati states that she is now possessed by a new demon for the first time: Kalu Yaka. What are the motives for suddenly bringing in this demon? Probably something in the context of the ritual was the cause of this new demon's intrusion. The dancing between the *Kapurāla* and the patient is a cultural enactment on one level: in almost all Sinhalese rituals the gods are honored with dances that please their minds. Here too the "spirits" dance before Lord Skanda. On the psychological level dance has other meanings. The Sinhalese word is *sellam* ("play") and has sexual connotations. Earlier, the god Skanda told the spirits "you must play." Psychologically it is a message from the *Kapurāla* to the girl; and carries a sexual connotation. The sensual quality of the dance is unmistakable—the *Kapurāla* holding her by the hair, the male and female facing each other dancing, her eyes shining. Somavati herself resisted this new force and went to her parents, but she is brought back into the dancing arena by the *Kapurāla*. Indeed the shaking of the hips and the lower part of the body seemed almost an attempt to achieve orgasm. Several times tears stream from Somavati's eyes when she is in this orgiastic state. The ritual has stimulated the sex drive, which was not crucial to the earlier states of possession. In a sense this was inevitable, for Somavati, who had enjoyed sex with her husband, had been deprived of it for over two years. Furthermore, the *Kapurāla* had just given her a branch of coconut flowers. Everyone in the culture knows what this action meant: Somavati is supposed to beat herself with it. This is obviously a powerful stimulus in Somavati's case, with her history of masochism. Immediately she says: "I am Kalu Yaka," the Sinhalese demon of lust, the Black Prince, who possesses women with lustful intentions! This illustrates dramatically how the motives of the individual determine the choice of a particular demon from the pantheon. This episode also shows how the ritual releases the inhibitions of the individual and taps deep unconscious feelings and impulses.

Note, however, that this sexual experience occurs with the *Kapurāla,* who is also the god Skanda, stern, but also (in mythology and in the images in the shrine) extremely handsome; and God in turn equals father, according to psychoanalytic theory. This equation—Kapurāla = god = father—is culturally recognized also insofar as Skanda, like other gods, is often addressed as father. He also acts like one in the ritual, cane in hand. But Skanda is different from other gods: he is handsome and rides a peacock, which means that a woman's oedipal fantasy of the beautiful father can be projected onto the god Skanda in the highly charged trance situation, where unconscious impulses are being released. Whether the further equation, father = husband, also occurs cannot be demonstrated, for there are neither overt cultural indications for this equation nor interview data to substantiate it. The only thing Somavati would say about her father is that she loves him, but he is stern. It was impossible to get interview material regarding oedipal relationships with the father, or the identification of husband with father.

The Exorcism Continued

Both persons are dancing (i.e., "playing") with coconut flowers in their hands. They face eath other.

Kapurāla: Most emphatically! Ha! Ha! Ha! Beef-eating demons, emphatically, I gave you the coconut flower to beat yourself with. Emphatically then——.

SOMAVATI: It can be done.

Kapurāla:	Then beat yourself with it.
SOMAVATI:	(curtly). Not now. (Looks towards audience at the yet unknown outsider.) Will you give me permission to hit him? Or will you hit him? Shall I hit him?
Kapurāla:	Most emphatically you have been asked not to hit just anyone; this flower is for hitting demons and demonesses.
SOMAVATI:	(threateningly). Then will you tell him to leave?
Kapurāla:	Emphatically! I am here to banish demons, the demon that is here must be beaten with the flower.
SOMAVATI:	Before you batter me, you must batter that fellow. Will you ask him to leave or no? Leave, leave. However much you ask I'll not leave. Why? I must chase *him* away!
Kapurāla:	Emphatically. Who is the demon that is activating this mortal body at this moment?
SOMAVATI:	Mahasona [Great Demon of the Graveyard].
Kapurāla:	For what reason have you been inhabiting this mortal body?
SOMAVATI:	(With a short laugh) I did not deliberately inhabit it.
Kapurāla:	Yes, who transferred you then?
SOMAVATI:	That Louis Kattadirala. He told this woman. You know who "this woman" is? This woman is Somavati.
Kapurāla:	What did he say?
SOMAVATI:	Requested that I break the neck and drink his [?] blood.
Kapurāla:	Yes? Mahasona, can you break someone's neck and drink his blood?
SOMAVATI:	(laughingly, in sarcastic tones). Well of course not! But since he did something unfair I wanted to do it.
Kapurāla:	Yes, emphatically, tell me which Lord Buddha has given you permission.
SOMAVATI:	(in lowered tones). The Lord Buddha did not give me permission to enter human bodies.
Kapurāla:	Yes!
SOMAVATI:	(sarcastically). Yes, but if requested I must come.
Kapurāla:	Yes, I know that if someone transfers you, you must go there. This is a transfer to be sure. This transfer has been done by exorcists some time back, but emphatically, in the light of dawn, with the ritual for the Mother[*māta*] Badra Kali, we will cut the evil sorcery and then will you leave this mortal body. . . .
SOMAVATI:	Yes, I will leave.
Kapurāla:	What proof can you give me?
SOMAVATI:	Proof? I will worship the Buddha, the gods.

Kapurāla: For certain?

SOMAVATI: And I'll worship the Kapumahatya [Mr. *Kapurāla*] and leave.

Kapurāla: Is this for certain?

SOMAVATI: Not only me . . . there are three of us.

Kapurāla: Yes. The chief of the host[*pirivara*] must know how to take his followers and leave. Yes. Otherwise emphatically the god of Alutnuvara, Dadimunda, will burn you from head to foot. Yes, remember that. Now do you want to play some more in this Dhammadvipa[the Island of Dhamma, i.e., Sri Lanka]? If so, this is the time.

SOMAVATI: Yes, I want a torch.

Kapurāla: Yes, you have been given a coconut flower, do you want a torch also?

SOMAVATI: I need a torch. (Pause. She sniffs the air.) But I smell the impurity of a burnt meat substance! Yes (turning toward audience), you will depart right now.

Kapurāla: (now genuinely anxious). What smell of impurity?

SOMAVATI: Someone has brought a bottle containing pork fat[*ūrutel*].

Kapurāla: Who?

SOMAVATI: Yes, I see him smiling!

Kapurāla: You have permission to pull him out (from among the audience).

SOMAVATI: (in triumphant tones). Ha! ha! ha! Aren't you leaving? Leaving? You[*tō*, as if to inferior or animal], aren't you going? I'll hit you for certain. Hit you I swear. Hit you, hit you, hit you, hit you . . . Mr. *Kapurāla* what do you say.

(Thus saying, she dances before the audience and points out a member of the audience, a dark, short man with a moustache, wearing a bright silk sarong and a shirt with black stripes. Somavati laughs in triumph and exultation.)

SOMAVATI: You say you've come here because there's a big crowd assembled. Aren't you leaving? Mr. *Kapurāla* shall I batter this man? Leave!

Kapurāla: I command the sorcerer who deals with spirits to leave this place immediately.

(Some persons in the audience threaten to molest the man, and he disappears into the darkness.)

SOMAVATI: (to audience in general, as she dances in the arena). Do
you think I am a woman, ha! Do you? Do you? Do you
think I am performing some gimmick? Do you know me
well? He is still within the bounds of this property. Ask
him to leave. I'll break his legs. (She continues to dance.)
This body can't dance any longer. I must go now.

(She looks exhausted suddenly. The *Kapurāla* gently leads her to the
mat and she lies down there.)

Exegesis

a.   The *Kapurāla* gives the coconut flower to the woman; but she
does not beat herself. Instead she is distracted by someone in the audience, as yet unidentified. It is obviously the same person referred to
earlier. Even the *Kapurāla* is puzzled by her request to hit him, and says
that she should hit the demons (i.e., herself).

b.   The woman then admits that Mahasona possesses her. In a previous exegesis I pointed out that Mahasona is associated with hitting
(and violence). This is confirmed here also for she, as Mahasona, wants
to hit someone in the audience (and also agrees to hit herself). Her
hostile rage is also expressed through Mahasona: she wants to break
the neck and drink the blood of Louis Kattadirala!

c.   Throughout the ritual the woman is permitted to act out, but
within the limits determined by the *Kapurāla*. The *Kapurāla,* or rather
Skanda, has the demon under control. The supernatural hierarchy is
established when the *Kapurāla* reminds the demon that the Buddha
hasn't given him permission to kill, but to accept substitutive offerings
from human beings. The myth of the Buddha's subjugation of the
demons is of course known to the audience. Having controlled the situation, the *Kapurāla* reminds the demons that in a special ritual to be
performed for Kali later on, they should leave the body of the patient.
Throughout the ritual, authority is established and reaffirmed: the authority of the gods over the demons, the *Kapurāla* over the patient, and
the Buddha above them all. The patient can act out; but she asks permission from the *Kapurāla*.

d.   The demons are threatened with punishment. According to Sinhalese myth the archpunisher of demons is Dadimunda, whose major
shrine is in Alutnuvara, fifteen miles from Kandy. Dadimunda is a minister of Skanda; and Skanda (through the *Kapurāla*) reminds the
demons that they should obey his will lest he order Dadimunda to
punish them.

e. The most interesting episode is the "pig fat" incident. It is obvious that Somavati had identified someone in the audience right from the start of the ritual, but the *Kapurāla* has not encouraged her, since this did not seem relevant to the standardized ritual. But the moment she mentioned "impurity" it alarmed the *Kapurāla*, since impurities, particularly pork fat, can invalidate the whole ritual. Thus Somavati got the attention of the *Kapurāla*.

What is the significance of "pork fat"? Note in an earlier incident in Somavati's life, she annulled the effect of the *Vishnu āgōra yantra* by saying that the exorcist's siblings had put pork fat all over her garden. This was an attempt at resistance and the wish not to be cured. Now Somavati feels the control of the *Kapurāla* (and the gods) being firmly established over her, and she makes a desperate attempt (as always unconsciously) to annul the effect of the ritual by saying that someone has brought in a bottle of pork fat. But why identify that particular person of all those present in the audience? And why the extremely aggressive reaction toward him? I felt that some unconscious identification was at work: the outsider resembled someone she knew. On a hunch I asked her during a later interview what her husband looked like. She said he was short, dark, had a moustache, and was fond of striped shirts! The likelihood is strong that she was expressing her rage against her husband, threatening to hit him, as he hit her, and an unknown person in the audience helped her (by his unwitting resemblance to her husband) to focus her rage. Thus the whole episode was overdetermined: the wish not to be cured (the pork fat idea) was linked with the identification of a member of the audience with her husband.

It is interesting to note the *Kapurāla*'s view of the episode. Why should anyone wish to bring pork fat in order to ruin the ritual he was performing? The *Kapurāla* says the man is an apprentice sorcerer who was envious of him and tried to spoil the ritual. The *Kapurāla* told me in an interview that he knows the man and asked him why he did it, but the man denied that he had brought pork fat to the ritual. "An obvious liar," the *Kapurāla* commented.

The Exorcism Continued

The pork fat episode was unexpected, breaking the tenor of the standard ritual. The ritual is resumed when the *Kapurāla* pulls Somavati by the hair: the invitation to "play." They dance in the arena for several minutes, the *Kapurāla* with a bunch of coconut flowers in his hand. Suddenly he beats his face with the coconut flower, whipping himself with its sinuous streamers. This whipping goes on for several minutes till the pieces of the whip break. He then touches her, somewhat gently with a new bunch of coconut flowers: she goes back to the mat and sits down. He takes a fresh bunch of flowers and hits himself with it, and then dances in mid-arena. This self-battering—always on the face— goes on for several minutes each time, and is performed several times, once inside the shrine before the images of the gods until the "whip" breaks into fragments. Now he dances gracefully before the gods.

He comes back into the arena, torch in hand, and dances before the seated patient—torch in one hand, the other hand clenched except for an index finger pointing out in a gesture of authority or command. Occasionally he lowers the torch, in an action indicating a blessing. He then extinguishes the torch by rubbing it on his hair. He is given another torch by an assistant. He now pulls the girl out and she dances with him. He keeps the torch on her head briefly and extinguishes it on his hair, and on his body. This is repeated. They dance more briskly; the drum increases its tempo. He calls me and my assistant into the shrine and delivers an "oracle": what's going to happen today will result in a successful piece of research! Then he comes into the ritual arena, and dances with Somavati.

SOMAVATI:	Hoo! Hoo! Hoo! Hooo! Hooo!
Kapurāla:	Who is it who is before me?
SOMAVATI:	Mahasona.
Kapurāla:	Emphatically! And his retinue? Yes these drum beats are for Mahasona. Speak up. . . .
SOMAVATI:	Hoo Hoo Hoo, Hoo, Hoo, Hoo! Riri Yaka [The Blood Demon]
Kapurāla:	And the rest?
SOMAVATI:	Why are you laughing? Do you know who the other one is?
Kapurāla:	Ha, ha!
SOMAVATI:	Kalu Yaka [Black Demon].
Kapurāla:	Ha! Ha!
SOMAVATI:	Ha! There are three *prētas* of the dead. Do you know who they are?
Kapurāla:	No, let me know who they are. . . . Is it a kinsman?
SOMAVATI:	I am no kinsman; I am someone who came from an outside village.
Kapurāla:	Yes, your name?
SOMAVATI:	Mary Nona.
Kapurāla:	Your village?

SOMAVATI: My village is Poruvendanda.

Kapurāla: For what reason have you possessed the mortal body of this young girl?

SOMAVATI: They brought me into the house of my granddaughter [i.e., the physician's young daughter]. Not only me, but three came along with me. Those three were mentioned earlier.

Kapurāla: Till such time as the Pure God of Alutnuvara, Dadimunda, arrives [later on] will you obey my command and desist from shaking the frame of this mortal woman?

SOMAVATI: I obey.

Kapurāla: Yes, most emphatically, you swear three times before the Lord Buddha—that you will not shake this mortal body till the arrival of God Dadimunda. Swear!

SOMAVATI: (goes to the Buddha shrine at the Bo tree and places her hands on the altar). I swear.

Kapurāla: Swear!

SOMAVATI: I swear.

Kapurāla: Swear!

SOMAVATI: I swear, by the gods, by the Buddha.

At this point the *Kapurāla* delivers a long homily to the audience in general. He allays the fears of the audience that the pork fat episode could have annulled the effect of the ritual. He says he is the god Skanda, and even a herd of pigs will not affect the ritual over which he presides.

Then the *Kapurāla* goes into the shrine and the altars outside and incenses them with resin. Somavati, responding to the drums, hoots and shouts in his "absence." The *Kapurāla* goes up to her, pulls her by the hair, and forces her to sit on the mat. He proceeds with his incensing, and goes into the shrine, takes a cane from the altar of the god Dadimunda and gives it to the girl seated on the mat. He then proceeds to bless other members of the audience.

Exegesis

a. Coconut flower: Why is it that coconut flowers are given to women to whip themselves with in many Sinhalese rituals? I am not concerned with the mythological significance of the coconut flower but its psychological significance. Two cultural ideas are obvious: it is beautiful, often used for decorations, and it is a whip. These two ideas are linked in the psychological meaning of the coconut flower: "It is beautiful to be whipped." This idea is also set forth by the *Kapurāla:* he invites Somavati to play and dances with her with the coconut flowers. After this extremely graceful dance, he suddenly starts beating himself with the coconut flowers. Then he hits her gently with it. Although he whips himself mercilessly on the face, no bloodstains or weals appear. This is because of divine protection, according to the cultural definition of the situation. To the female patient the message is: "It is beautiful to whip yourself with the coconut flower and is not as painful as you think." It should be noted, however, that Somavati did not respond to this message, for reasons that will be clear later on in the ritual.

b.   The torch episode has similar significance except that the girl is not given a torch, so she is not expected to burn herself. But the *Kapurāla* performs similar actions; as in the preceding episode, he gently blesses the girl with the torch then "burns" himself with it. The *Kapurāla's* explanation for this event is that if the demons are recalcitrant and refuse to leave they will be burned later in the ritual, by making the patient stand on a hot iron plate. This serves to prepare the patient for that eventuality.

c.   Finger pointing is a typical gesture of authority by the *Kapurāla* as he dances. All along he does two things: establishes authority over the patient and also permits the patient to abreact and act out. The latter has to be contained within the limits and control of his authority. This is necessary both for curing the patient and for maintaining his own charisma. After the demons and spirits admit who they are, the *Kapurāla* (Skanda) gives a command: they must be quiet till the god Dadimunda arrives in the arena. They (the demons in the patient) agree, but as soon as the *Kapurāla* is away incensing the altars, they become active and Somavati starts hooting and dancing. It is obvious that a feature of the standard ritual has broken down; Somavati cannot be contained. She has disobeyed the god. Psychologically this is due to the fact that these acting-out cathartic episodes are extremely rewarding for the girl and she is resisting since the pork fat incident failed; culturally, everyone knows that the demons (not so much as *prētas*) are deadly beings, and won't easily obey the deity when he is absent. True enough when the *Kapurāla* comes back, he makes the girl sit on the mat, and she remains there quietly till the next major episode, the arrival of Dadimunda, an hour later. Yet the fact remains that the demons have disobeyed the deity. Something has to happen to redress authority.

The Exorcism Continued: the God Dadimunda

The ritual recommenced at 12:20 a.m. and a new character entered the drama—an assistant of the *Kapurāla* named David—as the god Dadimunda. From this point I shall summarize these proceedings of the ritual, reproducing verbatim only those events I think are worthy of interpretation. To begin with, David as Dadimunda draws the woman who had been resting on the mat into the arena and they dance together. His treatment of her differs markedly from the *Kapurāla*'s; he is rough, brusque, and coarse as befits the deity he impersonates. He consistently addresses Somavati as *tō* (which I shall translate as *you,* but underline to show that it is not an ordinary personal pronoun, and is used toward extreme social inferiors). David holds a cane in hand: Dadimunda's weapon with which he quelled the demons according to myth. Let me quote parts of the dialogue between him and Somavati.

DAVID: Yes, do *you* know who I am?

SOMAVATI: I know you.

DAVID: Then why did you not recognize the power of the Buddha doctrine and Deva doctrine [*dharma*], when god Skanda asked you to surrender a while ago? Do *you* know what's going to happen to you?

SOMAVATI: I will be killed by you.

DAVID: I will not kill you, but burn you from head to foot.

SOMAVATI: (laughs, in the sarcastic tone she employs throughout this dialogue). Ha! Ha! . . . Ha! Ha! You are going to burn me, are you? Ha! Ha! Other exorcists have tried that before. Ha! Ha!

DAVID: I am the noble Dadimunda Devata Bandara [i.e., Dadimunda, chief of the lesser gods, or devatas] . . . I am chief of a host of 100,000. I brought demons from the eighteen provinces and made them break rocks, created worms in the bodies of those demons and demonesses, and in one night I cultivated sixty large stretches of rice fields, built the upper hall, and the lower hall, the long street and the short street. . . . I am the noble Dadimunda possessed of many virtues. You must remember that (in threatening tones).

SAMAVATI: Yes.

DAVID: I will not kill you.

SAMAVATI: (still sarcastic). Ha!

DAVID: Remember that I shall not kill you. Remember that you
              will suffer various tortures in my hands. If you want to
              play, play as much as you like now but afterwards leave
              this human body with honor (*nambu*) . . . today will end
              your habitation of the human body (*manu kanda*), remem-
              ber. Remember that you will be permitted to play as much
              as you want.

David now addresses the *Kapurāla* who is now in the area as Kapurāla,
not as deity, looking at what is going on.

DAVID: (facing *Kapurāla*). Remember that it is necessary to have a
              stream of fire (*agni jālava*). It is necessary, remember!
              Why, because the demons insulted the priest and cheated
              him; and they have possessed this body here causing many
              pains and tortures . . . these demons and demonesses
              must be singed and burnt, you must remember to re-
              member this! . . .

Exegesis

a.   The tone of the deity has changed completely: he has a rough,
coarse manner. This fits in with the personality of David who is a
rough, coarse person; it also fits the character of the deity he impersonates, the god Dadimunda who beats demons. The first few speeches of
the god are to scold her loudly for being recalcitrant in the previous
episode and not obeying the instructions of god Skanda, who is suzerain over him, Dadimunda. One of the acts that David must perform
as Dadimunda is to control Somavati. She is encouraged to "play," as in
previous episodes, but this play must be within the limits of his control—which he must establish.

b.   Who is this new deity that has entered the arena and what is his
psychological significance? Dadimunda's mythology is well known in
the culture: he built the temple at Alutnuvara, fifteen miles from
Kandy, by employing demons as his servants. He made them work by
beating them with his stick; he built streets and halls referred to in the
dialogue above, and made demons cultivate sixty paddy fields overnight. When they were recalcitrant he tortured them by infesting their
bodies with worms. Given these attributes of the deity, Somavati can
readily identify him with her husband, and provoke him in the manner
in which she provoked her husband. This comes out at the very begin-
ing, when Somavati tells David (the god) that she will be killed by him.

This is not the culturally anticipated response of the demon to the deity; gods never kill, they punish or beat the demons. But her husband threatened to kill her in his sadistic moods, and Somavati repeatedly told us in interviews that she feared he would kill her sometime. The more arrogant, sarcastic, and uncooperative she becomes, the greater the attempt on the part of David to affirm the greatness and punishing attributes of the god, which is exactly what Somavati wants to hear.

c. This section of the ritual also illustrates a personal problem that a *Kapurāla* faces: how to maintain one's charisma. David was irritated that he could not control Somavati; his charisma was threatened by her rebelliousness. He wants her to "surrender," but she continues to taunt him. It is this that makes David do something unusual (not part of the standard ritual); he goes up the the *Kapurāla* and tells him to prepare fire to burn the demons. The reference is to a ritual act that is rarely performed. If the demons are utterly recalcitrant, the *Kapurāla,* possessed by the goddess Kali, may ask the patient to stand on a red-hot iron plate. Although the decision to do this is made by the *Kapurāla,* never by the assistant, David fears that Somavati is getting out of control and this threat may help control her. Thus the priest is not simply playing the role of the deity; he is also affected as a person.

The Exorcism Continued

The *Kapurāla* realizes that David finds it difficult to control the demons in Somavati. He is already dressed up as the goddess Kali, the role he will play later in the morning. He decides to help David out of the situation; and both of them dance in the arena and confront Somavati. This is not a feature of the standard ritual; it was warranted by the necessity to control the intractable demons.

SOMAVATI: I will not go near anyone.

Kapurāla: Will these demons and demonesses leave this human body?

SOMAVATI: I will leave. . . .

Kapurāla: At what time will you leave?

SOMAVATI: At dawn. . . . I want to play once more. . . . I want to play once more in the morning.

Kapurāla: At what time?

SOMAVATI: Three in the morning.

Kapurāla: At three. Is that certain? You can't play with us in the way you played with other exorcists. If you don't go, we will put you in the fire and burn you.

SOMAVATI: (sarcastically). Oh dear, I have already finished stamping out your fire. You have burned us already, but you haven't chased us yet.

David then takes her by the hand to the altars of the deities inside the shrine, and pushes her head down in forced obeisance. Then the *Kapurāla* grabs her by the hair, takes her to the Buddha altar, and pushes her head down.

Kapurāla: Will you not even now leave this human body and depart?
SOMAVATI: I will leave.
Kapurāla: At what time?
SOMAVATI: At three.
Kapurāla: For certain?
SOMAVATI: I swear, swear, by the gods, by the Buddha, I will depart.
. . . At three I will depart, depart, depart.

The *Kapurāla* asks her what signs she will make as she departs.

SOMAVATI: I will hoot before the shrine, dance, spit, laugh, and leave. Leave.
Kapurāla: That won't do. Will you break a branch of a tree and then leave?
SOMAVATI: Yes I can . . . I swear by the gods, by the Buddha.

The demon agrees to break a branch of the large banyan tree on the shrine premises before leaving the body of Somavati. Meanwhile David is dancing in the background.

Now, an assistant brings into the arena a standard straight-backed chair. Both David and the *Kapurāla* dance around this chair for awhile. Then the *Kapurāla* grabs Somavati by the hair and forces her down in front of the chair. He has a cane in his hand and with it directs the woman to crawl under the chair. She crawls under the chair on all fours. "Get up—get to the other side," says David. She crawls under the chair in the opposite direction. This is repeated several times. David places the stick on her back and Somavati sprawls face down on the dusty arena floor. The *Kapurāla* with his stick and David with a coconut flower walk on the arena and Somavati, flat on the floor, crawls behind them, literally eating the dust. Then David holds her by the hands and drags her across the arena floor, still face down, all the way into the shrine, and from there to the inner sanctum (where we were not allowed to enter). There the god Dadimunda (David) beats her back mercilessly with his stick, then returns with Somavati, now in an upright position, to the other shrine. It is now 1 a.m.

The following dialogue ensues between Somavati and David.

DAVID: (in a brusque, loud voice). Why do *you* tell me lies? Why do you tell me such lies?

SOMAVATI: (in an appealing manner). I did not speak lies. Your lordship, please consider whether I have really told you lies.

DAVID: Why, after having given you permission, and made you swear you'd leave, why did you lie?

SOMAVATI: (in abject tones). Yes, I will look at the direction in which I'll depart and swear I'll leave. Swear, swear, by the gods, the Buddha, I'll leave.

DAVID: You must.

SOMAVATI: Yes.

DAVID: Obey my command.

SOMAVATI: Yes.

DAVID: Worship me, and this human body.

SOMAVATI: Yes.

DAVID: Redeem this human body.

SOMAVATI: Yes.

DAVID: And if you don't leave, do you know what kinds of punishment you will get? Therefore redeem this human body.

SOMAVATI: Yes.

DAVID: I am the Lord Devata Bandara Dadimunda, suzerain over 108,000 demons.

SOMAVATI: Yes.

DAVID: My command is such that.

SOMAVATI: (her voice is becoming quieter each time). Yes.

DAVID: You must yield.

SOMAVATI: Yes.

DAVID: Go three times [to each altar] and pay obeisance, and afterward you can go back and sit down. If not, this Dadimunda will punish you.

Somavati goes before the image of each god and worships them, as instructed by David. Then she goes outside and sits on the mat. David, with coconut flowers in his hand, gently touches her head with them blessing her. He hits himself on the face with the coconut flowers. He goes to the Buddha altar and hits himself; then goes into the shrine and facing the deities hits himself again. He leaves the flowers there and comes back and dances briskly for a long time in the arena. David then faces the girl and her mother seated beside her and gives Somavati an amulet and some "protective pins." He comes before the girl and speaks in firm authoritative tones. It is a long speech and goes on for about fifteen minutes. I shall quote excerpts from it, and summarize parts of it.

DAVID: Yes, yes, I am the noble, powerful god of pure Alutnuvara, Devata Bandara, courageous, leader of a host of demons. I succor thousands of persons fallen into unhappy plights, and provide a new dawn for them. Since I grew up near Gautama, the Buddha, the Father, I protect his *sāsana* [church] from 45,000 evil demons and demonesses and other cruel godlings [*dēvata*]. I got blessings [permission] from the Buddha for myself to be a Buddha in a distant eon . . . remember this often. I was born as the son of the demon Purnaka in the determination to avenge the insults that [Purnaka] hurled at the Father Buddha; I was born as Purnaka's son in order to split him in two, remember that . . . [the Lord Buddha] saw with his divine eye that I was about to split my own father in two. As he saw this, he created a huge darkness, preached me the five precepts [of Buddhist morality], and with a soft hand reached out for me and took me near him. He gave me permission to protect the *sāsana* for 5,000 years from demons and demonesses that trouble people, and acquire a little merit by those actions [thereby wipe out the sin of attempting to kill the father]. Therefore, remember I can torture, torment the demons that for many months and many days have taken over this mortal frame; put these demons in a mortar and pound them, split them in two, pierce their soles with burning pointed stakes. . . . Remember that I can bind demons who heed not the doctrine of the Buddha and the gods. . . .

Dadimunda, through David, then gives a series of instructions to the patient regarding what she should do after the exorcism is over.

1. Take the protective pins that you and your mother were given, and place them in an altar built inside your house, between the East and North side. Cover the wooden board used for making the altar with white cloth. Light three lamps with *mī* [a vegetable seed] oil. Place

three leaves of betel with the stems pointing towards the lamps, and the 'tail' pointing toward you. Place the two sets of protective pins [each set has four pins 1.5 inches and 1.3 inches long] on the altar, cover it with white flowers, and think of the Lord Ishvara. Then plant them in the eight corners, and the protection of Ishvara and his son Skanda will be assured. This must be planted in the four corners of the house—North, South, East, and West. One set an arm's length from the floor; and the other set an inch above the floor. This must be done the very next day before retiring. Many obstacles may arise, but you must be firm as a king of lions; plant these pins as instructed.

2. She must wear the *yantra* [amulet] given to her all the time. At home, before retiring, she may keep the amulet on the wood altar. But when leaving the house she must always wear it. It is forbidden to wear this at a polluted place.

3. She must light *mī* oil lamps for Ishvara for nine consecutive days. "Do not fear, have no doubts. . . . Remember you have to do it in the manner prescribed."

4. David goes to the other patient who had come to be cured and blesses her and utters a long homily. He comes back to Somavati and concludes his act with a short speech. The tone is now kind and reassuring.

You must remember carefully that I will send away the demons and demonesses that are insulting and abusing this mortal body, you must remember it well. As a result of these demons you think often that life is not worth it . . . but doubt not, fear not. They will not appear before your vision again, and I will remove those tortures, remember. Therefore think of the five precepts [of Buddhism] and live accordingly. . . . Remember this is my command [to the evil spirits] from me, Devata Bandara, Lord of the host of 140,000 demons. I will arrange everything for certain; I will open a path for you to lead a peaceful life. Remember this.

Exegesis

a. On the cultural level, the first part of the preceding episode deals with the taming of the recalcitrant demons by the superordinate god. On the psychological level, it is the attempt by the *Kapurāla* and his assistant to overcome Somavati's resistance and establish their control over her. The moment the *Kapurāla* enters the demons in Somavati agree to leave at 3 a.m., since she wants to "play" till then. She taunts the *Kapurāla;* in a later interview the *Kapurāla* called her (the demon's) attitude an *upahāra* (sarcasm) that could not be tolerated by the gods. She is even taunting the *Kapurāla* to burn her.

b. *Forced obeisance.* The taming of the demons comes in three acts. She is forced to pay obeisance to the deities and to the Buddha: the supernatural hierarchy threatened by the rebellious demons is reestablished; as is the authority of the *Kapurāla* over his patient. Under duress Somavati now agrees to leave at 3 a.m. When she says that she (the demons) will spit, hoot, and leave at 3 a.m., that is what *she* would like to do. But the *Kapurāla* asks the demon to break a branch of the banyan tree before leaving; this is the "proof" or vindication to the public that the demon has left. According to Sinhalese belief, departing demons break a branch of a tree as they leave the body of the patient; the *Kapurāla* would like this to occur to vindicate his charisma. (This never happened, and no one queried it, since there were ample dramatic vindications of the efficacy of the concluding ritual events.)

c. *Chair episode.* This episode, repeated later on in the proceedings, is of crucial psychological and cultural significance. On the cultural level, the demons have capitulated to the superior gods and acknowledged their power; the god waves his rod and the demons crawl on the floor. On the psychological level, it is Somavati's self abnegation; she literally grovels in the dust at the feet of the priests, and later of the deities. She is broken, humiliated, made abject, and made pliable psychologically.

d. *Beating episode.* In the final stage Somavati is dragged into the shrine and beaten by the god Dadimunda. On the cultural level, this is a repetition of the prototypical mythic event where the god Dadimunda beat the demons and subjected them to his will. On the psychological level, it is a repetition and reenactment of her relationship with her husband: as was pointed out earlier, she projects her attitudes towards her wife-beating husband to the demon-beating Dadimunda. Thus the psychological release and satisfaction that she derived from this episode must surely have been immense. She taunted the gods to do it (this was not part of the standard procedure) in much the same way as she taunted her husband. When they return to the arena Somavati is totally cowed, her resistance broken; the monosyllabical "yes" she utters, ever more softly, clearly indicates this. She is now *mella* ("tamed"), the *Kapurāla* told us later.

e. *The final speech of god Dadimunda.* In the first part of this speech the myth of the deity is proclaimed to the public. The fascinating oedipal myth of Dadimunda and the Buddha is not found in the Buddhist doctrines but is a popular invention. According to this myth a leader of demons, Purnaka, once tried to kill the Buddha. Dadimunda, in order to avenge this insult, was born as the son of Purnaka and his wife Erandati. Seven years after his birth he decided to kill Purnaka, but the Buddha saw this with his divine eye and created a dark cloud so that

Dadimunda could not see his father. Then Buddha stretched forth his hand, reached for Dadimunda, and took him near him. He delivered a sermon on morality and made him realize that killing his father was an eternal (*anantariya*) sin. The Buddha brought him up and later gave Dadimunda authority over all demons.

We must differentiate the psychogenesis of this myth from its psychological and social functions. The genesis of this myth can be related to one type of Sinhalese socialization experience where the son, in his preoedipal stage, has a fairly intimate and warm relationship with the father. Around age five, however, the father becomes more distant, and authoritarian. The myth expresses this beautifully: Dadimunda tries to kill the father at age seven, at the time the father has become a stern authority figure to him. But the Buddha, the idealized father imago, stretches out the nurturant hand and prevents this act. Psychologically this is a projection of the infantile conflict as it is found in the Sinhalese familial situation: the son would like to kill the father, but what prevents it is the fact that the father was at one time a loving person. In psychological reality—though not in cultural or social reality—it is likely that the Sinhalese relate to the Buddha as an idealized infantile father imago (as David does when he calls Buddha the Father). The attempt to regain the old father, a powerful Sinhalese wish, is expressed in the Buddha bringing up Dadimunda.

Yet we must distinguish the genesis of this myth from its significance in the ritual of exorcism for Somavati, for the problem here is how the patient uses the supernatural pantheon, and usage must be related to the motives of each patient. This myth may have meant a great deal to a male patient with a history of oedipal conflict and he would have identified with Dadimunda. Somavati, however, with a different set of problems, seizes on another feature of Dadimunda's character—his "sadistic" qualities rather than his oedipal history—and projects onto him her attitudes toward her husband. Different patients will adopt different aspects of a "standard" ritual performance, so that a standard ritual can incorporate a variety of psychological problems endemic to a group. Yet the myth as related by David is not devoid of significance to those assembled, including Somavati. On the cultural level, it affirms the primacy of Buddhist ethical values over pressing illicit and dark motives like the oedipal one—on no account must the father be killed, even if the father threatened to kill the Buddha, the most heinous "sin" in Buddhism.

f. *The protective pins.* David gives protective pins of two sizes to the patient and her mother with instructions to use them. They must be planted on the four points of the compass inside the house. The large set of pins is for the god Siva (Ishvara), and the smaller for his son, Skanda, who appeared in the ritual. This is to protect the house from intrusion by demonic spirits: the pins, charmed 108 times in the shrine, contain the essence of these gods. To protect her person Somavati must wear an amulet shaped like the trident (*trisūla*) of Siva. When she is in the house, she can place it on the altar; there is no need to wear it as the house is protected. Outside, however, she must always wear it, except in polluted places. Somavati in fact did everything as instructed the next day. Psychologically this act establishes some kind of ego control and executive autonomy in Somavati: she can deliberately control those demons by performing these divine prescriptions, rather than being controlled by them. Spiritually she establishes a relationship with the deities: the *mī* oil lamps that she lights for nine consecutive days is to establish a habit. She is expected to be a devotee of the gods forever, and light a lamp for them every day. Sociologically it is the first step in her relationship with the shrine and its officials and congregation: much as she can depend on the gods, she can also depend on the personnel of the shrine if she is in trouble again.

g. *The changed tone of Dadimunda.* At the conclusion of his last speech there is a marked change in Dadimunda's tone as he addresses Somavati. He is kind, almost gentle. As long as Somavati is recalcitrant, the god is stern; but self-abnegation and surrender to the father is part of the ideology of filial piety, and produces a change in the god's attitude.

The Exorcism Continued: the Goddess Kali

There is a long interval after the Dadimunda impersonation; people relax, have tea, and chat with each other. At 4:35 a.m. the exorcism resumes when the *Kapurāla* dresses up as the goddess Kali, with a gown, brassiere, anklets, and a red shawl in his hand. In the usual trance state he goes into the shrine and utters *gāthas* (prayers) in honor of the gods and the Buddha. Meanwhile an assistant places a large *puhul* ("ash melon") fruit before the other patient; a large fire is blazing in front of one of the temporary altars constructed in the compound for the gods of the four quarters. The *Kapurāla* comes out of the shrine, dancing, with two swords in hand; one he gives to the other patient, and the other to Somavati's mother. He then goes into the shrine and comes out with a cane (stick) in hand. All this time Somavati has been sitting on a mat quietly. The *Kapurāla* goes up to her and draws her by the hair into the dancing arena, then leads her by the hand into the shrine and points the stick toward the altar. She comprehends the sign and places her head on the altar before the Kali image, raising her head and lowering it on the altar several times in a limp movement, as if the head were performing the action independently of the body. She then worships the deities, hands folded, while the *Kapurāla* dances behind her with his cane. Then he holds her hair and leads her to the inner shrine and she follows, led by the signs he makes with the cane. He speaks to her in a commanding voice, his hands on her shoulder in an authoritative gesture.

Kapurāla: Emphatically, I am ready to expel with my power [the *prētas* who have inhabited this human body] and the three, Mahasona, Riri, and Kalu Yaka—but Mahasona who is leader of them all, are you ready to leave this human body?

SOMAVATI: Ready.

Kapurāla: Yes, emphatically are you ready to break a branch and leave as instructed by the priest [*gätiya*] of this shrine?

SOMAVATI: Yes.

Kapurāla: Yes, emphatically, can you do it?

SOMAVATI: I can.

Kapurāla: Otherwise, emphatically, you shall have to suffer in mountains of fire. . . . Thus, are you willing to dance as agreed by us and will you then leave for your own abodes? Otherwise. . . . Emphatically, are you ready to depart?

SOMAVATI: (almost eagerly). Yes, I am ready.

Kapurāla: Emphatically, will you come back to this body? Yes, will you ever again haunt or cast your malign eye on this body?

SOMAVATI: Never.

Kapurāla: Then, emphatically, I shall not torture you with punishments. . . . I Kali with eighteen other manifestations. . . . Emphatically, are you ready to depart to your own abodes?

SOMAVATI: (in eager tones). I am ready!

Kapurāla: (kindly). Yes, what do you want?

SOMAVATI: Nothing. (Then she changes her mind.) I want to play.

Drums beat and the two dance in the arena. An assistant blows a conch shell. After a few minutes the *Kapurāla* directs her to the shrine, where they dance before the deities and back to the arena.

Kapurāla: Yes.

SOMAVATI: Ha! Ha! Ha! Ha! I will leave, leave, leave!

(Conch shells are sounded and drums beat.)

Kapurāla: There is plenty of time for play. Yes, I shall give you permission to play as much as you like.

They dance. She throws up her hands and runs and dances all over the
arena for several minutes. The time is 5:00 a.m. Now the *Kapurāla* gestures to an assistant, who brings a chair into the arena. The *Kapurāla*
and *Somavati* dance round and round the chair, and the drums beat
louder as the dance increases in its tempo. The assistant stands on the
chair, cane in hand. The *Kapurāla* points a coconut flower at Somavati
and then at the chair. She crawls under the chair, up and down, up and
down, several times in both directions. The *Kapurāla* directs her with
the coconut flower; Somavati grovels under the chair and around it,
while the assistant continues to stand on the chair with the cane in his
hand. Then she contorts her body and crawls under the chair like a
snake in an almost impossible diagonal direction, and round the chair
again. She uses her elbows to crawl, face down; her whole body below
the waist is sprawled on the floor. She rises up, but the *Kapurāla* waves
the flower and she does it again and again, her face caked with dust
and tears. The *Kapurāla* gestures to the assistant, who removes the
chair. Somavati, now practically on the floor face down, drags herself
across the arena floor into the shrine, directed by the *Kapurāla,* and
crawls up to the images of the goddess and the other deities. The *Kapurāla* raises his hand; she gets up. He raises his hand and points to her
head. Following this order, she places her hands on her head and
worships the deities. Now she dances before the images of all the deities, while the *Kapurāla* dances behind her. It is 5:15 a.m. They come
back to the arena and dance there. He gestures to an assistant, who
summons the girl's mother. The girl's mother is in the middle of the
dancing arena, facing the girl and the *Kapurāla.* The *Kapurāla* holds the
girl by the shoulder.

Kapurāla: Say "never again will these demons come" and bow, touch
her feet, swear.
SOMAVATI: (bowing low, touches her mother's feet). I swear, swear by
the gods and the Buddha, that as long as life lasts and as
long as the world lasts, I will not come again. Swear, I
swear by the gods, the Buddha, and by my mother.
(The mother goes back and sits on her mat. The *Kapurāla* summons
David, who stands before her.)

Kapurāla: Now say: "I swear that as long as this body lasts and as
long as the wide earth lasts I will never again seek this

body," and worship the feet of the noble Dadimunda Devata Bandara, and ask forgiveness from his priest who is here by bowing before him.

(She falls down, worships David, and touches his feet.)

SOMAVATI: Swear, I swear by the gods, by the Buddha. . . .

(The father is summoned before the girl.)

Kapurāla: Yes, emphatically to your father say, "Never will I Mahasona come again to possess this person."

SOMAVATI: I swear, swear . . . by my brothers, my mother, my father. . . ."

(Drums beat, the conch is blown.)

Kapurāla: The time has come for the departure from the body. Yes, Mahasona . . . the three of you must leave this body wherein you dance. Emphatically, the time has come, and you can break the branch of the tree as you depart?

SOMAVATI: Yes, I can!

Kapurāla: (holding her by the hair). Then shake this mortal body and depart. . . . Yes, there the time is ripe, so emphatically, I say, hoot three times and leave this body. Otherwise, if you come back, you will be beaten with coconut flowers, yes, you will be placed on seven fires, emphatically, and placed on a red hot iron plate, and you will be conquered by eighteen fires. Now will you go worship the Great King, our Lord Buddha and then move over to the palace of the gods?

He points his finger at the Buddha altar and Somavati goes there and worships the Buddha. Then to the shrine and worships all the gods, again directed by his imperious finger. From here she moves into the inner shrine past the images of the deities and the Brasso cans used for polishing their ornaments. They come back into the arena, and there the two of them dance gracefully to the sound of conch and drum, her hands held aloft in worship as she dances, he with a bunch of coconut flowers in his hand.

Kapurāla: This is the final moment. Remember you can play for nine minutes longer [and then to me]. . . . You will see how the dark misfortunes caused by the demons are banished presently, and how the body will revert to its truly human form. . . . Emphatically, after they leave the body you will see how it truly looks. Watch these things with pleasure and expectation.

Drums beat and the conch sounds. She dances with her hands held aloft in worship. The *Kapurāla* draws a circle (*mandala*) on the floor with his cane. Somavati dances round and round in the circle for several minutes, never moving out of it. Then he draws a *trisūla* (Ishvara's trident) within the circle: she dances on it precariously, and if she tries to move out of the charmed circle, he directs her back into it with his flower.

Kapurāla: Emphatically, the time has now come, and so remember my command and your promise and it is good that you leave, or else die.

SOMAVATI: Hoo, hoo, hoo, (pause) hoo, hoo, hoo.

The girl dances for a few seconds within the circle and falls down in a faint. "The demons have left," the *Kapurāla* turns and tells me so, and then:

Kapurāla: Thus it ends. Leave, you who inhabited this mortal body, and go back to those who brought you here. Emphatically, never again will this girl be beset with such misfortunes as long as her body lasts, therefore, emphatically, all the misfortunes caused by demons and demonesses are over.

The *Kapurāla* sings and dances in the arena center, torch in hand. Someone has sprayed water on Somavati. She revives and goes back to her mat.

(After this the *Kapurāla* performs the melon-cutting ritual. According to Sinhalese belief, the effects of sorcery can be "cut" by cutting a charmed melon. Somavati participates in this rite, because it is part of the standard ritual, but it has little significance for her. It is, however, crucial to the other patient present, who was afflicted by the effects of sorcery.)

Exegesis

a. The *goddess Kali*. This personage is rarely worshipped in Sri Lanka, except in urban shrines. For my own purposes the important question is how does Somavati relate to the goddess? Kali is mother and is addressed as mother; but there are many mother goddesses, as there are father-gods. The question is what aspect of the maternal image is being represented here, and what is its psychological significance for Somavati? Kali is always referred to and addressed by Somavati in the formal terms used for mother, never in intimate style. Thus Kali is *mātā, māniyo* best translated as *mater*. By contrast the term *amma* which is the intimate term, is used along with the more formal terms, to address Pattini, another female goddess in the pantheon. The inference is that while Pattini is an approximation of the mother in her affective role, Kali is the cruel maternal imago (Carstairs, 1967, pp. 152–169). Somavati can easily identify the goddess Kali with the cruel aspect of her own mother, which is truly based on her early experiences. At this point in the ritual Somavati has been tamed by the *Kapurāla*, and offers no resistance to the commands given by the mother goddess. This ties in with the main "message" of this part of the ritual to the patient: the reestablishment of damaged authority relationships. The authority of the mother over the girl—so crucial in Sinhalese family structure—is affirmed. This time the patient does not protest. Since the patient is good, the *Kapurāla* allows her to "play." Thus a message is also given to the parents of the girl (whether it is effective is another question) which states: "this girl must be given an opportunity to 'play,' within the limits of parental authority." I believe that after seeing their daughter act out in such an extravagant manner, no parent could help but be more tolerant in the future. As we saw earlier, Somavati truly lets herself go, and runs about in the arena in abandon.

b. *Chair episode revisited.* The earlier chair episode was not part of the standard ritual but was introduced at that point to control the recalcitrant demons. The present chair episode is a standard procedure for all patients like Somavati who have been possessed by demons. What we have said earlier is applicable here too, but several additional comments are appropriate here. The control is being effected by Kali, the cruel mother, and it *is* a cruel treatment, extremely painful and humiliating to the patient. I believe that this extraordinary traumatic episode is analogous to a conversion experience, or to brainwashing and menticide, in that old cognitive maps are being erased and the "messages" of the ritual are being implanted into her consciousness. The fundamental message here is of control and authority: the gods have authority over demons, and the demons can do nothing as long as that authority is maintained; the parents have authority over Somavati; the *Kapurāla* and his assistants also have authority over her. The other message is "play": play is permitted within the limits of authority.

This establishment of external authority over Somavati is acted out immediately afterward when she asks forgiveness from her mother, David, her father, the gods, and the Buddha by prostrating herself before them. Given this context, it is no accident that the mother is the first person she worships. The whole possession episode has upset the traditional scheme of authority relations in the family and in the religious pantheon: these are now restored. As in any conversion the person who emerges from it is a different individual; the person is reborn. This rebirth idea is expressed in one feature of the chair episode: the *Kapurāla*'s assistant stands on the chair, cane in hand, and Somavati crawls under him. Symbolically she is being reborn as a child of the priests of the shrine. (The psychological meaning of this event for the priests is a fascinating problem, which cannot be pursued here.) Thus it is no accident that later on Somavati became a member of the congregation of the shrine.

c. *Word and gesture.* The language of the *Kapurāla* consists of a formal, highly Sanskritic diction, rather than colloquial, everyday usage. In a perceptive essay Tambiah has noted how the language of the priest suits the deity and the cult he represents. For example, spells pertaining to demons are a melange of Tamil, Telegu, Sinhalese, and Pali, whereas a more formal language is used in addresses to the gods of the pantheon (Tambiah, 1969). This is clearly exemplified in the present case. The deities impersonated by the *Kapurāla* have clearly defined identities in the religious tradition, and most of them come from the Sanskrit (Hindu) tradition. The formal, stylized, high sounding (e.g., "emphatically") language befits this tradition, as well as it suits the formal paternal role of this deity. This imperious vocabulary is matched with an imperious language of gestures—pointed finger, stick, and so on. Somavati's subservience to the diety is nearly complete when she has understood these gestural cues, and she obeys them implicitly. It should be noted that the *Kapurāla* does not use this language in everyday conversation. Also, in his trances he never speaks in tongues: probably the latter is used only when the identity of the deity is vague or unknown.

d. *The magic circle.* Historically the concept of a magic circle is derived from Tantrism. Renou says that the *mandala* is a circle "drawn on the ground to mark out a protected space in which the operator can safely attract or repel invisible forces" (Renou, 1962, p. 93). As adapted in this ritual, it is also something more. This "archetypal" image beautifully symbolizes the completeness of the control: Somavati dances within the circle drawn by the deity with his stick, symbol of his authority. She is enclosed within the circle of his authority, and this carries the signature of the presiding deity of the shrine, the trident (*trisūla*) of Ishvara. She faints within the magic circle: the demons flee, but the *Kapurāla* urges them to go attack those who brought them in, Louis the exorcist and his daughter!

V

AFTERMATH

In this chapter I have analyzed a spirit possession episode and the subsequent exorcism in psychocultural terms. The exorcism has a ready-made cultural framework, that is, the gods that are present and the rites practiced there are part of a "standard ritual." This ritual has not developed fortuitously; it can be presumed that it was designed to cope with the pressing psychological conflicts found in the local population. These conflicts are varied; and the standard ritual tries to deal with as many of them as possible. Thus all aspects of the ritual structure are not relevant for each patient, but some are for all. Sometimes the standard ritual may be modified to suit a particular patient, but such modifications are not great. Each patient's psychological problems must be expressed within the standard framework. We have tried to show how one patient uses this standard framework to express her psychological conflicts; another patient may use it differently. All these usages can be accommodated, since the psychological problems, though varied, are also finite: problems of repression of sex and aggression, oedipal conflicts, relationships with spouses, and so forth. These problems, generated by the culture, are combined in different persons in different ways: but the standard ritual has sufficient flexibility to cope with them. If it fails, the patient must go elsewhere.

Some concluding remarks are necessary regarding the effect of the exorcism on Somavati, since we followed her case up to September 1971, almost two years after her exorcism. The immediate effect of the exorcism was the eradication of all symptoms, both somatic and psychological. Her headaches, bodily pains, the nausea she often experienced before meals, and all signs of possession were eradicated, and remained so until our last interview with her. She also had total amnesia about the events of the exorcism, an ego defense that prevented her from remembering the unfeminine and humiliating behavior. This also ties in with the cultural explanation that these behaviors were the actions of a spirit (or spirits) having an identity and leading an existence separate from that of the patient. Yet important as the exorcism was, the aftermath was also crucial because it resulted in a change in Somavati's lifestyle.

From our point of view the cure did not end with the ritual; actually the critical period of the "cure" lies in the postritual period. The ritual itself was profoundly cathartic: Somavati abreacted and acted out her inner conflicts through a publicly intelligible ritual idiom. To use Wallace's terms, the "cathartic strategy" was contained within a "control strategy": the parental and supernatural authority was reestablished (Wallace, 1959). But this did not imply for Somavati, or for the others in my field notes, a reversal to the *status quo ante,* for the message of the exorcism impressed in her was "play," within the circle of control. But while Somavati wanted to "play," how could her parents be persuaded to allow her to "play"?

One of the immediate effects of the ritual was to draw Somavati into the circle of the powerful deities who could exercise such control over her and transform her. Over and above her parents were these deities, and the priests who impersonated them: she was a "convert" to the cult. The *Kapurāla* asked her to visit the shrine a week after the exorcism: during this visit he told her, in his trance state, that she has the Pattini *ārude* (trance) and is qualified to become a priestess of the goddess Pattini.

What are the implications of this revelation? *Āvēsa* is the term used to describe those possessed by evil spirits; *ārude* is for those "possessed" by a divinity. Psychologically they tap the same propensity: culturally they are radically different. She can now use this propensity to become a priestess, a veritable role transformation. Earlier she had been possessed by evil, troublesome demons; now the possibility exists for her to be possessed by the goddess Pattini, the ideal female in Sinhalese culture. The *Kapurāla* told her further that the deity would inform her later, in another trance state, of the date and time she could be inducted into her new role.

The effect of this was to draw the girl further into the circle of the deities. She came to the shrine often and sometimes stayed overnight watching other persons being exorcised. The parents had to relax their control over her: since this was a command of the gods, they could hardly oppose it. Thus Somavati traveled alone to the shrine, stayed overnight, and joined the other members of the congregation in group activities such as going on long pilgrimages. Some of the sociological consequences of her cult membership are therefore clear:

(a).   Her parents permit her to "play," since such play pertains to divine tasks.

(b).   The cult congregation acts as a substitutive kin group for Somavati, a group with whom she can interact freely and on whom she can depend. The latter is singularly important in Somavati's case and for

ESEKERE, G.

1970   "The idiom of Demonic Possession: A Case Study." *So
               cial Science and Medicine* **4**:97–111.

U, LOUIS

1962   *The Nature of Hinduism.* New York: Walker and Com-
               pany.

, MELFORD E

1967   *Burmese Supernaturalism: A Study in the Explanation and
               Reduction of Suffering.* Englewood Cliffs, N. J.: Prentice-
               Hall.

, M. E. and ROY D'ANDRADE

1958   "A Cross-Cultural Study of Some Supernatural Beliefs."
               American Anthropologist **60**:456–466.

BIAH, S. J.

1969   "The Magical Power of Words." *Man, Journal of the
               Royal Anthropological Institute,* n.s., **3,** (2):175–208.

LACE, A. F. C.

1959   "The Institutionalization of Cathartic and Control Strat-
               egies in Iroquois Religious Psychotherapy." In *Culture
               and Mental Health,* M. K. Opler, (Ed.), New York: Mac-
               millan, pp. 63–96.

others like her in urban Sri Lanka. For part of her life Somavati had lived among her kinsmen; then the vicissitudes of social change had pushed her family into other places of residence where they had few extended kin ties.

Meanwhile, the deity fixed a date for Somavati's induction as priestess about four months after her exorcism. Somavati went through a brief ceremonial in which she was elevated to the role of priestess, entitling her to have her own shrine and participate in some of the rituals of the cult. The principle involved here, often encountered in social life, is the role resolution of the psychological conflict or conflicts of the individual. The psychological problem of the individual is harnessed into social ends through a new role, which can utilize that problem in a new and positive direction; for example, when a homosexual is converted into a monk or berdache, or when Somavati's propensity for getting into a "trance" state is utilized for divine rather than demonic ends. Had it worked it would have elevated Somavati's social status and her own self-esteem; but Somavati simply could not take the role of priest, which was formally given to her in the ritual of investiture.

Her own reasons for her failure are partially satisfactory. If she were to become a priestess, she had to have a shrine in her own home, but this was not possible because of the crowded conditions in which she lived and her own poverty. Also I do not think she had the intelligence and resources required for the new role, as some others in the cult group had. Furthermore, she had a new but anticipated social problem: sex. The ritual had relaxed some of her sexual inhibitions: the new situation gave her freedom for "play." Within three months of the exorcism she had an "affair" with a young man who was a member of the cult group. In six months she had two other affairs, one with a priest of another shrine and a friend of the *Kapurāla*. She became pregnant and gave birth to a baby, but none of her lovers would acknowledge paternity. She now lives in her parents' house with her infant. It is interesting to note that the parents did not disown her or even reprimand her. They have recognized her right to "play." Moreover the *Kapurāla* interceded on her behalf, and met her parents about the possibility of getting her married to one of her lovers; the obstacle here was physiological paternity, which was very important to both lovers. The *Kapurāla* is optimistic that Somavati will eventually get married. What is important, however, is the *Kapurāla*'s fatherly role: the symbolic rebirth of Somavati as a child of the priests of the cult has a truly sociological dimension. The *Kapurāla* takes an interest in her future, and she finds comfort, security, and comradeship as a member of the cult group. Meanwhile the demons are quiet, perhaps waiting, as in all of us, ready to spring once again at an opportune moment.

POSTSCRIPT ON SOMAVATI: AUGUST 5, 1973

I interviewed Somavati once again in August 1973, when I visited Sri Lanka for summer research. She was more relaxed and communicative than I had ever known. She still lives with her parents, and her new child is well looked after and liked by them. Somavati has a new job: together with four other women, she cooks string hoppers (a noodle-like food) for the Vidyodaya University hostel nearby. The five women pool their resources and do the actual cooking at another woman's house. Although she works only four days a week, she earns about nine to ten rupees per working day, the largest income she has ever had. I was impressed by her enterpreneurial ingenuity. She gives most of this money to her mother for household expenses, but keeps some for her own use.

Somavati lights a lamp every evening for the goddess Pattini who, she says, is a mother to her. Pattini protects her, and she has had no demonic visitation. However, she has no intention of becoming a full time priestess, although she has the *ārude* (power) of the goddess Pattini. She visits the Nawala shrine often, and occasionally falls into a trance state in which she impersonates the goddess. Yet she still has no ability to utter prophecies. I saw her in one of these trance states during the annual celebrations of the shrine in August. Obviously her propensity for possession has been harnessed in a creative and meaningful way.

The *Kapurāla* told me that he is arranging a marriage for Somavati with one of his friends, a *Kapurāla* from another shrine.

NOTES

1. This research was a direct product of a larger project on healing rituals in Sri Lanka. The project was aided by a grant from the Foundations Fund for Research in Psychiatry (No. G. 67–363), for which I am immensely thankful. I am also indebted to my field assistants, Percy Livanage and Daya Jayasekera; and to Mr. Wijedasa of Wije-photo in Colombo, who took beautiful slides of the ritual. Above all my heartfelt gratitude goes to my friend, the *Kapurāla,* and to "Somavati" herself. (Somavati is a pseudonym used to maintain the informant's anonymity.)

2. Since this paper is not a comparative study, I ha[ ] erence to others who have written on "possession[ ] to read the excellent works by Bourguignon [ ] Messing (1959), Spiro (1967), Wallace (1959), an[ ] (1964). My own views on the "idiom of posse[ ] Obeyesekere (1970).

REFERENCES

ABERLE, DAVID
  1952   "Arctic Hysteria and Latah in[ ]
                  New York Academy of Sciences **5,**

BOURGUIGNON, ERIKA
  1965   "The Self, the Behavioral [ ]
                  Theory of Spirit Possession", I[ ]
                  Cultural Anthropology, Spiro, M. [ ]
                  Free Press, pp. 39–60.

CARSTAIRS, G. MORRIS
  1967   *The Twice Born.* Bloomington: In[ ]

DURKHEIM, EMILE
  1915   *The Elementary Forms of the Religio[ ]
                  Swain). London: George Allen a[ ]

FREUD, SIGMUND
  1957   *Future of an Illusion* (trans. by W. [ ]
                  York: Doubleday Anchor.

KARDINER, ABRAM
  1945   *The Psychological Frontiers of Society*[ ]
                  bia University Press.

KENNEDY, JOHN G.
  1967   "Nubian Zar Ceremonies as Psycho[ ]
                  ganization **26,** (4) Winter: 185–194.

KIEV, ARI (ED.)
  1964   *Magic Faith and Healing.* New York:[ ]

LAMBERT, W. W., TRIANDIS, L., and M. WOLF
  1959   "Some Correlates of Beliefs in the M[ ]
                  nevolence of Supernatural Beings:[ ]
                  Study." *Journal of Abnormal and Social*[ ]

MESSING, SIMON D.
  1959   "Group Therapy and Social Status i[ ]
                  Ethiopia." In *Culture and Mental Hea[ ]
                  New York: Macmillan, pp. 319–332.

Clive S. Kessler

Conflict and Sovereignty in Kelantanese Malay Spirit Seances

INTRODUCTION

Spirit possession is a complexly social, multidimensional phenomenon. Simultaneously at several levels, it reflects, addresses, and affects its social milieu. My concern here is with a fundamental but hitherto little recognized dimension of Kelantanese Malay possession seances: with the sociopolitical nature of the basic imagery, or idiom, whereby they characterize and manage psychosocial conflict. That idiom, then, is not exclusively an idiom of possession. Instead, it resonantly links illness and possession to other power-laden contexts from which it derives. Kelantanese healing seances thus enact an allegory of personality and polity; hence the title of this essay. In a specific sense "the personal is political" (as feminist theorists have insisted) among the Kelantanese.[1]

Politics, not possession, drew me initially to Kelantan. Under the joint impact of colonial rule and massive Chinese and Indian immigration, most of the sultanates of peninsular Malaya (West Malaysia) have undergone a profound economic transformation in this century. But in Kelantan, which borders with Thailand on the peninsula's east coast, a predominantly Malay population of peasant farmers and fisherfolk survives. Protected by its British administration (1909–1957) from any marked intrusion of alien populations or economic influences, Kelantan remains anchored in its past, a distinctively Malay state socially, culturally, and politically. In three elections between 1959 and 1969 the Kelantanese voted to power in their State Assembly the Pan-Malayan Islamic Party (PMIP), the main focus (until its absorption into a national coalition government in 1972) of Malay opposition to the interracial Alliance Party's dominance of Malaysian politics.

While seeking to discover the sources of support for the PMIP, both through an anthropological community study and by tracing the evolution of modern Kelantanese politics under colonial rule from those of the precolonial sultanate (Kessler 1974, 1974a), I also witnessed many Kelantanese possession seances, known as *main peteri,* and discussed them with their practitioners, spirit mediums known as *bomoh.* Apart from a theatrical excitement, these psychodramas also afforded insight into Kelantanese peasant society, culture, and personality. While my aim in this essay is to clarify the social basis and cultural idiom of these seances as well as the connection between them, I want also to elucidate what soon, if at first inchoately, became apparent to me in the field: these performances were not entirely unrelated to politics. I do not suggest that, like the Haitian *voodoo,* the *main peteri* was exploited as an instrument of political manipulation; rather that these seances are grounded in certain fundamental ideas which inform popular Kelantanese political understanding.

Since the *main peteri* and cognate rituals have been discussed by a number of writers (Clark, [1960]; Cuisinier, [1936]; R. W. Firth, [1967]; Gimlette, [1929, pp. 79–106]; Kramer, [1970]; Mohd, [1972]; Taib, [1972]; Sheppard, [1968, 1972, pp. 190–200]; Winstedt, [1961, pp. 56–63, 152–156]), I need not provide a full description here. Instead I offer only an outline sketch. But first, let me suggest their political aspect. These seances involve spirit mediumship and possession and are rites of exorcism. Usually their purpose is to cure a sick individual, often one afflicted with an obscure malady. But, as several writers (Cuisinier [1936, p. 97], R. W. Firth [1967, pp. 205–206], Gimlette [1929, pp. 98–100], Sheppard [1968; 1972, pp. 196–200] and Winstedt [1961, pp. 30–31, 63, 152]) have noted but never adequately explained, they are also occasionally but importantly performed for other beneficiaries: as "lustratory" or cleansing rituals, periodic or sporadic, to preserve or restore the spiritual well-being of a village, a district, or of the state as a whole; and as festive rites on notable royal birthdays, anniversaries, and weddings.

It is this connection I hope to explain by an analysis of the *main peteri* as a healing rite. To that end, in the three principal sections that follow, I outline the *main peteri* ritual form, provide data and case studies indicating the nature of the characteristic afflictions it is employed to treat, and discuss its cultural idiom as revealed in its principal underlying metaphor.

THE *MAIN PETERI* RITUAL: AN OUTLINE SKETCH

Though occasionally performed for a collective beneficiary, the *main peteri* is commonly employed to cure a sick individual. He or his family approach a *bomoh*, who may initially attempt a cure by lesser means— usually with privately administered libations of water consecrated by invocations to certain spirits. If this does not succeed, the patient may seek, or the *bomoh* counsel, more elaborate and public treatment through *main peteri*. Formerly, as Cuisinier (1936, pp. 38–83) and Gimlette (1929, pp. 73–77, 100–105) have noted, other forms of healing rite existed in Kelantan: *bageh, gebiah, belian, main mok pek,* and so on. These, however, are being replaced increasingly by *main peteri. Bomoh* now class all these rites under the generic term *main peteri,* of which the other forms, if mentioned at all, are characterized as subsidiary, even defunct, variants.

Depending upon the patient's condition and resources and the *bomoh's* assessment of them, the *main peteri* may be arranged for one, three, or even five evenings. The *bomoh* and his assistants arrive after sundown. They dine and converse with the patient's family, discreetly observe and discuss his condition, and then prepare for the performance, which generally lasts from about 9 p.m. to 3 a.m. In fishing communities the performance is usually held in a specially constructed outdoor pavilion; inland, among rice cultivators, it is generally held inside the patient's house, which is cleared to accommodate performers and spectators. Indoors or out, the arena set aside for the performance is clearly demarcated. A cloth (*langit,* literally "sky") is suspended over it, mats are laid around it, and spirit offerings (rice, eggs, betel nuts, fruit, etc.) are suspended or placed in trays on the eastern side. The *bomoh* and his "team" are seated on mats around the arena, he and his apprentices to the south, and the orchestra—players of the spike-

fiddle, gongs, drums, small metallic percussion instruments, and sometimes also a reed flute—to the east and north. The patient, and kin who
may offer aid and comfort during the performance, are located on the
western side.

The "tuning up" of the orchestra announces the performance, and
spectators, as many as a hundred, begin to arrive. Mundanely tuned,
the instruments must also be ritually attuned. With incense and incantations they are dedicated by the *bomoh*'s chief assistant, in fact cospecia-
list (R. W. Firth, [1967, p. 192] calls him "master of ceremonies"), the
spike-fiddle player or *mindok,* who both leads the orchestra and serves
as the *bomoh*'s foil and interlocutor, coordinating the musical and dramatic aspects of the performance.

Each phase of the *main peteri* is signaled and initiated by the *mindok*'s
playing of certain marker or "signature" (R. W. Firth, 1967, p. 192)
tunes. The performance proper begins with his solo playing of an initially subdued and plaintive chant. As the tempo increases the *bomoh*
rises, changes into a fresh sarong, ties colorful cloth bands around his
chest, dedicates himself with incense and invocations, seats himself
cross-legged, and begins to roll his head (*lupa,* literally to "forget" or
"go into trance") to the increasing tempo of the music, in which the
drums and gongs have joined. As his movements become more rapid
and agitated, the *bomoh* is said to become possessed by his familiar
spirit, or *penggawa.* Eventually he shrieks, signaling his *penggawa*'s overwhelming presence in him, throws parched rice to the four quarters
around him, and rises to dance, intermittently singing songs of the
spirits.

After his dancing and singing have built dramatically to a crescendo,
or to a series of mounting climaxes, the *bomoh* seats himself before the
mindok and their diagnostic consultation begins. Punctuated by further
singing and dancing to a variety of tunes, the *bomoh* several times takes
grains of parched rice and arranges them, two at a time, in four heaps
on a pillow before him. This divination (*raksi*) refers to the four elements—earth, water, fire and air—which constitute the cosmos and the
patient's person alike. The system of multiple divinations is inevitably
open-ended, leaving wide scope for expert discretion, and no matter
how the count comes up the *bomoh* will find warrant in it for his own assessment of the malady. This assessment is mainly suggested by the
mindok, who transmits it to the entranced *bomoh* both by cryptic verbal
allusions and by emphasizing, certain tunes as orchestra leader. For
these have different associations and emotional valence,[2] and patients,
even involuntarily, will give clues concerning their emotional state to an
observant *mindok* by responding to certain ones. An interesting point
here is that many, though by no means all, *mindok* are blind; these men,

with apparent justification, claim to be especially sensitive to changes in mood among those in their presence. On the basis of this diagnosis, the *bomoh* determines the appropriate spirit to effect the cure, and through his *penggawa* he summons the spirit to possess him. To heighten the drama several false starts may be made, and further divinations performed, before the right spirit is found to begin the cure.

Though certain important variations, to be noted later, exist in the method of cure, the essentials are identical. Ultimately it makes no difference whether the malady is broadly physical, psychosomatic, or psychological, for in Kelantanese thought there is no problematic separation of mind and body. All illnesses, psychic and physical, are caused by some spiritual weakness, or imbalance of the four elements, resulting in a lack of *semangat,* or spiritual essence. This permits malign spiritual forces capable of causing a variety of symptoms to invade the person. Though *bomoh* do make pragmatic distinctions between broadly physical and psychological ailments (some, indeed, specialize in the latter), the treatment is similar in all cases. In the dramatic encounter between the spirit invading the patient and the ideally stronger spirit summoned by the *bomoh,* the patient is led to accept responsibility for his diminished and vulnerable state. Either by his general attitude and demeanor, or perhaps by some unwilling act of ritual affront to a spirit (the patient is instructed), he has himself disrupted his inner balance, thereby inviting invasion and consequent illness. Only when he has acknowledged this deficiency and his own responsibility for it can it be redressed and the invading spirit driven out, by the combined strength of the spirit possessing the *bomoh* and the patient's own *semangat,* now refortified by the *bomoh*'s intervention. (Herein, incidentally, lies the saving explanation for the failures of *bomoh:* not their spiritual powers but those the patient had to summon were insufficient; the patient remains sick because at some level he wants to.)

In cases of obvious or specific affliction the *bomoh* will detect some spirit in the affected part of the patient's body, drive it down by manipulation and cajoling to the patient's big toe, and suck it out. If the music has thus far failed to induce trance in the patient, the *bomoh* seeks to provoke it by pounding the floor in syncopation with the orchestra's rhythm (cf. Needham, 1967). In trance, the patient rises and dances with the *bomoh,* demonstrating the ejection of the invading spirit and his own responsibility for the cure. Temporary alleviation of chronic and painful symptoms may thus result. Where no specific physical ailment is involved, the same routine is followed, except for the dramatic and metaphorical sucking out of the spirit from the affected part of the body. Instead, as will be seen, an alternative ritual procedure is followed.

The performance is then ended. The usually exhausted patient is advised how further to placate the afflicting spirit and the *bomoh*, after assuring their assent to these measures, dismisses the spirits summoned through his *penggawa*. With this final progression from invocation, divination, interrogation, and exorcism to envoi (*pelepas*, or "release"), the performance ends. But in concluding this outline of the *main peteri* ritual, an important variation must be noted.

In cases of specific affliction, offerings are simply made *in situ* to the benign spirits summoned by the *bomoh*. Sometimes the patient is additionally instructed to take certain offerings to some place purportedly inhabited by the invading spirit. (Jungle spirits, for example, may be appeased with offerings left at the edge of a village.) But in cases involving no obvious, specific or simple physical ailment—that is, in cases of psychological or diffuse psychosomatic illness—the ritual cure, or casting out, may be more elaborate. No invading spirit is sucked out. Instead, a *balai* (literally, "royal audience hall") is constructed. Built of bamboo in several tiers and gaily decorated with pennants, it is a model state or political domain. Its highest levels represent a royal palace (hence the name *balai*), the lower ones settlements and fields decorated with miniature inhabitants, human and animal, made of dough. At the conclusion of these performances offerings are arranged upon and about this *balai* to attract the spirits; afterward it is taken to some remote, uninhabited place beyond the village, or set adrift on a stream, or cast out to sea. Thus the *balai* is somehow an analogue of and substitute for the beneficiary. Those set adrift Gimlette (1939, p. 242) aptly terms "scapeboats." Significantly this ritual device is employed not only in cases of marked psychological and psychosomatic illness but also in those other performances mentioned earlier that serve to benefit a sociopolitical community—a village, a region, or the whole state. In both cases, individual and collective, the ritual, through the specific device of the *balai*, serves to ward off or drive out baneful influences (*tolak bala*) by displacement. Disruptive forces are coaxed from the beneficiary to a substitute, which is then jettisoned.

THE AFFLICTIONS AND TREATMENT OF
PATIENTS: TWO CASE STUDIES

General Observations

Before the meanings that may be attributed to these usages by the Kelantanese themselves or by the anthropologist can be further discussed, one must first consider the *bomoh*'s patients and their maladies. For *main peteri* is only one expedient in a repertoire of available cures, traditional and modern, for a variety of recognized illnesses.

Traditionally, all kinds of ailments, simple and complex, were referred to *bomoh*, then the only available medical practitioners. More recently, however, the Kelantanese have taken to Western medicine with considerable enthusiasm, but also selectively. They favor it in areas where it has been proven efficacious, and where its methods, as they have experienced them, do not conflict with their cherished values. (For an attempted outline of the relationship between traditional and Western medicine in Malaya see Wolff, [1965].) The Kelantanese deplore hospitalization, especially surgery, but for the alleviation and treatment of simple physical complaints they favor pills and injections (available through hospitals and clinics, from doctors in private practice catering to the wealthy, and from unlicensed local purveyors of "shots"; during 1967–1969 these illicit drugs originated mainly from U.S. medical supplies stolen in Vietnam and traded through Thailand.)

As a result of losing this clientele, *bomoh* are left with three kinds of patients: those with physical conditions Western medicine claims it can cure only by the unacceptable expedient of surgery; those with chronic, often terminal, physical illnesses which Western-trained doctors admit are beyond their powers to remedy; and those with psychological or psychosomatic illnesses whose symptoms Kelantanese hospitals may not acknowledge, or for which they can offer no cure. *Bomoh,* for their part, are not displeased with this contraction of their clientele, or have at least adjusted to it. They assert the complementarity and equality of their own knowledge with that of the "hospital doctors," and some are pleased to regard themselves as specialists in "spiritual" or psychological disorders. This enforced specialization renders all the more relevant to the Kelantanese case Raymond Firth's observation, based upon his Tikopia materials (1967a, pp. 325, 329), that "the phenomena of spirit mediumship may be regarded as a kind of idiom for the expression of ideas and emotions about social status, and about personal and social crises . . . an idiom for the expression of personal anxieties and conflicts."

Extending Firth's point, I. M. Lewis has more recently argued (1966, 1969, 1971) that the incidence of spirit possession is not random but follows certain social structural patterns or channels. It is generally concentrated among people of inferior, marginal, ambiguous, or problematic status, especially women. Possession provides a means whereby underlings, beset by social strain, may protest their inferior status, bid for attention or, by threatening to cause embarrassing disruption, induce their superiors to honor the obligations inhering in their admittedly unequal relationship. Thus the incidence of possession is a gauge of social strain and conflict, and of the psychological stress they occasion among those least able to deal directly with their causes. The cases I observed in Kelantan [3] confirm this argument.

Over twenty-one months I collected data concerning patients in ninety-eight *main peteri* performances. In seventeen of these I was unable to obtain a clear account of the patient's symptoms and personal situation, principally because of language difficulties early in my field work. Of the remaining eighty-one cases, thirty-five seemed to *bomoh* and me to involve some specific and chronic physical ailment such as malaria, tuberculosis, diabetes, ulcers, rheumatism, and so on. (In some doubtful cases I checked our assessment with a European doctor in the state capital who was sympathetically interested in local medical beliefs and practices.) The incidence of these cases shows no obvious social pattern. The remaining forty-six, however, seemed both to *bomoh* and me, in our different ways, to involve some psychological or psychosomatic complaint—to be, in his terms, cases of *angin* and *jiwa,* of psychological disturbance resulting from a humoral imbalance. Occasionally the patients themselves, consulted generally some time after the performance, were very articulate concerning the psychosocial origins and nature of their symptoms. These cases were not randomly distributed, but fell into five distinct categories consonant with Lewis's social stress hypothesis. The patients either occupied an inherently strained or ambiguous social position, or were making some difficult and stressful, even abruptly disjunctive, transition between social positions. As the case studies will suggest, moreover, recognition by *bomoh* of these five categories of patients and of the distinctive psychosocial basis of each was not simply ex post facto, conceded privately to the ethnographer, but was expressed at the time in the particular type of *main peteri* treatment adopted. The outside observer's more sociological characterization of the patient's predicament, I suggest, is congruent with, even contained within, the indigenous repertoire of symbols and related beliefs employed by *bomoh* to explain and cure illness.

Of these forty-six patients, thirty-seven were female and only nine male, a marked disparity consonant with Lewis's analysis. Therefore this essay will concentrate upon the female patients. Of the males it suffices to note that, like the females, they were beset by extreme, even unusual, pressure and anxiety deriving from a fundamentally ambiguous or conflicted social position. But unlike those of women which, given the nature of Kelantanese peasant society, stem basically from their relation to men and their status in the domestic realm, the insecurities of men arise from their relation to work and the status it affords in the world at large.

The anxieties of both categories of men were in fact connected with lessened status and esteem, with abrupt and disjunctive status transitions following the loss of prestigious and rewarding occupations. One category consisted of young men in their early or mid-twenties. After some initial success, they had failed in their aspiration to rise through education from peasant society into salaried employment, and were forced to return to their natal villages, humiliated yet denied the sympathy of neighbors to whom they had failed to prove themselves superior. The second category consisted of three middle-aged men from the coastal villages. Until recently all had been members of deep-sea fishing crews (R. W. Firth, 1966) but, no longer as strong and agile as before, had been replaced by young men despite their occupational skills and experience. Once mainstays of their community and its principal work groups, they had been forced to retire and spend their days among the women, children, invalids, and old people who constitute diurnal society among the fisherfolk. (A problem for aging fishermen, retirement presents no comparably abrupt transition to the inland rice cultivators. They can more gradually phase themselves out of agricultural labor and, even after their active participation has ended entirely, can still exert control over rice lands others cultivate for them; consequently their status is actually enhanced. Hence the confinement of cases of "retirement stress" to the fisherfolk, and further confirmation of the connection between status ambiguity or transition, stress, and possession.)

THE STATUS OF KELANTANESE WOMEN

The majority of patients, however, are women. Outside observers, whether Europeans or Malays from other states, have generally contended that Kelantanese women enjoy an economic independence, as well as freedom and equality, unmatched by women in other Malay and Muslim societies (Abdullah, [1967, pp. 47, 56–57]; Davison, [1889, pp. 86, 89], Graham, [1908, pp. 24–25]; Swettenham, [1948, p. 314]). But the status of Kelantanese women is not nearly as favorable as those casual observers have claimed, a fact that Rosemary Firth's research (1966) among the wives of the fisherfolk has suggested.

My own observations convince me that the situation of women inland, among the rice-cultivating peasantry, is even less favorable than among the fisherfolk of the coastal fringe. Among the generally impoverished fisherfolk, men do not easily attain a secure and high status, and the importance of conjugal cooperation, and of the earnings of women in household budgets, militate against any marked subordination of women to men. Among the rice cultivators this does not always hold true. With the poorer of them (whose situation in some ways resembles that of the fisherfolk) it may, but among the more secure peasant proprietors and petty rentiers the necessities of economic survival do not press so hard, or to the advantage of women. Even when they participate (which they do most importantly) in rice cultivation, peasant wives do not derive separate cash incomes, unlike the fishermen's wives who do so daily while their men are out to sea from the marketing of processed fish goods, a separate subsector of the economy they control. The efforts of many wealthier peasant husbands to restrict their wives' pursuit of some social and economic autonomy, and to confine them instead to unrewarded labor in the domestic realm, are marked and often the subject of local comment.

Outside observers, favorably impressed by the status of Kelantanese women, have been influenced primarily by the fact that much of the local marketing of subsidiary rural produce (fruit, vegetables, eggs, spices, etc.) is in women's hands. Yet married women who thus regularly derive an independent income do not dispose of it independently but contribute it to a joint household budget. This income, especially when it exceeds that provided by their menfolk (as it is likely to among the poor), may provide women with some leverage within the family and enable them to avoid the subordination that men generally attempt to impose (even if only the wealthy succeed or can afford to.) This avoidance of subjection, however, does not itself amount to freedom and equality.

Furthermore, many of the marketing women are widowed or divorced. The economic and social independence that they enjoy from any particular man is no indicator of equality, but actually the consequence of a general inequality between the sexes. Theirs is an enforced independence to fend for themselves in an attempt to avoid both subordination to a husband (who, with his rights to divorce, offers in exchange no long-term security) and a humiliating and difficult state of total dependence upon their kin.

There are no absolute barriers to a woman engaging in economic activity in Kelantan, or even to her surviving on her own. Upon divorce she can eke out a humble existence from marketing, and is not thrown back (as in some Muslim societies where women are domestically confined) into the power and uncertain charity of her male relatives. This precarious independence, resort to which may often be provoked by an unbearable assertion of male prerogative, is neither equality nor freedom. As will be seen, the effect upon women's social status and psychological security of male prerogatives to pronounce or refuse divorce is the central issue for many women resorting to illness and possession. It should be noted that the rate of divorce in Kelantan is high: in 1967 the Bachok District Kadhi's Office registered 548 divorces as against 797 marriages, a divorce-to-marriage ratio of 68:100; when 71 divorces later revoked are deducted, the ratio is 60:100. For all of Kelantan between 1957 and 1966, Roff (1968, p. 290) notes that, without allowing for revocations, divorces annually amounted to between sixty-one and eighty percent of marriages, the annual average being sixty-six percent. Over the preceding period 1948–1957, according to Gordon (n.d., p. 32), divorces in Kelantan as a whole amounted to seventy-seven percent of marriages, divorces not revoked to seventy-one percent.

Female main peteri *Patients*

Female *main peteri* patients fall into three categories. The larger two will be exemplified in case studies, to which a sketch of the third may serve as introduction. It comprises five cases of young women recently married for the first time. (For fuller accounts of Kelantanese Malay kinship and marriage see R. Firth, [1966], and R. W. Firth, [1974a]; on Malays more generally, see Djamour, [1959]; Swift, [1963]; Hashimah Roose, [1963].) First marriages among Kelantanese Malays are generally arranged marriages and rarely last long. For Kelantanese, as Muslims, but primarily for men, divorce is easily accomplished. Women cannot obtain a divorce directly, but can only induce their husbands to divorce them. This they can generally but not always do by "provoking" them privately with surliness and insult. But a possessive, jealous, or vindictive man may refuse to be provoked, forcing the woman to escalate from private measures to public humiliation. The latter is quite easily accomplished by older women of unequivocally adult status, but not by younger ones. Moreover, while subsequent marriages entered into by mature adults are contractual arrangements involving only the two principals, and hence more readily dissolved by them, first marriages, elaborately arranged by kinsfolk with a continuing interest in their duration, are less easy for the principals, especially the young wife, to terminate.

To counter an unwanted possessive husband and the unwillingness of her kin to countenance divorce before it seems inevitable, the reluctant young wife, unable directly to stage an embarrassing scene, has one principal recourse for ending her arranged marriage. She becomes sick, displaying persistent symptoms of depression, listlessness, and withdrawal requiring treatment by a *bomoh* through *main peteri*. *Bomoh*, for their part, while clearly recognizing this syndrome, are initially somewhat tentative and eclectic in their treatment of these cases. Once it becomes clear, however, that the woman is not merely conducting some tactical protest, but is determined upon divorce, the *main peteri* takes on the characteristic anti-male form discussed in the first case study below.

It is unusual, however, for a reluctant young wife to be driven to these extremes to escape an unwelcome arranged marriage. Having encountered only five cases, I would regard it as rare. Why then, among many arranged marriages that do not endure (and are generally not expected to) should the termination of some be so beset with obstacles that the woman is required literally to make herself sick? It seems significant that of these five women three were married off rather early (around age fifteen), and two, still single well beyond the normal age of marriage, had been hastily married off in their twenties by anxious families; that all five, somewhat unusually, were living with their husbands' families quite far from their own natal villages and close kin; that all were married to husbands considerably older than themselves, and into families markedly richer than those of their birth. Hence the pressure, especially from the wife's kin, that the marriage not be terminated until definitely proven unworkable. Consistent with Lewis's argument, cases in this category involve intersexual antagonism, an unusually stressful status, and status transition (as well as the attempt to reverse it).

The Case of Mek Mas, Wife of Awang Lah

If the difficulty of obtaining a divorce from their husbands prompts the illnesses of the reluctant young wives, it is the ease with which their husbands can divorce them that underlies the anxieties of a class of older *main peteri* patients, as the case of Mek Mas shows. This case, typical in most respects, is chosen to exemplify the largest category (nineteen cases) of *main peteri* patients—usually women in their middle to late thirties.

Mek Mas and her husband Awang Lah (like all personal names in these case studies, these are pseudonyms) had both been married previously, in late adolescence, but their marriages had neither lasted long nor produced children. Residents of neighboring villages, they were then married to each other, and for some years they subsisted primarily from their work on the land of Awang Lah's father and from the cultivation and sale of vegetables by Mek Mas. Three surviving children were born to them, the eldest of whom (since their marriage had now lasted about fourteen years) was approaching adolescence. Several years earlier Awang Lah's father had died, whereupon Awang Lah acquired full possession of about one and a half acres of rice land on which he had previously worked but of whose produce he had formerly enjoyed only a share. From part of the yield of this land Awang Lah, a shrewd speculator unlike his father, made loans to poorer peasant villagers, and when they defaulted he gained control of their lands. Now owning about three acres, Awang Lah had become a petty rentier landlord, and had begun to present himself in his village and its environs as a man of substance. As some of his neighbors had predicted, Awang Lah began to feel that, consonant with his newly asserted status, he should find a new wife—one younger than Mek Mas, satisfied to perform routine household chores, and showing no sign of years of toil in the rice fields.

Mek Mas felt her husband's growing aloofness and suspected that his commitment to her was waning. She realized that he now had the means to replace her, either partially, by taking a second wife (up to four being allowed a Muslim man at any one time) and relegating her to a secondary position (cf. Lewis, 1966; p. 314; 1971, p. 76), or even completely, by pronouncing divorce, perhaps requiring her to fend for herself and provide for their children without paternal support. (It is noteworthy that not only a long-term rise in affluence, as in Awang Lah's case, but also short-term seasonal fluctuations may predispose a man to consider divorce: figures for 1967 from the Bachok District Kadhi's Office indicate that divorce registrations reach a low during the hardship of the monsoon months from December to February, then rise, peaking at three times the January level in June, the period of relaxation and relative plenty following the rice harvest.)

Mek Mas faced a dilemma. She wished to forestall Awang Lah but feared to act, since pleas might dissuade him but, if not properly modulated, could also evoke what she most feared—a pronouncement of divorce. Her indecision, however, ended when her fears were confirmed: through her mother's sister rumor reached her that Awang Lah was displaying an untoward interest in a young divorcee in a neighboring subdistrict where he had recently acquired land. Action was now imperative.

Her objections, initially mild but increasing in forthrightness, were of no avail; Awang Lah was unmoved. Having pursued that avenue as far as she could without provoking him to intemperate action, Mek Mas relented. Seemingly apathetic and acquiescing in defeat, she soon began to display symptoms of melancholia, listlessness, and withdrawal. She described her condition in the usual terms: her food and drink were tasteless, and she could neither relax by day nor sleep at night. As she resisted the food and ministrations insistently urged on her by relatives whose attention was called to her plight, her symptoms became self-perpetuating, and after about two weeks her mother summoned Pak Weng, a *bomoh*, to examine her and offer appropriate libations and incantations. Hearing this, Awang Lah was unimpressed, and Mek Mas's listlessness and lack of affect increased.

As her disturbing condition persisted and intensified, Pak Weng was again summoned, and his suggestion that it be treated through *main peteri* was readily accepted. By this time Mek Mas's mother and aunt had informed and mobilized about a dozen of her kin, and they agreed to pay the costs of the performance (about $M 60 or $US 20 at that time all told, about half for the *bomoh* and his team and half for food and beverages) should Awang Lah refuse. They also offered to hold the *main peteri* in one of their homes should he be unaccommodating, although to hold it elsewhere would reduce its ability to sway him, and thus acknowledge that the marriage could not be saved.

By this time Mek Mas's condition was public knowledge and the subject of considerable comment. Her fellow villagers were agreed that the popular Mek Mas was an exemplary wife and neighbor deserving sympathy and support. Wishing therefore to avoid appearing callous and insensitive before his already somewhat unsympathetic kin and neighbors, Awang Lah agreed to provide for the *main peteri*. By now, moreover, exaggerated reports of Mek Mas's illness had reached the village of his prospective new wife, where Awang Lah was finding himself less welcome, not only by his intended in-laws (who would have been happy to see the marriage go through if it could have been accomplished smoothly) but also among a widening circle of associates of the man whom Awang Lah had dispossessed from his land. Awang Lah was already beginning to have second thoughts about taking a new wife.

As the *main peteri* began Mek Mas, assisted by several relatives, emerged from a side room to lie down at the edge of the arena. Apathetic and unresponsive, she was attended by her mother and aunt, who mopped her brow with cloths soaked in scented water. Behind and around them sat a large contingent of her relatives, men and women from several villages. Awang Lah, meanwhile, stood in semidarkness on the fringe of the audience accompanied by a few close associates. A number of his relatives were also present but, rather than gathering around him, they were dispersed among the crowd.

Mek Mas showed no interest in the early stages of the proceedings.

She did not even look at Pak Weng until the divination stage was reached, and only then when he pronounced her case one of *angin*. The core meaning of *angin* is "wind" or "air," and in this sense it is one of the four elements. By extension, *angin* may mean a humor or disposition; further, it connotes the emotions (an excitable person is said to be *berangin,* to have excessive *angin.*) Mek Mas's condition was thus identified as a spiritual or psychological one, whereupon (for reasons, or at least with apt associations, to be discussed later: see Table 1) the *mindok,* as orchestra leader, began concentrating on the *lagu perang* (war tune) and *lagu ulubalang* (warrior tune). These tunes, stirringly carried by the flute, are not specific to the *main peteri.* They derive from the musical repertoire of the Kelantanese *wayang kulit,* or puppet shadow play, where they accompany enactments of heroic battles in local versions of the Ramayana. (The close ritual connection between the *wayang kulit* and *main peteri* is discussed by Sweeney [1972, pp. 72–77]). Pak Weng began to dance to these tunes, repeatedly moving across the arena toward Mek Mas, and then retreating. Lapsing into trance, Mek Mas began responding to the music with spasmic movements of increasing intensity and frequency. After a half hour, apparently deep in trance, she rose and began circling the arena following Pak Weng, whose dance movements began to elide into the *bersilat* form.

Bersilat is a ritual dance performed by men (with the exception of *main peteri* cases such as this) and expressing certain idealized notions of masculinity. More than simply a dance, *bersilat* is regarded by Malays as their distinctive martial art originating from the old Malacca sultanate, as the ultimate accomplishment and hallmark of the classical *ulubalang* or warrior. But it is a martial skill highly mannered and formalized far beyond the practical demands of personal combat, for it represents, in floridly exaggerated form (cf. Wilkinson [1910, p. 27]), the basic movements in the use of the *keris* (sometimes *kris* or "creese"), or Malay dagger.

No longer used in *bersilat, keris* are employed decoratively in formal, (that is, courtly), Malay male dress. They are also worn by bridegrooms in the formal part (*bersanding*) of the wedding ceremony, which mimics royal enthronement rites. (The groom is thus termed *raja sahari,* "king for a day.") *Keris* are kept as heirlooms, and great practical attention and symbolic concern is lavished on them. The *keris* appropriately serves as the symbol of the main Malay political party—the UMNO, senior partner in the Alliance Party, which the PMIP opposed—and of Malay political aspirations and determination in general.[4] A Malay, no longer able to contain a humiliating grievance, traditionally killed his offender with his *keris* (and all bystanders as well, until he was himself felled) when he went *amok,* or "amuck" as the Malay term has passed into English. It was also the weapon typically used in the institutionalized *amok*—the *juramentado* or *parrang sabbil*—of the southern Philippine Muslims, whose usages provide further insight into the meaning of the *keris.*

Kiefer (1973) has discussed the paradoxical nature of these acts of vengeance against violators of the sanctity and dignity of Islam. The intending *sabbil* (as he was known) would prepare himself by performing the standard Islamic acts of ritual purification. He would then tightly bind his penis in the erect position (according to Tasker [1975, p. 11] the same custom survives among the southern Philippine Muslim rebels of today), even though this would normally invalidate the act of purification. Kiefer argues that the paradoxical conjunction of ritual purity and an erection unites the man of piety and of action, the normally separate realms of spiritual and military power, thereby combining "two otherwise contradictory values in a higher synthesis" (p. 123). *Parrang sabbil* thus permits the simultaneous realization of two routinely discrepant, even contradictory, facets of an idealized but elusive notion of masculinity.

The *keris,* then, is the symbol of vehicle par excellence of Malay male pride and self-respect. As Swettenham noted (1948, p. 146), "a Malay never moved without his *kris,* when he bathed he took it with him and when he slept it lay by his hand. He gave it more attention than his wife, and probably put a higher value upon it." Whether or not one is a strict Freudian, it should come as no surprise that traditionally a Malay bridegroom could absent himself from his own wedding simply by sending his *keris* as his ceremonial proxy (Hill, 1962, p. 16); or that, while no *keris* is employed, the *keris* dance, *bersilat,* is still typically performed as a ritual entertainment, primarily for male guests, at Malay village weddings.

Followed by Mek Mas, Pak Weng circled the arena in *bersilat* fashion. The predominantly evasive movements of *bersilat,* basically a form of self-defense, include, however, parry-and-thrust offensive sallies. With these Pak Weng goaded Mek Mas, drawing her ever further and more committedly into the enactment of combat. For while Pak Weng (a specialist in cases of this sort, as well as a *bersilat* teacher) merely feigned assault, Mek Mas pursued him with increasingly frenzied determination. She was also encouraged by the enthusiastic applause of the audience, especially her relatives. During more than a half hour of combat, Mek Mas managed to land some heavy blows upon Pak Weng, who reverted to purely defensive maneuvers, leaving her to carry the assault and therefore to attain a symbolic or fictive ascendancy. This continued until Mek Mas collapsed exhausted in the midst of her supporting relatives, and Pak Weng closed the performance with offerings and incantations.

For Mek Mas, and in the eyes of the audience, the performance was cathartic, serving to purge the emotions (*mengeluarkan nafsu*). By affecting a prototypically masculine form of behavior (cf. Lewis, 1971, p. 86), by invading a male prerogative, and by assaulting physically an arrogant and tauntingly provocative man, Mek Mas—most appropriately, given her illness and the dilemma from which it stemmed—expressed a fundamental intersexual antagonism and female resentment of male prerogative. (It is significant, I believe, that while there are active female *bomoh* in Kelantan, I never saw one treat a patient of this sort by *main peteri:* the point would presumably be lost.) Yet such performances are ambiguous. Despite his contrary pretenses, Pak Weng evidently remained in charge throughout, dictating the terms and even the tempo of Mek Mas's contrived and illusory triumph over him. The performance ended when, exhausted, she could no longer sustain the offensive against an adversary who acquiesced in a merely symbolic and easily avoidable defeat. Moreover, it remained uncertain whether Mek Mas's contrived, token victory would lead to success in her real and still unresolved struggle with Awang Lah.

At the symbolic level Mek Mas's was an ambiguous protest, but practically, and within limits, it was an effective one. For while men may enjoy prerogatives that are formally unequivocal, women, acting even in an ambiguous symbolic idiom, may show that their assertion and enforcement by men are not unproblematic. The already hesitant Awang Lah was thus dissuaded from taking a second wife at least for a while. He had seen how isolated he was at the performance, and what substantial support there was for Mek Mas, especially when her retaliatory assault was enthusiastically applauded. He also saw how solid the support was for Mek Mas among her relatives, who had rallied not simply around her symptoms, but to her in her predicament. As Werbner (1968, p. 130) remarks: "A possessed woman becomes the pivot around which her relatives, men or women, may mobilise highly specific or restricted congregations and compel declarations of responsibility and obligation to be made."

It came as no surprise to his prospective new wife and her parents (who soon heard news of the *main peteri*) when, some time later, Awang Lah sent a message cancelling his wedding plans. As for Mek Mas, on the morning after the performance she claimed to feel emotionally purged, and within a week she was again to be seen at her habitual place in the local market, busily engaged in trade and chatting animatedly with friends and customers. She pronounced herself cured, but (not unusual in cases of this kind) some weeks later a subsidiary ritual performance complete with *balai* was held, once more at Awang Lah's expense, to complete and confirm the treatment.

In this case, Mek Mas's contrived, symbolic victory over Pak Weng did translate into the practical defeat of her real adversary, Awang Lah. Yet, uncertain from the outset, and uncontrived, her victory in the real struggle was neither final nor definitive, merely a limited and short-term one; thus when it came, it was no less equivocal than the ritual form in which it was adumbrated. The basic sources of the conflict, though acknowledged, remained unaltered, and Awang Lah's neighbors (whose earlier predictions had been vindicated) were confident that within a couple of years he would try again, chastened by his earlier failure but more circumspect and effective because of it. Mek Mas's status stress was only alleviated, not eliminated, and the unwelcome status transition merely forestalled, not definitely stopped.

The case of Mek Mas indicates that trance—like drunkenness, to some extent, in our own society—may serve as a state of diminished social accountability. In extreme circumstances it permits the expression of things that cannot be said ordinarily or directly. Thus it serves as an "oblique strategy" (Lewis, 1971, p. 117) of protest, a covert mechanism of mobilization and manipulation for those denied the power to act directly. As Lewis notes:

By being overcome involuntarily by an arbitrary affliction for which they cannot be held accountable, these possessed women gain attention and, within variously defined limits, successfully manipulate their husbands and menfolk. . . . Hence, within bounds which are not infinitely elastic, both men and women are more or less satisfied: neither sex loses face and the official ideology of male supremacy is preserved. From this perspective, the tolerance by men of periodic, but always temporary, assaults on their authority by women appears as the price they have to pay to maintain their enviable position. . . . Thus . . . possession expresses insubordination, but usually not to the point where it is desired to immediately rupture the relationship concerned or to subvert it completely. Rather it ventilates aggression and frustration largely within an uneasy acceptance of the established order of things (1971, pp. 86, 120–21).

Through illness and trance Mek Mas sought, successfully in the short run, not to abrogate an unfavorable contract but to enforce it, to compel Awang Lah to respect it.

The Case of Mak Su Yam, Widow

Another category of *main peteri* patients (thirteen cases) consisted of women older than the reluctant brides and insecure wives. Widows and divorcees of middle age, they experienced a different predicament and their possession and treatment took a different form. But, as the typical case of Mak Su Yam shows, the underlying cause remains the same—the relation between the sexes in Kelantanese peasant society.

Mak Su Yam and her husband Pak Da Noor had lived together for about twenty years. Of their three surviving children, the two eldest had at marriage joined their respective spouses in a neighboring district. Some time later, when Mek Sah, their youngest, married a local man named Awang Soh, she remained in her natal village. Not long afterward her father died. His widow was now living in what had been her and Pak Da Noor's house with Mek Sah and Awang Soh. Until recently the manager of her own household, Mak Su Yam was now living as a subsidiary, even dependent, member of one managed by her daughter. Once a wielder of domestic authority, she quite suddenly was one no longer; once sexually active, she ceased to be so, but lived where she did with her daughter by virtue of her former sexual activity. Being a dependent and sexually inactive member of the household, she assumed a somewhat childlike status—an especially difficult transition to accomplish inasmuch as she had become, as it were, her own child's child.

Changes soon became evident in Mak Su Yam's behavior. Hitherto a diligent and competent woman, she became frequently forgetful and abstracted and, when her omissions were called to her attention, she laughed them off lightheartedly, almost irresponsibly. In addition, she began to display some of the characteristic features of the *latah* syndrome (cf. Yap, [1952]; Geertz, [1968]; Murphy, [1972]): sudden movements or sounds would elicit imitative actions and utterances from her or, startled, she would respond with a flood of coarse, even obscene, words.

Mak Su Yam and her daughter soon decided that treatment through *main peteri* would help, and they summoned Pak Mud, a *bomoh* regarded as particularly adept in cases of this kind. Before the performance began, Mak Su Yam (unlike Mek Mas in the previous case) mingled animatedly with the audience. Her behavior was at once childish and coquettish: her comportment suggesting a knowing and ironic parody of the blushing innocence of a young virgin, she also engaged several onlookers in bawdy banter and double entendre ripostes.

Though a violation of the fundamental Malay value of shame and modesty (*malu*), this behavior was "indulged" (*dimanjakan*), as one by-stander explicitly remarked, just as are the improprieties of the young who do not yet know better.

The performance began and Pak Mud proceeded quickly to the divination. From several counts Pak Mud singled out fire and earth as the dominant and recurrent motifs, and accordingly (cf. Table 1) pronounced Mak Su Yam's case as one of the Raja Dewa Muda. He then launched into the treatment phase, and the fact that he had brought with him all the special accouterments for this kind of performance indicates that he knew in advance what diagnosis he would make.

Performances of this kind consist of the enactment of selections from the *mak yong*, or Kelantanese folk opera. The patient, who generally retires at this stage to don the special *mak yong* royal garb, plays the leading role. The *mak yong* cycle comprises about one dozen principal stories concerned mainly with legendary royalty. From this repertoire only one is selected for enactment in these cases of *main peteri*, the story of the Raja Dewa Muda (or "Godling Prince"). It cannot be recounted in full here—see Sheppard's summary (1960, pp. 1–8), reprinted as appendix to Malm (1971, pp. 115–20)—but, in the light of the problematic status reversal and attendant identity dilemma of patients like Mak Su Yam, four principal elements stand out:

1. There is an initial ambiguity concerning the identity of the Raja Dewa Muda's parents.

2. This impels the Raja Dewa Muda to leave the palace. He encounters a magical princess who, by depriving him of his *keris,* causes him to be injured, apparently slain, until the princess herself, disguised as a *bomoh*, revives him and returns his *keris* to him, inscribed with instructions as to where he may later find her.

3. Awakened, and suspecting that the *bomoh* is really the princess in disguise, the Raja Dewa Muda challenges her to a series of feats in which he believes a woman cannot match a man. But his strategem fails: she outperforms and outwits him, and then disappears.

4. Distraught with loss and longing, the Raja Dewa Muda notices the instructions on his *keris* and follows them. He rejoins the princess in her father's palace where, to protect him from further injury, she keeps him by day in the form of a flower, permitting him to resume his normal form at night—except that he remains unaging, handsome, and loving.

These four motifs—the ambiguity of parenthood; the control by women over the *keris*, sexuality, and independence of men; the question of the equality of the sexes; and a woman's stopping the clock, so to speak, upon a young, attractive, devoted, and essentially captive man—resonantly articulate the identity dilemma of women like Mak Su Yam.

One further point should be noted concerning sexual antagonism and its symbolic expression. The *mak yong*, whose forms are borrowed here, involves sexual inversion. Save for two clowns, low characters repeatedly subjected to humiliating beatings by the principals, all of the actors are female, including the main one whose role, that of a princely male, is played by the *main peteri* patient. Moreover, much of the *mak yong* humor, sustained during comic interludes by the two clowns, is earthy and scatological; this finds its counterpart in the explicitly sexual utterances and allusions of the *main peteri* patient. This is especially the case with patients (like Mak Su Yam) who go into deep trance during the performance. Responding to the *lagu bokbong* (the tune takes its name from a small field rodent that I cannot identify precisely but which is characterized as playful, irresponsible, and sexually voracious), these women usually cavort suggestively, raising their sarongs above their knees, and accost men in parodied form by brandishing large bananas before them.

As a result of her treatment, Mak Su Yam claimed several days later to feel emotionally purged. At least temporarily, her affliction was dispelled; her *latah* symptoms subsided, and her behavior became less erratic. But what Mak Su Yam, like other patients in this category, derived from *main peteri* was simply catharsis. Conflict is only acted out, not removed. The fundamentally ambiguous social position from which the symptoms of these patients stem is, unlike that of the newlyweds and the insecure wives, redefined neither by the ritual itself nor by any course of mundane events which the *main peteri* sets in motion. Since the underlying conflict remains, pressures may build up again and the symptoms of affliction return. For this reason presumably, like many women in her situation, Mak Su Yam became a repeater, arranging *main peteri* therapy at regular intervals thereafter to dispel the symptoms of conflict and restore emotional "tone."

In Mak Su Yam's case illness and possession are again demonstrably related to the stresses of social status and status transition, in this case the difficult transition to an inherently ambiguous status. To remain in that status is to endure continuing and irremovable conflict, yet the only alternative to it is remarriage, and to many women this expedient is unwelcome. Thus the incidence of possession among all three categories of women patients derives from and also quite openly expresses the problematic relation between the sexes in Kelantanese peasant society. The cases of the newlyweds involve the freeing of a woman from the control of a particular man; those of the older women articulate the dilemma of women atypically unrelated through marriage to any particular man. More pointedly, the cases of women like Mek Mas involve a woman's attempt to exert a measure of control over a particular man, her husband, and to extract a continuing commitment from him, to hold him to his contract. Thus it is not surprising that the ritual therapy of the insecure wives provides the most overt and dramatic expression of sexual antagonism and of resentment against sexual inequality.

THE RITUAL SYMBOLISM OF THE *MAIN PETERI:*
THE MAIN METAPHOR

The analysis so far has related sociologically the incidence of psychological and psychosomatic symptoms, and their treatment through trance and possession, to the strains of conflicted social positions or status adjustments. It has also suggested that these stresses detected by the outside observer are in some measure recognized within the idioms of Kelantanese culture itself, specifically in the forms of treatment employed by *bomoh*. We can now consider directly those indigenous idioms, beliefs, and symbols, central to which is the *balai* device, the model palace and realm generally employed in cases of psychosocial stress illness.

The question of the *balai* and its meaning can best be discussed in a broader context. Following the unsatisfactory attempts of earlier scholars of Tylorean inspiration such as Skeat (1900) and Annandale (1903, 1903a, 1904, 1904a, 1909) to provide a systematic account of Malay supernatural beliefs in terms of souls and animistic essences, Sir Richard Winstedt, doyen of twentieth century Malayanists, insisted (1961, 1961a) that Malay "magic" displayed no system or order, only an inchoate *mélange* of indigenous animistic, Hindu and Islamic (mainly Sufi) ideas. (Winstedt's predecessor Wilkinson held the same idea, though perhaps less emphatically, contending [1908, p. 64] that Malay culture consisted of "a sort of museum of ancient customs—an ill-kept and ill-designed museum in which no exhibit is dated, labelled or explained.") Reacting against this view, however, later scholars such as Cuisinier (1936, 1951) and Endicott (1970) have again claimed to detect in Malay beliefs an overall system of order: the former, in a parallelism between the macrocosm of the universe and the microcosm of the person (1951, pp. 250–251); the latter, in the relations between spirit and matter, and especially in the ritual maintenance and manipulation of the boundaries of material receptacles of spirit in varying degrees of concentration and individuation.

Both Cuisinier and Endicott seem to me largely correct as far as they go, but they do not go far enough. As Geoffrey Benjamin, in a sympathetic review of Endicott's book, has remarked (1970, p. 15), it raises many further questions, including that "of the relationship between magic and traditional Malay political ideology". To pursue this suggestion one must ask how the *balai* device fits into Cuisinier's scheme of macrocosm and microcosm, and into Endicott's of material receptacles employed in the ritual manipulation of spiritual essences. And if the *balai* serves as a mediating middle term between microcosm and macrocosm, we may further wonder why the material vessel employed to transfer spiritual essences between person and cosmos is specifically a sociopolitical model. The answers to these questions concerning the *balai* may enable us to understand better not only the healing seances of the Kelantanese but also their connection with the state, district, and village cleansing rites mentioned at the outset.

It has been a significant omission that while scholars since Skeat have industriously collected Malay magical texts and incantations, and have traced out their complex connections with Javanese, Sanskritic and Islamic ideas, few have been concerned with the primarily political symbolism of the body and person that is dramatically enacted in actual healing performances. The concern here, therefore, is not to provide a comprehensive analysis of Malay magicomedical ideas, but only to highlight this one hitherto neglected aspect of them.

An analysis of the political dimension of Kelantanese healing seances may begin with a consideration of language. As in their other varied ritual activities, *bomoh* employ in these seances a special or "secret" language. Since Malay special vocabularies serve primarily in discourse with or concerning, royalty, this in itself insinuates a political tone into the *main peteri*. *Bomoh* call this special language *bahasa dalam* ("inner language"). The term is evocative of the *sejarah dalam,* the inner or "real" history of important but secret dealings and strategies within the palace between the ruler, his relatives, and advisors—the story of how power is really exercised behind the external appearances generally taken as reality. Both cases, the verbal and the historical, are aspects of the fundamental Malay dichotomy between the outward (*lahir*) or phenomenal appearances of things and their true though disguised inner (*batin*) nature. The truth and superiority of the "inner" history, in contrast to conventionalized epic historiography, reside in the fact that its form and dynamic derive not from artificial ex post facto constructions upon the meaning of action, but from the actual motivations of the principals. *Bomoh,* exponents of "inner" language in healing, must also penetrate outward appearances and reach a correct and unobscured understanding of real though hidden motivation. Healing thus resembles statecraft, since the prerequisite for both is an identical, or at least analogous, understanding. But the similarity goes further, beyond motivation to power. Because of its congruence with real motivation, the form of *sejarah dalam* corresponds with the forms and actualities of power. The true, inner form is therefore itself powerful, and to understand, to have access to it is to deal in power. Analogously *bomoh,* reaching beyond outward appearance to deep motivations through the powerful forms of a language congruent with them, are dealers in power. As in Java (see Anderson, 1972), power, somewhat circularly, consists of the access to power, through arcane knowledge and ritual management of outward verbal forms corresponding with its inner nature.

The meaning of this may become clearer if we consider not merely the fact of a special language, but the details of that actually employed. These details suggest that the *bomoh* not only, if metaphorically, deals in power but is also (again metaphorically) concerned with the management of a realm, is the exponent of a kind of statecraft. The relationships I collected from *bomoh* and have set forth in Table 1 (Cuisinier, [1936, pp. 18–19] offers a similar table, but its details differ somewhat from those presented here) provide a convenient entry into these matters. The table of correspondences indicates that each of the four elements has a bodily counterpart, and is also associated with a category of spirits identified by the colors black, green, yellow, and red. These same colors in another framework also symbolize, in slightly varying classical and folk versions, the four principal offices or institutional mainstays of the characteristic Malay political form, the sultanate. (The treatment in the first case study above of Mek Mas's *angin* affliction with war tunes, the ritual enactment of combat and mimicry of a warrior's behavior may be recalled here.) A basic parallelism, a metaphorical identification, of the body personal and the body politic is suggested. Further evidence of this identification occurs within the ritual idioms of the *main peteri.*

During the *main peteri* performance, especially in the dialogue between *bomoh* and *mindok,* the patient and his body are cryptically described in "inner" language as a palace or realm. He is often denoted as *anjong tujoh istana lima* (a palace of "seven porches" or "outer rooms" and "five inner rooms.") The five inner rooms (cf. Cuisinier, [1936, pp. 20–26]; Winstedt, [1922]) are the heart, liver, spleen, and two lungs. The seven outer porches are variously the seven senses (hand, foot, taste, sight, hearing, smell, and genitals), the seven sentiments (wishes, faith, longing, perception, affection, desire, and contemplation), and the seven points (brow, palms, knees, and feet) on which the body rests during prayer.

With these same associations the body or person of the patient is also designated as a *sifat tujoh gemelan satu,* a unified yet sevenfold manifestation or assemblage of attributes. He is also *jalan empat simpang tiga,* "four roads and three intersections," again totaling seven and denoting the four limbs, the underarms, and the crotch. Alternately, there are nine roads (*jalan sembilan:* eyes, ears, nostrils, mouth, anus, and urethral opening) and nine gates (*pintu sembilan:* mouth, nose, eyes, ears, fontanelle, navel, anus, genitals, and palms) associated with nine provinces (*sembilan desa:* arms, forearms, thighs, calves, and trunk.)

Despite or transcending these and other numerological variations (different *bomoh,* and even the same one at different times, may offer different versions), the body is a realm, at once unitary and multiplex. Its various components are ideally coordinated and integrated, subordinated to a governing center, the palace of personality, the head. Since this conception of the body as a realm is not merely abstract and static, it permits illness or disorder within the person to be presented in political terms. Sickness, as was noted earlier, is regarded as the result of some imbalance or lack of regulation between the constituent humoral elements of the person, and the fundamental political image of such disorder is anarchy or civil war—the absence of effective rule. The body and its provinces are a disarticulated realm, a realm in chaos, lacking harmony and integration. As the *bomoh* and *mindok* declare in a recurrent refrain, *dalam negri huruhara: tiada nyata dalam anjong tiada tetap dalam istana*—"throughout the land there is disorder: in the outer porches there is no clarity, in the inner councils no stability." Order and clarity, embodied in the counterimage of *saorang raja, sabuah negri* ("a single ruler in an undivided land"), that is, definitive sovereignty, must be restored.

Toward this end the efforts of *bomoh* and *mindok* are directed, practically and symbolically. Their interlocution consists in large part of allusions to or recitations of stories (rather like the Raja Dewa Muda story involved in the case of Mak Su Yam, except that the four other categories of patients do not themselves enact the plots.) These stories tell of wrongly outcast or changeling princes, of realms without proper rulers, and rulers separated from their rightful realms. In short, they are parables of lost sovereignty, a metaphor for the patient's turmoil and illness. By performing these allegories, *bomoh* and *mindok* act out for (and before) the patient his own contrary tendencies and inner conflicts. As they do so, taking their parts from the patient's own inner drama, they address each other with royal pronouns and courtly titles.

In identifying through their divination the nature and source of the patient's affliction, *bomoh* and *mindok* liken the assemblage of four humoral elements to a realm, asking: "in what district, and in what village" (*dalam negri mana, kampong apa*) does the disorder lie? The matter, they declare, resembles that between slave and ruler, subject and sultan (*pasal hamba dengan raja, rakyat dengan sultan*). The land, they observe, is fouled (*kotor*) with strife (*susah gadoh dalam negri*). They compare the patient to a battlefield (*medan perang*) or arena of conflict (*bom, gelenggang*), and liken their own intervention to a royal audience or council (*medan majlis*) where rivals are reconciled or restrained by a superior will. Thus the evening's business, they say, is like that of a strong ruler—to promulgate law and orderly custom (*malam ni nak jatoh hukum, meletak adat*), restoring authority and curtailing strife. Since the patient's inner imbalance and illness, it will be recalled, stem from a lack of inner strength, they must fortify his spiritual essence (*membuat semangat*). This task, in the political idiom of the *main peteri,* is characterized as and treated coterminously with the *perangkatan daulat,* the custom at Malay royal installations and state ceremonies of "raising" the spiritual strength that ensures a ruler's legitimate sovereignty and the integrity of his realm. Ultimately this is accomplished when the enactment of the parable of lost sovereignty reaches its happy conclusion and definitive authority, the basis of universal harmony and contentment, is restored.

Beset by social pressures and psychic conflict, the patient is aptly depicted as an arena of factional dispute, of rival tendencies. But why this political confusion, this lack of effective authority and control? Within the person, as in political society, the potentiality for discord and dissension is endemic. Disorder erupts not because these potentialities exist but because they have not been checked. Who then, within the person, is the ineffectual ruler, the incompetent authority? In *main peteri,* it was noted, the patient is purged of disruptive emotions (*nafsu*) that have grown beyond control. Like animals, humans are moved by *nafsu,* but unlike animals they also, by their very nature, have the means to temper and regulate their *nafsu.* This means is *akal,* or reason (cf. Siegel, [1969, pp. 98–133]; Rosen, [n.d.]; Kessler, [1974, pp. 302–306; 1974a, pp. 339–351].) If *nafsu* has increased, causing imbalance, then it is reason, rationality, self-knowledge, and self-control which have failed, permitting civil strife to erupt within the person. And it is the sovereignty of reason that the *bomoh* seeks to restore through the accretion of *semangat* and the expulsion of *nafsu*. The realm is righted by the reassertion of authority in the palace—the head and mind.

For Kelantanese the person is, at least metaphorically, a miniature state, an arena of contending forces, some dominant, others usually subordinate but always having the potential to mount insurrection and foment strife. The Englishman's home is reputedly his castle; the Kelantanese is himself his own realm, his mind its palace, his embattled reason its precarious sovereign.

The logic of this underlying political metaphor inspires the use of the *balai* device, a model palace and realm, as a surrogate for the patient. The argument is clinched by a detail reported by Cuisinier (1936, p. 112): an adjunct ritual device to the *balai* and in some contexts its ritual substitute, the *saka* (which is fashioned from a young coconut with its top open set upon a stake) represents simultaneously the pillars of a house and a human skull or head. In the words of the Kelantanese charm recorded by Winstedt (1922, p. 263; 1961, p. 78), "The intention of 'the house' is the body. The body is the place of the spirit. . . ." Thus—turning the analogy back upon itself—if, by treating the person in *main peteri* as a political realm, definitive sovereignty and authority can be enhanced and baneful and disruptive influences dispelled, then the logic of employing *main peteri* to foster peace and dispel disorder at the political level, with an entire community or its symbolic leader as beneficiary, is also clear. In the person of the ruler the two bodies meet, in his palace, two domains.

This implies that the use of the *balai* involves not simply a twofold parallel between person and cosmos, as Cuisinier would have it, but a fourfold analogy: between the person, the idea of the state as concretized in the *balai*, the state as an institution, and the cosmos. Of these four the middle terms, the state in its symbolic and actual forms (which Cuisinier neglects in her analysis), invest the analogy with its dimension of power. Hence, mediating between person and cosmos, the state, in its concretized conceptual form as the *balai*, provides the appropriately potent instrument or receptacle (as Endicott puts it) for ritually manipulating and transferring powerful, and therefore potentially dangerous, spiritual essences.

Mainly covert and implicit, and expressed largely in arcane language (though with dramatic concreteness in the *balai*), this political metaphor, when it has been extracted and understood, explains certain other linguistic features of the *main peteri*. Two of these will be noted briefly here.

The *bomoh*'s familiar, it will be recalled, is know as *penggawa*, a term which has another and far more common usage in Kelantan. It denotes a subdistrict headman, the intermediary between villagers and their local leaders on the one hand, and the district head, the state administration and sultan, on the other. I accorded no special significance to this coincidence until I attended a seance at which the *mindok*, on hearing the *bomoh*'s customary preliminary announcement that he would have to call his *penggawa*, retorted: "If you can manage it, get a state assemblyman instead. Since we began to have elections, *penggawa* are useless. To get anything done at all, you've got to work through elected officials!" Apart from its sociological acuity, inappropriate for discussion here, this remark (and I later heard many others like it) suggested to me the permissibility of making a connection between the two senses of the term *penggawa*.

On the basis of this connection I came to understand better what *bomoh* meant when they insisted (as they did from the outset of my inquiries) that *main peteri ini merupakan satu politik*, that *main peteri* is a kind of politics. In making this assertion, subsequent discussion revealed, *bomoh* were not simply insisting on the connection between knowledge, especially knowledge of "inner" forms and power, nor were they merely alluding to the intermediary political level in the analogy between person and cosmos. The personal, political, and cosmic levels, they maintained, were linked not only conceptually, by analogy or isomorphism, but also ritually and practically by their own role and activities. Just as the administrative *penggawa* connects village folk to the sultan through district and state officials, so too do *bomoh*, through their spiritual *penggawa* who possess them, serve as low-level functionaries in a hierarchy of cosmic administration ultimately under Allah. Like appointees of the civil administration, and with a separate but cognate jurisdiction, they discharge duties necessary for the maintenance of peace, law, and order. "We, too, are magistrates," said one.

As for the second linguistic point, there has been much fanciful and inconclusive speculation (Cuisinier, [1936, pp. 93–96]; Sheppard, [1972, pp. 196–197]; Winstedt, [1961, pp. 63, 152–155; 1961a, p. 27]) concerning the origins of the term *main peteri*, which means literally "princess play." (The term *mak yong* also means princess.) Whether or not the choice of the feminine form is adequately explained by the large proportion of women among the patients treated, or by reference to the legends of female rulers characteristic of northeast Malayan traditions, the appropriateness of a royal idiom to these metapolitical seances is nevertheless clear. Indeed, certain traditions cited by Cuisinier (1936, p. 94) do trace the *main peteri* back to Kelantan's legended if not legendary female ruler, Tuan Puteri Sakdong, but no less significant than her sex is the fact that her story, the tale of a betrayed ruler and a subverted dynasty that will return one day, is a copybook parable of "lost sovereignty."

It should be noted here that only in Kelantan are these seances called *main peteri* and embellished with royal trappings. Elsewhere in Malaya these rites, less elaborate in form, are known simply as *main berhantu* ("spirit play"). I suspect, but cannot argue here, that this may be related to matters I have discussed elsewhere (1974a, pp. 41–51)—to peculiar geographic circumstances that long inhibited the emergence of a strong, centralized sultanate in Kelantan and rendered it an area of recurrent insurrection, secession, and civil war.

CONCLUSION

Several conclusions emerge from this analysis of the *main peteri*. First, Lewis's hypothesis concerning the connection between stress, illness, and possession is confirmed. Second, explication of the underlying political metaphor indicates that, cast in the idioms of Kelantanese culture, Lewis's theory is largely understood by *bomoh* and is expressed by them in the ritual therapy they employ. Third, although Winstedt was content (1961, pp. 35–37, 152–166; 1961a, pp. 64–68) to regard Malay shamanistic rituals of state and the enthronement rites of marriage simply as Tantric Hindu residues or survivals, it is clear that whatever its origins (and they may be diverse), the political idiom shared by a variety of Malay rituals has been fully domesticated and—no mere residue—has become a fundamental organizing idea or motif of Malay culture.

This raises a fourth issue: whether any coherent order is to be found in Malay magical ideas. Finding the arguments of Winstedt and Wilkinson both nihilistic and arrogantly prejudiced, I have sided with Cuisinier and Endicott, even while suggesting certain omissions and shortcomings in their work. With considerable justification, however, R. W. Firth (1974, p. 190) finds Endicott's analysis too formalistic, abstract, and rigid (cf. Kessler, 1971), and in personal discussions he has expressed similar reservations concerning Cuisinier's work (1936). In criticizing the rigid formalism of closed systems, Firth correctly emphasizes the pragmatic aspect of magic, the experimental attitude, even skepticism, that may inform its use, and the manner in which contextual factors (no less than formal intellectual or cultural patterns) may shape the choice and implementation of ritual procedures. But as long as one is neither a committed nihilist nor a monistic formalist, the argument is perhaps a false one. Certainly the formal patterns abstracted from reality by the ethnographer may take varying phenomenal forms and be quite idiosyncratically realized by different individuals, but this does not deny the existence of some underlying formal structure accessible to detection (cf. Barnes, 1974). Thus the empirical and formal approaches are not necessarily opposed or incompatible, and the latter, for all its apparent rigidity, need not be so. As Cuisinier remarks (1936, p. 93), "one should acknowledge the extent to which this apparently rigid system is in fact endowed with elasticity" (author's translation). Thus in this account of the *main peteri* I have taken neither an exclusively formalist nor a strictly empirical approach. Instead I suggest the analysis that comes closest to the truth is one which proceeds as *bomoh* themselves do—which seeks, in a flexible yet not arbitrary manner, to bring the formal and the empirical together and enables them, meaningfully but not mechanically, to address each other.[5]

TABLE 1.   Some Symbolic Classifications Made by *Bomoh*

Element	Temper	Bodily Equivalent: Primary, secondary (and main organ)	Color of Elemental Spirits	Associated by Honorific Color with	
				i. In classical theory	ii. In folk scheme
Earth (*tanah*)	Cold/dry	Skin, hair (heart)	Black	Chancellor (*temenggong*)	Spirits of state, nobility (*dewa*)
Water (*ayer*)	Cold/wet	Flesh, blood (lungs)	Green	Treasurer (*bendahara*)	Minister (*menteri*)
Fire (*api*)	Hot/dry	Bone, sinew (spleen)	Yellow	Ruler (*raja*)	Ruler (*raja*)
Air (*angin*)	Hot/wet	Spirit, genes (liver)	Red	Commander (*laksamana*)	Warrior (*ulubalang*)

Finally, and briefly, one other issue: the recent and growing interest in the symbolism of the human body. In many familiar cases such as the Ndembu (Turner, 1968), the Fipa (Willis, 1967) and, in European culture—from John of Salisbury's classic medieval metaphor of the body politic and Hobbes's Leviathan to the organic analogies of Spencer, Durkheim, and Radcliffe-Brown—society is depicted in the image of the human body. But, as Mary Douglas observes (1970, p. 65), fundamentally "the social body constrains the way the physical body is perceived." Thus, as the case of the Kelantanese *main peteri* sharply indicates, if an analogy between "the two bodies" is to be culturally asserted, society may, as readily as in the reverse case, provide an image of the human body.

NOTES

1. This essay is based upon research conducted in Kelantan from August 1967 to October 1968, and from January to July 1969. For supporting my research I acknowledge my gratitude to the London Committee of the London-Cornell Project for East and Southeast Asian Studies (financed jointly by the Carnegie Corporation of New York and the Nuffield Foundation) and to the Senate and Faculty of Arts of the University of Sydney (which awarded me the Hannah Fullerton Post-graduate Travelling Research Scholarship). I note again an immeasurable debt toward those Kelantanese into whose lives I intruded, and on this occasion also record my indebtedness to *bomoh* and ritual experts who explained and permitted me to observe their activities: Pak Da Mjah of Teratak Pulai, Daerah Gunong Timor; Pak Sein of Kampong Tempoyak, Daerah Bekelam; Pak Peing bin Mat of Kedai Jelawat; Che Limah Anak Rimau of Pulau Melaka, Kedai Lalat; and Awang Mek Mas of Kedai Jelawat. I am grateful also to Joan Vincent for her helpful comments on an earlier presentation of this material. Hester Eisenstein has made a number of valuable suggestions concerning matters of both substance and style, for which I thank her.

2. For an ethnomusicological discussion of the music of the Kelantanese *mak yong* or folk opera—many of whose tunes, as will be seen below, also feature in the *main peteri*—see Malm (1969, 1974). A recording prepared by Professor Malm is also available (*The Music of Malaysia, Ma'yong Theatre Music of Kelantan,* Anthology Records AST 4006).

3. The numbers and categories of *main peteri* patients cited from my work by Raybeck (1974, p. 240), being based only on a preliminary analysis of incomplete data, differ slightly from those presented in this chapter. Raybeck's discussion of stress and its expression in Kelantan usefully complements the analysis presented here.

4. A precursor of the PMIP, the radical Pan-Malayan *Kesatuan Rakyat Indonesia Semenanjong* (Union of the Peninsular Indonesian People), gloried in the acronym KRIS, by which it was popularly known.

5. In a personal communication Professor Firth has kindly commented on my characterization of his position in the preceding paragraph. Though his

response (through no fault of his) reached me too late to permit any emending of the text, I would like to clarify my remarks. In citing Firth's reservations concerning uniformitarian accounts of intellectual systems, I was far from including him among those who would deny any basic order to Malay beliefs. Rather, I sought to suggest a convergence of our positions. A nonabsolutist concern (such as his) with the variability of actual behavior informed by broad cultural ideas and an equally nonabsolutist concern (such as mine) with those ideas as they inform actual behavior in specific situations are, I was trying to suggest, compatible. Unlike the partisans of either extreme, we may agree that the formal and empirical approaches are not mutually exclusive, but complementary.

REFERENCES

ABDULLAH BIN ABDUL KADIR

1967   *The Voyage of Abdullah: being an Account of his Experiences on a Voyage from Singapore to Kelantan in A.D. 1838* (A. E. Coope, trans.). Singapore: Oxford University Press.

ANDERSON, B. R. O'G.

1972   "The Idea of Power in Javanese Culture." In *Culture and Politics in Indonesia,* C. Holt, B. R. O'G. Anderson and J. T. Siegel, Eds. Ithaca, N.Y.: Cornell University Press, pp. 1–69.

ANNANDALE, N.

1903   "Primitive Beliefs and Customs of the Patani Fishermen." In *Fasciculi Malayenses I,* N. Annandale and H. C. Robinson, Eds. Liverpool: Liverpool University Press, pp. 73–88.

1903a   "Religion and Magic among the Malays of the Patani States." In *Fasciculi Malayenses I,* N. Annandale and H. C. Robinson, Eds. Liverpool: Liverpool University Press, pp. 89–104.

1904   "Religion and Magic among the Malays of the Patani States: Part II." In *Fasciculi Malayenses IIa,* N. Annandale and H. C. Robinson, Eds. Liverpool: Liverpool University Press, pp. 21–57.

1904a   "Customs of the Malayo-Siamese." In *Fasciculi Malayenses IIa,* N. Annandale and H. C. Robinson, Eds. Liverpool: Liverpool University Press pp. 61–89.

1909   "The Theory of Souls among the Malays of the Malay Peninsula." *Journal of the Asiatic Society of Bengal* (n.s.) 5: 59–66.

BARNES, R. H.

1974   *Kédang: a Study of the Collective Thought of an Eastern Indonesian People.* London: Oxford University Press.

BENJAMIN, G.

1970   "Review of An Analysis of Malay Magic by K. M. Endicott." *Triple Crown* **1:** 14–15.

CLARK, K.

1960   "Puja Pantai." In *Straits Times Annual for 1960.* Singapore: Straits Times Press, pp. 72–75.

CUISINIER, J.

1936   *Danses Magiques de Kelantan.* Travaux et Mémoires de l'Institut d'Ethnologie de l'Université de Paris, 22. Paris.

1951   *Sumangat: L'Ame et son Culte en Indochine et en Indonésie.* Paris: Gallimard.

DAVISON, W.

1889   "Journal of a Trip to Pahang, &C with H. E. the Governor, August 17th. to 27th., 1889." *Journal of the Royal Asiatic Society, Straits Branch* **20:** 83–90.

DJAMOUR, J.

1959   *Malay Kinship and Marriage in Singapore.* London School of Economics Monographs on Social Anthropology, 21. London: Athlone Press.

DOUGLAS, M.

1970   *Natural Symbols: Explorations in Cosmology.* New York: Pantheon Books.

ENDICOTT, K. M.

1970   *An Analysis of Malay Magic.* London: Oxford University Press.

FIRTH, R.

1966 (orig. 1943)   *Housekeeping Among Malay Peasants.* 2nd edit. London School of Economics Monographs on Social Anthropology, 7. London: Athlone Press.

FIRTH, R. W.

1966 (orig. 1946)   *Malay Fishermen: Their Peasant Economy.* 2nd. edit. London: Routledge & Kegan Paul.

1967   "Ritual and Drama in Malay Spirit Mediumship." *Comparative Studies in Society and History* **9:** 190–207.

1967a   "Individual Fantasy and Social Norms: Seances with Spirit Mediums." In *Tikopia Ritual and Belief.* Boston: Beacon Press, pp. 293–329.

1974   "Faith and Scepticism in Kelantan Village Magic." In

Kelantan: Religion, Society and Politics in a Malay State, W. R. Roff, Ed. Kuala Lumpur: Oxford University Press, pp. 190–224.

1974a "Relations between Personal Kin (*waris*) among Kelantan Malays." In *Social Organization and the Applications of Anthropology: Essays in Honor of Lauriston Sharp,* R. J. Smith, Ed. Ithaca: Cornell University Press, pp. 23–61.

GEERTZ, H.

1968 "Latah in Java: a Theoretical Paradox." *Indonesia* **5:** 93–104.

GIMLETTE, J. D.

1929 (orig. 1913) *Malay Poisons and Charm Cures.* 3rd edit. London: J. & A. Churchill.

1939 *A Dictionary of Malayan Medicine,* H. W. Thomson, Ed. London: Oxford University Press.

GORDON, S.

n.d. "Malay Marriage and Divorce." *Intisari* **2**(2): 23–32.

GRAHAM, W. A.

1908 *Kelantan, a State of the Malay Peninsula: a Handbook of Information.* Glasgow: James MacLehose & Sons.

HASHIMAH ROOSE

1963 "Changes in the Position of Malay Women." In *Women in the New Asia,* B. E. Ward, Ed. Paris: UNESCO, pp. 287–294.

HILL, A. H.

1962 *The Malay Keris and Other Weapons.* 2nd. edit. Malayan Museum Popular Pamphlets, 5. Singapore: Government Printer.

KESSLER, C. S.

1971 "Review of An Analysis of Malay Magic, by K. M. Endicott." *Man* (n.s.) **6:** 148–149.

1974 "Muslim Identity and Political Behaviour in Kelantan." In *Kelantan: Religion, Society and Politics in a Malay State,* W. R. Roff, Ed. Kuala Lumpur: Oxford University Press pp. 272–313.

1974a Islam and Politics in Malay Society: Kelantan 1886–1969. Unpublished Ph.D. thesis, University of London.

KIEFER, T. M.

1973 "Parrang Sabbil: Ritual Suicide among the Tausug of Jolo." *Bijdragen tot de Taal-, Land- en Volkenkunde* **129** (1): 108–123.

KRAMER, B. H.

1970   "Abstract of Psychotherapeutic Implications of a Traditional Healing Ceremony: the Malaysian Main Puteri." *Transcultural Psychiatric Research Review* 7: 149–51.

LEWIS, I. M.

1966   "Spirit Possession and Deprivation Cults." *Man* (n.s.) 1: 307–329.

1969   "Spirit Possession in Northern Somaliland." In *Spirit Mediumship and Society in Africa,* J. Beattie and J. Middleton, Eds. New York: Africana Publishing Corporation, pp. 188–219.

1971   *Ecstatic Religion: an Anthropological Study of Spirit Possession and Shamanism.* Hamondsworth, England: Penguin Books.

MALM, W. P.

1969   "The Music of the Malaysian M'yong." *Tenggara* 5: 114–120.

1971   "Malaysian Ma'yong Theatre." *TDR/The Drama Review* 15 (2 [incorrectly numbered 3]): 108–114, with two plot summaries appended, 115–121.

1974   "Music in Kelantan, Malaysia and Some of its Cultural Implications." In *Michigan Papers on South and Southeast Asia 8.* Ann Arbor: University of Michigan Center for South and Southeast Asian Studies, pp. 1–46.

MOHD. TAIB BIN OSMAN

1972   "Patterns of Supernatural Premises Underlying the Institution of the Bomoh in Malay Culture." *Bijdragen tot de Taal-, Land- en Volkenkunde* 128 (2/3): 219–234.

MURPHY, H. B. M.

1972   "History and the Evolution of Syndromes: the Striking Case of Latah and Amok." In *Psychopathology: Contributions from the Biological, Behavioral and Social Sciences,* M. Hammer, K. Salzinger, and S. Sutton, Eds. New York: Wiley, pp. 33–55.

NEEDHAM, R.

1967   "Percussion and Transition." *Man* (n.s.) 4: 606–614.

RAYBECK, D. A.

1974   "Social Stress and Social Structure in Kelantan Village Life." In *Kelantan: Religion, Society and Politics in a Malay State,* W. R. Roff, Ed. Kuala Lumpur: Oxford University Press, pp. 225–242.

ROFF, W. R.
1968   "Review of The Muslim Matrimonial Court in Singa-
                    pore, by J. Djamour." *Bijdragen tot de Taal-, Land- en
                    Volkenkunde* **124** (2): 286–291.

ROSEN, L.
n.d.   Bargaining for Reality: a Study of Male-Female Relations in
                    Morocco. Unpublished manuscript.

SHEPPARD, M. C.
1960   *The Magic Kite and Other Ma'yong Stories.* Singapore:
                    Federal Publications.
1968   "Feast for the Sea Djinns." In *Straits Times Annual for
                    1968.* Kuala Lumpur and Singapore: Straits Times
                    Press, pp. 38–41.
1972   *Taman Indera: Malay Decorative Arts and Pastimes.* Kuala
                    Lumpur: Oxford University Press.

SIEGEL, J. T.
1969   *The Rope of God.* Berkeley: University of California
                    Press.

SKEAT, W. W.
1900   *Malay Magic.* London: Macmillan and Co.

SWEENEY, A.
1972   "The Shadow Play of Kelantan: Report on a Period of
                    Field Research." *Journal of the Royal Asiatic Society, Ma-
                    laysian Branch* **43** (2): 53–80.

SWETTENHAM, F. A.
1948 (orig. 1906)   *British Malaya.* 3rd edit. London: John Lane/The Bod-
                    ley Head.

SWIFT, M. G.
1963   "Men and Women in Malay Society." In *Women in the
                    New Asia,* B. E. Ward, Ed. Paris: UNESCO, pp.
                    268–286.

TASKER, R.
1975   "Cotabato: Marcos' Offensive." *Far Eastern Economic Re-
                    view* **87** (8), 21 February: 10–12.

TURNER, V. W.
1968   *The Forest of Symbols.* Ithaca: Cornell University Press.

WERBNER, R.
1968   "Correspondence concerning Spirits and the Sex War."
                    Man (n.s.) **3:** 129–130.

WILKINSON, R. J.

1908   *The Incidents of Malay Life*. Part I of Life and Customs, Papers on Malay Subjects, 1st Series. Kuala Lumpur: Government Printer.

1910   *Malay Amusements*. Part III of Life and Customs, Papers on Malay Subjects, 1st Series. Kuala Lumpur: Government Printer.

WILLIS, R. G.

1967   "The Head and the Loins: Lévi-Strauss and Beyond." *Man* (n.s.) **2:** 519–534.

WINSTEDT, R. O.

1922   "A Malay Pantheist Charm." *Journal of the Royal Asiatic Society, Straits Branch* **86:**261–267.

1961 (orig. 1925)   *The Malay Magician*. Rev. ed. London: Routledge & Kegan Paul.

1961a (orig. 1947) *The Malays: a Cultural History*. 6th edit. London: Routledge & Kegan Paul.

WOLFF, R. J.

1965   "Modern Medicine and Traditional Culture: Confrontation on the Malay Peninsula." *Human Organization* **24** (4): 339–345.

YAP, P. M.

1952   "The Latah Reaction: its Pathodynamics and Nosological Position." *Journal of Mental Science* **98** (413): 515–564.

Esther Pressel

Negative Spirit Possession in Experienced Brazilian Umbanda Spirit Mediums

UMBANDA BACKGROUND, BELIEFS, AND RITUALS

Umbanda is a modern syncretic spirit possession religion composed of cultural elements from the three continents which contributed most to Brazilian lifeways—Africa, South America, and Europe. Historically, indigenous Indian religions and African religions later brought by slaves to Brazilian sugar plantations included trance and spirit possession as important features of their beliefs and rituals. Over the years Amerindians and Africans syncretized their religious practices with Catholicism, producing the well-known Candomblé cult in Bahia, Xangô in Recife, Batuque in Belém, and Macumba in the more southerly areas of Rio de Janeiro and São Paulo. Bastide (1960) provides an excellent survey of the literature describing these and other Afro-Brazilian religions. For the most part, these religions served the needs of the lower class and largely racially mixed or nonEuropean populations.

In the nineteenth century some members of the traditional middle and upper classes, looking to France for their intellectual models, introduced the French spiritism of Allen Kardec to Brazil (Warren, 1968). Eventually, in typical Brazilian fashion, spiritist concepts from Kardecismo were added to the Brazilian religious mélange. During the past fifty years, cultural traits derived from these religions of widely diverse geographic and cultural origins have been in the process of being regrouped into new patterns in Umbanda.

Umbanda is largely an urban phenomenon. It apparently evolved from the Macumba cult in the large Brazilian metropolitan areas, such as Rio de Janeiro and São Paulo in the 1920s (McGregor, 1967, p. 169). Macumba, as a distinct cult, seems to have been replaced by Umbanda and its negative counterpart Quimbanda. Umbandists like to emphasize that they have purged their religion of the *magia negra* (black magic) of Macumba. They claim that Macumba's bad reputation in this area has been passed on to Quimbanda, which deals heavily with evil *exu* spirits. The term "macumba" remains, and is sometimes used as a generic term for Afro-Brazilian religions. It also has a derogatory connotation in many areas of Brazil. For this reason, Umbandists do not like outsiders to use the word. They will, however, call each other "macumbists" in a friendly joking situation.

Today one can easily find Umbanda *centros* (centers, i.e., places of worship) as far south as Pôrto Alegre (Lerch, personal communication),[1] as well as several thousand miles to the northwest in Belém (Leacock and Leacock, 1972). It is my impression that Umbanda's emergence and subsequent expansion were linked to social and economic changes leading to the replacement of regional political strongholds by a stronger central goverment and an increased sense of nationalism. It is interesting to note that Umbanda is now in the process of spreading to the smaller cities and towns in the interior of Brazil as these become integrated into the national socioeconomic structure.[2]

Umbanda is a religion with wide appeal to persons in all parts of the socioeconomic spectrum. Members are frequently recruited among those who think of themselves in terms of upward mobility. Generally they are in the upper lower and middle classes. Their ethnic origins are as diverse as the cultural elements that constitute the beliefs and rituals of Umbanda. In São Paulo, where I conducted the major part of my research,[3] fifty percent of the membership is Euro-Brazilian. Some Japanese-Brazilians also participate. In the Umbanda centers I visited, between sixty and seventy-five percent of the total number of mediums were women. Men, however, participated in other ways; for example, by playing the African drums, or by acting as "directors" assisting the cult leader in practical matters of money and organizational skills.

The great popularity Umbanda enjoys is directly related to its emphasis on spiritual *consultas* (consultations). The possessing spiritual entities diagnose and treat illnesses and help solve a myriad of personal problems for the believers, who may come to the two weekly public sessions in search of spiritual assistance. Ritual activities during these consultations, as for the entire spirit session, revolve about two principal sets of religious beliefs. One set of beliefs has to do with five major types of spirit. The second involves a theory of spiritual "fluids," which Umbandists have apparently borrowed from Kardecismo. After outlining Umbanda beliefs, I shall describe the physical setting of the centers and the typical ritual activities conducted in them.[4]

There are five major types of spirits in Umbanda. As we shall see, four of the types are fairly common and appear with regularity at Umbanda centers in São Paulo. These spirits can be either male or female. Both men and women may be possessed by spirits of either sex, and each medium is possessed by all four spirits. Although I shall outline the general characteristics of each spirit type, it should be noted that each individual spirit has its own particular personality. The general role of each of these four spirit types is learned by every Umbanda medium; the more specific personality traits of each spirit seem to stem from the medium and his interaction with others.

The *caboclo* spirits possess the mediums once each week. The particular night they arrive is regular for each center; however, one center will feature *caboclos* on Monday, whereas another may have these spirits come on Thursday nights. They are said to be the spirits of dead Brazilian Indians. While possessed by a *caboclo,* a medium will display protruded lips, furrowed brows, and eyes that slowly open and close, staring into space. A few may beat their chests and jump into the air, landing in a position ready to shoot an imaginary arrow. *Caboclos* like to puff on a cigar. They also prefer to drink beer, although this is not always permitted in public sessions. These spirits project a personality that is somewhat stern and aloof. If an individual should argue with an Indian spirit, the *caboclo* would quickly reprimand him. *Caboclo* spirits are appreciated for their advice in situations requiring quick and decisive action, such as obtaining or maintaining a job.

The *prêtos velhos* possess mediums at the second weekly session. Regarded as spirits of dead Afro-Brazilian slaves, they are stooped and bent over from many years of hard labor and tremble from old age.

The *prêtos velhos* speak in slow and quivering voices as they smoke their pipes. These spirits like to sip red wine. The *prêtos velhos* are very gentle and easy to approach. Seated on their low stools and conversing with someone who has come for help, they are almost grandfatherly in manner. The *prêtos velhos* seem to have infinite patience. They are adept at handling long and drawn-out intricate personal problems, such as familial difficulties or love affairs. Furthermore their extensive knowledge of herbal remedies is useful in treating illnesses. Although Umbanda stores that carry special herbs and other ritual paraphernalia are found throughout São Paulo, it is just as probable that a *prêto velho* will send a client to a pharmacy to purchase a modern drug for his illness.

The *criança* is the third type of spirit, the spirit of a child who died between three and five years of age. Spirits of this type usually appear only once each month. The playful and innocent child spirit is more accessible than the other spirits. It skips, rolls, and tumbles throughout the entire Umbanda center, approaching members of the audience to ask for sweets and soft drinks. Even a fifty-year-old medium possessed by a *criança* is high spirited. Everyone present loves this extroverted creature. Unlike the *caboclo* and the *prêto velho,* the *criança* spirit is not so stringently defined by race and culture. If one asks for the child's ethnic origins, the *criança* spirit will usually describe them. Ordinarily however, the child is thought to be Brazilian, that is, without a specific ethnic identity. One can apparently ask the child spirit to help with any illness or personal problem, since it does not seem to specialize as the other spirits do.

The fourth type of spirit is the *exu* and his feminine counterpart, the *pombagira.* These are spirits of people who led especially wicked lives. *Exus* are frequently foreigners, and I personally encountered *exus* with such diverse backgrounds as French, Mexican, and Japanese. In addition to these, my informants indicated that they knew of *exus* who were German, Italian, and Portugese. I also found some *exus* who were Brazilian, but with special regional backgrounds. The *exu* spirits are antisocial characters who seem to enjoy exhibiting their base nature through cursing, off-color stories and songs, and bad manners in general. The more wicked *exus* may specialize in performing antisocial acts, such as breaking up marriages and crushing business competitors. "Good" *exus,* said to be more spiritually evolved, may be used to counteract the evil magic of the "bad" *exus.* *Exu* spirits are usually present in Umbanda centers one night each month.

Three of these four spirit types—the *caboclo, prêto velho,* and *criança*—had led rather good lives and at death passed on into *aruanda* (heaven). Therefore they are thought to be with a spiritual, or heavenly, "light."

The *exus,* in contrast, had led especially wicked lives. Since they failed to make it to heaven, they are usually said to be without "light." The spirits of persons who commit suicide automatically become *exus.* The *exus* spend much of their time in cemeteries, which are regarded as particularly dangerous places for mediums with undeveloped spiritual abilities.

Because of the somewhat negative connotations associated with *exus,* some Umbandists claim that they do not work with this type of spirit. Furthermore, some Umbanda centers do not hold public *exu* sessions. A closer inspection of the situation, however, revealed that these centers do conduct smaller, private *exu* spirit meetings, and all Umbandists I met eventually admitted that they did indeed have an *exu* spirit.

Most Umbandists like to make a distinction between the more spiritually evolved *exus* they practice with and the more base *exus* said to be found in the Quimbanda cult. To move into a higher spiritual plane and be regarded as a "good" Umbanda *exu,* the spirit has to perform a number of good works to counteract the *magia negra* of the Quimbanda *exus.* Since what is regarded as white magic by one person may be thought of as being black magic by another, the matter of good versus bad *exus* is resolved more in terms of personal inclination. Thus there is a continuum of sorts between Quimbanda and Umbanda.

Exus differ from the other spirit types in another important way. They usually demand some sort of payment, either in money or material goods, before performing a service for a client. A bottle of rum will nearly always please an *exu.* The *pombagira* loves expensive perfume. In contrast, the other spirit types do not insist on prepayment for services performed. The emphasis in these cases is on *caridade* (charity). However, if a client is satisfied with the assistance he has received from a *caboclo* or *prêto velho,* it is quite proper to offer a small gift such as flowers, candles, tobacco, or any other ritual paraphernalia used by Umbandists.

The preceding four spirit types represent the more ordinary spirits that possess Umbanda mediums. They are the spirits that usually diagnose and help cure illnesses and other personal difficulties that clients may bring to a center. The fifth spirit type, the *orixá,* is thought to come from a more elevated realm. In the West African Yoruba religion, the *orixás* were spirits of deities that possessed humans. During the period of Brazilian slavery the *orixás* were syncretized with Catholic saints; for example Oxum, goddess of calm fresh waters, became identified and equated in some regions of Brazil with the Virgin Mary. Even today the saint's name and that of the *orixá* are regarded as two terms for the same entity. As Umbanda evolved from earlier syncretic cults, the *orixás* became more remote from man on earth.

Umbandists believe these deities are so powerful that a medium would explode if possession were to occur. For this reason the *orixás* send spiritual envoys to possess Umbandists. These envoys are very highly evolved spirits of the dead—close to the saints or deities themselves. The *orixás* or, more accurately, their envoys do not communicate directly with clients. Instead they may offer a blessing through very limited gestures. These spirits very rarely appear in Umbanda centers; when they do possess a medium, they are regarded with awe.

Orixás are important as guardian spirits. Each Umbandist is a *filho(a)* (son, daughter) of a specific deity. After paying a fee to a cult leader for the necessary divination, an individual can learn which *orixá* protects him. However, this does not always occur, and friends of the medium speculate about the matter. This is entirely possible because it is believed that an *orixá* exercises a certain amount of influence over the personality of his *filho(a)*. For example, if a medium (male or female) behaves in a suave, very feminine manner, his friends may guess that he is protected by the goddess Oxum.

The *orixás* are important in the larger Umbanda belief system in that they head the seven major *linhas* (lines) of the spiritual hierarchy. Umbandists loosely organize all of their spirits under these seven *linhas,* each of which is subdivided into seven *falanges* (phalanxes). In turn, each *falange* is further subdivided into seven *legiões* (legions) of spirits.

As mentioned earlier, spirits less evolved than the *orixás* (i.e., the *caboclos, prêtos velhos, crianças* and *exus*) are commonly consulted when personal difficulties arise. The consultation is based on a theory of special supernatural fluids, a theory apparently borrowed from Kardecismo that provides the major cultural link between these two spirit-possession religions in Brazil. Although Umbandists place a great deal of emphasis on a theory of supernatural fluids, they have not developed a well-codified cosmology that goes beyond describing the relationship between supernatural fluids and the behavior and well-being of an individual. The rank and file of Kardecismo, who tend to be more intellectually oriented than Umbandists, seem to have a better sense of how the theory of fluids fits into their cosmology.

Supernatural fluids are spiritual emanations that surround one's body and affect one's well-being. They are believed to emanate from three sources: (1) one's own innate spirit; (2) the spirits of the dead, which are floating about freely; and (3) spirits of living persons close by. Bad fluids are often associated with the *exus.* An individual surrounded by bad fluids is sickly and trouble-ridden. A healthy individual free from anxiety is said to have good fluids. Illnesses are classified etiologically by Umbandists. Camargo (1961, pp. 100–102) has drawn up the following list of five commonly recognized causes of illnesses, to which I have added a sixth, the "evil eye."

1. Sickness as a consequence of religious negligence or ignorance. When a medium fails to perform certain *obrigacões* (obligations) he owes to his *orixá* or to other lesser spirits, sickness or other personal problems may occur. The specific duty usually includes leaving some food or drink in a particular place for the spirit.

2. Magical etiology of illness. A *coisa feita* (thing done) refers to an *exu* work of black magic performed in Quimbanda. It frequently involves blocking the paths of the client's competitors in business or love. Bringing illness is one means of accomplishing this aim.

3. Perturbations provoked by spirits. An unhappy disincarnate spirit may agitate the "fluids" in an individual, bringing illness or various kinds of personal problems. In some cases a spirit may come to disturb an individual to get revenge for actions committed in a previous incarnation. In other instances the spirit is merely perverse and/or ignorant, thus disturbing the life of an innocent victim. The latter type of spirit needs to be enlightened in an Umbanda center as to its proper behavior.

4. Karmic illnesses. In a previous incarnation a spirit may have led a somewhat wicked life. Death and subsequent reincarnation in another individual may bring trials in the forms of illnesses and other disorders to this person. It is believed that these difficulties may serve to redeem sins committed in the former life. The concept of Karmic illnesses is found in Kardecismo, from which it was probably borrowed by Umbandists.

5. Illnesses resulting from undeveloped mediumship. This category represents a general catchall and tends to overlap any of the other causes in this list. When no other easily discernible cause can be determined, undeveloped mediumship may be cited. Through developing his mediumship, an individual learns how to interpret spiritual realities as well as to defend himself against them.

6. Illnesses caused by the "evil eye." As in other parts of the world where this folk concept exists, children are especially defenseless against the evil eye. Umbandists also believe that adults with strong innate mediumistic tendencies are very receptive to the influences of the evil eye. Therefore such persons should develop their mediumship as a precautionary measure to resist bad fluids passed along through the evil-eye mechanism.

Although the preceding list tends to be focused on illnesses, I found that Umbandists lump together personal difficulties and illnesses under the term "spiritual disorders." I believe that they are successful in treating clients because their system of causes takes into account the link between psychological problems and physical illness. Umbandists, however, view the common underlying cause as spiritual, and not as psychological or biological. They also recognize purely mental and physical illnesses, but do not normally attempt to cure them. The following summary will clarify for the reader the Umbanda concepts of illness:

	Mental Illness	Physical Illness	Spiritual Disorders
Causes	Psychological	Biological	Spiritual
Examples	Depression	Headaches	Depression and/or headaches
Cured by	Psychologists, psychiatrists	Medical doctors	Umbanda spirits

The preceding summary shows that spiritual problems and illnesses may mimic the more common psychological and biological difficulties. Thus a person suffering from headaches, on failing to obtain relief from a medical doctor, may turn to an Umbanda spirit for supernatural assistance. Umbandists also enjoy citing examples of individuals who were dismissed as incurable by psychologists and were later cured by spiritual means. The classification of a patient's disorder as spiritual, instead of mental or physical, seems to depend on finding a spiritual cause and ascertaining that the patient can again become an adequately functioning member of his society.

In assigning one of the six causes Umbandists generally regard headaches or other physical symptoms as secondary, since the same symptom may appear in all six categories. What is usually taken into account instead is the behavior of the patient or of persons with whom he has social relations. This is especially true when assigning causes 1, 2, 3, and 6. If such behavioral signs are absent or unknown to the diagnostician, category 5 (i.e., undeveloped mediumship) is designated as the cause of the client's spiritual disorders. Even after the patient's mediumistic abilities have been successfully developed, personal difficulties and illnesses may remain. In such instances, category 4 (i.e., Karmic causes) may be used to explain these more chronic states of poor health and problems.

Most consultations with spirits occur within the context of public Umbanda sessions. Umbanda centers are usually located in the middle-class and working-class districts in São Paulo. Some are housed above stores or in abandoned garages; however, most either rent or own their own building near the business district or in an ordinary residential neighborhood.

Outside the main entrance of many centers is a small, inconspicuously placed "altar" dedicated to the *exu* spirits. Before entering the center, an individual may pause briefly to pay homage at the *exu* altar. With fingers interlaced and palms extended downward, the individual softly repeats the word *"exu"* several times. The altar is inside a small box in which offerings of food and drink are placed to satisfy the demands of these spirits. Hopefully this will permit spiritual sessions in the center to proceed without the interference of the potentially malefi- cent *exus*.

On entering the center, one usually finds it illuminated by glaring electric lights. There is often a table at the door at which several men sit. These are the "directors" of the center, who have been selected by the cult leader and who look after the more mundane aspects of run- ning the center. Sometimes, the Candomblé term *"ogan"* is used to refer to a director. Their functions vary but primarily they attend to fi- nancial affairs. At the table they collect the monthly dues of the associ- ates if they care to pay. They may also see to it that each person who enters signs his name in a guest book. Somewhere near the entrance there may be a bulletin board on which various items have been posted: a notice of a fund-raising picnic; a reminder that women are not per- mitted to wear slacks in the center; and perhaps a few photographs of members possessed by their spirits, taken at a religious *festa* (celebra- tion, i.e., special ritual event held in honor of an *orixá*).

Umbanda centers are divided into two major parts by a railing. Those who have come to ask for spiritual assistance sit in the rear half on wooden benches arranged in two rows. The two sexes, about equal in number, sit on opposite sides of the room. Depending on the size of the center, there may be as few as 30 or as many as 300 persons who have come for the session. There is frequently a sign on the wall re- minding one that "silence is a prayer," but it is ignored as friends from opposite sides of the city gossip about their daily affairs. A few people may carry bouquets of roses, carnations, or gladioli that they will present to a favorite spirit.. They may also bring cigars for *caboclo* spirits and pipe tobacco for *prêto velho* spirits.

The front half of the center is devoted to the ritual activities of the spirits. The major piece of furniture here is the *conga* (altar), which is covered by a white drape. Statues of the *orixás, caboclos,* and *prêto velhos* are found on the altar. The *orixás*, or saints, nearly always present on the altar are the blessing Christ with open arms, the Virgin Mary, and

St. George on a white charger. Usually there are statues of Cosmas and Damian, the saints who represent the *criança* spirits in Umbanda. The large altar also holds flowers, candles, and a glass of water. The water is considered a necessity since it is supposed to aid in drawing off evil spiritual fluids from any *exu* spirits that may appear in the center. Two or three *atebaques* (drums), which "call" the spirits to possess the mediums, are off to the side of the altar. Although men usually play the drums, in a few centers women may also participate.

On the night of a public session one may observe the mediums entering the dressing rooms of a center from about 7:30 p.m. on, where they change from street clothing into their ritual garments. They have prepared for the session by avoiding heavy foods and alcohol during the day. Before coming to the center they took an ordinary bath followed by a ritual bath of seven herbs in their homes. As the rear half of the center fills up with those who have come to seek assistance, the mediums gradually begin to wander into the front section. Men and women stand at opposite sides of the altar.

Although the ritual garb of the mediums is nearly always white, colored clothing may be seen in a few centers that are more African in cultural orientation. Women wear blouses with a simple round or square neckline and billowing midcalf length skirts. Underneath are as many as five stiffly starched petticoats, which partially cover ankle-length pantalettes. A small triangular kerchief is tied behind the head. Yards of lace have been sewed through all the items. The men wear white trousers and shirts. Both sexes wear white tennis shoes, and everyone carries a white hand towel embroidered with the symbol of the center and edged with lace; it is used to wipe off perspiration and occasionally to help control a wild spirit that may appear. Some cult leaders require mediums in their centers to wear a ribbon diagonally across the chest or around the waist, usually the symbolic color of the leader's *orixá*. The most important single items of the ritual costume are the *guias*, or strands of beads, which represent the spirits of each medium. The number of strings of beads is limited only by what the medium is able to afford and the number of spirits that possess him.

At about 8:30 p.m., when a sufficient number of mediums have assembled in front of the altar, the cult leader opens the *gira* (turn-around, i.e., the session). The drummers begin to beat the *atebaques* as the mediums sway or dance counterclockwise to the rhythm. The audience joins in the singing of songs to various *orixás* and to the other, lesser, spiritual entities. An assistant brings in a silver censer suspended from a long chain that contains smoldering perfuming herbs and is used for the *defumacão* (perfuming and purification). The assistant carries it to the altar, to the drums, to each of the mediums, and finally to the members of the audience. A wave of the hand brings the fumes closer to purify the body and to offer protection against evil fluids brought to the center. Then each medium goes to *saravá* (salute, i.e., prostrate himself) the altar as the cult leader blesses him and extends a hand to be kissed. In some centers it is customary to pay homage to, then send away through songs, any *exus* that may be lurking around.

After more drumming and singing, an assistant may take up a collection from the audience. The cult leader or an assistant may then give a brief sermon in which the mediums are reminded of the Christian virtues of love and charity, and of the superiority of the works of Umbanda—small today but grand tomorrow. The faults in the ritual behavior of the mediums may be pointed out. Prayers are offered to Oxalá (Jesus Christ) and to other spiritual entities for the sick and troubled, and then permission is asked to open the *trabalho* (work, i.e., session of spirits who will "work" that night).

Some mediums begin to spin around rapidly, and as their heads and chests jerk back and forth in opposing directions, the spirits *baixam* (lower) themselves into their *cavalos* (horses, i.e., mediums). The hair of some female mediums becomes disarrayed. Since it is the night of the Indian spirits, the facial expressions of what had been smiling mediums are transformed into the stern countenances of the *caboclo* spirits. Some of the Indians may move about as if they were shooting an imaginary arrow. They shout in the *lingua* (tongue) of their "nation." The spirits may dance for a few minutes, greeting each other by touching each other's right and left forearms. When the drumming stops, they find their places and wait for members of the audience to come for the consultations during which requests for help are made. The hands of the mediums rest behind their bodies, palms outward and fingers snapping impatiently, waiting for members of the audience to approach them.

On entering the sacred front area, a person is directed to one of the spirits by an assistant. If an individual wishes to speak with a specific spirit, he must wait his turn in line. The cult leader's spirit may be quite popular, and it may be necessary for a person to pick up a numbered tag at the entrance door. This encourages people to come early so they can get a low number and not need to wait until eleven or twelve o'clock for their consultation.

The *consulta* may cover any illness or personal problem that one could imagine—*qualquer coisa* (anything), as my informants put it. There are the usual aches and pains, nervous tension, fatigue, as well as "heart" and "liver" ailments. When people wish to emphasize the spectacular, they cite cases of cancer cured by the spirits or refer to the several centers that specialize in spiritual "operations." There is always the problem of getting and/or keeping a job. However, it is not just working people who bring their problems. Some businessmen also feel in need of assistance from the "good" Umbanda *exus,* who can break a spell cast on them by some practitioner of black magic. Family quarrels, difficulties in love affairs, and even poor scholastic grades are brought to Umbanda centers.

Each personal problem or illness requires and receives individual attention from a spirit. In addition to giving advice for the specific difficulty, a spirit may tell one to purchase from an Umbanda store herbs for special baths at home or candles to burn while praying to an *orixá.* Before taking leave of a spirit the person is rid of his bad fluids, which are giving him difficulty. This ritual is known as *passes.* The spirit passes his right hand over the person's body, pulling out the bad fluids. With each downward stroke the spirit flicks his wrist and with a snap of his fingers disposes of the fluids. Before sending the person away, the spirit may ritually blow smoke over him for added protection from evil fluids. After a final embrace from the spirit, the person returns to his seat.

Drumming and singing continue off and on during the consultation period. A spirit may occasionally possess a member of the audience, causing the individual to shriek and shake violently. The cult leader or an assistant will walk back to the possessed and gently quiet him. If the uninvited spirit should insist on remaining, he will be led to the front part of the *centro.* The cult leader tells the spirit that his *cavalo* needs to attend sessions regularly to develop his mediumistic capacities. After the spirit has left, the individual himself is told that he must return for further spiritual development.

As the crowd gradually thins out, a few spirits not occupied with consultations begin to converse with each other. Others may dance a bit, as long as they do not disturb the session. Several *caboclos* may decide to leave early and hand their unfinished cigars to an assistant.

To avoid leaving his medium *carregado* (loaded, charged) with evil fluids accumulated during the "passes," the spirit shakes the clothing of his medium and makes passes with his hand over the body. Particular attention is paid to the head. As the spirit begins jerking the head and chest of its medium with opposing motions back and forth, someone steps near to assist the medium if necessary.

Some mediums fall backward into the arms of the assistant as the spirit leaves. They squint their eyes as if not accustomed to the bright light, wipe away perspiration, and may accept a glass of water. Disoriented, they may put a hand over their eyes.

As the lines shorten in front of the more respected and developed spirits, the assistants and those mediums whose spirits have already left may go to consult with a *caboclo*. The sessions usually last three hours. As the few who remain in the rear begin to yawn, an assistant moves among the spirits, quietly letting them know that the end of the session is near. The remaining spirits leave together as a special song is sung. The spirits may be dancing at this point. While everyone joins in singing the closing song, each medium again prostrates himself in front of the altar and the cult leader gives him a final blessing.

The mediums return to the dressing room. After changing into street clothing, they leave with friends or relatives who have remained until the end. Later in the week the mediums return to the center for another night of spiritual "works." However, instead of the *caboclos*, it is the *prêtos velhos* who possess them. Usually the *crianca* spirits and the *exus* appear at an Umbanda center only once a month.

NEGATIVE POSSESSION STATES IN EXPERIENCED MEDIUMS

In the preceding section I mentioned that a spirit occasionally possesses a member of the audience at public Umbanda sessions. The possession may be induced during a consultation, or it may happen spontaneously while the medium is still in the audience. In either case the uninvited spirit is frequently unruly, exhibiting inappropriate behavior or speech. Generally such possessions occur in inexperienced mediums. The cult leader will strongly urge the individual to return for the purpose of "development of mediumship." In practical terms, this means learning to control the disruptive behavior of one's spirits.

Some Umbanda centers have special nights set aside for mediumship instructions. Novices may learn some limited Umbanda doctrine as well as more practical matters, such as learning to call and dismiss spirits at will. In other centers, the cult leader may conduct brief learning sessions during the regular public sessions each week. In either case an experienced medium sees to it that the novice enters a light trance, which appears to be similar to a hypnotic state. This is achieved by various techniques, such as turning the individual around many times, followed by passing the hand rapidly in front of the novice's face and simultaneously snapping fingers or clapping hands. Polyrhythmic drumming may also help induce the altered state of consciousness. Sometimes a more quiet technique of concentration is utilized. The novice focuses on a lighted candle. In all cases the person in charge makes suggestions for the spirit's behavior while the novice is in the light trance.

The duration of the learning period varies from a few weeks to a year, depending on the requirements of a specific center and on the capabilities of the novice. The novice does not have to enter into a period of extended seclusion, and continues at his or her regular place of employment in office, factory, or home.

Umbanda mediums in São Paulo ideally learn to be possessed by, and to control the behavior of, the four spirit types—*caboclo, prêto velho, criança,* and *exu*—which ordinarily appear at public sessions. Interestingly, some of the behavior learned in connection with spirit roles is carried over into behavior outside of the religious context. An individual's personality may be weakly developed in a behavioral trait typical of one of the spirit types. After learning to play the role of each spirit, the novice may extend that personality trait into his own everyday behavior. For example, an extremely impatient woman I knew felt that she had learned to be calm from her *prêta velha* spirit.

The sequence of events just described fits rather nicely into what Lewis (1971) has divided into two major phases of the medium's behavior in spirit possession. In Lewis's "primary phase," a spirit medium's behavior is characteristically involuntary and uncontrolled. Some possession religions regard the spirit as pathogenic, and exorcism is required. Other religions, such as Umbanda, may find the spirit acceptable in varying degrees but unruly and in need of being tamed. In either case, the possession fequently is regarded as an illness requiring therapy. In Umbanda the cult leader or another experienced medium will attempt to diagnose the spiritual disorder according to one of the six categories listed earlier. The medium enters the possession cult in which he learns to control his disorderly spirits. This represents Lewis's "secondary phase," during which possession gradually becomes voluntary and controlled (Lewis, 1971, p. 55, 92–93, 122, 126).

Lewis (1971, p. 55) has pointed out correctly that his terms, namely, primary and secondary phases of spirit mediumship, are somewhat similar to the labels used by Bourguignon (1968, p. 9), who distinguishes "negative" and "positive" types of spirit possession. I have found the terms of Bourguignon and Lewis useful in thinking about Umbanda mediumship. In examining the behavior of experienced Brazilian mediums, however, it seemed to me that Lewis (1971) tended to emphasize the idealized progression through two phases of spirit mediumship and to overlook the fact that negative, uncontrolled, and unsolicited possessions may occur in experienced mediums during stressful periods. In the remaining part of this chapter, then, I consider two examples of experienced Brazilian mediums who, at times, exhibited unexpected negative and uncontrolled possession. I also examine the mechanisms they used to handle such deviations from idealized spirit behavior.

Cecília was in her early fifties when I met her in São Paulo in 1967. She was a highly respected spirit medium, having developed her mediumship for over twenty years. Hardly a day went by that someone did not drop by to ask Cecília for spiritual assistance with personal problems or illnesses. Generally she would ask them to talk about their difficulties, and would then suggest that they attend a public Umbanda spirit session to talk with one of her spirits. If it appeared that the individual's problem would require more attention than could be given in the usual ten to twenty minutes allowed for "spirit consultations" at public meetings, Cecília frequently suggested a private session, lasting several hours and including two to five mediums. Spirits usually enjoyed themselves more at these sessions, since they were not under the watchful eye of an Umbanda cult leader.

Cecília had not, however, participated in Umbanda in such an active manner in earlier years. Indeed, she had resisted becoming a medium in her late twenties and early thirties, when she had experienced a number of "spiritual disorders" herself. I shall discuss this "primary phase" of possession behavior for Cecília after considering her childhood experiences with the spirit world.

Cecília was born in 1915 in a small town in the interior of the state of São Paulo. She was reared on a large farm where her father had been the head cook, and her mother was a seamstress. Cecília's formal education was limited to two years of primary schooling. She said that her first experience relating to the spiritual world occurred when she was eight years old. She saw an image of a woman from the waist up in a pool of water. Her mother told her that it was only her eyes playing tricks on her as the children were romping about in the water. Cecília today believes the image might have been her *orixá* spirit, Nanã. When she was several years older, Cecília began to think seriously about the nature of spiritual forces. Her mother had been nervous and quite ill, losing consciousness and breaking out into a cold sweat for periods of ten to fifteen minutes. The family called in a Syrian to bless the sick woman. He told Cecília that whenever her mother became nervous and ill, she should pray because she had the right forces to help her mother. Cecília turned the man's words over in her head. It must not be physical force he was talking about, for she could not possibly lift her heavy mother. She decided that the man was talking about some sort of spiritual force she had. She added that she used this inner strength several times when her mother attempted suicide. Later in her life, Cecília came to believe that her mother's difficulty had been due to undeveloped mediumship. There had been no Umbanda center in their small town to which her mother might have been taken. Cecília did not learn about such places until she was fourteen, when her family went to visit relatives in Rio de Janeiro.

When she was seventeen, Cecília moved to São Paulo, where she worked as a cook in a wealthy home—the same occupation as her father's, she added. She remembers the great fun she had going to the *bailes prêtos* (dances for blacks) at that time. Cecília married when she was twenty years old. Her husband had a pushcart from which he sold ice cream, and gradually worked his way up until he was operating a bar. The young couple had three children—a girl when Cecília was twenty-five and mixed twins the following year.

Then a series of events occurred to upset their secure family life. Cecília's husband began acting strangely. He fought with and fired his employees, and soon lost his bar. The older girl died when Cecília was twenty-eight, and the boy was killed by an automobile the following year. Also, at this time, Cecília's husband took a mistress. It was at this point that a friend suggested that Cecília go to a center for spiritual help. There, a spirit advised that she needed to think seriously about her mediumship, for her dead mother had a mission to fulfill through her. This news made her sad because she had never wanted to become involved with spirit possession. Cecília left temporarily for the nearby port city of Santos, to bathe in the ocean waters. She believed this helped to prepare her spiritually. After returning she attended a session that was a mixture of Kardecismo and Umbanda. At the table of Kardecist mediums, Cecília was possessed by her mother's spirit. She learned that her mother's suffering in life had been due to undeveloped mediumship, and that the spirit could evolve through Cecília's own spiritual development. Later, the group of mediums passed to another room in which they were possessed by Umbanda spirits. Cecília received a *caboclo,* and at a later session was possessed by Father Agostinho, a *prêto velho.*

There was never any doubt in Cecília's mind that spirits existed, but she was reluctant to become a medium. Still, several strange events seemed to have pushed her in this direction. One night she dreamed that she and her husband were fleeing through a wooded area. Pursuing them was her Indian spirit, carrying a spear. After catching up with them, the *caboclo* attempted to seize her from her husband for the purpose of sexual relations. There were some other unusual events, which she related as follows:

One day I was cooking beans, and I took a little bit of meal and mixed it with the beans and fried it together with some meat I had drying in the house. I took some in my hand and sat down on the floor to eat it. It was so good! When I finished eating, I looked at the corner in the kitchen and I saw this face and neck, sweating! Oh, how the sweat rolled off his face. His hair was falling. Loose! With sideburns. Beard. I said, "Our Lady! What can this be?" I wasn't troubled by his presence. He didn't want to incorporate. I was alone in the house with my daughter. She was still small. And I wasn't even troubled by him.

Several days later when day broke and I awakened, I had a head the size of a clothes closet. I tried to go outside, but I just ran into the door. I vomited. I vomited what I didn't have in my stomach. I hadn't even eaten yet! I had only taken some coffee. That coffee had turned into something like you find in a chamber pot in my stomach. So, I went running, feeling terrible, running to the house of my *mãe de santo* [mother in sainthood, or holy mother, a term used by Umbandists for a female cult leader]. And I told her, "Look mother, for the love of God, help me! I don't know what has taken hold of me today, but I can't stand it. I'm really sick. Help me!" And she said to me, "Well, good for you! You deserve what you've got. I'm not going to hurry just for this. First, I'm going to take my bath, and then I'm going to take my ritual bath with herbs. And only then will I see you." Then I begged her, "For the love of God, see me *now*, for I can't stand this any longer." And that which I felt in my stomach, my head—such heaviness—left me. But my face stayed fixed in a strange manner and my arms were open. At that point she became more calm. She knew what it was. She also knew that I didn't like it! That I wanted none of this. So she had been tormenting me.

As she started talking with me I received a Japanese spirit. He said that every time I didn't want to go to the center, he was going to come and strike me with these things. And then he told the story of his life. That he had been a prisoner of war. He had hidden children in a tunnel so they wouldn't get killed. He was discovered and put into solitary confinement. A room so small he could only stand up in it. They threw hot water on his head until he was forced to tell what he knew at times. He then said that all of the symptoms I felt were his. And that he was going to stay by my side. That he was one more light that would be by my side while I practiced spiritualism. He bid the *mãe* goodbye and left. And then I received the *boiadeiro* [cowboy, the spirit she had seen in her kitchen earlier]. When he left, I received an old boyfriend who had died in an accident.

He said that he wanted to possess me, because he also needed to evolve spiritually. But that he wasn't going to stay with me. He had come only this one time. He said that while he was still alive, he had wanted me very much, but now he was staying only to protect me: that he was going to open the road for me so I would have some luck; that I had found someone who would care for me just as he would have done if alive; that he had come only to ask for a pardon for certain things. He had courted me but had liked another girl. He did wrong by the other girl. I knew it and separated myself from him. He didn't want me to leave. Thought that I should marry him, even with things as they were. But I said to him, "Why should I make the other girl unhappy? I don't have to. I'm free. I'm still young. Marry the other girl." I didn't want him anymore. Then he tried to attack me but even at this I still told him that I didn't want him anymore. I really didn't want him. Even now I like him less because he wanted to come against me. He followed me around to all the places I went. Where I'd go, he'd follow. So his spirit had come this time to ask for pardon. That he was wrong. And after he left, my uncle's spirit came. All of this in one day!

In addition to these rather strange spiritual events in Cecília's life at about age thirty, her husband was believed to be experiencing the effects of a bad *exu* spirit. He had had a mistress who had become dissatisfied with him. She supposedly had paid an *exu* spirit to bring harm to him. Cecília claimed that as a result, he had gone berserk, selling his possessions, smashing his car with his bare fists. (At this time he was a taxi driver.) Her neighbors told her that she should urge him to go to a center for help. When he refused to go for a spiritual consultation, Cecília went herself. Again the cult leader told her that she would have to develop her mediumistic abilities, this time to help her husband overcome his spiritual problems. Cecília had been reluctant to do this, but the fate of several spirits of the dead and the solution of her family problems seemed to rest upon her willingness to become a medium. She believed that it was the will of God and that she could no longer ignore her destiny.

It seems likely that certain of Cecília's early experiences with possession states can be linked with particular difficulties she was having in her family and with her marriage. Over a period of two or three years several things occurred in Cecília's life that might have led her to question her roles as mother and wife. For example, two of her three children died, which might have made Cecília doubt her abilities as a mother. Her husband behaved in a peculiar manner, firing his employees, and ruining the business he had built up. Later he sold his possessions and smashed his taxi. These things probably caused Cecília to feel financially insecure, especially since she was no longer working herself. There was also the matter of her husband's mistress, and this must have brought questions to Cecília's mind regarding her role as a wife. For a year or so, she attended spirit sessions, asking the spirits of other mediums for advice, and sometimes becoming possessed herself. This was done on an irregular basis, for Cecília had no intention of becoming a spirit medium at that time. Then, within a period of several days, a number of different spirits—Japanese, cowboy, boyfriend, uncle—came to her. These were what I would regard as spontaneous, as opposed to ceremonial, or controlled, possessions.

The spontaneous possessions that I observed in Brazil frequently (but not always) occurred outside a formal religious setting of public sessions. They were generally uncontrolled outpourings of things normally kept bottled up. Sometimes the spirits said things that a medium would not admit even to himself. In such possessions, it was as if the dimension of time were somehow erased as past and future were melded into the present. In a normal situation, an individual relies a great deal on his past experiences to tell him how to act and/or what he can say without future negative consequences. It is interesting to note that the common denominator in the cases of spontaneous possession trance recorded in my notes is psychological conflict, frustration, and anger. Depression may also be present, but this is regarded by many psychologists as anger turned inward on the self. Similar types of altered states of consciousness precipitated by psychological stress and frustration have been reported by Paul (1967) for Guatemala and by Freed and Freed (1964) for India.

It seems to me that in terms of its apparent lack of time dimension, the spontaneous type of trance is related to some other forms of altered states of consciousness. In a fascinating article contributed by an anonymous author in Tart's *Altered States of Consciousness*, a comparison is made of various altered states: emotion-filled psychotherapy sessions, meditation, daydreaming, ecstasy, anger, lovemaking, and certain states produced by marijuana. All share the common denominator of an absence or alteration of time experience (Anonymous, 1972, p. 349).

Although spontaneous possessions obviously occurred, Umbandists preferred more controlled spirit activities in public sessions. During the first twenty minutes or so of controlled ceremonial possession, the medium focused on the stereotyped spirit role he was playing. Voice, gestures, and facial expression were that of the possessing spirit. The medium's eyes tended to stare straight ahead. But as most mediums became more involved in their consultations, facial expressions, voices, eyes, and gestures tended to return to a more normal state, although they were said to be possessed over a longer period of two or three hours. A good consultation requires forethought and evaluation. It seemed as if most mediums moved from their earlier state of light trance to a state more closely approximating their ordinary behavior. Perhaps this shift occurred because most mediums required the time dimension in their consultations.

I bring up this matter of controlled Umbanda possession for the purpose of having the reader contrast it with Cecília's spontaneous possessions during her early phase of mediumship. It seems to me that her possessing spirits at that time tell us a great deal about her pent-up feelings. For example, the Japanese spirit, like Cecília, was concerned with keeping children from dying. The war in which this spirit was involved seemed to be something like the personal war Cecília found herself in. He was a prisoner, perhaps as Cecília felt herself to be—confined in her apartment and in a marriage that had temporarily gone sour. Finally the Japanese kept all his secrets to himself until forced, under the pressure of hot water thrown on his head, to tell all he knew. This was similar to Cecília's keeping everything bottled up inside until, in the heat of anger that sometimes leads into the trance state, she (the Japanese) exploded with all she (he) knew.

Two other spirits appear to speak to her need to be recognized as a desirable woman during this period when her husband had taken a mistress. First, the *caboclo* spirit, who chased her for the purpose of sexual relations in her dream, seems to indicate this need. Second, and I think most fascinating, is the possession by an old boyfriend. He reassured Cecília that she had made the right choice in marrying her husband.

I earlier noted that Cecília's economic security was probably threatened to some extent by her husband's difficulties. This, combined with Cecília's other problems, no doubt gave her cause to question her relatively helpless state of being. After all, she had been reared in an independent rural atmosphere and had supported herself by working as a cook when she first moved to São Paulo. In light of this, it is interesting that Cecília's spirits during this early period of her mediumship were nearly all male—the *caboclo, prêto velho, boiadeiro,* the Japanese, her former boyfriend, and her uncle. The only exception was her mother's spirit. It is possible that the preponderance of males here was a reversal of sex roles to gain some sense of control that Cecília evidently felt she needed. During the period of field work, Cecília came across as a strong personality, but as one who handled power in indirect ways. She was strong in a nurturant manner. Some other mediums observed that Cecília was like a "mother" to them, and for this reason they half-seriously, half-jokingly referred to her as the *mãe de santo* of their private session.

Today Cecília's husband faithfully spends most of his nights at home, having given up his mistress. Cecília says that she now recognizes three periods in a man's life: youthful love and courtship; a period of middle-age dissatisfaction and a turning to other women; and a final period of satisfying love with one's wife in older age. Cecília and her husband appear to have a very loving relationship in which he, at least superficially, maintains an authoritarian status. Umbanda provides Cecília with a means of meeting a wide variety of people outside her home. She feels that her mediumship has made her a "free woman"—

to use her term—for as long as she tells her husband she is at Umbanda sessions, he allows her to stay out until 2 and 3 a.m. Nor does he become upset if the Umbanda people she is with are men. In fact, Cecília's husband seems to enjoy listening to Cecília's recounting of intimate details of the problems clients bring to her spirits! This suggests, of course, that the trance state that Cecília experiences during possession is normally not very deep, and that she recalls what occurs during possession.

Cecília very strongly believed that once a person has developed his or her mediumship, a certain degree of control is expected to be exercised over the spirits. She would tell younger mediums that they could ask their unruly spirits not to possess them until a regular spirit session. One example was a young man who claimed that his spirit wanted to throw him in front of moving buses. Another case involved a young woman who said that her female *exu* spirit made her behave in an unladylike, sexy manner in front of men. Cecília also said that a medium could ask his spirit not to behave inappropriately at Umbanda sessions. During the entire year of field research, I never observed Cecília's *regular* spirits behaving improperly. Interestingly, during periods of special stress, Cecília was possessed by a *new* and somewhat difficult to handle *caboclo* spirit.

The first uncontrolled possession that I observed in Cecília occurred at a public session during which Cecília exhibited excessive perspiring and a total lack of conscious recognition of her surroundings. Her spirit did not dance in the usual counterclockwise fashion, but wandered in and out of the circle of dancing possessed mediums. At one point the spirit half vaulted and half fell across the room toward a small closet in which the cult leader stored an elaborate feathered costume worn only on special occasions by her Indian spirit, "Green Feather." When Cecília's possessing spirit began to enter the closet, several assistants pulled him away. Wildly flailing Cecília's arms about, the possessing spirit then moved to a wall where he severely pounded her head several times. For a few seconds, Cecília appeared to return to normal, her eyes aware of the events in the Umbanda center. Then she swayed and returned to the deeper trance state. During the remaining part of the Umbanda session, Cecília continued to wander aimlessly about. It was highly unusual that Cecília's spirit should exhibit this type of uncontrolled behavior.

The reasons for this very disorderly and unsolicited possession became clearer the following night when Cecília and several other mediums held a private spirit session for a friend of theirs. The same spirit possessed her, this time announcing that he was not her regular

Indian spirit, and giving his name as "White Feather." Speaking in a very loud and angry voice, he told us that he was not happy with his medium because she did not want him to possess her. He claimed that he would cut Cecília's life in half if she continued to oppose his possessions. White Feather next began to complain about the Umbanda center at which Cecília practiced, saying that the cult leader made the spirits put their heads between their legs, that is, be humble and obedient. Pointing out that the spirits were not allowed to smoke, drink, or say what they pleased at the public sessions, White Feather then proclaimed that he was going to make his medium urinate at the next public session in front of everybody to show his displeasure.

White Feather concluded his harangue by shouting that he was an important Indian chief, and that he wanted to be the head of an Umbanda center. At this point, the spirit violently threw down his glass of beer, smashing it on the floor. Immediately, White Feather left. Cecília, still in a trance, collapsed on the floor. Several persons at the session managed to lift her into a sitting position on the floor. But her eyes stared straight ahead, and none of the movements of the others attracted her attention. Attempts to get her to speak were also unsuccessful. She remained in this catatoniclike state for three minutes. Finally Cecília returned to normal, stood up while clutching her abdomen, and drank some water.

On the day following this outpouring by White Feather, I talked with Cecília, who told me that she ached a great deal because the spirit had been extremely rough with her. She had put hot compresses on her arms and shoulders. Cecília confessed to being ashamed of the things White Feather had said the night before, and expressed a strong preference for her regular Indian spirit. Cecília explained that it had been White Feather who had possessed her two nights before at the public session. She speculated that White Feather, who wants to be the head of a cult center, was jealous of Green Feather and had gone to the open closet looking for the cult leader's green feathered costume.

Several especially stressful events occurring a few days earlier may help explain White Feather's appearance and Cecília's inability to control this new spirit. First, a week before White Feather's first possession at the public session. Cecília's daughter gave birth to a baby girl with a cleft lip. Although it was successfully operated on, the family worried a great deal. Second, since her daughter, son-in-law, and their three children lived with Cecília and her husband, the birth of the baby meant more work for Cecília, who cared for her grandchildren—all under five years of age—while their parents worked. Third, a teenage niece from the country moved into the crowded apartment, so that she could attend school in São Paulo. Cecília never linked White Feather's appearance with family problems and financial strain resulting from the two recent additions to the household. It does seem possible, however, that Cecília's unconscious desire for power to control her personal life was expressed in the symbolic form of White Feather. As the head of an Umbanda center, White Feather could have placed Cecília into a position of authority and power. To some extent such an elevated position might have helped Cecília's financial situation, too. Interestingly, not long before, the *mãe de santo* at a second Umbanda center where Cecília practiced spiritism on a semiregular basis had asked her to become the cult leader's major assistant. This position would have required more time and effort than Cecília was able to give, and she therefore did not accept the offer. It may, however, have helped to plant the idea of becoming a cult leader in Cecília's mind.

White Feather appeared a third time, much later, during the year of my field work. By this time Cecília was complaining to friends about her ne'er-do-well son-in-law. This intensified when he was out drinking with friends instead of baby-sitting on the nights Cecília wanted to attend sessions of Umbanda. (At this time, his wife was working the 3 to 11 p.m. shift as a nurse's aid.) Also, Cecília was beginning to admit to close friends that she would like to be a cult leader. She would always add that her husband wanted a wife, and not a *mãe de santo*. At this point she would laugh about Green Feather's comment that his medium (the cult leader) no longer had sexual relations since her initiation as a *mãe de santo*. Cecília added that she had explained this situation to White Feather, hoping that he would understand. When he did possess Cecília again, White Feather was considerably more subdued and gave her no difficulty. Moreover, he did not appear to behave in a manner significantly different from that of her regular *caboclo* spirit. It seems to me that this change in White Feather's behavior might have been helped by Cecília's open and frank recognition of her displeasure with her son-in-law, as well as of her desire to be the head of an Umbanda center one day.

The exact reason for White Feather's third appearance is still unclear to me, but there are three possibilities. First, the private session being held that day was for an important local man, the operator of a small Italian pasta factory. The owner of the building had ordered the man to pay more rent or move out. White Feather boasted to this man of being the head of a line of spirits. Perhaps then, the difficult spiritual task at hand had required a spirit more "evolved" and more "powerful" than Cecília's regular *caboclo*.

Second, the session was held on a Sunday afternoon because Cecília's husband had temporarily grounded her late-night activities at private sessions. Although he was a very understanding husband and never complained about Cecília's being away until 2 or 3 a.m., she always had to inform him of her activities and whereabouts before leaving the house. As she had forgotten to do this, he had taken away her house key for three weeks. She did not overtly blame him, but seemed more annoyed with herself at having forgotten to tell him. The session was therefore held on a Sunday afternoon, and possibly White Feather appeared as a symbol of domestic power.

Third, Cecília's *māe de santo* was having an elaborate ritual goat sacrifice the following week. Perhaps Cecília's covert jealousy of her cult leader was symbolized in White Feather's appearance. After all, White Feather had been jealous of Green Feather at an earlier time. Cecília said that she did not understand White Feather's reason for possessing her this third time. She was, however, happy because he seemed to accept her familial obligations and inability to become a cult leader immediately. She was pleased that he was no longer giving her so much trouble.

Cecília is a very good example of a medium who views possession behavior in two ideal stages. The initial, or primary, phase involves degrees of unsolicited and uncontrolled spirit possession. Various illnesses may also be present. Such negative experiences can be overcome through the *desenvolvimento* (development) of one's mediumship capacities. Cecília so firmly believed that a developed medium should have only controlled, voluntary, and positively valued possession experiences, that she had to invent a new spirit at the unconscious level. It simply would not have been proper for her regular *caboclo* spirit to deliver hostile words about Cecília's *māe de santo,* or to be jealous of Green Feather. On the other hand, it was all right for the more elevated (head of a line of spirits) and less controlled White Feather, who wanted to head an Umbanda *centro* with Cecília as his medium, to be annoyed with the *māe.* This particular strategy used by Cecília to handle negative possessions within the secondary phase of spirit mediumship was not the only one I observed.

The second case study to be discussed in this chapter involves a thirty-three-year-old man whom I call João. He had worked with spirits off and on for ten years. Although most of his spirits were controlled, there was one female spirit who frequently made João behave inappropriately. Interestingly, when this happened, a second regular spirit would possess João, either to help him get out of the awkward situation or to castigate him for having failed to control the first spirit!

When I first met João, he was a waiter in the boardinghouse where I lived briefly. On the surface João was a mild person. Physically he was small and delicate, with almost feminine mannerisms and speech. To all his friends it was clear that he was protected and influenced by the *orixá* deity, Mamãe Oxum. Mamãe Oxum, equated with the Virgin Mary by some Umbandists, is the most feminine of all the *orixás*. As goddess of the fresh waters, Mamãe Oxum is quiet, suave, delicate. It is sometimes said she loves rich things. Whenever Oxum possesses one of her *filhos* (children), her behavior contrasts with that of the great undulating Iemanjá, whose domain is the ocean waters.

I found it extremely difficult to learn much about João's background. There were great gaps in his life history. Friends of a specific individual under study were usually able to verify for me the data collected from that person or to fill in new material. None of his friends were able to do this for João's background. I know only that he was born in 1934 in the northern state of Alagoas; that in João's Catholic family one of his brothers was a spirit medium; that João had had two years of primary school; and that later he had attended a religious school (Catholic) for three years. João's family moved to São Paulo in 1950, when he was sixteen. His father worked as a carpenter, and João had been unsteadily employed at various jobs. Recently he had worked as a waiter.

When João was twenty-three years old, his friends suggested that he begin developing his mediumship. He said that at that time he was suffering both at home and at work. He was not willing, however, to explain the particular details. João remained in Umbanda for about one and a half years. When he was twenty-five, half of his family joined the Pentecostal church. João was also baptized into this Protestant church. Five years later he had more personal difficulties of an unspecified nature, and friends directed him to the Umbanda center where Cecília practiced spiritism. João had not become as experienced a medium as Cecília, either in terms of years or in having the special kind of insight into human relations required for successful spirit consultations. João was able, however, to control most of his spirits, with the exception I shall now discuss.

The shy and mild-mannered person I first met was apparently a superficial João. What his friends regarded as his more gross feminine characteristics erupted in the form of Margarida, a female *exu* spirit. João, and everyone who knew him, recognized his homosexual tendencies. Everyone agreed that this behavior was due to the overwhelming influence of Margarida. The first time I saw Margarida was on a sidewalk beside the main throughfare in a middle-class district at about 12:30 a.m. It was early in the year of field work and that evening I had

attended a public Umbanda session. Afterward Cecília, João, a third
medium whom I shall call Juvenir, and I had gone to a local restaurant
for pizza, beer, and rum. João discussed his current problems at the
boardinghouse where he worked. The servants had not been paid, and
most had left that day. This meant that João had had to cook the large
meal by himself. As he continued to talk, Cecília was leafing through
the pages of a book the cult leader had lent me. It was filled with pictures of people dressed in the elaborate costumes of the *orixás*. Cecília
gave special attention to a photograph of a man dressed as Oxum Maré
(Oxum of the tides, different from Mamãe Oxum). She read aloud the
caption, which described the bisexual nature of Oxum Maré. Everybody laughed.

Continuing the conversation, Cecília brought up a male homosexual
who for a short time had been a medium at the Umbanda center where
she practiced. She then moved on to discuss what she believed to be the
great masculinity of Brazilian men. Cecília claimed that they were all
quente (hot) and looked at women only from the waist down. She speculated that what gave Brazilian men this great aspect of their tempera-
ment must be *feijão* (beans). The laughter continued as we consumed
more rum and, after more conversation, all of us except João shared in
paying the bill. Abruptly, João jumped out of his chair and ran to the
door. Juvenir followed close behind. When Cecília and myself came
outside a minute or two later, João was sitting on a retaining wall beside
the sidewalk. Margarida had spontaneously possessed him. Margarida,
in "her" high-pitched voice, was cursing quite a bit. She said that her
horse was a son-of-a-bitch and sexually wanted two men who were
walking by. Cecília replied that Margarida's horse should put such
things out of his mind or things would be black. There was a bit more
conversation in which Margarida spoke with agitation and Cecília with
deliberate calmness. Cecília suggested to Margarida that her horse
should come to Cecília's home to discuss his problems. She told the
spirit to leave, and with a few jerks of head and chest, João was again
normal.

The four of us then walked about half a block to Cecília's apartment
building where she bid us goodnight. A taxi picked up João, Juvenir,
and me. During the short ride to the boardinghouse João began to jerk
his head in the manner of initiating possession and reached for Juvenir, who held his hand for a few seconds and then asked if he were
all right. João replied that he felt better. As the driver stopped a block
from the boardinghouse, João took out some money to pay the fare.
Suddenly, his facial expression changed, and he began to giggle in a
high-pitched voice. Margarida had returned, and since women do not

usually pay taxi fares, "she" began to fold up the money and put it back into João's pocket. Margarida stuck out her tongue at the driver, who by this time had turned around to look at the scene. He asked João if he were *louco* (crazy, masculine). With a flirtatious nod of the head Margarida responded that no, she was *louca* (crazy, feminine). Then João became normal again, although still somewhat inebriated. With some difficulty he walked to the house, taking each step carefully and biting his lower lip. Later in the year I came to know João better. He told me that when he finally reached his room that night, his *prêto velho,* Father Joaquim, was annoyed by his behavior with Margarida. The *prêto velho* proceeded to castigate João by violently throwing him under the bed.

João's difficulties at work grew worse. All the servants had left except João, who was now working very long hours without pay. He remained at his job for eleven days more after his experiences with Margarida and Father Joaquim. João's behavior changed slightly; he became more aggressive, sometimes flailing his arms about. He talked in louder tones and laughed at a high pitch. This behavior was attributed to Margarida's being nearby. At times João became extremely nervous. This was especially apparent two nights after Margarida's sidewalk possession, when the group had gathered for an evening of conversation at Juvenir's apartment. João's arms, hands, and legs trembled. He drew attention to himself by teasing and shouting *"chequei!"* ("I arrived!"). This is a phrase some spirits use to announce their act of possessing a medium. The others in the room knew that João was planning to quit his job, but had no prospect for a new one. As his cries became louder, Cecília quietly tried to talk with João. Eventually Cecília was able to calm João sufficiently to initiate a spirit session. *Caboclo* spirits possessed João and Cecília. João's *caboclo* said that he wanted to talk with Juvenir privately, and the two retired to another room for about fifteen minutes. I was never able to learn the content of that conversation. As soon as the two returned to the group, both *caboclos* left. Cecília then received a "hick" spirit from the country, who entertained the group. Finally, some playful child spirits possessed Cecília, João, and Juvenir. After these spirits left, João appeared to be less tense and, to some degree, returned to a more subdued state.

About a week later, João quit his job and found temporary employment in a barbershop. Within a month, however, he had another job as cook and waiter in an exclusive beauty salon. Soon after, João's friends visited his combination living room-bedroom at the beauty salon one Sunday afternoon. They held a special spirit session to signal an auspicious beginning for João. He liked his new occupation and was still working there the last time I heard from him, two years later.

The possessions I have just described for João fall into two general categories: (1) the three spontaneous, uncontrolled, and negative experiences with Margarida (outside of the restaurant and in the taxi) and with Father Joaquim (later, in João's room); and (2) the slightly more controlled and positively valued possessions by João's *caboclo* and child spirits in Juvenir's apartment. The three earlier spontaneous possessions occurred at a time when he was required to work harder and without pay in the boardinghouse kitchen. More importantly, these possessions happened before João had time to "sort things out" for himself. His anxiety level was probably raised by the prospect of losing his job and having to look for another one, while the triggering device was his inability to help pay for the restaurant check and taxi fare. The fact that Margarida, instead of another spirit, possessed him was possibly due to the nature of the earlier conversation in the restaurant about sex as well as to the custom of women not normally paying bills. Although João's somewhat hysterical behavior during the next few days was said to be caused by Margarida, it did not go beyond the bounds of propriety. Margarida did not possess him directly, nor did she cause him to shirk his culturally dictated employee responsibilities. There was no need, therefore, of Father Joaquim's presence to castigate João, as he had done the night Margarida put in her appearances. It is striking, I think, that once the points of stress were symbolized by means of a spontaneous possession, João seemed to become more aware of his problems. Although his difficulties continued for a week or so, and his mood had not entirely subsided, he had better control of his spirits at the private session two days later. Moreover, the fun-making child spirits may have helped João forget some of his fears temporarily.

We should not overlook the fact that João's spontaneous possessions occurred when he was under the influence of alcohol. Alcohol is not usually an important part of the Umbanda setting for trance and possession states, and one might be tempted to regard João's spontaneous possessions as simply inebriated behavior. Whatever the case may be, alcohol was not involved sometime later in the year when a double possession by Margarida and Father Joaquim occurred again, this time in Juvenir's apartment. Juvenir and his apartment-mate, Renato, had invited Cecília, João, and me for Sunday afternoon tea and sandwiches. Juvenir was wearing very brief shorts, and João continuously made remarks about them. I perceived that João was perhaps stimulated by Juvenir's sensuality. His general behavior suggested to the others that Margarida was nearby, influencing his actions. Someone teased João about this, and he pretended to be annoyed while thoroughly enjoying the attention.

That afternoon the group wanted to listen to the tape-recorded version of the private spirit session they had held the night before at Maria's home. My notes follow:

We go into the living room to listen to the tape of the night before. The *prêtos velhos* are first. Cecília and João get up to dance to the taped *prêto velho* music several times, then sit down. During the music, João is suddenly and violently seized by one of his spirits. Seated on the sofa, he suddenly curls up in what is almost a fetal position. He squirms in this position for about thirty seconds while we watch with some alarm. When João returns to normal, his face is very red and he utters a long sigh, for he has been holding his breath. A few minutes later he gets up to dance again to the *prêto velho* music. While he is dancing, his *prêto velho*, Father Joaquim of Angola, possesses him in a normal manner.

A stool is brought out for Father Joaquim to sit on. Someone lights a pipe for him, and a newspaper is laid on the floor for him to spit on. I turn off the tape recorder, but Juvenir and Cecília tell me to record Father Joaquim, who later tells us the story of his life. João's body continuously trembles, especially his feet, hands, and head. As the session progresses, the trembling alternately stops and starts. Father Joaquim tells Juvenir to go change from his shorts into long pants. Juvenir complies. Father Joaquim calms down somewhat, and Cecília receives her *prêto velho*.

In this instance of spontaneous possession, I am not aware that João was under any particular stress other than the probable psychological conflict stemming from his homosexual nature. It appears that João was sexually stimulated by Juvenir, which was interpreted half seriously and half jokingly by the others present as Margarida's influence over João. However, it is more difficult to say that João's behavior on the sofa—referred to as *choque* (shock)—was linked to sexual behavior. Finally, he told Juvenir to change into trousers. Evidently this was done so that Margarida would become less interested in Juvenir's appearance. I might add that the trembling exhibited by Father Joaquim is normal behavior that is acted out by the medium when possessed by these rather elderly (seventy or eighty years old) spirits of the dead.

To summarize, Umbandists, like mediums in many other possession religions, ideally view spirit mediumship in terms of two major phases. The two case studies presented in this chapter, however, indicate that especially stressful experiences can sometimes precipitate involuntary and unmanageable spirit behavior in a normally controlled medium.

The strategies that experienced mediums use for handling such spontaneous and often negative possessions vary. I observed a few developed Umbanda mediums who totally disregarded admonitions that their normally controlled spirits should not be used for personal reasons; for example, one medium not described here used her regular spirit to ask that a loan of money be repaid to her. Generally Umbandists question the authenticity of this sort of spirit behavior in a developed medium. João's excessive use of Margarida's possessions would seem to fit this category of overuse of spirits for one's personal convenience; however, since his other spirit, Father Joaquim, corrected Margarida's behavior, we actually have a somewhat different strategy in which Margarida ultimately was controlled. Finally, in Cecília's case, we have a very experienced medium whose spirits were regarded by others, as well as by herself, as always being controlled. Thus, when involuntary and unacceptable spirit behavior occurred, Cecília had to present the case for White Feather's being a new and more elevated spirit than she normally was able to manage. Additional data on other Umbandists and on mediums in other spirit possession religions would tell us whether we are examining idiosyncratic behavior for João and Cecília, or regular strategies that developed mediums utilize for explaining uncontrolled spirit behavior in stressful situations.

NOTES

1. Patricia Lerch is presently (1975) doing research on Umbanda in Pôrto Alegre for her doctoral dissertation at Ohio State University. Levy (1968) and Camargo (1961) have made studies of Umbanda in São Paulo. Brown (1974) conducted her work on Umbanda in Rio de Janeiro.

2. Umbanda is something of a "national folk religion," an interpretation I have discussed elsewhere (Pressel, 1974).

3. This research was conducted during an eleven-month (1967) field study in São Paulo, Brazil. The work reported in this paper is part of a larger study that was supported by U.S. Public Health Service Research Grant MH 07463 from the National Institute of Mental Health. The project, entitled Cross-Cultural Studies of Dissociational States, was under the direction of Dr. Erika Bourguignon, of the Department of Anthropology, Ohio State University.

4. Parts of the descriptive material presented here have appeared elsewhere (Pressel 1973, 1974). The reader should keep in mind that Umbanda beliefs and rituals are variable, and that a visit to any given Umbanda center is bound to yield some traits that differ from the description given here.

5. The names of mediums used in this paper are fictitious.

REFERENCES

ANONYMOUS

1972   "The Effects of Marijuana on Consciousness." In *Altered States of Consciousness*, Charles T. Tart, Ed. Garden City, N.Y.: Doubleday & Company, Inc.

BASTIDE, ROGER

1960   *Les Religions Africaines au Brésil.* Paris: Presses Universitaires de France.

BOURGUIGNON, ERIKA

1968   "World Distribution and Patterns of Possession States," In *Trance and Possession States,* Raymond Prince, Ed. Montreal: R. M. Bucke Memorial Society.

BROWN, DIANA

1974   *Umbanda: Politics of an Urban Religious Movement.* Unpublished Ph.D. dissertation, Columbia University.

CAMARGO, CANDIDO PROCÓPIO FERREIRA DE

1961   *Kardecismo e Umbanda: Uma Interpretação Sociológica.* São Paulo: Livraria Pioneira Editôra.

FREED, STANLEY A., and RUTH S. FREED

1964   "Spirit Possession as Illness in a North Indian Village." *Ethnology* 3:152–71.

LEACOCK, SETH and RUTH LEACOCK

1972   *Spirits of the Deep: A Study of an Afro-Brazilian Cult.* Garden City, N.Y.: Doubleday Natural History Press.

LEVY, MARIA STELLA

1968   *The Umbanda Is for All of Us.* Unpublished M. A. thesis, University of Wisconsin.

LEWIS, I. M.

1971   *Ecstatic Religion.* Harmondsworth, Middlesex: Penguin Books, Ltd.

MCGREGOR, PEDRO

1967   *Jesus of the Spirits.* New York: Stein and Day.

PAUL, BENJAMIN D.

1967   "Mental Disorder and Self-Regulating Processes in Culture: A Guatemalan Illustration." In *Personalities and Cultures,* Robert Hunt, Ed. Garden City, N.Y.: The Natural History Press.

PRESSEL, ESTHER

1973   "Umbanda in São Paulo: Religious Innovation in a Developing Society." In *Religion, Altered States of Conscious-*

ness, and Social Change, Erika Bourguignon, Ed. Columbus, Ohio: Ohio State University Press.

1974   "Umbanda Trance and Possession in São Paulo, Brazil." In *Trance, Healing, and Hallucination,* Felicitas D. Goodman, Jeannette H. Henney and Esther Pressel. New York: John Wiley and Sons.

WARREN, DONALD

1968   "Spiritism in Brazil." *Journal of Inter-American Studies* **10:**393–405.

Joan D. Koss

Spirits as Socializing Agents: A Case Study of a Puerto Rican Girl Reared in a Matricentric Family

A wide variety of belief systems include spirit beings who interact with children, but very little has been written on the roles these beings play in the developing intrapsychic economy of the child. In one of the few discussions of this subject, Spiro (1967) suggests that Burmese village children are motivated to believe in *nats* (punitive spirits), witches, and ghosts (malevolent beings) through displacement of perceived hostility of parents and their own deep rage against parental rejection. These children come to believe in spirits because their earliest experiences, mediated by their private fantasy systems, are isomorphic with their society's religious "fantasies" regarding the quality and nature of interpersonal and interbeing relationships. Spiro makes the important point that for the believing individual "religious beliefs are true, not only because they are transmitted with the authority of tradition," but also because one has personally experienced their truth (1967, p. 72).

From another perspective, Bourguignon (1965) describes how spirit beings are incorporated into the self-related roles of Haitian children when they are encouraged in their play at possession by the *loa* deities. The play develops patterns of activities associated with alternate identities, as the children learn to refer to themselves in the third person and dissociate their identity as a child from their identity as a deity. This then is a way of directly experiencing a society's beliefs so that a culturally constituted reality that includes ever-present other-than-human beings subjectively becomes part of the individual's reality (Hallowell, 1955).

How children come to believe in the existence of spirit beings becomes an even more interesting question when one considers that religious belief systems are comprised of command patterns through which the normative idioms of a society are transmitted as lessons for infants and reinforcement of correct behavior for their adult socializers. All societies must provide ways to structure their members' egos so that they are motivated to behave according to socially prescribed rules, and all societies have backup systems that serve as additional emphases by demonstrating the negative consequences of denying cultural prescriptions to try to insure that most people will behave as expected. Spirit beings commonly assume roles as judges of conduct and sources of malevolence, but how do children come to appreciate these beings subjectively as moral arbiters and negative sanctioners?

In Puerto Rico spirit beliefs function to convey, interpret, and reinforce moral injunctions, particularly with reference to intimate family relationships that are highly valued and so charged with personal significance as to assume an almost sacred quality. Reports of the appearance of spirits of deceased relatives, especially father or mother, are common and seem to occur when individuals encounter difficult situations of inter- or intrapersonal conflict. A deceased father appeared to a boy to admonish his mother's actions because she was neglecting to provide her children with time and love. A recently deceased mother appeared to a distraught man with marital conflict and other misfortune and offered supportive encouragement that his problems would soon be over. Adherents to the special set of beliefs and ritual practices known as *Espiritismo* (Koss, 1970, 1974, 1975; Garrison, 1972; Seda Bonilla, 1964) conduct family séances in which spirits possess a relative who has developed mediumistic powers to communicate with the spirit world. These family rituals are often used to enforce the authority of women whose power in the family may be de facto but not de jure since, traditionally, only male authority is legitimate (Fernandez, 1968).

This chapter will describe in detail the life events of a young Puerto Rican woman reared by five maiden sisters whose need for male authority was fulfilled by calling upon their deceased father at regular family séances. Her case is noteworthy because she is presently deeply involved in a relationship that is considered highly immoral; she is living with her father as his wife, without apparently the least pang of guilt or intrapsychic conflict over the inappropriateness of their actions given definite social, moral, and legal proscriptions against incestuous relations. As will be noted later she does suffer from anxiety that arises from her "marital" problems, but the aspect of her marriage that would be universally labeled as incestuous, and negatively sanctioned in extremis, has no personal relevance to her motivations or conduct. As will be clear when her life story is reviewed, her deceased grandfather, in spirit form, was her paternal authority and the ultimate referent for her most basic notions of "correct" behavior. She met her biological father when she was already an adult of twenty-one years, and although she calls him "father" she does not relate to him in the ways considered proper and respectful for Puerto Rican father-child relationships, which include a heavy taboo on any and all expressions of sexuality.

ANNA'S EARLY YEARS

I met Anna when she applied for a job as a research assistant on a project investigating *Espiritismo* among middle-class Puerto Ricans. She explained that she wanted to understand more about her childhood experiences with spiritist rituals and that her father's family was prominent in the spiritist movement since its first decades in Mayaguez, Puerto Rico. She was then twenty-seven, divorced, and had a young son about six years old. She was endeavoring to obtain an undergraduate degree in psychology, which she had delayed at the time of her first marriage at nineteen. As noted above, she was living with her son and her father in an apartment not far from the university, and she exchanged frequent visits with her mother. Anna rarely spoke of her first husband but, as I got to know her better, was quite upset about her relations with her father. In exploring these problems with her the intensity of the relationship became obvious, and I discovered that as a child she had never lived with him but was reared by her mother and the latter's four sisters, none of whom were married. Anna had been conceived out of wedlock and her father's identity hidden from her until her curiosity, after her marriage, forced her mother to reveal clues that enabled Anna to find her biological father.

Before marrying, Anna had lived in a household of women and only had contact with males occasionally, and never in an intimate way.

Anna describes her earliest memories:

I was reared up by my aunts, four of them. My mother was the youngest, and she used to go out to work; she worked with the government. I never saw her during the day, only in the evenings. I didn't behave very well at home; I didn't have much friends either, never, till I got to high school. I didn't make many friends because they weren't allowed in the house. I was not allowed to go out and play. My only outings were with my mother, when she took me to the movies and to the circus when it was in town.

She seems to have been very protected as a child and confined to her home much of the time. Her rebellion against this isolation from other children seems to have caused her aunts much consternation over her unruly (relatively speaking) and often disruptive behavior. Anna recalls: "All I can remember [of her preschool days] was that I was in the home all day, making noise; that I didn't want to eat. They had to force me to eat and I had these tantrums and all that, and they were awful."

These actions seemed confined to her aunts (the two eldest who stayed at home to keep house), for when "my mother got home everything quieted down. I remember her reading me the comics because I couldn't read then. I fight a lot; I had a lot of arguments with my aunts."

The child's boredom and loneliness must have been acute because she was not allowed to play with or see other children. Anna recalls: "There were other kids but I was not allowed to play with them. Never! . . . I couldn't go out to the balcony alone, I couldn't!" The reasons given by the aunts were that the other children were children "of the streets" who had bad habits, and they were afraid Anna would be "spoiled" like them. Moreover they were "very much scared that I would hurt myself or someone else would hurt me. I couldn't go out to the balcony alone either. I couldn't."

These themes of misbehavior continued through her early school years. Anna related that she always had good grades except in "conduct." She was known as a child who would make trouble for her teachers. "I was always fighting with the teachers." She did manage to make friends at school but was not allowed to visit their homes until she was in sixth and seventh grade. Even then, she had to be picked up and delivered by her friend's parents. But, Anna remembers, "My aunt kept phoning all day long to see how things were going." She was allowed to visit her friends' homes once every two or three months. Still later, her aunts changed a bit and permitted her to bring a few school friends home, one at a time. Even in her teens she was never allowed to mix with neighborhood children.

The "family" consisted of the five sisters, ruled over by the eldest, Elena, who ran the household. The second sister sewed at home for a living, and the youngest three, including Anna's mother, worked in offices. Their parents had died before Anna was born, but the main family goal, promoted mainly by the eldest maiden sister, was to keep the family together in the family home. Her difficulties in this effort must have been great because she insisted on extreme prohibitions that excluded outsiders whenever possible. The only visitor permitted was an older male cousin who, as Anna remembered, only visited about once a year. Anna's early childhood isolation was enhanced by this woman's prohibition of visits from anyone whom her younger sisters might manage to befriend—a most unusual situation for a Puerto Rican family, since the norm is to open one's house to many relatives and intimate friends and enjoy a constant flow of persons. Anna remarked: "Every time that one of my aunts got a boyfriend . . . there were awful arguments in the home because she didn't want them to go out with them. She wouldn't allow them to visit them in the home either. They [the younger aunts] were prisoners. All they could do was to go out to work and come back at a fixed time . . . or she would say that they were doing wrong in the streets."

One aunt found a boyfriend, a man who rented an apartment over their garage. He would take her to and from work, but one night she came home late, yet before dark. Elena was furious and threatened to take this younger sister to a doctor to see if she was still a virgin. Anna recalls: "They were afraid of her [Elena]. When she would fight or opened her mouth, it was so displeasing. It was awful, the things she said . . . she threatened that she was going away . . . would kill herself. They [her sisters] were afraid because they didn't want to hear her speak like that."

Elena, orphaned at almost forty and a spinster, had become head of the household. She dominated her four sisters (ranging in age at that time from eighteen to thirty-three years) by fiat, by threatening to leave the natal home, by not eating, by throwing terrific tantrums, and by threatening to kill herself. Relative to her intense needs, her parents (Anna's grandparents) were deferred to as authorities for family affairs, and their wishes for family continuity carried out at all costs.

(Anna once commented that even now the aunts could not speak of their beloved parents without crying.) Elena seems to have used this extreme sense of closeness to their parents on the part of her sisters to forward her plans for eternal family unity.

She apparently found her best weapon in *Espiritismo*. As long as Anna could remember the sisters held séances among themselves behind locked doors for fear that neighbors would find out. She related: "One of my aunts began to develop her spiritual powers, and she was in that state for about a year. And she had to stop working because she was really sick. She spent the whole day in bed—the whole day. About five or six o'clock in the afternoon she got up and she was possessed, and that went on up to about three or four o'clock in the morning. . . . And she changed physically, she got all swollen; the spirits communicated through her." When asked who the spirits were, Anna remembers, "Most of the time my grandparents were the ones who communicated, and relatives of them that I didn't know. They died before I was born; and friends of them from their youth. All I could remember was that they painted a good picture; everything was going to be okay. The financial matter would be fine. They had to be calm, have patience, and all those things."

The family medium, Rosa, was the sister most in trouble with Elena because of friendships with men; it was she who had the alliance with the man in the garage apartment. She remained an old maid for many years claiming that she was unable to marry because of "spiritual causes." Some years after Anna left to marry, this sister finally managed to overcome the difficulties and marry at the age of forty-two. I asked Anna how she overcame the "causes" which are not at all uncommon among women who develop mediumistic powers when young. (The ideological rationale is that a purer vessel, free from the taint of sexuality has a better chance of communicating with higher, more enlightened spirit beings.) She replied that this aunt got rid of the spiritual causes, "with time, with patience and with prayer, and with arguments she had in the family." Anna's reply expressed her own intense reaction to her ruling aunt's severe restrictions on intimate relationsips with the opposite sex. As will be clear from details of Anna's own earlier experience with *novios* (serious boyfriends) and at present (both discussed below), Anna's love life can be viewed as an exquisite rebellion against norms imposed by her aunts, morals reinforced by her mother's fear of scandal, and valued behavior sanctioned by spirit beings.

Although Anna remembers many spirits of her grandparents' acquaintances appearing at the table during her aunts' séances, the very special—one could infer, latently incestuous—relationship they had with their father was perpetuated to Anna. When asked about her memories of her grandparents, she replied rather hastily, "I cannot remember anything . . . I didn't meet them! I can only say what they told me. My aunts, my mother, everyone in the house told me they were very good parents . . . they love them very much. . . . They were well liked in their neighborhood. My grandfather was a very poor man. He only studied until third grade, and he made a fortune all by himself. He lost it afterward . . . but he was a self-made man. And my grandmother loved him very much. She was very quiet; she never interfered in the household and she let him take care of everything."

When asked, "What kinds of thoughts did you have about your grandfather when you were little?", she replied, "I thought I would have liked to have meet [sic] him and, I thought he was a great man. I haven't changed that. . . . I remembered when he communicated they always brought me to him. I mean to him—he was always talking through my aunt (*fulana*), and she embraced me. Supposedly he was speaking, and he told me, "Oh my little grandniece (sic), I love you so much and I am always protecting you, and things like that."

Anna's impressions of her grandfather came from another important source in addition to her aunts' descriptions and her contacts with his spirit during the family séances. She recalled that: "I saw that man seated in that rocking chair, and when I called my aunt she told me, 'It's my father, so it's your grandfather.' And that time is not a particular time because it was just like all the rest of my childhood. I think I was on vacation, summer vacation, because I know it was in the morning. And there was nothing particular about that time as I can remember. Nothing had happened. . . ." When asked if she was sure there wasn't anyone actually there, she replied, "No man ever set foot in my home so I had to [faltering]. He was not there definitely. There was no one in my home except my aunts."

Not only were these experiences of her grandfather's spirit usual (and not "particular", i.e., "special") but they were interpreted by her principal caretakers as valid experiences of her long dead grandfather, experiences that were expected. Their intensity and vividness must have been remarkable because she recalled quite clearly the details of what she saw as a child: ". . . I didn't see his face. I mean his face was in darkness, shadow. I saw his body and he was sitting with his legs crossed. I thought he was a tall man, and he was seated there quietly like . . . observing or resting. That was all. And I *saw* him [her emphasis] there. I'm sure I saw someone. In fact that was what I told my aunt because there was nobody there. I knew no one visited us except women friends."

These experiences of grandfather's spirit were not part of a dissociated state; they could be accounted for (from the perspective of our "scientific" orientation of the world) as the result of heightened suggestibility, given the intensity and interest in their father by her major caretakers—who literally ruled over her by attempting to control her movements, select her literature, and even regulate her experiences. But the appearance of her grandfather was certainly real for the child and accepted as such by her aunts, given *their* behavioral reality, that includes the possibility of seeing spirit beings in one's home, if the spirits have a specific purpose in being there. Although Anna was probably not aware of it as a child, one might well suppose that her aunts and mother considered the spirit presence of their father as "natural" in view of their struggle to conserve family unity and handle family affairs without the presence of a much-needed male authority as the final judge of female actions. The spirit-grandfather's daytime appearances were probably considered proof that his appearance at the table during the evening séances was genuine (i.e., it wasn't a lower spirit impersonating him). The very fact that Anna could see him as he had been described to her and appeared in photographs must certainly have reinforced her belief in his continued existence as well as her recognition of the role the spirit-grandfather continued to fulfill in the family as the "father" of her aunts and mother, and as her surrogate father. Yet she did not think of him as being alive; he appeared as a spirit might appear, with some shadowy aspects; that is, his face was hidden to the extent that she could not define his features. Although in such spirit appearances in Puerto Rican culture it is common to converse with the spirit, to verify its identity, in this case there seemed no need for verification by conversing; it was as if the spirit-grandfather's presence was expected by the maiden sisters who were Anna's caretakers.

Grandfather's hidden face, when he appeared as a spirit, may well have had another meaning for Anna. She lived out her early years in a world without intimacies with men, never able to indulge the first stirrings of attraction by feeling their physical presence or by being touched or held by them. While there is no doubt that she acquired a concept of "father," it seems to have included only ideas with regard to his presence as an arbiter of female actions, as supportive, and as a source of spiritual love and concern. In short there could not have been, and was not, any sensuality of physical attraction that could later be denied, projected, or displaced. In answer to questioning about whether she felt he was attractive as a man she replied: "No! [emphasis followed by a pause] Well he was very tall, really. He was like six feet two or something. And then, let's say that he had an air of elegance about him, but his face was not very good looking. I have seen his pictures and he was not very good looking, really."

ANNA'S LATER YEARS

The loneliness and resultant rebellious behavior of the early years of Anna's childhood diminished in the preteen and teen-age years, when she was permitted to develop friendships with her female peers. She recalled a "good adjustment" and good grades until the fifth year, when her grades began to be poor. This indicates some problems in the period of growing interest in the opposite sex, but the memory of this time in her life was not brought out spontaneously as were other memories. She remembered that she managed to have some "boyfriends," but saw them only in school to avoid her aunts' condemnation. During this period the younger aunts were dating, and Anna recalls:

The boyfriends of my aunts that *could* get into the house, they were friendly with me, and in spite of the fights with *my eldest sister* [my emphasis], when my aunts could go out with their boyfriends usually my mother would accompany either one who it was, and they took me along; they were very nice with me. I mean I always liked everybody who went into the house; I always liked all of them. Only *my eldest sister* [my emphasis] was the one who didn't like them.

Thus the young girl did have some contact with intimate male-female relationships that were characterized by aspects of "love" and romance. Anna's statements about these memories are especially interesting, because she refers to her mother's eldest sister, the family's matriarch, as *her* sister, a key to the strength of her very close identification (in the sense of introjection) with her mother. (It seems less than fortuitous that she made this "slip" in view of their sharing a "father," and, at the time of our conversations Anna had the same lover her mother had enjoyed more than twenty-eight years earlier!)

Though her memories of it are poor, it appears that this stage in her psychosexual development was not at all unusual. Anna had a great interest in movie stars, read some of the romantic novels, and attended occasional dances at her all-girls high school. When asked, "What happened the first time they [the aunts] found out you had a boyfriend?" she replied, with an elongated shriek, "Ohhhhh, [gasp] it was awwful! I mean they were so upset, and they said my mother was the guilty one because she hadn't taught me what decency was, that I was in the wrong way, that I was to be a prostitute when I was older, and that I was following her [mother's] footsteps."

This was the first and only mention Anna made of how the sisters reacted to her mother's illegitimate pregnancy. It seems clear that Anna's mother was emotionaly blackmailed for her immoral act, and Anna seems to have been all too painfully aware of the sisters' condemnation. Given her mother's inferior position in the household, she did not serve as a source of authority for Anna; rather, this position, as an example of a woman who had sinned, must have caused great pain for her daughter. No doubt Anna's verbalized hatred for her eldest aunt included her resentment of the aunt's attitude toward her mother.

Despite the restrictions on intimacy with men, and on extrafamilial intimacy in general, Anna did manage to attract and hold a suitor whom she met at a high school dance when she was seventeen. "I met him there and he kept coming to my home and all that. At first I had trouble with my aunts because they didn't want me to fall in love or anything. I had fallen in love before; I had boyfriends and all that, but they were never happy about that. I just had to do it in spite of what they thought or did." Thus Anna's normal attraction to the opposite sex gained ascendency in her late teens, and she married when she was in her first year of college. One year later she gave birth to a son.

Anna was reluctant to speak about her relationship with her ex-husband except to say that he was a nice person, but that she was not very happy with him. Oddly, her curiosity about her biological father surfaced strongly at the time of her marriage. She recalls that she questioned her mother diligently when the marriage bans were published in church. She was concerned with the fact that she was registered as having the same paternal and maternal last names. The Hispanic custom is to give the child his/her paternal last name and the last name of his/her mother's father as well. Since her last names were identical, Anna's mother explained that the father had been her first cousin and that he died overseas when Anna was an infant. Apparently this did not satisfy the bright young woman, and she probed until her biological father's true identity was revealed. She then searched him out. He was still married when she met him, and her younger half-brother was still living at home. Although he had not legally recognized her and given her his name, he readily acknowledged his paternity and seemed aware of her existence. In her version of their meeting, they almost immediately fell in love and three weeks later had sexual relations. Subsequently both were divorced from their respective spouses and began to live together, known as father and daughter to the world. She reports that he wants to marry her but that she chose this kind of relationship "to avoid hurting my mother."

LIFE WITH "FATHER"

What is it like to manage impressions as a father and daughter, and what are the psychic and social consequences of such charades given a couple who are really lovers? These questions are faced by Anna and her father almost daily. Three years ago Anna went to see a psychiatrist, an affinal relative, and questioned him regarding her desires to live with her father as his wife. She recalls that he said that the possible social consequences of their arrangement did not matter as much as her feelings; that as long as she was comfortable and happy with their relationship she should live with him as they both desired. Other family members appear to accept them as a "father-daughter"; both her mother and her father's sister accept the situation on its face value but give her the kind of advice they would give a married couple. One young couple, an intimate girlfriend of Anna's and her husband, know about the situation and go out with them socially. This couple mediates their arguments as they would for any married friends.

The presence of Anna's young son presents some problems. Her father has offered to adopt him, but they have to work at keeping their intimacy from him. They are optimistic, however, that this is simply a matter of adequate rooms in their house and adjoining bedrooms. When asked about her sexual relationship, particularly because of her father's advanced age Anna replied quite frankly, "I have no problem that way." She even implied that her sex life was very good, much more enjoyable than when she was married to her son's father.

Relations with her mother were observed to be quite good. Her mother had left the "family" and was living alone in a small apartment, visited by a lover whom she acquired some time ago. Anna's mother was present at all holiday celebrations and seemed to support and approve the arrangements of Anna and her father. Their relationship did have its problems, however, which related mostly to their inability to present themselves as married or as lovers and therefore bound to each other and to no one else. A series of very destructive arguments began when he thought that Anna reciprocated the attentions of men, among his friends, who regularly asked her to dance at parties or asked her to go out with them. He began to be especially sensitive to her independent activities, and would only allow her to attend parties at the university if he accompanied her. He monitored all of her activities and expressed his suspicions by staying out late without her and arguing with her about money matters. This state of affairs became very serious when he threatened to withdraw money from their joint bank account, and she said many harsh things and threatened to move out of the apartment they shared. She also consulted a psychiatrist, who did not encourage her to leave home.

Probably some of the turmoil was encouraged by Anna herself as a way of reassuring herself of her father's love. In the course of her arguments with her father, she was involved in an automobile accident with extended ramifications in court. The driver of the other car was a young man who was attracted to her, and she admitted encouraging his attention to make her father "jealous and angry." She succeeded too well and bitterly repented her actions. When her father would not forgive her, she packed her things and found a small apartment but was so unhappy that she pleaded with him to let her stay. This coincided with Valentine's Day, so she put an ad in the lovers' column that stated in large letters: "Papa: Forgive a loving fool. I love you more than ever." In her anguish she consulted a detective who, she said, tried to proposition her and even suggested that she was in love with her father! She reported that at one of his consultations, after showing her a vial of liquid, he said, "I will put a few drops of a drug on your vagina and lick it off." She was somewhat embarrassed by his vulgarity, but did not report that it shocked or upset her. It was as if she expected men to respond to her in this heavily sexualized way without the proper respect that men accord to "good women."

Her pleading and strong desire for her father's love had the very familiar ring of a distressed wife, and she admitted that he is "naturally jealous" because he is "ninety percent husband" and she *does not like him as a father* (my emphasis). She repeated often that "I don't care how much longer he lives, a year or until he is a hundred years, *I can only have happiness with him* [my emphasis], even if he is so difficult and no one but me can get along with him . . . I thank God that he is that way or maybe he wouldn't stay with me."

This marital upset blew over in a few weeks, and Anna never moved away from her father. They made up, as all true lovers do, and he promised her a long summer's trip to South America. It is noteworthy that at no point during their quarrel did any material come out that indicated either one had changed the nature of this love from conjugal to paternal and filial. Their intense interest in each other as lovers was obvious to anyone listening to a recitation of their problems although, admittedly, I heard only one side. And Anna showed no feelings of distress or guilt over the fact that she loved her father; she once even purchased a button that read, "Incest is for all the family," and would have proudly worn it if her father hadn't objected. Once she remarked that the most distressing thing about their relationship was that she couldn't bear any children for him; she had gotten pregnant three times, but had undergone abortions in order not to disturb the impression of their relationship as father-daughter that they so carefully maintained.

DISCUSSION

One might ask if this case could really be called "incestuous." Doubtless both Anna and her father acknowledge their biological relatedness but do not relate to each other as father and daughter, for it would appear that he has no significance for Anna as a psychological father, at least in her conscious awareness. She never knew him as a child, never had the opportunity to feel attracted to him and experience the ambivalence on his part as he felt attracted to her but then inhibited his impulses and rejected her passion in a fatherly way. Moreover, she never enjoyed the opportunity of expressing these kinds of feelings toward any man, not even a surrogate father. In Anna's case the surrogate father was pure spirit; she appears never to have experienced him as a sex object even in fantasy. Is it possible that Anna's conceptual and affective appreciation of "father" is limited to a "father" without physical-sexual attributes? Could her own, apparently normal sexuality develop without a beginning in a forbidden paternal love, despite Freud's suggestions that this is necessary? Or could her longing for her actual flesh and blood father have rendered him so exceedingly attractive that the emphatic taboo on conjugal love between father and daughter (which they both acknowledge) is strongly suppressed? Before considering the possible explanation for this guiltless and relatively comfortable incestuous relationship, data on aspects of both their personalities obtained from the California Personality Inventory (CPI) will be considered.

Since the CPI has not been standardized for middle-class Puerto Ricans, only impressionistic conclusions can be drawn, based on United States middle-class norms established by Gough (1957) and other investigators. These considerations are interesting, however, despite the limitations of analysis. A look at the profile configurations for Anna and her father reveals a curious difference between them; Anna's profile shows only four areas of problems (four scale scores below the median out of eighteen while her father's profile shows twelve areas of problems! One might conclude that Anna is better adjusted than her father according to this rough indication. The father's profile, however, although showing many scores below the median, is not very low. Rather it shows scale scores just below the median in all but three scales. Both could be said to be "well-adjusted," "socially effective" persons in general terms.

Of five factors calculated by Gough, Factor 2, gives an indication of the individual's social poise and interpersonal effectiveness. Here again Anna scores higher on all scales except the one that indicates the level of well-being. Her father's scores, though lower, are only relatively low on the scale that equates with self-confidence and vivacity in social transactions, which fits with his personality as I observed him. Looking further into their profiles, both score somewhat above the median on the scale that equates with the trait "sensitivity to others," meaning that they are both well above average in being able to assess others' feelings toward them. Although this may be a key to their seemingly successful impression-management of a highly unusual relationship, it also indicates that they are not simply too dense to sense others' feelings, so that their actions stem from lack of capacity to appreciate normative expressions in their social milieux. Also, both score above the median on the scale "good impression," which indicates a fairly great concern about how another will relate to oneself. In contrast, both Anna and her father score a bit below the median on the socialization scale, which equates with the trait of "propriety," "an acceptance of rules, proper authority, and custom." Neither of these scales is unusually low, however, only low in relation to their other scale scores. Thus there is no indication that either Anna or her father are extremist social rebels; merely that their degree of social maturity is not exemplary compared to established U.S. norms although they might be for Puerto Rican society. (They are not "rebels" at all if their profiles are plotted against Italian norms. They appear there as very "well-adjusted.") Both of them also score relatively low on the scale for "communality," where the trait equivalents are "similarity to others" and "seeing things the way most people see them." As in the case of the socialization scale, however, these scores are not exceptionally low.

Summarizing the impressions gained by a very general look at the personality inventory data, a blind analysis would not yield the impression that Anna or her father were unusual in any way or had special emotional problems. This merely confirms the kind of impression one gets upon direct acquaintance with them, which is a very positive one, of two aware, intelligent people: in Anna's case the impression is that of a very socially adept individual, fairly attractive in appearance, with a good sense of humor and a definite air of practicality as well as a "down-to-earth" quality. In her father, one might observe an older man who appears fifteen years younger than his chronological age, quite dapper and solid but also young in his outlook and views.

The intriguing questions remain: Is Anna's present mate psychologically a father? And, as a corollary, what is the psychological significance of the spirit grandfather for Anna? Beyond these questions lies the need to understand the full meaning of possession rituals to cultural neonates in Puerto Rican society. Are they projective systems in the usual Freudian sense, in that forbidden desires can be expressed and satisfied through them and by reference to their created realities? Or do these rituals provide an objective reality for the young in societies where possession trance is institutionalized in family settings and deals with familial roles?

If possession rituals provide a culturally patterned projective system in Puerto Rico, Anna's denial that her present mate is psychologically a father could be explained as a true blanket denial (in the sense of negation) of her established relationship to him on both her conscious and unconscious levels of awareness. She has obvious, crucial personal reasons for denying that relationship. She could hardly avoid being impressed with her aunts' condemnation of her mother for giving birth to an illegitimate child; her denial of her relationship to her biological father effectively denies her fatherless state and the painful emotions that must have been aroused when her aunts reminded her mother of her immoral behavior. Anna appears to have been identified with her mother by the aunts as soon as her apparently quite normal sexuality began to appear. Any attempts she made to express it were accompanied by warnings not to be like her "bad" mother. In the sense proposed by Melanie Klein (Money-Kryle, 1974), her introjection of the bad mother would lead to guilt feelings whenever she was involved with men in an intimate sexual way. Therefore intimacy with her father avoids this pain; he is not outside the family circle and therefore not a forbidden love object. She also identified with a warm, loving "good" mother who satisfied her whims and nurtured her when she suffered from her aunts' cruel restrictions. Thus she is also reproducing her "good" mother's actions by mating illicitly with a male of whom her aunts would never approve if they knew about their actions, and effectively denying their harsh judgment of her "good" mother, whom she remembers as never defending herself against these slings and arrows. By taking her father as her lover-husband, she is effectively resolving what may be hypothesized as a host of conflicts stemming from her illegitimacy: her controversial and painful existence as the result of well-advertised immorality on her mother's part; the extreme restrictiveness on sexual intimacy imposed by her maiden-aunt socializers; and her desire for a physical father due to a fatherless childhood brought about by her mother's wrongdoing.

This kind of analysis has an intuitive "fit" if we are equipped with the basic assumptions that go with Freudian and neo-Freudian notions about psychodynamics. But if we take another position, one which I believe is more faithful to a Puerto Rican culturally constituted reality (cf. Hallowell, 1955), and still assumes the necessity of identifying (introjecting) with "father" for normal female psychosexual development, Anna's choice of a lover can be related to the very special kind of spirit father she experienced. This view would consider the real possibility that the spirit grandfather did take on an objective existence for Anna as a child. In Puerto Rico and numerous other societies in which the cultural ethos is not Western-scientific, spirits exist. Many Puerto Ricans who do not practice spiritist rituals will say, "Yo no creo [in Spiritism], peros los que hay que hay." ("I don't believe in that, but what exists is.") The spirit grandfather, as a principal socializing agent in Anna life, reinforced the strict morality imposed by her maiden aunts and became the source of her conceptualization of "father," since he was "father" to all the women around her. If this kind of ethereal "father" did take on an objective psychological reality for the child, is it not possible that she internalized a "father" figure who was not characterized by physical love and intimacy? Thus for Anna, although she may recognize her culture's definition of "father," the man with whom she is now living has none of the attributes of a "father" as she experienced those attributes during her tender years. Moreover, she never had a chance to experience physical intimacy with an adult male until well past puberty, since such an intangible father surrogate could never be a lover. None of the feelings of attraction and its inhibition were mediated by him during her childhood or by any other man, nor did she observe intimate behavior between males and females in the family setting.

The great physical attraction that Anna and her father felt for each other upon meeting for the first time may not be at all related to their concepts regarding fathers and daughters but may instead, by some happy circumstance, have satisfied their concepts regarding lovers. That they were related through his paternity may have had some relevance for him but perhaps none at all for her. On the unconscious level, Anna may need a lover who is a fatherlike individual in his supportive (financially) and protective qualities, especially since her "spirit-father" offered very little that was tangible in this regard. On his part her father may enjoy recreating the youthful relationship he had with her mother at a time when his present marriage and life has aged. (This is hardly uncommon.) His very great jealousy over his young and attractive mate may be just the antidote Anna needs as protection against a world of evil, predatory men who, she was taught, would suddenly take her away from the blanketing protection of her old aunts' household if she failed to observe the aunts' restrictions against strange men. It is hardly coincidental that their ideal man was incorporeal!

REFERENCES

BOURGUIGNON, ERIKA

1965   "The Theory of Spirit Possession." In *Context and Meaning in Cultural Anthropology,* Melford Spiro, Ed. New York: Free Press.

FERNANDEZ, FRANK

1968   "Spiritism and the Puerto Rican Migrant Family." Manuscript.

GARRISON, VIVIAN

1972   "Espiritismo: Implications for Provision of Mental Health Services to Puerto Rican Populations." Paper read at the Eighth Annual Meeting of the Southern Anthropological Society, Columbia, Mo., February 24–26.

GOUGH, HARRISON G.

1957   *Manual for the California Psychological Inventory.* Palo Alto, Calif.: Consulting Psychologist Press.

HALLOWELL, A. I.

1955   *Culture and Experience.* Philadelphia: University of Pennsylvania Press.

KOSS, JOAN D.

1970   "Terapeutica del Sistema de una Secta en Puerto Rico." *Revista de Ciencias Sociales* **XIC:** 259–278.

1974   "Religion and Science Divinely Related." Paper read at the Annual Meetings of the American Anthropological Association in Mexico City.

1975   "Thereapeutic Aspects of Puerto Rican Cult Practices." *Psychiatry* **XXXVIII:** 160–171.

MONEY-KRYLE, T. E.

1974   "The Kleinian School." In *American Handbook of Psychiatry,* 2nd edit. S. Arieti, Ed. N.Y.: Basic Books.

SEDA BONILLA, EDWIN
    1964   *Interacción Social y Personalidad en una Comunidad en Puerto Rico.* San Juan: Editorial Edil.

SPIRO, M.
    1967   *Burmese Supernaturalism.* Englewood Cliffs, N.J: Prentice-Hall.

Vivian Garrison

The "Puerto Rican Syndrome" in Psychiatry and *Espiritismo* [1]

One hot Friday afternoon in July 1968, Maria, an attractive 39-year-old, married Puerto Rican woman, was sitting at her bench in a handbag factory in New York's garment district, where she had worked for four years. Suddenly, to the surprise of those around her, she began to scream and tear her clothes from her chest. She ran to the window, apparently trying to throw herself through it. When restrained, she fell to the floor in an unconscious or semiconscious state, with her whole body twitching.

This bit of behavior set off a chain of events involving Maria, her place of work, her extended family, general medical practitioners, psychiatrists, *Espiritistas*, and this anthropologist. It invoked interpretations that range in the psychiatric literature from malingering in an immature personality, through various neurotic reaction pattern diagnoses and, apparently, once it was known she also believed herself to be "possessed," paranoid schizophrenia. In the Puerto Rican subculture, she had had a well-known experience, an *"ataque de nervios"* (nervous attack). It was interpreted by the *Espiritista* as *obsesión* (possession) by three misguided spirits sent against her by works of witchcraft. She was also told by the *Espiritista* that she was vulnerable to these works of witchcraft because she was in a process of "developing spiritual faculties."

This chapter will follow this chain of events in the subcultural context in which they occurred in order to uncover the "meaning" of spirit possession in the biological, sociocultural, and psychological realities of Maria's life. The concept of "spirit possession" as used here is an etic term used by anthropologists to refer to an altered state of consciousness which is explained within the culture or cultures under consideration as caused by or related to the presence of spirits. The Puerto Ricans I studied do not often use the term "poseido" (possessed). *Obsesado* (obsessed) is the nearest equivalent, but this has a meaning which is not accurately translated in English by a single gloss and it is only one of many states believed to be caused by the presence of spirits. The primary purpose of this chapter is to discriminate the variety of states and different meanings of those states interpreted as spirit possession among Puerto Ricans in New York. This will be done by reporting the discriminations of these states made by the *Espiritista* throughout the course of Maria's illness and treatment, and comparison of these with psychiatric and psychological judgments that were or might have been made at the same time. This comparison of folk and medical concepts of these states may also help to clarify some of the confusion in Anglo-american psychotherapeutic practice with respect to the diagnosis and treatment of some of these states, particularly the *"ataque de nervios,"* or "the Puerto Rican Syndrome," as it is known in the psychiatric literature. It will serve to elucidate the interface of these two symptoms of healing (the folk and the modern) as they impact reciprocally upon a single client-patient.

Maria was followed over a six-week period from the Monday following this Friday episode, during which she was treated continuously in a Spiritist *centro*, evaluated by a psychiatrist, and interviewed formally and informally at intervals by the anthropologist. She was followed-up three weeks later and again five years later.[2] Maria's case can be considered a "typical" illustrative example of (1) the *"ataque de nervios"* as a clinical entity, and the confusion of American psychiatry with respect to this either culturally specific or culturally colored dysfunction, and (2) the Spiritist short-term treatment of acute psychological reactions and the long-term treatment projected, but not necessarily followed, for approximately fifty percent of Spiritist clients. It should not be construed as an exhaustive description of the belief system, concepts of disorder, or treatment practices of the *Espiritistas,* however, and Maria should not be considered typical of the Spiritist treatment population. There is great richness and variety in the Spiritist diagnostic and treatment systems, which is not fully reflected in this single case. Similarly, the range of presenting problems and the range in type and degree of severity of psychiatric disorder among the Spiritist clients is equal to the range found in the general population and in a psychiatric clinic population, that is, from no significant disorder to acute and chronic schizophrenia (Garrison, to be published).

As a whole person (or as a case among the 150 studied) Maria is unique and inconsistent, although her *ataque* may be considered typical. Psychiatrically she presents herself alternately as hysterical, possibly psychotic, hypomanic, phobic, hypochondriacal, and as a relatively mature, self-assertive, and competent, although manipulative, woman who uses hysterical mechanisms provided by the culture as an acceptable means of coping. Her premorbid or basic personality structure is not yet clear despite approximately thirty hours of observation and formal and informal interviewing. She cannot be considered a "typical Puerto Rican" or an example of Puerto Rican modal personality. I do not presume to make a full analysis of Maria's personality dynamics or to proffer an accurate psychiatric diagnosis. What I will do is describe Maria briefly as background and then throughout the episode from four only partially congruent perspectives: her own, that of her peers within her own family and subculture (including the *Espiritista*), that of the psychiatric literature and of the clinicians who saw her, and that of my own observations of her.

Throughout this description I will point out possession states that are interpreted differently by both *Espiritistas* and psychologists or psychiatrists, and at its conclusion I will attempt a partial equation of these two systems of interpretation of similar phenomena in a review of "levels of possession" recognized. My use of the term "levels of possession" is arbitrary and does not follow a consistent theoretical schema of "levels" in any conventional system of analysis. These levels are, however, related, on the one hand, to the progression of the Spiritist's attention to the condition of any client and, on the other, to levels of psychological significance in psychoanalytically oriented psychotherapy. Once the parallelism of the two systems of belief and practice of curing are understood, it is possible to compare the folk and the professional treatments of similar conditions.

BACKGROUND

Maria was born in a small rural town in Puerto Rico, the fourth of seven living children, six girls and one boy. The boy was the fifth child and the *hijo predilecto* (favored child) of both parents. Maria reports that her childhood "was very happy"; they all "got along very well"; they were "financially comfortable" and "didn't have any problems." The whole family moved to New York when she was eight years old. She attended school in New York until she was sixteen and in the second year of high school, at which time she married and left school. She was married to her first husband for approximately six years and bore a son toward the end of that marriage. She divorced her first husband "because he was alcoholic and beat her." She soon married her second husband, Carlos, a longshoreman, "because," she said, "he was a good man and a good provider." She has never professed any love for Carlos but insists that he has always been a "good man" and "a good husband," and that she has "been good with him." There were no children of this marriage and Maria was frank in admitting that she has used contraception to avoid having another child "because it costs a lot of money to raise a child properly." She attempts to conceal the fact, however, that her one son was not a product of this marriage, and that her husband, for whom it was the first marriage, is therefore childless. She "does not know" how he feels about that.

At the time of her *ataque* Maria was living with her second husband and sixteen-year-old son in a six-room apartment in one of the better Hispanic neighborhoods of New York City. The apartment was nicely furnished in lower middle-class style and was well above average in comfort. It was equipped with air conditioning, a stereo system, and a lightly stocked bar. She explained that the bar was for her husband and for the parties she "loved to give." Maria drinks very little herself. Maria's mother and father, then in their seventies, and her brother and his family lived in the same neighborhood within a two-block radius and there was constant visiting among them. Maria contributed ten to twenty dollars a week to her parents' support. Maria's sisters were living in California, Ohio, Miami, and Puerto Rico, but at the time of Maria's *ataque* her two sisters from California (Paz) and Ohio (Gloria) and their families were in New York visiting because their father was ill and in the hospital. Maria's mother has a history of *ataques de nervios*, and her sister Gloria has a long history of what appears to be hysterical conversion reactions. It is said that she had been treated for six months in a clinic for paralysis of an arm, that they wanted to amputate her arm, although "the doctors found nothing wrong," and that she was subsequently "cured" by an *Espiritista*.

Maria, according to both herself and other members of her family, had no history of *ataques* or other "nervous" problems prior to about one year before the *ataque*. Details of her personal, family, and medical history are, however, thin and suspect, largely because she denied any past difficulties or any possible precipitants of the *ataque*. She was preoccupied at all contacts, including the five-year follow-up, with immediate problems (principally somatic complaints) and she avoided giving information and concealed essential facts. In this respect she is characterized by a guardedness and suspiciousness that far exceeds subcultural norms.

Maria characterized herself as, above all, "lista" (clever, shrewd) and the Puerto Rican research assistant and secretary working with me on this project, as well as the *Espiritista,* agreed with this characterization. She is upwardly mobile, or at least upwardly aspirant, and in some aspects of her life she is openly self-assertive and aggressive. She had worked steadily, although this was not a necessity and not usual among married Puerto Rican women at her economic level, throughout her second marriage to provide greater "security" for the family. She is fluent in Spanish and English and her speech in either language suggests greater education than she has. In contrast to many Puerto Rican women, and in contrast with the apparently hysterical nature of her symptoms, she does not value passivity or suffering. She prides herself on being *independiente* (independent), not *timida* (timid) and on being able "to defend herself." She is extremely manipulative, as we will see in the five-year follow-up interview, but she is not seductive in manner.

Maria says she had been *"enferma de los nervios"* ("sick in her nerves") for approximately one year prior to her *ataque*. We know retrospectively that her "nerves" were intimately connected with periods of illness suffered by her husband. His problems began according to Maria "suddenly one Sunday afternoon in November, 1965." He went into the bathroom, got sick, and came out "unable to breathe." He was admitted to a hospital for one month where he was treated, she says, for asthma. "Then he got sick in his stomach," and was admitted to another hospital, where he was treated "for ulcers, the doctor told me." This is when she first began to *padecer de los nervios* (suffer from her nerves). She went to the doctor the same day that Carlos was admitted to the hospital for the second time because "It is natural isn't it with what had happened to me." She was given Librium, which she took until a month before her *ataque*.

In the spring of 1968 Carlos was hospitalized again, either from an accident or for another operation (Maria is vague about it), and he was out of work for three months. He had returned to work during the week of the *ataque*, only to have another injury, this time to a hand, and he was again out of work. In retrospect we also know that Maria's husband was in and out of the hospital during that year and from then until spring of 1970, when he died of what Maria imagines to have been cancer. She says "the doctors never told me what he had—except asthma, ulcers, something in his pancreas, and something about his blood." Maria already suspected that Carlos had cancer at the time of the *ataque*. She had also been avoiding sexual intercourse with him during this year because, she says "I didn't know what he had—whether it was contagious."

Within her own subculture Maria is not seen as mentally or psychiatrically ill. *Locura* (craziness) or *enfermedad mental* (mental illness) is considered to be a very serious chronic condition equatable only with organic brain syndromes or chronic process schizophrenia in the psychiatric nosology. *Locura* is believed to be an organic, irreversible condition, which is greatly feared. Even the most severe chronic schizophrenics studied by Rogler and Hollingshead (1965) in Puerto Rico did not refer to themselves, nor were they referred to by their families, as "loco," instead they were "afraid of becoming *loco*" or "as if *loco*." The psychiatrist is seen as the medical specialist who treats *locura*. This is often strongly contrasted with a variety of "nervous conditions" that are considered medical but not psychiatric problems. Maria, and many other Puerto Ricans studied protest: *"Estoy nerviosa* (or *soy nerviosa*) *pero no soy loca!"* ("I am in a nervous state [or I am a nervous person] but I am not crazy!")

To be *enferma de los nervios* (sick in the nerves) or to *padecer de los nervios* (suffer from nerves), as Maria says, are generally considered temporary states of illness that are medical and not psychiatric. They may refer to a constitutional predisposition to be easily affected by environmental events, in which case it is believed most often to be a matter of "caracter" (character), which cannot be changed. The *ataque de nervios*, is also generally considered to be a medical problem, but not a psychiatric one. It is recognized in the culture that these are provoked by external stresses and are related to the individual's constitutional ability to resist. The *"ataque de nervios"* is culturally prescribed behavior in some rural areas of Puerto Rico (LaRuffa, 1971, pp. 69–71), and probably within the Puerto Rican lower classes more generally (Rothenberg, 1964), in certain circumstances. It may be expected of a "good woman" at the death of a very close relative, or upon witnessing an act of aggression which she is powerless to stop (cf. Trautman, 1961), such as her husband beating the children. The *"ataque"* in the first situation is the ritualized grief reaction familiar to anthropologists. In the second it often serves to stop the husband from beating the children. He is also given the opportunity to reflect on the impact of his actions on both his wife and his children, while not having his authority over the children challenged or undermined in their presence. The "secondary gains" of this kind of *ataque* are clearly recognized—with approval—among the Puerto Ricans with whom I have discussed it. Whether or not the secondary gains are recognized by the *ataque* patient is another matter, which is essential for psychiatric diagnosis and treatment, but one on which it is difficult to get information.

This culturally defined, sometimes approved, mechanism for dealing with less-than-ideal circumstances with less-than-ideal behavior depends for its success upon a culturally agreed upon fiction that the *ataque* is involuntary behavior of an alarming nature, the cause of which is to be found in the environment or in the behavior of others. In this context it is a culturally recognized, acceptable cry for help or an admission of inability to cope, and family and friends are required by norms of good behavior to rally to the aid of the *ataque* victim and relieve the intolerable stresses. If the stresses are not great enough by cultural standards to merit the *ataque*, the person will be said to have "weak nerves" or to be *"enfermo de los nervios."* Women particularly, but men as well, are thought to be susceptible to certain kinds of stresses. If they do not succumb to some emotional display under these prescribed circumstances, they are considered to be "insensitive" and "to have no heart." Among psychologically sophisticated middle or upper class Puerto Ricans, as well as Angloamericans, this may be seen as either hysterical or immature behavior, but the fact is that it is also a culturally accepted means of coping and one that can be expected to "work" within that cultural context.

The *"ataque de nervios"* has been described extensively in the psychiatric literature with varying interpretations. As a clinical phenomenon the descriptions are varied but quite consistent. It is generally characterized by a transient state of partial loss of consciousness, convulsive movements, hyperventilation, moaning and groaning, profuse salivation, and aggressiveness to self or to others in the form of biting, scratching, or striking, and it is of sudden onset and termination—a few minutes to two days (Rubio et al., 1955). Its behavioral manifestations range from complete flaccidity or catatonic posturing with mutism to agitated, assaultive hyperactivity with screaming. It may be manifested in impulsive suicidal or homicidal acts (Trautman, 1961) or be accompanied by transient hallucinations, delusions, and other disturbances of perception or thought (Fernandez-Marina, 1961). All conscious motivation and memory for the event are characteristically denied once the brief *ataque* has passed. Causality is then frequently attributed to "spirits" or to a vague undefined "they," suggesting persecutory delusions. It is not uncommon for the *ataque* patient to disrobe and run nude into the street. Within this variation the essential identifying features of the *ataque* or "the Puerto Rican Syndrome" are the bizarre seizure disorder, and its brief duration.

The *ataque* has been interpreted in the psychiatric literature as evidence of a high rate of organic brain syndrome among Puerto Ricans (Ramirez de Arellano et al., 1956); as a culture-specific syndrome such as *Hsieh-Ping* of Formosa, *Koro* of Malaya, and *Arctic Hysteria* Maldonado-Sierra and Trent, 1960); as an hysterical mechanism which gives cultural coloration to any disease syndrome from malingering to schizophrenia (Mehlman, 1961); and as a dissociative reaction resulting from minor stress that simulates more severe psychopathology in patients with "basic overly dependent, emotionally unstable personalities" (Rubio, et al., 1955). Most writers agree that it is an hysterical mechanism or syndrome, usually a dissociative reaction, but its relation to underlying psychodynamics are disputed. Fernandez-Marina (1961) sees it as an hysterical mechanism that may also serve as a basic ego defense against a psychotic break, or as regression in the service of the ego. Both Mehlman (1961) and Rothenberg (1964) emphasize its relationship to the management of anger and the anxiety and guilt generated by feelings of anger in a culture which requires repression and suppression of anger. To summarize, then, from a psychiatric point of view it would appear that the basic psychodynamic feature of the *ataque*, regardless of the presence or absence of more severe psychopathology, is dissociation in an attempt to disown undesirable impulses associated with anger and/or aggression (Rothenberg, 1964; 1971), as well as sex (Thomas and Garrison, 1975).

Maria's *ataque* occurred, if my reconstruction is accurate, at a time when her husband was seriously ill, or she thought he was; she had denied herself sexual outlet for approximately a year; her father, who was in part dependent upon her, was in the hospital; her sister was also ill; and all had rallied to the bedside of her father. She was now required to work as a result of her husband's illness in a subculture in which women are not expected to work, to support a man she had married without love because she thought he would be a good provider. She was also resentful, as we will see, of her father's dependency and, apparently, of her son's growing independence. Additional burdens were placed upon her by the visiting relatives who had to be housed and entertained and, in the case of her sister Gloria, "cared for." She was very angry with all of them, but in this situation there was no one with whom she could legitimately be angry and her culture strongly sanctions the direct expression of anger.

With this background then, that was not available to any of the specific parties with the possible exception of Maria at the onset of her episode, I will proceed to describe how it unfolded and how the two alternative systems of care (the folk and the professional) impacted upon this process. For the first four days we have only retrospective accounts from Maria herself, her family and the *Espiritistas;* through these, however, and observations of other cases the process can be reconstructed fairly well.

MARIA'S EPISODE

Initial Medical Assessment

After Maria's *ataque,* described above, the factory foreman called her home and talked with her sixteen-year-old son. He in turn called his uncle, Maria's brother, and in approximately one hour Maria's brother, a sister, and a brother-in-law arrived at the factory and took Maria home. Both Maria and her brother report that she was "all right then," but they took her to a nearby clinic "because she had to go anyway." The fact that no ambulance was called to the factory, as well as the verbal reports, indicates that none of the observers at the time considered the matter a very serious medical emergency.

In the clinic Maria sat silently and let her brother speak for her, denying any memory of the *ataque.* Her brother explained that she had had an *ataque* and that a little while back she had found some *porqueria* (dirty stuff) at her door and that "she thought she had a 'work' done against her." She was given a psychotic diagnosis, probably paranoid schizophrenia, and was referred to Bellevue Hospital for psychiatric hospitalization. Her brother agreed to transport her there.

Records of this examination have not been procured, as Maria was very angry with the clinic for the referral and would not give me permission to contact the examining physician or to consult the record. She said "that would make me very *nerviosa.*" Rothenberg (1964) has suggested that *"nervios"* among Puerto Ricans means "anger." For Maria "nerviosa" often means exactly that.

Regardless of what was actually said to Maria in the medical consultation, she received two messages: (1) there was nothing organically wrong with her, and (2) they thought she was *loca*. The first message functioned as a referral to an *Espiritista*. The second message was a severe blow to Maria's self-esteem and clearly taxed further her already overwhelmed defenses. That she "had been referred to Bellevue" had become her "chief complaint" by the time she reached the *Espiritista*.

With respect to the first message, there is an all-pervasive belief among Puerto Ricans in New York—although it is held more strongly by some than by others and becomes more credible to all in times of emotional disturbance—that there are "spiritual causes" of conditions that may explain any symptoms, organic or psychological, "when the doctor can't find anything" to explain the pains or symptoms one is experiencing. For Maria, and for many Hispanics in New York, the *Espiritista* is just one more specialist in the health, mental health, and welfare systems. Area surveys in New York and San Juan (Garrison, 1972; Lubshansky, et al., 1970; Rogler and Hollingshead, 1965) have shown that between thirty-one and eighty percent of Puerto Ricans (depending upon the ethnicity, sex, and attitude of the interviewer) will admit to an unknown interviewer in a standardized interview that they have sought the help of a spiritist at some time, despite an equally widespread tendency—particularly among the middle class—to deny any spiritist involvment, or even any knowledge of its existence (Garrison, 1972; Koss, 1975; Wakefield, 1957).

Nearly half (24) of fifty clients studied in depth in the spiritist *centro* attended by Maria had "gone to the doctor" or "gone to many doctors," and in their perceptions, "the doctors could find nothing wrong" before they presented their complaints to the spiritist. Twenty-nine of the fifty go to doctors with those somatic complaints that they consider "material," and to the spiritist for personal and interpersonal problems, mood and feeling states, and other somatic complaints that they consider "spiritual." By the same token, all but two of thirty-four (94%) consecutive Spanish-speaking admissions to a psychiatric outpatient clinic located in the same neighborhood had also been to a spiritist about the same problems that brought them to the clinic, twenty-six (76%) had some belief in "spiritual causation" of their current psychiatric difficulties, and seventeen (50%) had come to the psychiatrist only after they were unable to find a spiritist that could help, spiritist interventions had failed, or a spiritist had said either that they had a spirit "too strong to work" or that the person was "too weak to work the spirits." At least ten (29%) continued to see spiritists for their "spiritual problems" while attending the clinic for the "material problems." Thus a folk healing system which, for the medical professionals, is something completely separate and totally distinct, actually intersects through the folk concepts of disease with the professional treatment system so that there is a naturally occurring referral network between and among the emergency services, medical-surgical clinics, spiritists, and the mental health professions, which often bypasses the psychiatric services for all but the most severe mental disorders. In the folk system, Maria's referral to a psychiatric hospital was reinterpreted as a statement that the doctor had found nothing medically wrong and, therefore, as a referral to an *Espiritista*.

The family, rather than taking Maria to Bellevue as instructed, took her home and on the following Monday took her for a *consulta* with an *Espiritista*, Rosa, with whom I had been doing field work for some time.

The First Spiritist Contact

Rosa's is one of fourteen spiritist centers known to me in a ten-census-tract area of the South Bronx.[3] Eleven of these are located in store-fronts, and are clearly identifiable from the street. Three, including Rosa's, are located in unmarked basements and are known only through word of mouth. There are also seven *botánicas* (religious object stores that sell herbs, perfumes, candles, statues of saints, indios, congos, and other ritual objects of folk Catholicism, Spiritism, and *Santeria*). Spiritist *consultas* are often given or referrals to *centros* may be made from these *botánicas*. There are also an unknown number of *Espiritistas, Santeras, Santeros, Babalawos* and other types of healers working out of apartments that have not been identified for purposes of this study. To my knowledge there is only one gypsy "Spiritual Reader and Advisor" of the kind more often found in other American inner-city neighborhoods. There are also thirty-five Spanish-speaking Pentecostal churches or storefronts in this area that have healing services and trance 'possession' (again, not an emic term) by the Holy Ghost. These are, however, very different from the spirit medium cults and, although many of their members were involved in *Espiritismo* prior to their conversion to Pentecostalism, this sectarian religion demands exclusivity of membership. They in no way enter into the case of Maria.

Espiritismo is a spirit medium cult of a type found widely distributed throughout the world, apparently among peoples at a preindustrial, urbanized, state level of sociocultural development, as attested by the case studies of this volume and the cross-cultural studies of Bourguignon, et al. (1973). Specifically, *Espiritismo* traces its origins to the mid- and late nineteenth century writings of a Frenchman, whose nom de plume was Allan Kardec. Kardec was an engineer and an adept of mesmerism and he attempted to rationalize the folk beliefs in spirits then popular in Europe in concepts of nineteenth century science, psychology, and philosophy within the prevailing "psychicist" theories of mental health and illness. He attributed his insights, however, to "enlightened spirits" that dictated this wisdom through him as medium. For history, development, and diffusion of *Espiritismo* specifically, see Macklin (1975), and for its history and development in Puerto Rico, see Koss (1974). For more complete ethnographic descriptions of *Espiritismo* among Puerto Ricans, see Garrison (1972), Koss (1973, and 1975). For descriptions and interpretations of the therapeutic practices of *Espiritistas* see Bram (1958), Koss (1975), Lubchansky, et al. (1975), Rogler and Hollingshead (1961, 1965), and Seda Bonilla (1969).

Today in New York City the beliefs and practices of *Espiritismo* derived from Allan Kardec are syncretized with beliefs and practices from *curanderismo* (itself a syncretism of folk Catholicism, sixteenth century European medicine, and earlier Mesoamerican and Caribbean Indian practices), and with *Santería,* an Afroamerican syncretic cult which evolved under this name in Cuba and is now spreading rapidly among Puerto Ricans and American Blacks in New York City. *Espiritismo* and *Curanderismo* are essentially Euroamerican in their social structure and world view. *Santería,* on the other hand, like related Vodun in Haiti, Shango cults in Trinidad, Macumba in Brazil, and others, is essentially Afroamerican in social structure and world view. Rosa is both an *Espiritista* and a *Santera,* and also considers herself "Apostolic Catholic" by religion. She holds *Espiritista reuniones* (public meetings) in the basement of one of the three buildings she owns, and her *Santería* practices are based in her *"fundamento"* (the residing place of her particular saints) in her apartment upstairs in the same building, where she also does Spiritist *consultas* (private consultations). She refers people to the Catholic church to say masses, light candles and, sometimes for baptism and to get holy water for use in Spiritist rituals. In traditional *Santería* there are no public meeting places (churches) or congregations, rather all functions take place at the *fundamentos* of initiates in their homes and are organized through a network of fictive kinship reminiscent of the lineage systems of West Africa. In contemporary New York some *centros* have introduced *Santería* practices into the functions of the Spiritist *reunion,* others hold *Santería* ceremonies at distinct times.

The fourteen Spiritist centers studied are organized and licensed as "churches" and have a president, secretary, and treasurer on paper at least and, in theory, a membership of individuals paying dues of two dollars per month. Actually membership lists are rarely kept, dues are not paid, and in all but two *centros* where there are worship services as well as healing sessions, they function strictly as healing cults and not as an alternative religion. The great majority of those who attend spiritist *centros* in both area surveys and in the *centro* client sample report their religion as Roman Catholic. Only three of the fifty Spiritist clients studied in depth consider *Espiritismo* to be their "religion." Koss (1974) has shown that the relative importance of *Espiritismo* in Puerto Rico as either sectarian religion or as healing cult has varied with historical periods and varies now by class. In the largely lower-class Puerto Rican neighborhood studied, *Espiritismo* is folk psychotherapy and not a religion in opposition to Catholicism. Maria's contacts with an *Espiritista* during her episode were in one of these *centros* dedicated almost exclusively to healing and not to worship or metaphysical study. Later she chose to attend, as a preferred form of practice, a *centro* where philosophical teachings in Spiritism classes are emphasized and healing is minimized—a *centro* in the more middle-class Spanish-speaking neighborhood where she lives.

Rosa's *centro,* like most of the small, intimate basement or storefront *centros* (9 of the 14) have a *"Presidente de la mesa"* (head medium who presides at the table), who is in effect the cult leader and single, stable organizational figure, and a small group (3 to 5) of relatively fixed auxiliary "fully developed mediums," who also sit at the table and "work" the spiritual problems of others. Other "fully developed mediums" visit the *centro* periodically and "work at the table," thus developing and practicing their skills under a variety of *"presidentes"* and keeping themselves informed of the practices of others. In addition, there will always be a varying number of "mediums in development" who sit at or near the table and are in "the process of developing their spiritual faculties." Beyond that there is a rotating group of "members" and "visitors" who have come to seek help for a problem, "for curiosity," or simply because they "like it." The mediums in these *centros* assume; "If they come they have a problem or they would not have come." The majority (176 of 180 members and visitors over a six-month period in the *centro* studied in depth) cease to attend when the immediate problem has been relieved (one to six weeks), only to return again when the next problem occurs (92 of the 180 (51%) were returnees).

In all of these healing cult *centros* there are two essential types of service performed: the *reunión,* or public meeting, and the *consulta,* or private consultation. Each *centro* schedules *reuniones* one or two nights a week, and sometimes more, and most presidents schedule specific hours during the week when they are available for private *consultas.* Attendees can present themselves for the first time for either a *reunión* or a *consulta;* whichever it is, however, the president usually refers them to

the other, and the usual course of spiritist attendance involves participation in both *consultas* and *reuniones*. Maria was brought first by her
family for a *consulta*.

Maria and her family (her husband, brother, one sister, and a
brother-in-law) did not select this particular *centro*. Instead, they were
looking for a male medium they had once known in the same neighborhood and arrived at Rosa's apartment door by "chance," or what
they considered possibly to be "divine guidance."

If this contact followed the most common format I have seen repeatedly, Rosa ushered them in and invited them to sit around the kitchen
table while she completed other things she was doing. This provides
some delay, during which Rosa has an opportunity, although this is not
part of her theory of what she does, to observe and overhear the informal interactions of the family before beginning her ritualized *consulta*.
When Rosa was ready to attend to their requests, she first found out
which of them was to be considered the client, and what the relationships were among those present. They volunteered the information
that Maria had had an *ataque* at work on Friday and that the clinic had
referred her to Bellevue. She then ushered them into the *cuarto de los
santos* (saints' room). She asked Maria to sit at a small table under the
altar opposite her and wrote Maria's name upon a slip of paper. She
then placed the paper under a fishbowl of water. She lit a cigar to invoke her Congo protections, breathed deeply, made a few jerking
movements with her body, indicating the presence of the spirits, and
then began to speak in a series of affirmative statements about symptoms and complaints that Maria was presenting. It is understood in advance that Maria is only to confirm or deny the truth of these statements and not to volunteer further information. Among the symptoms
which Rosa so divined and Maria confirmed were: she "had not slept
for many nights"; "she felt very nervous and did not know why"; "she
felt she had something in her head"; "her mind goes blank"; and "she
was afraid she was going to become *loca*." Judging by many actual
transcripts of such *consultas*, Rosa probably also named a number of
somatic complaints, including headaches (*dolor de cabeza* and *dolor de
cerebro* [4]), pains in the abdomen or ovaries, blurred vision, and feeling
weak. Difficulties in the home and difficulties between her and Carlos
were most certainly mentioned as well, but at that time Maria was denying any such difficulties.

Rosa then, having divined what the psychiatrist would call the "presenting complaints," or the symptoms that the client or patient would
herself volunteer if she were asked why she had come, told her that
"what she had" was "spiritual" and not "material" and reassured her

that there was no need to go to the hospital. Rosa then told her that what she had was a *trabajo de brujería* (work of witchcraft) against her to make her go crazy. Maria confirmed that she had found a penny and some *porquería* (pig things) at her door and that she had herself suspected a "work." Rosa then, inspired I believe by the fact that the *ataque* took place at work, asked if anyone at her place of work had *"envidia"* (envy or jealousy [5]) of her. Maria confirmed that there were three women at work who were envious of her. Rosa summed up (as she did for me later, but with the qualification to me that that was not all of it): "That's it, you have a work against you by someone where you work who wants to see you sick, who wants to make you crazy." Three *espíritus obsesores* had been "sent against her." *Espíritus obsesores* are, according to Rosa, "spirits of darkness that fill your mind with base, material, ignorant thoughts, and impulses that you can't get rid of." Someone had purportedly "hired" by *brujería* (black magic) the services of low-grade, poorly developed, disincarnated spirits to make Maria *loca*.

This is the first level of possession (*obsesión* through *brujería*) diagnosed for Maria (discussed below). Note that the symptoms caused are the presenting complaints, and the explanation for it is the displaced, projective explanation that the client might also have given at that time. The Spiritist diagnosis of a recent *"trabajo de brujería"* appears to refer most often to an immediate situation in which there is some actual interpersonal tension. These spirits are considered to be the easiest to "lift." Also, in Maria's situation, adoption of this "explanation" provides her psychologically with the defense mechanism of "displacement" of her frustration and anger at husband and family (unacceptible) to others at her place of work (acceptable). It does not reinforce denial of her anger but encourages its expression at a "safe" object. Causality, however, is "projected."

Maria was then fumigated with the smoke from the cigar of the Congo to *despojarla* (relieve her) of some of the effects of the spirits, was told to say the "Prayer for Light for the Suffering Misguided Spirits," and to use a certain perfume which is repellent to the malevolent spirits, in order to "soften up" the *espíritus obsesores* and to return the next evening to the Spiritist *centro* to have her *causas* (molesting spirits) *trabajadas* (worked) or *levantadas* (lifted) in the *reunión*.

"*Causa*" means both "cause" in the general English sense and can refer to either "material" (natural) or "spiritual" (supernatural) causes; more specifically it refers to disembodied spirits that molest the living. One medium alone in a *consulta,* with the help of *guías* (spirit guides), can discover the *causas* of a client and can *limpiar* or *despojar* (clean) the person spiritually, but the working or lifting of the *causas* must optimally be done in a *reunión* where there are a number of mediums present so that one can "mount" the causa, another can "interrogate" it, and there will always be other mediums present to help the medium in trance in case the spirit is "too strong," "too rebellious," or otherwise destructive to the medium.

The First Reunion

The following evening at the *Centro* Maria appeared with her husband, two sisters, two brothers-in-law, and two nieces. This was my first direct contact with Maria. She was clearly in a very anxious, agitated, and probably depressed state. She sat tense, rigid, silent, and motionless except when she was disruptive. She was able to attend and respond appropriately when addressed directly, but was unable to attend to what was happening around her, or to retain any of the immediate events in her memory. I had made arrangements with her prior to the *reunión* to call her the following morning in connection with my research. She disrupted normal center ritual three times during the opening scriptures and prayers to ask me when I was going to call, exactly what time I would call her, and would I be sure to call again if she didn't answer, because "sometimes I feel nervous and I just have to get out of the house."

The usual *reunión* in a Spiritist *centro* consists of three distinct segments. The first is the "preparation of the atmosphere," or the "development of union of thoughts," during which Spiritist scriptures and prayers are read and all concentrate upon God and call silently upon their protecting spirits. The second is the "working of the *causas*," during which the spirit mediums as a group divine the "causes" or reasons why the people have come, and "mount," "reeducate," or "give light to" troublesome spirits that are discovered. The third segment is *"despojos"* or cleansing ceremonies in which everyone participates.

On this particular evening in Rosa's *centro* there were three fully developed mediums besides Rosa (1 woman and 2 men), three mediums in development (2 women, 1 man) and twenty-four members and visitors (10 women, 9 men, and 5 children), including the six adults and two children in Maria's party. Before the opening of the reunion, as is usual, there was a great deal of informal interaction among those present. The story of Maria's *ataque,* her subsequent referral to Bellevue, and the *consulta* was told and discussed. All present agreed that Maria did not have to go to the hospital, that her problems were spiritual.[6] The opening of the *reunión* proceeded as usual with one of the visitors ritually opening *The Scriptures According to Spiritism* (Allan Kardec) randomly to a passage that is expected to be particularly appropriate to the problems of that person or to the problems to be "worked" in the *centro* that evening and the reading of this scripture and a number of standard prayers (see *Colección de Oraciones Escogidas de Allan Kardec y Otros Autores* (Anonymous). The lights were then turned off and the president and each of the fully developed mediums *"pasó un protector"* ("passed a protector," i.e., went into trance with one of their guiding spirits). The spirit guides blessed the *centro* and the *reunión* and "prepared" the material bodies of the mediums to "work" the malignant spirits. The mediums in development each tried "to pass their protection." One succeeded in passing a *madama* (a *curandera* spirit) who could not yet speak through the medium. The other two only *"cogieron fluidos"* ("caught fluids"). *Fluidos* are the ectoplasm of the incarnated or disincarnated spirit and also the sensations a medium *feels* from the presence of a spirit. The *"fluidos"* of a "low grade spirit" are hot and often painful; those of an "enlightened protection" or good spirit are cool and fresh. Etically, these are states of possession experienced by mediums to be discussed below as fifth and sixth level possessions ("mounting protections" and "mounting the *causas* of others").

The mediums directed themselves to the problems of those present. The second stage of the *reunión* began.

The mediums first turned their attention to Maria. It is customary for the president of the table, if she knows the client from a previous *consulta* or from previous visits to the *centro,* to leave divining of the cause of a client to other mediums who do not know that client, thus giving *"comprobación"* (consensual validation) of what the client has already been told by the president-medium. In this case Rosa asked a male medium at the table to call upon his *"Indio de transporte"* (an Indian spirit with the "faculty of transport") and to work this woman. The faculty of "transport" is that which is needed for the spirit to go to the place where a *brujeria* has been left to retrieve it. The male medium demurred, saying that he had not completed his obligation to his protections for some months and could not "work" the *causa,* but he did give Maria an *"evidencia"* or vision. He saw a figure standing behind Maria. Rosa then asked her, in the form of an affirmative statement to be merely confirmed or denied, as in the *consulta:* "When you are in the street, you feel like someone is walking behind you? Maria answered: "I walk like a sleepwalker." Rosa continued: "When you are alone you feel like someone calls your name, and no one is there?" Maria answered: "I think I hear the telephone, and when I answer it no one is there." The male medium then began to describe more about what he saw in the figure behind Maria: it was half black and half white. It was a saint that

wanted to help her, but there was something that impeded it. He asked
her if she didn't have periods in which she felt alone and cried, and
others in which she felt happy. At this point the president interrupted
the medium to say: "*A ti te pasa lo mismo, verdad?*" (The same thing happens to you, right?). He confirmed this, and continued to Maria: "You
have to go into complete solitude, complete retirement for a period.
You must wear black with a little bit of white—a great sacrifice." (This
would be a fifth level possession for Maria, but the other mediums did
not pursue the interpretation made by this medium.)

The president and other mediums then turned their attention to
others present, including one of Maria's two sisters, Gloria, who had a
"*causa* in her stomach." [7]

About halfway through the *reunión*, the president's attention was
refocused on Maria. At this time Rosa said, "This spirit is not going to
pass tonight. It is too strong." Maria was told that she had to *despojarse
la casa* (do spiritual cleansings in the home), say the "Prayer of the
Necesitados" for seven days to "soften up the spirits," to pray, to put on
perfume every night, to put something at her door to keep the influences away, and return the following week to have the *causa levantada*
(spirit lifted).

The session continued with the "work" on behalf of others. At one
point Rosa asked: "Who on this side of the room has a pain in their
right side?" (She was supposedly feeling that pain herself from the
presence of a *causa* that came with someone sitting on that side of the
room.) Maria's husband, Carlos, stood holding his left side and said it
was he. Other attendees pointed out that that was not his right side, but
his left. Rosa then indicated to another woman: "It is you, true?" and
the lady confirmed it, but Rosa immediately switched her attention
back to Carlos as follows:

ROSA: Your food tastes bitter, is it true?
CARLOS: Yes.
ROSA: It repeats on you?
CARLOS: True.
ROSA: You feel distended and gaseous after eating?
CARLOS: That's right.
ROSA: Come to the table and put your hands over the bowl of holy
           water.

Carlos moved to the table. Then, with all the mediums' attention upon
him, Rosa continued:

ROSA: Do you believe in the *obra espiritual* [spiritual work]?
CARLOS: Yes.
ROSA: Have you gone to a doctor?
CARLOS: Yes.
ROSA: And they don't do anything for you?
CARLOS: (Demurs.)
ROSA: Ay, Diós mio! (Shudders.)

The medium then asked him in the same format but with a greater implication that there was a guiding spirit giving her the information, if he had pains in his gall bladder, kidneys, back, and head. To all he responded positively. Then she asked if he had clouding of vision, to which he also said yes.[8] The medium then told him that he needed glasses and that he must wear them daily, but also that he had a *causa espiritual* causing his defective vision. She then said: "You think that you are going to die?" Carlos nodded acquiescence.

Then one of the other fully developed mediums went into trance. Everyone recited the Lord's Prayer and Hail Mary to give the spirit strength to come into the medium. The spirit in the medium proceeded directly to *despojarse* (cleanse itself) over the fountain of water before it. The president reprimanded the spirit for not greeting the table and ordered it to give a greeting. The president rang the bell to give the spirit clarity. Finally the spirit spoke, saying, "They didn't want to let me even enter." The president continued to ring the bell. The spirit then spoke further: "I am going to give my greeting to the table and go. . . . Let the peace of God be here. . . . There are others behind me. . . . I wasn't supposed to do any of this . . . ," and the voice faded; the medium emerged from trance. Maria's husband sat down, knowing that he had a number of spiritual *causas,* none of which had been fully "worked" and that he would have to return to the *centro* to have each *levantada,* or lifted from him. The spirit that does not confess why he has been causing harm and repent will return and have to be worked again and again until he does repent. The implication of the behavior of this spirit for the believers present was that it was trying to *"engañar"* (deceive) by complying with what they expected of it while it was actually answering to someone else: "I wasn't supposed to do any of this." Notice that it is a fully developed medium and not Carlos himself who is "possessed" by the spirit that affects him. The nature of this "possession" for Carlos is ambiguous, but for the medium it is called *"montando o pasando la causa"* (mounting or passing a molesting spirit), or what we will consider below as a sixth level possession.

During the third stage of the *reunión*, and *despojos* (cleansings), Maria again received special attention. She had to be cleansed by three separate mediums. These cleansings followed diverse ritual patterns but the theory of all of them is that in bringing the *fluidos* (fluids, ectoplasm, vibrations) of the good spirit protectors of the mediums into contact with the *fluidos* of bad spirit *causas,* the bad *fluidos* are absorbed by the good. Sometimes the bad spirit itself is removed in this way without being "worked," but usually this only removes the lingering effects of the presence of the bad spirits. All that have been "in the presence of all of this dead" during the course of a *reunión* must be *despojado* before leaving the centro.

During the *despojos,* Maria was also told by a protecting spirit in the president that she was *"en desarrollo"* (in development). This is a very important communication, which means that Maria has mediumship faculties that she must develop. It is not sufficient for her to simply be relieved of the *causas* currently bothering her, because she is in a particularly vulnerable state in "a period of spiritual evolution" during which she will continue to be vulnerable until she develops her own abilities to communicate with her own spirit guides, thus being "protected" and able to help herself and others. A person in a period of spiritual development, or a medium in development, must continue to come to the center, must learn to work the spirits, and must work the spirits, or they will invariably fall ill and troubled again. This is the second level of possession diagnosed for Maria (to be *en desarrollo*). Notice that it refers to Maria's own state of being, and implies she must develop her abilities to achieve at will the fifth and sixth levels of possession (mediumship).

To summarize briefly what happened in this *reunion* from the observer's point of view: it seems that the two mediums in the beginning disagreed on what their protecting spirits were "giving them" about Maria. Rosa, by prior indications, had wanted to treat it as a *trabajo de brujería,* while the auxilliary male medium had gone directly to more fundamental personality issues specifically mood fluctuations resulting from a relationship with a saint that "wanted to help" but was impeded by something (a fifth level possession—a troubled relationship with a *proteccion*). This medium had previously admitted to not being in good relations with his own guides, and Rosa treated this *evidencia* as if it were a projection of his own problems to the client (A ti te pasa lo mismo, verdad?) in a way reminiscent of the analysis of countertransference in the supervision of a psychiatric resident. The two interpretations are not irreconcilable, and, as we will see, they are both used before the process is complete. For this evening, however, it was decided that whatever Maria's problem was, it was "too strong to work" [9] that evening. So Maria's "cure" was postponed, while *causas* were worked for one of Maria's sisters and for her husband. The sister was divined to have a consistent set of somatic complaints in the digestive system, and was diagnosed as having a *causa* in her stomach related to arguments and dissatisfaction in her marriage. Carlos was divined to have many somatic complaints, primarily in the digestive system, but also in his vision, and one clearly psychological symptom, fear of dying. This spirit did not repent and say why he was doing what he was doing, so it is a certainty that it will have to be worked again before it is "enlightened" and "lifted." there is no indication of where this spirit came from or why. It is a spirit with the husband, but it also represents a problem central to Maria's difficulties, one that Maria had previously denied— her husband's illness and his (and her) fears of his dying.

Despojando la Casa (Cleansing the Home)

The following day, Rosa went to Maria's home to *despojarla* (cleanse it). Again, I was not present, but cleansing the home usually consists of sweeping the house with a cluster of branches from special aromatic bushes, which have been dipped in a mixture of holy water and perfumes, particularly those dedicated to *paz en el hogar* (peace in the home), and sometimes ammonia and other effective cleansing agents. The house is thus swept from the innermost corner to the outside door. During the ritual cleansing, a pragmatic cleansing is also performed if necessary, and a great deal of informal, nonstylized discussion of the matters at hand takes place between the medium and the client. [10]

When not in trance or ritually invoking their spirit protectors the mediums are "humilde" (humble). They will say: "I am nobody; I have nothing—it is just what 'they' [referring to the spirit protectors] give me." Thus the mediums are able to go back and forth with the client between an egalitarian and an authoritarian role relationship. In the egalitarian role they are able to discuss, evaluate, and interpret to the client "what the spirits have said." But in trance the "enlightened" spirits "tell" the person what the person does not know. The wisdom of these "enlightened" spirits may be questioned by other mediums in the *reunión* and it may be decided that it is not a very wise spirit after all (*uno que engaña;* one that deceives or *una causa que intenta pasar como protector;* a low-grade spirit that tries to pass as a wise one), but this rarely happens with a "fully developed medium." Sometimes the mediums themselves remember what the spirits said ("conscious" or "semiconscious trance,") and sometimes they remember nothing ("unconscious trance"). In the latter case they may require the client to recall for them what the spirits said. This double style of communication is an essential feature of spiritist therapy. Rosa used this "cleansing of the home" much as the health and welfare agencies use "home visits"—to glean information about the client and family that is not easily elicited in the consulting room or in the ritual setting—and as an opportunity to interact with Maria in a pragmatic one-to-one earthly frame of reference.

Immediately after this home cleansing, Rosa left the city with Maria's sister, Gloria, to go to Cleveland, Ohio. Gloria was afraid to drive her own car so Rosa was to drive her, do cleansings in her home, and to "work" another spirit of Gloria that had been identified (probably an *esposo de existencia,* see third level possession below) and to "cure" some other people there, returning by air at the family's expense.

I visited Maria at her home the following day. The apartment was impeccably clean and neat. Maria joked that her son had removed the plastic covers from the furniture when he heard I was coming. With this, the boy, who appeared rather quiet and timid anyway, disappeared into the bedroom not to emerge again.

Maria appeared to be much improved but was in a forced, excessively good humor. She said that she was much better; that she had not slept for nine nights before she went to the *centro,* but the last two nights she had slept well; that because she didn't sleep she didn't eat and had lost ten pounds, but now she was also eating. She repeated her complaints, "I am nervous and I do not know why"; "I have a good huband and a good son—neither give me any problems—but I am nervous." She pointed out how good her son was: "He is putting on records now to make me feel happy." She talked a great deal about how she had always liked music, dancing, and parties, and what "a happy girl" she had always been until now. She said the "nervousness" had begun about three weeks before, and during this time she had had many "attacks" of "just nervousness," until the Friday at work when she had the first real *"ataque de nervios"* in her life. At this time she remembered her *ataque* and explained it this way: She began to feel pressure and constriction in her chest; she felt that she could not breathe, that she was going to be asphyxiated. She opened the buttons of her blouse and went to the window to open it to get some air, and others thought she was trying to throw herself out the window.

Again she became very angry, shook noticeably when she talked about the doctor at the clinic, and told me several times not to contact him because that "would make me nervous." She was, however, very willing to visit another doctor with me. She also became very angry and shook when she spoke of her father. She said: "He acts like a baby—and he is not as sick as I am!"

Maria gave me the impression during this and subsequent interviews that she depended more and made more demands upon her brother than upon her husband or other members of her family. It was her brother who came for her at the factory, who took her to the medical center, who drove her to the psychiatric consultant the following Monday, and whom she said she counted upon most. As I was administering the Cornell Medical Index (CMI) she asked me several times to wait until her brother got there, "so he can tell me how to answer." Her brother never came to the *centro*. Five years later, she gave as one of her reasons for attending Spiritist centers only sporadically: although "they have helped me a lot," "I have a brother that doesn't believe in that, so I can't go." She never mentioned her mother, her sisters, or her husband.

In discussing the possible causes of her *ataque*, Maria mentioned not sleeping and not eating; she thought it might be from malnutrition. And, she said, "It might be a 'work' too, I always think about that." She was apparently not totally convinced by the diagnosis given her by Rosa. Most of my probes in this direction, however, ended up with her questioning me about the extent of my beliefs in spiritism. She wanted to know what I wanted to hear before she would speak. (This characteristic showed up clearly in the five-year follow-up, in which, while I was out of the room brifly, she asked my research assistant how much I believed in Rosa, what she should say about that, and what she "had to say in order to get me to help her.")

The thrust of Maria's presentation of self throughout this interview was to show me how much improved she was and, therefore, how she did not need to go to the hospital. She simply denied all problems with the exception of a few somatic complaints and her vague "nervousness." Any causal factors that were elicited had to be inferred indirectly, more from what she didn't say than what she volunteered. She did not specifically give credit to the *Espiritista* for her improvement or deny it either. She had gotten better the same way she had gotten worse—inexplicably.

There was, however, no evidence that I could discern of thought disorder, delusions, or hallucinations; in short, no evidence of schizophrenia or acute psychosis, other than the elated mood and the massive denial. It was impossible to get any information from her about possible precipitating factors in the current episode, and it was very difficult to get any history. Although she had no chronic diseases and no specific acute organic disorder, with the exception of an intestinal parasite, she was currently in treatment and had been seen during the preceding month in five separate medical facilities for various vague somatic complaints.

The Psychiatric Consultation

The following Monday, ten days after the *ataque,* Maria's brother drove Maria and me to the hospital for a psychiatric evaluation I had arranged. En route the brother briefly, and only on probe, gave me his version of what had happened. He thought that some time before a neighbor had done a work against his sister—she had found *porquería* at her door—and this had caused her nervousness. He had no idea of what might have caused the *ataque* that Friday afternoon. He was totally uncommunicative about himself.

Maria was interviewed by the psychiatrist (who had been given all the background information that I had) in my presence. Maria's initial statement of her problem was: "I am nervous and I don't know why. I haven't any problems. I have a good husband and a good son, who never give me any trouble." "I used to be such a happy girl." She described herself as a meticulous worker and homemaker who is forever on the go, starting several tasks and flitting from one to the other until all are done. She described how she always had friends in the house, how she liked music and dancing and missed her parties.

At first, she denied any memory of the *ataque* and deferred to me to describe it to the doctor. When I referred the question back to her, she described it as she had done for me the day before. In the beginning she denied any similar prior episodes, but as the interview progressed she admitted to several similar periods of "nervousness," all milder, for which she also had no explanation. The family and psychiatric history elicited was essentially the same as that I have presented above. The connection between her husband's illnesses and Maria's nervousness emerged, but she made no connection between her husband's accidents and illnesses and her own anxiety. She did speak somewhat bitterly about how his income was unreliable and how she had to work.

She admitted to the psychiatric consultant that her decision to have only one child had been quite deliberate, explaining that it takes a lot of money to bring up children properly. She had used various birth-control measures throughout their marriage, although her husband would like to have another child. She concealed the fact that her one child was not the son of her current husband.

At the conclusion of the interview, the psychiatrist reassured Maria that she was much better and that she also saw no need for her to be hospitalized. Afterward Maria said that the doctor was "very, very, very nice" and that "she examines differently from other doctors." Maria's referral for psychiatric hospitalization had now been "undone" medically as well as spiritually. My purposes for Maria had been served and her interest, although not her willingness, to participate in my research fell off immediately.

The psychiatric opinion given reads in part as follows:

Mental Status:

Mrs. M. is a short, slight, attractive Puerto Rican woman of 39 years; as neat as a pin, casually dressed except for black lace stockings. She is friendly, polite, talked spontaneously and profusely. She smiles and gesticulates a great deal, mood is moderately elated. Her answers are relevant, coherent, at times circumstantial. Delusions, hallucinations were not elicited. Oriented in all spheres, memory intact, judgment fair to good, insight questionable.

We don't have enough material to arrive at a clear-cut psychiatric diagnosis, particularly as cultural factors complicate the picture. There is no doubt that Mrs. M. presents as a hypomanic: hyperactive in every aspect of her life and behavior. She used the hyperactivity to cope with her great chronic anxiety. She also uses massive denial of whatever problems are causing her anxiety, e.g., mother's failure to provide nurturing, husband's inadequate performance as a provider for the family.

She is very suspicious of all people all the time in spite of her overtly pleasant, friendly and very social behavior.

When her defense mechanisms prove to be inadequate to control her underlying anxiety, anger and depression, she resorts to projection and hallucinations, i.e., suffers an acute psychotic break.

DIAGNOSTIC IMPRESSION: Borderline Schizophrenic; hypomanic, recovering from acute psychotic episode.

In discussion afterward the examining psychiatrist talked with me at length about the great difficulties of treating a patient like Maria, who utilizes denial as her primary defense, with traditional techniques of psychotherapy. She told me that if Maria had come to this clinic as a patient seeking treatment, she would have medicated her with Librium and left the door open for her to return whenever she felt the need, but that she would not have attempted psychotherapy with Maria. She said that "no one would refer this lady for psychotherapy" for the following reasons: (1) The existing bias that low-income groups are not disposed to insight therapy; (2) She probably would not go, or would not return, because of her primary defense of denial. (She is not likely to follow through any prolonged treatment because the threat of becoming attached to anybody is too great. She would probably come for about three sessions, and that would be it until the next crisis.) (3) "To be therapeutically effective, we would have to unleash Maria's anger at her husband—we would not try to uncover the basic conflict—and Maria would probably not let that happen, or if she did, she would decompensate and would not come back to be patched up again." If Maria had arrived at the clinic in her acute state she might have been admitted to the hospital and discharged within a few days. Had she returned for treatment to the innovative clinic where she was evaluated, the doctor said, "I might have tried to bring her husband in to get a clearer picture of him and what she has to cope with. She would probably resist it and, if she did, I would let it go, unless she had another acute attack, when I would insist upon it."

The Second Reunion

The following Tuesday evening Maria came to the *centro* accompanied by her husband, her son, her sister, Paz, Paz's husband, and their two children. There were only a small number of people (19) in the *centro* that evening, and immediately after the scriptures and prayers the mediums' attentions were directed to Maria and her husband. There was some discussion among them as to whether this spirit would come tonight. The medium who had given Maria the *evidencia* the week before was not present this evening. Instead there were, besides the president, two other fully developed mediums and one medium in development working at the table.

Rosa first asked Maria if she had sometimes dreamed that she was flying through the air. Maria confirmed that she had. Rosa then asked her if she had cold sweats and hot flashes in her body sometimes. Maria also confirmed this. Rosa then prescribed that she cleanse herself with certain plants—three flowers, holy water, flower water, and the perfume that Rosa had given her before—for three consecutive days.

Soon Esmeralda, one of the mediums, said to Maria: "I don't know why, but I see in you thoughts of this place and thoughts of another place outside of this country." The mediums discussed this *"evidencia"* and it was decided that there were two "works" against Maria, one done by someone in this country—the work she had found at her door—and another by someone far away. One was sent to break up her home and both were "working her mind", or trying to make her go crazy. The one from far away was the stronger. The persons responsible for these works were not identified. Then Rosa, in a trance with a protecting spirit, addressed herself to Maria, saying, in part: "You sometimes want to break up your home and just go and keep on going. You feel hateful toward [indicating Maria's husband]. He repulses you and he doesn't do anything for you [sexually]. You don't feel anything with him. Sometimes you get livid [*te dan rabietas*] with him." Maria volunteered that sometimes she has a desire to chop his head open with a meat cleaver. Rosa continued: "This spirit wants to see you alone without him and without anyone. You have never been happy with any man, isn't it true?" Maria assented. "Sometimes it doesn't even matter to you that you have a child, true?" Maria confirmed.

Then Rosa, still in trance, began to laugh and sing, saying, "It comes singing such a pretty song." The song was largely unintelligible, but the attitude assumed was one of frivolous unconcern and merriment, a burlesque of the hyperactivity, denial and fun-loving orientation Maria had exhibited with me the week before, with the psychiatrist the day before, and probably with Rosa at the time of the *despojo de la casa*. Rosa then emerged from trance.

The third medium, Laura, then said: "I want to run out of here." Rosa told her not to be afraid of the spirits. "I am not afraid of any spirit." Then Laura went into trance with this *causa* of Maria. The *causa* said: "Why do you bring me here. I don't want to come here!" Then to Maria directly, "Let's get out of here. You don't belong here." The medium had risen in her chair and was moving toward the door. Rosa reprimanded the spirit: "Here, you can't do whatever you want to do," and demanded that it seat the medium again. The spirit said: "She must come with me." The whole group said the Lord's prayer, and Rosa demanded that the spirit give a greeting to the table. The recalcitrant spirit did not, and the whole group said the "Prayer for the Poor Unhappy Beings." The spirit in Laura began to tremble and, finally, putting her hands over the bowl of holy water, said: "Let the peace of God be here." The group answered, "Now and forever." Rosa began then to instruct the now repentant spirit: "You must take note that you are a spirit and until today you have been misguided. You wanted to put her into an asylum, you wanted to kill her." The spirit confessed "They put . . . in the door. . . ." Rosa interrupted the spirit, telling it that this couple forgave it and to make a medium of transport to go there and see what there was in the door. After a silence, indicating the time it took the spirit to go and return, Laura started tapping her hands over the bowl of water, saying: "Here I bring what was in the door." Rosa demanded of the spirit: "Listen whose is this doll?" There was no answer. Then Rosa directed herself again to Maria: "You sometimes have pulsating in your abdomen. Sometimes you have pains in your waist and hips. And in your kidneys. Clean your legs, your knees and your ankles!" The *causa* in Laura then said: "Now I am going to leave, for the sake of my own spirit, because I was in darkness. I knew not what I was doing." Rosa reiterated that the *causa* had to realize that it was a spirit, and that it was meant for better things, that it has a mission. The *causa* then retired from the body of Laura saying, "peace and justice," and one of Laura's protecting spirits entered and made passes over Maria to cleanse her of all that the spirit had left on her.

Shortly thereafter Rosa went into trance with the second *causa* of Maria. It arrived saying: "Cowardly traitor! My companion has abandoned me." This was a very "strong" spirit, and it took a great deal of "interrogation" before it repented. It first gloried in the fact that it had her sick and that it was going to get her into an asylum. It rejected the "light" it was offered and blasphemed the crucifix put before it and denied belief in anything, including God himself. It also said that it wasn't alone because there was still one more besides it. Finally this spirit also repented, and began to confess the ills it had caused Maria and her husband. It addressed itself primarily to Maria's husband telling him, "as much damage as I caused her, I also caused you." It took responsibility for having caused him stomach problems, fears of death, desires for death, headaches in the frontal and occipital lobes, pains in the kidneys, clouded vision, and turning of the right ankle. The spirit begged their pardon, they each forgave it, and it retired in the same manner as the previous *causa,* having deposited all the bad in the bowl of water. A protecting spirit of the medium took it off to a "spiritual school" and another entered the medium to continue the cleansing process. (When a causa has been with a person as long as this one had been with them the effects (*fluidos*) of this spirit have "penetrated deeply" and it takes time to clean away these effects after the spirit itself is gone).

Maria and her husband were also given extra special attention during the evening's general *"despojos."* Maria was made to walk up and down upon the prone body of Laura in trance with the Guardian of the Cemeteries.

During this final period Rosa gave Maria a *receta* (prescription) for a bath, which I had never heard before and have heard only once since. She was told to bathe herself at midnight this evening and for two subsequent evenings with chilled water from the refrigerator, to be thrown on her suddenly by her husband. Rosa also told her to put a *collar* (necklace) of *Obatalá* (one of the Seven Powers in *Santería*) on her son to prevent an accident in which she (Rosa) was seeing him.[11]

To recapitulate, this evening Maria had been worked for two *causas de brujería* (first level possession below). One, the more immediate in time and space, (a recent *brujería*) claimed responsibility for her somatic complaints, her *ataque,* and her anger, hatred, revulsion, and frigidity with her husband. At the same time this spirit pointed out that she had never been happy with any man (reference to a third or fourth level possession, to be clarified below). The second *causa*, from some unnamed source more distant in time and space (an old *brujería*) also claimed responsibility for her anger, negativism, blasphemy and, additionally, all the harm it had caused her husband. They were both made to explicitly forgive this spirit. Maria was left to ruminate, if she would, on the possible source of this spirit. Both spirits enacted Maria's reluctance to come to the *centro* to be "enlightened" (resistance to insight or lack of motivation for treatment?). The first mimicked and mirrored her "pretty song" (denial?), and not only succeeded in securing an admission of her anger at her husband but also a spontaneous admission of homicidal fantasies. Note that these spirits have gone beyond the "presenting complaints" in pointing out other feelings and behavior patterns of which Maria may or may not have been aware. They are also beginning to point out repetitious patterns of behavior and feelings; for example, she "has never been happy with any man." The mediums also succeeded in unleashing Maria's anger at her husband—the sine qua non for an effective therapy according to the psychiatrist who evaluated her. The psychiatrist had also believed that this would be impossible.

The Third Reunion

The third week Maria and her husband appeared at the *centro* with the same group of relatives as the week before, plus another couple who were neighbors and friends. This evening Rosa was the only fully developed medium (capable of manifesting the *causas* of others—sixth level possession) working at the table. Although there were mediums in development who could interrogate the spirits once they were manifested, this limited the possibilities for the psychodramatic "working of the spirits."

This evening Maria and Carlos were not the central or first focus of attention. Instead Maria's eight-year-old niece (Noni), daughter of Paz, was the first called to the table by a spirit speaking through Rosa calling for "my daughter." This child was "nervous" and "overactive", according to the "spirits" and the parents in previous sessions. She was said to be "in development" and to be destined to work both the spirits and the saints. The spirit in Rosa explained that she had been Noni's mother by the same father in a previous incarnation (a third level possession), and that she was concerned about her daughter and wanted them to take better care of her. The spirit chastized the actual mother for not paying attention to things as she should, for being forgetful. Paz admitted it. The spirit mother then pledged herself to be a helpful and not a harmful presence. Relating to Noni, the spirit asked, "Do you see me in your dreams?" The implication in spiritist thought is that this spirit is now a "protection" and "guide" for Noni that will be there to help her when she needs help and will help her to help others when she develops her spiritual faculties (fifth level possession).

Then a spirit in Rosa called Carlos forward, saying: "You often have horrible headaches, do you not? You wake up often every night, do you not? You often feel that your mind becomes blank, true?" He responded "Yes" to each of the spirit's questions. Then Rosa's visage began to change and her body jerked forward and backward slowly, indicating that another spirit (the *causa*) was entering the medium. She began touching his hands and laughing in a vulgar and sardonic way saying, "What do you bring me over here for?" An auxiliary medium began the interrogation process of confronting the spirit with God and the fact that he is only a spirit and for his own spiritual development he must stop inflicting harm upon this man. In the process the spirit said, among other things: "I want to murder you. I want to see you dead. I hate you. You have to go to die in a hospital. You had a very serious operation, did you not? And you will have another one. Your wife is hiding that from you, does she not?" There was a long silence after this revelation, which the spirit finally broke by saying, "Speak. If you do not talk I will go away." With that, Maria got up and moved to the table beside her husband. The spirit began to repent: "I have been very mean to you. I want to ask my Guardian Angel for help. I want him to get my mind out of darkness. Forgive me." Maria and her husband expressed forgiveness. Rosa emerged from trance with the bad spirit and passed into trance with a protecting spirit who said to them "You both have to give your full cooperation. Consult the doctor who treated you the first time. The bad spirit is not here any longer. Put a small bucket filled up with water and a veil on top of it underneath your bed. You will dream." The spirit then cleansed them both with holy water and perfume.

The *reunión* continued, focusing consecutively on others present, and toward the end of the evening Rosa's attention came back to Maria: "Do you see? You no longer have headaches. *Despójate!* (Cleanse yourself!) Pray the Prayer to the Guardian Angels. Next week you will sit with those *"en desarrollo"* (in development) at the table. But you will have to wear a white dress."

Maria protested "But I don't have a white dress." Rosa responded:
"That is a small question. You can get a wash-and-wear dress for

three dollars." Then, changing the subject, "How is your son? Pray The Prayer of the Children Blessed by their Parents and put some holy water in his room."

The spirit coming with Maria's husband from an unknown source and treated this evening sounds like the superego of a depressed man (cf. Lubchansky, et al., 1970). This spirit, essentially his, also affects Maria, as the spirit that was essentially hers worked the week before affected him. Maria spontaneously joined her husband at the table when this spirit accused her of deceiving him about the gravity of his illness.

The Fourth, Fifth, and Sixth Reunions

The following weekend Rosa took Maria with her to her *finca* (farm) in New Jersey for a "little rest," as she had been planning to do since much earlier in the episode. It is not clear whether these plans had been made while Maria was most upset and only deferred because of Rosa's trip to Ohio and other things that intervened, or if Rosa had deliberately waited for Maria's acute episode to be relieved. By this time Maria had recovered fully by observation and she reported that she felt much, much better, but she still had her "days" of not feeling so well. Rosa's attitude was that she was fully "cured" and her role on that day of "rest" was to help Rosa with the chores of the *finca*, particularly helping her gather the plants which Rosa would use later for cleansing others at the *centro* and for preparing herb baths. They had a long confidential talk about Maria's problems with her husband, which both Maria and Rosa remember and refer to five years later. I have no details of this conversation, except that Rosa learned that Maria and her husband had sexual relations "maybe once in a year." I know from long experience with Rosa's involving herself in my own private life and observations of her with clients that she avoids nothing. She definitely works frankly with individuals around their sexual problems of the most intimate nature, including doing works specifically to cure impotence or frigidity, works to attract the opposite sex, homosexuality, overattachments bordering on incest between parents and children, and other problems. She also works with people around their aggressive impulses, for example their desires for "vengeance," "lack of control," and "faults of character." But Rosa tells me, "those are personal things of the person that you cannot publish." Reassurances of confidentiality and anonymity have not influenced her to violate her code of confidentiality. She does discuss these matters with me when I am involved in the treatment process and have more than a research need to know as, for example, when I have taken psychiatric patients to her for consultation. In this case I did not hear, and Rosa did not tell me, exactly what transpired in their conversations on this trip, which may have been the psychotherapeutic highpoint of Maria's spiritist therapy—perhaps the "working through" of the "insights" provided by the spirits.

The following Tuesday, Maria and her husband came to the *centro*. Maria was dressed in white as instructed, and she sat at the table to begin the process of "developing her spiritual faculties." This process involves possession at the fifth and sixth levels that we have seen only in the developing and fully-developed mediums in the *centro*, and which will be clarified below. During this evening Maria was not addressed as a sufferer by any medium, and she took no part in the working of others except in the ritual recitation of prayers and cleansings in which all present participate. At the conclusion of the *reunión*, Rosa was selling baths that she had prepared from the herbs collected the Sunday before by Maria and herself.[12] Maria purchased one for herself and one for her son.

The following week, or fifth week after the *ataque*, Maria came to the *centro* accompanied by a friend (Isabel) who lives in the same building. They both sat at the table. Although Isabel claimed to have never attended a *centro* previously, Rosa identified her as a medium and had her sit at the table. This was one of those evenings when there are no new attendees with acute problems and Rosa devotes more time to developing the faculties of the mediums than to working the *"causas"* of sufferers. There were four partially developed mediums at the table in addition to Maria and Isabel and, again, no fully developed mediums other than Rosa. As we have seen, it is customary for each of the mediums at the table at the conclusion of the scriptures and prayer reading to manifest their principal protecting spirit to prepare the medium for working the *causas*. This evening there was a partially developed medium who was having difficulty passing his protection because he had a *causa* getting in the way, and two who had "retired" from the "work." A medium who is supposed to work the spirits and does not, it is believed, may be punished by *causas de prueba* (spirits that come with them throughout this incarnation to put "tests" on the person for their spiritual development), or the protecting spirits, feeling neglected or resentful, may simply turn their backs on the person and leave him vulnerable to any bad influence that may come along. Rosa helped all of these mediums to manifest their "protections," working two *causas* in the process. As usual, she encouraged everyone present to speak up about whatever they might "see" or "hear" about someone. She also gave Maria her first instructions in trancing: "Put perfumed alcohol on your hands and put them over the table. You must put your hands on the table. And concentrate upon God and call your protection." Maria put the perfumed alcohol on her head, neck, and hands, as she had seen other mediums do, and put her hands on the table. Maria made no further movements toward assuming the medium role and Rosa did not insist that she do so.

Before this session began, I had asked Maria how she was feeling and she had responded that she had been sick again on Saturday and Sunday and, in the same breath and sentence said, "My father is sick." When Rosa mounted a protecting spirit that could be questioned by anyone present, Maria asked the spirit about her sickness. The spirit answered: "I have told you already, you have to go to a doctor. What you have now is material. It is not spiritual."

During the general *despojos*, Maria was cleansed, but was not encouraged to pass a protection as were the other developing mediums present. During this period Isabel went unexpectedly into a mute trance which was completely aberrant in terms of the usual patterns of trancing in the *centros* of the South Bronx. She sat rigidly, eyes open but glazed, staring fixedly into space. Her only movement was prescribing circles in the air with one hand. This state alarmed everyone present. The mediums asked the spirit what it wanted, and after some time it succeeded in delivering a message (a prescription for someone) in sign language and retired from the medium to everyone's great relief. I drove Maria and her friend home and learned that Isabel had just recently arrived from Cuba, where she had probably learned other patterns of trancing. She claimed total amnesia during the trance state and was frightened about the "something" that had happened to her.[13] Above all, she was concerned that Maria not tell anyone they knew that this had happened. Neither wanted to talk about it. Maria's confidential reaction expressed to me was that "she is crazy," and "I don't know her very well." Later Rosa also confided to me that she did not understand what had been going on with Isabel.

Maria purchased another bath for her son at the end of this session. Rosa asked her how he was, and Maria said that the baths had done him a lot of good—"he stays in more now," and he "takes care of me very nicely."

The next week Maria attended the reunion, again with her husband, for the sixth and last time. Maria sat near but not at the table. Neither of them were worked, nor was Maria encouraged and coached in passing spirits.

Follow-up

Three weeks later, when Maria had not returned to the center, I attempted to call her and discovered that her phone had been disconnected. I went to her house and, finding no one home, inquired among neighbors who said that the family had "gone to Puerto Rico." There was no indication that they intended to return. I had fantasies of a second honeymoon inspired by midnight iced baths, or at least a new life begun on the basis of new understanding and greater sharing of both their problems as revealed by the spirits.

Follow-up five years later, however, indicated that any improvement in Maria's coping or in her relationship with her husband that might have been brought about by the *Espiritista* was, at best, only temporary.

Maria was still living in the building where she had lived for sixteen years. She avoided talking with me on my first two visits. Then, much to my surprise, I received a message in my office that she had called, that she was "very nervous" and that she thought that I may have "been sent by providence to help her."

I went to visit her. Her apartment was not as spotless and orderly as it had been earlier. The bar was empty and pushed against the wall. Carlos had died three years before, leaving his property in Puerto Rico and his savings account in a trust for his sister and her children. Maria, although his legal wife, had been left with nothing. Apparently, for technical reasons, she was not entitled to any death benefits from a pension plan or other insurance. She was living on disability for which she had been certified by a private psychiatrist whom she had seen twice. According to Maria he then told her that he did not want to treat her, that there was nothing wrong with her, and that she should go to work.

Immediately upon my arrival Maria had begun to impress upon me that she was "unable to work because she could not go out of the house or travel on the subway alone." She would get "too nervous." She "had to have a friend accompany her." Then she would get to the job and "get nervous, not be able to breathe, feel pressure in her chest, think she was going to be asphyxiated, and would be able to stay only one or two days." She insisted that she did want to go to work but could not because of her illness, her *"nervios."* As the interview progressed it became increasingly clear and, finally, explicit that what she wanted from me was help to find a part-time job "in entertaining work," which she would not have to report, so she would not lose her disability check and could go back to school for her high school equivalancy diploma. She had already started in this program.

Maria had continued to *"padecer de los nervios,"* but she had not had another *ataque* or another episode of the same severity. She had become ill again when her husband entered the hospital for the last time and had not returned to work since. She was collecting $127 a month in disability payments and at the same time had developed a small business in her home selling pantyhose, sweaters, and other garments in the neighborhood. Far from being unable to leave the house alone, she was in fact selling merchandise on credit and making her own collection calls in a neighborhood where many fear to leave their homes, to say nothing of entering other buildings. She was aggressively pursuing restitution of her husband's estate through the courts in both Puerto Rico and New York. She claimed to have an active sex life, discreet but gratifying. Male underwear drying in the bathroom lends credence to her claims. She planned to marry again, but not until her case in court had been settled. She believed, probably rightly, that she would prejudice her rights if she changed her name prior to that settlement. She says she is better now in general; she "eats well, is more tranquil," she "doesn't have headaches or fainting spells, and sleeps well, "except I am tired when I wake up, and why would that be?" "But when I am with people, I am fine. It is when I am alone that I feel badly, and I don't think about anything." She also knows: "Physically I don't have anything wrong, nothing, nothing, nothing. They have checked my heart, my lungs . . . (she named every organ system) and they don't find anything wrong." She has visited many, many doctors, and everywhere she goes they tell her there is nothing wrong. But she also says, "My disease is so very, very, very rare that I can't explain it."

She is very angry with doctors "who deceive me with medicines that don't do anything for me" (Librium, Equanil, Valium) and "don't tell me the truth." She says: "It is natural if one doesn't feel well and goes to a doctor, and the doctor says there is nothing wrong, or gives you medicine and there is nothing wrong. It is natural to think that you have something that he doesn't want to tell you." She quotes a doctor as saying, "What do you want me to do: tell you you have cancer or something terrible like that when you don't have it?" She insists: "My nerves have to come from somewhere, whether it is from loneliness, from lack of a companion, from malnutrition, from something I went through in childhood . . . they have to come from something, and what I want is for them to tell me the truth."

She said that Rosa and the many other *Espiritistas* she had seen in the interim had "helped her a lot" but she doesn't go consistently because "it is far away," "I can't go alone," and "my friend goes once and then doesn't go for a while," and "my brother doesn't believe in that."

She thinks of the episode documented as one in which she was "passing through the problems that my husband had." She does not retain the witchcraft explanation of this episode.

Talking again of marriage toward the end of the interview, Maria said: "For now, I want another happiness: I want to work, get completely well and in good health, get myself a little house—I am learning to drive . . . and then get married when I can find a good, reliable man. I don't want to just take a man to have a man, because this you can always find, and I don't want to marry one who then mistreats me and I have more troubles." Toward the end of this interview she said: "The most that I have is that, I am, like *un señor* (referring to an *Espiritista*) told me, when I want something and I can't do it, it makes me angry (*me da rabia*); because, for example, I wanted to learn to drive (she gave an example of how she got exasperated with her errors in trying to learn to drive), then I feel badly, and when I feel badly, I get nervous."

If we take this summary of "the most of it" as Maria herself sees it, her "nerves" come from anger, frequently generated by frustration of her upwardly mobile strivings. This is not to suggest that I also think this is "the most of it" for her. Maria's most salient characteristics as I see them are her very transparent manipulativeness and the apparently shallow and superficial quality of all her interpersonal relationships. Yet I do want to indicate that she has healthier ways of presenting herself than would be expected in a patient who presents herself initially as primarily phobic, hypochondriacal, or hysterical. On closer examination she appears to be a relatively independent, socially striving woman in a culture that does not reward aggressive self-assertiveness in women, and does provide a number of culturally institutionalized hysterical mechanisms through which valued ends might be achieved.

THE MEANING OF POSSESSION IN THIS CONTEXT

We have noted six distinct states of the sufferers and the healers in the process of treatment of Maria and those around her that fall into the anthropological category of "possession" beliefs and behaviors. These are not the only types of possession recognized by the spiritists, but they are the most frequent, and most of the spiritist interpretations of mental status and altered states of consciousness are variations within one or another of these six general types. As stated earlier, my use of the expression "levels of possession" is arbitrary and does not follow any conventional scheme of levels of analysis. These "levels" are, how-

ever, related on the one hand to the progression of the spiritists' attention to the *ser* (being or spirit) of a client in the processes of *trabajando
las causas* (working the molesting spirits) and *desarrollo* (the unrolling of
mediumship faculties) and, on the other, to levels of psychological significance in psychoanalytically oriented psychotherapy. I do not wish to
suggest that these states are directly equatable from one system to another. The terms in Spiritism, as in psychodynamic theory, take their
meanings from the total complex of concepts that make up one or the
other of these systems of thought. Thus no term from either system
can be directly equated with a term from the other. Nonetheless there
are significant similarities as well as differences in the ways that spiritists and psychodynamically oriented psychotherapists conceptualize,
diagnose, and treat "spiritual" or "mental" states which a third-party
observer can recognize as similar on the basis of empirically observable
behaviors and verbalizations that invoke these concepts.

In order to draw these parallels, I need three languages: one, the
emic concepts of the *Espiritistas;* two, the emic concepts of the psychotherapist, and, three, a set of etic concepts with which to describe the
phenomena as objectively as possible. For the first language I will use
the Spanish terms of the *Espiritistas,* most of which have been defined
or at least glossed in English above. Where I use these concepts in English translation I will enclose them in double quote marks (". . ."). For
the second language I will use the psychological and psychiatric terms
in common use in the two clinics where I did my research, rather than
any single comprehensive statement of the theory and practice of psychoanalytically oriented psychotherapy. These terms will appear enclosed in single quote marks ('. . .'). For the etic terms I will use anthropological concepts insofar as these have been developed, ordinary
English, and arbitrary symbols.

As background for the analysis of the six states of possession involved in the spiritist treatment of Maria, Table 1 presents a schema-
tized comparison of the self and world view of *Espiritismo* and of psychodynamic theory. Comparison of these models of self and world
reveals that there are certain basic similarities in the conceptualizations
of the psyche and its relationships to external reality, but there are also
essential differences. These similarities and differences are the following:

1. The division of the experience of reality into "invisible," "visible
and invisible," and "visible" on the one hand, and 'unconscious,' 'preconscious,' and 'conscious' on the other. In both systems of thought
there are areas of experience and motivation, the sources of which are

unknown to the one experiencing them. These areas of experience are better known to some ("developed mediums" on the one hand, and the 'insightful' or 'the fully analyzed' on the other). They can become better known, in either system to those who are "in development" on the one hand, or those who are 'appropriate for psychoanalytically oriented psychotherapy,' on the other, if they will go through a long-term process called *"desarrollando facultades"* (developing, literally unrolling, one's faculties) in the spiritist system or 'psychoanalysis' or 'insight psychotherapy' in the psychodynamic system.

2.   The division of the self into three basic divisions. Two of these (A and C in Table 1) are largely in the realm of the unknown ("invisible" or 'unconscious') and are in perpetual opposition. The third (B in Table 1) is known ("visible" or 'conscious') and is the integrator. In *Espiritismo* there are the *protecciones* (wise, helping, but also punishing spirits), the *causas* (ignorant molesting spirits), and the *propio ser* (one's own spirit in whatever state of ignorance or wisdom it has achieved across successive incarnations). The *propio ser* is the seat of one's individuality and one's *carácter* (character). In psychodynamic theory these three 'structures' are the 'superego,' the 'id,' and the 'ego.'

3.   There are fundamental similarities in the functions attributed to the paired concepts of positions A, B, and C, as indicated in Table 1. A (the "protections" and the 'superego') is the repository of social and moral rules. A embodies the functions of guidance and psychological punishment or guilt in both systems. B (the *propio ser* and the 'ego') has the functions of integrating and managing the conflicting directions of A and C. In the spiritist system, B is the repository of one's intellectual functions, one's "individuality," one's "character," and one's *"facultades"* ("faculties"). *Facultades* are abilities that one may or may not have to communicate with the spirits, such as the ability to see or hear the spirits, to enter trance, to have inspiration, to be an observer, to write, and so on. In the psychodynamic system, B is also the repository of one's 'intellectual functions,' one's 'personality,' although not one's 'character,' and the so-called 'ego-functions.' The *propio ser*, or ego, is often characterized as either "strong" or "weak" in both systems.

4.   There are equally fundamental differences in the two conceptualizations of self and world represented in Table 1. The most all-pervasive and significant is to be found in the physical location attributed to these concepts. A and C in the spiritist system of thought (the *protecciones* and the *causas*) are usually located outside the skin and are free floating. In the psychodynamic self and world view, A and C (the 'superego' and 'id') are located inside the skin of the individual. Psychodynamic theory assumes the location of these structures within the or-

Table 1
Self and World View

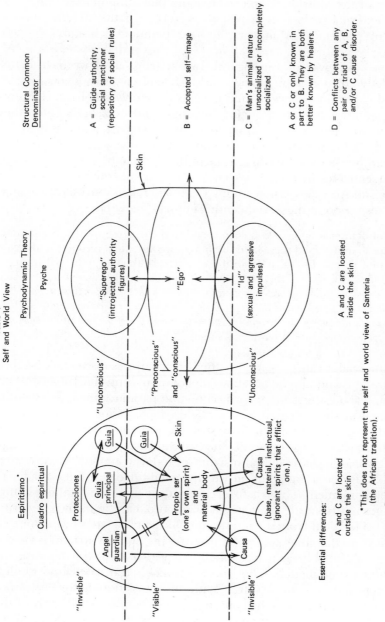

Espiritismo*

Cuadro espiritual

"Invisible"

"Visible"

"Invisible"

Guia
Guia
Guia principal
Protecciones
Angel guardian

Propio ser
(one's own spirit) and
material body

Skin

Causa
(base, material, instinctual,
ignorant spirits that afflict
one.)

Causa

Psychodynamic Theory

Psyche

"Unconscious"

"Preconscious"
and "conscious"

"Unconscious"

Skin

"Superego"
(introjected authority
figures)

"Ego"

"Id"
(sexual and aggressive
impulses)

Structural Common
Denominator

A = Guide authority,
social sanctioner
(repository of social rules)

B = Accepted self–image

C = Man's animal nature
unsocialized or incompletely
socialized

A or C or only known in
part to B. They are both
better known by healers.

D = Conflicts between any
pair or triad of A, B,
and/or C cause disorder.

Essential differences:

A and C are located
outside the skin

*This does not represent the self and world view of Santeria
(the African tradition).

————— Broken line indicates that the dividing point is variable.

A and C are located
inside the skin

ganism of the individual, and to attribute them to other individuals or other external realities is at best to make use of the 'defense mechanism' of 'projection' or, at worst, to have 'paranoid delusions.'

In my own way of viewing the two systems, until we have better knowledge of the biophysiology and biochemistry of consciousness, A, B, and C are only concepts that have as their only empirical referents their manifestation in thoughts, feelings, and behavior. Thus, they have no location in space, either internal or external, and this is a matter of faith in both theoretical systems.

Freud himself saw this difference in the location of 'psychic forces' as the essential difference between psychoanalytic theory and earlier theories of spirit possession. In his 1923 paper, "A Neurosis of Demoniacal Possession in the Seventeenth Century," he wrote:

Cases of demoniacal possession correspond to the neuroses of the present day; in order to understand these latter we have once more had recourse to the conception of psychic forces. What in those days were thought to be evil spirits to us are base evil wishes, the derivatives of impulses which have been rejected and repressed. *In one respect only do we not subscribe to the explanation of these phenomena current in mediaeval times; we have abandoned the projection of them into the outer world, attributing their origin instead to the inner life of the patient in whom they manifest themselves.* (p. 92) (emphasis mine)

If the reader can suspend, for the balance of this discussion, his own assumptions and judgments about the location of psychic forces and his thinking about the issues of projection and paranoia, the following discussion will show that what is considered possession by some corresponds not only to the "neuroses of the present day" as asserted by Freud, but also to some of the psychotherapeutic processes, ego strengths, and 'psychological insights' of today.

There is one more point on which I would like to ask the reader to suspend judgment. This is a difference in the two systems of thought that emerges not from the comparison of the two, each in its own integrity, as in Table 1, but from the intersection of the two systems when one element from the other system (in this case the Spiritist system) is viewed as it would appear as a part of the viewer's system (in this case the psychodynamic model). The word *"espíritu"* is translated into English language and thought as 'spirit.' With this translation, however, come a number of adhesions to the concept that are not necessarily part of the concept in their native language system. Thus 'spirit' in modern Western medical science denotes a belief of "primitive' people in 'supernatural beings' that are anthropomorphized. The usual Western clinician would not doubt the 'concrete' nature of this belief in 'spirits,' and he would probably be right in the case of Angloamerican patients that presented beliefs in 'spirits.' In the Puerto Rican spiritist system, however, the belief in spirits may be no more and no less 'concrete' than the beliefs in 'ego,' 'superego,' and 'id' among modern Western psychotherapists. Mediums dispute among themselves the existence and exact nature of the spirits, bringing all the behavioral and experiential evidence they have at their disposal to bear upon the points they are making. One medium I knew was fond of saying, "The spirits, if they exist. . . ." Another, a president of a *centro,* once said to me, "It is very ignorant to believe that you are possessed by evil spirits, but sometimes you have to enter into the person's ignorance with them to gradually bring them out of it." Certainly few, if any, spiritists would say emphatically that the spirits do not exist, but a psychotherapist would also find it difficult to say that the superego, ego, and id do not exist. These are all concepts that are more or less reified. As reader then, do not give the concept of "spirit" a concrete reality which it may or may not have in the belief system of an *Espiritista.*

First Level Possession: Brujeria

The first spiritist diagnosis made for Maria was one of a recent *brujeria* ("witchcraft"), or sorcery, in anthropological systems that distinguish witchcraft and sorcery (Evans-Pritchard, 1937). The spiritist theory is that a *brujo* (witch), or "one who works the bad," can be hired by anyone to go to a cemetery and/or perform other rituals to, in turn, hire or bribe the disincarnated spirit of a recently deceased person that has not yet passed from limbo, a spirit that died before he had completed his mission in his last incarnation and does not want to accept that he is dead, or any low-grade, poorly developed spirit, to do his bidding. This spirit is then "sent against" the sufferer to cause illness, fights in the home, separation, divorce, business failures, *locura,* or other misfortune, and sometimes death. Such "works of witchcraft" are usually attributed to motives of *venganza* (vengeance) by someone who feels wronged or to *envidia* (envy) by anyone. The perpetrator of the "work" is not usually identified by the mediums; it is up to the client to volunteer the possible identity of the perpetrator.[14] The "cure" of a *brujeria,* similarly, does not depend upon an identification of the perpetrator or any acts of witchcraft or counterwitchcraft in retaliation. The spiritist theory of cure of this condition is to "mount" the molesting spirit in the body of a medium, "interrogate it," "find out why it is causing the difficulty," and "give it light" or "educate it." The spirit is confronted with

God in the figure of Christ on the Cross and convinced that he is *equivocado* (mistaken), that he has no business doing this person harm, that he "was meant for better things," and that "for his own spiritual progress" he must cease and desist and retire to the spirit world—often to a spiritual school in the spirit world. The client must then "work on his own head" to "cleanse" himself of the lingering effects or fluidos (fluids, ectoplasm) of the molesting spirit, and "protect himself" against the influence of such spirits in the future, either by wearing *resguardos* (amulets) as protection or by "developing" his relationships with his own guiding spirits so that these misguided spirits cannot find *"entrada"* (entrance).

In Maria's case the first diagnosis was that three *espíritus obsesores* ("low-grade spirits of darkness that possess the mind and fill it with dark thoughts") had been hired by three envious women in the factory where she works. Later, when these "spirits" were "worked," they were reinterpreted as one recent *brujería* from someone close by (this time coworkers were not mentioned) and another, older, from someone far away (also not identified).

It is usual for the spiritist to distinguish between "recent *brujerías*" and "old *brujerías*." As we have seen in the case of Maria, and this is confirmed by analysis of the 180 consecutive spiritist *centro* attendees, the recent *brujería* explains the immediate 'presenting complaints' or those symptoms and discomforts of which the person is fully aware upon presentation. The source of the *brujería* is usually also attributed to an actual or potentially hostile relationship in the client's immediate interpersonal relations. The most common are the husband's other woman, an in-law, or the ex-spouse from a recent separation or divorce. The older witchcraft, as in the case of Maria, usually explains recurring patterns of symptoms or behaviors similar to those currently being suffered, such as Maria's "never having been happy with any man." The older witchcraft diagnosis is pointing to patterns of behavior of which the client may or may not be aware. The source of the old *brujería* is usually attributed to the time of the first occurrence of the behavior alluded to. The most common is the *brujería* regardless of who perpetrated it that caused the breakup of the client's first marriage. The older *brujería* is a diagnosis already at a deeper level of psychological significance than the new *brujería*. The new *brujería* seems to be associated with and refer to what the psychotherapist would rate on 'problem appraisal' as a 'social relations disturbance,' while the old *brujería* refers to a recurrent pattern of upsets or of self-defeating behavior that the psychotherapist would probably consider, examples of 'psychoneurotic' patterns, or 'character disorder.'

By the time these same spirits "arrived" mounted in a medium, their referents were again changed to a still deeper level of psychological significance (See sixth level possession, below.) They represented Maria's 'unconscious' or 'repressed feelings of anger,' her 'guilt' about this anger, her reluctance to change, and her 'preferred defense mechanism' of 'denial.'

The diagnosis of a new witchcraft in Rosa's practice usually appears to be what the psychodynamically oriented would call a 'projective defense,' either 'suggested' or 'reinforced' by the mediums, that serves to reduce the immediate anxiety and is then immediately undone again by the ensuing ritual which removes the 'projected' cause of the symptoms. In Maria's case, the first witchcraft diagnosis appears to represent a defense of 'displacement' more than 'projection.' Her anger at husband, father, and other family (unacceptable and guilt-producing) was displaced from them to the women at her place of work, thus permitting her expression and 'catharsis' of at least some of her repressed anger in a safe way at a safe 'object.' Before this *causa* was manifested and lifted, however, she was confronted with her feelings about the illness of her husband as these were brought out before her during the "working" of him, and the second diagnosis had been made of an old *brujeria* that referred to her long-term anger at all the men in her life, including not only her husband but her son as well. Thus the previously displaced anger was directed back to appropriate objects. The *evidencias* (visions) of this spirit also identified her sexual frustrations in the form of the classic Freudian dream symbolism of "flying through the air," and in an admission of sexual unresponsiveness, if not frigidity. The "working of" this spirit allowed Maria to express her rage freely at her husband, the sine qua non for effective psychotherapy, which the examining psychiatrist had considered an impossibility with Maria. Causality was still 'projected,' but the feelings and behaviors were not 'denied.' The spirit (manifested in the medium—level six possession) actually pantomimed Maria's 'denial' and her 'resistance' or, at least, 'her reluctance to accept therapy.' These motives were 'role played' before her for her to 'identify with' and 'reincorporate' as she was able. The second *causa de brujeria* mounted in the medium assumed responsibility for causing as much damage to Carlos as to Maria, thus also 'externalizing' Maria's 'guilt' for her to 'identify with' and 'reincorporate,' as she was able. Both husband and wife were required to forgive this spirit genuinely before they could be free of it.

Once these spirits are identified, "worked," and "lifted" completely, the individual is solely responsible for seeing that they are not permitted to manifest themselves again. Thus, from a psychoanalytic point of view, causality is 'projected,' but 'responsibility' for the future remains with the individual.

Psychologically the *causa de brujería* is the most superficial of the diagnoses made by the mediums; it is also, in their estimation, the easiest to cure. In spiritist thinking the new *brujería* can be "lifted" completely and irrevocably, often at a single session with some ritual *despojos* following. The old *brujería* is more difficult; it has been around longer and the *"fluidos"* of those spirits have "penetrated deeply" into the person. The spirit is also very "attached to" the person having been with him so long. These spirits may have to be "mounted," and "interrogated" repeatedly before they finally take leave, and if the person reverts to doing the same things again that caused these spirits to be sent originally, those spirits will again come back to punish him. In psychodynamic thinking, it is also easier to relieve immediate symptoms than to alter 'psychoneurotic patterns.' The latter require more 'insight' and more 'working through.'

Second Level Possession–Vulnerability of Those "In Development"

The second type of spiritist diagnosis made for Maria was that she was "in development."

A "medium in development" who has "not yet developed his or her spiritual faculties" is *débil* ("weak") and vulnerable to all kinds of "low-level," "ignorant," "base" spirits in which the "material impulses dominate." These spirits may want to possess a body for any of a number of reasons. They may have died a violent or untimely death in their last incarnation (e.g., an accident or a dread disease such as tuberculosis or cancer), in which case they will give the person thoughts of the accident or thoughts of death, and the symptoms of the disease of which they died. These spirits may be *"espíritus obsesores"* like the one "hired" in the work of witchcraft against Maria. These are just "base, low spirits that possess the mind" with "bad thoughts" that "the person cannot get rid of." They are often spirits that change their form into those of animals, such as "a monkey that plays with one's mind" *como le da la gana* (however he pleases), or a spirit that is a house cat one minute and a tiger the next. People may see them in their dreams or when awake. They may tell people to do things they don't want to do. There is no specific "explanation" given for the presence of any of these spirits; they are just there because of the person's "undeveloped" condition.

Also, a "medium in development" who has not yet developed his or her "spiritual faculties" will often be punished by his or her own "guardian spirits" for not doing what he or she must do. Each developing medium has "a mission in this incarnation," which includes "learning to work the spirits" and "to progress in his spiritual development by helping himself and helping others, by doing good." *Pruebas* (trials or tests) of their spiritual development will be put upon them by the "spiritual order." Through these trials "they improve and develop their spiritual strength." Mediums who do not follow these mandates may be either punished by their guardians, or their guardians may simply turn their backs on them, leaving them vulnerable to any base, undeveloped, ignorant spirit that wants to make use of them.

The spirits that molest those "in development" are "mounted", "interrogated" and "lifted" in the same way as *causas de brujeria* when they are identified specifically; for example, *un espiritu que se transforma en animal* ("a spirit that transforms itself into an animal"), or *un espiritu enganador* (a deceptive spirit), but generally the "cure" for those "in development" is "to develop." (See fifth and sixth level possessions below.)

This diagnosis is made for almost all adolescents who come to the spiritist *centro* and for approximately half of all of those who are "worked." These spirits appear to represent what psychotherapists might simply call 'immaturity,' or 'weak ego,' 'primitive impulses,' or sometimes 'psychotic symptoms,' such as 'thought disorders,' 'mood disorders,' or 'hallucinations.' They may also be dramatic, symbolic statements of feelings and sensations as they might be reported by an 'hysterical personality.' Further analysis of these data is needed to specify more exactly the referents of the spiritist diagnosis of "in development," but it is clear that it has a deeper level of psychological meaning than the *brujeria* as it refers to the state of the individual's own *propio ser* and is a lifelong condition which requires lifelong attention.

Third Level Possession: Causas de Otras Existencias (Spirits from Other Incarnations)

In spiritist theory, one's *propio ser* develops across as many lifetimes as it takes for one to develop from the base, ignorant, materialistic state dominated by instincts, in which all spirits are created, to the formal, wise, spiritual being guided by sentiments (of which love is the highest) as represented in the high-level and pure spirits. Since this development is continuous throughout successive generations, errors and unresolved interpersonal relationships from previous incarnations can endure into the present one and must be resolved before one can "progress."

This kind of spirit was seen during the working of Maria only as one came up in treatment of her niece, Noni (her "mother in another existence"). This spirit mother placed responsibility directly upon the present mother for being lax in the care of her daughter. This spirit is a "protection" of the daughter, but had been afflicting the mother. When this spirit is satisfied, it will cease to molest the mother and will be an ever-present helpful presence for the daughter. This was an unusual case of possession.

The most usual type of "spirit from another existence" is the *espíritu de familia* (family spirit) or the *espíritu de cadena* (a spirit that comes enchained with the whole family). Such spirits are passed from parent to child and affect the whole family. These are the spiritual interpretations that frequently sound clearly analogous to psychological interpretations, as for example, when a spirit that troubled the mother "fell more heavily on the child because the child was weaker and undefended." We have not, however, seen a spirit of this kind during the working of Maria and those around her.

Another usual type of "spirit from another existence" is the *"marido o esposa de otra existencia"* (husband or wife in another existence). If a man or a woman treated a spouse or suitor badly in another existence, this spouse will seek reparation and stay around and try to keep the mate from being happy with anyone else. These spirits, like one later diagnosed for Maria from another source, get in bed between the couple and cause repugnance between them. They cause quarrels and all kinds of havoc in the home. A spirit of this kind will come around when the spouse is not there and make the person feel good; then it will come around when the spouse is there and make him or her angry and resentful. It will also, for example, make a woman reject men who are good for her and accept men who are bad for her.

The "cure" of this kind of spirit possession is to mount the spirit and interrogate it, until it tells what it was the person did (usually abandonment, neglect during a time of need, or failure to keep a commitment) that causes it to seek reparations. Alternately the spirit expresses feelings of longing and feelings of rejection, angry feelings and loving feelings. When this spirit is fully worked, it ends up forgiving the person and the person in turn forgives it the damage it has been causing. These spirits do not leave easily, and one should regularly say prayers for them.

The spouse from another existence represents the person's 'ambivalence' in relationships with the opposite sex. It represents more enduring personality characteristics than the *brujería* and more specific undesirable traits than the general state of vulnerability of those "in development." It appears in analysis of the fifty spiritist cases, for which I also have psychiatric assessments to be associated with a psychiatric diagnosis of hysterical personality or hysterical neurosis. Gladys Egri, (private communication) suggests it is analogous to the 'unresolved oedipal conflict.'

It is interesting that this interpretation, available to Rosa for use with Maria, was not used for her. Instead, it was understood that what caused her problems with husbands, beyond those of *brujería*, was a *causa de prueba* (level four).

Fourth Level Possession: Causas de Prueba (Spirits of Test or Trial)

Maria, Rosa believed, although she did not say this to Maria during the *reuniones* described, had a *"causa de prueba"* that would "not let her be happy with any man." Note that the effect is the same as that for the spirit of the old *brujería* and also that which might have been diagnosed at level 3, but there is a difference in the etiology and the implications for change.

This kind of spirit "comes with one from birth" particularly anyone who is born with the "mission" in this existence "to develop himself or herself materially and spiritually." It is a spirit sent by the spiritual order to cause the individual "suffering and affliction" through which he can develop his moral, material, and spiritual fiber and "progress" in his "mission."

Causas de prueba cause all kinds of problems: financial problems, family problems, diseases, sexual perversion, anything you can name. They make both "material" and "spiritual" "tests" of the person's strength. Material "tests" are to be resolved by material means if possible. If the "material tests" cannot be resolved by "material" means, they have to be *"aguantado"* (born with patience and resignation), one must learn *paciencia* (patience) and *control* (control) and *"a hacer la caridad"* (to do charity or spiritual work for others).

These spirits are "worked" repeatedly in all of their manifestations, but it is not clear (to me or to the spiritists themselves) whether one can ever "get rid of them" or not. Sometimes however, one can, convert them into *guias* (spirit guides) or helping spirits. (See level five.) The "cure" is "to develop" and to go on "working the causes."

Analysis of the 180 cases shows that *causas de existencia* or *causas de prueba* are frequently diagnosed in the presence of symptoms probed by the mediums that a psychotherapist would recognize as indicative of depression (inability to sleep, lack of appetite, difficulty in concentrating, crying a lot, feeling alone and unloved, thoughts of suicide, feeling "as if" going crazy). Such symptoms of depression can, however, also be attributed to *brujería* to *causas de familia* or any *causa*. The spirit, when mounted in the medium, arrives angry at that individual and tells him why he is angry. This kind of a spirit usually says it wants to see the person dead from a disease, dead by his own hand, or by the hand of another, it is irrelevant, he wants to *"acabar con el"* (put an end to him) in any way. In psychodynamic thinking, the spirit 'confronts' the individual with the 'anger at self' that is assumed to underlie 'depression.' *Causas de prueba,* rather than providing or reinforcing projective or paranoid defenses, may provide the individual with psychological insight into the dynamics of his symptoms of depression. The spirit worked for Carlos at the first session is an example of this kind of possession, although it was not made totally clear during the *reunión* exactly where Carlos' spirit came from or what kind of spirit it was.

Fifth Level Possession: Las Protecciones (The Protections)

Every "medium in development" or "person with *facultades* not yet developed" is expected to try to develop relationships with his or her own particular protecting spirits. During the treatment of Maria we have seen tyro mediums, including Maria, make their first attempts to achieve trance with their *guía principal* (principal guide). We have seen partially developed and fully developed mediums "pass their protection" before beginning the "working of the causes." We have seen fully developed mediums sitting at the table questioning sufferers with respect to information purportedly provided to them by "spirit guides." We have also seen mediums report *"evidencias,"* or visual pictures of the spiritual state of the sufferer, also purportedly provided through the "spiritual *facultad"* to see such things. We have seen fully developed mediums pass fluidly from a state of possession by a *causa* of a sufferer to possession by their own "spirit guides." These are the *"facultades"* that the individual is expected to develop; they are referred to in the literature of Spiritism and Spiritualism by the terms "trance," "clairaudition," and "clairvoyance." There are other *facultades* some of which we have seen and others that we have not seen. *Transporte* ("transport") is a *facultad* in which the spirit of the medium (or a guardian spirit of the medium—it is not clear to my subjects or to me) leaves the body of the medium and goes to another place to retrieve something put there, or to look at the conditions there. *Inspiración* ("inspiration") is when the medium has ideas that he or she "does not know where they come from." *Observación* ("observation") is when "the spirits give the person the gift to watch and see things that others do not notice." *Presentimientos* (presentiments) enable the medium to anticipate or warn against future events.

The *facultades* appear to me to be ordinary human faculties elaborated with the cultural idea that they have a superior human (deceased high-grade human) "spiritual source." These are, of course, more highly developed in those who work on their development. Literate spiritists would not agree to calling the spirits a "supernatural source," as they believe spirits to be a part of nature and subject to empirical investigation through the "science of spiritism." Less literate spiritists consider the *facultades* and *protecciones* as "supernatural." From a psychodynamic point of view the *facultades* appear to be ordinary 'ego functions' thus elaborated in the cultural belief system.

The *protecciones* are the spirits with which the medium communicates using these *facultades,* and the source of the superior wisdom, enlightenment, judgment, the higher sentiments, and spiritual strength. They are the superior human beings from whom the mediums can obtain these superior qualities through exercise of their *facultades.* The "protecting spirits" are of two kinds: the guardian angel and the spirit guides. Everyone has a guardian angel, who helps and protects you, but you do not often know when or how, even if you are a medium. No one, including mediums, communicates with the guardian angel directly, but mediums often recognize the intervention of the guardian angel on their behalf, particularly in keeping them safe from harm. The guardian angel, among other things, protects the medium's "material" from harm when it is lent to another spirit in trance.

Guias or spirit guides, are the disincarnated spirits with which a medium or a medium in development is in direct communication. The *guias* do not "possess," but "help" the medium. They talk to the medium, protect the medium from *causas*, and mount the medium in trance to talk to and help others. These spirits have valued personality characteristics, and represent strengths present in, needed by, or desired by the medium. Such *protecciones* are often Catholic saints (*San Lázaro, San Miguel,* etc.), the Yoruban powers of *Santeria* (Obatalá, Chango, Yemaya, etc.) folk heroes (Joan of Arc), idealized ethnic types (the *Madama,* the *Congo,* the *Indio,* the *Hindu,* the *Negro Africano*), a physical type (a strong black, an old man or woman), a professional type (priest, doctor, missionary), a deceased relative of the individual, or a relative from another existence, but they may be any individually delineated character and, once they become known to the medium, they are individually delineated. They are not perfect beings, but they are "enlightened, elevated spirits." The saints cannot be corrupted, but the others can. They all have their compensatory strengths and weaknesses. The *"madama,"* for example, is a black slave woman who has learned Spanish as a second language, so she speaks very precisely. She is usually very humble, but she can also love diversion and be very frank in her speech, saying things a modest woman is not supposed to say, such as talking about the pleasures of sex. Her special skill is curing with plants. Within the broad outline of the stereotype, each of the *guias* of a fully developed medium becomes a very individual character to those who get to know them.

In my view of the world, the *protecciones* together with the *causas* symbolize the actual and the ideal social order of the plural, stratified, largely preindustrial society of Puerto Rico. The *protecciones* represent for the individual idealized part-selves. In psychodynamic thinking, they often enact the 'superego functions' (Lubchansky, et al., 1970). They also represent some 'ego functions' such as 'judgment' and 'intellectual processes.' They may, in addition, however, represent the 'libido' as, for example, when a *madama* or a *conga* likes "to talk frankly" about the pleasures of sex.

A trance state interpreted as one involving possession in the anthropological sense by a spirit guide is, unlike the levels of possession we have discussed so far, a desired state, which is actively sought, taught, practiced and "developed." It is what anthropologists have called "controlled" or "voluntary" possession (Lewis, 1971; Oesterreich, 1966) or "desired possession" (Bourguignon, 1973). But the distinction between "desired" and "feared" or "voluntary" and "involuntary" possession is not always so clear. "Protectors" punish one ('superego function') and may be the cause of illness and suffering (level four possession). Some "protections" "need light" or are "poorly developed" themselves. Sometimes *causas* come "masquerading as protections" (level two possession). Protections are sometimes "crossed with *causas.*" As we will see below, these less desirable states of possession by protections are commonly seen in the "medium in development."

Maria did not persist in her efforts to become a medium, but 'dropped-out' once her immediate distress was relieved. Nonetheless it is significant that this was the 'treatment modality' ultimately prescribed by the spiritists for Maria, and it is therefore worthwhile to review how this process might have taken place as observed in the other mediums present and in other cases where the process has been observed.

The process of *desarrollo,* or of developing mediumship *facultades,* appears to follow fairly clear stages which are recognized by the mediums in evaluative adjectives modifying the term "mediumship." There are "people with *facultades* not developed" (or "mediums not developed" or "mediums in development"), "partially-developed mediums," and "fully-developed mediums." Among "fully-developed mediums," the abilities of the mediums are further evaluated in terms of the number and quality of the *protecciones* and the "style of working" both the *protecciones* and the *causas*. A fully-developed medium may be said to *"trabajar muy linda"* (work very prettily). In greater detail, as observed, these stages involve:

1. The "person with *facultades"* who "must develop" sits at or near the table "to have the protection" of the guiding spirits of the other mediums while in the vulnerable state of being "in development" (level two possession), and is encouraged to use his *facultades* in whatever way he can. Specifically, in Rosa's *centro,* this usually means that he is encouraged to participate in "interrogation of the spirits", "to say whatever he can see or hear" about others present, and "to call upon his protections" and try to "manifest" his *guía principal.* These are three distinct but concurrent processes.

a. "Learning to interrogate the spirits" is learning to play the roles of the auxiliary mediums. Interrogating the spirits amounts to questioning the molesting spirits manifested about their reasons for molesting the person, and instructing them in the rules of correct behavior in accordance with the doctrines of *Espiritismo.* The developing medium usually begins only by using the standard phrases spoken in unison, such as, "Until today, good spirit," or "May God forgive you," while more senior mediums do the more individualized "interrogation." It takes some time for a developing medium to learn the role of interrogating the spirits. This, I suggest, may be a process by which the 'superego functions' are standardized to those of the group.

b. Learning to say "whatever he can see or hear" about others, is also called learning to "give *evidencias.*" The developing medium usually begins very tentatively and timidly "to say what they (referring to the spirits) give me." They usually begin by saying what they have "seen" or "heard" only after a senior medium has already said it, then they say, "I saw it too, but I didn't know whether it was just mine," or "I didn't dare say it." This is all right, it is called *"comprobación"* (confirmation) and the medium is encouraged to continue. He may be told "not to hold anything that they give him," because "anything that they give him he has to say or he will get sick." Then they may start adding depth or detail to *evidencias* already made by a senior medium. When they begin to volunteer *evidencias* not previously suggested, they often begin with a qualifying phrase such as, "With the permission of the table, I don't know whether this is something that they give me or if it is something of mine (*cosa mía*), but I see. . . ." The senior mediums then either give *comprobación* of the *evidencia,* or they expand and modify it; or they may, as in the case of the male medium at the first session

Maria attended, be told that that is their own problem (*cosa suya*). Learning to give *evidencias* is also a long process and it is a skill that is continuously elaborated over the practicing lifetime of a medium. It is a skill that is developed more by some mediums and less by others.

In my way of viewing reality, this is a process through which the person is encouraged and learns to 'identify with' others, 'introspect,' and then 'project' his own thoughts and feelings back to the other to be confirmed or denied by the client and by the supervising mediums. It is a process by which the medium gains, through consensual validation or rejection, the ability to evaluate his intuitions about others. It is a process that resembles the 'analysis of countertransference' in the 'supervision' of a psychotherapist in training.

c. Learning to "manifest" one's *protecciones* is the first step in learning the *facultad* of "trance." All who have *facultades* that they must develop are encouraged, like Maria, to go into a trance with their *guia principal*. This is the sine qua non of "mediumship," at least in Rosa's practice. But before one can manifest his *guias*, he must be free of *causas*. Most "developing mediums" are "afraid of the spirits" at first and are reluctant to go into trance. Most mediums have, in fact, deferred "developing" from some earlier time when they were told they were "in development," before they actually "develop." The "developing medium," using *pases* (rapid movements of the hands and arms around the head), alcohol rubbed on the temples and back of the neck, cigar smoking, hyperventilation, spinning, strong suggestion, concentration, and/or other less immediately apparent techniques of trance induction enters an 'altered state of consciousness' that the "fully developed mediums" appraise as being "a manifestation of a *causa*", a *protección* crossed with a *causa*", "a *protección* that needs light", and so on.

I use the term 'altered state of consciousness' with no actual knowledge of the state of consciousness, and great doubt about whether there is any actual 'altered state of consciousness' other than 'regression' in these uncontrolled trance states and 'regression in the service of the ego' in the controlled trance states. Observationally, what I see usually is that a medium in development begins to breathe heavily; arms, first gyrating around the head, are subsequently extended upward in which position they merely quiver, the neck is often jerked a few times, the medium usually rises from the chair and may or may not lunge about the room making violent movements or pelvic thrusts, being caught and prevented from falling by the others present or falling to the floor. Usually an unintelligible utterance emanates from the medium. It may be sighs or shrieks, but it is most often just a prolonged tremulous vocalization with no meaningful content. The spirit may be completely mute or it may say: *"Que la paz de Dios sea aquí"* (Let the peace of God be here.") The medium may "be thrown to the floor," where he or she may roll around, pound the floor with fists, or merely lie quietly trembling. Some of these trance states look more 'sexual' in the movements of the body. Others look more 'aggressive.' Some look either both or neither 'sexual' nor 'aggressive,' but merely 'hyperkinetic.' The mediums say "what kind of a spirit is there." If it is a *causa,* or a *"protección* crossed with a *causa,"* the spirit will be ordered to leave the body of the medium in development immediately and the *causa* will subsequently be mounted in the body of a "fully-developed medium" and "worked" in the view of the developing medium in the same way all *"causas* are worked." If it is a *"protección* that needs light" or a *"protección* poorly developed," the medium will be required to say prayers and to read passages from the *Scriptures According to Spiritism* and to continue coming to the *centro* "to work *la obra"* (spiritual work), and *hacer la caridad a los demás* (do charity to others).

It is my guess, although it would require more observations to test this hypothesis, that when the trance is 'aggressive' the mediums say it is a *"causa,"* and when it is 'sexual,' it is a *"protección* that must be developed."

2. The person becomes a "partially developed medium" as soon as he or she can manifest an enlightened *guía.* The trance state with an enlightened *guía* never involves the violent "throwing of the medium around the room or onto the floor." The partially developed medium may use the same techniques of trance induction, but he or she goes quietly into trance, usually stays seated in the chair and the spirit speaks kindly and formally. In the beginning the spirit guide will only speak standard phrases (e.g., "Let the peace of God be here!) or make the typical sound (e.g., the ululation of the Plains Indian, if it is an *Indio*). Later the spirit guide may make full sentences, and will address itself eloquently and fluently to a problem of anyone or all present. The "partially developed medium" mounts at least one of his *guías* at each *reunión* unless he has a *causa* troubling him, or has failed to complete his obligations to the protections and is not in a good relationship with them (like the male medium in the first session with Maria). The mediums must be able "to pass a *protección"* "to prepare the body" before they can "mount a *causa"* of another. As long as or as often as the medium continues to have problems, these problems will be "worked" by other mediums in the same way that other clients are "worked." This will probably last throughout the lifetime of the medium, since no one is ever completely free of problems. Thus there is no clear distinc-

tion in the *centros* between 'sufferer' and 'healer' (cf. Frank, 1961). Approximately fifty percent of the 'sufferers' are 'healers' "in development" and the 'healers' are also 'sufferers.' The "partially developed medium" has usually learned the role of interrogation of the *causas,* his *protecciones* speak and instruct the clients and the bad spirits in "enlightened" ways, and he may have "developed" several additional *"guías"* so that he has a repertoire of helping spirit roles and can usually mount some, if not all, of the *causas* that are presented (sixth level possession).

The "partially developed medium" is instructed and expected to visit a number of *centros* ("not just one, but not too many either") in order "to develop" and "practice" his *facultades* with various mediums in different places. But he is also expected to participate most often in one that "is comfortable and congenial for him."

3. A "fully developed medium" has a versatile repertoire of *protecciones* that he or she can manifest at will. Rosa has twenty-seven *guías,* each with its own particular individuality and special talents. These spirits come and go with little or no use of the objects and gestures of trance induction. A series of small jerks of the neck and possibly some fluttering of the hands are the usual evidence of the entry of the spirit. Its presence is known more by the change in style and content of speech of the medium than by body movement.

The medium becomes a "fully developed medium" only when he or she also has a versatile repertoire of *causas* (sixth level possession) that he or she can also manifest at will. As Rosa said during the working of Maria, "I am not afraid of any spirit."

Sixth Level Possession: The Causas Manifested by Mediums in Trance

The last skill learned by a medium (and one with which he or she will always exercise some caution) is the manifestation of the *causas* of others as these are presented by clients in the *centros.* Some mediums will always remain afraid to manifest certain kinds of *causas* that are very strong and very ugly. (There is an example in Esmeralda's reluctance to mount one of the *causas* of Maria. As we have seen in the "working" of Maria and her husband, these *causas* come expressing anger, hatred, and resistance to "light." They act out and express the unacceptable impulses, thoughts and feelings that in psychodynamic terms would probably be called 'id impulses' and 'repressed' and 'suppressed' memories, motives, and feelings. They sometimes cry and lament their fates. They sometimes "throw the medium on the floor" in a trance state that resembles the first trance states of a "medium in development" or, possibly, the *"ataque de nervios."*

Mediums are not supposed to manifest *causas* when they are alone, but only in the presence of other mediums who can "help them" if the *causa* is "too strong" or "gets out of control."

I believe that the trance states in which a fully developed medium has mounted a *"causa"* is, like the trance state with a "protection," nothing more or less than 'role playing' within the cultural interpretation that the ability, again, is a "spiritual faculty." It is 'regression in the service of the ego.' They can go in and out of 'primitive,' or 'unconscious,' or 'preconscious' states at will. They have added these 'primitive' or, if uncontrolled, then 'psychopathological' mental states to their repertoire of roles in the same way that they have assumed a number of "guiding spirit" or 'superego' and 'ego' roles. Rosa tells me: "Now, very often I do it without any spirit on me; very rarely do I actually have a spirit on me." This is not to say that she is deceitful or a charlatan. She knows how these spirits manifest themselves and can enact them whether or not they actually come. She does not tell this to her clients, but in her opinion (and in mine) this is not actually deceit; it is merely a necessity for the treatment situation—it is the 'professional role.' Rather than a blank face to provoke transference, the medium assumes the role of a mirror for one to see into his own psyche (or "spiritual picture") in a more direct way.

In my view of the world, again, it takes a very intuitive person (or a great deal of clinical experience) to be an effective medium. The medium looks at someone and, with the minimal observations and verbal cues present, "divines" the 'presenting complaints.' She does not, however, attempt to "divine" the "cause" without first having "discovered" and had confirmation of the 'presenting complaints,' and usually some history. It also takes a very empathetic person to set up the psychodramatic events that constitute the "working of the causes" in the *reunion*. It would also take, I should think, a strong ego, or strong sense of self to role play *causas* of others. In my opinion this cannot be done without considerable objective awareness of self and others—an awareness achieved through the mediumship training process and practice.

The "Ataque": Another Level of Possession?

Notice that in the working of Maria and those around her, none of those who were interpreted as possessed (in the anthropological sense) actually went into a trance state with the spirit purportedly possessing them. Rather these spirits were manifested in the feelings and behaviors of the client, but were mounted only in the body of a "developed medium" while the "possessed" client looked on.

It does happen rarely that a client does go into a trance state that is interpreted as a manifestation of the *causa* of that person. This happened only three times during the observations of 180 cases, and I have seen it under only two circumstances. The first is when a client present in the *centro* for the first time, seated in the audience with no attention from the mediums, suddenly and without apparent provocation, goes into a violent trance state in which "the spirit throws him or her around the room or onto the floor." This kind of trance looks very much like the *"ataques de nervios"* that I have seen in the clinical setting. The person staggers around the room arms flailing, body jerking, and voice wailing until he or she ends up on the floor quivering and silent, or beating the floor with fists and crying in what looks like either an infant's or a child's temper tantrum. These trance states may look more or less sexual but they are more aggressive than sexual.

The other circumstance under which the client may manifest his own *causa* is in the case of a developing medium who, in the process of trying to "mount a protection," mounts instead a *causa* or a "protection crossed with a *causa*." These trance states may also look more or less sexual, but I think it is the aggressive element that cues the mediums to interpret it as a *causa* rather than a protection.

When this happens, in either circumstance, the spirit is exorcised immediately in the most direct way—it is confronted by an enlightened protection that confronts it with goodness and orders it out of the body of the medium. The spirit submits to this superior moral force, and is subsequently mounted in "the material" of a developed medium who then enacts the behaviors previously observed in the client, with corresponding verbalizations. The "possessed" is at this point, as in the other states of possession, "worked," witnessing his own possession in the body of another.

These possession states, and only these of the many that are seen in the spiritist *centros,* appear most possibly to be what Breuer and Freud (1893) described as the "hysterical attack." This is a very significant point in view of the fact that much of the psychiatric literature on possession states assumes not only that the condition is hysterical but that spirit medium cult practices owe their popularity to the acceptance of hysterical conversion reactions and the encouragement of hysterical dissociative reactions. In fact, these hysterical reactions seem to be treated as ailments by the spiritists as much as by the modern Western physician.

Had I included this form of possession in my scheme of "levels of possession," it would have had to have come first for a number of reasons. First, in following the course of events in Maria's episode, this state came first. It is the state that preceded the spiritist diagnosis of a "work of witchcraft." Second, while it is never initiated or encouraged by the mediums, if it occurs it gets first attention in the form of immediate and direct exorcism. Actually it falls outside this scheme of "levels" because it is considered a symptom and not a state of possession. Its occurrence, however, is enlightening with respect to the spiritist's treatment of the phenomenon known to psychiatry as the 'Puerto Rican syndrome.'

The *ataque* (or 'Puerto Rican syndrome') is generally agreed, as we have seen above, to be an hysterical syndrome, but it is an hysterical syndrome with particular distinctive features related to specific culture patterns, particularly child-rearing practices, but also possibly other historical circumstances, such as colonial domination as well (Rothenberg, 1964). The child-rearing patterns that Rothenberg considers most important are the widespread use of bottles and pacifiers by which the child is taught to repress and suppress anger. He sees the *ataque* primarily as a discharge of repressed and suppressed anger. Fernandez-Marina (1961) sees the fondling, caressing, and handling of the infant by different persons, before the differentiation of the zones of the arousal system (the 'polymorphous pervert,' in Freud's terminology),[15] as the most significant factor in the child-rearing practices that bring about this particular Puerto Rican type of hysterical reaction. Fernandez-Marina explains:

A normal infant-mother relationship is anaclitic—that is, adequate, consistent, predictable, and predicated to one identifiable other—and within it the instincts which depend on the ego for expression develop with the necessary organization for correct action. The discharge of tension for keeping homeostasis is performed in an effective manner so that the ego is kept intact without being greatly disturbed. As Freud postulates, if this anaclitic dependency on the mother is not established, a narcissistic fixation, with all of its consequences, follows.

For the Puerto Rican infant, a variation of this relationship occurs which I would like to call a *heteroclitic* dependency. When the polymorphous pervert is fondled, caressed, and handled excessively by different persons, this stimulation fixes tension discharge mechanisms polymorphously at this primitive level. The heteroclitic pattern of relationships enables the infant to discharge tension, with a heteroglyphic or 'blurred' object, and with defectively integrated oral-anal-phallic zones. The ego itself, however, may develop sufficiently in most of its functions to deal adequately with reality and so escape a narcissistic fixation. Sometimes, if the predominant mothering one is schizophrenogenic, the narcissistic fixation does occur. Nevertheless, the development stimulated through heteroclitic relationships with other persons leaves the person with a better functioning arousal and tension discharge mechanism, which protects him from extreme regression.

The polymorphous pervert, since he shares his sleeping quarters with others, is frequently exposed to primal scenes which tend to increase tension, and then uses the mimetic device of a hyperkinetic discharge for achieving a vicarious orgasm. As an adult, the same person regresses to this polymorphous primitive discharge if either the threshold of other anxiety-discharging mechanisms is surpassed quantitatively or these mechanisms are not adequate qualitatively.*

Fernandez-Marina is impressed with the absence in Puerto Rico of the extremely regressed backward patient found in mainland hospitals, and he attributes this to the function of the *ataque* "which can also function as basic ego defenses against psychotic breaks, or as limits to extreme regression or total disorganization of the ego." Similarly, Rothenberg argues that Puerto Ricans use hysterical symptoms for restitution of psychotic processes in instances where the continental would be more apt to use obsessive-compulsive symptomatology. There is no essential conflict between the interpretations of the *ataque* by Fernandez-Marina and Rothenberg. Fernandez-Marina deals with the etiology of the specific form of the hysterical attack, and Rothenberg deals with the inadequacy of other mechanisms of discharge of aggressive impulses which result in the manifestation of the *ataque* in the adult. Both recognize that it occurs in people with different personality structures and serves different functions for different people, but that it has positive functions for some in preventing more severe disorder.

It would seem that the spiritist system of treatment capitalizes on this natural restitutive process. I would like to suggest that spirit mediumship development is a process in which the *"ataque"*, as an involuntary regression (sometimes to this polymorphous-polyclitic stage and sometimes not), becomes retrained to serve as regression in the service of the ego. The "medium in development" is encouraged to go into trance ('to regress to whatever stage of development at which his discharge mechanisms are fixed'); the mediums then differentiate the *causas* and the *protecciones* (aggressive drive states or sexual drive states) and the "level of development" of the *protecciones* ("undeveloped," "poorly developed," "needing light," "developed," etc.). (If there is any correlation of the "levels of development" of the spirits with the 'oral-anal-phallic-genital' levels of development recognized in psychoanalytic theory, it is something I simply cannot say anything about as yet on the basis of the analyses that have been done, but it is a possibility.) The spirits thus identified, if they are *causas*, are mounted in the body of another medium to be viewed, identified with, and reincorporated if

* Reprinted by special permission of the William Alamson White Psychiatric Foundation, Inc. (Copyright 1961) from *Psychiatry* 24 (1961): 79–82.

the subject is capable. The protecciones thus identified are then "pullido" (polished), "given light," "educated" and "developed." The medium in development is progressively trained to manifest both *protecciones* and *causas* at all levels of development. It seems to me that this could be a process whereby not only the drive states are differentiated but also 'objects' and 'zones.' Here, however, I have gone far beyond the data available. In any event, mediumship training is a "development process' (in spiritist terms) or a 'growth process' (in the terms of some psychotherapists). The spiritists appear to have a potentially effective means of treatment, both short- and long-term, of a syndrome that professional psychotherapy, drawing as it does largely upon insights from people of different cultures than the Puerto Rican, with different basic self and world views, finds difficult to manage with traditional techniques.

SUMMARY

It appears to me that the two types of healers (the folk and the professional) interpret the same feelings and behaviors in similar ways, that they have similar treatment goals and, to some extent, similar treatment techniques; but they talk about what they see and do within very different systems of conceptualization of the self and world. The conceptual systems are, in fact, diametrically opposed in that the locus of the illness is inside the self in one system and outside the self in the other. Or, one might equally say that the self extends beyond the body in one system and is contained within the skin in the other. In any event, the boundaries of self and nonself are drawn differently. The psychotherapeutic and the spiritist ways of viewing the self and world are closer if one considers sociodrama, family therapy, or any of a number of interactional theories of personality rather than classical psychoanalytic theory; in general, however, the folk and modern systems are antithetical, and the interface of the two systems as they impact upon the single individual must almost necessarily be reciprocally antitherapeutic.

If we look merely at the pattern of interaction between the healers, Rosa and her auxiliary mediums, and the client, Maria, and the impact of the healers' messages upon Maria's ego defenses of the moment, what in fact was done was not that different from what would have been done in any psychiatric facility. Rosa actually did what the psychiatric consultant projected but believed herself unable to accomplish with Maria.

Maria was treated for a six-week period in what would be analogous to 'individual, group, and family treatment modalities,' and the techniques of 'crisis-intervention' in the mental health clinic. Rosa first sought to relieve Maria's acute anxiety with 'reassurance' that she was not "*loca*," and by providing her with an alternative explanation of an easily curable condition—"a new witchcraft" (first level possession). (In the clinic to which she was taken for assessment by the researcher, her immediate symptoms would have been relieved with similar reassurance and medication.) At the same time, however, Rosa confronted Maria with the denied fact of her husband's illness and their mutual fears of his death. A week later, when the intense anxiety was relieved, Maria was first confronted with her sexual frustration, then provoked to 'abreact' her anger at her husband and admit her anger at her son. She was required to accept responsibility for never having been happy with any man. She was confronted with a parody of her denial (her "pretty song") and with her resistance (the spirit that wanted "to get out of here"). Her presenting complaints were "lifted" (removed by 'suggestion'?). A second spirit (an older *brujería* confronted her with her negativism and her "denial of everything" and the problems that she had caused her husband. Husband and wife were given a mutual *receta* (prescription) for a bath. During the third week the attentions of both were focused upon the illness of Carlos and this was redefined as a problem for both of them; all of the "spiritual problems" were removed and they were referred back to the doctor and told they both had "to give full cooperation." Apart from these 'group sessions' Rosa had two long 'individual sessions' with Maria, one during the first week (the "*despojo de la casa*") and the other during the fourth week (the visit to the *finca*). We do not know exactly what happened in either of these individual sessions, but we do know that the two women in an egalitarian role relationship discussed the messages and meanings of the messages of the spirits in a pragmatic way.

During the first week's session, Maria was also told that she was experiencing all of these symptoms (*brujerías*, etc.) because she was in a vulnerable state ("*en desarrollo*") (second level possession). Maria was believed to have an *espíritu de prueba* (spirit of test/trial) (fourth level possession) which would be with her all her life and would subject her to future episodes of similar and different "tests" of her "spiritual strength," unless she "developed" and improved her "spiritual faculties" ('ego functions'?). In this respect, the spiritist *centro* offered Maria long-term developmental treatment which was not a possibility for her in the average mental health clinic.

The fact that Maria failed to avail herself of this opportunity is equally significant in both systems. In the psychiatric system it is attributed to her heavy reliance upon 'denial' as her primary defense, her 'lack of insight' and her 'fear of getting too close to anyone.' The psychiatric consultant said she would not try to uncover the basic conflict. Rosa, at the conclusion of Maria's treatment episode, considered her "cured" of the immediate spiritual problems (the *trabajos* and *causas* that caused the *ataque*, the unnecessary pains of both husband and wife, and the marital discord). She did not, however, anymore than a psychotherapist would, consider that her basic personality structure or the problems that had led her to this episode had been affected. Rosa, tells me in confidence (not to be shared with the client) that Maria has a *"falta de carácter"* (character defect)—she is an *ingrata* (one ungrateful to the spirits)—once she was "cured" she ceased to come to pay her debt to the spiritual helpers and to complete her "mission." Unless she comes seeking help, there is nothing Rosa can do, and she will be ill again.

It is my opinion, although I can document this only with negative evidence, that Rosa shares with the psychiatric profession the reluctance to uncover the basic conflict with Maria. Maria was not given a diagnosis at the third level of possession (a *causa de otras existencias*—the *causa de familia*, or the *causa de cadena*—those spirits related to one's family history and development). Furthermore, Rosa never probed with Maria (unless possibly in the individual sessions not witnessed) her relationships to her family of origin or her early history, although it is common for her to do so. Furthermore she never explored, in public at least, Maria's relationship to her first husband, which is even more common in Rosa's practice. Also, Rosa never really encouraged Maria to go into trance or to participate in the development of mediumship fully during the six weeks she was in the *centro*. She may have been postponing this, or she may have felt about Maria, as she has about others, that while she needs to "develop *facultades*," she really does not have the capacity to do so.

Again it appears that the two types of healers classify the same feelings and behaviors in similar ways as illness or health and have similar treatment goals. To a lesser extent they have similar treatment techniques, but they view these within very different systems of conceptualization of the self and world. These different systems of interpretation of the self and world in part reflect the different cultures of which the systems are each a part (Puerto Rican vs. general American). In part they also reflect different levels of sociocultural development (preindustrial state societies vs. modern Western industrialized state societies), and levels of socioeconomic status within culture (lower or working class vs. professional class). Generally they mirror a difference in popular thinking even within general American middle-class culture and the subculture of the mental health professions. It is not my purpose here to define the extent of distribution of this particular view of self and world, but it does extend beyond the Puerto Rican spiritist, and thus the implications of these findings are generalizable beyond this population. The extent of that generalizability, however, is suggested by the contributions to this volume, the distributional studies of Bourguignon (1968), studies of preindustrial societies in general and of lower classes within modern industrial societies. In any event, it is a great oversimplification and ethnocentrism to consider the one system (the spirit medium cult) "magical" and the other (modern Western psychoanalytically oriented psychotherapy) "scientific." It is also a great oversimplification to equate possession beliefs and behaviors with any one or two categories from the psychiatric nomenclature.

NOTES

1. From 1966 to 1969, this research was supported under NIMH Grant RO 1 MHO2308-02 to Lincoln Hospital Mental Health Services, a division of Albert Einstein College of Medicine (Harris B. Peck, M.D., and Elmer L. Struening, Ph.D., Coprincipal Investigators), and from 1972 through 1975 under NIMH Grant RO 1 MH22563-01 to Columbia University, Department of Anthropology (Vivian Garrison, Ph.D., and Alexander Alland, Ph.D., Coprincipal Investigators), located by collaborative arrangement at Bronx State Hospital. During the interim period (December 1969 to June 1972) kind support was provided by Yale University, Department of Psychiatry, and the Connecticut Mental Health Center, New Haven, Connecticut, where Garrison was then Assistant Professor and Staff Member of the Program Information and Assessment Unit. The assistance of Gladys Egri, M.D., as psychiatric consultant, and Eugenia Pizarro, as Research Assistant, on Grant RO 1 MH22563-01, and of many of the staff and faculty of all three institutions are gratefully acknowledged. Special thanks to Edward Hornick, M.D.; C. Christian Beels, M.D.; Pedro Rodriguez, M.D.; Angel Mercado, M.S.W.; Irene Labourdet, M.D.; Raymond Prince, M.D.; and Dorothy Ludwing, M.D., for consulting on this and similar cases and for reading and making helpful comments on previous versions of this paper. The help of the many mediums and clients is also acknowledged with particular gratitude; above all, to Loreta Colon, my key informant on Spiritism and *Santeria*. All names used in this report are pseudonyms to preserve the anonymity and confidentiality of the informants, although fully informed consent has been obtained from all and the paper itself has been read to, and commented on, by the medium called Rosa.

2. Although this paper will deal exclusively with the case of Maria, the interpretation of this case is made in the context of a larger study involving participant observations in over twenty *centros,* intensive long-term participant observations in two *centros,* standardized interviews with presidents of nine *centros* and with approximately 250 people in the following six groups: (1) a random sample of the Puerto Rican population in the study area, (2) a consecutive sample of admissions to the mental health clinic in the study area, (3) everyone who attended a selected *centro* during a one-week period, (4) a selected representative sample of those who attended another selected *centro* over a six-month period, (5) a consecutive sample of Spanish-speaking admissions to a second mental health clinic (Tremont Crisis Center), and (6) an 'interface sample' of fifty people who had been treated by both mental health professionals and by *espiritistas.* The investigator also lived in the home of a spiritist *centro* president on two occasions for eight months and three months respectively, to observe the informal interactions between the healer and her clients.

3. Figures on the numbers of healers and churches were established as of one point in time (December, 1966), since these are continually changing.

4. *Dolor de cabeza* is a frontal or temporal headache, while *dolor de cerebro* is a dorsal or occipital pain. The "meaning" of the latter, literally translatable as "mind ache," in the concepts of modern medicine and psychiatry is not clear. But in a previous analysis I did of CMI date compared for Puerto Rican random normals and for psychiatric patients, it was found to be significantly more frequent among psychiatric patients.

5. *"Envidia"* is not well translated by the English envy or jealousy. *"Envidia"* as it is used among the people I am writing about has a much broader meaning which, I believe, refers to any hostility or competition, expressed or projected. *"Envidia"* can be used to refer to any competitiveness, to "bad vibes," to overt directed hostility, which may or may not be motivated by coveted attributes or qualities, and to the diffuse impersonality and competitiveness that characterizes a city. Maria says: *"Envidia*—that is what most characterizes New York City."

6. This is not always the case. On rare occasions spiritists do refer clients to psychiatrists or for psychiatric hospitalization.

7. *Causas del estomago* (spirits in the stomach) seem, on analysis of data from the 180 cases, to be related to symptoms of anxiety and tension and are also attributed to witchcraft. Further, they seem to be associated with marital difficulties in the case of women and with alcoholism and sexual promiscuity and/or impotence in men.

8. Three items on the Cornell Medical Index indicating clouding of vision and other symptoms about the eyes proved to be the strongest discriminants out of 196 symptom items between Puerto Rican male psychiatric clinic and random normal samples (p. 001). This is apparently one of the first ways in which Puerto Ricans, both male and female, manifest and express emotional disturbance, regardless of the specific nature of the disturbance.

9. *"Causas* that are too strong to work" are rarely identified in the spiritist *centro*. Among the clinic patients studied, however, such a spiritist diagnosis was reported much more frequently.

10. A black American *Santera,* who is particularly knowledgeable in Western psychological thinking as well, pointed out to me the significance of this ritual for "depressed women": "She comes to us, and what she wants is a work to get her husband back for her. Well, we can't get her husband back for her, but what we can do is go to her house and get her cleaned up and get the house cleaned up. Then, if he does happen to come around, or if another man comes around, she will be more attractive to him."

11. Putting a *collar* or *collares* (beads) on someone is an overnight ritual in *Santeria* that provides the person with some "protection" by the *Orisha,* or saints and establishes a fictive kinship relationship between the *Santera* as *madrina* (godmother) and that person as *ahijado* (godchild). Rosa would assume a godmother role to Maria's son and a coparent role to Maria with respect to her son when she performed this ritual.

12. This selling of baths in the *centro* is a very unusual practice, and this is the only time I have seen it done in this or any other *centro!* It is reminiscent, however, of other unique ego-building tasks I have seen Rosa assign to other clients, such as a young student who had temporarily dropped out of the High School of Fine Arts who was enlisted in painting murals on the *centro* walls and given a great deal of praise for his talents; or a depressed woman who had had to give up her occupation as a hairdresser because of arthritis in her hands who was involved in setting Rosa's wigs, which Rosa subsequently wore in the *centro,* proclaiming the beauty and fine work on her wigs done by the client. These tasks are also reminiscent of rehabilitation therapy.

13. The Spiritists say mediums can be "conscious, unconscious or semiconscious" when in trance and will, accordingly, remember or not remember the messages given by the spirits. It is my impression that this woman did not remember what had happened and that it was the deepest altered state of consciousness that I have seen in these centers.

14. Although the perpetrator of the witchcraft is not usually named by the mediums, many of those who seek spiritual help test the mediums' abilities by asking for such explicit identification. Also, many testimonials of spiritist believers include accounts of how spirit mediums have accurately identified individuals in their past by name.

15. Freud, S. "On Narcissim: an introduction." In *Collected Papers* **4**:31-59; London, Hogarth, 1937: p. 44, cited by Fernandez-Marina, *op. cit.,* p. 82.

REFERENCES

ANONYMOUS

1966   *Colección de Oraciones Escogidas de Allan Kardec y Otros Autores.* New York: Studium Corporation.

BOURGUIGNON, E.

1968   "World Distribution and Patterns of Possession States." In *Trance and Possession States*, R. Prince, Ed. Montreal: R. M. Bucke Memorial Society.

BOURGUIGNON, E. (ED.)

1973   *Religion, Altered States of Consciousness and Social Change.* Columbus: Ohio State University Press.

BRAM, J.

1958   "Spirits, Mediums, and Believers in Contemporary Puerto Rico." *Transactions of the New York Academy of Sciences* 20:340–347.

BREUER, J. and S. FREUD

1966   On the psychical mechanism of hysterical phenomena: preliminary communication (originally published 1893). In S. Freud and J. Breuer, *Studies on Hysteria.* (Transl. from the German and edited by James Strachey.) New York: Avon Books.

EVANS-PRITCHARD, E. E.

1937   *Witchcraft, Oracles, and Magic among the Azande.* New York: Oxford University Press.

FERNANDEZ-MARINA, R.

1961   "The Puerto Rican Syndrome: Its Dynamics and Cultural determinants." *Psychiatry,* 24:79–82.

FRANK, J. D.

1961   *Persuasion and Healing: A Comparative Study of Psychotherapy.* Baltimore: The Johns Hopkins Press.

GARRISON, V.

1972   Espiritismo: Implications for Delivery of Mental Health Services to Puerto Rican Populations. Paper read at the Eighth Annual Meeting of the Southern Anthropological Society, Columbia, Mo., February 24–26.

KARDEC, ALLAN

1964   *El Evangelio Segun el Espiritismo.* Mexico, D.F.: Editorial Diana, 12th Edition. (First published in French, 1864, translator anonymous.)

KOSS, J. D.

1973   "Artistic Expression and Creative Process in Caribbean
               Possession Cult Rituals." Paper prepared for the XI In-
               ternational Congress of the Anthropological and Eth-
               nological Sciences, Chicago, September, 1973. To be
               published in *The Performing Arts, Music, Dance and The-
               ater,* J. Blacking, The Hague: Mouton.

1974   "Religion and Science Divinely related: a Case History of
               Spiritism in Puerto Rico." Paper read at the 73rd Annual
               Meeting of the American Anthropological Association,
               Symposium on Spiritism in Latin America, Mexico City,
               November 19–24, 1974.

1975   "Therapeutic aspects of Puerto Rican cult practices."
               Psychiatry **28**(2):160–171.

LA RUFFA, A. L.

1971   *San Cipriano: Life in a Puerto Rican Community.* New
               York: Gordon and Breach.

LEWIS, I. M.

1971   *Ecstatic religion: an Anthropological Study of Spirit Posses-
               sion and Shamanism.* Baltimore, Md.: Penguin Books.

LUBCHANSKY, I., G. EGRI, and J. STOKES

1970   "Puerto Rican Spiritualists View Mental Illness: the
               Faith Healer as a Paraprofessional." *American Journal of
               Psychiatry* **127**(3):313–321.

MACKLIN, J.

1975   "Belief, Ritual and Healing: New England Spiritualism
               and Mexican-American Spiritism Compared." In *Re-
               ligious Movements in Contemporary America,* I. I. Zaretsky
               and M. P. Leone, (Eds.) Princeton, N.J.: Princeton Uni-
               versity Press, pp. 383–417.

MALDONADO-SIERRA, E. D. and R. D. TRENT

1960   "The Sibling Relationship in Group Psychotherapy with
               Puerto Rican Schizophrenics." *American Journal of Psy-
               chiatry* **117**:239–244.

MEHLMAN, R. D.

1961   "The Puerto Rican Syndrome." *American Journal of Psy-
               chiatry* 118:328–332.

OESTERREICH, T. K.

1966   *Possession, Demoniacal and Other, among Primitive Races, in
               Antiquity, the Middle Ages and Modern Times.* Secaucus,
               N.J.: University Books. (Orig. publ. in German, 1921).

RAMIREZ DE ARELLANO, R., M. RAMIREZ DE ARELLANO, and L. GARCIA

1956   *Attack, Hyperkinetic Type: The So-Called Puerto Rican Syndrome and its Medical, Psychological and Social Implications.* San Juan: Veterans Administration Report.

ROGLER, L. and A. B. HOLLINGSHEAD

1961   "The Puerto Rican Spiritualist as a Psychiatrist." *American Journal of Sociology* **67:**17–21.

1965   *Trapped: Families and Schizophrenia.* New York: John Wiley & Sons.

ROTHENBERG, A.

1964   "Puerto Rico and Aggression." *American Journal of Psychiatry* **120**(10):962–970.

RUBIO, M. M. URDANETA and J. L. DOYLE

1955   "Psychopathologic Reaction Patterns in the Antilles Command." *U.S. Armed Forces Medical Journal* **6:**1767–1772.

SEDA BONILLA, E.

1969   *Interacción Social y Personalidad en una Comunidad de Puerto Rico.* (Segunda Edicion Revisada), San Juan, Puerto Rico: Ediciones Juan Ponce de Leon.

THOMAS, C. S. and V. GARRISON

1975   "A General Systems View of Community Mental Health." In *Progress in Community Mental Health.* Vol. III. L. Bellak and H. Barten, (eds.) New York: Brunner/Mazel.

TRAUTMAN, E. C.

1961   "The Suicidal Fit: a Psychobiologic Study on Puerto Rican Immigrants." *Archives of General Psychiatry* **5:**96–105.

WAKEFIELD, D.

1957   *Island in the City.* New York: Corinth Books.

Index